Nāgārjuna in Context

Nāgārjuna in Context

Mahāyāna Buddhism and Early Indian Culture

JOSEPH WALSER

MOTILAL BANARSIDASS PUBLISHERS
PRIVATE LIMITED • DELHI

First Indian Edition: Delhi, 2008

ISBN : 978-81-208-3260-2

MOTILAL BANARSIDASS
41 U.A. Bungalow Road, Jawahar Nagar, Delhi 110 007
8 Mahalaxmi Chamber, 22 Bhulabhai Desai Road, Mumbai 400 026
203 Royapettah High Road, Mylapore, Chennai 600 004
236, 9th Main III Block, Jayanagar, Bangalore 560 011
Sanas Plaza, 1302 Baji Rao Road, Pune 411 002
8 Camac Street, Kolkata 700 017
Ashok Rajpath, Patna 800 004
Chowk, Varanasi 221 001

PRINTED IN INDIA

BY JAINENDRA PRAKASH JAIN AT SHRI JAINENDRA PRESS,
A-45, NARAINA, PHASE-I, NEW DELHI 110 028
AND PUBLISHED BY NARENDRA PRAKASH JAIN FOR
MOTILAL BANARSIDASS PUBLISHERS PRIVATE LIMITED,
BUNGALOW ROAD, DELHI 110 007

For my father, Joseph Walser III,
for teaching me a love of learning

Contents

Acknowledgments ix

Introduction 1

1. Locating Mahāyāna 16

2. Locating Nāgārjuna 59

3. Mahāyāna and the Constraints of Monastic Law 89

4. Mahāyāna Sūtras as Monastic Property 123

5. On the Parasitic Strategies of Mahāyāna 153

6. *Abhidharma* and Sectarian Identity 188

7. Nāgārjuna and the *Abhidharma* 224

Conclusion: Toward the Outline of a Career 264

Appendix: The Authorship of the *Ratnāvalī* 271

Notes 279
Bibliography 339
Index 357

Acknowledgments

THE PROCESS OF WRITING this book has been rather long and often difficult, and I could not have done it without the help of both friends and family. First and foremost, I am enormously grateful to my wife, Radha Subramanyam, who was a constant source of advice and inspiration for this book. Radha has provided emotional support while never compromising on her standards of what constitutes good scholarship. Her critical and scholarly eye was invaluable to the final product, one that I would never have begun it, let alone finished, without her. I also thank my family on both sides of the ocean for their help throughout my studies and through the crafting of this work. Their love and assistance over the years has been a large factor in the completion of the project.

In addition, I am grateful for the generous efforts of those scholars who read and commented on drafts of the book. In this category, especial acknowledgment is due to Jim Egge, who must have read four different drafts (without complaint!). I also thank Aloka Parasher Sen of University of Hyderabad, for her astute and extensive comments on the sections dealing with archaeology and early Indian history. Leonard Priestley agreed to read and comment on several drafts of the last two chapters. His expertise in the rather difficult Pudgalavādin material was a godsend. Furthermore, his keen eye for both philological accuracy and philosophical nuance in some instances forced me to completely rethink my approach.

I also appreciate the assistance of many other people who proofread drafts. I am especially grateful to Lydia Francis, who spent hours with me checking my translations from the Chinese. I also extend my gratitude to Wendy Lochner at Columbia University Press, who guided the book through the long journey to publication. I would also like to thank Debra E. Soled, who did an excellent job of editing the final draft as well as to the anonymous readers for Columbia University Press and Oxford University Press, whose comments were invaluable. I further acknowledge Ananda Abeysekhara, Gary Leupp, Ikumi Kaminishi, and Jim Ennis for their help and comments on specific chapters, and Parimal Patil, George Bond, Todd Lewis and Beth Burton for being generally supportive throughout the process.

Finally, I offer my appreciation for those professors who have mentored me over the years. Although there are too many to name all of them, three deserve special mention. I am eternally grateful to Adolf von Wuertenburg for sharing with me his love of Sanskrit, to David S. Pacini who, in his own way, opened my eyes to the joys of scholarship, and to Isshi Yamada, who showed me by his example what is possible. I sincerely hope that this book lives up to the standards they have set.

Nāgārjuna in Context

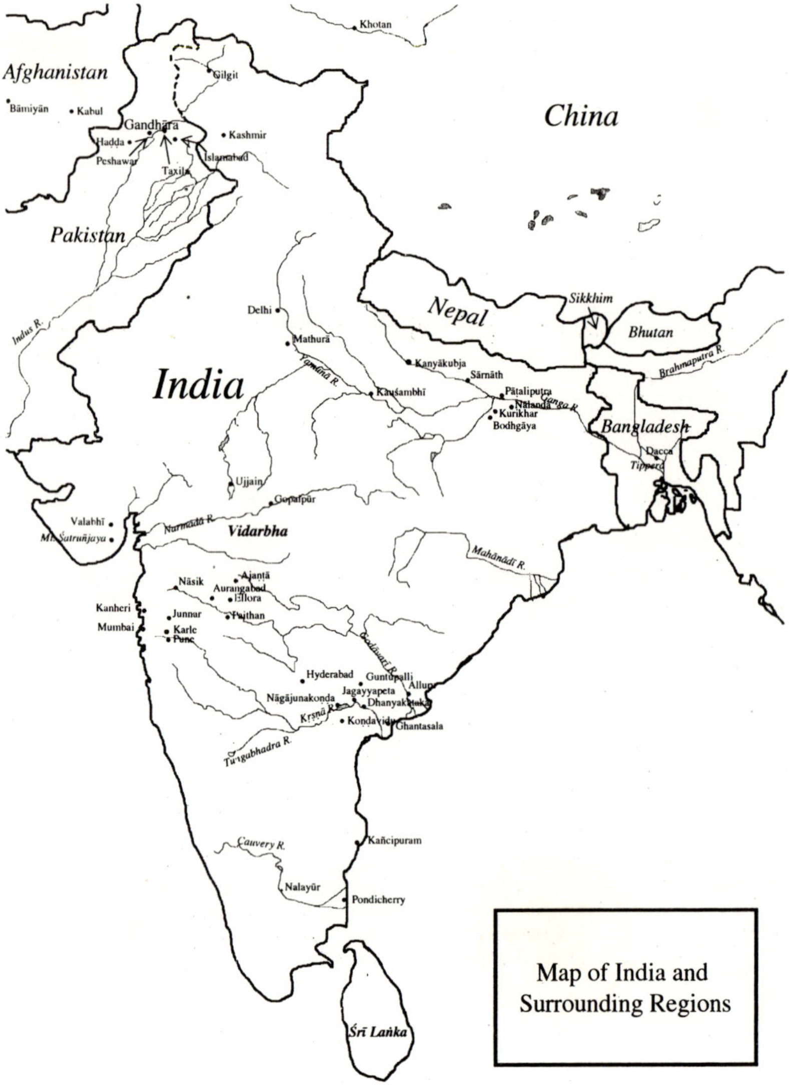

Map of India and Surrounding Regions

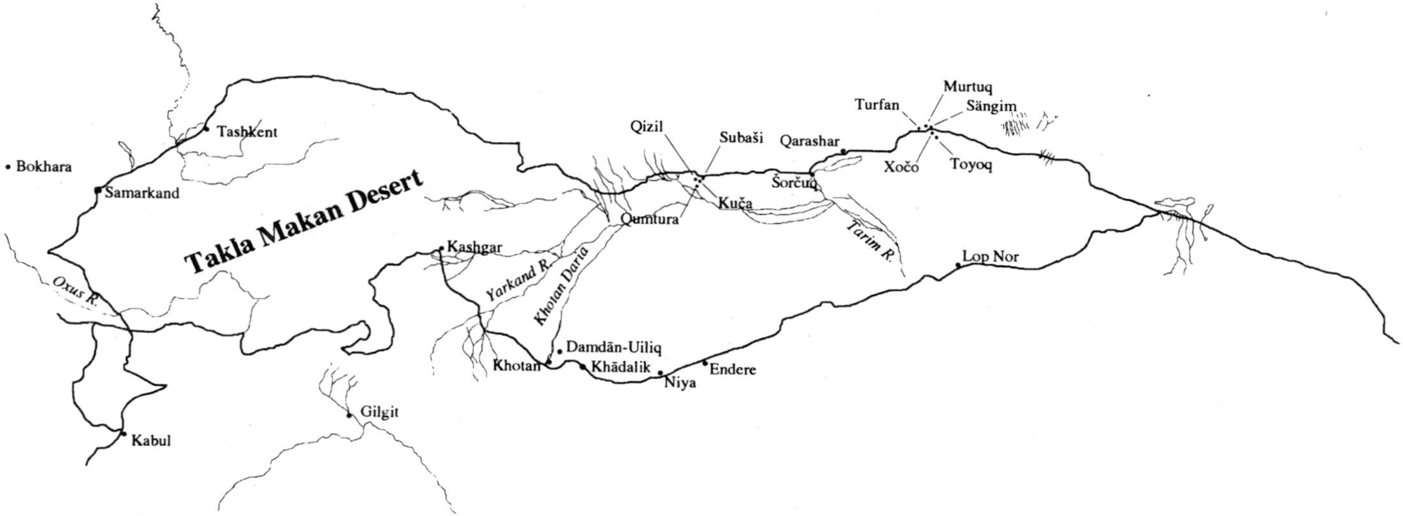
Bokhara
Samarkand
Tashkent
Takla Makan Desert
Oxus R.
Kabul
Gilgit
Kashgar
Yarkand R.
Khotan Daria
Khotan
Damdān-Uiliq
Khādalik
Niya
Endere
Qumtura
Qizil
Subaši
Kuča
Qarashar
Šorčuq
Tarim R.
Turfan
Murtuq
Sängim
Xočo
Toyoq
Lop Nor

Introduction

THIS BOOK IS A STUDY of Nāgārjuna, a Buddhist philosopher of the second century and a key figure in the development of Mahāyāna Buddhism in ancient India. Few figures in the history of Buddhism stand out more prominently than Nāgārjuna. In Mahāyāna hagiographies, Nāgārjuna is among the earliest of the great saints mentioned. Nāgārjuna is prominently represented in the transmission lineages for both the Zen tradition and the various Tantric traditions. He has been cited as a source of authority by personages as diverse as Tsongkhapa in Tibet and Dōgen and Shinran in Japan. As a measure of his authority, in the eighth century the Tibetan king Khri Srong lDe brTsan declared, "Everyone should follow the teachings of Nāgārjuna and engage assiduously in the practice of morality and the perfections."[1]

To find someone of comparable stature in other religions, one would have to look to Augustine of Hippo or, perhaps, to Moses Maimonides. Yet such a comparison with Augustine and Maimonides would soon expose a serious deficiency in our knowledge about Nāgārjuna. Scholars of Augustine, for example, have not only examined his arguments against Pelagius but also have investigated his institutional role as the bishop of Hippo. Similarly, scholars of Maimonides study his *Thirteen Articles of Faith* and *Guide for the Perplexed* but also examine and debate his other roles as a chief justice (*dayyan*) and as the physician to Saladin. Indeed, it has become common in scholarship of Western religious figures not merely to study the ideas of the author but to look at what those ideas meant in the social and institutional context in which the author wrote.

By contrast, despite great scholarly interest concerning Nāgārjuna's contributions to Mahāyāna doctrine, a similar level of interest in his social and institutional contexts has been absent. This absence is particularly unfortunate in light of the fact that Nāgārjuna, along with Aśvaghoṣa, is one of the earliest-known figures in Mahāyāna Buddhism. Any study, therefore, that successfully uncovers his indebtedness to his contemporaries as well as his contributions to the larger Mahāyāna movement would also reveal a great deal about Mahāyāna Buddhism at a time when its doctrinal and institutional boundaries were being negotiated.

This book aims to achieve such a recovery. The traditional focus of Nāgārjuna studies here shifts from viewing him as a philosopher to viewing him as an early champion of the nascent Mahāyāna movement. This shift draws the focus away from strictly doctrinal concerns and the logical viability of his arguments to questions of the imprint of social and institutional forces on his works. The center of the work, then, is not so much Nāgārjuna's teaching on emptiness but the rather strange way that he goes about arguing for it.

Nāgārjuna is perhaps best known in the West for his employment of apparently logical arguments to arrive at counterintuitive conclusions. For example, the first verse of the first chapter of his *Mūlamadhyamakakārikā* posits, "At nowhere and at no time can entities ever exist by originating out of themselves, from others, from both (self-other), or from lack of causes."[2] In the same vein, chapter 10 examines the relationship between fire and fuel and comes to the conclusion that "fire is not wood, nor is it in something else than wood. Fire does not contain wood. There is neither wood in fire nor fire in wood." From this he concludes, "Insofar as I am concerned, those who speak of the reality of entities and who assign them distinct essences cannot be considered truly knowledgeable of the (Buddha's) teachings.[3] My investigation of Nāgārjuna is less concerned with the validity of these arguments than with the question: "Why this particular argument and not some other?"

It is my contention that many of the peculiarities of Nāgārjuna's writings can be more adequately understood if read as strategies devised to respond to the specific demands of the social and institutional contexts in which he wrote. This thesis entails two separate, though intertwined, tasks. The first requires bringing these contexts into relief by locating Nāgārjuna historically, socially, and institutionally. The second is to uncover the ways in which Nāgārjuna's writings reveal a strategy to secure the needs of Mahāyāna Buddhism within this context.

By focusing on strategies implicit in Nāgārjuna's writings, this book takes an unusual approach to Nāgārjuna. There is an enormous amount of

Western scholarship on Nāgārjuna, stretching back almost a hundred and fifty years. Most of it takes his writing as exemplary of "Mahāyāna philosophy." In so doing, these works assume that his intended audience was either his Mahāyānist supporters or his philosophical opponents (i.e., the Sarvāstivādins, the Sāṃkhyas, etc.). Neither of these scenarios provides a sufficient explanation. Rather, what is elided by such arguments is a third and functionally more important audience—those monks and laypeople in control of the resources that the Mahāyānists needed. The members of this audience would probably not have been affiliated with the Mahāyāna per se (they may even have been opposed to Mahāyāna), but neither would they have been the opponents that Nāgārjuna attacks in his writings. If we assume that Nāgārjuna needed to win over this third audience, we might speculate that the opponent Nāgārjuna engages in his arguments is someone whom the third audience had an interest in defeating.

By refuting these opponents, Nāgārjuna secures an alliance with his spectator audience and thereby secures a place for Mahāyāna within their monastery. One of the primary goals of Nāgārjuna's strategy was the incorporation of Mahāyāna texts into the monastic industry of text reproduction and preservation. But if Nāgārjuna had argued against the position of monks in his home monastery, the monks of succeeding generations would have lacked any impetus to recopy the text that had proved their school wrong.

Examination of internal and external evidence relevant to Nāgārjuna suggests a plausible (if, at times, diaphanous) picture of his career. Although much remains to be filled in, two parts of his career are treated in this book: his early period as a monk in a Mahāsāṅghika or a Saṃmitīya monastery, perhaps around Mathurā; and a later move to coastal Andhra Pradesh, where he was an adviser to a king. Throughout his career, Nāgārjuna appears to have been not so much a founder of a specific school of philosophy as a champion of Mahāyāna more generally. The image presented here of Nāgārjuna, while somewhat less extraordinary than the traditional legends of him, is a far more complete portrait than scholars have drawn previously. Nāgārjuna, far from being an ivory-tower philosopher, stands out as not only as a brilliant thinker but also a sincere and shrewd champion of the Mahāyāna cause.

In this regard, I focus specifically on his strategies to ensure the transmission and preservation of Mahāyāna sūtras—a necessary and crucial factor in the successful spread of Mahāyāna Buddhism. Nāgārjuna labored to demonstrate how Mahāyāna texts fall within the category of texts that non-Mahāyāna monasteries had a prior legal commitment to preserving. Moreover, by showing that Mahāyāna does not deviate from the teachings contained in the *Tripiṭaka* of his host monastery, Nāgārjuna was able to ensure the survival of Mahāyāna in a hostile monastic environment.

Theoretical Matters and the Scope of the Project

Thus far, I have referred to Mahāyāna Buddhism as the Mahāyāna *movement.* My choice of words is intended to highlight the social focus of my inquiry. Although one may refer to "Mahāyāna Buddhism" as a doctrinal system, the designation "Mahāyāna movement" refers specifically to the social and institutional *apparatus* of Mahāyāna Buddhism. Mahāyāna Buddhism does not exactly qualify as a "social movement" in the modern sense of the term. Nevertheless, a comparison between the Mahāyāna movement and certain theoretical discussions of modern social movements further delimit the features of Mahāyāna Buddhism that constitute the target of my inquiry.

A brief comparison between Mahāyāna and social movements indicates what is *not* investigated here. Sociological theories of social movements arose as an attempt to explain social protest movements in Europe and the United States. Hence, most definitions of social movements apply primarily to social protest movements. As such, the element of grievance and the attempt to rectify it for society as a whole form a common part of the definition. Suffice it to say that, from the standpoint of correcting social grievances, it is not clear that Mahāyāna constitutes a "social movement" at all since it is not clear from what, if any, grievances the movement arose. Furthermore, it is not clear that Mahāyāna constituted a social movement *organization,* in view of the lack of evidence that it was organized in any meaningful way. Finally, although social protest movements seek overall change in the societies from which they spring, it is not clear that Mahāyānists expected or even wanted all the monks in their monasteries (much less all laypeople) to become *bodhisattvas.*

Nevertheless, while Mahāyāna may not fit the definition of a social movement, reference to the work on social movements of the past three decades sheds some light on the social dynamics behind Nāgārjuna's writings as they pertain to early Mahāyāna. According to John Lofland, social movement organizations are "associations of persons making idealistic and moralistic claims about how human personal or group life ought to be organized that . . . are marginal to or excluded from mainstream society—the then dominant constructions of what is realistic, reasonable, and moral."[4] I have chosen this definition, not because it necessarily represents a consensus, but because it contains several features that are useful in thinking about Mahāyāna. The first feature is the opposition between the movement in question and the "dominant construction." At the very least, we know that the "idealistic and moral" claims of Mahāyāna raised a few eyebrows, and as argued in Chapter 1, at least some Mahāyāna communities appear to have been "marginal" or "excluded" on the basis of their affiliations. The other useful part of the definition concerns the term "mainstream society." Lofland defines mainstream society as "a set of institutions and their authoritative decision-makers that can and do maintain public order, dominate economic activity, and provide plausible rationales for exercising power and authority in such matters."[5] He goes on to point out that some agents in the mainstream society have more of a hand in constructing normativity than others. Finally, he shows that the construction of normativity is *pari passu* the construction of marginality.

In the case of Mahāyāna Buddhism, we have to consider two mainstream societies: the society consisting of laypeople (Buddhists, non-Buddhists, kings, ministers, foreigners, etc.) and the society consisting of non-Mahāyānist monastics. The most immediately important mainstream society for the Mahāyāna Buddhists who lived in monasteries (monastic Mahāyānists are the primary focus of this book) comprised the other monks of the monastery. Again, as shown in Chapter 1, there is no evidence for the existence of a purely Mahāyāna monastery as early as the second century, when Nāgārjuna was writing. This means that the relevant Buddhist mainstream would have consisted of the established Buddhist sects, such as the Sarvāstivādins, the Mahāsāṅghikas, and the Dharmaguptas. As a matter of course, agents of these sects authorized certain doctrines, texts, and rules of behavior both through their own actions of promotion and through the punitive powers of the institution. For reasons that this book explores, Mahāyāna was perceived to challenge the normative doctrines, texts, and rules of behavior and was marginalized to the point that even the earliest records of Mahāyāna register a kind of defensiveness about its doctrines.

As seen in Chapter 1, sometime between the first and fifth centuries what perhaps began as cursory attempts at doctrinal or literary innovation became institutionalized and references to Mahāyāna monasteries began to appear. If, as argued in Chapter 2, Nāgārjuna writes at the end of the second century, then he is writing at a crucial juncture in the development and institutionalization of Mahāyāna. If Mahāyāna were a movement marginalized from the mainstream by those "authoritative decision-makers that can and do maintain public order, dominate economic activity, and provide plausible rationales for exercising power and authority,"[6] then an investigation of Nāgārjuna, specifically focusing on his strategies, may reveal how Mahāyāna survived and eventually came to thrive in such an environment. It is the *survival* of Mahāyāna, as opposed to its *origins,* that forms the central focus of this book.

Several prominent social movement theories address the question of what makes one social movement succeed and not another. One theory, in particular, deemphasizes the role of grievances in the formation and success of social movements. The "Resource Mobilization Theory" of John McCarthy and Mayer Zald asserts that the relative success or failure of a movement has more to do with the movement's ability to mobilize resources than with the magnitude of its members' grievances. A movement's ability to access and direct resources forms the heart of the theory.

> Each [social movement organization] has a set of target goals, a set of preferred changes toward which it claims to be working. . . . The [organizations] must possess resources, however few and of whatever type, in order to work toward goal achievement. Individuals and other organizations control resources, which can include legitimacy, money, facilities and labor. Although similar organizations vary tremendously in the efficiency with which they translate resources into action . . . the amount of activity directed toward goal accomplishment is crudely a function of the resources controlled by an organization.[7]

Application of this theory would shift the emphasis of the study of Mahāyāna from an emphasis on doctrine to one on how Mahāyānists managed to secure the resources of money, labor, legitimacy, and media access to perpetuate that doctrine. And in this respect, McCarthy and Zald point out an important, if obvious, fact. These resources are often not in the control of movement members. They are most likely to be under the control of the mainstream culture. This premise leads to the other features of the theory, which McCarthy and Zald summarize as follows:

> **Support base**
>
> . . . Social movements may or may not be based upon the grievances of the presumed beneficiaries. Conscience constituents, individual and organizational, may provide major sources of support. And in some cases supporters—those who provide money, facilities, and even labor—may have no commitment to the values that underlie specific movements.

Strategy and tactics

> The concern with interaction between movements and authorities is accepted, but it is also noted that social movement organizations have a number of strategic tasks. These include mobilizing supporters, neutralizing and/or transforming mass and elite publics into sympathizers, achieving change in targets.

Relation to larger society

> Society provides the infrastructure which social movement industries utilize. The aspects utilized include communication media and expense, levels of affluence, degree of access to institutional centers, preexisting networks, and occupational structure and growth.[8]

What light might this theory shed on our study of Mahāyāna? If Mahāyāna was to be successful, it needed to have a certain amount of discretionary use of resources that were under the control of other groups. Any investigation of the success of Mahāyāna must investigate its strategies in relation to those resources. The Resource Mobilization Theory posits that social movements must rely on nonmembers as well as on mainstream infrastructure for at least some of their resources. This means that a movement's tactics in securing cooperation from nonmembers are just as important as its tactics for recruiting and training members. The tactics will, of course, vary depending on whether the agents in control of the resources are sympathetic nonmembers ("conscience constituents"), neutral nonmembers ("the bystander public"),[9] or actual opponents. In the case of Mahāyāna, the resources in question would be under the control of either their host monastery or the outside, lay society. The bulk of this book examines the different strategies employed by Nāgārjuna to secure resources from precisely these two sources.

McCarthy and Zald's article was, of course, not the last word on the topic of resource mobilization. The theory has been criticized and defended from various angles.[10] One key development that is useful in an exploration of Mahāyāna concerns the structure of the resource base from which the movement must draw support and the institutional infrastructure on which it must depend. Although much of Resource Mobilization Theory focuses on the internal strategies that movements use to mobilize their followers and to disseminate their message, several theorists began to focus on the influence of the mainstream political and institutional context on the formation of movement strategies. In 1986 Herbert Kitschelt coined the phrase "opportunity structure." According to his definition, "Political opportunity structures are comprised of specific configurations of resources, institutional arrangements and historical precedents for social mobilization, which facilitate the development of protest movements in some instances and constrain them in others."[11] He goes on to explain that "political opportunity structures influence the choice of protest strategies and the impact of social movements on their environments."[12] As such, in contrast to other Resource Mobilization theories, the emphasis of Kitschelt's analysis is "on relating the strategic choices and societal impacts of movements to specific properties of the external political opportunity structures that movements face."[13]

An opportunity structure is a political, institutional, or legal structure consisting of laws or bylaws governing the allocation of resources, the recognition of institutions, the ways that laws are to be formed and the ways in which dissent is to be handled. According to Kitschelt, "These rules allow for, register, respond to and even shape the demands of social movements that are not (yet) accepted political actors. They also facilitate or impede the institutionalization of new groups and claims." For example, most governments and institutions have a mechanism through which grievances may be aired and changes introduced. The accepted mechanism for change may well determine the form and the strategies that social protest takes to the extent that the use of that mechanism for change constitutes one of the goals of the movement.

Article V of the U.S. Constitution, for example, stipulates that an amendment may be appended to it if, and only if, that amendment is approved by two-thirds of the House of Representatives and the Senate or if the amendment is ratified at a constitutional convention. The National Archives and Records Administration then publishes a draft of the amendment for consideration by the state legislatures. The state legislatures vote on the amendment, and if three-quarters of the states ratify the amendment, it becomes part of the Constitution.[14] The framers of this article probably did not have the Temperance League in mind when they wrote the provision, but the Temperance League certainly had the mechanics of Article V of the Constitution in mind when it organized the Temperance movement.

The political and institutional rules that constitute the political opportunity structure describe the mechanisms through which reform may become established, institutions recognized, officials elected, and resources distributed. In so doing, these rules also form a threshold that any agent of change must reach in order to succeed. If the movement in question does not meet that threshold, it must either adopt a different strategy or fail trying. Furthermore, the overall disposition toward change can affect the movement strategies more globally. Again, according to Kitschelt,

> when political systems are open and weak, they invite *assimilative* strategies; movements attempt to work through established institutions because political opportunity structures offer multiple points of access. In contrast, when political systems are closed and have considerable capacities to ward off threats to the implementation of policies, movements are likely to adopt *confrontational,* disruptive strategies orchestrated outside established policy channels.[15]

Mahāyāna Buddhism was never a unitary phenomenon, and much of its diversity in its early years can be ascribed to the different strategies used by Mahāyānist groups to respond to the different political and legal structures in which they were enmeshed. This book studies the writings of one particular author as this kind of strategy, exploring aspects of Nāgārjuna's writings as strategies to secure the resources necessary for the survival of Mahāyāna. The focus is on those strategies that specifically target the part of the mainstream (non-Mahāyāna) audience that served as agents of the legal and administrative apparatuses of the local monastic and civil communities.

From Philosophy to Context

In discussing Nāgārjuna's role in securing resources for the Mahāyāna movement, my intention is to supplement, not to replace, philosophical studies of Nāgārjuna's writings. It is undeniable that the majority of the works that can most securely be attributed to Nāgārjuna are *prima facie* works of philosophy and that the depths of the philosophy contained in these writings have yet to be plumbed. Still, while modern scholarship on Nāgārjuna's philosophy tends to overlook his social and institutional affiliations, the philosophical issues themselves beg a host of questions concerning precisely these affiliations. For example, many scholars assume that Nāgārjuna's opponents were Sarvāstivādins, and many modern works investigate his arguments against this opponent. Yet no one has so far given a plausible reason why he singled out the Sarvāstivādins for refutation and not, say, the Theravādins. The above discussion of Resource Mobilization Theory highlights the fact that the audience that Nāgārjuna was writing for was probably much more crucial to the well-being of the local Mahāyāna community than the scholars against whom he was writing.

Even Nāgārjuna's most philosophical treatises can yield important insights into the strategies of Mahāyāna if we take a slightly different perspective on the role of philosophical arguments. What may serve as a *descriptive* statement from a philosophical point of view can simultaneously be understood as having an *injunctive* function from an institutional point of view. Arguments carry a workload, and often they do so on many different levels. Sometimes the work they do is an expression of the author's intention, sometimes not. Regardless of the author's intention, there is some work that all arguments must do. To clarify what I mean by workload here, it may be useful to distinguish writing from publishing. One is completely free to write anything to oneself in order to prove something to oneself. Indeed, one may write a philosophical proof on the back of a napkin simply for personal pleasure and hide it away under the mattress with impunity. Publication (i.e., "making public"), by contrast, is always a social phenomenon with tangible social rewards. At a minimum, the work that a published argument must do is to ensure its own production. To this end, it may be less important for an author to convince the readers of an argument's correctness than to convince them to reproduce the argument, although the acceptability of an argument is usually an important factor in its publication.

Publication is often tied to other rewards. Thinking of the modern context, consider how often some kind of institutional payload is tied to a particular target audience's judgment regarding a published work. That reward may be something as simple as a passing grade in a class, the acceptance of an article in an academic journal, or votes in an election. In some arguments, the very livelihood of the author is at stake—hence, the oft-heard dictum in academia, "publish or perish." In modern academia the acceptance of an argument is tied to books being published, getting tenure, and so on. Authors tend to be very aware that they do not write in a vacuum. They write to imagined audiences and attempt to anticipate the desires and criticisms of those audiences. Works meeting certain criteria are published, and those that do not meet them are not. Authors write with these stipulations in mind and try to make their manuscripts conform to the form of a publishable text. It is likely that in this regard the professional lives of monks as authors in the Indian Buddhist monasteries of the second and third centuries were little different from those of modern writers.

Here, it is important to note another important difference between my project and that of the sociologists involved in research on social movements. Social movement researchers have many tools at their disposal that are not available to someone conducting historical research. I believe that our understanding of Mahāyāna in general and Nāgārjuna in particular will be greatly enhanced if we, following Kitschelt, relate "the strategic choices and societal impacts of movements to specific properties of the external political opportunity structures that movements face." However, unlike Kitschelt, we do not have recourse to interviews of the movement organizers to ask what their strategies were. The best I can do is to look at the opportunity structures comprised in legal literature, compare then to what Nāgārjuna wrote, and from there infer his strategies. The danger in this method is that it is easy to infer strategies where there may be none. To this objection, I can only say that there are no smoking guns here. Any kind of historical work involves a degree of uncertainty. Nevertheless, I do believe that the attempt to come up with a plausible reading of the available evidence sheds an important light on the subject.

Nāgārjuna's writings are mostly about Buddhist practice and its goals. In this he is not in any way duplicitous. His writings are, however, multivalent in that they also can be read to have strategic implications. The first strategic layer of Nāgārjuna's writing, then, must be the strategies that he, as a Mahāyānist,[16] employs to ensure that his own writings will be acceptable and, hence, published. This strategy is related to his strategy to ensure the survival of the movement as a whole. The strategies that he uses to ensure the reproduction of his own texts also argue for the legitimacy of all Mahāyāna texts.

It is from the standpoint of the authorization of textual production that I wish to reopen the discussion of the Buddhist "canon." As has been pointed out by Steven Collins, word "canon" has two meanings.[17] The first simply denotes a collection of texts (either oral or written) that is considered authoritative without being the sole textual authority. The second signifies a collection of texts that is closed (i.e., no new texts may be added to it and none may be taken away).

In early Buddhist materials many different terms are used to convey a sense of canonicity (at least in the sense of an authorized body of texts). The term that best conveys the sense of the authority of Buddhist scripture is *buddhavacana* (word of the Buddha). Superficially, this term ties the authority of individual texts to the authority of the source—ostensibly the Buddha himself, although, as seen later, the term is much more inclusive. Other terms are descriptive of the canon's content. The earliest of these is probably *Tripiṭaka* (Three Baskets), consisting of the *Sūtra Piṭaka* (the collections of the sermons of the Buddha), the *Vinaya Piṭaka* (the collections of monastic rules), and the *Abhidharma Piṭaka* (the doctrinal digests of the different Buddhist "schools"). In the same vein, other Buddhist texts discuss a "nine-limbed scripture" or a "twelve-limbed scripture."[18]

These categorizations of scripture appear quite early, but Collins argues that, even though they are often taken to refer to the content of the canon, before the advent of written scriptures, it is more likely that they refer to genres of literature rather than to a fixed collection of texts.[19] Even after the advent of written Buddhist texts, it is still debatable whether the canon was ever closed in fact. Vasubandhu, both in his *Abhidharmakośa* and in his *Vyākhyāyukti,* mentions discrepancies in the contents of the canons used by different schools as well as the existence of different recensions of the same texts.[20] Similarly, it is clear that new texts continued to be introduced into the authoritative collections of early schools. Thus there is a degree of uncertainty as to the specific collection that Nāgārjuna would have considered "canonical." Nevertheless, that Vasubandhu has to point out that the *Tripiṭaka* differs from place to place and school to school indicates that many assumed that it was fixed and therefore could argue against potential heretics as if the *Tripiṭaka* constituted a complete and closed canon. It is from this perspective that Collins argues that the perception or the idea of the Pali canon is more important that the actual contents of the canon as possessed by any given monastery.[21] It is the "very idea" that the canon was closed in a given monastery that would lead to resistance to the reproduction of Mahāyāna texts in Nāgārjuna's time.

Indeed, Collins claims that Mahāyāna itself may have been the catalyst for the closure of the canon, at least among Theravādins. He suggests that the closure of the Theravāda canon coincides with the advent of Mahāyāna at the Abhayagīri monastery, which he places in the third century.[22] He sees both the writing and the fixing of the canon to coincide with the creation of Ceylonese *vaṃsa* literature (a kind of genealogy of the religion) since these texts define orthodoxy and scriptural integrity through a description of heresies.[23] As a Mahāyānist who defends the status of Mahāyāna sūtras, Nāgārjuna would have been at the heart of the debates over what was and was not canonical. Whether the canonical catalogues were in fact fixed during his lifetime, "the very idea" that the canon *should* be closed to at least some texts lies at the heart of what Mahāyānists were arguing for.

One of the key resources needed by Mahāyānists was the media. Again, Mahāyāna Buddhist texts should be seen not just as an aggregation of philosophical ideas but as ideas whose survival requires processes of production. Whatever else Mahāyānists may have required, there could be no Mahāyāna without the continued presence of Mahāyāna texts (either oral or written). The production of Mahāyāna sūtras involved both labor and material resources—resources that would have been under the control of the "mainstream" community, not the Mahāyānists themselves. As discussed in Chapters 3 and 4, the procedures and rules governing the reproduction and preservation of monastic texts was already in place for mainstream Buddhist texts. The monastic laws covering textual reproduction serve as a kind of "political opportunity structure" against which Mahāyāna's strategies would be devised. Here it is important to note that there are no monastic rules in any of the *vinayas* that specifically target Mahāyāna. Rather, the legal infrastructure established in the *vinayas* sets forth a set of standards governing what is to be learned, preached, recited, and copied. Mahāyānists knew that if they met these standards, their activities in these matters would have to be tolerated. By the same token, if their activities did not meet these standards, they would be liable to disciplinary sanctions even if no one actually brought suit.

The standard for doctrinal and textual acceptability, as shown in Chapters 3 and 4, was legally determined by the textual precedent set in the monastery. In other words, the preservation of a text might be assured if it was like the texts that the monastery was already committed to reproducing. Thus the importance of canonical precedent within the monastery would determine how the laws in the *vinaya* would apply to a particular text newly introduced into the monastery. Although all monasteries were committed to reproducing what they understood to be canonical (functionally speaking, "word of the Buddha" or *Tripiṭaka*), it is apparent that some monks resisted the inclusion of Mahāyāna texts in that category. So, the idea of the *Tripiṭaka* as a legal category (not as a specific catalogue of texts) becomes both the site and the goal of Mahāyāna's struggles.

Consequently, an important strategy for Nāgārjuna was to show that Mahāyāna texts shared the same authority as those already contained in the *Tripiṭaka* and should therefore be included in the canon. Following the example of other Mahāyāna texts, Nāgārjuna made characteristically Mahāyānist propositions and arguments while couching these arguments in clandestine (and not-so-clandestine) allusions to doctrines, texts, and laws that were already part of the *Tripiṭaka*. In doing so, he demonstrated the Mahāyāna sūtra's contiguity with sources already contained in the *Tripiṭaka*.

The demands of production, then, come to determine the final form of Mahāyāna texts. The result is that many early Mahāyāna *sūtras* and *śāstras* have come down to us marked by a kind of hybridity. Early Mahāyāna texts therefore should be regarded not as pure representatives of Mahāyāna difference but as the hybrid products of institutional negotiation. On one level, the very reproduction of texts is at stake, yet, on another level, what is being negotiated is Buddhist identity itself. "Mahāyāna" and "non-Mahāyāna," then, should be read not as fixed identities but as hybridities arising out of the process of identity negotiation. As Homi Bhabha has written:

> Terms of cultural engagement, whether antagonistic or affiliative, are produced performatively. The representation of difference must not be hastily read as the reflection of pre-given ethnic or cultural traits set in the fixed tablet of tradition. The social articulation of difference, from the minority perspective, is a complex, on-going negotiation that seeks to authorize cultural hybridities that emerge in moments of historical transformation.[24]

In Nāgārjuna's works is visible the negotiation of Mahāyāna identity through its engagement with well-established and financially endowed Buddhist sects. The syncretic strategies of Mahāyāna that Nāgārjuna employs consist of a range of devices aimed at maximizing Mahāyāna's authority while minimizing its apparent difference from the norms of his host monastery. What Mahāyāna teaches is in many ways new, but it is packaged as merely a rearticulation or elaboration of an old and already authoritative tradition. The result is that Mahāyāna texts are neither entirely canonical nor entirely innovative. For the period under consideration in this book, much of Mahāyāna literature occupies a hybrid space, and this condition lasts until it achieves authority of its own.

Chapter Breakdown

The present work therefore places Nāgārjuna's writings in the milieu of early Mahāyāna, identifies the obstacles facing early Mahāyāna and discusses the strategies he used to overcome these obstacles. Chapter 1 discusses the geographic range and institutional viability of Mahāyāna in India during the first few centuries of the Common Era (C.E.). Mahāyāna's lack of independent institutional support may have been responsible for its virtual invisibility in the archaeological record until the fifth century. Chapter 2 narrows the study of Nāgārjuna to the Eastern Deccan. This chapter reviews the available evidence relevant to Nāgārjuna's date and place of residence and considers the likelihood that, while he wrote the *Ratnāvalī,* Nāgārjuna lived in a Mahāsāṅghika monastery in or near an urban center in the Lower Krishna River Valley in modern Andhra Pradesh.

The remaining chapters investigate Nāgārjuna's strategic use of three sources of textual authority in Buddhism: the *vinaya piṭaka,* the *sūtra piṭaka,* and the *abhidharma piṭaka.* To this end, Chapter 3 contends that, under

Mahāsāṅghika law, a monk teaching Mahāyāna doctrine would be liable to the charge of causing a schism and would have been exposed to various legal sanctions, both from the monastery and from secular authorities. The chapter also examines Nāgārjuna's strategies in the *Ratnāvalī* to limit Mahāyānists' liability to this charge. Chapter 4 addresses the issue of property rights and the legal and economic implications of the presence of Mahāyāna in a Mahāsāṅghika monastery for the production and reproduction of Mahāyāna texts. For Nāgārjuna's community of Mahāyānists, the most efficient way to get their texts reproduced may well have been to camouflage them as the kind of texts that the monastery had a prior commitment to reproducing.

Chapter 5 examines the precedent for camouflage in other Mahāyāna sūtras and examines how Nāgārjuna incorporates this strategy into his foundational work, the *Mūlamadhyamakakārikā*. Mahāyāna manipulation of common Buddhist texts inserts new interpretations into the interstices left open by the prior textual tradition, and the new Mahāyāna teachings stay well within the doctrinal boundary of texts acceptable for reproduction.

Chapters 6 and 7 look at the ways in which Nāgārjuna forges alliances with the Buddhist sectarian interests represented in *Abhidharma* literature. Chapter 6 presents an overview of Buddhist sectarian material (*abhidharma*) that may have been available to Nāgārjuna and addresses the issue of what Mahāsāṅghika *abhidharma* materials would have looked like. Chapter 7 examines arguments of the *Mūlamadhyamakakārikā* for alliances that Nāgārjuna forged between Mahāyāna doctrines and important sectarian interests of his day.

This book argues that Nāgārjuna belonged to a minority Buddhist movement that was still in its early stages in the second century. Nāgārjuna's ostensibly philosophical works reveal strategies to ensure the material reproduction of Mahāyāna manuscripts. It lays out the specific constraints and threats to Mahāyāna as well as the textual tactics for navigating this terrain. In the end, Nāgārjuna's strategy for the survival of Mahāyāna is one of syncretism, hybridity, and purported conformity with the assumed canon. Although his texts are addressed to an obvious opponent, they actually target a "home audience"—an audience to whom he is declaring loyalty and solidarity in order to secure a place for Mahāyāna Buddhism in a potentially antagonistic environment.

I
Locating Mahāyāna

To present Nāgārjuna's role in the development and spread of Mahāyāna, we must first explore the contours of Mahāyāna in India around the time that he lived. The present chapter examines Mahāyāna's development on two fronts: its institutional development and its geographic diffusion. To that end, I present evidence for Mahāyāna's development in the first centuries of the Common Era through an examination of inscriptions, Mahāyāna *sūtras*, records of Mahāyāna translators, Chinese pilgrims' accounts of Mahāyāna, and Buddhists' own histories of their religion.[1] The preponderance of this evidence suggests that Mahāyāna was a relatively small, in some places embattled, movement within Buddhism with no independent institutional status. This state of affairs seemed to persist until at least the fourth or fifth centuries.

A fair amount of discussion has recently taken place over the very definition of Mahāyāna as well as over the degree to which Mahāyāna Buddhism should be distinguished from non-Mahāyāna Buddhism. The problem lies in the diversity of Mahāyāna sources. The issue is summarized by Jan Nattier:

> Thus we find one scripture (the *Akṣobhyavyūha*) that advocates both *śrāvaka* and bodhisattva practices, propounds the possibility of rebirth in a pure land, and enthusiastically recommends the cult of the book, yet seems to know nothing of emptiness theory, the ten *bhūmis*, or the *trikāya*, while another (the *P'u-sa pen-yeh ching*, 菩薩本業經) propounds the ten *bhūmis* and focuses exclusively on the path of the bod-

hisattva, but never discusses the *pāramitās*. A Mādhyamika treatise (Nāgārjuna's *Mūlamādhyamika-kārikās*) may enthusiastically deploy the rhetoric of emptiness without ever mentioning the bodhisattva path, while a Yogācāra treatise (Vasubandhu's *Madhyānta-vibhāga-bhāṣya)* may delve into the particulars of the *trikāya* doctrine while eschewing the doctrine of *ekayāna*. We must be prepared, in other words, to encounter a multiplicity of Mahāyānas flourishing even in India, not to mention those that developed in East Asia and Tibet.[2]

In order to accommodate the diversity within the phenomena of Mahāyāna in India, I adopt different strategies of definition in this book. The purpose of this chapter is to examine the contours of "Mahāyāna" in the broadest sense. Hence, as evidence it uses primarily items in which the word "Mahāyāna" is actually included. One could certainly argue that by the time the word "Mahāyāna" enters the historical record, it had already become something of a brand name to which a diverse set of authors, practitioners, and so on wished to attach themselves.[3] A brand name does not necessarily denote a single product, manufacturing plant, or location, and yet the name suggests the idea of a unity. Subsequent chapters employ a narrower definition of Mahāyāna to apply more specifically to the Mahāyāna of Nāgārjuna's community.

Many prominent theories in scholarly literature relate to the social context of early Mahāyāna. The theories relevant to the social context of early Mahāyāna have appeared mostly in discussions of "the origins of Mahāyāna." Although Mahāyāna's origins per se are not directly relevant to this study (Mahāyāna was already well under way by the second century), these theories of Mahāyāna's origins relate to both Mahāyāna's social context and the trajectory of its spread.

There are three divergent views of the social context of early Mahāyāna. The first view is simply that Mahāyāna arose in and remained ensconced within already established Buddhist sects, such as the Sarvāstivāda and the Dharmagupta. According to this view, the word "Mahāyāna" may never have applied to a separate Buddhist institution. Mahāyāna would simply denote a specific doctrinal predilection among a smaller cohort of monks within of one of the existing sects. This theory proposes that Mahāyāna should be seen as a *vāda,* that is, a "school" or a "philosophical movement" (i.e., a body of doctrine), as opposed to a *nikāya,* which denotes the full institutional apparatus, both material and ideological, of affiliated monasteries. This hypothesis is the least controversial of prevailing theories and plays a central role in the argument presented here. According to this view, regardless of Mahāyānists' specific beliefs, they would have taken the same vows, lived in the same monasteries, and received the same ordination as any other Buddhist monk. This view has been accepted by some of the most prominent scholars to research early Mahāyāna, including Junjirō Takakusu, Auguste Barth, Louis de La Valée Poussin, Jean Prysluski, and Heinz Bechert.[4] For evidence, these scholars primarily cite the travel accounts of Yijing and Xuanzang, both of whom mention monasteries in which Mahāyānists and non-Mahāyānists lived and studied together. Furthermore, these scholars have also noted that few inscriptions in India used the word "Mahāyāna" as an adjective to describe a monastery or a *saṅgha*. Finally, according to Bechert, if Mahāyāna had formed a separate sect, there would first have to be a schism. Yet he reads Buddhist legal literature to define a "schism" as a rift over interpretation of Buddhist law—not Buddhist doctrine. He concludes that the creation or adoption of Mahāyāna as a separate doctrinal system would not have constituted a schism.

Some advocates of this view, such as Bechert and Paul Williams, claim that Mahāyānists lived peacefully among other monks in their monastery. Others, such as Stephen Kent, argue that although Mahāyānists may have lived among non-Mahāyānists (and hence did not form a separate *nikāya*, or particular Buddhist sect), there was considerable tension between the two groups.[5] Because of this tension, Mahāyānists endured constant antagonism at the hands of their fellow monks. It was this constant persecution that led to the "embattled mentality" found in such Mahāyāna texts as the *Saddharmapuṇḍarīka*. This latter view has been championed by Gregory Schopen, who argues that "one strand of the early Mahāyāna in India was institutionally located within the larger, dominant, established monastic orders as a marginal element struggling for recognition and acceptance."[6]

The second view is that early Mahāyāna was fostered not so much by the monks as by the laity. Akira Hirakawa has been the primary exponent of this position, and his paper expounding this view remains a classic forty years even after it was written. In it he sets forth arguments connecting Mahāyāna's origin to the laity and to *stūpa* worship. His arguments tying the origins of Mahāyāna to the laity follow from his close readings of early Mahāyāna *sūtras*.

Hirakawa begins by arguing against any simple identification between Mahāyāna and any one *nikāya*. Although some common Mahāyāna ideas (among which he mentions the transcendence of the Buddha and the ten *bodhisattva* stages) can be found in the literature associated with the Mahāsāṅghika sect, others (such as the notions of *vinaya* and *abhidharma* found in the Mahāyāna *Mahāprajñāpāramitopadeśa*) clearly come from that of the

Sarvāstivāda.[7] Hirakawa then connects Mahāyāna explicitly to the laity by pointing out that, in Mahāyāna texts, the Buddha addresses his audiences not as "householder" or "monk" (the common forms of address in *Tripiṭaka* literature) but as the ambiguous *kulaputra/-duhitṛ* (= "son/daughter of a good family"), which could refer to either laity or monks.[8] Next, he argues that the earliest versions of the six *pāramitā,* such as that found in the *Daśabhūmika Sūtra,* the *Aṣṭasāhasrikā Prajñāpāramitā,* and the *Ugradattaparipṛcchā,* explain the perfection of morality as the *daśabālaśīla.* Hirakawa claims that these ten precepts are identical to the *dasasīlas* of the Pāli *nikāyas*—precepts that were originally lay precepts, not monastic ones.[9] He shows that even the earliest Mahāyāna *sūtras* seem to categorize Mahāyānists together with the laity since they make a distinction between *bodhisattva,* on the one hand, and *bhikṣu* or the *śrāvaka-saṅgha,* on the other.[10]

The next part of Hirakawa's argument is perhaps the most interesting and the most controversial. He contends that the institutional basis that fostered Mahāyāna was the *stūpa.* This argument has five parts. First, he illustrates the centrality of *stūpa* worship through early Mahāyāna *sūtras* in which *stūpa* worship is extolled.[11] In particular, he points out the structural similarities between the description of *Sukhāvatī* in the *Smaller Sukhāvatī Sūtra* and the description of a *stūpa* from the *Mahāsāṅghika-vinaya.* Having made the initial connection between Mahāyāna and *stūpas,* he shows that the *stūpas* were considered a space separate not only from both the mundane world of the laity but also from the monastery. Hirakawa believes that the early Chinese translations of these *sūtras* suggest that early Buddhists regarded *stūpa* not just as the mound in which the relics are buried but as the whole *stūpa* compound in which devotees (read *bodhisattvas*) could gather for worship. To show that this space was not an exclusively monastic space, he points out that worship at the *stūpa* involved music and dancing. Because both activities were proscribed for monks, he argues, such worship must have been performed by the laity. Furthermore, although the *stūpas* were recipients of fabulous amounts of donated wealth, the *vinayas* are unanimous that *stūpa* property formed a property category separate from other categories of property in the monastery, and that the *saṅgha* had the obligation to maintain *stūpa* property, but did not have the right to dispose of it regardless of the circumstances.[12]

Most of the *vinayas* teach that the merit earned from donations to the *stūpa* was inferior to that made by donations to the *saṅgha*—the only exception to this rule being found in the *Dharmagupta vinaya.*[13] Hirakawa surmises that the privileging of one kind of benefaction over another was a reflection of the resentment by monks against those who attended the *stūpa*.[14] He then notes that the early translations of the *Ugradattaparipṛcchā Sūtra* (an early Mahāyāna *sūtra*) describe the *bodhisattva* renunciant as living at the *stūpa* and that the later translations move him into the monastery.[15] Finally, he observes that whereas *nikāya* Buddhism revolved around the *saṅgha*, Mahāyāna must have revolved around the Buddha. Hirakawa's argument is multifaceted, but its central thesis is that Mahāyāna developed among the laity in the context of *stūpa* worship. As such, he regards the antagonism sometimes found in Mahāyāna *sūtras* as a reflection of the antagonism of monastery-centered Buddhist traditions against laity-centered Buddhist traditions.

The third view of early Mahāyāna, explained more recently by Reginald Ray, is an extension of part of Hirakawa's argument. Following Hirakawa's lead, Ray points out the distinctions that early Mahāyāna *sūtras* make between monks and *bodhisattvas*. Ray highlights the numerous discussions of asceticism in the same texts and contends that Mahāyāna originated in and was fostered by communities of "forest-dwelling monks" (*āraṇyakas*). These monks were, according to Ray, initially critical of monastic life and only became "monasticized" (his term) well into the Common Era. The movement he describes sought to contrast the *bodhisattvas* (whom he considers forest monks) with the *bhikṣus* (monks living in monasteries), who, in turn, are depicted by the Mahāyānists as too caught up in scholasticism and debate to really seek liberation. In contrast to a Mahāyāna centered on worship of the Buddhas (Hirakawa's "Buddha-centered" Mahāyāna),[16] Ray's Mahāyānists are critical of settled monastic life insofar as it detracts from the life of meditation.

Gregory Schopen has further suggested that the forest strand of Mahāyāna was a parallel development to the "embattled Mahāyāna monks" of the monasteries. Schopen argues that a Mahāyāna that was geographically marginalized in this fashion could account for the dearth of paleographic evidence relating to Mahāyāna before the fifth century.[17]

Another fruitful line of inquiry has revolved around the question of the geographic spread of Mahāyāna. Three authors in particular have written in this vein. In 1921, Charles Eliot was perhaps the first to suggest a northwest Asian influence on (and possible origin for) Mahāyāna. Although he notes that many features of Mahāyāna are also present in Hinduism—thus ruling out a foreign origin for Mahāyāna—he does indicate that some peculiar features of Mahāyāna have more in common with Persian religion than Indian. Following the line of inquiry begun by Sylvain Lévi, who argued for a Tokharian origin of the *bodhisattva* Mañjuśrī,[18] Eliot points to the similarities between the Mahāyāna Buddha, Amitābha, and the Zoroastrian god Ahura Mazda. He writes that both Ahura Mazda and Amitābha are deities residing in a paradise of light. In both cults, the practitioner is led to this paradise of light after reciting the name of the deity. Finally, Eliot remarks on the homophony between the names of Amitābha's paradise (*Sukhāvatī*) and the name of Ahura Mazda's abode (*Saukavastan*).[19] He summarizes his findings as follows:

> Thus all the chief features of Amitābha's paradise are Persian: only his method of instituting it by making a vow is Buddhist. It is true that Indian imagination had conceived numerous paradises, and that the early Buddhist legend tells of the Tushita heaven. But Sukhāvatī is not like these abodes of bliss. It appeared suddenly in the history of Buddhism as something exotic, grafted adroitly on the parent trunk but sometimes overgrowing it.[20]

Almost a century later, the hypothesis of a Persian origin for Buddhas such as Amitābha and Kṣitigarbha has yet to be either confirmed or refuted as there remains so little evidence for a cult of either of these Buddhas in India.[21]

In 1954 Etienne Lamotte offered his own study of the geographic provenance of Mahāyāna.[22] Lamotte considers the evidence from the *Kathāvatthu,* from Candrakīrti, and from the Tibetan doxographers Tāranātha and Buston, each of whom locate early Mahāyāna in Andhra Pradesh. Lamotte finds reasons to reject all this evidence. Lingering on the question of Nāgārjuna's place of residence, he considers and then rejects a south Indian origin.[23] Lamotte then turns to the northwest and shows that Mahāyāna texts, such as the *Mañjuśrīmūlakalpa,* the *Mahākaruṇāpuṇḍarīka,* and the *Mahāprajñāpāramitopadeśa* (which, at this point in his career, he believed was composed by Nāgārjuna), all contain specific references to the geography and peoples of northwestern and central Asia. He notes that despite the numerous traditions placing Nāgārjuna in the south, the *Mahāprajñāpāramitopadeśa* was clearly written in the north,[24] suggesting that we take seriously Kalhaṇa's *Rājataraṅgiṇī* and its placement of Nāgārjuna in Kashmir.[25] Finally, Lamotte surveys the records of Faxian and Xuanzang, emphasizing that, "One can no longer doubt the important role played by the Kuṣāṇa states in the formation of the Mahāyāna if one is willing to take a good look at the census of the monasteries and the monks drafted at the beginning of the fifth century by Faxian and of the seventh century by Xuanzang."[26] Lamotte combs through the travel accounts of these two pilgrims to tabulate the results of their census. His numbers reveal a predominance of Mahāyānists in the north and virtually none south of Magadha.

The last scholar under discussion here whose work sheds light on the geographic concentration of Mahāyāna is Xinru Liu, who explores the connections between Roman trade with China and the development of Buddhism. Liu cites a passage from the *Mahāvastu* that mentions "seven jewels": "*suvaṇa* (gold), *rūpya* (silver), *vaiḍūryā* (lapis lazuli), *sphāṭika* (crystal or quartz), *muktā* (pearl), *lohitikā* (a red precious stone or coral), *musāragalva* (ammonite, agate or coral)."[27] These texts also mention silk, which at that point could have only come from China. In addition to silk, she mentions coral (of Roman manufacture) and lapis (the only lapis lazuli deposits are in Afghanistan)—commodities whose respective provenances describe the arc of an ancient trade route between Rome and China. She argues that all seven items were among the luxury goods traded between Rome and China during the Kuṣana dynasty. On this route, the later Kuṣanas became wealthy by acting as middlemen transferring goods from central Asia, through Kashmir, Taxila, and finally to Barygaza on the coast of Gujarat. This route allowed the Romans to circumvent the Sassanian empire and trade their goods through Ethiopia. Although these items are not found exclusively in Mahāyāna *sūtras,* they play a prominent role in Mahāyāna *sūtras* (Liu cites the *Saddharmapuṇḍarīka,* in particular), suggesting that Mahāyāna *sūtras* containing references to these items were composed somewhere along that route and addressed to an audience for whom these commodities would be significant. This would place the composition of these *sūtras* in the corridor from central Asia, through Afghanistan or Kashmir, Taxila, Nāsik, and on to Barygaza.

To summarize, the scholarly consensus seems to be that Mahāyāna had not developed into a fully independent Buddhist institution in the first few centuries of the Common Era. On the contrary, it either existed as a movement within established Buddhist sects or in sectors of society outside of Buddhist institutions altogether (i.e., among the laity or as "forest monks"). The consensus also seems to be that Mahāyāna began as a movement in the northwest and moved southward as it developed. To further ground this consensus, I will review the evidence from four sources central to the study of early Mahāyāna: Mahāyāna *sūtras,* inscriptions, Chinese pilgrims' accounts, and Buddhist doxographies. In order to avoid the complications involved in defining Mahāyāna by identifying a few characteristic features, the discussion here is limited to evidence in which the word "Mahāyāna" is actually used. My concern in this chapter is not to define Mahāyāna, but to attempt to reveal something of its institutional configuration, prominence and geographical spread.

To the social contexts proposed by Schopen, Hirakawa, and Ray this chapter adds a fourth context that is crucial to our understanding of Mahāyāna sources, in general, and those relating to Nāgārjuna, specifically. The evidence suggests that the status of some Mahāyānists may have changed around the fifth century, when it appears that they began to occupy more privileged positions in selected monasteries. The implications of Mahāyāna's early embeddedness, its spread and its subsequent emergence are developed in subsequent chapters.

Sūtras

The hypothesis that Mahāyāna was embedded in Buddhist *nikāyas* is supported by the Mahāyāna *sūtras* themselves. The very earliest Mahāyāna *sūtras* translated into Chinese by Lokakṣema (working between 169 and 189 C.E.) do not appear to be the works of one *sect* opposing another. Examining the contents of these eleven texts, Paul Harrison writes that the movement responsible for these texts refers to itself as "Mahāyāna" only rarely. In these texts, the term "mahāyāna" occurs only about twenty times.[28] Equally rare is the term *bodhisattvayāna,* and the term *hīnayāna* is used even less frequently (a total of four times). Furthermore, when these texts are compared, something other than sectarian identity appears to be at stake. Harrison concludes that the distinctions they are primarily concerned with are not sectarian but, rather, doctrinal.

> The rarity of the terms *mahāyāna* and *bodhisattvayāna* already invites the conclusion that at this stage there is no rigid division of the Buddhist saṅgha into two hostile camps to the extent that the modern understanding of the terms "'Mahāyāna" and "Hīnayāna" implies. . . . Rather than speak of the Mahāyāna, they chose to address themselves to those substantive issues which we have come to associate with that movement, i.e., the doctrines of emptiness (*śūnyatā*), the perfection of wisdom (*prajñāpāramitā*), and the five other perfections, skill-in-means (*upāyakauśalya*) and, above all, the career of the bodhisattva, the aspirant to awakening or buddhahood.[29]

Contra Ray, many Mahāyāna *sūtras* seem to be perfectly comfortable with settled monastic life. For examples, we might turn to the *Maitreya Mahāsiṃhanāda Sūtra,*[30] the *Ugradattaparipṛcchā,* or the *Upāliparipṛcchā*—each of which seem to *assume* settled monastic life. The *Ratnarāśi Sūtra*[31] not only depicts Mahāyāna as thoroughly ensconced in monasteries, it also presents the forest-dwelling monk as holding an important position *in the monastery itself.*[32] Finally, Hirakawa himself points out that by the time of the *Bodhisattvabhūmi,* it was assumed that Mahāyānists were taking monastic (*prātimokṣa*) vows *before* taking the bodhisattva vow.[33] Hirakawa explains this away by asserting that Mahāyānists moved into the monasteries later in the movement. However, Shizuka Sasaki has taken Hirakawa to task on this point and has demonstrated exhaustively that, although Mahāyāna texts criticize *śrāvakas,* none of the Mahāyāna texts Hirakawa presents criticize the *bhikṣus* of sectarian Buddhism.[34] Sasaki argues that, whereas Mahāyāna texts pit *śrāvakas* against *bodhisattvas,* Hirakawa is wrong to equate the former with *bhikṣus* and the latter with the laity. Given this problem with Hirakawa's argument, we are left to assume that the term *bodhisattva* in early Mahāyāna texts may include both monks and laypeople.

Even if one asserts the monastic context of early Mahāyāna, there is no reason to deny the existence of other contexts. It is undeniable that the *sūtras* cited by Hirakawa and Ray distinguish between the *bodhisattvas* and monks, and others may stress an ascetic life outside the monasteries. Although both Ray and Hirakawa argue that, over time, Mahāyāna moved into the monasteries, this does not preclude some Mahāyānists from living in monasteries, while others were forest-dwellers and still others were laypeople. Mahāyāna was probably never unitary, but differed from region to region. Indeed, many scholars have suggested that each Mahāyāna *sūtra* may represent a distinct "Mahāyāna" community. According to Hajime Nakamura:

> Unlike the various recensions of the Hīnayāna canon, which were virtually closed by the early centuries of the common era and which shared, at least ideally, a common structure . . . the Mahāyāna scriptures were composed in a variety of disparate social and religious environments over the course of several centuries, diverge widely from each other in content and outlook, and were in many cases meant to stand as individual works representing (it has been conjectured) rivals to the entire Hīnayāna corpus.[35]

In this reading, *sūtras* such as the *Saddharmapuṇḍarīka* may well be the work of communities that actually were embattled, while the *Ratnarāśi sūtra* was produced and used by a monastic community in which there was little tension, and the *Raṣṭrapālaparipṛcchā* was produced by a community of forest-dwellers.

Location

The sheer number of Mahāyāna *sūtras* combined with the enormous difficulties involved in determining the geographic origin of texts precludes any sweeping claims about the northern origins of Mahāyāna based on the provenance of Mahāyāna *sūtras*. The best that we can say is that several prominent Mahāyāna *sūtras* betray a northwestern origin. In addition to the *sūtras* mentioned by Lamotte and the Amitābha, Kṣitigarbha, and Mañjuśrī texts discussed by Eliot and Lévi could be added those texts mentioning the products of trade with China. A cursory list of Mahāyāna *sūtras* that mention either the "seven jewels" or one of the trade items manufactured outside India during the second century (such as silk or coral) includes the *Saddharmapuṇḍarīka*, the *Pitaputrasamāgama*, the *Bodhisattvapiṭaka*, the *Tathāgataguhya Sūtra*, the *Śatasāhasrika Prajñāpāramitā*, and the *Aṣṭāsāhasrikā Prajñāpāramitā*. This list *sūtras* is not exhaustive, but it suggests a loose correlation between the provenance of Mahāyāna authors and the northern trade route between Rome and China.

The most often cited counterevidence to a northern provenance of Mahāyāna is the *Gaṇḍavyūha* chapter of the *Avataṃsaka Sūtra*. According to Nalinaksa Dutt:

> The Gaṇḍavyuha, a work of about the 2nd or the 3rd century A.D., speaks of Dhānyākara as a great city of Daksinapatha and a seat of Mañjuśrī, who lived in an extensive forest at Mala-dhvājavyūhacaitya and converted a large number of Nāgas and other inhabitants of that place.[36]

In one of his early works, B. S. L. Hanumanathan Rao cites this passage from Dutt and uses it to argue for a southern stronghold of Mahāyāna in Andhra Pradesh.

> The *Gaṇḍavyūha* of about the 3rd century A.D. informs that Mañjuśrī lived in a monastery at Dhānyakaṭaka and converted a large number of Nāgas and others of that place to Buddhism. It further mentions that a certain Sudhana visited a number of places which were seats of Bodhisattva practices. Most of them are in South India and the most important of them was Dhānyakaṭaka . . . From these accounts the following points become clear: (i) Mañjuśrī lived for a long time in Andhra and Dhānyakaṭaka was the centre of his activi-

ties. (ii) Dhānyakaṭaka and other places in Andhra, probably under the influence of Mañjuśrī, became the seats of Bodhisattva practices.[37]

Using the *Gaṇḍavyūha* to argue for the early presence of Mahāyāna in Andhra Pradesh presents many problems. First, the word "Dhānyakaṭaka" occurs nowhere in the *Gaṇḍavyūha,* nor does Dutt claim that it does. Dutt points out that the Sanskrit text describes a city named "Dhāny*ākara*" not "Dhānya*kaṭaka*." Nevertheless, Lamotte makes the same identification as Rao when he writes: "Mañjuśrī appears in the Deccan near Dhanyākara (*Kiao tch'eng* [覺城], or *Fou tch'eng* [福城]), the present day Dharanikot, in the district of Guntur."[38] Although the eagerness to identify the places mentioned in the *Gaṇḍavyūha* with archaeological sites is understandable, we have to proceed with caution. In a more recent discussion of Dhānyakaṭaka, Rao notes:

> The earliest epigraphical reference to the place as *Dhaṃnakaḍa* occurs in the 3ṛd century B.C. The other variants of the term are *Dhaṃnakaḍaka, Dhānakaḍaka—Dhānyakaṭaka*. Pallava Simhavarman's inscription mentions *Dhānyaghaṭa*. Medieval inscriptions refer to the place as *Śrīdhanyakaṭaka, Śrīdhānyaghata* and *Dhānyāṅkapura*. *Mañjuśrī Mūlatantra* prefixes the honorific and calls it as *Śrīdhānyakaṭaka,* whereas *Sēkōddēsaṭīka* epitomizes the term simply into *Śrīdhnya*.[39]

Although historically there have been variations of the name "Dhānyakaṭaka," the variations of the first part of the name revolve around Sanskrit versus Prakrit pronunciations of either *dhanya* (Prakrit, *dhaṃna*) meaning "bringing or bestowing wealth, rich . . . fortunate,"[40] or *dhānya,* meaning "produce of the fields, a share of which was payable to the king or landlord."[41] *Kaṭaka* denotes a camp or capital.[42] Thus the name might be translated as something like "the Fortunate Capital" or "the Capital of Grain-taxes" (I am sure that this sounded more appealing in the second century), while medieval inscriptions refer to it as "the Pot [*ghaṭa*] of Grain-Taxes." "Dhānyākara" (the Place of Grain-Taxes) does not ever appear to have been used by the locals as a variant for Dhānyakaṭaka. Granted, Dhānyākara and Dhānyakaṭaka do sound similar. This homophony might be significant if all the place names mentioned in the *Gaṇḍavyūha* corresponded to actual place names. The author was clearly familiar with south India, and even if a few place names are invented, they are made up by someone with knowledge of the region. For example, the text mentions a district called Nalayur, which is clearly a Tamil word (*nalla* ["beautiful" or "good"] + *ūr* ["place"]).[43] This may plausibly be identified with the ancient city of

Nallūr in Tamil Nadu. The problem is that many of the other places mentioned in the *sūtra* appear to be fictional, and even the southern direction that Sudhana travels seems to be more symbolic than geographic. Sudhana is always told to travel southward and yet he somehow ends up in Magadha *after* visiting Laṅka.

The problems are compounded by the Chinese translations. Two Chinese translations of the *Gaṇḍavyūha* date from the late fourth or early fifth centuries. The first, *Luoma gajing* 羅摩伽經, is a partial translation by a Chinese monk named Shengjian in which the passage in question is absent. The second occurs as the last chapter of the *Avataṃsaka Sūtra* translated by Buddhabhadra, a monk from central India, sometime between 408 and 419 C.E.[44] When we turn to the section in question, we find that Buddhabhadra translates the place name as 覺城 (*juecheng*, the "City of Realization").[45] Although it is tempting to regard the extant Sanskrit text as original (as Lamotte does) and to simply assume that 覺城 is the proper translation of Dhānyakaṭaka, it is difficult to see how this could have happened. In Buddhabhadra's translation, 城 could translate either *ākara* or *kaṭaka*. But the character 覺 has nothing whatsoever to do with grain, donation, or taxes. Neither the meaning nor the etymology nor the phonology of 覺 has anything in common with *dhānya*. All its definitions relate to cognitive events, like learning or understanding. Unless the character in Buddhabhadra's translation can be explained as a mistake, we have no choice but to assume that Buddhabhadra's original read something like "Bodhipura" (probably a made-up name) instead of "Dhānyakaṭaka." It is not until Śikṣānanda's eighth-century translation that we find a possible match for Dhānyakaṭaka.His translation (in T. 279) translates the place name as *fucheng* (福城). Here, 福 works well for either "fortunate" or a gift or a donation.[46] Hence, it is likely that the name Dhānyākara began to appear in manuscripts only after the eighth century. Although the third-century author may have had his or her eye on south India, it is unlikely that Dhānyakaṭaka was in any way singled out by the author of the *Gaṇḍavyūha* as a stronghold of Mahāyāna.

Mahāyāna *sūtras* present us with not only literary evidence about early Mahāyāna but physical evidence as well. The Mahāyāna *sūtras* themselves give the impression that Mahāyānists were numerous. This picture is tempered by the archaeological record. The physical record of Mahāyāna manuscripts suggests that, although Mahāyāna may have begun in the Kuṣāṇa era, it may not have become established until approximately the fifth century. Kuṣāṇa-era Buddhist manuscripts have been found spanning the length of the Silk Route from Merv in the present-day Turkmenistan, Haḍḍa and Bāmiyān in Afghanistan, Qizil, Subaši and Šorčuq, on the northern route and around the Takla Makan desert, and at Kohmārī Mazar and Niya on the southern route.[47] Most of these manuscripts have been *abhidharma* texts, *kavya* works, fragments of the *prātimokṣa,* or *sūtras* and their commentaries.[48] Yet, of all the Kuṣāṇa-era manuscripts found on the Silk Route, only one manuscript of a Mahāyāna *sūtra* has so far been found.

This lone Mahāyāna *sūtra* manuscript is a copy of the *Aṣṭasāhasrikā Prajñāpāramitā* smuggled out of Bāmiyān, now in the Schøyen Manuscript collection. According to Lore Sander, the paleography of this piece places it in the second half of the third century due to the similarity of its letters to those of the succeeding Gupta type.[49] This is the earliest manuscript identified so far from this collection. The collection of manuscripts to which this piece belongs contains a continuous series of paleographic types including the "square-upright" Kuṣāṇa Brahmi of the *Aṣṭasāhasrikā* (third century), the early western Gupta style of the fourth century, and the Gilgit/Bāmiyān type I of the fifth or sixth century. The collection also contains several other Mahāyāna texts that Sander considers a script "introducing the local development to Gilgit/Bāmiyān type I" (fifth to sixth centuries).[50]

Although more Mahāyāna manuscripts may eventually turn up from the Bāmiyān region, the absence of any Mahāyāna *sūtras* elsewhere on the Silk Route before the fifth century is remarkable, and its paucity requires an explanation. The earliest Mahāyāna *sūtras* translated into Chinese refer to their own copying and preservation in books. The monks who brought the first Mahāyāna *sūtras* to Luoyang in the second century must have acquired or memorized or at least transported Mahāyāna *sūtras* in the same regions where other Buddhist monastic collections have been unearthed. It is therefore difficult to believe that there were no written Mahāyāna texts in this region before the third century. Why, then, do we find no Mahāyāna books from this period when we do find other Buddhist books? Since other *sūtras* do exist in the collection of manuscripts recently acquired by the British Library, dating to the same period, the absence of corresponding Mahāyāna *sūtras* at these sites becomes more poignant. According to Richard Salomon:

> Although it would be premature at this point to draw detailed conclusions about the doctrinal positions of the tradition represented by the British Library fragments, it is worth mentioning that the preliminary studies carried out to date reveal no clear traces of Mahāyāna ideas or tendencies . . . In general, the fragments seem to concern issues and subjects that are typical of "mainstream" (i.e., pre- or non-

> Mahāyāna) Indian Buddhism. . . . on the whole it appears that the manuscripts come from a time and place in which Mahāyāna ideas had not come into play at all, or at least were not being reflected in scholastic texts. This issue is of particular interest because these texts come from a period and region—first-century A.D. Gandhāra—which, according to some views at least, played a central role in the origins of Mahāyāna. . . . as matters stand at this point, the British Library scrolls do not offer any support for the hypothesis of a relatively early origin for Mahāyāna Buddhism.[51]

There are a number of sites along the Silk Route whose manuscript collections cover the same range of paleographic types as that found in the Schøyen collection. For example, Qizil near Kuča on the northern route contained Buddhist manuscripts dating from the second through the eighth centuries. The catalogues of the German expeditions to this site include a total of four identifiable Mahāyāna manuscripts—three unidentified fragments (one in early Turkestani Brahmī, one in northern Turkestani Brahmī, one unlisted), and part of the *Kaśyapaparivārta* in southern Turkestani Brahmī. All are written on paper and are probably no earlier than the sixth century.[52] To the east, at Šorčuq near Qarashar we find the same pattern. The manuscript remains recovered from that site date from as early as the third century and form a continuous series stretching into the eighth century, when the site closes. Yet the earliest Mahāyāna manuscript found at the site is a copy of the *Saṃdhinirmocana Sūtra* dating from the late fifth century.[53] Fourteen other Mahāyāna manuscripts have been identified from that site, and here, too, none of them date back earlier than the sixth century.

In fact, apart from Bāmiyān, no Mahāyāna *sūtra* manuscripts dating from before the fifth century C.E. have been recovered from any of the sites on the Silk Route where Mahāyāna manuscripts have so far been recovered—Gilgit, Šorčuq, Toyoq, Qizil, Sängim, Xočo, and Murtuq on the sorthern route[54] and at Damdān-Uiliq, Khādalik, Niya, Endere, and Dunhuang on the southern route.[55] The Bāmiyān manuscript seems to be the exception to the rule. By contrast, the fifth and sixth centuries appear to have been a watershed for the production of Mahāyāna manuscripts. In addition to the *Saṃdhinirmocana Sūtra* mentioned above, a fifth- or sixth-century Sanskrit manuscript of the *Saddharmapuṇḍarīka Sūtra* has been discovered in Xinjiang province, China.[56] Some important Mahāyāna *sūtras* have also been recovered in Old Khotanese translation. Among Mahāyāna works surviving in Old Khotanese, Oktor Skjærvø lists: the *Anantamukhanirhāra-dhāraṇī*, the *Bhaiṣajyaguruvaiḍūryaprabharāja*, the

Karmavibhaṅga, the *Kāśyapaparivarta*, the *Saṅghāṭa sūtra*, the *Śūraṅgamasamādhi sūtra*, the *Suvarṇabhāsottama*, the *Vimalakīrtinirdeśa sūtra*, and the *Book of Zambasta* (an original Khotanese composition, not a translation).[57] Indeed, one wonders whether a cultural shift signaled by the shift from the use of Prakrit (an Indic language) for everyday interactions to Khotanese ("close to the 'Old Middle Iranian' type")[58] in the fifth century might have played a role in the general acceptance of Mahāyāna in that region.

Absence of evidence is not, of course, evidence of absence. Countless manuscripts have presumably been destroyed over the centuries. Furthermore, many of the manuscripts in the central Asian manuscript collections have yet to be identified, and it is possible that more Mahāyāna manuscripts like the Bāmiyān *Prajñāpāramitā* text may turn up. If and when that happens, the following observations may have to be revised. Nevertheless, the relative dearth of Mahāyāna manuscripts in existing collections would still require an explanation. If one asserts that Mahāyāna manuscripts existed at these sites, but were subsequently destroyed, then there must be an explanation as to why Mahāyāna *sūtras* were *selectively* destroyed. If more Mahāyāna manuscripts come to light, then we must still explain why Mahāyāna appears in so few monastic libraries and not in the majority of such libraries. Again, there may be a great deal of evidence that we do not have, but we can only construct our theories on the evidence that we do have.

Inscriptions

One salient fact that all three hypotheses discussed at the beginning of the chapter attempt to explain is the virtual invisibility of Mahāyāna in the archaeological record. As mentioned above, plenty of Mahāyāna *sūtras* were composed before the second century, so this situation stands in stark contrast to the dearth of Mahāyāna manuscripts that have been found.

The same situation applies to inscriptions. Inscriptions using the word "Mahāyāna" raise almost as many questions as they answer. According to Gregory Schopen:

> epigraphically—the "beginning of the Mahāyāna in India is not documentable until the 2nd century A.D., and that even as "late" as that it was still an extremely limited minority movement that left almost no mark on Buddhist epigraphy or art and was still clearly embedded in the old established purposes of earlier Buddhist groups. What is even more surprising still is the additional fact that even after its initial

appearance in the public domain in the 2nd century it appears to have remained an extremely limited minority movement—if it remained at all—that attracted absolutely no documented public or popular support for at least two more centuries. It is again a demonstrable fact that anything even approaching popular support for the Mahāyāna cannot be documented until the 4th/5th century A.D., and even then the support is overwhelmingly monastic, not lay, donors.[59]

The second-century document to which Schopen refers is a lone inscription from Mathurā dated to 104 C.E. that labels the image on which it appears as "Amitābha Buddha." The inscription does not mention Mahāyāna by name nor have there been any other examples of a cult of Amitābha elsewhere in Indian art of this period.[60]

Although Schopen's statement about the lack of support for Mahāyāna still stands per se, it needs to be nuanced in light of more recent work by Richard Salomon. The earliest inscription actually mentioning Mahāyāna by name occurs in a recently discovered Kharoṣṭhī inscription from Endere in modern-day Xinjiang. Richard Salomon notes: "it is fairly likely that the king [referred to in the inscription] was Aṃgoka and that the inscription was written during the earlier part of his reign, that is, sometime around the middle of the third century C.E."[61] Salomon translates the inscription as follows:

> In the year . . . of the lord, the great king, the king [of kings, the great, victorious, pious . . .], crusher of his enemies, who is his own army, whose (name is [well]-received), who is wor[shipped by gods and men], who has set forth on the Great Vehicle [mahayana], who is fixed in the true dharma, of great majesty, [the great king Aṃgoka] . . . The names of the supervisors [?] of ? [are] Okaripa, Śirṣa, [and] Kutre.[62]

Since Aṃgoka, "who was probably the most powerful of [the kings of Shan-shan] had . . . set forth on the Great Vehicle," Salomon concludes, *contra* Schopen "there is every reason to think that the Mahāyāna, rather then being a persecuted heterodox sect, was prominent and enjoyed royal patronage in Shan-shan."[63]

Salomon finds confirmation for this suspicion in a letter inscribed on wood found at Niya on the southern Silk Route dating to the mid-third century.[64] It dates to a few decades after the Aṃgoka inscription[65] and belongs roughly to the same period as the *Aṣṭāsāhasrikā Prajñāpāramitā* manuscript of the Schøyen collection. According to Burrow's translation:

> At the feet of the great *cozbo* Ṣamasena, beloved of men and gods, honoured by men and gods, blessed with a good name, who has set forth in the Mahāyāna, who is of infinitely pleasing aspect, the *tasuca* . . . makes obeisance, and sends the health of his divine body, much, immeasurable. And for that reason first I am pleased that . . . hearing that, you should be pleased. This is what I have to say: The tax there . . . Pideya came . . . called Suvaṃniya . . . here again . . . this matter.[66]

Burrow stops translating halfway through line six. The rest of the line reads *u tha suvaṃniya nama sutra*. We can only guess at the import of the letter, but a few of its elements are suggestive. First, this is a letter from a local official to a Great Governor (*cozbo*) in Kroraina—hence, a letter from a layperson to another layperson. The recipient of the letter is one who has "entered into Mahāyāna" (*mayāyāna saṃprasti*[*thi*]*ta*). The sender refers to a tax and then twice uses the word *Suvaṃniya,* the second time in the context of a *Suvaṃniya nama sutra.* Although, as F. W. Thomas points out, there is a *sūtra* in the Tibetan *bka' 'gyur* named *gser gyi mdo*[67] (*Suvarṇa Sūtra*),[68] it is probable that this passage refers to a version of the *Suvarṇabhāsottama Sūtra* (*Sūtra* of Golden Light), an early Mahāyāna *sūtra*. The *Suvarṇabhāsottama Sūtra* contains rather lengthy sections of advice to kings, and it is possible at least that the author of this letter is referring to the discussion of the king's responsibility to uphold the law to stress the need to uphold the local tax law.[69] Since none of the other letters at Niya indicate that the author is himself as a Mahāyānist, we may tentatively assume that Mahāyāna texts such as the *sūtra* mentioned above were generally known in certain lay circles even outside the groups that considered themselves Mahāyānists.

The last of the early sources relating to Mahāyāna in the far north occurs in a fragment of an Avadāna found in the Schøyen collection. According to Salomon, this Sanskrit fragment "is written in northwestern Gupta Brahmī of about the fourth century A.D.,"[70] and thus is later than the Niya and Endere records. This fragment refers to the Kuṣāṇa emperor Huvikṣa, as one who "has set forth on the Great Vehicle." Again, Salomon sees in this fragment the possibility that Mahāyāna had secured official patronage in the northern regions.

> Thus, the new fragment almost certainly provides, to my knowledge for the first time, an explicit statement to the effect that a Kuṣāṇa emperor was—or more precisely, was claimed as—an adherent of Mahāyāna ideals, and this in a text which may have been composed during

> the Kuṣāṇa period, or at the latest, not long after it. The only other early documentary reference to a king in such terms, namely in the aforementioned Endere inscription, dates from around the middle of the third century or slightly later, and hence is likely to be roughly contemporary with the text represented in the Schøyen fragment. . . . Since the Endere inscription comes from a culture which was within the sphere of influence, if not under the direct domination, of the Kuṣāṇas . . . these two new references imply a pattern of royal adherence to Mahāyāna ideals during the later part of the Kuṣāṇa period, possibly dating back, at least, to the time of Huvikṣa.
>
> In this connection it is interesting to recall that the earliest clear and unambiguous epigraphic reference to Amitābha, and hence, by implication, to the Mahāyāna, comes in an inscription from Mathurā dated during the reign of Huviṣka, in the twenty-sixth year of the era founded by Kaniṣka. . . . This convergence around Huviṣka of early allusions to Mahāyāna concepts might be mere coincidence, but new material seems rather to suggest that the time of Huviṣka was a pivotal one in the development of the Mahāyāna.[71]

We now have five examples of early Mahāyāna artifacts from the second and third centuries; the Amitābha statue from Mathurā, the *Prajñāpāramitā* manuscript from Bāmiyān, the Aṃogha inscription from Xinjiang, the Niya letter, and the Bāmiyān *avadāna* mentioning Huvikṣa. These three artifacts suggest, at a minimum, that Mahāyāna existed in three places at that time: Mathurā, Bāmiyān, and the ancient kingdom of Shan-shan. What can we make of the evidence so far? On the one hand, Salomon (albeit tentatively) points in the direction to a pan–northern frontier patronage of Mahāyāna. On the other hand, we are still left with the fact that Mahāyāna manuscript collections are noticeably lacking in monasteries in this region. Furthermore, the two artifacts from Shan-shan identify two laypeople as Mahāyānists. There are no inscriptions indicating monks or *śramāṇas* to be Mahāyānists. The only evidence for monks with a Mahāyāna affiliation remains in the Bāmiyān manuscripts. As for the Bāmiyān *avadāna* fragment, Salomon quite rightly points out that the document tells us that the author wanted the audience to believe that Huvikṣa was a Mahāyānist, not that Huvikṣa necessarily thought of himself in that manner. Until more evidence comes to light, we are better off accepting the assertion that Huvikṣa was a Mahāyānist as the wishful thinking of its author.

For their part, inscriptions from India, Pakistan, and central Asia have yet to reveal a Mahāyāna monastery before the fifth century. This confirms the thesis of Gregory Schopen, who demonstrates that the archaeological record shows no evidence that monks received any donations *as Mahāyānists* until the fifth century. Only at that time is the word used in votive inscriptions. Furthermore, one is struck by just how few such inscriptions there are even among later inscriptions. After searching through a rather voluminous collection of archaeological reports from the nineteenth and twentieth centuries, Schopen could find only fourteen inscriptions in which "Mahāyāna" is mentioned by name.[72] The inscriptions are: one from Ajaṇṭā,[73] one from Nālanda,[74] four from Bihar,[75] two from Bengal,[76] one from Mādhya Pradesh,[77] three from Sārnāth,[78] one from Valabhī,[79] and one from Chittagong.[80] Out of these, the inscription from Ajaṇṭā can no longer be considered as Mahāyānist in light recent work on it by Marilyn Leese and Richard Cohen.[81] The inscription from Nālanda dates from the time of Mahipāla I (r. 977–1027 C.E.) and records the gift of a *paramopāsaka* originally from Kauśāmbhī who "traversed in the great Mahāyāna."[82] The four Bihar inscriptions are all from the eleventh and twelfth centuries. Of the two Bengal inscriptions, one is early (506 C.E.) and one is late.[83] The inscription from Gopalpur, Mādhya Pradesh, again dates from the eleventh to twelfth centuries. The inscription from Sārnāth is from the eleventh century, while the inscription from Valabhī in Gujarat dates to 404 C.E.

Although it is difficult to know how much we can infer from these inscriptions, some provisional observations can be made on the basis of Schopen's sample. First, it is striking how few inscriptions bearing the word "Mahāyāna" have been discovered out of the thousands of inscriptions found in India. Schopen did not look at every inscription discovered in India, but he did examine a large sample, representing over a thousand years and covering most states of India, Pakistan, and Bangladesh. If the word "Mahāyāna" had been prominent in inscriptions in any of these areas, he would most likely have been aware of it. Hence, it is probably not unreasonable to state that inscriptions bearing the word "Mahāyāna" were rare.

The second observation concerns the relative ages of the Mahāyāna inscriptions. Although most of our inscriptions date from the tenth through the twelfth centuries, only two votive inscriptions date from the fifth to sixth centuries. The earliest of these inscriptions was found at Valabhī (Vallabhipur in Gujarat). It records a donation by Dharasena IV from 404 C.E. Bhandarkar translates as follows:

> Shrī Dharasena, the great Māheshvarā, the great lord, the king of kings . . . [etc.] commands all whom it may concern: Be it known to

> you that for the increase of the religious merit of my mother and father. I have (assigned) to the assembly of the reverend mendicant priests of the Mahāyāna (school) coming from the four quarters to the monastery constructed by Divira-pati Skandabhaṭa in the village of Yodāvaka in Hestava prāhāra in Surāshtra, the four divisions of the same village of Yodhāvaka: viz. three for the purpose of [providing] clothing, food, [means of] sleeping, sitting . . . and medicine; for the purpose of [providing] the means of worshipping and washing the glorious Buddhas.[84]

Unfortunately, Bhandarkar does not include the text of the inscription in his article, but we can assume that the phrase "the assembly of the reverend mendicant priests of the Mahāyāna (school) coming from the four directions" represents something like *āryamāhāyānika-caturdiśabhikṣusaṅgha*. The second earliest Mahāyāna grant (505 C.E.—this one from Tippera, Bengal) similarly records a king making a gift of land to a *Māhāyānika (?)–Vaivarttika-bhikṣusaghanām*.[85] The artifacts from Shan-shan might provide the earliest physical evidence that anyone considered himself a Mahāyānist, but only in these two inscriptions do we find evidence that monasteries were known by their benefactors as Mahāyānist.

Much of the evidence that Schopen culls from paleographic evidence was leveled as a critique of Hirakawa's argument that Mahāyāna began and was fostered as an *exclusively* lay movement revolving around *stūpas*. Of all of the inscriptions using the word "Mahāyāna," the earliest two use the word to describe the monastic *recipient* (either an individual or a monastery), while the later inscriptions use the word to describe the *donor* (usually a layperson). In fact, the earliest occurrence of the word is used to describe monks and only later described the lay donors. Furthermore, if the laity had given birth to Mahāyāna in and around the *stūpas*, why do inscriptions recording donations by the laity on *stūpas* make no mention of Mahāyāna until quite late? The inscriptions that Schopen examines even call into question Hirakawa's contention that worship of *stūpas* was primarily the provenance of the laity.

Inscriptions from *stūpas* recording the names and titles of donors begin to appear in India as early as 150 B.C.E. If Hirakawa were correct and *stūpa* worship were primarily the concern of the laity, then we should expect virtually all the donations to come from the laity. Yet, in 1985, Schopen demonstrated that a significant percentage of donations made to *stūpas* (he gives the example of 40 percent of the Barhut inscriptions and 40 percent of the Kharoṣṭhī inscriptions edited by Konow)[86] were made by Buddhist monks and nuns. Indeed, donations to *stūpas* by monks and nuns have been recorded throughout India. By Hirakawa's reasoning, there should be no such donations. Finally, in a 1975 article Schopen demonstrates that—contrary to Hirakawa—there are Mahāyāna *sūtras* that elevate what he calls "the cult of the book" (i.e., worship of a Mahāyāna *sūtra*) *over* worship of a *stūpa*.[87] According to this reading, many of the early Mahāyāna *sūtras* were actually in competition with *stūpa* worship. Hence, while the Endere and Niya inscriptions suggest that Mahāyāna was accepted among the laity, there is no corroborating evidence for this in other inscriptions from the laity.

Earlier Mahāyānists? The Śākyabhikṣu Debate

A point should be made here concerning inscriptions mentioning a group called *Śākyabhikṣu/Śākyabhikṣunī*. Although that the earliest inscriptions mentioning Mahāyāna by name occur only in the sixth century, Schopen claimed that Mahāyānists may have gone under another name before that time.

> in none of the inscriptions which refer to Mahāyāna by name does the name Mahāyāna occur alone: with one exception, it is always joined either with the title *śākyabhikṣu* (three times) or with the title *paramopāsaka* (nine times). We can also restate the same set of facts by saying that twelve of our inscriptions explicitly call both *śākyabhikṣus* and *paramopāsakas* "followers of the Mahāyāna" (*mahāyānānuyāyin,* etc.) and that these are the only individuals to be so called. Second, in none of the approximately forty inscriptions in which the names of the various non-Mahāyāna schools—Sarvāstivādin, Mahāsāṃghika, etc.—occur does the title *śākyabhikṣu* or the title *paramopāsaka* occur.[88]

Schopen concludes that, even though the name Mahāyāna only appears at the beginning of the sixth century, the same group that called itself "Mahāyāna" in the sixth century also called itself *Śākyabhikṣu/-bhikṣuṇīs* or *paramopāsaka/-opāsikas*. Although this places the first public appearance of Mahāyāna a century earlier, the evidence regarding these inscriptions still belies Hirakawa's hypothesis. In a 1985 article, Schopen notes that, of all the inscriptions bearing the above terms and recording donations to stūpas and on images, more than 70 percent were donated by monks and nuns.[89] Again, the earliest evidence concerning the term *Śākyabhikṣu* indicates a monastic context for Mahāyāna and not a lay one.

To date, the status of the *Śākyabhikṣu/Śākyabhikṣunī* has yet to be resolved. On the one hand, some inscriptions mention donations to a *Śākyabhikṣu saṅgha* where no other sect is named, suggesting that the term may have designated an independent sect in some locations. Nevertheless, Schopen's identification of the *Śākyabhikṣu* with Mahāyāna has been criticized. Tillman Vetter, in particular, has questioned Schopen's use of statistics to correlate *Śākyabhikṣu* with Mahāyāna on the grounds that his sample is far too small to support his conclusions.[90] Yao-ming Tsai points out that Schopen's identification of *Śākyabhikṣu* with Mahāyāna is based on the fact that the two words occur together in three out of fourteen inscriptions (the term *paramopāsaka,* however, occurs in conjunction with *mahāyāna* in nine of the fourteen inscriptions). On the contrary, Tsai gives an alternate explanation of the title *Śākyabhikṣu* in these inscriptions. He posits that, in those compounds, just because the term "Mahāyāna"

> tells us the *yāna* affiliation of the donor, the term Śākyabhikṣu does not necessarily do so—any more than the term "Buddhist" in the English compound "Mahāyāna-Buddhist" does . . . An understanding of the epithet Śākya aids us in further looking into the *yāna* status of the term *śākyabhikṣu.* Shih Tao-an (釋道安, 312–385), almost in the same epoch as the earliest of the extant epigraphs in question, proposed the epithet Shih (釋; Śākya) to be the surname of all ordained members of the Saṃgha regardless of their nationality, sectarian affiliation, social status, and the like—a proposal widely adopted not only in China but also in Annam (*thich*), Korea (*sŏk*) and Japan (*shaku*). The *Ekottarāgama* also attests to the practice of using the epithet *śākya* as a substitute surname. For example, it reads: "Just as, when rivers flow into the sea, they lose their respective names and distinct flavors, so the various clans, once they have left the household and entered upon the Path of the Buddha, become equally members of the Śākya clan" (T. 125, vol. 2, p. 658b–c). . . . Logically, historically and doctrinally, such epithets as *śākyabhikṣu* do not display any segmentary characteristics of the *yāna/vāda.* Instead these epithets appear to be created and used in order to transgress or minimize the segmentation within the Buddhist tradition.[91]

Richard Cohen has taken the inquiry much farther in his examination of the *Śākyabhikṣu* inscriptions at Ajaṇṭā. He argues that those who identified themselves thus saw themselves as the Buddha's adoptive sons, thereby identifying with Rāhula. Cohen argues that *Śākyabhikṣu* should be identified with the term *bodhisattva.*[92] Cohen's study is important and should lead to further inquiry along these same lines. His most recent article still does not clinch the connection between *Śākyabhikṣu* and Mahāyāna such that we could say that all *Śākyabhikṣus* were Mahāyānists. Nevertheless, he examines the relationship between these terms in the fifth-century sources. Yet, in support of Tsai's argument that *śākyabhikṣu* is not necessarily a marker of Mahāyāna affiliations, Cohen points out that Vasumitra (a Sarvāstivādin *par excellence*) is also said to be a *Śākyabhikṣu* in the preface to his *Samāyabhedoparacanacakra*.[93] Cohen points out that this attribution is lacking in the earliest translation, but it can be found in the seventh-century translations that correspond to the point when Mahāyānists began to consider Vasumitra a Mahāyānist.[94]

For our purposes, two points need to be highlighted. First, no inscriptions mentioning *Śākyabhikṣus* have been found as early as the second century. Second, it does not appear that the *Śākyabhikṣus* formed their own sect, with its own ordination lineage and *vinaya* rules. While Schopen claims that "in none of the approximately forty inscriptions in which the names of the various Nikāya schools—Sarvāstivādin, Mahāsāṅghika, etc.—occur does the title *Śākyabhikṣu* or the title *paramopāsaka* occur," Cohen has found one inscription from Ajaṇṭā where an Aparasaila monk is labeled *Śākyabhikṣu*.[95] Along these same lines, he also notes that all the *Śākyabhikṣus* at Ajaṇṭā belonged to the Mūlasarvāstivādin *nikāya*.[96] Thus the label does not appear to be an identifier of membership in a particular *nikāya,* so even if it were a marker of Mahāyāna identity, that identity did not necessarily constitute a separate institution.

Each of the three hypotheses discussed at the beginning of the chapter attempts to explain the absence of inscriptions mentioning Mahāyāna. These attempts met with varying levels of success. Hirakawa's thesis that Mahāyāna begins with the laity explains the lack of Mahāyāna inscriptions in monasteries, but fails to explain why there are no inscriptions using the word at *stūpas*. Ray's hypothesis that Mahāyānists were forest-monks circumvents this problem by placing Mahāyānists in places where there are few inscriptions. Although Ray's point seems plausible, Schopen's explanation that Mahāyānists were an embattled minority within the monasteries fighting for recognition seems more persuasive. Mahāyānists in this scenario may have been able to write *sūtras*, but may not have had the clout to get the name of their movement carved in stone.

The evidence from inscriptions gives no indication that Mahāyāna was ever an independent institution in the way and on the scale that the other Buddhist *nikāyas* were. The Valabhī and Tippera inscriptions do, however, suggest that some Mahāyānists began to receive a degree of recognition (and money) *as Mahāyānists* at the start of the fifth century. The evidence amassed by Schopen is consistent with Mahāyāna being a movement (a rather minor one at that) taking place primarily within the monasteries. Under this interpretation, Mahāyāna was relatively invisible (archaeologically speaking) for the first few centuries because Mahāyānists did not need to receive donations *as Mahāyānists.* What Mahāyānists there were would have benefited from donations made to the *nikāya* affiliated monasteries in which they lived. It should also be pointed out that there are no inscriptions mentioning Mahāyāna by name south of the Valabhī inscription. Indeed, in the extreme south, there is no evidence of Buddhism of any kind until the fourth century.[97] Thus according to the paleographic record alone, it would appear that Mahāyāna began in central Asia (Xinjiang and Niya), relocated to the southern frontier regions of midlatitude India (Gujarat and Bengal/Bangladesh), and only later became established in more central areas like Sārnāth and Nālanda.

Chinese Pilgrims: Mahāyāna, Hīnayāna, and "Mixed" Monasteries

Viewing the paleographic record in isolation from other evidence is misleading. For example, in support of the hypothesis that Mahāyānists were also members of the various *nikāyas,* most authors have turned to the accounts of the Chinese pilgrims Faxian, Yijing, and Xuanzang, each of whom describe monasteries that were a mixture of Mahāyāna and non-Mahāyāna throughout north and central India. Further, *contra* Ray, none of these pilgrims report large numbers of Mahāyānists living in the forest.

Faxian, who traveled to India in the years 399–414 C.E., specifically mentions two Mahāyāna monasteries. The first reference occurs during his visit to Khotan, where he describes, "a monastery called Gomati, of the Mahāyāna school."[98] Legge's translation "mahāyāna *school*" is misleading for our purposes since the English "school" is sometimes used to translate 部 (*bù,* sect). The Chinese 寺 (*sì*) here simply means "A Buddhist monastery."[99] Faxian mentions another Mahāyāna monastery in Pāṭaliputra next to the Aśoka *stūpa.* Here he uses a more phonetic 摩訶衍伽藍[100] (*Mohe-yangalan,* lit. *Mahāyān* [*Saṃ*]*ghārā*[*ma*]), but the fact that he understood the term "Mahāyāna" as applicable to a physical monastic structure comes through quite clearly. If Faxian encountered this monastery between 399 and 414, then his testimony comes from the same time period as the Valabhī inscription referred to above.

Faxian's account significantly augments the information provided by the archaeological record alone. He also mentions Mahāyāna in contexts where the Mahāyānists apparently do not have their own monasteries. When Faxian traveled through 羅夷 (Luóyí, in modern-day Afghanistan), 毘荼 (Pítú, Bhida in modern-day Punjab), and 僧伽施 (Sēnggāshī, Saṅkāśya, modern-day Samkassam, near Kannauj, Uttar Pradesh), he mentions monasteries where the monks were "students of (both) Mahāyāna and Hīnayāna" (大小乘學).[101] Apparently, while some Mahāyānists lived in monasteries that could be identified as such, many shared monasteries with non-Mahāyānist monks. Where this would have been the case, we can see why Mahāyānists would not have left much of an impression in the archaeological record.

We should not make too much of Faxian's report since, although he was apparently aware of the tradition of the "eighteen Buddhist sects," he classifies the monasteries and monks whom he encounters *only* as Mahāyānist or Hīnayānist.[102] He does not make the same sectarian distinctions that we find in the archaeological record (e.g., between a Sarvāstivādin monastery and a Mahīśāsika monastery), and hence we should examine what he saw as the identifying features of Mahāyāna. In this regard, Faxian does not tell us much. He certainly did not mean that a Mahāyāna monastery is one that employs ordination and *pratimokṣa* rules distinctive of the Mahāyāna, since it is in a Mahāyāna monastery in Pāṭaliputra that he finds the copy of the *Mahāsāṅghika-vinaya,* which he later translates and which will occupy much of Chapters 3 and 4. At the Mahāyāna monastery called "Gomati," he describes a kind of *Rātha Yatra* festival centered on the image of the Buddha and Bodhisattvas, but he gives us no indication that these are distinctively Mahāyāna practices.[103] The one place where he does make a defining distinction between Mahāyānists and other Buddhists is in regard to Buddhist worship in Central India. His comments here are illuminating.

> Where a community of monks resides, they erect topes to Śāriputtra, to Mahā-maudgalyāyana, and to Ānanda, and also topes (in honour) of the Abhidharma, the Vinaya, and the *Sūtras*. . . . The bhikshuṇīs for the most part make their offerings at the tope of Ānanda. . . . The Śrāmaṇeras mostly make their offerings to Rāhula. The professors of the Abhidharma make their offerings to it; those of the Vinaya to it. Every year there is one such offering, and each class has its own day for it. Students of the mahāyāna [lit. 摩訶衍人[104] = Mahāyānists] present offerings to the Prajñā-pāramitā, to Mañjuśrī, and to Kwan-she-yin.[105]

In this description, Faxian is writing about a single community and the ritual distinction of the different textual specialists within that community. Tentatively we might suggest that a "Mahāyānist" was seen as a textual specialist—a vocation within the monastery on par with the *sūtradhāra*, *vinayadhāra*, and *mātrikadhāra* mentioned in other sources.

We get a clearer, if later, picture in the travel account of Yijing. In his 南海奇歸内法傳 (*Nánhǎi qíguī nèifǎzhuàn*, T. 2125, written in 691 C.E.), he explains the difference between the Mahāyāna and Hīnayāna as follows: "Both adopt one and the same discipline (Vinaya), and they have in common the prohibitions of the five *skandhas* ('groups of offences'), and also practice of the Four Noble Truths. Those who worship the Bodhisattvas and read the Mahāyāna *Sūtras* are called the 'Mahāyānists,' while those who do not perform these are called the Hīnayānists."[106] Putting this statement together with Faxian's account, we can explain why the Mahāyāna monastery at Pāṭaliputra was using the *Mahāsāṅghika-vinaya*—according to Yijing, Mahāyāna and Hīnayāna employ the same *vinayas*. Yijing also claims that the characteristics that distinguish the Mahāyāna from Hīnayāna are worship (here *bodhisattvas* vs. Faxian's worship of texts) and the use of Mahāyāna texts.

Yijing explains the relationship between the *-yānas* and the sect names that appear in Indian inscriptions. He claims, "There exist in the West (i.e., India) numerous subdivisions of the schools which have different origins, but there are only four principal schools of continuous tradition."[107] These schools are the Mahāsāṅghika Nikāya, the Sthaviravāda Nikāya (Theravāda), the Mūlasarvāstivāda Nikāya, and the Sammitīya Nikāya. Although each of these is said to have numerous subdivisions, Yijing says, "which of the four schools should be grouped with the Mahāyāna or with the Hīnayāna is not determined."[108] In short, for Yijing there is Mahāyāna and Hīnayāna; there are also different sects (ideally eighteen, but in actuality only four), but there is no simple correspondence between the two systems of classification.

Xuanzang (who traveled from China to India in the seventh century) describes what the relationship between Mahāyāna and Hīnayāna might have looked like. Like Faxian, Xuanzang reports that there were some monasteries where all of the monks studied and practiced Mahāyāna.[109] Elsewhere, however, Xuanzang tells us that monks in many regions studied both Mahāyāna and non-Mahāyāna doctrines within the same monastery. Unfortunately, the exact nature of the sectarian affiliation of these monks remains unclear in his writing. For instance, he tells us that there were a thousand monks at the Mahābodhisaṅghārāma who memorized or recited (習學) the *dharma*, the rules and the ceremonies of the 大乘上座部

(*dàshéng* [*Mahāyāna*] *shàngzuò* [*Sthavīra*] *bù* [sect]).[110] Xuanzang also uses this designation to describe monks in Bodhgāya, Kaliṅga, Surat, Bharukaccha, and Śrī Laṅka.[111]

In his treatment of the distribution of Mahāyānists in India, Lamotte has some difficulty explaining how the two adjectives *dàshéng* and *shàngzuò* relate to each other. In Lamotte's tabulation of Xuanzang's "census" of Buddhist monasteries, "Mahāyāna-sthavira" becomes a subcategory of the Sthavira sect proper. Lamotte explains this categorization as follows: "'Bhikṣus 'studying both the Hīna- and Mahāyāna': these were probably Mahāyānists living in former Hīnayānist monasteries, whose rules they continued to observe."[112] This explanation does not always work. For instance, at Kanyakubja, Xuanzang tells us that at one of the monasteries, "there were 3,000 additional people who simultaneously labored (兼功) to memorize the Mahāyāna *and* Hīnayāna."[113] Since no conjunction is necessary in the Chinese, we have to rely on other indications that Xuanzang is talking about "Mahāyāna *and* Hīnayāna" and not "a Mahāyāna *kind of* Hīnayāna." Here, the term 兼 (*jiān*, translated here as "simultaneously") gives the sense both of combined effort and concurrent action, which would only make sense if there were two distinct *-yānas* at play here. If it is not plausible to argue that Xuanzang's 大乘小乘 (Mahāyāna Hīnayāna) denotes a special, "Mahāyāna" kind of "Hīnayāna" (especially since the term 兼 implies two things), there is no reason why the phrase "Mahāyāna Sthavīra sect" at the Mahābodhisaṅghārāma cannot mean there were a thousand people who studied the *dharma* and so on "*of both the* Mahāyāna and the Sthavira sects." Certainly, the *vinaya* law would have been common between the two (and hence, they could live in the same monastery), but by the Chinese pilgrims' accounts it was precisely in the area of scripture (*dharma*) and liturgy that the two differed. Lamotte would only be justified in his reading of this passage if there were some reason why one monastery could not contain monks of two different *yāna* affiliations. Yet this seems to be precisely what our pilgrims are telling us was the case at certain localities.

From the Chinese pilgrims' accounts we learn a number of important features of early Indian Buddhist sectarian organization. It appears that early Indian Buddhist identity was twofold: monks and nuns had an *ordination/pratimokṣa* affiliation (classified in terms of the *vinaya* adhered to) as well as a *yāna* affiliation. There seems to be no necessary correlation between the two. The former would have been an affiliation to one of the ordination lineages corresponding roughly to the four schools that Yijing mentions. The latter would have been a doctrinal/liturgical affiliation to either the Mahāyāna or Hīnayāna. We also know that in some regions, monasteries were of a single *yāna* affiliation, while at many other locations the population of a given monastery may well have been mixed. Finally, while each of the pilgrims refer to monasteries that were exclusively Mahāyānist, it appears from their accounts that most Mahāyānists lived in monasteries that were not predominantly Mahāyānist—illustrating Schopen's point that Mahāyānists were in the minority even as late as the seventh century.

One last point needs to be made here regarding the geographic spread of Mahāyāna according to the pilgrim's accounts. The first has been made by Lamotte, namely that the pilgrim's accounts find Mahāyāna to be primarily a northwestern phenomenon.[114] Furthermore, it should be noted that, despite the fact that Xuanzang finds Mahāyānists as far south as southern Kośala, he does *not* find any Mahāyānists as far south as Dhānyakaṭaka (modern-day Amaravatī).

Early Buddhist Doxographies

Evidence from inscriptions indicates two important facts. One is that Mahāyāna before the fifth century was largely invisible and probably existed only as a minority and largely unrecognized movement within the fold of nikāya Buddhism. The other is that, after the fifth century Mahāyāna began to be a recognizable category by donors—although still on a small scale. The following discussion shows through Mahāyānists' histories of their own religion that they did not conceive of Mahāyāna as having any independent institutional status until roughly the fifth century—that is, the same time that they began to receive donations as Mahāyānists.

The testimonies of the Chinese pilgrims are invaluable for their perspectives on Buddhism during the centuries in which they visited. For sources predating Faxian, however, we have to turn to indigenous Indian sources for information concerning the status of Mahāyāna. Like the archaeological record, non-Mahāyāna sources display no awareness of the existence of Mahāyāna before the fifth century. Looking at early Buddhist doxographies or histories of the "eighteen schools," we may conclude that the Mahāyāna monasteries that Faxian describes may have been a fairly recent development. Indeed, there is a noticeable parallel between the absence of any mention of "Mahāyāna" in the archeological record and a corresponding absence of it in early Buddhist historical records.

The kind of information early Buddhist chronicles provide should be clarified. Perhaps as early as the second century, Buddhists began to write histories of their religion and its development since the death of the Buddha.[115] One of the primary interests of these works is to explain and chronicle the controversies and schisms that led to the creation of the diverse Buddhist sects as the authors of these texts knew them. Although not all the sect names listed in the chronicles have been found in the extant inscriptions in India, the opposite is also true—all sect names found in Indian inscriptions can be found in these lists. We can assume, then, that the lists contained in the chronicles reflect the sectarian constitution of Buddhism as their authors knew it.

Another defining interest of these texts seems to be an attempt to convey the authority of tradition. A very early tradition set forth the founding myths (legends of the first Buddhist councils, of Mahādeva, etc.) and also set the number of Buddhist sects at eighteen. In order to be added to the list, a sect would have had to become sufficiently prominent to warrant writing its origins into a pre-existing tradition. What the historical development of the chronicles shows us, then, is the point in time when the Buddhist group reached a threshold of prominence warranting a historical revision. Mahāyāna seems to have reached this minimal threshold at about the same time as monasteries begin receiving donations under the name "Mahāyāna." If we take into account all of the extant Buddhist doxographies, the best we can say is that its sectarian status seems to have been superfluous until the sixth century, since there does not appear to be any awareness of Mahāyāna as an institution in the Buddhist histories of their own tradition until this point.

The two earliest extant Buddhist chronicles are the *Śāriputraparipṛcchā*[116] (anonymous) and the *Samayabhedoparacanacakra* attributed to Vasumitra.[117] The *Samayabhedoparacanacakra* was probably written in the second century if we can assume that the same Vasumitra who is mentioned in the *Mahāvibhāṣa* wrote it. In any case, it was translated three times. The first translation was completed sometime in the Qin dynasty of the Sixteen Kingdoms period (351–431 C.E.) and is sometimes attributed to Kumārajīva (cited below as the Qin translation).[118] André Bareau assigns the text to c. 350 C.E. without any discussion.[119] However, since the *Śāriputraparipṛcchā* contains virtually the same account (at least in outline) and was translated between 317 and 420 C.E., we can assume with a degree of certainty that the tradition reflected in both of these texts dates to at least the third century.

These two histories do not differ substantially from each other and record a sequence of events leading to the origin of the "eighteen Buddhist schools," which forms the core narrative for all subsequent Buddhist accounts of its own history. Both begin with a legend (also recorded in the *Mahāvibhāṣa*)[120] of a council convened at Vaiśālī during which Buddhists divided into eighteen sects. According to the *Samayabhedoparacanacakra*, the schism occurred over the "five theses" propounded by the monk Mahādeva.[121] At this meeting the group which accepted all five theses—the majority—called themselves the *Mahā-sāṅghika*, while those who abstained called themselves the *Sthaviras*. The five theses called into question the complete otherworldly nature of the Arhant (i.e., Mahādeva held that Arhants can have erotic dreams, can still learn things, etc.). The chronicles take this as the starting point to discuss the further divisions of the Buddhist *saṅgha* into eighteen sects, grouping all the sects into subsects of these two. The *Śāriputraparipṛcchā* begins in roughly the same manner, but the schism occurs because of an attempt by some (who later became the *Sthaviras*) to increase the number of *vinaya* rules.[122]

Nowhere in the *Samayabhedoparacanacakra* is the word "Mahāyāna" used, nor is there any indication that its author knew of its existence. This is especially interesting given that two of the translators of Vasumitra's text into Chinese were Paramārtha (sixth century) and Xuanzang (eighth century). Each translator was a strong proponent of Mahāyāna in his own day. Surely, if any of these texts had any hint of Mahāyāna in it, one of these Mahāyāna scholars would have translated it and commented on it. This is even more certain if the first translation was done by Kumārajīva, since his translations often insert his own notes into the text. The word "Mahāyāna" is similarly absent from the *Śāriputraparipṛcchā* and from the account of the schism in the *Mahāvibhāṣa*. We must conclude, then, that the *Samayabhedopacaranacakra* and *Śāriputraparipṛcchā* were written before Mahāyāna had come into general awareness as a separate Buddhist institution or at least at a time when Mahāyāna could safely be passed over without comment.

A slightly different version of the origin and differentiation of Buddhist sects was compiled in the Pali *Dīpavaṃsa* and *Mahāvaṃsa*. The *Dīpavaṃsa* is the earlier of the two, and it ends with the reign of Mahāsena (276–303 C.E.) providing us with a *terminus ante quem* for its authorship. Both works contain a version of the narrative sequence found in the *Samayabhedopacarana*. Both texts record a story of a group of twelve thousand monks from Vesali called Vajjiputtas, who adopted ten heretical theses. They were ultimately excommunicated by Aśoka, but returned later to form a Great Assembly (*mahāsaṅghika*). According to Hermann Oldenberg's translation of the *Dīpavaṃsa:*

> The Bhikkhus of the Great Council settled a doctrine contrary (to the true Faith). Altering the original redaction they made another redaction. They transposed Suttas which belonged to one place (of the col-

> lection), to another place; they destroyed the (true) meaning and the Faith, in the Vinaya and in the Five Collections (of Suttas). Those Bhikkhus, who understood neither what had been taught in long expositions nor without exposition, neither the natural meaning nor the recondite meaning, settled a false meaning in connection with spurious speeches of the Buddha; these destroyed a great deal of (true) meaning under the colour of the letter. Rejecting single passages of the Suttas and of the profound Vinaya, they composed other Suttas and another Vinaya which had (only) the appearance (of genuine ones) [= *patirūpā*]. Rejecting the following texts, viz.: the Parivāra which is an abstract of the contents (of the vinaya), the six sections of the Abhidhamma, the Paṭisambhidā, the Niddesa, and some portions of the Jātaka, they composed new ones. Forsaking the original rules regarding nouns, genders, composition, and the embellishments of style, they changed all that. . . .
>
> All these five sects, originating from the Mahāsaṃghikas, split the (true) meaning and the Doctrine and some portions of the Collection; setting aside some portions of difficult passages, they altered them. Forsaking the original rules regarding nouns, genders, composition, and the embellishments of style, they changed all that.[123]

Since the monks of the Mahāsāṅghika allegedly altered texts and composed new ones, and since Mahāyānists were sometimes charged with writing new texts (i.e., the Mahāyāna *sūtras*), it is tempting to assume that the Mahāsāṅghikas (and their subsects) described in the *Dīpavaṃsa* were, in fact, Mahāyānists. We must, however, be very clear about what this passage does and does not say. Nowhere in the *Dīpavaṃsa* is the word "Mahāyāna" used, and, in any case, there is simply not enough information here to conclude that Mahāyāna *sūtras* are intended here, since even the Sarvāstivādins could be said to have a different *abhidharma*, and so on.

The account goes on to describe the schism that took place among the Theravādins. Eleven sects split off from the Theravādins. Among these eleven, the Mahīśāsaka sect seems to have had nothing whatsoever to do with the Vajjiputaka monks, and yet they are *also* accused of "[splitting] the (true) meaning and the Doctrine and some portions of the Collection; setting aside some portions of difficult passages, [and altering] them. Forsaking the original rules regarding nouns, genders, composition, and the embellishments of style, they changed all that."[124] In other words, the charge of changing scripture seems to be an accusation that the *Dīpavaṃsa* levels at all "heretical" sects and therefore cannot be considered a specific charge against Mahāyānists.

As in the Sanskrit chronicles, the word "Mahāyāna" does not appear in either Pāli chronicle. However, many scholars point out that these chronicles do mention Mahāyāna under a different name—*vetullaka*. According to John Holt,

> The first fairly certain indication of Mahāyāna teachings at the Abhayagiri monastery occurs during the reign of Vohārika Tissa (A.D. 214–236) when the king appointed his minister Kapila, according to the *Nikāya Sangrahāya* . . . , to decide whether or not the Mahāvihāra's claim that Sanskrit *Vaitulyapiṭaka sūtras* being used at Abhayagiri were truly the teachings of the Buddha. Kapila found in favor of the Mahāvihāra monks, the Vaitulya *sūtras* were burned, and the Vaitulya (meaning "dissenting") monks were disrobed and banished.[125]

Indeed, Holt's interpretation of Pāli histories seems to reflect the prevailing trend.[126] However, if we pay close attention to the dates of Holt's sources, there is sufficient reason to question the presence of Mahāyānists before the fifth century in Śrī Laṅka. Holt says that the first mention of the Vetullavādins relates to events of the third century. Since this information is found only in the *Nikāya Saṅgraha,* which was written sometime in the fourteenth century, we may dismiss its testimony. Indeed, the term *vetulla* does not occur in the *Dīpavaṃsa* at all, but appears to have been introduced into the doxographical lexicon only in the *Mahāvaṃsa.*[127] Nevertheless, even in the *Mahāvaṃsa,* the name *vetullavāda* appears nowhere in the lists of Buddhist sects. The only clue that we have as to their identity occurs in the story of a certain Dhammarūcci, a Tamil monk who belonged to the Vajjiputaka sect. The fact that the *Mahāvaṃsa* gives Dhammarucci a sectarian affiliation *and* describes him as a *vetullaka* can only indicate that in the fifth century, when the *Mahāvaṃsa* was written, the term *vetullaka* itself was not a sectarian designation.

Finally, it is significant that although Faxian stayed in Śrī Laṅka for two years (c. 410 C.E.)[128] and mentions the Abhayagīri monastery (the monastery most associated in the Pali *vaṃsa* literature with the *vetullaka* controversy), he never mentions encountering any sign of Mahāyāna on the island. Since Faxian makes a point of mentioning Mahāyāna when he encounters it elsewhere,[129] we may surmise that there was nothing in Śrī Laṅka recognizable to Faxian as Mahāyāna at the time of his visit. It is somewhat doubtful, then, that the Pāli chronicles were aware of Mahāyāna as an independent sect before Buddhaghosa in the fifth century.

The evidence from the early Buddhist chronicles adds to our understanding of the geographic distribution of Mahāyāna. Although Faxian encounters Mahāyāna monasteries in the early fifth century, the Buddhist doxographies written before that time seem to have been unaware of Mahāyāna in any institutional capacity at all. Since we know, from other evidence, that Mahāyāna existed as early as the second century, we must conclude that these Mahāyānists were ensconced in non-Mahāyāna monasteries to such an extent that an ancient historian of Buddhism could pass over them without comment.

Mahāyāna Chronicles

Mahāyānists wrote their own doxographies, but even these do not present Mahāyāna as an independent monastic entity in any way until the sixth century. The earliest Mahāyāna chronicle, the *Mañjuśrīparipṛcchā*, roughly follows the narrative provided by Vasumitra. It is the earliest extant chronicle to mention Mahāyāna by name and is itself a thoroughly Mahāyāna text. The *Mañjuśrīparipṛccha* was translated into Chinese by Saṅghabhara, who traveled to India between 506 and 520 C.E. A quotation from this text has been added to the beginning of the *Samayabhedoparacanacakra* of T. 2032 (the Qin dynasty translation). Although it is possible that the quotation was added by the original translator, it is more likely that Paramārtha added it onto the text in the early sixth century as the note placed at the end of the text by its eighth-century editors seems to indicate.[130] All this indicates that the text was written after Vasumitra's text (possibly even after the first translation), but before the sixth century.

Its rather brief discussion of Mahāyāna reveals an important clue to the nature of Mahāyāna before the sixth century. In it, Mañjuśrī asks the Buddha:

> At that time Mañjuśrī said to the Buddha. "World Honored one, after the Buddha has entered into Nirvāṇa, how will your future disciples distinguish the sects? What are the original sects?" The Buddha told Mañjuśrī, "In the future, my disciples will have twenty sects able to teach in this dharma realm. Members of those twenty sects may equally obtain the four fruits (of the Buddhist path). The *Tripiṭaka* is equally peaceful without inferior, middling, and superior. Just as there is no distinction in the taste of the ocean water, or just like the man who has twenty children (loves them all the same). What is ultimately true is word of the Tathāgata. The two original sects arise out of the Mahāyāna, arise out of the *Prajñāpārami*[*tā*]. Śrāvakas, Pratyekabuddhas, and all Buddhas all of them arise out of the *Pra-*

jñāparami[*tā*]. Mañjuśrī, just like earth, water, fire, wind, and empty space are where all living beings reside. Just like this, the *Prajñāpāramі*[*tā*] and the Mahāyāna are that from which all Śrāvakas, Pratyekabuddhas, and Buddhas arise.[131]

Like the *Samayabhedoparacanacakra*, the *Mañjuśrīparipṛcchā* begins with a statement that all the sects are equally potent to induce enlightenment, and all contain the Buddha's word equally. But while the essence of the Buddha's word (*buddhavacana*) for Vasumitra was the four noble truths,[132] for the *Mañjuśrīparipṛcchā, buddhavacan* is equated with the ultimate truth, which includes and is epitomized in the Mahāyāna and *Prajñāpāramitā*. The *Mañjuśrīparipṛcchā* treats truth embodied in the Mahāyāna as prior to all Buddhist sects, which are "equally capable of attaining the four fruits." What is important here is that, in this ostensibly Mahāyāna text, Mahāyāna is not presented as a school, nor is it discussed in the context of the creation of the eighteen schools. Highlighting its importance, the *Mañjuśrīparipṛcchā* positions Mahāyāna as the necessary condition for the arising of any of the schools. While we may see in this a strategy to present Mahāyāna as a kind of "*ur*-Buddhism" (and therefore above all reproach), we must also acknowledge in the same strategy an unawareness of the institutional status of Mahāyāna. As such, it cannot be insignificant that this text was written before the first monasteries received and disposed of funds under that name.

By the same token, it cannot be a coincidence that the first discussions of Mahāyāna's institutional status occur in the sixth century—roughly a hundred years after the earliest Mahāyāna inscription at Valabhī. Mahāyāna as a distinct form of Buddhist belief and practice creatively interpolated into the (by that time) classical account of the genesis of Buddhist sects is first found in Paramārtha's commentary on the *Samayabhedoparacanacakra*. Although the original of Paramārtha's commentary no longer survives intact, significant portions of it have been quoted by Jizang (549–623) in his *Sanlun xuanyi*[133] and the commentary on it by the Japanese monk Chūkan in 1280.[134] The portions translated by Demiéville show Paramārtha negotiating a place for Mahāyāna within an already existing Buddhist history.[135] To make this negotiation convincing, he has to rework preexisting elements in a way that will seem plausible to an audience already familiar with the story absent the Mahāyāna.

Most of the Sanskrit histories, beginning with that of Vasumitra, attribute schisms among Buddhist schools to a legendary figure named Mahādeva.[136] The *Mahāvibhāṣa* attributes the split between the Sthaviravādins and the Mahāsāṅghikas during the reign of King Aśoka to him, while the *Samayabhedoparacanacakra* attributes to him the split within the Mahāsāṅghika itself (200 A.N.) into the Caityaśaila, Aparaśaila, and Uttaraśaila sects. In both texts, the schism is said to occur as the result of his proposal of five heretical theses. It is clear that what we have here, rather than two historical personages named Mahādeva, is a (purely?) literary figure named Mahādeva, along with his five theses serving as a trope for heresy and schism in general.

In keeping with that tradition, Paramārtha inserts a discussion of the Mahāyāna into his discussion of both these events—and is perhaps the first person to do so. In his discussion of the schism caused by Mahādeva at the time of Aśoka, Paramārtha tells us that the Mahāyāna *sūtras* themselves were composed at the behest of Mahādeva. Paramārtha has Mahādeva telling his disciples that, since the Parinirvāṇa of the Buddha, there were many capable of teaching the *dharma* and that they could also write their own *sūtras*.[137] Those who accepted these new *sūtras* were the Mahāsāṅghikas (the group that also accepted and defended his five theses), while those who did not were the Sthaviravādins. Although Paramārtha does seem to indicate a special affiliation between Mahāyāna and Mahāsāṅghika that is missing from any other source, we are nevertheless still not justified in making any simple equation between the two.

Paramārtha further tells us that there was controversy over the Mahāyāna within the Mahāsāṅghika itself some two hundred years after the Buddha. According to Jizang's version:

> During the two hundred years (that is to say, from the second century after the Nirvāṇa of the Buddha), from the Mahāsāṅghika school there arose again three schools. This school was then transferred to the country of Aṅguttara (?) to the north of Rājagṛha because of Mahādeva. Taking the Avataṃsaka, the Prajñā and the other *sūtras* of the Mahāyāna, this school recited them by incorporating them into the Tripiṭaka. There were those people who believed in them and others who did not believe in them at all. This is why it formed itself into two schools. The non-believers said that only the Tripiṭaka recited by Ānanda and the two other masters was deserving of faith, and that the *sūtra* of the Mahāyāna outside of the Tripiṭaka did not merit belief. As for those who believed in the Mahāyāna, they cited three reasons: they declared it to be worthy of faith first of all because in this epoch there are still to be found some people who have personally heard the Buddha dictate the Dharma of the Mahāyāna. Next because, if a person reflects in the principles of

> the Way (in the logical principles, *tao li: siddhānta, nyāya*) by themselves, it follows that the Mahāyāna exists. And finally, because they believe their teachers.[138]

This rather short passage tells us a great deal about Mahāyāna as Paramārtha perceived it. According to his commentary, the Mahāsāṅghika school moved to the north of Rājagṛha two hundred years after the Buddha's nirvāṇa, due to the heresy of Mahādeva, and began to discuss whether the Mahāyāna *sūtras*[139] should be incorporated into the *Tripiṭaka*.[140] The Mahāsāṅghikas were divided over the issue, with some embracing the Mahāyāna *sūtras*, and others holding that only the *sūtras* recited by Ānanda, Upāli, and Maudgalyana at the first council were authoritative.[141] Consequently, the Mahāsāṅghikas broke into three groups (the Ekavyāvahārika, Lokottaravāda, and the Kaukūlika), but Paramārtha never identifies which (if any) among these adopted Mahāyāna *sūtras* into the *Tripiṭaka*. We are left to assume that each of the three subsects contained both proponents and opponents of the Mahāyāna *sūtras*. Paramārtha simply tells us that the monks who upheld the Mahāyāna *sūtras* did so for three reasons (identical in both versions). First, the Mahāyāna monks claimed to have heard the Mahāyāna *sūtras* directly from the Buddha's lips (presumably in a trance).[142] Second, they claimed that anyone who reflected on logical principles would know that the Mahāyāna exists.[143] Finally, they believed in the Mahāyāna *sūtras* out of faith in their gurus.

In the context of the creation of the Bahuśrutīya school, Paramārtha again raises the issue of dissent within the Mahāsāṅghika over the status of the Mahāyāna *sūtras*. Here, however, the formation of a new sect is more clearly related to the adoption of Mahāyāna texts. According to Chūkan's version, a certain Arhant named 祠皮衣 (Cípíyī)[144] lived at the time of the Buddha and practiced meditation on top of a snowy mountain (Himalayas?) for two hundred years. When he came down from the mountain he found that the *Tripiṭaka* of the Mahāsāṅghikas only taught the conventional truth, and not the ultimate truth. Hence:

> in the Mahāsāṅghika school this Arhat recited completely the superficial sense and the profound sense. In the latter, there was the sense of the Mahāyāna. Some did not believe it. Those who believed it recited and retained (these teachings). There were in the Mahāsāṅghika school those who propagated these teachings, and others who did not propagate them. The former formed a separate school called "Those who have heard much." . . . It is from this school that there

has come the *Satyasiddhiśāstra*. It is why a mixture of ideas from the Mahāyāna are found there.[145]

Paramārtha tells us that the Bahuśrutīya school was formed in order to embrace both the teachings of conventional and of the ultimate truth—the latter being allegedly absent from prior Mahāsāṅghika versions of the *Tripiṭaka*. It should be noted in this regard, however, that even Paramārtha is not willing to completely identify this school with Mahāyāna. Noting that this school produces the *Satyasiddhiśāstra,* he says that "for this reason [because the Bahuśrutīya revere teachings of conventional and ultimate truths], it [the *Satyasiddhiśāstra*] is mixed, implicating Mahāyāna ideas."[146] Although the Bahuśrutīya school was probably experimenting with Mahāyāna during Paramārtha's lifetime, there is no indication from Vasumitra's text that they had adopted Mahāyāna *sūtras* at that time. All that we are told is that they held that the teachings of suffering, impermanence, emptiness, selflessness, and the peace of nirvāṇa are supermundane.[147] This in and of itself is hardly a Mahāyāna position. Furthermore, while Paramārtha is correct to say that the *Satyasiddhiśāstra* has distinctly Mahāyāna ideas in it, some of these ideas come from Nāgārjuna's disciple Āryadeva,[148] and so we cannot assume that the text represents a typical Bahuśrutīya position at the time of Nāgārjuna.

The only school that Paramārtha unequivocally identifies with the Mahāyāna is (surprisingly) the Dharmgupta school, which Paramārtha claims had a canon consisting of five "baskets" (*piṭaka*) instead of three.[149] In addition to the *Tripiṭaka*, the Dhamaguptakas also had a *mantrapiṭaka* (咒藏)[150] and a *bodhisattvapiṭaka* (菩薩藏).[151] Paramārtha's description of the Dharmguptaka school probably comes closest to what we may consider a straightforward Mahāyāna sect, and yet Paramārtha gives us frustratingly few details and never actually uses the word "Mahāyāna" to describe them. Furthermore, if some Mahāyānists had been Dharmaguptakas during Paramārtha's lifetime (which is quite possible), it is uncertain when they began to be so. On the one hand, the collection of manuscripts in the British Library collection hailing from a first-century Dharmguptaka monastery is remarkable in its lack of any reference to Mahāyāna. Furthermore, the *Dharmagupta vinaya* never mentions any scripture collections beyond the standard *Dīgha, Mādhyama, Saṃyukta,* and *Ekottara Āgamas,* although Mahāyāna itself is mentioned briefly.[152] The absence of any mention of a *Bodhisattva Piṭaka* in this *vinaya* is perhaps even more significant when it is considered that Buddhayaśas, the translator of the *Dharmaguptaka vinaya,* was himself a Mahāyānist.[153] On the other hand, the fact that Buddhayaśas was a Mahāyānist along with the fact that the preface to the *Dharmagupta vinaya* states that the Dharmagupta sect had assimilated 體, the Mahāyāna *Tripiṭaka*,[154] suggests that some Dharmaguptas were Mahāyānists by the fifth century.

Thus, while Paramārtha's commentary on the *Samayabhedoparacanacakra* contains discussions about the origins of the Mahāyāna *sūtras* and discusses several schisms, he seems to be at a loss as to how to bring the two together. This reflects a state of affairs in which the place of Mahāyāna as a separate institution needed explanation, but whose actual place was not entirely obvious, even to an indigenous observer.

Two other sixth-century authors who seem to have been aware of the question of Mahāyāna's sectarian status were Bhāvaviveka and his commentator, Avalokitavrata. As Peter Skilling has pointed out, Bhāvaviveka, in his *Tarkajvāla*, states that the *Siddhārthikas* of the *Mahāsāṅghika-nikāya* use a *Vidyādhāra-piṭaka*, the Pūrvaśailas and the Aparaśailas both use a *Bodhisattva-piṭaka*, while the Bhadrayānīyas use a *Vaipulya-piṭaka*.[155] In the same vein, Avalokitavrata, in his commentary (*ṭīkā*) on Bhāvaviveka's *Prajñāpradīpa*, writes:

> At this point, those who belong to the Śrāvakayāna say: "Mahāyāna is not Word of the Buddha because it does not belong to the eighteen schools, Just like Sāṃkhya, etc." The objective of that (argument) is not established. Since the heart of the Mahāyāna which is said to be the so-called *Great Āgama Piṭaka* (*sde snod kyi gźi chen po*) of the Mahāsāṅghikas themselves also pertains (to the eighteen schools). Hence, the Mahāsāṅghika scriptures give rise to the characteristics (*mtshan ñid*) of the *Daśabhūmika sūtra* and the *Pāramitā*. (Finally) because Mahāyāna *sūtras* like the *Prajñāpāramitā* etc. are chanted by the Aparaśailyas and the Pūrvaśailyas of the Mahāsāṅghika (Mahāyāna is established as Buddhist).[156]

Here, the opponent explicitly states that Mahāyāna is not one of the eighteen sects, implying that it is heterodox like the brahmanical Sāṃkya school. Avalokitavrata counters that although Mahāyāna is not one of the eighteen schools, its *sūtras* have also been employed by at least two of the Mahāsāṅghika schools; the Pūrvaśailyas and the Aparaśailyas. At this point, we see an about-face. In the accounts of the Chinese pilgrims, we find Mahāyānists sharing monasteries with those of the Buddhist sects. Here, Avalokitavrata claims that both the Pūrvaśailyas and the Aparaśailyas are the Mahāyānists since they use Mahāyāna *sūtras*. It would be wrong to think that Avalokitavrata was describing something that had always been the case (we have no reason to suspect that the Pūrva/

Aparaśailyas as a group were necessarily reading the *Prajñāpāramitā Sūtras* during Nāgārjuna's lifetime). Rather, we should take his statement as an indicator of Mahāyāna's growing visibility and influence during the sixth century, when Bhāvaviveka and Avalokitavrata were writing.

Mahāyāna in the Early Historical Landscape

Summing up the evidence so far, we know from the Chinese translations that Mahāyāna existed at least as early as the first and second centuries of the Common Era, and yet there is a remarkable paucity of Mahāyāna manuscripts before the fifth century. There are two artifacts from the kingdom of Shan-shan indicating that high government officials were Mahāyānist and yet no indication that there were any Mahāyāna monks or monasteries in this area until Faxian's travel account from the fifth century. Add to this the fact that Mahāyānists themselves do not seem to have identified Mahāyāna with any particular Buddhist sect until the sixth century, and it is difficult to avoid the conclusion that the movement was present but does not seem to have received much recognition within India until the fifth century. Clearly, this conclusion is revisable, for reasons stated above. Yet even, as noted above, if a hoard of second-century Mahāyāna manuscripts are found, scholars will still have to explain why those *sūtras* appear in that monastery and not in other libraries of the same time period. Indeed, while the hypothesis of Mahāyāna's minority status relies on the weight of what may be circumstantial evidence, the opposite hypothesis—that Mahāyāna enjoyed equal status in the monasteries or that there were Mahāyāna monasteries before the fifth century—has very little evidence to support it so far. For this reason, the remainder of this book assumes that the Mahāyāna of Nāgārjuna's day was a minority movement.

The reason for Mahāyāna's lack of recognition in its early days cannot be adequately explained by Hirakawa's theory that Mahāyāna was exclusively a lay movement, for the reasons that Sasaki has pointed out. Furthermore, not all Mahāyānists could have been forest-dwellers, as Ray suggests, because many Mahāyāna *sūtras*, such as the *Ratnārāśi,* take settled monastic life for granted. The best explanation for the lack of recognition by non-Mahāyānists can be explained by the fact, as seen from accounts of the Chinese pilgrims, that most Mahāyānists lived in "mixed" monasteries and had to fight for recognition (as Schopen has argued). As shown in Chapter 3, it may well have been in the best interest of Mahāyānists in these monasteries to keep a "low profile" until they formed a majority within the local *saṅgha.* Local politics would therefore have been a key factor in the emergence of Mahāyāna, and therefore the "rise of Mahāyāna" would have occurred at different times in different places. The evidence further suggests that Lamotte's thesis of a north or northwestern origin of Mahāyāna may be correct, and that it spread southward until reaching Śrī Laṅka in the fifth century.

Mahāyāna does not seem to have experienced the same fate everywhere throughout the time period under discussion. It seems to have been an upper-class phenomenon in Shan-shan, though not necessarily accepted by the monks. By the fifth century, there were a few monasteries that were predominantly Mahāyānist, although, according to Chinese pilgrims' accounts, many Mahāyānists lived in monasteries that were not exclusively Mahāyānist. One question is yet to be addressed. If Mahāyāna had been so well accepted among high government officials (as Salomon suggests), then how can we explain the lack of Mahāyāna manuscripts in early manuscript finds in this region? The first possible explanation is that, apparently, the monks of Shan-shan may not have lived in monasteries.[157] If this is indeed the case, then any existing Mahāyāna *sūtras* would not have been stored in one place and hence would be harder to find. This does not explain the absence of Mahāyāna *sūtras* farther west, such as Khotan. Here, in anticipation of Chapters 3 and 4, it should be noted that the legal authority of the monastery may have allowed the monastery to restrict both lay donations to Mahāyānists as well as the production and dissemination of Mahāyāna texts even if the king had a predilection for Mahāyāna ideas.

As for donations to Mahāyānists, it should be remembered that the engraving of one's name and donation onto a rock was an action taking place in a public sphere. With the exception of certain royal inscriptions (the Valabhī inscription would be one such exception), votive inscriptions were not carved by the donor solely from personal initiative. The relative uniformity of artistic hand at the *stūpas* and of "handwriting" in the inscriptions indicate that donations were probably solicited by the monks, and the votive messages dictated to the artisan by the monk in charge of construction, not directly by the donor. Vidya Dehejia describes this process in relation to the construction of the *stūpa* at Sāñchī.

> One can but speculate on the actual process by which the Sāñchī stūpa was raised. It would appear that when the community of monks at [Sāñchī] decided to enlarge their stūpa, face it with stone and further enhance its surroundings by adding stone railings, sculptured gateways and a stone pillared assembly hall . . . one of their most important tasks was fund-raising. Monks presumably traveled to numerous towns and villages collecting subscriptions. When the

> inhabitants of a particular township, for instance Nadinagara or Madhuvana, gave money for a series of coping stones or for slabs to pave the *pradakṣina patha,* the Construction Supervisor ensured that their names were engraved on their gifts. There was, however, no random cutting of stones, and donors could not gift finished pieces from their local workshop. Rather, it was necessary to adhere to the clear-cut plan of the Sāñchī architect.[158]

Dehejia's speculation is probably not too far off. One of the monastic occupations appearing in many *vinayas* and inscriptions is the *navakarmika*—the monk in charge of construction projects, as implied by the Chinese translation of 營事比丘 (building-duty monk) in the *Mahāsāṅghika vinaya.*[159] Whereas many of the details of the day to day running of the monastery have yet to be sorted out, the existence of a formal office such as this suggests that all donations and votive messages were to be processed by an official intermediary. In other words, the appearance of the word "Mahāyāna" in an inscription reflects not just an individual whim but, to some extent, the tacit acceptance of the institution as a whole.

Thus in the Valabhī and Tippera inscriptions we know that the donor was aware that s/he[160] was giving to a Mahāyāna monastery and wanted others to know that s/he was giving to Mahāyāna monks. But the mention of Mahāyāna in these inscriptions may also indicate that the monastery itself had solicited these funds under the auspices of Mahāyāna. These examples show two monasteries asking for and receiving endowments as Mahāyānists for the purposes of providing the needs of their fellow inmates and for maintaining the rituals of the monastery. If they could receive donations under those auspices, then presumably they could also dispose of these funds under the same. Mahāyāna appears to have been recognized by the laity as the kind of entity capable of receiving and disposing of those funds in the fifth century.

Curiously, we cannot say the same for the later inscriptions. In all the inscriptions mentioning "Mahāyāna" from the tenth through the twelfth centuries, "Mahāyāna" describes the donor and not the recipient. Each of these inscriptions uses the phrase *pravara-mahāyāna-yāyayikaḥ paramopasaka* (Great layperson who follows the distinguished Mahāyāna). It apparently was more important for a donor to be known as a Mahāyānist than to be known as the patron of a Mahāyānist. Whatever the reason, none of these inscriptions mention the affiliation of the recipient of the donation, and so we cannot conclude much about the identity of monasteries from these later inscriptions.

Regarding the monastic control over the dissemination of texts, although Faxian mentions finding a Mahāyāna monastery in Khotan and despite the fact that Khotan comes to be a Mahāyāna stronghold in later centuries, there is an anecdotal account of legal maneuvers against the spread of Mahāyāna texts in Khotan. Possibly the earliest account of Buddhism in Khotan can be found in the story of Zhushixing in *Jusanzang jiji* (Collection of Notes Concerning the Translation of the Tripitaka).[161] Zhushixing travels to Khotan to get a more reliable copy of a 真式 (*zhēnshì*, "true law")—presumably the 25,000-line *Prajñāpāramitā* later translated by Mokṣala. His pupil was prevented from bringing it back to Luoyang because, according to *Jusanzang jiji*, "the Hīnayāna students of that land told the King not to release the text since, although there are śramaṇas among the Han, it is a brahmin book and [the Chinese] might distort its true words [*zhēnyán*]."[162] From this brief account, it is difficult to determine exactly what the Hīnayānists' objection was. Was their objection that the Mahāyāna text was a "brahmin [i.e., non-Buddhist] book" and therefore the king should not allow it to spread? Or did they actually believe the Mahāyāna text to have some power and were worried that the Chinese would mispronounce its words, thereby incurring great danger? (真言 would, by the time of Xuanzang, come to translate "mantra.") Zürcher dismisses this story because that the fire ordeal appears to be a stock element of the story and appears in a number of other stories.[163] This objection does not mitigate the fact that the author of *Jusanzang jiji* thought it plausible to tell a story about Khotan in which not only was Khotan predominantly Hīnayānist but those Hīnayānists were prominent enough to be a serious obstacle to the spread of Mahāyāna. As Mark Twain pointed out, "Truth is stranger than fiction, but it is because Fiction is obliged to stick to possibilities. Truth isn't."[164] If this story contains even a kernel of truth in it, then it was at least plausible that a monastery might appeal to a king to prevent the transmission of a text that they considered to be heretical. The legal issues are taken up at length in Chapter 3.

It is perhaps not a coincidence that the question of Mahāyāna's sectarian status arises as late as the sixth century, since this would coincide with the time when we can safely say that that Mahāyānists begin to receive and spend wealth *as Mahāyānists*. In other words, it is only when Mahāyānists begin to receive donations as Mahāyānists that we can safely assume that they were in control of their own resources. The invisibility of Mahāyāna during its all-important formative years was a function of its relationship to the sects of Buddhism that were already established. It could remain below the radar, as it were, so long as it was not an independent Buddhist institution. Stating this does not mean that Mahāyāna and sectarian Buddhism were synonymous. Rather, the relationship between Mahāyāna and its host monasteries was one of both legal and economic dependence. Legal dependence stemmed from the fact that all monks living in a given monastery would take exactly the same ordination vows and, hence, would be accountable to the same rules. Economic dependence resulted from the fact that, being ensconced in monasteries already affiliated with one of the established sects, Mahāyāna could not develop itself as a "brand name" that the laity could associate with meritorious donations. Hence, there is little evidence before the fifth century that Mahāyānists commanded a source of funding independent of the rest of the monastery.

It was precisely this situation that may have led to a diversity of "Mahāyānas" reflected in Mahāyāna *sūtras*. We may speculate that in monasteries where the number of Mahāyāna adherents was small, the monks would have to be careful not to attract attention to themselves lest they incur legal sanctions for their activities. Furthermore, Mahāyāna monks who found themselves in the minority would have had some difficulty in acquiring the material goods that they needed to propagate Mahāyāna (most notably,. the scriptures themselves). In places where the division between Mahāyāna and non-Mahāyāna Buddhism in a given monastery was even, or where Mahāyānists outnumbered their non-Mahāyānist brethren, there would be considerably more freedom to preach and write what they wished. As seen in Chapter 2, such was not the case for Nāgārjuna, whose writings are very much a part of the milieu of the embattled Mahāyānist minority community.

2
Locating Nāgārjuna

THE INTRODUCTION STATES my intention to examine the social constraints on Nāgārjuna's writings in order to highlight his strategies to further the cause of Mahāyāna. The discussion of Mahāyāna in Chapter 1 should make it apparent that the social constraints on Mahāyāna and the strategies necessary to overcome those constraints differed from one region to another and from one century to another. Being a Mahāyānist probably would have been much easier in fifth-century Khotan than in second-century Andhra. An examination of Nāgārjuna's works yields fruit only if we can narrow the geographic area and the historical period in which he may have produced them. This chapter attempts to circumscribe a range of dates and places of composition for one of Nāgārjuna's works—the *Ratnāvalī*.[1] The date and provenance of this text provides a benchmark for the rest of the investigation.

Unfortunately, scholars have had difficulty saying anything conclusive about Nāgārjuna's life. In 1923 Max Walleser surveyed all the material that was then available to him about Nāgārjuna and concluded:

> The systematic development of the thought of voidness laid down in the *Prajñāpāramitā Sūtras* is brought into junction with the name of a man of whom we cannot even positively say that he has really existed, still less that he is the author of the works ascribed to him: this name is Nāgārjuna.[2]

Eighty years later, the situation has not improved. Surprisingly little new evidence or new interpretation has been brought to bear on the question of his dates and location in recent scholarship, although some works have summarized the available data. In the most recent of these summaries, Ian Mabbett provides an excellent survey and analysis of much available scholarship to date. The abstract to his article minces no words in its evaluation of the current state of Nāgārjuna scholarship.

> Nāgārjuna, the founder of Madhyamaka, is an enigma. Scholars are unable to agree on a date for him (within the first three centuries A.D.), or a place (almost anywhere in India), or even the number of Nāgārjunas (from one to four). This article suggests that none of the commonly advanced arguments about his date or habitat can be proved; that later Nāgārjunas are more likely to have been (in some sense) the authors of pseudepigrapha than real individuals; that the most attractive (though unproved) reading of the evidence sets Nāgārjuna in the general area of Andhra country in about the third century A.D.[3]

The rather intractable problem with which scholars have been struggling becomes apparent in Mabbett's account of the sources. Although there is no lack of literary sources discussing Nāgārjuna, almost all the elements contained therein are mythical at best and conflicting at worst. Furthermore, very few details contained in these sources can be corroborated with external evidence. Most of this material comes from accounts that were written with hagiographical interests ahead of historical documentation. Clearly, for those who like certainty, any kind of "proof" of Nāgārjuna's dates and place of residence is still a long way off.

Part of the problem is that, in scholarship on India, "absolute chronologies" (i.e., a set of dates that can be translated into Gregorian dates) have largely been worked out only for empires and their political administrators. In order to connect Nāgārjuna to a Gregorian year, we must first connect him to an Indian monarch for whom the dates are known. To make this kind of connection, we need to find evidence relating to practices or events that leave their mark in the archeological record. Unfortunately, Nāgārjuna's *magnum opus,* the *Mūlamadhyamakakārikā,* focuses so exclusively on classical Buddhist doctrine and logical issues that it has few such cultural references that would help us date it.

Mabbett's conclusions, however, need not be the end of the story. It is the purpose of this chapter to argue that if we are willing to accept a fallibilist proof, or an analysis based on partial information, we can come to some kind of solution, albeit a tentative one. Given the pressing need to take some sort of stand on this issue, even a tentative solution is preferable to the present impasse.

The following discussion puts forward two propositions that could have a bearing on the date of Nāgārjuna. The first is that Nāgārjuna's patron, to whom he wrote at least two letters, was a Sātavāhana king. The second is that, within the Sātavāhana domain, the motif of the Buddha on a lotus pedestal that Nāgārjuna mentions in one of his letters (the *Ratnāvalī*) only occurs in the Eastern Deccan at the end of the dynasty. There is a long tradition of identifying Nāgārjuna with the Sātavāhana dynasty. Unfortunately, this information by itself is hardly helpful (the dynasty spanned several centuries and covered the whole of the Deccan). Nevertheless, if we correlate information about this dynasty with sculptural references found in the *Ratnāvalī,* then it is plausible that he wrote the *Ratnāvalī* within a thirty-year period at the end of the second century in the Andhra region around Dhānyakaṭaka (modern-day Amaravati). My interpretation not only supports Mabbett's "most attractive reading" of third-century Andhra, but upgrades it to the most likely reading, given our current state of knowledge.

Nāgārjuna's *Dānapāti* Was a Sātavāhana King

We can begin to date Nāgārjuna by examining the evidence indicating that his *dānapati* and benefactor was a Sātavāhana king. Many factors support this thesis. First, the earliest and latest dates for Nāgārjuna coincide almost exactly with the range of dates for the Sātavāhana dynasty. Second, early translators and commentators give every indication that Nāgārjuna's *dānapāti* was a Sātavāhana. Third, the way that Nāgārjuna's hagiographies appear to have developed provides us with sufficient reason to doubt stories of Nāgārjuna's connection to other kings and to other places.

Earliest and Latest Dates

That Nāgārjuna lived during the reign of a Sātavāhana king must be admitted as a possibility when the factors establishing his earliest and latest dates are considered. Obviously, Nāgārjuna is writing at a time when the early Mahāyāna *sūtras* have already been written. Because the earliest *Prajñāpāramitā sūtras* are estimated to have been written around 100 B.C.E., we may take this to be a general *terminus pro quem* date for Nāgārjuna.

On the other end, the earliest datable external sources mentioning Nāgārjuna are several translations of the *Daśabhūmikavibhāṣa,* attributed in their colophons to Nāgārjuna. According to Lamotte:

> the Chinese catalogues list among the works translated by Dharmarakṣa at Ch'ang-an, between A.D. 265 and 313, a *P'u-sa hui-kuo ching* [菩薩悔過經]. This translation is noted in the *Ch'u* (T 2145, ch. 2, p. 8b 17), and the *Li* (T 2034, ch. 6, p. 63a 23) which remark: "The colophon says that this is an extract from the *Daśabhūmikaśāstra* of Nāgārjuna." It therefore results that a work by Nāgārjuna had already reached China about A.D. 265.[4]

Whether or not Nāgārjuna actually wrote the *Daśabhūmikaśāstra* does not change the fact that two catalogues (both from the sixth century C.E.) record the existence of a colophon of a work translated in 265 C.E. listing Nāgārjuna as an author. If we can assume that this was not some other Mahāyānist named Nāgārjuna, then 265 C.E. may be a *terminus ante quem,* by which time Nāgārjuna must have been an established scholar.

A third-century date is confirmed in the writings of Kumārajīva and his school. Kumārajīva indicates a third-century date for Nāgārjuna's death in a statement at the end of his translation of Nāgārjuna's *Biography,*[5] which claims, "From that leave taking [i.e., from Nāgārjuna's death] until today one hundred years have passed."[6] Arguably, the "today" referred to is the time of Kumārajīva's translation of the text. According to Richard Robinson:

> It would be hard to defend every item in the *Biography,* but it is easy to show that in substance it represents Kumārajīva's account. Seng-jui mentions the *Indian Chronicle(s)* (*t'ien-chu-chuan*), which probably means the biographies narrated by Kumārajīva. Hui-yuan's biographical sketch of Nāgārjuna in his Preface to the *Great Perfection of Wisdom Treatise* agrees with the *Biography* and many of his allusions are intelligible only with a knowledge of it. Seng-jui mentions the existence of temples to Nāgārjuna and Aśvaghoṣa, unfortunately without the date that occurs in the *Biography.* But the literary form and style of the *Biography* are typically Chinese. It has the standard opening, which states the man's native region and class, and then indicates that the child was precocious and received a good education. The laudatory clichés are purely Chinese and transparently do not stand for Indic originals. Insofar as it is genuine, this *Biography* must consist of Kumārajīva's oral account as worded by his disciples. . . .

In this case, the point one hundred years after Nāgārjuna's death would be sometime during Kumārajīva's residence at Ch'ang-an (A.D. 401–13). Thus Nāgārjuna would have flourished in the third century A.D.[7]

The other set of dates for Nāgārjuna comes from a disciple of Kumārajīva named Sañ-jwei (So-yei), who places Nāgārjuna at the end of the time of the 象法 (*xiàngfă = dharma pratirūpaka,* or "Semblance dharma").[8] Correlating this information with the dates of Āryadeva recorded by another disciple of Kumārajīva, Ui Hakuju comes up with a date of about 113–213 C.E. for Nāgārjuna.[9] Although this testimony relies on some rather strained calculations, it does suggest that Nāgārjuna may have lived in the third century C.E.[10]

Although none of the evidence so far presented is unimpeachable, there is no real evidence that Nāgārjuna lived before 100 B.C.E. or after 265 C.E. The period between the first century B.C.E. and the third century C.E. roughly corresponds to the dates for the Sātavāhana dynasty (the dynasty ends sometime in the first two quarters of the third century). Hence, that Nāgārjuna lived during the time of Sātavāhana dynasty is a strong possibility.

Translators and Commentators

The oldest extant sources testifying to Nāgārjuna's connection with the Sātavāhana dynasty surround two works: the *Suhṛllekha* and the *Ratnāvalī*. According to tradition, Nāgārjuna wrote these as letters to his patron king. The translations into Chinese and Tibetan are fairly consistent in naming this king. The earliest extant translation of the *Suhṛllekha* was translated by Guṇavarman sometime after 431.[11] Presumably, it is Guṇavarman who gives it the title 龍樹菩薩為禪陀迦王說法要偈(The Essential Verses [*gāthā*] on Dharma Explained by the Bodhisattva Nāgārjuna to King *Chantaka*).[12] This name for the *Suhṛllekha's* addressee can also be found in the seventh century in Yijing's *Nanhai jigui neifa chuan,* where the king is named 市寅得迦 (Shiyindeka).[13] Although not as close as we might like, it is possible that both Chantaka and Shiyindeka translate the place name "Dhānya[ka]ṭaka" (near modern-day Amaravati), which is the name of an important Sātavāhana site in the Eastern Deccan. If this is the case, Guṇavarman and Yijing are telling us important information concerning the king's capital. Yijing also claims that this king is a Sātavāhana (娑多婆漢那, *Shaduopohanna,* which he translates as 乘士國).[14]

Between 560 and 570, Paramārtha translated the *Ratnāvalī* into Chinese, though he does not name the author.[15] He does, however, mention its addressee. The title of this translation in Chinese is 寶行王正論 (*Bǎoháng-wángzhènglùn*, "Treatise on the Row of Jewels [Delivered to] King "Righteous"). In this same vein Xuanzang's use of 引正 (Yǐnzhèng, "leading to righteousness") a century later to translate the Sanskrit name Sātavāhana (娑多婆訶, Shaduopohe),[16] suggesting that Paramārtha may also be using the character 正 (*zhèng*, "righteousness") as a (spurious) translation of *Sāta* (reading it as somehow being derived from the Sanskrit *sat* = "truth" or "righteousness") to designate the king to whom the *Ratnāvalī* is addressed as King *Sāta*[vāhana]. A better explanation, though a more complicated one, is that although Paramārtha uses the character 正 to translate the sound "sata," this indicates not the Sātavāhana dynasty but, rather, one of the many Sata (Prakrit = "Sada") kings. Quite a few Sata/Sada kings are mentioned in inscriptions found in inscriptions from Andhra Pradesh. Inscriptions and coins mentioning these kings have been found at Chebrolu, Dhānyakaṭaka, Ramatīrtham, Guntupalli, Vaddamanu, Nandayapallem, and Velpur.[17] The identity of these kings is a matter of some debate. Some scholars consider the kings whose last name ends in "Sada" to be rulers in the Sātavāhana lineage. Others consider them to belong to another dynasty. The debate over this issue seems to revolve around an inscription found at Guntupalli, a village in west Godāvarī district. The inscription reads as follows:

Mahārājasa Kalinga(Ma)–
Hisakadhipatisa Mahā–
Mekhavāhanasa Siri Sadasa lekhakasa Culago–
Masa maḍapo dānaṃ

—"Gift of a *Mandapa* by Cula Goma, the scribe of Mahārāja Siri Sada who belonged to the dynasty of Mahāmeghavāhana and had the title Kaliṅga–Mahiṣakādhipati"[18]

This inscription clearly establishes a connection between the Sata kings and Mahāmeghavāha Khāravela of the Hathigumpha inscription and mentions the extent of his kingdom (namely, the area of Kaliṅga). D. C. Sircar suggests that the name was Sāta, indicating that this king was born to a Sātavāhana princess, but the form *Sada* often appears on Sātavāhana coins and hence is not necessarily a matronym. However, if we include the Sata kings in the Sātavāhana dynasty, we have to posit a collinear rule. Whether they were independent from or under the suzerainty of the Sātavāhanas, the Sata kings seem to have been confined to coastal Andhra throughout their reign, which was roughly coterminous with that of the Sātavāhanas.[19] For our purposes of finding a date and location of Nāgārjuna, it does not matter much whether his patron king was a Sata king or a Sātavāhana, as the time period and geographic range coincide with the most important evidence from the *Ratnāvalī* (discussed below). Furthermore, it is likely that Paramārtha, being from Ujjain, would have had access to important texts from coastal Andhra Pradesh since the two areas were culturally well connected and well traveled since at least the second century. He also would have passed through Kaliṅga on his way to China (he took a sea route).

In the Tibetan translations of these works, the addressee of these letters is translated as *bDe spyod* (good conduct) in the *Ratnāvalīṭīkā* by Ajītamitra,[20] as well as in the colophon to the Tibetan translation of the *Suhṛllekha* by Sarvajñādeva.[21] The meaning of this word is so close to Xuanzang's translation for Sātavāhana ("leading right") that one cannot overlook the possibility that it also translates Sātavāhana.[22] Most scholars take this to translate the name "Udayāna," following Scheifner,[23] but in the absence of any Sātavāhana kings by that name, either in the Purāṇic accounts or in any inscription discovered so far, it is more likely that it is a translation of the name of the dynasty itself.

Thus, from the colophons of these translations, we have Nāgārjuna's patron identified as one of the Sātavāhanas whose personal name was something like "Jantaka." This personal name of Nāgārjuna's king is quite common in later Tibetan literature. Although Mabbett believes that this may be a version of the surname Sātkarṇi, so common among members of the Sātavāhana dynasty,[24] this reconstruction cannot account for the fact that both Guṇavarman and Yijing explicitly represent a nasal sound in their transliterations. Again, it is more likely to be the place name, Dhānya(ka)taka. In any case, the colophons that tell us the dynasty of the recipient consistently name the Sātavāhana dynasty, and no colophons contradict this attribution.

The Elements of Nāgārjuna's Hagiography

This general agreement among the translators of Nāgārjuna's letters about the identity of Nāgārjuna's patron king needs to be placed in the larger context of legends about Nāgārjuna. Since none of the translators lived during the life of Nāgārjuna, we must consider the possibility that their sources of this attribution are the legends about Nāgārjuna that were circulating at the time of translation. Therefore, we must assess the hagiographical tradition surrounding Nāgārjuna before we can assess the testimony of these translators who likely drew upon it.

The earliest extant legends about Nāgārjuna are compiled into Kumārajīva's biography of Nāgārjuna, which he translated into Chinese in about 405 C.E. After that, legends proliferate in Buddhist, Hindu, Siddha, and Jain sources. The following is not an exhaustive review of all the legends told about Nāgārjuna. Much of the bibliographic spadework and analysis of this material has already been done by Mabbett and others.[25] This discussion offers, instead, a new interpretation of the evidence already collected by these scholars.

Legends of Nāgārjuna were compiled for over a thousand years in Sanskrit, Chinese, and Tibetan. When these legends are taken as a group, the diversity and range of the stories is daunting. Even if we look to these legends only for information about Nāgārjuna's patron or place of residence, we are left with a number of problems. Although most of our sources mention that Nāgārjuna's patron was a Sātavāhana,[26] there are two dissenting voices in this regard. The first, the *Kathāsaritsāgara* (eleventh century) by Somadeva Bhaṭṭa, is a reworking of an earlier *Bṛhatkathāmañjārī* of Kṣemendra (also eleventh century), and the second is *Rājataraṅgiṇī* by Kalhaṇa. The former work seems to be oblivious to any connection between Nāgārjuna and a Sātavāhana king insofar as it has one section of stories devoted to King Sātavāhana and a separate section for stories related to Nāgārjuna, who in turn is the associate of a King Cīrāyus ("Long-Life"). No place name is associated with Nāgārjuna in this work. The *Rājataraṅgiṇī* by Kalhaṇa is a court history of Kashmir that is often discussed in modern works on Nāgārjuna. Kalhaṇa mentions Nāgārjuna as living at *Ṣaḍarhadvana*[27] during the reign of either Huṣka, Juṣka, or Kaniṣka.

When we come to the issue of Nāgārjuna's place of residence, the legends are much more diverse. Kumārajīva's translation of Nāgārjuna's legends mentions a rather vague "south India" (presumably "Dakṣinapāṭha") a number of times and also mentions that he spent a brief period in the Himalayas.[28] Some (fifth-century) versions of the *Laṅkāvatāra Sūtra*[29] (and the *Mañjuśrīmūlatantra*)[30] claim that a monk whose name sounds like *Nāga* will live in Vidarbha.[31] Xuanzang has Nāgārjuna living 300 *li* southwest of the capital of southern Kośala at a mountain called "Black Peak," or "Black Bee."[32] Candrakīrti in his commentary on Āryadeva's *Catuḥśataka* says that Āryadeva became Nāgārjuna's disciple after traveling in south India, perhaps indicating that Nāgārjuna lived there too.[33] The Jain tradition[34] (which is also echoed by Al-beruni)[35] consistently places Nāgārjuna at Mt. Śatruñjaya in Gujarat,[36] while the Buddhist and Siddha traditions consistently place him at Nālanda, Śrīparvata,[37] Kañcipūram,[38] Dhānyakaṭaka,[39] Godāvarī,[40] and Vidarbha. If we add Kalhāṇa's assertion that Nāgārjuna lived in Kashmir, then we have to admit that Nāgārjuna could have lived virtually anywhere in India.

Indeed, the range of dates and the conflicting traditions concerning Nāgārjuna's residence and royal patronage have led many to dismiss some of these sources or all of them. For instance, Etienne Lamotte complains:

> Concerning the tradition that makes Nāgārjuna a subject of the Śātavāhana kings, one can contest the testimony of the Kashmiri chronicle that connects him to the kings Turuṣka in the Northwest, Juṣka and Kaniṣka and assigns to him as a residence the Wood of the Six Arhats near Hārwan in Kashmir. Southern Kośala is not the only spot to have a Śrīparvata, that is to say in Sanskrit, a Sacred Mountain. It is a toponym extremely well known that the Mahābhārata, and the Purāṇas apply to numerous mountains and which designates notably one site in Kashmir. In that which concerns Nāgārjuna, *it is scientifically incorrect to resign to their context, to group them artificially and to pretend a connection to the country of Andhra. The biographies and notices which are devoted to him swarm with legends, each one more stupefying than the next and which concern at least four different Nāgārjunas.*[41]

If the reports of the later traditions conflict, the question at this point is what to do with the testimony as it has come down to us in these traditions. Contemporary Buddhist scholars lean toward a kind of academic agnosticism when it comes to looking for historical evidence among legendary materials. As in Christianity's "Search for the Historical Jesus," the "Search for the Historical Buddha," has told us much more about the early compilers of the Buddhist *sūtras* than about the Buddha himself.

In order to interpret these legends, the most productive position is to assume that all pieces of information in the legends were included for a reason. In general, hagiographers compose their stories with two purposes in mind: spiritual edification and institutional legitimation. Elements of hagiographies inserted for the purpose of spiritual edification tend to echo or illustrate themes found in scripture, such as acts of altruism (Nāgārjuna offering up his head upon request in a number of these legends echoes the kind of radical giving found in the *Vessantara Jātaka* and several Mahāyāna *sūtras*). Elements of hagiographies inserted for legitimation are sometimes more difficult to spot. These fall into two groups. In some stories, the character of Nāgārjuna is placed in juxtaposition to a person, place, or theme that is independently famous. For example, Nāgārjuna is often said to reside at a place called Śrīparvata. Śrīparvata was already famous as a powerful and auspicious place by the time Nāgārjuna legends were being written. By locating Nāgārjuna there, the character of Nāgārjuna takes on some of the (in this case, magical) legitimacy already associated with the site. Legitimation also works in the opposite direction. After Nāgārjuna became famous, his association with pilgrimage sites lent an air of legitimacy (and antiquity) to those sites (we may speculate that this is partly responsible for Nāgārjuna's association with Nālanda in some of the post-tenth-century legends).

If this description of the rationale for the composition of these stories is correct, then we have a tool with which to dismiss spurious details about Nāgārjuna's life. Any detail present in a legend for the purposes of spiritual edification or for purposes of legitimation may be hypothesized to tell us more about the needs of the compilers of the legend than about the subject of the legend itself. Note that the existence of such a literary device does not *prove* that there is no factual basis; an element of a story may serve the plot and also happen to be true. Nevertheless, the presence of such devices should make us question the historical accuracy of the information until we have some reason to think otherwise. By the same token, if an element of the Nāgārjuna legend proves to be an early element in the tradition, and if it does not have an obvious role in edification or legitimation, then we have no choice but to assume that it was included into the hagiographies because it was "common knowledge" to the compilers of these texts. This does not mean that the information is objectively true but, rather, that the compilers assumed that it was a fact that their readers probably already knew. To contradict this information even in a legend would probably be equivalent to someone writing a legend about George Washington in which he becomes a benevolent ruler of Thailand. Few would accept it because it goes against common knowledge. The following argues that Nāgārjuna's association with the Sātavāhana king and Andhra country cannot be dismissed as a mere plot device and that his association with any other king or any other part of the country do appear to be mere plot devices.

The Nāgārjuna legends are diverse, but the diversity seems to stem from only a few factors. Nāgārjuna legends were legitimated by four sources. The first two are traditions, originally independent of the Nāgārjuna legend, that were drawn into the Nāgārjuna legend. The other two sources are thematic elements that can be found in all of Nāgārjuna's legends, which take on a life of their own. Almost every element that occurs in Nāgārjuna legends can be attributed to at least one of these four sources, while some of the stories have multiple determinations.

Other Nāgārjunas

Other scholars who have tried to sort out the details of the Nāgārjuna legend have attempted to solve the problem by postulating more than one Nāgārjuna, or many authors using "Nāgārjuna" as a *nom du plume:* one Nāgārjuna who was a Mādhyamika philosopher, one who was a tantric adept, and one who was a medical practitioner. Although this hypothesis should not be accepted without question, it also cannot be completely dismissed.[42] Many people over the course of Indian history answered to the name Nāgārjuna. But this does not mean that these "other Nāgārjunas" were operating under a pseudonym, any more than is the modern Telugu actor named Nāgārjuna. Nāgārjuna is still a common name in Andhra Pradesh.[43]

The fact that there were many later Nāgārjunas, does not, however, help us sort out the details of Nāgārjuna's hagiography. We cannot claim that all the tantric/alchemical elements of Nāgārjuna's hagiography belong to a seventh-century "tantric" Nāgārjuna when these same elements appear in Kumārajīva's fourth- or fifth-century *Biography.* Furthermore, works ascribed to a Nāgārjuna, such as the *Yogaśataka* and the *Rasendra Maṅgala,* do not claim to be written by the same author as the *Mūlamadhyamakakārikā*[44] and are easy to distinguish. Thus, for the most part, the assumption of other Nāgārjunas does not help us much in sorting out the details of his hagiography.

However, one other early Nāgārjuna (a Jain) who lived in the early fourth century C.E. was incorporated into the Nāgārjuna legend translated by Kumārajīva. The Jain legend could be a source for Nāgārjuna's association with Surāṣṭra/Gujarat in Jain sources as well as a source for the stories of Nāgārjuna's role in compiling the Mahāyāna *sūtras*. Kumārajīva's account of Nāgārjuna living with a monk in the Himalayas shows evidence of a borrowing from Jain traditions of the (Jain) Third Council. This part of Kumārajīva's story occurs shortly after Nāgārjuna is ordained and has mastered the *Tripiṭaka.*

> Then [Nāgārjuna] sought other texts, but completely failed, so he went to the Himalayas. In those mountains there was a pagoda, and in that pagoda there was an old bhikṣu who gave him the Mahāyāna texts.[45]

It is conceivable that this brief detail of Nāgārjuna's biography was assimilated into the story from the (Śvetāmbara) Jain Ardhamāgadhī canonical text, the "Nandi sutta," where a Jain Nāgārjuna (unrelated)[46] is said to be the disciple of a master named "Himavat."

> 35 Homage to Nāgārjuna the teacher who was an able *śramaṇa* of Himavant, and who was the memorizer of the earliest (holy texts) and was the memorizer of the interpretation of the Kālika scriptures.
>
> 36 Homage to Nāgārjuna the canter, who taught the *Ogha śruta*, who attained the ability to recite in proper order and who was perfectly acquainted with subtlety and subtle things.[47]

In the Jain tradition, as in the Buddhist tradition, there were four "councils" to determine or confirm the scriptural tradition. The third of these councils was held at Valabhī (modern-day Valabhīpur in Gujarat) in the first half of the fourth century and presided over by a monk named Nāgārjuna. This Nāgārjuna, according to the "Nandi sutta" passage quoted above, had been the student of a certain "Himavat" ("Snowy"), who entrusted Nāgārjuna with the memorization of the early Jain texts and the *Kālika śruta* (texts that are to be read at a specific time). The "Nandi sutta" was probably composed sometime in the fifth century,[48] but the story obviously dates back to the third Jain council itself. From the above, it seems likely that the Buddhist tradition (recorded by Kumārajīva) that Nāgārjuna received an important set of scriptures (the Mahāyāna *sūtras*) from a monk in the "Himalayas" (lit. "Snowy Mountains") is borrowed from the Jain tradition that a Nāgārjuna, who was a student of "Himavant," memorized two important sets of texts: the *Kālika śrutas* and the *Pūrva (śrutas)*. If the Jain legend of Nāgārjuna is indeed the source of the tradition that places the Buddhist Nāgārjuna in the Himalayas, then we have grounds to question the claim that Nāgārjuna was there. In later hagiographies of Nāgārjuna, the connection with the Himalayas is dropped and Nāgārjuna is said only to have received these texts from the *Nāga* kingdom. Nevertheless, the element of the story that claims Nāgārjuna to be the bearer of an important class of religious texts remains.

In terms of the effect of this connection, the character of Nāgārjuna receives some authority by a partial merging with the character of the more recently famous Jain Nāgārjuna. At the same time, Kumārajīva's story demotes the status of the Himalayan monk Himavantācārya, thereby taking legitimacy away from the Jain tradition even as it borrows legitimacy from a Jain saint. Nāgārjuna learns what he can from this monk, but is dissatisfied and looks for other Mahāyāna *sūtras* elsewhere.

The *Mahāmegha* Prophecy and Related *Sūtras*

One of the best ways to grant legitimacy to a Buddhist saint is to have his birth and career predicted by the Buddha. This was certainly the idea behind the prophecy about the monk "whose name sounds like *Nāga*" in the *Laṅkāvatāra Sūtra*. There is another prophecy that may have factored into the construction of the Nāgārjuna legends—a prophecy that, in its original context, was unrelated to Nāgārjuna but was conscripted into the Nāgārjuna legend at least by the time of Candrakīrti (seventh century). Like the Jain Nāgārjuna, this prophecy may also be a source for the legends locating Nāgārjuna's residence in Gujarat. However, we must consider whether this prophecy could also be the source for the tradition associating Nāgārjuna with a Sātavāhana king. In his *Mādhyamakāvatāra,* Candrakīrti relates the following prophecy about Nāgārjuna:

> Also from the *Mahāmegha* (Great Cloud) Sūtra in 12,000 [verses]: "Ānanda, this Licchavi youth called 'Joy-When-Seen-By-All-Beings,' when 400 years after my *parinirvāṇa* have elapsed, will be a fully ordained monk named *Nāga* [who will] spread widely my teaching. Finally, in the world realm called the 'Pure Illumination,' (Prasannaprabhā)[49] he will become an arhant, a Samyaksambuddha, named 'Jñānākaraprabhā.'"[50] Therefore, by means of this *āgama* [Nāgārjuna's prediction] has been necessarily, and unmistakably established.[51]

The section of the *Mahāmegha Sūtra* to which Candrakīrti is referring has the Buddha talking about the past and future lives of a certain Liccavi youth named Sems can thams cad kyis mthoṅ na dga' ba ("Pleasant-to-See-by-all-Sentient-Beings"). Versions of the prophecy concerning the lives of this youth also appear in the *Mahābherīhārakaparivarta Sūtra* and the *Suvarṇaprabhāsottama Sūtra*.

The problem with this prophecy insofar as Nāgārjuna is concerned is that, although the earliest translation of the *Mahāmegha* into Chinese[52] does mention that a Licchavi youth will be reborn as the monk who will protect the dharma, it does not mention the monk's name. The closest that this translation comes is to say that the Licchavi youth was formerly a mysterious *nāga* king,[53] named Mahāvīrya*nāga*rāja (大精進龍王).[54] The Licchavi is, however, associated with a Sātavāhana king in a future life.[55] The Buddha foretells that, twelve hundred years after his death, the Licchavi youth will be reborn to a brahmin in the kingdom ruled by a great south Indian king named Sātavāhana (娑多婆呵那, *Soduopohena*), whose kingdom is called 須賴吒 (*Surāṣṭra,* modern-day Gujarat). He will be born in a village called 善方使 (Shànfāngshǐ) on the river 華鬘 (Huáhuán). During this lifetime he will become a monk who, among other things, teaches the *Vaipulya sūtras* of the Mahāyāna, supports and lifts up the Dharma, and distributes this (the *Mahāmegha*) *sūtra* throughout the world.[56] Thus, whoever this person is, he is associated with western India and a Sātavāhana king. Given the existence of many different versions of the *Mahāmegha Sūtra*, we cannot rule out the possibility that Candrakīrti is actually quoting from the version that he knew, a version that is no longer available. However, in view the fact that Nāgārjuna's name does not appear in any other version of this prophecy,[57] it seems more likely that Candrakīrti's statement reflects more of the reading practice of the Buddhist community that he represents than an actual textual variant.

Mabbett takes another of the *Mahāmegha's* prophecies to refer to Nāgārjuna. This is the prophecy that occurs at the very end of the *sūtra* and discusses a certain princess who will be the daughter of a "Sātavāhana" (his reconstruction of 等乘) king on the south bank of the river "Kṛṣṇa" (黑闇) in a town called "Dhānyakaṭaka" (執穀).[58] He concludes, "the *Mahāmegha Sūtra* therefore offers us a '*Nāga*' and a '*Nāga*rāja,' named in proximity to a prophecy about a Sātavāhana ruler at Dhānyakaṭaka."[59] Mabbett may be reading this *sūtra* too much through the lens of later Tibetan sources. Bu-ston and the other Tibetan historians do place Nāgārjuna at Dhānyakaṭaka, but the version of the *Mahāmegha Sūtra* that Mabbett (through Demiéville) cites does not. The "proximate prophecy" to which Mabbett refers occurs many pages after the prophecies attributed to Nāgārjuna by classical sources with nothing to link them. Furthermore, it is clear from the text that the Dhānyakaṭaka story is a prophecy relating a future birth of the *devī,* who is a character in the story unrelated to the future-Bhikṣu/present-Licchavi/past-*Nāga*rāja.

Not all traditional authors were convinced that the "*Nāga*" to whom Candrakīrti alludes in this prophecy refers so unmistakably to Nāgārjuna. Bu-ston, for one, provides an extended quotation from the *Mahāmegha Sūtra* contextualizing Candrakīrti's citation, and then adds, "So it is to be read, but it is not clear, whether (this passage) really refers to Nāgārjuna."[60] From the passage that Bu-ston quotes, it is clear that his version differs from Candrakīrti's, insofar as in Candrakīrti's version the monk is named *Nāga,* whereas in Bu-ston's version, the monk bears the name of the Buddha (presumably some form of "Śākya-"). Bu-ston explains that others have made this misattribution based on the fact that Nāgārjuna's ordained name is said to have been "Śākyamitra."[61] Nevertheless, he remains skeptical.

Because this prophecy probably had nothing to do with Nāgārjuna initially, the question of how its subsequent association with Nāgārjuna was justified in the minds of its interpreters becomes more significant. Why *this* prophecy? Was Nāgārjuna associated with this prophecy because it has a monk associated with a Sātavāhana king, or is Nāgārjuna associated with a Sātavāhana king because he is associated with this prophecy? In order for Candrakīrti to make his interpretation of the text plausible, we have to assume that some element of the future Licchavi's life corresponded to information that was already known about Nāgārjuna. Unlike the prophecy in the *Laṅkāvatāra Sūtra* that gives specifics of the monk's philosophical activities, this prophecy does not tell us anything about the future monk's affiliations except that he is an advocate for the Mahāyāna and propagates the *Vaipulya sūtras*. This monk is not named, so the attribution cannot be on similarity of name. *Nāgas* play a big part in the *Mahāmegha Sūtra* (a factor discussed further below), but, unlike the *Rājataraṅginī*, the particular story in the *Mahāmegha* that is associated with Nāgārjuna is not a story about *Nāgas*, except insofar as the monk had been a *Nāga* king two births earlier. Neither of these factors alone should have been enough to identify Nāgārjuna with this particular monk. The attribution of Nāgārjuna to the prophecy about the Licchavi youth crosses the threshold of plausibility only when these two elements are taken together *with the association with the Sātavāhana king*. The future, unnamed monk who in a past life was a *Nāga* king, who will teach the Mahāyāna, and who will associate with a Sātavāhana king in his future life, probably did sound like Nāgārjuna to Candrakīrti. Thus, we should see information about Nāgārjuna and the Sātavāhana king as leading to the association of Nāgārjuna with this prophecy, not that Nāgārjuna is associated with this prophecy and therefore becomes associated with the Sātavāhana king.

Nāgas

Every story related to Nāgārjuna contains recurring elements, though some elements recur infrequently. The discussion below examines two of these elements—*nāgas* and alchemy—in relation to his association with particular kings and place names.

Every account of Nāgārjuna has some etiological myth related to his name, that is, relating to *nāgas,* or snakes. Without detailing all the cultural significance of *nāgas* in early India, it suffices to say that *nāgas* were considered creatures of great magical power, who were often conscripted into the service of Buddhism in Buddhist legends. Nāgārjuna's connection to *nāgas* usually involves his receiving some gift or boon from a *nāga* king. In the *Harṣa-Carita,* this is an antidote to all poisons, a gift from the moon. In Kumārajīva's *Biography* and in the Tibetan historical tradition, the gift is the *Prajñāpāramitā Sūtras.* These myths demonstrate an attempt to tie the character of Nāgārjuna to some other element desirable to the hagiographer (such as alchemy or Mahāyāna Buddhism) through the instrument of his name.

Other associations made with *nāgas* are more complicated. Phyllis Granoff has identified this theme as one of the threads unifying all Jain biographies of Nāgārjuna.[62] These stories are replete with *nāga* associations. The most obvious of these is the fact that in Jain hagiographies Nāgārjuna's father is the *nāga* king, Vāsuki. Subtler use of the *nāga* connection is made in Nāgārjuna's association with, Stāmbhana Tīrtha. According to Granoff:

> What makes Nāgārjuna's association with Stāmbhana Tīrtha possible is the sinuous snakes. Stāmbhana was in fact revered for being the locus of a magical image of the Tīrthamkāra Parśvanātha. Now biographies of Parśvanātha are unanimous in pointing out connection between this Tīrthamkāra and the snake god Dharanendra. Nāgārjuna is said to have brought the magical image of Parśvanātha to Stāmbhana in the advice of his father the snake king, in order to make his elixir, in an act that now must seem almost natural in the associative world of these texts: the son of the snake God brings to the holy site the image of the *tīrthamkāra* protected by the snake deity.[63]

As we have shown above, *nāgas* are a contributing factor in Candrakīrti's association of Nāgārjuna with the *Mahāmegha Sūtra.* This *sūtra* is primarily a vehicle for transmitting a rain-making mantra. As such, the role of *nāgas* as both listeners of the *sūtra* and as characters in the story is emphasized. In addition to the Sātavāhana connection, Candrakīrti's association of Nāgārjuna with the Licchavi youth was probably aided by the youth's past life as the *Nāga*rāja (one cannot help but notice the play-on-words with "Nāgārjuna") Mahāvīrya.

The *nāga* connection played a more critical role in the assimilation of the Nāgārjuna legend into the chronicles of Kashmir in the *Rājataraṅgiṇī.* In this work, Nāgārjuna and his Mahāyāna followers are credited with leading good brahmins away from the rites of the *Nīla[mata]purāṇa,* with the result that the *nāgas* sent the snows to destroy the people. Those who did not adhere to Buddhism and still performed the rites were magically spared, whereas all the Buddhists were destroyed. The snows only abated when a certain brahmin, Candradeva, practiced austerities to please Nīla, "lord of the [Kashmir] *nāgas* and protector of the land." This Nīla subsequently reestablishes the rites previously revealed in his *purāṇa*. The story is then summarized: "As the first Candradeva had stopped the plague of the Yakṣas, thus the second brought an end in this land the intolerable plague of the Bhikṣus."[64] The entire story is a reworking of an older legend contained in the *Nīlamata Purāṇa*[65] with Nāgārjuna imported into the beginning of the story to explain why the *nāgas* were angry. That there were Buddhists in Kashmir was certainly common knowledge. The detail of Nāgārjuna at the head of the Buddhists seems to have been added as a poetic way to connect Mahāyāna Buddhists (we can assume that by that time it was common knowledge that he was a Mahāyānist) with a story about *nāgas*. However; unlike in the Jain stories, Nāgārjuna is the villain who is antagonistic to the *nāga* king, Nīla. Thus, pending any discovery to the contrary, the associations of Nāgārjuna with both Stāmbana Tīrtha and Kashmir should be regarded as serving a legitimating function in their legends and not as fact.

Alchemy

Another element common to all traditions concerning Nāgārjuna is that he was an alchemist. At the time that these legends were first composed (c. fifth century), alchemy was of great interest in the courts and monasteries in India as well as in China. Whether one is trying to sell the Nāgārjuna legend to an Indian audience or whether one is trying to export the legend to a Chinese audience, claiming that the saint is an alchemist would have ensured the audience's attention. Although the Jain tradition is perhaps the first to actually use the term "rasayāna siddha" ("alchemist")[66] to describe Nāgārjuna, this idea clearly has roots going back to Kumārajīva's stories of Nāgārjuna. In Kumārajīva's *Biography*, Nāgārjuna is credited with making an "elixir" (藥) of invisibility. In the story, he and some friends go to a magician for the formula. The magician, wanting them to remain dependent on him, does not give them the formula, but gives them pills that they are to grind to a paste and put on their eyelids. Nāgārjuna smells the resulting paste and guesses its seventy ingredients along with their quantities. The theme of Nāgārjuna detecting the formula for an elixir appears again in the *Prabandhacintamāṇi*, in which it is an ointment for flying that he smells under the ruse of washing his master's feet (the ointment works when applied to the feet).[67] In Xuanzang, Bu-ston, Tārānātha, and the *Prabandhacintamāṇi,* Nāgārjuna is credited with turning rocks into gold.[68] In Xuanzang's account, this is done in order to help a Sātavāhana king out of financial difficulties, whereas in Tibetan accounts, it is done to feed the *bhikṣus.* Xuanzang reports, "Nāgārjuna had the secret to long life,"[69] though the source of this long life is not mentioned. In Bu-ston, Tārānātha, the *Bṛhatkathāmañjāri,* the *Kathāsaritsāgara,* and Jain sources, he is credited with producing an elixir of longevity. In the *Prabhāndhacintāmaṇi,* this is in order to prove his perfection of charity. In Bu-ston and Tārānātha this elixir is shared with the Sātavahāna king, whose life is thereby prolonged.[70]

That Nāgārjuna is consistently associated with alchemy explains some details that we find in biographies of him. Granoff points out that Nāgārjuna is associated with Padaliptācārya by virtue of the fact that the Jain master was "the best known of all wizards in the Jain tradition."[71] Of course, the *nāga* connection also played a role in the association, insofar as Padaliptācārya was the boon of the snake goddess Vairothya to his barren parents. Furthermore, according to the *Prabandhakośa,* Padaliptācārya was really named "Nāgendra."[72] Nāgārjuna's connection to Padaliptācārya may be one of the rationales behind his association with Gujarat in general and Mt. Ḍhaṅka in particular. Padaliptācārya is associated with the mountain, and Nāgārjuna is associated with the *ācārya.*[73]

The alchemical connection is also the inspiration for the story in the *Bṛhatkathāmañjarī* and the *Kathāsaritsāgara,* where the king is named "Cīrāyus" ("long-life"). Clearly, the king's name is merely a function of a story about Nāgārjuna's alchemical feat of producing an elixir of immortality. Finally, it is worth considering whether Nāgārjuna's association with Śrīparvata may be one made by his biographers solely through his association with alchemy, as the name "Śrīparvata" had strong associations with the study of alchemy dating to at least the fifth or sixth century (when some of the earliest biographies were written). Nāgārjuna's association with this site may be nothing more than the association of his alchemy with the most famous alchemical site.

In fact, the numerous stories about Nāgārjuna's alchemical prowess may even confirm his south Indian origin. This is because, despite the many hagiographical details associated with alchemy, curiously, no evidence exists that Nāgārjuna *was* an alchemist. Although many works survive in the Tibetan canon that are ascribed to Nāgārjuna, according to David White, "Of the fifty-nine works attributed to Nāgārjuna and translated, in the twelfth through thirteenth centuries C.E. into Tibetan in the

Tanjur, none contains any alchemical material."[74] This is a strange circumstance for a figure who became the alchemist *par excellence* not only in his own religious tradition but in the Hindu and Jain traditions as well. No other Buddhist figure has been so widely renowned for alchemy and appropriated into other traditions as an alchemist. Thus the origin of the alchemical association requires some explanation.

Kumārajīva's *Biography* contains three examples of Nāgārjuna's magic (only the first of these feats is alchemy proper). The first story is Nāgārjuna's mishap with the invisibility potion, the second is his magical battle with a brahmin, and the third is his conversion of the south Indian king. At the beginning of each of these stories is something indicating that he is in south India. In fact, of the four times south India is mentioned, three of these introduce a story about his alchemy or wizardry. Although no Indian sources from the fifth century explicitly mention alchemical practices, alchemy was already firmly ensconced in the popular imagination of the Chinese for whom Kumārajīva was writing. In fact, in Ge Hong's *Baopuzi* (c. 320 C.E.) there is a discussion of an invisibility potion.[75] It is quite possible that the early associations of Nāgārjuna with alchemy came from Kumārajīva in an attempt to appeal to Chinese interests. The question remains as to why this practice would be associated with south India. The answer could be as simple as south India being a vast unknown region to Kumārajīva and hence the appropriate location for exotic heroes. Yet, by the time that Kumārajīva is writing, the trade routes between north and south are well traveled and the exotic south does not seem to be a major theme in the literature and drama of the day. Furthermore, some sources (such as Candrakīrti's *Catuḥśatakavṛtti*) connect Nāgārjuna to south India apart from any mention of alchemy.[76] Taking all this evidence together highlights the possibility that, for Kumārajīva, Nāgārjuna's south Indian origin may have been primary whereas his association with alchemy was strategic.

So where does all this leave us? Tracing the literary connections in the various legends of Nāgārjuna has led us to question the validity of Nāgārjuna's associations with Kashmir, the Himalayas, Mt. Ḍhaṅka, Stāmbhana Tīrtha, and Śrīparvata. Similarly, the stories associating Nāgārjuna with King Cīrāyus, and with Huṣka, Juṣka, and Kaniṣka, have also been called into question. The only element of these stories that does not seem to have been put there for specific sectarian, institutional, or ideological motivations is Nāgārjuna's association with the Sātavāhana king. As far as his residence is concerned, we are left with three names that occur prominently in Nāgārjuna legends: Nālanda, Vidarbha, and possibly Dhānyakaṭaka.

Nālanda cannot be taken seriously as a possibility for three reasons. First, it was not a strong monastic center until about 425, that is, after Kumārajīva's report that Nāgārjuna had been dead more than a hundred years.[77] Second, Nāgārjuna's associations with Nālanda are confined to Tibetan Buddhist sources that are concerned with placing him in the transmission lineage for the *Guhyasamājatantra,* a text that was important in the curriculum at Nālanda. Third, Xuanzang and Yijing both spent considerable time at Nālanda and studied Nāgārjuna's texts there. It is strange that they would have spent so much time there and yet chose not to report any local tales of a man whose works played such an important part in the curriculum.

Although absence of evidence cannot be taken as evidence of absence, the silence of the pre-tenth-century sources about a north Indian origin for Nāgārjuna should be carefully examined. Kumārajīva was born in Kuča and, at the age of nine, went with his mother to Kashmir, where he received his early schooling. Presumably, it was in Kashgar that he studied and memorized the texts of Nāgārjuna.[78] If he was between fifty and sixty years old when he translated Nāgārjuna's *Biography* in Chang'an and testified that Nāgārjuna had been dead for nearly a hundred years, we may assume that Nāgārjuna had been dead considerably less time than that when he first studied his texts before the age of twenty. Given this, it seems unlikely that he would not have heard any news of Nāgārjuna's having lived on the same trade route as the places where he (Kumārajīva) studied. By the same reasoning, Xuanzang, Yijing, and Huichao traveled to India during the sixth through eighth centuries and spent considerable time at Nālanda University; none of them report stories connecting Nāgārjuna with north India or with a north Indian king, whereas all of them (Kumārajīva included) heard stories connecting Nāgārjuna with south India and two of them heard of his association with a Sātavāhana king.[79]

The two remaining sites are in south India. Furthermore, the sites of Vidarbha and Dhānyakaṭaka (provided this latter attribution does not come from the *Kālacakra sūtra*) do not seem to be connected to stories about alchemy or *nāgas* and should be taken seriously as possible sites for Nāgārjuna's residence.[80] Because these two sites had strong associations with the Sātavāhana dynasty, these sites may also lend their weight to the connection between Nāgārjuna and a Sātavāhana king.

The Sātavāhana connection finds further support in the fact that, whereas all the elements in the Nāgārjuna hagiography discussed so far have some connection to either *nāgas* or alchemy, the Sātavāhana dynasty does not have strong connections to either. This is especially noticeable in the *Kathāsaritsāgara,* where the legends of Nāgārjuna and those of Sātavāhana are separated. All the stories about alchemy and *nāgas* are associated with Nāgārjuna, but none of these elements are contained in the story of Sātavāhana. The Sātavāhana king is mentioned in the *Mahāmegha* legend, however, as seen above, it is unlikely that the *Mahāmegha* is the source of this information. In short, Nāgārjuna's connection to a Sātavāhana king seems to have occurred independent of any hagiographical patterns of legitimation discussed thus far. In later hagiographical literature, it is not uncommon for a saint to have interactions with a king, but in most of these legends, the king is unnamed. It does help the legitimacy of a saint to be associated with a king, but if this association were made up, we would not expect to see unanimity as to the name of the king. The diversity of the legends about what Nāgārjuna did with this king rule out a single, *ur-* source for this information. Hence, we are still pressed to explain why Nāgārjuna is associated with *this* dynasty. Although many legends exist about Kaniṣka as a great patron of Buddhism, the only stories about a Sātavāhana king being a benefactor of Buddhism occur in conjunction with legends of Nāgārjuna. As far as the early Indian literary imagination was concerned, the Sātavāhana dynasty was probably not the best dynasty to which to attach your saint. Until another explanation can be offered, we simply have no choice but to consider that Nāgārjuna's hagiographers assumed this information to be common knowledge. Alternatively, we can find good reasons to discount stories claiming Nāgārjuna's association with any dynasty but the Sātavāhana and with any part of India but the Deccan. Thus, through a long process of elimination, the best reading of the information available points to Nāgārjuna's residence in the Deccan during the reign of a Sātavāhana king.

The *Ratnāvalī* and the Sātavāhana Dynasty: The Image of the Buddha

How does Nāgārjuna's association with the Sātavāhana dynasty help narrow down his date or place of residence? Simply put, Nāgārjuna's *Ratnāvalī* instructs the king to say a certain ritual formula three times a day in front of an "image of the Buddha" and to construct images of the Buddha "positioned on lotuses." If the arguments concerning Nāgārjuna's patron are valid, then the *Ratnāvalī* would have to have been written:

1. during the reign of a Sātavāhana king
2. at a time and in a region where Buddhas sitting on lotuses were a motif in use

3. at a time and in a region where Buddha images were available as distinct objects of veneration and/or propitiation, and
4. to a king who could have had access to an appropriate Buddha image to recite Nāgārjuna's twenty verse prayer.

Although anthropomorphic images of the Buddha had wide currency around Gandhāra and Mathurā as early as the first century, during most of the Sātavāhana dynasty anthropomorphic representations of the Buddha were absent in the Deccan. In fact, very few Sātavāhana kings were alive at a time and a place to meet all the above criteria for the *Ratnāvalī's* addressee.

The *Ratnāvalī* contains three verses in which Nāgārjuna mentions images of the Buddha.[81]

231 You should respectfully and extensively construct
Images of Buddha, Monuments [*stūpas*] and temples
And Provide residences, abundant riches, and so forth.[82]
232 Please construct from all precious substances
Images of Buddha with fine proportions,
Well designed and sitting on lotuses,
Adorned with all precious substances.[83]
465 Therefore in the presence of an image [of the Buddha][84]
Or monument [*stūpa*] or something else
Say these twenty stanzas
Three times every day[85]

The context indicates that these verses refer to actual images of Buddhas (as opposed to Buddhas to be visualized in meditation). Verses 231 and 232 begin a long list of construction and public works projects for the king to perform. Nāgārjuna is clearly not talking about meditation in this section. It is also likely that the image referred to in verse 465 was a physical image, as this practice of using physical images in a Mahāyāna ritual context has been found in other sources contemporary with the *Ratnāvalī*.[86] If Nāgārjuna lived at some distance from the king, we might refine our criteria further by stating that the motif of a Buddha on a lotus had to have been available at a time and in a place where Nāgārjuna could refer to it, and the king had to have access to an image of such a Buddha (preferably one not embedded in a narrative context), in front of which he could perform this ritual. I am, of course, assuming that Nāgārjuna would not have suggested that the king stand in front of an anthropomorphic image of the Buddha, knowing that such a thing was not in vogue where the king lived.

The Buddha Image in the Deccan

For a Sātavāhana king to be able to stand in front of an anthropomorphic image of the Buddha (as opposed to an iconic representation) and recite a formula, he would most likely have to have lived in the Eastern Deccan sometime *after* the first century C.E. Although the Western Deccan sites of Nāsik and Paithan were centers of Sātavāhana political activity until at least the reign of Yajña Śrī Sātakarṇi (170–198 C.E.) virtually no anthropomorphic images (sculpted or painted) of the Buddha have been found anywhere in the Western Deccan during the Sātavāhana dynasty.[87] Most scholars place the beginning of anthropomorphic representation of the Buddha in the Western Deccan much later, during the reign of Harisena (c. 450–500 C.E.) of the Vākāṭaka dynasty.[88] Thus, even if A. M. Shastri is right in claiming that Kumbha Sātakarṇi, Karṇa Sātakarṇi, and Śaka Sātakarṇi were the last three rulers of the Sātavahāna dynasty who ruled from Vidarbha right up to the beginning of the Vākāṭaka dynasty, it is still unlikely that any of these were Nāgārjuna's patron, because none of them would have had access to a Buddha image in that region.[89] For this reason, any king who could have been Nāgārjuna's patron would have had to live in the Eastern Deccan.

Only a few places in the Eastern Deccan were home to Sātavāhana kings. It appears that Puḷamāvi, Sivamakaskandha Gautamiputra, and Yajña Śrī Sātakarṇi may have ruled from Dhānyakaṭaka and Vijaya ruled from Nāgārjunakoṇḍa (also known as Vijayapūra). It is not known from where the last two Sātavāhana kings listed in the Purāṇas, Candraśrī and Puḷumāvi II, ruled. It is possible that Candraśrī continued to rule from Nāgārjunakoṇḍa as the one inscription mentioning him comes from Kodavoḷu in Godāvarī district. Using this same reasoning, however, we would have to place the last Sātavāhana king far west of Nāgārjunakoṇḍa, because Puḷumāvi II's only surviving inscription was found at Myakadoni in Bellary district, Karnataka.[90] The discussion below explores the art history of these regions to determine which of these kings would have had access to an image of the Buddha.

At this point it is useful to discuss the nature of art historical evidence available. All the work that has been done on the relative chronology of art in India during the period under consideration has been on art carved in stone. The reasons for this are obvious. Images made of materials that decay or break simply have not survived. The Buddha could be represented in other media, such as paintings and wooden or clay sculptures. The earliest mention of the figure of the Buddha refers to a painting.[91] Similarly, literary evidence for the representation of the Buddha on cloth can be found in the *Rudrāyanāvadānam* of the *Divyāvadānam,* where there is a legend that King Bimbisāra allowed the Buddha's image to fall on a piece of cloth in order that it might be painted.[92] Such portable images of the Buddha were popular at the time of Yijing, who reports the use of portable drawings of the Buddha by traveling monks.[93] Finally, M. K. Dhavalikar notes that some caves at Kanheri have wall sockets for installing wooden images.[94]

The varieties of artistic representation are relevant here because the the *Ratnāvalī* passage quoted above may well refer to a painting and not a sculpture. Verses 231–232 contain three verbs relating to the construction of the image. Unfortunately, both the Tibetan *mdzod pa* and *bgyis pa* and the Chinese 成立 seem to translate some form of the rather generic Sanskrit verb √kṛ ("to make"). The Narthaṅ and Peking versions of the Tibetan canon have *brgyan pa bgyid du gsol,* which simply means "to completely adorn." The third verb in verse 232, however, is more specific. Both the Chinese and Tibetan translations indicate that the images of the Buddha are to be "drawn" or "painted" (Paramārtha, 畫; Tibetan, *bris pa*). Both of these terms could translate the Sanskrit √*likh* (lit. "to scratch," but also "to write" or "to draw"). Although, it is possible that the *Ratnāvalī* is referring to the practice of scratching a line drawing of the subject on the rock before sculpting,[95] if the *Ratnāvalī* were referring to a sculpture, we would expect Paramārtha to use a different character, say 雕 (to sculpt) or 刻 (to chisel, to engrave). Whether anthropomorphic paintings of the Buddha existed during Sātavāhana times is at present difficult to prove. Paintings from Sātavāhana times have been found in the Western Deccan, but none of the Buddha. Nevertheless, unless there is some special explanation of why the anthropomorphic image of the Buddha (on a lotus, no less) should be portrayed in nonstone artworks when it is consciously avoided in stone sculptures, we may assume that the appearance of the lotus pedestal motif in sculpture would have been contemporaraneous with its appearance in other media.

Our task, then, is to determine when the motif of the lotus pedestal first appears in the Eastern Deccan. In the Eastern Deccan, the most thorough scholarship of the art history has focused on two sites: Amarāvatī and Nāgārjunakoṇḍa. The discussion below covers some of the relative dates of images from these sites and assumes that the sequence was the same at other sites in the region in the absence of a reason to think otherwise. A considerable amount of work has been done on the art sequence at the Amarāvatī *stūpa,* known in ancient times as Dhānyakaṭaka. The most recent work is that of Anamika Roy, who has thoroughly investigated the epigraphy, art, and architecture of that site in order to determine its chronology. On the basis of her findings, she divides the development of the site into four distinct phases.[96] The first phase is from about the third century B.C.E. to the first century C.E. During this time, although quite a few Buddhist narratives are portrayed in sculpture (narratives from the life of the Buddha as well as his past lives), an anthropomorphic image of the Buddha is conspicuously and uniformly avoided. In its place is the Buddha represented symbolically by the Bodhi tree, the *dharma cakra,* and so on. This avoidance of representing the Buddha anthropomorphically seems to be a Deccan-wide phenomenon and not confined to any particular sect in the Deccan during this period.

The second phase spans the first century C.E. and includes the first anthropomorphic representations of the Buddha. Roy lists two examples of this early form of the Buddha in catalogue numbers 187 and 188 of the Madras Government Museum.[97] These are both hybrid representations of the Buddha; images that use both symbolic representations and anthropomorphic depictions. Significantly, both depictions of the Buddha from this period have the Buddha sitting on either a throne (*paryaṅka*) or a long seat (*āsandi*) in *abhāya-mudrā.*[98]

The third phase marks the height of Buddhist art at Amarāvatī and lasts roughly until the second half of the second century. It is during this phase that the majority of the *Jātaka* tales were carved on the rail copings. In this phase, no new anthropomorphic representations of the Buddha appear, and the style again reverts to symbolic manifestations.[99] Nevertheless, there is no evidence to suggest that the previously installed Buddha images were taken away during this period.

The Sātavāhana kings who might have ruled over the area during these two artistic periods (and hence would have had access to an image of the Buddha) were Puḷumāvi I, Vāsiṣṭhīputra Sātakarṇi, Siva Śrī, and Sivamakasada. Possibly Gautamiputra Sātakarṇi was late enough to be included in this list, although all inscriptions bearing his name locate him in the Western Deccan.

It is unlikely, however, that any of these kings was the one to whom the *Ratnāvalī* was addressed because this artistic phase shows no evidence of the existence of the lotus throne (*padmapīṭha*) motif in the Deccan area this early. Even at Gandhāra and Mathurā during the Kuṣāṇa dynasty, wherein the anthropomorphic depiction of the Buddha begins quite early, the vast majority of Buddhas are depicted as sitting on three-tiered rectangular platforms whose flat front face served as a place for an inscription or an additional motif.[100] Buddhas depicted on lotus thrones in that region tend to be dated to the third century or after.[101] At Mathurā, sometime toward the end of the second century, *kuśa* grass cushions were added to the simple pedestal on which the Buddha sits, but no lotus thrones.[102] Coomaraswamy places the advent of the lotus throne motif sometime in the second century, but does not offer any more precision as to the time or the place of its advent.[103] Unfortunately, this precision is necessary to date the *Ratnāvalī* from its mention of a lotus base (*padmapīṭha, padmāsana,* or *kamalāsana*). If, however, we assume that a Sātavāhana king ruling over either Dhānyakaṭaka or Nāgārjunakoṇḍa patronized Nāgārjuna, then we need only to look for a rough date of the first *padmapīṭha* in this area to find a lower limit for the composition of the *Ratnāvalī.*

Roy does not discuss the advent of the lotus pedestal motif in the art of Amarāvatī, but a review of the documented sculptures from Amarāvatī containing this motif reveals that each of them belongs to her fourth phase of sculpture and to the second part of the fourth epigraphic phase. Relatively few sculptures from Amarāvatī exhibit this feature. It is found on a pillar (Madras Government Museum [MGM] 247), a frieze decorated with alternating Buddhas and *stūpas* (MGM 256), a drum slab (British Museum [BM] 79), and a railing pillar (BM 11). All of these are dated by Roy as from the third century or afterward (Roy's fourth phase), as they all share stylistic features common to whose Buddha images date from the second half of the third century.[104] The fourth and final period of Amarāvatī art, according to Roy, was marked by a change in artistic style. The human forms are noticeably more elongated. Fortunately, there is also a change in epigraphy that corresponds to this stylistic change. The epigraphy becomes more ornate, characteristic letters being a notched *ba* and a *pa* with a descending hook.[105] The latter development distinguishes the writing style of Śiva Skandha's Amarāvatī inscription from that of his immediate successor, Yajña Śrī.[106] Of the four images depicting a Buddha on a lotus from Amarāvatī, three have inscriptions. The inscription on MGM 247 is of little help in dating the image.[107] The inscriptions on BM 79 and MGM 256, however, do seem to belong to the same period as their sculptures, and Roy assigns both of these inscriptions to the second part of the fourth epigraphical phase (c. third century C.E.). Although the drum slab (BM 79) containing this motif has an inscription, Roy is somewhat uncertain of her dating of it. Her best guess is that it belongs to the fourth phase of epigraphy at Amarāvatī:

> BM no. 79 . . . : Half of the inscription is chipped off. Out of the remaining few letter forms, only one word *Bhadanta* is intelligible and

on the basis of these few letters, we may tentatively date it in the late 2nd or early 3rd century A.D. (Fourth phase).[108]

The inscriptions must, however, be more recent than the sculpture, because parts of the inscription continue between the heads of the uppermost figures of the frieze. Hence, Robert Knox's comments on the date of the sculpture are relevant.

> The extreme, fleshy naturalism of the carving of this relief places it at once in the Amarāvatī High Period. In the tightly packed, nervously energetic decoration of the slab it falls easily into the 2nd phase of the 3rd century A.D.[109]

With all the examples of the lotus pedestal placed in the fourth epigraphic and sculptural phase of Amarāvatī, the writing of the *Ratnāvalī* can reasonably be placed within the same period, because only during this phase is the motif of Buddha standing and sitting on lotus flowers.

To what extent can we translate this correlation into a range of dates? Of key importance to this study is the fact that, on epigraphical and stylistic grounds, the dome slab with the Buddha standing on lotuses discussed above belongs to the same epigraphic phase (Roy's IV.2) as the dome slab mentioning the reign of Yajña Śrī Sātakarṇi.

The latter inscription is not by Yajña Śrī himself but from an *upāsaka* from Ujjain.

> Sidham rājño Gotamapu[trasya] Śrī-Yajṭa-[Sa]-takaṇisya
> saṃvatsare . . . vāsa-pa 5 divase 8 Ujjayini-upasakena
> Jayilena . . . mahācetiye. . . kāritam . . .
> 3 . . . Dhanakaṭa-cetiya[110]

Unfortunately, although the inscription indicates that it was donated on the eighth day of the fifth fortnight of the monsoon, the regnal year is missing. Thus, all we know is that this was inscribed sometime during the reign of Yajña Śrī Sātakarṇi (which, by Purāṇic accounts, lasted twenty-nine years). As the sculpture on which the inscription is found still uses a nonanthopomorphic representation of the Buddha, we might assume that it was carved near the beginning of the fourth phase of Amarāvatī art and that it predates our Buddhas on lotuses discussed in the *Ratnāvalī*. This allows us to date the *Ratnāvalī* no earlier than the reign of Yajña Śrī (last quarter of the second century).

The reigns of the three Sātavāhana kings succeeding Yajña Śrī were fairly short (Vijaya six years, Candra Śrī three or ten years, and Puḷumāvi III seven years). Hence, if Nāgārjuna wrote the *Ratnāvalī* during the reign of a Sātavāhana king and during a time when the *padmapīṭha* motif was available, it would have had to be written within a period of fifty-two years. However, not all these kings ruled from Dhānyakaṭaka/Amarāvatī. We know from an inscription found at Nāgārjunakoṇḍa that Vijaya Sātakarṇi had moved the capital to that site, about a hundred kilometers away.[111] Although the Buddha image (with or without lotuses) continued to be produced at Amarāvatī, upstream at Nāgārjunakoṇḍa, artists or patrons appeared reluctant to use anthropomorphic images of the Buddha at all. In fact, the first images of the Buddha at this site can be dated only to the reign of Māṭharīputra Vīrapuruṣadatta (236–260 C.E.) or later.[112] The first Buddha in a nonnarrative context (i.e., carved for the purpose of worship) comes into existence only during the time of Ehuvala Cāṃtamūla (261–285 C.E.).[113] Thus, while images of the Buddha on a lotus existed in the Deccan during the reign of these last three Sātavāhana kings, it is unlikely that such an image was available to any king living at until the time of the second Ikṣvāku king (i.e., long after the Sātavāhana dynasty was over).

Although the location of the other two kings is uncertain, it appears from the location of their inscriptions that they were not at Dhānyakaṭaka/Amarāvatī either.[114] Until more is known about the reign of these two monarchs, it would be dangerous to speculate about the availability to them of Buddha images. The only surviving inscription mentioning Puḷumāvi II comes from the eighth year of his reign and is located at Myakadoni in Bellary district in Karnataka. If Puḷumāvi II had in fact relocated to that area, then it is unlikely that he would have had access to an image of the Buddha. Nevertheless, we cannot rule out either of these two kings as possible patrons for Nāgārjuna simply because we do not know enough about them. If, however, further investigation uncovers evidence that they continued Vijaya's rule from Nāgārjunakoṇḍa, they would be unlikely candidates for Nāgārjuna's king. By process of elimination, this leaves Yajña Śrī Sātakarṇi (c. 175–204 C.E.) as the most likely candidate for Nāgārjuna's patron, with Candraśrī (c. 210–213 or 210–220 C.E.—the *purāṇas* do not agree about the length of his reign) and Puḷumāvi II (c. 213–220 or 220–227 C.E.) as other possible candidates. If Nāgārjuna's patron had been a Sata/Sada king (as suggested by Paramārtha's translation of the *Ratnāvalī*), the date would not change because the few images of the Buddha found elsewhere in coastal Andhra probably do not predate those of Amarāvatī. Therefore, the best determination of the composition of the *Ratnāvalī* has to be between 175 and 204 C.E. or between 210 and 227 C.E., somewhere in the Lower Krishna Valley, with the earlier dates more likely than the latter.

Conclusion: Nāgārjuna's Monastery

In view of the discussion concerning Nāgārjuna's date and location, and the evidence from inscriptions, Chinese pilgrims, and Buddhist doxographies discussed in the introduction, it is highly unlikely that Nāgārjuna could have lived in an exclusively Mahāyāna monastery. It is much more likely that he lived in a mixed monastery. If we look at the inscriptions from the Andhra area, we must concede that in the lower Krishna Valley toward the end of the second century there simply were no Mahāyāna monasteries, either under the name "Mahāyāna" or under the name "Śākyabhikṣu."

Eleven Buddhist sects are mentioned in the Deccan inscriptions from this period: the Pūrva[mahāvina]śailas (at Amarāvatī and Alluru), the Apara[mahāvina]śailas (Nāgārjunakoṇḍa, Vengi, Kanheri, and Ghantasala), the Rājagīrika (Amarāvatī), the Caityaka (Nāsik, Junnar, and Amarāvatī), the Mahāsāṅghikas (Karle and Nāgārjunakoṇḍa), the Bāhuśrutīyas, the Mahiśāsakas (all at Nāgārjunakoṇḍa),[115] the Uttaraśailyas (Jaggayapeta), and (in the mid- to late fourth century) the Theravādins (Nāgārjunakoṇḍa and at points in north-coastal Andhra).[116] Despite the temptation to claim that the Pūrvaśailyas and Aparaśailyas were Mahāyānist based on Avalokitavrata's, discussion, it must be remembered that Avalokitavrata is writing in the sixth century and his account cannot be viewed as reflecting the situation four hundred years earlier without corroborating evidence. Inscriptions of other sects such as the Rājagīrikas, the Mahāsāṅghikas (as such, not as a subsect), the Mahīśāsakas, and the Uttaraśailyas appear too late to have been present during Nāgārjuna's time. Inscriptions mentioning the Bhadrānīyas (a subsect of the Vatsīputrīyas) can be found at Nāsik and Kanheri, but they do not seem to have ever been a presence in the east. The Bahuśrutīyas and the Dharmaguptakas, who, according to Paramārtha, were most likely to have been open to Mahāyāna ideas, both resided primarily in the north. If inscriptions are any indication, the Dharmaguptakas were confined primarily to Mathurā and the northwest around the Gandhāra region (modern-day Peshawar).[117] The Bahuśrutīya inscriptions are not confined to the north, but none have appeared as far south as the Deccan until the reign of Māṭharīputra Vīrapuruṣadatta (c. 250–275).[118]

In fact, the earliest inscriptions in the Eastern Deccan offering any possible indication of a financially independent Mahāyāna monastery date only from the fifth through the sixth centuries. The earliest is the Tummalagudem copperplate inscription of Govindavarman I (r. c. 420 C.E.). This inscription records the gift of two villages to an unnamed monastery. The inscription does, however, mention Mahāyāna notions such as *mahābodhicitta*, the eighteen *āveṅika* dharmas of the Buddha, and the three vehicles.[119] Hence, while we do not necessarily know that the monastery was Mahāyānist, we do know that Govindavarman I wanted to be known as one. Another possible candidate is found in an inscription among the Koṇḍavidu copperplate inscriptions of Prithivī Śrī Mūlarāja (fifth to sixth centuries).[120] Although this inscription says little about the beliefs of the inhabitants of the monastery, it indicates that the gift was made to a *Śākyabhikṣusaṅgha*, a possible epithet for a Mahāyānist.

Thus, the extant evidence points to the most likely scenario as being that Nāgārjuna probably lived in a Pūrvaśailya, Aparaśailya, or Caityaka monastery during the time he wrote the *Ratnāvalī*. If this is the case, then he wrote it in a time and at a place lacking any evidence that Mahāyānists received or disposed of money as Mahāyānists there or even though there were enough Mahāyānists present to constitute a proper movement. The consequences of Mahāyāna's minority status for Nāgārjuna's writing are the subject of Chapter 3.

3
Mahāyāna and the Constraints of Monastic Law

CHAPTERS 1 AND 2 argue that the preponderance of evidence points to two theses: in general, Mahāyāna was probably not well established, either institutionally or financially, in India until the fifth century; and Nāgārjuna was likely to have been living in a Mahāsāṅghika monastery in Andhra Pradesh when he wrote the *Ratnāvalī*. Chapter 3 addresses the implications of these for the interpretation of Nāgārjuna.

Few who have read Nāgārjuna's works have failed to be struck by his unusual writing style. Nāgārjuna's rhetorical idiosyncrasies, far from being merely adventitious, are part of a larger strategy to legitimate a budding Mahāyāna Buddhism in the Andhra region of India. Strategies arise as a response to specific constraints. Understanding the strategies that Nāgārjuna employs necessitates understanding the constraints those strategies were meant to overcome.

Chapter 1 discussed Gregory Schopen's thesis that, for ordained Mahāyānists, "early Mahāyāna in India was a small isolated, embattled minority group struggling for recognition within larger dominant groups."[1] Although Jan Nattier and others have argued that at least some Mahāyānists did not find themselves in conflict with their fellow Buddhists, the picture of Mahāyāna that Nāgārjuna develops in the *Ratnāvalī* and the *Mūlamadhyamakakārikā* was in conflict with fellow Buddhists.[2] This chapter develops Schopen's thesis about the tension between Mahāyāna and non-Mahāyāna as it is presented in chapter 4 of the *Ratnāvalī*.

In a recent article on early Mahāyāna, Schopen calls Nāgārjuna's *Ratnāvalī* an ideal vehicle to illustrate the nature of early Mahāyāna since it provides us with a "contemporary characterization" of the movement.[3] I would only add to this observation that the *Ratnāvalī* is one of the earliest extant sources written by an identifiable Mahāyānist whose date and location can be ascertained—thus, its "contemporary characterization" is also among the oldest.[4] For Schopen, the weakness of the Mahāyānists' position in the monastery is illustrated by the tenor of Nāgārjuna's rhetoric:

> The tacit admission (in *RĀ* 4.85) of the rejection of the Mahāyāna is perhaps the one unifying theme of the entire discussion in chapter IV of the *Ratnāvalī,* and although Nāgārjuna—or whoever wrote the text—does occasionally actually muster arguments in response to the perceived rejection, the response is most commonly characterized not by the skill of a dialectician, but rather by the heavy-handed rhetoric typical of marginalized sectarian preachers.[5]

Schopen points to three features of Nāgārjuna's rhetoric, which indicate that the Mahāyāna of Nāgārjuna's community was in a position of weakness. The first feature is the fact that Nāgārjuna has to defend Mahāyāna texts and teachings as authentic "word of the Buddha."[6] For Schopen, this is a tacit admission that his audience did not accept Mahāyāna as authentic. The second feature is Nāgārjuna's resort to slander. Nāgārjuna has little good to say about the opponents of Mahāyāna in the *Ratnāvalī.* As a group, he accuses them of being "ignorant" about Mahāyāna and of basing their opposition to Mahāyāna entirely on "anger." The third rhetorical feature indicative of Mahāyāna's weakness occurs in *Ratnāvalī* verses 88–89, in which Schopen sees a virtual admission of defeat:

> But the real weakness of the position of the Mahāyāna is perhaps most strikingly evident, in a series of verses where our author gives up any attempt to argue for the acceptance of the Mahāyāna, and—playing off of the old Buddhist ideal of *upekṣā*—argues instead that it should at least be *tolerated.* . . .
>
> > Since it is indeed not easy to understand what is declared with intention by the Tathāgata, when one vehicle and three vehicles are declared, one should be careful by remaining impartial (*ātmā rakṣya upekṣayā*)
> >
> > There is indeed no demerit through remaining impartial (*upekṣayā hi nāpuṇyam*). But from despising there is evil—how could

> that be good. As a consequence, for those who value themselves despising the Mahāyāna is inappropriate.

This has the smell of a retreat.[7]

The following discussion holds that, while Schopen has got the setting right (Mahāyāna does appear to be an embattled minority in the *Ratnāvalī*), he has perhaps mistaken the tactical elements of the letter for signs of defeat. Much more needs to be said about the tactics and strategies on both sides of the conflict. A careful analysis of this section of the *Ratnāvalī* in light of the early Indian legal milieu reveals a set of shrewd legal maneuvers concealed behind the apparently shrill rhetoric—maneuvers that, in the long run, allowed the Mahāyānists a modicum of success.

How would the Mahāyānists of Nāgārjuna's community have been distinguished from any other Buddhists? To answer this question, I propose a functional definition of Mahāyāna. What is it that Mahāyānists do that other Buddhists do not? At minimum, a Mahāyānist is someone who identifies with *the idea* of Mahāyāna, however inchoate or polythetically defined. In light of the *Ratnāvalī* quotation above, we can further say that the Mahāyāna relevant to Nāgārjuna's community was constituted by those Buddhists who produce and replicate teachings understood to be labeled "Mahāyānist" (and, again, in the *Ratnāvalī,* the word "Mahāyāna" appears to need no definition—even for the king to whom it is addressed). By this definition, Mahāyānists would stand out as a distinct group to a greater degree in communities in which there was resistance to this activity of production and reproduction of Mahāyāna teachings.

Let us consider the majority position. Schopen says that Mahāyāna was "embattled." What were the weapons of this battle? The first and perhaps most obvious weapon for opponents of the Mahāyāna was the law. From the vantage point of a monk, the law in ancient India had a three-tiered, segmentary structure consisting of civil law, sectarian law, and local monastic rules. The overarching legal category and the final authority was civil law as exemplified in the various *Dharmaśāstras*. Sectarian monastic law of the Buddhist *vinayas* was subsidiary to civil law.[8] Finally, each individual monastery had a set of "house rules" (*kriyākarma*) to supplement the *vinaya* rules.

A note concerning *vinaya* rules themselves. Ever since the appearance in 1991 of Schopen's influential article "Archaeology and Protestant Presuppositions in the Study of Indian Buddhism," scholars of early Indian Buddhism have been trying to wean themselves away from an overreliance on textual sources.[9] Schopen questions the usefulness of scholar's use of *vinaya* texts to describe ancient monastic life. He then takes some famous archaeologists to task for grounding their interpretation of archaeological finds in an assumption (presumably derived from a reading of *vinaya* texts) that monks could not possess money. For Schopen, the problem with giving primacy to the written *vinaya* texts is that these texts may not have ever been implemented.

> There appears to be, however, no actual evidence that the textual ideal [in the *vinayas*] was ever fully or even partially implemented in actual practice; at least none is ever cited. And even though the mere existence of rules against it might suggest that monks did own personal property, and even though it is clear that in the textual ideal itself the infraction of those rules was a "minor offense," and even though it is almost certain that in a strictly legal sense "the monk might retain the ownership of the property that he had abandoned," still all material evidence that monks did have personal property must be explained away: Bühler's "they must have obtained it by begging," Lüders' "Probably, we have to suppose [they that they collected the money . . . by begging it from their relatives or acquaintances]."[10]

Any facile attempt to portray monks in ancient India as renouncing all wealth appears feeble in light of archaeological finds such as the coin mold that was found in a monk's cell in a monastery at Nāgārjunakoṇḍa.[11]

As a result of these observations, many scholars today tend to read Buddhist *vinaya* texts as interesting pieces of literature, but not necessarily as legal documents that were put into effect—despite the fact that Schopen's later work on the *Mūlasārvāstivāda vinaya* strongly suggests that the authors he criticizes simply had not understood the complexities of the *vinaya* laws concerning wealth.[12] Although a corrective was certainly necessary in order to mitigate an overliteral reading of *vinaya* texts, recent trends dismissing *vinaya* texts as having no legal teeth do not account for all the evidence either. The best approach is to take a middle path. It would be difficult to prove that every monastery followed and enforced every monastic rule to the letter (and easy to find examples where they did not), yet there is no reason to assume that *the idea* of the *vinaya* was not a governing force in the monastery. Consider an analogy from modern society. The modern nation-state is governed by thousands of laws. The average citizen is aware of a handful of these laws (e.g., "murder is prohibited") and is probably not aware of the majority of them (e.g., "spitting on the sidewalk is prohibited"). As a result, while most of us are careful not to violate the laws carrying the severest penalties, on a given day a person might violate a score of minor laws and be completely unaware of it. The local government might be aware that these transgressions take place and simply not consider it worthwhile or not have the means to prosecute the offenders. The law as written nevertheless serves as an *opportunity structure* for all interested parties. It is a resource available to facilitate one's own actions or to constrain someone else's actions *should one choose to appeal to it.*

This chapter and chapter 4 take Indian legal texts seriously. In so doing, they do not assume that these texts were always followed to the letter, any more than they assume that all citizens of modern nation-states follow the law to the letter. On the contrary, the chapters describe evidence for a legal infrastructure governing the allocation of resources, the recognition of institutions, the formation of new laws, and the handling of dissent. Because the ancient legal texts referred to appear to be the only sources offering a structure for such regulation, these documents should be regarded as providing a common legal recourse *on the occasion of a dispute.*

Classical Indian jurisprudence understood religious orders like Buddhism as a kind of *samaya,* or group brought together by compact under a group charter. As such, they were to be treated in the same manner as other kinds of internally ordered social groups, such as guilds. The charter of each group defined its institutional structure and defined membership by adherence to the group's internal rules. Violation of these rules could result in sanctions applied either internally or (in severe cases) by secular authorities. Because membership is constituted by conformity to rules, those found in violation could be stripped of membership. These charters were meant to supplement, not supercede, the dictates of civil law.

For Buddhism, the *vinayas* of the various Buddhist monastic sects were understood as their legal charter. They were therefore a matter not just of internal concern but of public record.[13] The *prātimokṣa sūtra* of the Mūlasarvāstivādins even makes explicit the connection between the Buddhists' *prātimokṣa sūtra* and the charters of guilds, saying, "this great treaty consists of articles of precepts for the monks which are like a guild of merchants."[14]

Buddhist monastic law itself has two levels. The first level consists of sectarian law, or the law applicable to all monasteries affiliated with a particular sect. For example, all Mahāsāṅghika affiliated monasteries would follow the *Mahāsāṅghika vinaya,* all Mūlasarvāstivāda monasteries, the *Mūlasarvāstivāda vinaya,* and so on. The second level consists of the local monastic rules (called *kriyākarma*) instituted by each individual monastery. Again, these rules appear to be supplementary rules, added on to those of the *vinaya.*

It is a remarkable feature of the extant *vinayas* that they are aware not only of their own legislative power but also of the need to situate this power in relation to both civil authority and local monastic authority. For example, in its description of the first "council" (*saṅgīti*, lit. "recitation") in which the *Tripiṭaka* was first compiled, the *Mahāsāṅghika vinaya* (the *vinaya* tradition into which Nāgārjuna was most likely ordained)[15] relates an account of Upāli's recitation of the *Vinaya Piṭaka*. Upāli's very first statement about the *vinaya* begins by laying out the five potential sources of law (here best translated as either "law" or "rule of comportment"):

> There are five pure dharmas, according to dharma, according to *vinaya*, which lead to happiness. Those which are not in accord with the dharma and *vinaya* must be opposed. What are the five? The first is purity of local monastic ordinance (制限 *kriyā karma*); the second is purity of local (civil) law (方法); the third is purity of discipline (戒行 *śīla*); the forth is purity of the elders (長老 *āyuṣman*); the fifth is the purity from (prior) worldly comportment (風俗).[16]

The definitions of these five are discussed below, but for the time being it suffices to say that the first three *dharmas* correspond to the three basic levels of law outlined above.

As shown below, these various levels of law were written so as to be binding in very real and practical terms. They should be seen as a potential constraint to Mahāyāna activities in monasteries where its interpretation and application were in the hands of a non-Mahāyāna majority. To the extent that Mahāyānists were seen as a threat (or merely a nuisance), they would have to negotiate their way through monastic polity while being vigilant about any legal pitfalls along the way. Any perceived breach of the standard procedure of the monastery might direct unwanted attention to the Mahāyānists and would leave them open to sanctions ranging from general disapproval to censure of their preaching.

This chapter focuses specifically on the nexus of civil, sectarian, and local laws and its implications for what a monk is and is not free to communicate. It should be remembered that philosophy must be communicated and that there was nothing like unrestricted freedom of speech for ordained monks in ancient India. At the sectarian level, monks in the Mahāsāṅghika order took 202 vows governing acts of body and speech. Any reading of Nāgārjuna must take this legal context into consideration. If Mahāyānists were indeed in the minority, then all their preaching and writing activities would have been vulnerable to sanctions under the law as adjudicated by those in a position to do so. It will be crucial for our interpretation of Nāgārjuna's writing to take into consideration the laws that could potentially apply to Mahāyāna, as his writing would have to take these laws into account. As Leo Strauss notes in his *Persecution and the Art of Writing:*

> Persecution cannot prevent even public expression of the heterodox truth, for a man of independent thought can utter his views in public and remain unharmed, provided he moves with circumspection. He can even utter them in print without incurring any danger, provided he is capable of writing between the lines.[17]

Clearly, if Nāgārjuna were writing under fear of censure then not only what he says at face value but also to what he says "between the lines" are critical. A close examination of his work demonstrates a careful articulation of philosophical innovation *vis-à-vis* the negotiation of material and institutional constraints.

The *Vinayas,* the Majority, and the Charge of "Splitting the *Saṅgha*"

Let us begin at the level of sectarian law as found in the *vinayas.* Early Mahāyānists living in non-Mahāyāna monasteries faced two obvious hurdles. The first was that their lectures and sermons would not have conformed to those preached by their brethren, and the second that the *sūtras* they wanted copied, studied, and preached from would not be understood to conform to the *sūtras* in use by the rest of the monastery. For both reasons, Mahāyānists were vulnerable under Buddhist monastic law to the charge of instigating a schism. The accusation of fostering a schism (*saṅghabheda*) had potential legal repercussions that were quite severe and would have to be a great concern to any budding religious movement.

Although Buddhism in India never had a central ecclesiastic institution with the authority to decide matters of doctrine or law comparable to the "Congregation for Doctrine and Faith" in the Catholic Church, this is not to say that a functional "orthodoxy" did not exist at the local level. In matters of dispute, the law code in the *vinayas* emphasized consensus brokered through the scriptural hermeneutics offered by local experts in contrast to any authority held by a single monastic office. The importance of consensus was built into the very fabric of the monastic apparatus and therefore limited the degree to which Mahāyāna could deviate from the norm and still receive institutional support or recognition.

Because all the monasteries in the lower Krishna River Valley during the time of Nāgārjuna belonged to the Mahāsāṅghika, it will be worthwhile to examine the rules restricting a monk's doctrinal affiliation in the *Mahāsāṅghika vinaya.*[18] The importance of monastic unity can be seen in the seriousness with which schismatics are treated in Buddhist monastic law. From the standpoint of Buddhist law, one who is guilty of instigating a schism is guilty of a *saṅghātiśeṣa* offense. On a practical level, a *saṅghātiśeṣa* offense requires censure and a probationary period—a fairly hefty punishment as monastic sanctions go. On a karmic level, however, the consequences are quite severe. Causing a schism is a sin with immediate retribution of a rather nasty variety (on par with killing one's mother and father, killing an *arhant,* etc.).[19] The *Abhidharmakośavākya,* by Vasubandhu, for example, says that a person found guilty of such a crime will have to endure a cosmic age in Avīci hell![20]

This offense as it is worded in the *Mahāsāṅghika Prātimokṣa* is defined as:

> Whatever monk should proceed toward a division of a *saṅgha* which is harmonious, or having taken up a legal question conducive to a schism, and should persist in taking it up, that monk should be spoken to thus by the monks: "Do not, O Venerable One, proceed toward a division of a *saṅgha* which is harmonious, or taking up a legal question conducive to a schism, persist in taking it up. Let the Venerable One come together with the *saṅgha,* for the *saṅgha* is harmonious, united, on friendly terms, without dispute, and dwells comfortably under one rule, like milk and water, illuminating the Teaching of the Teacher." And should that monk . . . abandon that course, this is good. If he should not abandon it, that monk should be questioned and admonished by the monks up to three times for the abandonment of that course . . . Should he not abandon it. . . . and persist in taking it up, that is a *saṅghātiśeṣa.*[21]

Notice here that weight of this rule lies in the contrast between one monk's behavior and the idealized image of the *saṅgha* as "harmonious, united, on friendly terms, without dispute, [which] dwells comfortably under one rule, like milk and water." This ideal stands in stark contrast to the allegations by Mahāyānists that there was considerable acrimony within some monasteries toward the very idea of Mahāyāna. The passage seems to be saying that a monk who finds himself advocating a controversial position should abandon that position for the sole reason that it may threaten the unity of the *saṅgha.*

The rule that follows in the *prātimokṣa* prohibits other monks from following a schismatic, and in this rule we glimpse a different criterion surpassing even the majority consensus for determining whether a teaching is heretical.

> If there are one, two, three, or many monk-comrades of a schism-minded monk, who take his side and follow him, and these monks together with men should say to those [other] monks, "Do not, O Venerable Ones, say anything good or bad about this monk. This monk speaks according to the Dharma and this monk speaks according to the Vinaya." . . . These monks [siding with the schism-maker] should be spoken to thus by the [other] monks: "Do not, O Venerable Ones, speak thus. This monk does not speak according to the Dharma and this monk does not speak according to the Vinaya." . . . Should they not abandon it, having taken up that course, and persist in taking it up, that is a *saṅghātiśeṣa*.[22]

This passage places the authority of the text over that of the monks. It uses a formula that is common in *vinaya* literature, "If there are one, two, three, or many [monks doing something wrong] . . ." The use of this phrase is an indication that sheer numbers alone do not vouchsafe a heretical position. Rather, the accusation is that any monk who follows someone not teaching *dharma* and *vinaya* (i.e., someone who is not *dharma-vādī/vinaya-vādī*) is culpable to the charge of following a schismatic regardless of how many other monks follow suit. The benchmark of monastic authority is not the number of people involved but, rather, the authority of the *dharma* and *vinaya* itself, as it has been received by the monastery in question. In the traditional four methods for resolving conflicts in a monastery, the position of *dharma* is assumed to be given and immutable, and it is assumed that, since all monks wish to be in accord with it, they will quickly reform when confronted with a better interpretation.[23] Yet even here textual authority boils down to authoritative interpretation determined by a formal act of the *saṅgha*. Thus, the "Sāmagāma sutta" of the *Majjhima Nikāya* states:

> And how is there removal of litigation by confrontation? Here bhikkhus are disputing: "It is Dhamma," or "It is not Dhamma," or "It is Discipline," or "It is not Discipline." Those bhikkhus should all meet together in accord. Then, having met together, the guideline of the Dhamma should be drawn out. Once the guideline of the Dhamma has been drawn out, that litigation should be settled in a way that accords with it. Such is the removal of litigation by confrontation.[24]

Mahāyāna's Liability

If Mahāyānists were in the minority, to what extent would they have been liable to this charge of "splitting the *saṅgha*"? The *Majjhima Nikāya* passage dismisses the possibility of a dispute over doctrine in the Buddhist *saṅgha* and assumes that the only tension that will arise in the *saṅgha* will be a dispute over the interpretation of monastic rules. If this were the case, the *saṅghabheda* rule would not necessarily have applied to Mahāyāna. Indeed, the prevailing trend among scholars is to take the terms *dharma* and *adharma* in the rules concerning schisms as referring to the monastic rules alone. This interpretation sees the monastic rules concerning schisms (*saṅghabheda*) as splits exclusively over legal issues and not over points of doctrine. It is presumably for this reason that Prebish translates the word *adhikaraṇa* (issue or topic) as "legal question," in his translation of the *Mahāsāṅghika Prātimokṣa,* and why Ñāṇamoli translates it as "litigation" despite the fact that the term can also refer to a topic of philosophical debate. The first to argue for an exclusively legal interpretation of *adhikaraṇa* was Heinz Bechert:

> Here, "*bhikkhū adhammaṃ dhammo ti dīpenti* . . ." has been understood as referring to the teaching of the Buddha in general. This interpretation is, however, wrong, because in this context within vinaya regulations *dhamma* means the "law of the Buddha" as issued in the Vinayapiṭaka for the Sangha and nothing else. This is corroborated by a series of synonyms used in many vinaya passages, e.g. in the passage following the above quoted definition of *saṅgharāji* and *saṅghabheda* (Vinaya II, 205): "*ayaṃ dhammo ayaṃ vinayo idaṃ satthu sāsanaṃ*" (this is the law, this is the rule of discipline, this is the teacher's order"). . . . It is now clear that *saṅghabheda* does not mean "schism" in the sense known from Christian Church history, where it nearly always implies dissentions in the interpretation of dogma. In Buddhist tradition, "splitting the Sangha" always refers to matters of monastic discipline.[25]

Quoting the last part of the above passage, Paul Williams points out the implications that this has for our understanding of early Mahāyāna.

> This [i.e., Bechert's thesis] is important. Schools and traditions might differ on doctrinal matters, and of course, doctrinal differences

> might arise after schism has occurred . . . Nevertheless, *differences of doctrine as such are a personal matter. In theory a monastery could happily contain monks holding quite different doctrines so long as they behaved in the same way—crucially, so long as they adhered to the same monastic code.*[26]

There is, however, some reason to question the applicability of Bechert's interpretation for all Mahāyānists. Bechert makes his conclusion about the practice of Buddhist law from the reading of one example from the Theravāda tradition alone. Even within the Theravāda tradition *Cūḷavagga* VII 5.2, for example, attributes splits in the *saṅgha* to the existence of debates within the monastic community.

> *Saṅghabheda, Saṅghabheda,* tell me Sir in what respect is the *Saṅgha* split? Here, Upāli, monks teach dharma to be what is not the dharma, they teach what is not the dharma to be the dharma. They teach what is not the *vinaya* to be the *vinaya.* They teach what is not the *vinaya* to be the *vinaya.* They teach that what was not said, was not uttered by the Tathāgata was said and uttered by the Tathāgata. They teach that what was said and uttered by the Tathāgata was not said and uttered by the Tathāgata. They teach that what was not habitually practiced (*āciṇṇa*) by the Tathāgata, was (actually) practiced by the Tathāgata. They teach that what was actually practiced by the Tathāgata was not practiced by the Tathāgata. They teach that what was not ordained (*paññatta*) by the Tathāgata, was ordained by the Tathāgata. They teach that what was ordained by the Tathāgata was not ordained by the Thatāgata. They teach that what is an offence (*āpatti*) is not an offence.[27]

Buddhaghosa's commentary on this passage defines *dharma* and *adharma both* in terms of law and in terms of religious practice.

> "They teach what is dharma to not be dharma . . ." concerning the eighteen topics leading to schism etc., the ten skillful karmic paths are "dharma" according to the mode used in the Suttantas (*suttantapariyāyena*). The ten unskillful karmic paths are "not dharma." Thus, the four foundations of mindfulness, the four right efforts, the four bases of spiritual power, the five sense faculties, the five powers, the seven enlightenment factors, the noble eightfold path and the thirty-seven dharmas which are the limbs of awakening are called "dharma."[28]

Here, the ten unskillful karmic paths might be roughly interpreted to fall under the auspices of the *vinaya* code, but the thirty-seven limbs of awakening cannot. The religious practices embodied in the thirty-seven *bodhipakṣa* fall within the domain of the *sūtra piṭaka,* not the *vinaya piṭaka.* Indeed, the discussions of the *bodhipakṣa* are otherwise virtually absent from Theravādin *vinaya* literature outside the commentaries. Even if Bechert is correct regarding Theravāda, his conclusion does not apply to other *vinayas.* Jan Nattier and Charles Prebish have pointed out that early scholastic accounts of the Vaiśālī schism disagree as to whether its cause was a dispute over law or a dispute over doctrine.

> we find that the breakdown is according to sectarian affiliation: the Theravādin and Mahāsāṅghika sources cite the Vinaya as the source of the schism, while the Sarvāstivādin works (as well as Paramārtha, a Mahāyānist whose work is based on the Sarvāstivādin tradition of Vasumitra) all attribute the schism to matters of doctrine.[29]

Although the *Śāriputraparipṛcchā* (an early Mahāsāṅghika doxographical work) claims that the Vaiśālī schism occurred over matters of the *vinaya,* the *Mahāsāṅghika vinaya* clearly points to debates over doctrine in addition to debates over law as a potential source of schism. The commentary on each of the *prātimokṣa* rules begins with a *nidāna* (origin story) explaining the situation that gave rise to the rule. The incident that gave rise to the *saṅghabheda* rule in the *Mahāsāṅghika vinaya* is recounted as follows:

> At that time, Devadatta desired to split the harmonious, unified *saṅgha* and thus strove to facilitate an issue conducive to the splitting of the *saṅgha.* Concerning the twelve sūtra, the *nidāna* (戒序), the four *parājikas,* the thirteen *saṅghātiśeṣa* offences, the two *aniyata* dharmas, the thirty *nisārgika* offences, the ninety-two *pāyantika,* the four *pratideśanīya* dharmas, the *śaiksa* dharmas, the seven *adhikaraṇa-śamatha* dharmas and the (six) *anudharma,*[30] he instituted what had not been instituted. Those (rules) that had already been instituted, he conveniently disclosed, so that householders and monks could follow the dharma. The nine classes of scripture are: sūtra (修多羅), *geya* (祇夜), *vyākaraṇa* (授記), *gātha* (伽陀), *udāna* (優陀那), *itivyūtaka* (如是語), *jātaka* (本生), *vaipūlya* (方廣), and *abhūtadharma* (未曾有法). From these nine kinds of scripture, he further authored (作) different sentences, different words, different flavor (異味; *anya rasa*), and different meanings. (He taught) each (monk) to recite and study (the

> Buddhist scriptures) in a different script (異文) and in his own language. Retaining it this way he also taught others to retain it thus.[31]

The *Mahāsaṅghika vinaya* thus presents the origin of the *saṅghabheda* rule from two distinct activities of Devadatta. The first is that he added rules to the *vinaya*. The second is that he corrupted the transmission of the nine sections of the *sūtra piṭaka*. It is evident from this passage that the "splitting of the *saṅgha*" rule applied not only to disagreements over the *vinaya*, as Bechert and Williams contend, but to disagreements regarding the *sūtra piṭaka* as well. The schism that Devadatta instigated was not just a disagreement over an interpretation of a monastic rule—more fundamentally, it stemmed from a disturbance in the institutional mechanism for scriptural reproduction. To the extent that the teachings of the Buddha form the very fabric of monastic life, flaws in the reproduction of his teachings may well have constituted a threat to the whole monastic project. Interestingly, this rule against splitting the *saṅgha* is the only rule in the *Mahāsaṅghika vinaya* that applies to someone who intentionally introduces change into the scriptural tradition. We may wonder then whether the Mahāsāṅghikas saw textual corruption as the *saṅghabheda* offense *par excellence*.

Hierarchy of Appeals

By the time of Nāgārjuna, monasteries had a corpus of texts already authorized (though this corpus was not necessarily identical from monastery to monastery).[32] It does not take too much imagination to see that some monks might have accused the Mahāyānists in their midst of introducing change into the scriptural corpus because they interpreted scripture differently or because they employed different texts. These monks had cause under Mahāsāṅghika monastic law to accuse the offending monks of attempting to introduce a schism. How would the monks so offended proceed to address the problem? In practice, the need for unanimity in order to settle matters of dispute could provide pressure enough. Although it took place later and perhaps was not typical, an example of the pressures to conform is provided in Yijing's (late seventh-century) account of an assembly at Nālanda monastery.

> If the monks had some business, they would assemble to discuss the matter. (衆僧有事集衆平章 令其護寺) Then they ordered the officer, Vihārapāla to circulate and report the matter to the resident monks

> one by one with folded hands. With the objection of a single monk, it would not pass. There was no use of beating or thumping to announce his case. In case a monk did something without the consent of all the residents, he would be forced to leave the monastery. If there was a difference of opinion on certain issue, they would give reason to convince (the other group). No force or coercion was used to convince.[33]

The Chinese character that Lahiri translates as "business" is 事, which is often translated as *adhikaraṇa* in *vinaya* literature. Hence, the situation described by Yijing is an official monastic assembly called to settle a matter of dispute (which could be doctrinal or legal). Two points are important here. First, the matter was not considered settled until all were in agreement. Second, (ideally) neither the Vihārapāla nor the other monks were to coerce those who did not agree.

Yijing was primarily familiar with the *Mūlasarvāstivāda vinaya*. The *Mahāsāṅghika vinaya*, however, does contain a provision for using various degrees of coercion. In the section addressing the pacification of disputes (*śamathādhikaraṇa*) in the *Mahāsāṅghika vinaya*, most cases describe an errant monk being approached by another monk and asked to change his ways. Although a monastery could always resort to the *vinaya* definitions and punishments for *saṅghabheda*, it was probably better for the unity of the *saṅgha* (not to mention the image of the *saṅgha* in the eyes of the laity) to put pressure on a monk through a more informal confrontation. The *Mahāsāṅghika vinaya* states that, when a recalcitrant monk refuses to concede to the majority, the arbitrating monk (if he deems himself unequal to the task) may appeal to a hierarchy of authorities to intervene.

> The Buddha told Upāli, "He who wishes to settle an argument should first assess his own strength of body, strength of virtue, strength of eloquence [辯才], and bravery. Know how the issue arose. A monk first reflects on (himself) regarding required strengths (mentioned above). When the argument arises again, it will not take long before his heart softens and the argument easily disappears. If, after self-reflection, the monk realizes that he does not have the above strengths, the debate has been on-going for a long period of time, (and) the opponent is too strong to be vanquished, then he should ask a monk of great virtue [大德] to help him settle the dispute. If there is no monk of great virtue, he should ask a "well-versed" [多聞, *bahuśrutīya*] monk. If there is no such well-versed monk, then he should ask a forest-dwelling monk [阿練若]. If there is no forest-

> dwelling monk, he should ask an influential lay-person. After that disputing monk has seen the lay-person, he will be ashamed of this dispute and will settle easily. If again there is no such *upāsaka,* he should ask the king and other such powerful officials. When that disputing monk sees witnesses their great power, he will become awe inspired and the dispute will be settled easily.[34]

This passage presents a hierarchy of appeals that may be used to coerce agreement on issues of dispute. At this point it will be useful to inquire as to what kind of leverage each of these figures wielded. The "monk of great virtue" and the "well-versed" (*bahuśrutīya*) monk represent honorific titles given to monks of either great virtue or great learning, respectively. The *bahuśrutīya* also seems to have been something of a functionary within the monastery, whose role is parallel to the rabbi in Judaism.[35] The forest-dwelling monk (*āraṇyaka*) is also commonly listed among monastic vocations and is a monk who practices meditation outside the monastery. The monk of great learning is perhaps the more practical choice of the two since he will be better able to present a convincing interpretation of scripture. Yet the monk of great virtue and the forest-dwelling monk are emblematic of the Buddhist monastic profession as a whole and as such have the respect of monks as well as the laity. The pressure they bear is of a more charismatic sort—something like being asked by Mother Theresa to behave.

Appeals to the laity and to the king constitute leverage of an entirely different order. The laity (in the late second century) were the primary source of income for the monastery. The extent of their donations to a given monastery would have been partly determined by the extent to which the resident monks were considered to constitute a "field of merit." To have a recalcitrant monk confronted by a pious layperson (piety being determined largely by the layperson's reputation for charity [*dāna*]) posed a threat to the monk's reputation—with possible economic consequences for the monastery as a whole. Appeal to the king to settle a dispute was a last resort. There are, of course, some prominent examples of such royal intervention. King Aśoka's intervention in an early Buddhist monastic dispute leading to the expulsion of a number of monks was certainly well known and could not have been very far from the minds of any would-be schismatics.[36]

Aśoka's purge of the *saṅgha* in the third century B.C.E. reflects provisions made in the early Indian law code for royal intervention into sectarian disputes. In *Dharmaśāstra,* religious associations like Buddhist monasteries are seen as voluntary groups (*samaya*) held together by compact (*saṃvid*). As mentioned above, one name for such groups in India legal literature is *samaya*. It is not coincidental that the title of Vasumitra's work is the ***Samayabhedoparacanacakra*** (the Splitting of the Samaya), rather than the ***Saéghabhedoparacanacakra*** (the Splitting of the Saṅgha). For the most part, *Dharmaśāstra* recommends letting such groups govern themselves according to their own rules. According to P.V. Kāne,

> Yāj[ñavalkyasmṛti] II. 192 prescribes that the king should respect the usages and conventions of occupational guilds, merchants, heretical sects, and groups (corporations &c.) and allow them to pursue the course of action they had followed from ancient times. Nārada (samayasyānapākarma, verses 2–6) and Bṛhaspati quoted in the Vīramitrodaya (vyavahāra) contain very important directions as to what conventions of guilds the king should respect and what he is not bound to respect. Nārada says that the king should enforce the conventions agreed upon by heretic sects, naigamas (merchants), śreṇis and other groups residing in the country or the capital. . . . the king should prohibit (out of their usages and conventions) such as are opposed to the king's interest, or are disapproved of by the people in general, would be ruinous for the king. *The King should not tolerate their creating factious groups among themselves, taking up arms for a purpose detrimental to the State, and causing injury to one another.* The king should especially curb those who cause dissentions among the several groups; if they are connived at in these activities they might cause terrible danger.[37]

Aśoka's purge of the *saṅgha* is usually presented as a rather extraordinary event—a potential threat though not a common one. Yet the passage from the *Mahāsāṅghika vinaya* cited above suggests that monastic disputes could be taken to the king as a matter of course. Although corroborating evidence for this practice is scanty, it appears that kings could, and sometimes did, play quite an active role in managing the monastery. A more detailed example of the complex relations that could develop between the Buddhist monastic sects and the state is represented in a third-century letter from the king of Krorainia (modern-day Loulan)[38] to a district magistrate in Niya, an early administrative center and one of the oases on the Silk Route:

> Regulations for the community of monks . . . to be carefully kept . . .
> In the 10th year of his majesty the great king, Jiṭugha Mahagiri, son of heaven, in the 12th month, 10th day . . . the community of

> monks in the capital laid down regulations for the community of monks in Caḍ́ta. It is heard that the novices do not pay attention to the elder, they disobey the old monks. Concerning this these regulations have been laid down by his majesty in front of the order of monks. The elders Śilaprabha and Puṃñaṣena (are to be) in charge of the monastery (*viharavala*). They have to administer all the activities of the community. (Disputes) are to be examined in accordance with the law. All the activities of the community of monks are to be administered by them . . . so that the community of monks shall be content in mind (*atanaṃna*). Whichever monk does not partake in the activities of the community of monks shall pay a fine of one roll of silk. Whichever monk does not take part in the *posatha* ceremony, his penalty is (a fine of) one roll of silk. Whichever monk at the invitations to the *posatha* ceremony enters in a householder's dress, shall pay the fine of one roll of silk. Whichever monk strikes another monk, (in the case of) a light (blow the fine is) five rolls of silk, (in the case of) a moderate (blow) ten rolls of silk, (in the case of) an excessive (blow) fifteen rolls of silk.[39]

Several points need to be highlighted here. This is a letter from a king to his district magistrate, that is, from one secular authority to another. The letter was occasioned by an apparently fractious local group of monks: some of whom showed disrespect to the monastic hierarchy, some fought among themselves (sometimes violently), some did not bother to wear monastic robes, or attend the bimonthly recitation of the *prātimokṣa*. The community of monks in the capital wished the monks in Niya to conform to the standards of discipline. The rules that are to be applied are the *vinaya* rules devised by the pan-Buddhist community,[40] and yet it is the king who not only appoints monks to administer the rules but also levies fines upon their abrogation. By this letter, the district magistrate is empowered to enact the provisions of the *vinaya* rules of the community of monks in the capital and to administer the fines. In sum, the Buddhists devise their own law in the *prātimokṣa*, but the teeth of that law ultimately rest with the state.

Acts of Suspension

Accusing another monk of *saṅghabheda* was perhaps the most severe accusation that could be leveled against a monk with errant views and threatened the most severe sanctions. A less severe measure was to impose a suspension (*utkṣepanīyakarma*) on the monk until he recanted his views. The origin story for this rule in the *Mahāsāṅghika vinaya* is virtually identical to that of the Pali *Cūḷavagga* (I.32). The story concerns a monk named Ariṣṭa (阿利吒),[41] who makes the following claim: "The dharma that Tathāgata taught (in the *suttānta*) I understand (to be thus:) the World Honored One taught that (certain) *dharmas* are a hindrance to the path. (But) practicing these *dharmas* does not hinder the path."[42] Later in the same section, the *Mahāsāṅghika vinaya* explains that Ariṣṭa regards the five desires arising from sight and possessing desire for bodily form not to be a hindrance to the attainment of the four *dhyānas*.[43] At this, the other monks tell him not to slander the *sūtras*. They admonish him many times, publicly and privately, but he refuses to renounce this view. Ultimately, the Buddha makes the following rule:

> All of the monks should instruct him (as follows:) A monk makes this speech: Āyuṣman, don't slander the Bhagavat. Slandering the Bhagavat is not good. The Bhagavat did not teach this. The Bhagavat taught there are hindrances to the path of dharma that really are hindrances to the path. Abandon this sinful issue [事 *adhikaraṇa*]! All of the monks should (so) instruct this monk. Then if he still clings to this view and does not relinquish it (then they should) accordingly (reprimand him) a second and a third time. If he relinquishes the view, good. If he does not relinquish the view then the *saṅgha* should perform an act suspension (*utkṣemanīyakarman*), after that he obtains a *pacāttica* (an offense requiring confession).[44]

The consequences of suspension are defined in the *Prātimokṣa sūtra* of each school. In the *Mahāsāṅghika vinaya* this rule can be found at *pācattika* no. 46:

> Whatever monk should knowingly eat, dwell, or lie down in the same house with a monk who has been sent away [*utkṣiptaṃ,* i.e., suspended] by the harmonious *saṅgha* in accordance with Dharma and in accordance with Vinaya, and who, acting as he speaks, has not abandoned that evil view [*pāpikām dṛṣṭiṃ*] and has not made Anudharma, that is a *pācattika*.[45]

The effect of this rule is effectively to ostracize the errant monk until he recants his former views and adopts the views of his brethren. Presumably, if this ostracization was not effective, the monastery could resort to the more draconian measures mentioned above.

The Definition of Authoritative Scripture

Given the seriousness with which infidelity in the reproduction of scripture was treated in the *Mahāsāṅghika vinaya,* there can be no question that Mahāyānists could have been liable to the charge of instigating a schism. As noted above, such liability entailed vulnerability under both monastic and civil law. Liability does not, however, always result in prosecution. To prevent such a prosecution, the Mahāyānists needed only to create the *impression* of compliance. By conforming their teachings to the letter of the law, they could coerce their *confrères* to acquiesce to the presence of Mahāyānā. The degree of Mahāyānist culpability boils down to how the concerned parties defined *dharma* and *vinaya* and how they defined "deviation." It is precisely the first two categories that become contested in Mahāyāna writings, so we now turn to definitions of *dharma* and *vinaya*.

Mahāyāna would not have survived if Buddhists had defined their "canon" (the *Tripiṭaka*) with a fixed list of sermons claimed to have been uttered by the Buddha. Happily, the definitions of scriptural authority in early Buddhist texts are much more complicated.[46] Because the authority of scripture was so central to monastic administration, the issue of how to determine scriptural authority was addressed early in the Buddhist tradition. Both the *sūtra* collections and the *vinayas* have definitions of which texts and teachings are to be considered authoritative. All traditions accept that a sermon did not have to be uttered from the physical lips of the Buddha in order to qualify as a statement of *dharma*. Because, in the *Mahāsāṅghika vinaya,* Ariṣṭa is said to have "slandered the *sūtra*" (謗契經), the text uses Ariṣṭa's apostasy as an opportunity to define *dharma*:

> *Dharma* is that which the Bhagavat said and that which the Bhagavat has approved. *What the Bhagavat has said* is what the Bhagavat says himself. What the Bhagavat approves is what the Buddha's disciples and others say, of which the Buddha approves.[47]

This echoes a statement made earlier:

> That which is *dharma* is that which the Buddha said (*buddhavacana*) and that which the Buddha has approved. *Buddhavacana* is what the Buddha's mouth elucidates. What the Buddha approves is what the Buddha's disciples and others say of which the Buddha approves.[48]

In Buddhist literature generally, the term "word of the Buddha" becomes a metonym for any authoritative utterance representing the *dharma* of the Buddha. Realizing the difficulties posed by allowing statements by beings other than the Buddha to have authority, early texts include a set of criteria, called the "four great teachings" (*mahāpadeśā*), which serve as tests to determine whether a sermon has the status of "word of the Buddha."[49] These criteria can be found in both the Pāli and Chinese canons.[50] Regardless of whether the sermon was heard from the lips of the Buddha himself, from a group of elders and leaders (*sathero sapāmokkho*), from a large group of monks, or just one monk, it is to be "placed beside *sūtra* and compared with *vinaya*."[51] Consider Maurice Walshe's translation of one passage from The "Mahāparinibbāṇa sutta" of the *Dīgha Nikāya:*

> Suppose a monk were to say: "Friends, I heard and received this from the Lord's own lips: this is the Dhamma, this is the discipline, this is the Master's teaching," then, monks, you should neither approve nor disapprove his words. Neither approving nor disapproving, his words and expressions [*padabyañjanāni*] should be carefully noted and compared with the Suttas and reviewed in the light of the discipline. If they, on such comparison and review, are found not to conform to the Suttas or the discipline, the conclusion must be: "Assuredly this is not the word of the Buddha, it has been wrongly understood by this monk," and is a matter to be rejected. But where on such comparison and review they are found to conform to the Suttas or the discipline, the conclusion must be "Assuredly this is word of the Buddha, it has been rightly understood by this monk." This is the first criterion.[52]

The same procedure is repeated three more times, substituting "a group of elders and leaders," "a large group of monks," and "one monk" for "the Lord's own lips." The qualifications stated for the "large group of monks" and for the "one monk" are that they be very learned (*bahussuto*), those to whom scripture has been handed down (*āgatāgamo*), and who memorize sermons (*dhammadharo*), monastic rules (*vinayadharo*), and the topical lists of the *abhidharma*.[53] In the context of this passage, the epithets *bahussuto,* and so on, are merely honorific adjectives commending the learning of the monk or monks who are the reputed source of the *sūtra* in question—something on the order of the term *trepiṭaka*[54] (one who knows the whole *Tripiṭaka*) in certain inscriptions or the title *caturvedi* in Brahmanic Hinduism. The point of this passage is that a monk should not be swayed by the reputation of the reputed source of the *sūtra*, but should acknowledge the authority of the text only to the extent that its content conforms to what he already knows. At least theoretically, the authority of any text can be thus reevaluated by any monk.

The four great teachings have some practical implications as presented in the *Dīgha Nikāya*. These teachings describe how a newly introduced text may be authorized as the "word of the Buddha" in the local monastic community. The fact that the sermon in question is "to be placed beside" the *sūtras* (*sutte otāretabbāni*) and is to be compared to the monastic rules (*vinaye sandassetabbāni*)—both future passive constructions—indicates that the text in question is not already among the *sūtras* or *vinaya*. The legitimization of a new text becomes a question of how to interpret textual precedent, which will presumably be a function of the new sermon's structural and doctrinal similarity to the corpus of accepted sermons used in one's own community. The great teachings did not, however, merely stipulate the structural features of textual precedent. They also defined *who* would determine that precedent. Given that these sermons were in the memories of textual specialists, they would be the ones asked to pass judgment on the authority of a text. Thus the door to canonicity was guarded but not closed. In Herbert Kitschelt's terms, the legal opportunity structure of Mahāsāṅgika monastic law as it pertained to scriptures authorized for reproduction was relatively "open and weak" (see the introduction). Depending on how the law was administered in a given monastery, it could easily accommodate assimilative strategies so long as Mahāyānists crafted their strategies carefully.[55] Even so, the road to authentication for new texts and doctrines had to run the gauntlet of the old guard, as it were. Yet any text successfully navigating this road could be considered "word of the Buddha" so long as it remained within the boundaries circumscribed by more veteran texts.

Sometime in the early centuries of the Common Era, a third criterion for textual authenticity was added: that it has to be "in accordance with truth" (*dharmatā*). This criterion for "word of the Buddha" does not appear in the *Dīgha* passage or in the *Aṅguttara*. It does, however, figure prominently in most of the later discussions of *buddhavacana*. The criterion can be found in the *Mūlasarvāstivāda vinaya*[56] as well as in Vasubandhu's *Abhidharmakośa* and the commentary on it by Yaśomitra. In his refutation of the Vatsīputrīyas, Vasubandhu quotes a scripture in order to contest the existence of the *pudgala* (literally, "the person," a self or a pseudo-soul). The opponent counters that the scripture cited by Vasubandhu does not have authority because it is not read in their sect. To this Vasubandhu responds that their response is not valid because (1) "all of the other sects read this *sūtra,*" (2) "it does not contradict the *sūtras,*" and (3) "it does not contradict *dharmatā.*"[57] Yaśomitra comments as follows:

> *This is certainly not the word of the Buddha*. By this it is meant that these sūtras are apocryphal. *In all the sects* (means) in the sects such as Tāmraparṇīya etc. *And does not oppose the sūtra* (means it) does not oppose the heart of the *sūtra* nor does it cause contradictions to the heart of the *sūtra*. *Nor does it oppose dharmatā* (means) the *dharmatā* which is dependent-origination.[58]

The original says *na dharmatā bādhate*. It seems, however, that the definition was open to variation. In their discussion of the same criterion, the *Mahāyānasūtrālaṃkāra*, the *Bodhicāryāvatārapañjika*, and the *Netti Pakaraṇa* all use *avilomati*. The introduction of this third criterion represents an important shift in the Buddhist notion of textual authority and would prove crucial for the Mahāyānists. According to Ronald Davidson:

> Its presence as one of the three criteria of acceptance in the *Mūlasarvāstivāda-vinaya* and other texts indicates both the developing fascination with dependent-origination and the desire that the Buddha's teaching remain acceptable to the perceptive observer. Its presence also indicates the intrusion, for the first time, of a philosophical argument into the criteria. . . . Virtually all later textual justifications, particularly those of the Mahāyāna, would be conducted on the basis of philosophical argument.[59]

The four great teachings not only describe the operative criteria for determining the authenticity of *sūtras,* but were equally important in determining correct behavior as well. Though apparently minor, the local monastic rules (*kriyākarma*) could carry a lot of weight. For the Mūlasarvāstivādins, these local monastic rules could be a key factor in determining one's inclusion in the rain retreat. According to Gregory Schopen:

> The first part of the *Varṣāvastu* lays out the procedures and ritual forms which are to be used by any group of Mūlasarvāstivādin monks who wish to enter into the rainy season retreat at any given locality or *āvāsa*. Not surprisingly, one of the first procedures concerns and determines membership in the group or—most simply put—who is in and who is out. Somewhat more surprising, perhaps, is the fact that membership in the group is not explicitly determined by the acceptance of a specific monastic code, or even the *Vinaya,* but by the

> acceptance of what are technically known as *kriyākāras,* or—to use a gloss—"local monastic ordinances." . . . It is . . . clear that they were concerned with a very wide range of activities. One, for example, barred nuns from entering the local *vihāra;* another made it an infraction for one who used the privy not to leave the equivalent of sufficient toilet paper for the next guy. The specific content of such ordinances is not so important here as the fact that they were local, and that the acceptance of them was required to be counted as a member of the group that was undertaking the rain retreat in that specific location.[60]

The *Mūlasarvāstivāda vinaya* is in many respects quite different from the *vinayas* of the Mahāsāṅghikas, the Mahīśāsakas, the Sarvāstivādins, and the Theravādins. Indeed, the parallel speeches commencing the rain retreat found in the *Mahāsāṅghika vinaya,* the *Mahīśāsaka vinaya,* and the *Sarvāstivādin vinaya* make no mention of accepting the *kriyākarma* as an element of admission into the rain retreat.[61] Nevertheless, in the *Mahāsāṅghika vinaya,* local monastic rules, civil law, and monastic law all must be subjected to the four great teachings. This can be seen in Upāli's speech about the five pure *dharmas*. The definitions of these five pure *dharmas* are explained in the *Mahāsāṅghika vinaya*:

> There are five pure dharmas, according to dharma according to *vinaya* which lead to happiness. Those which are not in accord with the dharma and *vinaya* must be opposed. What are the five? The first is purity of local monastic ordinance [制限, *kriyākarma*]; the second is purity of local (civil) law [方法] the third is purity of discipline [戒行, *śīla*]; the forth is purity of the elders [長老, *āyuṣman*]; the fifth is the purity from (prior) worldly comportment [風俗]. Purity of local monastic ordinance (means) all the monks residing in a *vihāra* author the ordinance. Regarding the four great teachings [四大教, *mahāpadeśā*]:[62] those [local monastic ordinances] in accordance with them can be used. Those not in accordance should be rejected. This is called purity of local monastic ordinance. Purity of civil law (means) according to the law of the country [國土]. Regarding the four great teachings: those [civil laws] in accordance with them can be used. Those not in accordance should be rejected. This is called purity of civil law. Purity of discipline (means) that I see a certain vow-holding monk enact a law [行是法]. If [this law] is in accordance with the four great teachings, it should be adopted. That which is not in accordance should be rejected. This is called purity of discipline. Puri-

ty of elder (means) that I see an elder monk, an honored one (such as) Śāriputra or Maudgalyāyana enact a law. If it is in accord with the four great teachings then it should be used, if not then it should be rejected. This is called purity of elders. Purity from (prior) worldly comportment (means) not acquiring (requisites) according to the previous worldly dharma (i.e., to one's comportment prior to ordination). (Or), untimely eating of food and drinking or having sex. Like this, everything that was previously (appropriate) is conventionally pure. Without leaving the family [these acts] are pure. This is called purity of lay comportment.[63]

A monastery can apparently enact any local rule that it wants, but only to the extent that the rule is agreed upon by the entire monastery and provided that it is in conformity with textual precedent as read by the leading authorities of the monastery. As a legal device, the creation of additional rules allowed for monasteries to accommodate local circumstances while maintaining coherence with the larger sectarian movement. The same device was also the basis for the creation of subunits within the monastery. Groups of monks could take on special disciplinary obligations, such as the thirteen *dhūtaṅgas* for periods of time. The *Mahāsāṅghika vinaya* section on miscellaneous rules contains a rule concerning the adoption of these additional disciplinary obligations:

> There are two monks who make a rule [制限, *kriyākarma*] that they should receive a scripture together, and that they should a recite the scripture together. Again, the one who does not receive or recite [it] obtains a *vinayātikrama*.[64]

This rule deals with an instance in which a subunit of monks (here, two monks) take on an extra obligation, namely, that they will commit a certain *sūtra* to memory. Not only does the *Mahāsāṅghika vinaya* allow for such additional vows, but it even provides sanctions for their abrogation. Chapter 1 examined the reports of Mahāyānists residing in the same monasteries as non-Mahāyānists. Here is a rule that may indicate how Mahāyāna as a legal entity might have been construed *vis-à-vis* Buddhist monastic polity. Indeed, it may be that the earliest institutional formation of Mahāyāna (at least as far as *coenobitic* Mahāyāna is concerned) consisted of such a vow taken between a group of monks within a monastery to take on additional obligations such as the studying, recitation, and veneration of a group of Mahāyāna *sūtras* (e.g., the *Bodhisattvapiṭaka*) and the adoption of additional ethical standards.

An Example from the *Yogācārabhūmi*

The *Bodhisattvabhūmi* (ostensibly authored by Asaṅga, c. fourth or fifth century) provides an image of what this might have looked like. It contains a description of the ritual procedure to become a Mahāyānist. According to Mark Tatz's translation, the process begins as follows.

> The bodhisattva, whether lay or monastic, who aspires to train himself in this threefold aggregate of ethics that is the bodhisattva training, who has made the resolve for supreme, right and full awakening, should first fall at the feet of a bodhisattva who is a co-religionist in that he also has made the bodhisattva resolve, who has taken and knows the vow, and who is capable of grasping and understanding the meaning of its verbal communication, and then entreat him as follows: "I seek to receive from you, *kulaputra,* the bodhisattva vow-of-ethics obligation. If it be no importunity, may it suit you to hear me for a moment and to grant it, out of pity."[65]

The aspirant is then instructed on the advantages of adopting the *bodhisattva* vow and then worships the Buddhas of past, present, and future and the *bodhisattvas* of the ten directions. The aspirant is then asked by the preceptor whether he or she is now a *bodhisattva* and has resolve for enlightenment.

> Thereupon, he [the aspirant] should be addressed thus: "Will you *kulaputra* so-and-so, receive from me all the bodhisattva bases of training and all the bodhisattva ethics—the ethics of the vow, the ethics of collecting wholesome factors, and the ethics of accomplishing the welfare of sentient beings.[66]

Here the postulant "receives" the *bodhisattva* precepts *śikṣāpada* from another *bodhisattva* in a similar manner to the way a layperson receives the five or ten precepts from a monk on an *uposaṭha* day or the way that a monk receives the full set of *vinaya* rules upon ordination. Indeed, the *Bodhisattvabūmi* makes explicit comparisons between the *bodhisattva* precepts and those of the *prātimokṣa* and, in so doing, asserts the superiority of the *bodhisattva* precepts. It claims, "No *prātimokṣa* vow undertaking can approach even a hundredth part of this vow-of-ethics undertaking . . . in regard to the acquisition of merit."[67]

Unlike the five lay precepts or the precepts contained in the *prātimokṣa* vow, the *bodhisattva* precepts are not enumerated because they are innumerable. Instead, the *bodhisattvas* are asked to determine their own correct behavior as Mahāyānists based upon their study of Mahāyāna scriptures.

> The bodhisattva who has been established in the bodhisattva vow-of-ethics obligation should on the one hand deduce again and again for himself, "This is fitting for the bodhisattva to do; this is not the fitting thing for the bodhisattva to do," and he should thenceforth perform his actions and train himself in accord with just that. Listening conscientiously, on the other hand, to the collection of bodhisattva scriptures or to this contraction that is the code of the bodhisattva collection, he should train in accord with just that, in order to accomplish the many thousand fold bases of training promulgated by the Lord for bodhisattvas in those various scriptures.[68]

If the additional strictures on behavior placed on the *bodhisattva* are viewed as *new teachings,* the statement that they should be in accord with Mahāyāna scripture is simply a new twist on the four great teachings. However, instead of comparing the new practice to the (non-Mahāyānist) *Tripiṭaka* as instructed in the *Dīrgha Āgama,* the *bodhisattva* measures his or her actions against the *bodhisattva* scriptures or the code of the *bodhisattva* collection.[69]

The specific activities of these Mahāyānists appear to be the legal equivalents of a group of monks taking a vow among themselves to recite a special group of scriptures. *Bodhisattvas* are to perform "daily worship to the Tathāgata or to a shrine that represents him, to the Doctrine or to doctrine in the form of a book—the collection of *bodhisattva* scriptures or its code—or to the Community—the community of high stage bodhisattvas of the ten directions."[70] In this regard, the *Bodhisattvabhūmi* stresses that the *bodhisattva* is to follow the *bodhisattva śikṣāpada* only so long as they do not violate an "internal rule of the community" (*kriyākara*) or the "thought of the majority" (*prabhūtatarānāṃ cittam*).[71] In the latter case, the *bodhisattva* must bow to the will of the majority. Presumably, such conformity could entail the end of the recitation and study of Mahāyāna *sūtras* in that monastery.

According to the *Bodhisattvabhūmi's* description of Mahāyāna practice, at least for ordained Mahāyānists, Mahāyāna consisted of a set of values, forms of worship, and textual traditions that were adopted in addition to the monastic precepts listed in the *prātimokṣa.* These practices, if formalized, would fall into the category of internal or local rules (*kriyākarma*).

But even local rules were to be held up to the standard of the four great teachings, that is, they were to be compared with the *sūtra* and were not to conflict with *vinaya*. This would not be a problem in monasteries (like Asaṅga's) in which the majority of monks already revered Mahāyāna *sūtras*. It would be a big problem, however, in monasteries in which Mahāyāna *sūtras* were considered heretical. Nāgārjuna's monastery was more likely to fall into the latter category.

Nāgārjuna's Defense of Mahāyāna in the *Ratnāvalī*

With the preceding as background we are finally ready to address Nāgārjuna's defense of Mahāyāna in chapter 4 of his *Ratnāvalī*. Schopen argues that the weakness of Mahāyāna's position is indicated by three parts of Nāgārjuna's defense: (1) his defense of the authenticity of Mahāyāna teachings as "word of the Buddha"; (2) his resort to slander; and (3) his request for tolerance of Mahāyāna (instead of its acceptance). Although Schopen is substantially correct, details must now be added to his analysis. In light of the *Mahāsāṅghika vinaya*, these rhetorical moves by Nāgārjuna might be seen as constituting a legal gambit to avoid sanctions against Mahāyāna coming from his own monastery as well as the civil authorities.

Nāgārjuna begins his explicit argument for the authenticity of Mahāyāna teachings in verse 80.

80 The Great Vehicle has a nature of giving patience effort, concentration, wisdom and compassion. Hence, how could there be any bad explanations in it?

81 Others' aims are [achieved] through giving and ethics. One's own are [achieved] through patience and effort. Concentration and wisdom are causes of liberation. These epitomize the sense of the Great Vehicle.

82 The aims benefiting oneself and others and the meaning of liberation as briefly taught by the Buddha [in Hīnayāna] . . . Are contained in the six perfections. Therefore these are the word of the Buddha [*tasmād bauddham idaṃ vacaḥ*].[72]

"The aims of benefiting oneself and others and the meaning of liberation," which Nāgārjuna claims to be "briefly taught by the Buddha," are most likely a reference to the "Sukavagga" of the *Aṅguttara Nikāya* (although this phrase occurs elsewhere in the *Aṅguttara* as well). There, in a sermon which seems to have been a favorite among Mahāyānists, the Buddha states that both the monk who has mental obscurations (*āvila*) and one who has no mental obscurations (*anāvila*) are to "know their own aim and others' aims, and are to know the way [*netaṃ*] to directly experience the highest, which is distinguished by the noble knowing and seeing."[73] By showing the Six Perfections to be parallel to this formulation, Nāgārjuna is "placing a disputed text beside the *sūtra*" as instructed in the four great teachings. The result can be seen in his conclusion: "Therefore, these [the Six Perfections] are the word of the Buddha."

Schopen is certainly correct from the standpoint of later Mahāyāna. Nāgārjuna's rhetoric here is surprising. Not once in Nāgārjuna's defense of Mahāyāna in the *Ratnāvalī* does he claim that Mahāyāna *sūtras* present a doctrine that is superior to any other form of Buddhism. On the contrary, he consistently argues only for Mahāyāna's equivalence. Without taking into account the legal context outlined above, this maneuver would be hard to explain. It would be something on a par with Augustine's arguing that Christianity was really teaching the same thing as Manichaeism. In the context of avoiding censure under monastic law, however, his tactic makes sense. If Nāgārjuna in any way indicated that Mahāyāna was superior to the Buddhism followed by the rest of his monastery, he would be asserting its difference from the accepted "word of the Buddha." Furthermore, if the teaching and copying of Mahāyāna texts were construed by his *confrères* as deviating from what they considered "word of the Buddha," the Mahāyānists could be charged with corrupting the transmission of the Buddhist teaching. Nāgārjuna and his compatriots would then have been liable to the charge of "splitting the *saṅgha*" (*saṅghabheda*). The only way to avoid this charge was to establish Mahāyāna teachings as "word of the Buddha" and hope for the best.

In chapter 4, verses 86–88, discussed by Schopen, Nāgārjuna claims a doctrinal equivalence between the Mahāyāna doctrine of "emptiness" and the common Buddhist doctrine of "cessation of outflows."

> 86 The non-arising [*anutpādo*] that [is taught] in the Mahāyāna—that emptiness [*śūnyatā*] is the "extinction" [*kṣaya*] of others [i.e, of other Buddhists]. Hence be accepting [of Mahāyāna] because of the unity of the meaning/purpose [*artha*] of cessation and non-arising![74]

Again, Nāgārjuna is clearly attempting to align Mahāyāna doctrine with that of the "word of the Buddha." Yet, as is often the case in Mahāyāna works, the equivalence (*ekyam arthaḥ*) that he urges on the reader is somewhat problematic. The problem stems from the term *artha,* which can mean both "meaning/referent" and "purpose or goal." "Non-arising/emptiness," in this verse, is claimed to have either the same meaning/referent as the term "extinction" or the same purpose/goal. In non-Mahāyāna *sūtra* literature, the term "extinction" (*kṣaya* = Pāli, *khaya*) is quite common. This term is most often used to denote the destruction of the "corruptions" or "defilements" (*āśrava*), which amounts to becoming an *arhant.* A typical use of this term in the canon can be found in the "Cakkavatti Sīhanāda sutta" of the *Dīgha Nikāya:*

> And what is power for a monk? Here, a monk, by the destruction [*khaya*] of the corruptions, enters into and abides in that corruptionless liberation of the heart and liberation by wisdom which he has attained, in this very life, by his own super-knowledge and realization. That is power for a monk.[75]

The term "emptiness" (Sanskrit, *śūnyatā;* Pāli, *suññatā*) is also used to denote a psychological state reached at the end of a series of meditations wherein defilements are extinguished. Thus, in the *Majjhima Nikāya:*

> When it was evening, the venerable Sāriputta rose from meditation and went to the Blessed One. After paying homage to him, he sat down at one side. The Blessed One then said to him: "Sāriputta, your faculties are clear . The colour of your skin is pure and bright. What abiding do you often abide in now, Sāriputta?" "Now, venerable sir, I often abide in voidness [*suññatā*]." "Good, good, Sāriputta! Now, indeed, you often abide in the abiding of a great man. For this is the abiding of a great man, namely, voidness."[76]

A non-Mahāyānist would, of course have to agree with Nāgārjuna's statement insofar as the referent (*artha*) of the terms "emptiness" and "extinction" (*kṣaya*) is roughly the same in non-Mahāyāna *sūtras.* Both terms denote a state of mind achieved through meditation in which there are no defilements. The problem is that these two terms are no longer equivalent in Mahāyāna texts. Consider the following passage from the *Kāśyapaparivārta:*

> Furthermore, Kāśyapa, the real investigation of dharmas, does not make dharmas empty because of emptiness, [rather] dharmas are already empty. [It] does not make dharmas signless due to the signless [rather] dharmas are already signless. [It] does not make dharmas wishless due to the wishless [rather] dharmas are already wish-

less. . . . Similarly, insofar as there is no essencelessness of dharmas as an essence [in itself] and insofar as no essence is found, such indeed is the investigation, O Kaśyapa, that is said to be the true investigation of dharmas and to be the middle way.[77]

Here the term "emptiness" (along with its companion terms "signlessness" and "wishlessness") is no longer used to describe a psychological state but has shifted to describe the *dharmas* themselves. Under this interpretation, *dharmas* would presumably also include the defilements, whereas the emptiness of the emptiness gate applies to nirvāṇa—which is presumably the antithesis of all defilements. Whereas the realization that all *dharmas* are empty may lead to the subsequent destruction of defilements, emptiness in its Mahāyāna usage does not mean the same thing as the mental state in which all defilements have been destroyed.

This passage raises the important issue of the sources of the terminology with which Mahāyānists construct their doctrines and the uses to which that terminology is put. Although they may have felt free to proliferate Buddhas and Buddha fields, the core ontology taught by those Buddhas had to appear fundamentally the same so long as they were beholden to a non-Mahāyāna majority. Early Mahāyānists were careful not to introduce new vocabulary when it came to this one area. Hence, to speak of a "proto-madhyamaka in the Pali canon" as Luis Gómez does,[78] or to assert, as David Kalupahana does, that "Nāgārjuna [is] merely. . . a grand commentator on the Buddha-word," does not get to the heart of the issue.[79] The similarities between certain parts of Nāgārjuna's works and the Pāli canon that these two authors expose were probably intentional, and, if so, were also strategic. As discussed in Chapter 5, Nāgārjuna also plants these allusions to the canon in his *Mūlamadhyamakakārikā* to promote a specifically Mahāyāna agenda.

Nāgārjuna protects Mahāyāna against the charge of "splitting the *saṅgha*" on two fronts. The first, as mentioned, is to claim that Mahāyāna doctrine is "word of the Buddha" and therefore is protected speech under monastic law. What Schopen identifies as "name-calling" is Nāgārjuna's second strategy. Nāgārjuna does not label his opponents "stupid" merely to insult their intelligence. Rather, the discussion in which he questions the intelligence of his opponents occurs in the context of pointing to the reason why they do not see Mahāyāna as "word of the Buddha." Similarly, Nāgārjuna's complaints that only anger or hatred motivates the opponent can also be read as a legal defense of Mahāyāna. These accusations occur in a series of verses (chapter 4, verses 6–71 and 89), where Nāgārjuna claims that those who deride the Mahāyāna do not understand it and are motivated by anger.[80] The theme of "hatred" in this argument works on several different levels. First, in verse 70 Nāgārjuna emphasizes the sinful nature of hatred by pointing out that those who hate Mahāyāna will burn (in hell).[81] Nāgārjuna is accusing his opponents here of having not just hateful thoughts but a hateful temperament.[82] He then points out that if even those of a faith type are burned (in hell) then how much more so those of the hatred type![83] More important, by identifying the opponents' motivation as anger, Nāgārjuna can turn the tables on his opponents and accuse them of an abrogation of a different *prātimokṣa* rule. According to the *Mahāsāṅghika Prātimokṣa:*

> Whatever monk, ill tempered, corrupt, and angry because of malice, should accuse another monk of a groundless *saṅghātiśeṣa* dharma, that is a *paryāntika* [an offense requiring confession of wrongdoing].[84]

A groundless charge of "splitting the *saṅgha*" (especially one arising out of anger) would be a proper application of this rule since it is a *saṅghātiśeṣa* offense. If Nāgārjuna's first tactic (showing that Mahāyāna is "word of the Buddha") is successful, then he is justified in claiming that his opponents are "stupid" (insofar as they do not see that Mahāyāna is "word of the Buddha"). If his opponents acknowledge the equivalents that he points out and yet persist in their objections then they will have accused the Mahāyānists of a *saṅghātiśeṣa* offense out of malice. It is then Nāgārjuna's opponents who must make a public confession of wrongdoing—thereby publicly vindicating Mahāyāna's status as "word of the Buddha."

Clearly the king would not have been subject to the *pācattika* rule discussed above. Therefore a different explanation must be sought for Nāgārjuna's appeal to gain the king's tolerance of Mahāyāna. Schopen claims that Nāgārjuna's request for tolerance (as opposed to acceptance) in verse 86 constitutes a "retreat." Let us examine this verse in the light of Buddhist monastic law. Verse 86 ends with Nāgārjuna's request that the king be tolerant of Mahāyāna because of the equivalence between Mahāyāna and Buddhist "orthodoxy." As discussed above, disagreements in monasteries—especially when they threatened schism—were open to royal intervention. Recall that the *Ratnāvalī* is a letter written to a king, and as such it also addresses matters of civil law. Because of his warnings about the karmic consequences of hatred, Nāgārjuna alerts the king:

388 What the Tathāgata has taught with a special intention
Is not easy to understand.

Therefore, since he taught one as well as three vehicles,
You should protect yourself through neutrality (upekṣā).
389 There is no fault [*pāpaṃ* = "sin"] with neutrality, but there is fault
From despising it. How could there be virtue?
Therefore those who seek good for themselves
Should not despise the Mahāyāna.[85]

In this context, the word "neutrality" (*upekṣā*) should be interpreted as Nāgārjuna telling the king *not to take sides* (neither the side of the "Śrāvakayāna" [Nāgārjuna's term] nor the Mahāyāna). Ajitamitra's commentary on this verse seems to concur with this reading. He explains the term *upekṣā* (*btaṅ sñoms*) as follows: *btaṅ sñoms ni mi 'jug pa'o* (*upekṣā* means not to *'jug pa*). The term *'jug pa* is a fairly common in Tibetan. Among the relevant translations, according to Chandra Das, are "to enter," "to be converted," "to appoint," and "to settle."[86] Perhaps the best translation of this sentence would be "*upekṣā* [means] not to enter [into the dispute]." In other words, Nāgārjuna is telling the king to stay out of it. Ajitamitra's commentary on the following verse conveys the same meaning: "by maintaining *upekṣā* concerning [what is or is not] Word of the Buddha, [the king] does not decide [for either side]."[87] Here, Ajitamitra identifies the crux of the dispute between Mahāyāna and non-Mahāyāna as an argument over what is to be considered "word of the Buddha" (*saṅs rgyas kyi bka'*).

Upekṣā in *Dharmaśāstra* and the *Ratnāvalī*

Nāgārjuna's strategy in this passage, therefore, is not limited to giving the king spiritual advice. Indeed, the term *upekṣā* as a technical term is found in the *Dharmaśāstra,* and it is likely that Nāgārjuna is also using it in this sense. *Upekṣā* is listed in the *Matsyapurāṇa,* the *Agnipurāṇa,* the *Viṣnudharmottara,* and the *Mahābhārata* as one of the royal *upāya* or strategies for resolving conflicts. According to Kāne, "*Upekṣā* consists in not preventing a person from doing what is unjust or being addicted to some vice or engaging in a fight and is illustrated by king Virāṭa's connivance at the death of Kīcaka [*Kām.*{*andakīyanītisāra*}, XVII. 55–57]."[88] Hence, by telling the king to maintain *upekṣā,* Nāgārjuna is acknowledging that although there may be internal dissension within the monastic community, the appropriate policy for the king to follow is that of neutrality. Nāgārjuna's strategy of asking for the king's neutrality (instead of asking for the king's commitment to Mahāyāna) makes sense only in the context of a dispute within the monastic community about Mahāyāna itself. Indeed, from the king's point of view, the offense of "splitting the *saṅgha*" would certainly have been considered "internal dissension" as addressed by the *Nāradasmṛti* passage discussed above.

Conclusion

If Schopen's main thesis that early Mahāyāna was in a minority position is correct, then Nāgārjuna should be read as fighting, not to compete with non-Mahāyānists, but to be included among them. In such a context, there is nothing to be gained by competition, whereas inclusion would guarantee continued access to monastic resources. Indeed, Nāgārjuna's defense of Mahāyāna in the *Ratnāvalī* is quite different from later defenses of Mahāyāna. Perhaps Nāgārjuna's strategies are characteristic of *early* Mahāyāna alone, since they seem to differ radically from later Mahāyāna apologetics. To take one prominent example, Asaṅga (ostensibly from fourth-century Peshawar) also defends Mahāyāna's status as "word of the Buddha" in the *Mahāyānasūtrālaṃkāra*.[89] In this work, he addresses the same four great teachings discussed above. The opponent makes the following objection:

> This is the characteristic of *buddhavacana:* that which manifests in *sūtra,* appears in *vinaya* and does not contradict *dharmatā*. And that is not Mahāyāna because [it] teaches that all dharmas lack essence. Hence, it is not *buddhavacana*.

To this objection Asaṅga replies:

> It does manifest—in *its own* Mahāyāna *sūtra* and it appears in the *vinaya of its own kleśas*. The *kleśas* of bodhisattvas are spoken of in the Mahāyāna. The bodhisattvas have the *kleśas* of discrimination [*sic. kleśasya vinayaḥ*]. and because they have great and profound characteristics. And it does not contradict *dharmatā* because *dharmatā* is for the purpose of attaining great enlightenment *(mahābodhi)*.[90]

Here Asaṅga sidesteps the objection that Mahāyāna texts do not manifest in the known *sūtra* literature by stressing the existence of more than one canon: one for Mahāyānists and one for non-Mahāyānists. Asaṅga's strategy of presenting Mahāyāna as independent and superior to non-Mahāyāna is clearly different from Nāgārjuna's strategy presenting Mahāyāna as equivalent. The difference stems from the contexts in which they are writing. Asaṅga appears to be writing from a monastery in which his own authority is unquestioned and the authority of the Mahāyāna as "word of the Buddha" is equally unquestioned. Asaṅga would then be free to assert the superiority of Mahāyāna because no one in his own order could bring against him the charge of "splitting the *saṅgha*." By contrast, Nāgārjuna's arguments in the *Ratnāvalī* seem to be directed toward the king and the monks in his own monastery. If Nāgārjuna were in a minority position, these monks could very well bring that charge against him and his followers. If the Mahāyānists persisted in upholding the Mahāyāna, the issue could be brought to the king—hence, Nāgārjuna's letter could be read as an impassioned request for royal clemency.

4
Mahāyāna Sūtras as Monastic Property

EARLIER CHAPTERS discussed the legal limitations that Mahāyānists may have encountered upon teaching their doctrine. This chapter investigates a related factor, equally crucial to Mahāyāna's survival: the reproduction and preservation of Mahāyāna texts. The continued presence of Mahāyāna in any given monastery would require the reproduction and preservation of Mahāyāna *sūtras*. *Sūtras* are not just bundles of ideas; they are manufactured goods produced by monasteries. As such, their (re)production would have required the allocation of the resources of time and labor, pens, paper, and ink. Furthermore, storage space had to be devoted to their preservation, and each text had to be copied periodically before it deteriorated. All of this necessitated established institutional practices to ensure that a designated collection of texts would be copied, memorized, and preserved as a matter of course. For the purposes of this chapter, a Mahāyānist is defined as someone who engages in the legitimation and replication of self-consciously Mahāyāna texts.

The history of textual reproduction forms the hidden backbone of the history of Buddhist philosophy itself. For the most part, philosophers of religion occupy themselves with the ideas of philosophy, but it should not be forgotten that the (premodern) Buddhist philosophy available to modern scholarship is coextensive with what has been preserved textually. Nāgārjuna may have written in the second century, but the only reason his writings are still available is that copyists reproduced his text generation after generation, up to Hodgeson's seventeenth century Nepali manuscript. Although it is common to think that the constitution of philosophical traditions lies solely in the exchange of ideas, most philosophical debates—especially those that occur over time—have a significant material component. The debates among Buddhapālita, Bhāvaviveka, and Candrakīrti took place over at least three centuries. These debates, which occupy a central place in Indo-Tibetan Mādhyamika, did not occur among contemporaries but were writings of men arguing against ideas that they most likely had read in books. In short, philosophy cannot exist in the abstract—to exist in history it must take corporeal shape in the form of a written document. This material component of philosophy has its own history developing in tandem with the history of the ideas it transmits. The following discussion demonstrates the close relationship between the ideological contents of a Nāgārjuna's texts and the productive processes to which they were subjected.

Institutional Procedures— An Example from Gandhāra

Although much is known about the practices of textual reproduction in Rome and China in the early centuries of the Common Era, scholars are just beginning to piece together details of the book culture of ancient India. Thus the procedure for copying religious documents in Mahāsāṅghika monasteries remains obscure. For some reason, the authors of the *Mahāsāṅghika vinaya* did not find it necessary to explain the procedures of scriptural reproduction. While the version of this *vinaya* translated by Faxian contains numerous references to writing, bookkeeping, carvers of inscriptions, pens, and paper, it contains only one reference to copying scripture:

> After swallowing food, when applying eye medicine, when reading sūtra, reciting sūtra, copying sūtra [寫經], during walking meditation, or while giving or taking *prasāda*. At all these times one should not bow.[1]

This passage tacitly acknowledges that *sūtras* were being copied in *Mahāsāṅghika* monasteries, yet it is completely silent about what this process would have looked like. The most likely explanation for this relative silence is that its authors simply took for granted the process of scriptural reproduction.

In general, Buddhists transmitted their *sūtras* orally at an early date and began writing and copying these *sūtras* into scrolls or books as early as the first century B.C.E.[2] Large collections of early (i.e., Gupta dynasty and earlier) manuscripts have been recovered at very few archaeological sites in south Asia. Those that have been found are primarily from the far north (Pakistan, Afghanistan, and China). No manuscripts have been found from Nāgārjuna's time period as far south as Andhra Pradesh, so no physical evidence is available to help determine the textual practices of second-century Andhra. Nevertheless, if the physical evidence from the north is combined with evidence from Mahāsāṅghika law and both are correlated with internal evidence from Nāgārjuna's own works, an outline of the relevant textual practices can be discerned.

The earliest collection of Buddhist manuscripts discovered so far is a cache of twenty-nine birch-bark scrolls written in Kharoṣṭhī script that was received by the British Library in 1994. This collection has been studied intensively by a team of scholars headed by Richard Salomon and Collett Cox of the University of Washington. The first report of their findings was published in *Ancient Buddhist Scrolls from Gandhāra*. On paleographic grounds, the provenance of these scrolls can be traced to first- or second-century Afghanistan—probably from a Dharmagupta monastery located in the Gandhāra region (modern-day Peshāwar Valley in or around the village of Haḍḍa).[3] Evidence from the scrolls shows that, even at this early date, the copying, storage, and disposal of Buddhist texts was an organized and officially sanctioned procedure in the monastery. The scrolls are all made of birch-bark that has been rolled into "cigars" and placed in pots.

Two important points arise from the findings of the University of Washington team. First, although the scrolls clearly deteriorated during the almost two thousand years of their interment, Salomon notes that many of the texts were already damaged before being placed in the jars. Salomon discusses similar finds from Haḍḍa and Taxila, in which *sūtras* placed in pots were discovered in *stūpas* and beneath images at the main gate of a monastery.[4] He concludes that these buried texts were copied after having been damaged and ritually buried in pots along with other relics in a religiously auspicious location in the monastery. According to Salomon, "This [practice of ritual burial] implies that written texts were perceived to have some sanctity or spiritual power comparable to that of the relics of deceased holy persons; or rather, they were considered as a sort of relic themselves."[5] Presumably other kinds of texts were produced in the monastery (letters, financial registers, etc.) that were not accorded the same respect and hence were not preserved. The physical placement and treatment of the scroll strongly suggests the scrolls' status *vis-à-vis* other documents.

The second point concerns the method of copying the scrolls. The scrolls in the British Library collection show the distinct handwriting of twenty-one different "scribes."[6] Five of these manuscripts (accounting for three different scribal hands) have the word *likhidago* (it has been written) scrawled over the previous writing—something that they have in common with other manuscript finds from the region. The use of the word *likhidago* is telling. To whom was this notation written? There are two possible scenarios. One is that the notation was intended for the monk who was in charge of burying the texts, indicating a division of labor between those who copied and those who buried the texts. The second possibility is that this is the copyist's notation is to himself, which would indicate that the copyists were responsible for a large number of texts. Obviously, these two scenarios are not mutually exclusive. In either case, the presence of this interlinear marker may indicate a fair degree of routinization. According to Salomon,

> Although the selection of the pieces that have survived is a matter of chance, there is internal evidence to suggest that the process of the recopying and disposing of old texts was an orderly and planned activity. . . . the manuscripts with the later copyist's notations form a coherent group in that not only were they originally written by the same two scribes but also the later annotations on them are, in six out of seven cases, in an identical third hand. This means that these manuscripts not only originally constituted a distinct set of texts but also were recopied as a unit. This in turn suggests that they constituted part of a "library" in the proper sense of the term, that is, of an orderly and systematic collection of texts as opposed to a more or less randomly accumulated pile of manuscripts. Furthermore, the fact that they were evidently recopied as a group indicates that the preservation of written texts was also an organized and systematic activity.[7]

Not all the documents found in the British Library collection reflect this kind of routinization. The *avadāna* texts in the British Library collection contain seven instances of an abbreviation formula such as *vistare sarvo karya,* "The whole [story] is to be done [i.e., recalled] in full," or *vistare janidave siyadi,* "[The story] should be known [i.e., recalled] in full." Salomon concludes from this that:

> These notations, which resemble similar formulae in other Buddhist texts in Pali and Sanskrit, as well as the overall brevity, sometimes extreme, of the avadānas give the impression that the texts are merely skeletons or outlines, which were evidently meant to be filled in and

expanded by the reader or reciter. In this respect they resemble the similarly abridged avadāna and jātaka texts in the Bairam Ali manuscript from Merv in Turkmenistan.[8]

If documents like these were used as a mnemonic or as lecture notes, they indicate an overall textual practice wherein the written document serves as a kind of index to the memorized corpus. In contrast to the *likhidago* texts indicating routinized reproduction, the lecture notes were probably private copies. Hence, from this one collection alone, evidence suggests that (1) certain genres of religious manuscripts were treated with an esteem similar to that accorded to religious relics; (2) documents of certain genres were copied in a routinized fashion using a division of labor and were perhaps owned corporately; and (3) some texts appear to have been private copies. Arguably, the *avadāna* texts were seen (at least by their authors) as possessing the same status as the *sūtra* texts, since, so far, only religious texts have been found copied on the *verso* side of the *sūtra* manuscripts and not documents like personal letters.

Work on the newly discovered Buddhist manuscript collections from Central Asia is still quite young, and much remains to be done. Furthermore, very little of the new manuscript collections has been properly edited and published. For this reason, the relevance of the evidence from the British Library collection would be questionable without corroboration from other sources.

Scriptural Preservation in Monastic Law

One obvious "other source" is, of course, Buddhist monastic law itself. Unfortunately, as mentioned above, there is only one, rather vague reference to copying scripture in the *Mahāsāṅghika vinaya*. The situation improves considerably, however, if we take into consideration the fact that the graphic copying of scripture is only one factor in the larger enterprise of textual reproduction. To clarify matters the discussion below distinguishes between the scriptual reproduction and textual reproduction. The remainder of this chapter uses the word "text" to refer to the content of a treatise regardless of the medium in which that treatise is found. Hence, a text can be instantiated either in a book or in the memory of a person who has memorized it. The word "scripture" refers specifically to texts that are inscribed onto a physical medium (i.e., in a book, inscription, etc.). Whereas scriptural reproduction forms a part of textual reproduction, not all textual reproduction is scriptural reproduction—especially in cultures where textual recitation and memorization are important. In fact, the practices and procedures for scriptural reproduction may well have arisen from other practices aimed at the preservation of a certain textual tradition. Three aspects of the Buddhist enterprise of textual preservation examined below, primarily through the lens of the *Mahāsāṅghika vinaya:* education, recitation, and graphic inscription.

In the view of the *Mahāsāṅghika vinaya,* the tasks of a monk are to maintain the discipline, to learn Buddhist doctrine, and to meditate. The work includes a rather lengthy section detailing which activities, if unperformed, constitute the abandonment of the Buddhist discipline. Among these, education in Buddhist doctrine is one of the benefits of monkdom that the monk is forbidden to abandon.

> What is the abandonment of common benefit [共利]? There are two kinds of common benefit: The first is the benefit of dharma. The second is the benefit of robes and food. The benefit of dharma means studying [*svādhyāya*] and question and answer [sessions]. The benefit of robes and food means: receiving one donation in common. The benefit of dharma and the benefit of robe and food together comprise the common benefit. If a monk says, "I abandon this benefit." This is called abandoning the discipline. Like in the above [discussion] abandonment of the Buddha, [abandonment of discipline] has been explained extensively. If [the monk] says, "[I] abandon the benefit of dharma." This is called the abandonment of the discipline. He is guilty of a heavy offense [偷蘭罪, *sthūlāpatti*].[9]

The *Mahāsāṅghika vinaya* defines learning as not only a right but an obligation—to abandon the study of Buddhist doctrine constitutes a serious violation. Buddhist learning has two components: studying (*svādhyāya*), which consisted of the recitation and memorization of texts, and question and answer sessions in which the finer points of doctrine could be clarified. This monastic education occurs as part of the relationship between preceptor and disciple.

> What should be taught to a resident disciple (*sārddhevihārasmiṃ*) by his preceptor (*upādhyāya*)? After having received full ordination, the disciple should learn[10] both sections of *vinaya.* If (the disciple) can't master (that), he should learn one section. Again, if he can't master one section, he should learn at length five sūtras of the *vinaya.* Again, for the one not capable mastering five sūtras, he should learn four (chapters) or three (chapters) or two (chapters) or one chapter in de-

tail. (If) one sūtra is not learned, then the thirty are to be learned, along with the rest of the frequently heard verses (*śiṣṭakam abhīkṣṇa-śrutikāyo gāthāyo ca*).[11] If he does not learn the two *aniyata* rules, then (at least) the four *parājikā* violations have to be learned. The one who is to be trained should be instructed morning noon and evening. In the evening, (he is to be instructed) with either the *abhidharma* or the *abhivinaya*. "*Abhidharma*" means the nine genres of sūtra (namely): the *sūtra*, the *geya*, the *vyākaraṇa*, the *gāthā*, the *udāna*, the *itivṛttaka*, the *jātaka*, the *vaipulya* and the *adbhutādharmmā*.[12] "*Vinaya*" means the *prātimokṣa*. (These are to be taught) in brief and at length.

If (the student) is not able to enumerate (*uddiśituṃ*) (the rules of the *prātimokṣa*, at least) the (*vinaya*) transgressions are to be learned, as are the sūtra, the aggregates, the sense spheres, dependent-origination, and when to stand and when to not stand. He is to be trained in (good) conduct (*ācāraṃ*), and to restrain bad conduct. In this, he should instruct (his disciple). This is instruction for him: studying (*svādhyāyati*[13]), dwelling in the forest, entering into abandonment. To the extent that this is to be taught, he will accomplish a sense of shame. If he is not so instructed (the preceptor) is guilty of transgressing the *vinaya*. The preceptor who does not teach his resident disciple like this transgresses the *abhisamācārikā* dharma.[14]

This is the first clear discussion of Buddhist education as a process for textual transmission. For the first five years after ordination, each monk has a preceptor. It is the responsibility of the preceptor to teach the monk the *Sūtra Piṭaka* and the *vinaya*. The passage also seems to acknowledge that not all monks will be able to learn such a mass of material, and so it also sets a rather minimal standard for learning. Although the ideal is to learn the entire textual corpus, the monk must at least know a handful of the most serious *vinaya* offenses, basic conduct in the monastery, and the most important doctrines: the aggregates (the *skandha*), the sense spheres (*āyatana*), and dependent-origination (*pratītyasamutpāda*).

Individual tutelage was not the only method of textual transmission described in the *Mahāsāṅghika vinaya*. It also mentions monks teaching texts through group call and response:

The Buddha was staying at Aṭavī Village. . . . At that time there was a building-duty monk [營事比丘] who taught all the youths the *Pārāyaṇa* (chapter of the *Sutta Nipāta*) sentence by sentence. At that time a certain brahmin thought: Where is (this) superior [善勝] dharma? I should be ordained in that. After having this thought he

> then set off for the Aṭavī *vihāra,* aspiring to be ordained. He saw a Bhikṣu teaching and all of the youths learning to recite. It is just like the youths who sit in school learning to chant these words. At that time the brahmin thought: "Today I aspire to the highest dharma according to that mendicant, but (in there it sounds like nothing but) "wei wei,"[15] just like children in school learning to make chanting sounds. Furthermore, I can't tell who is the teacher and who is the student." Having seen that person (teaching the pupils in such an unseemly fashion), he lost faith. In the end, he did not see the Buddha and thereupon immediately returned home. He did not moreover, become a monk. . . . (The Buddha said:) If a monk teaches an unordained person to recite a word of dharma, that is a *pāccatika* (offense).[16]

The pedagogical context described here is different from the preceptor/disciple relationship. Here a single monk teaches a group to recite a scripture. Although the monk is at fault for teaching in this manner, the fault does not lie in the fact that he is not their preceptor. Rather, in this story he is at fault because his pupils have not received full ordination and therefore do not know proper comportment—hence, the raucous chanting. In the subsequent rule, the Buddha forbids a monk to teach unordained pupils. Nowhere does he state that this transmission is to take place only between the preceptor and disciple—the passage here simply takes for granted that this kind of formal group recitation sessions exist. Hence, it appears that Mahāsāṅghika monasteries had two mechanisms for textual transmission/preservation: transmission from preceptor to disciple and transmission to a group of monks.

This passage forms the preamble to *Pācattika* rule number six: "Whatever monk should speak Dharma, step by step, to an unordained man, that is a *pācattika.*" The commentary that follows clarifies the rule, although not nearly as much as one might wish.

> If a monk teaches one who has not yet received all the precepts a sentence of dharma, that is a *pācattika* (offense). "A monk": this has been explained at above. "One who has not yet received all the precepts [*anupasaṃpanna*]," (means someone) other than monks and nuns. Although nuns receive the complete set of precepts, they do not get to teach. "Dharma sentence." If sentence, syllable and phoneme are recited together [i.e. the teacher and the pupils recite them simultaneously]. "Dharma" means "*Buddhavacana*" and that to which the Buddha has given his approval." "*Buddhavacana*" [佛所說] means

what the Buddha himself has said. "That to which the Buddha gives his seal of approval [佛所印可-, *Buddhāvadhāraṇa*]" means words, heard by disciples extending to those things other people say to which the Buddha gives his approval. All *kuśala dharmas* up to nirvāṇa; these words should be regarded as "Dharma." "*Dictation*" [教] means in order to teach, speech is manifested. "*Pācattika*" has been explained above. If a monk teaches one who has not yet received the precepts, to say the syllables [聲, *svara*], "the eye is impermanent," together (chanting the syllables) in rising tone, together in falling tone, together stopping. Joining (the syllables) together for happiness without interruption,[17] that is a *pācattika* offense. (The teachings of) hearing, tasting, smelling, body (touch) and sight, the eighteen sense spheres (*āyatana*), the five aggregates (*skandha*), up to "all dharmas are suffering, empty, impermanent and not self" are also like this. . . . If monks recite together, the senior monk should recite (while) the junior monk (should) follow along silently in his mind. If the senior monk recites what is not correct the junior monk should recite. The senior monk (then) should follow along, chanting silently in his mind. Even the female lay disciples (*upāsikā*) [should be instructed like this].[18] If in the *saṅgha*, there is simultaneous chanting, [the monks] do not get to chant a single verse together. They are allowed to chant simultaneously with each one speaking a different *gātha*.[19]

This rule may be interpreted in two ways. A "strong reading" takes both the story and the rule as prescribing who may and may not be taught to memorize authorized Buddhist *sūtras*. The *vinaya* stipulates that the texts covered by this procedure are, in fact, to be "word of the Buddha" texts. Indeed, the commentaries on this rule are one of the few places in Buddhist legal literature where "word of the Buddha" is defined. By prohibiting monks from teaching the laity to memorize Buddhist *sūtras*, this rule asserts the memorization and transmission of "word of the Buddha" texts to be the sole perogative—and hence responsibility—of ordained monks and nuns. Indeed, this is how the rule is applied today in Theravāda monasteries. A monk may not teach a layperson to memorize a Buddhist *sutta* in Pali.[20]

Still, this rule should be open to other interpretations. It is difficult to know to what extent such a prohibition contained in this rule was applied. The problem with this interpretation is that the apparent prohibition against teaching the laity at the beginning of this passage is undermined by the statement at its end stating that the monk should teach in this manner to all disciples "down to the female lay-disciples." Outside evidence also suggests that some laypeople knew and transmitted Buddhist *sūtras*. As Sylvain Lévi points out, *vinayas* from other schools contain a rule in which a monk is allowed to leave the rain retreat if an educated layperson who has learned a sūtra wishes to impart that sūtra to a monk before it gets lost.[21] The text does not say how the layperson learned the text, but it is perhaps significant that, even here, the *Sarvāstivāda vinaya* inserts a list of eight texts that a layperson may learn. But a comparison of pages 450c–451a of the *Mahāsāṅghika vinaya* with the *varṣāvastu* section of the other *vinayas* shows that the latter include references to a layperson finding a text and teaching it to monks while the former does not.[22]

A "weak reading" of this rule places the interpretive weight of the interdiction on the phrase "step-by-step" (or, better yet, "word for word" [*padaśaḥ*]), rather than on "to speak." This may be one of those cases in which the original intent of the rule aimed in one direction and the interpretation of the rule changed as the needs of the community changed. In this case, the original intent may well have been to make the preservation and transmission of Buddhist texts the sole prerogative of ordained Buddhists. Nevertheless, the *vinaya* as now available is concerned primarily with preserving the decorum of the process of textual transmission while allowing for the transmission of texts to the laity. *Sūtras* would be transmitted in a "call and response" fashion, rather than by the teacher and pupils reciting together. The monk was "to say the syllables 'the eye is impermanent,' together (chanting the syllables) in rising tone, together in falling tone, together stopping."

Two points should be made here regarding this rule as well as the rule concerning what and how students should be taught. The first is that the two processes of individual tutelage and group education are not only for the cultivation and training of the individual but also one of the central mechanisms for textual preservation in the monastery since the memorized textual corpus is coextensive with the corpus the monastery can claim to have preserved. The second is that both of the *vinaya* rules discussed above display definite standards for the kinds of texts to be preserved. In the sections dealing with what a preceptor should ensure that his pupils learn, the standard is set out in terms of the nine genres of *sūtra* and the *vinaya*, while in the sections dealing with *pācattika* rule number six, the category of "word of the Buddha" serves as the standard for textual preservation. Neither of these denote a fixed list of texts. On the contrary, they serve more as an index to those texts for which there was an institutional commitment to reproduction and preservation.

Memorization was an indispensible form of monastic labor. In the eyes of both the laity and of other monasteries, nothing less than the doctrinal identity of the monastery was at stake. Furthermore, memorization was a labor whose productive capacity was limited by the time it takes to memorize a text accurately and by the mnemonic capacity of the monks engaged in this activity. Since the limitations of time and the capacity of each individual's memory constrain the number of texts a given monastic community can retain, the community has a stake in ensuring that no monk shirks his duty and that labor is not wasted on unauthorized texts. For this reason, the *vinayas* also state that there are certain kinds of texts that a monk must *not* memorize. This concern comes out clearest in the *Mahīśāsaka vinaya:*

> All the monks were reciting heretical books. All the white-robed (*upāsakas*) scolded them saying: these *śramaṇera Śākyaputras* are not sincere in the joys of *brahmacarya*. (They have) forsaken the Buddha's sūtras and the discipline (in) chanting these heretical books. All the monks accordingly informed the Buddha. The Buddha said, "This is not permissible." There are various monks who have received heretical path *śāstras* and who do not know shame. Smṛti said, "The Buddha permits us to chant heretical texts (we) do not incur this shame." The Buddha said. "In order to subdue heretical paths it is permissible to chant heretical books. However, one may not follow a book (if it) gives rise to views."[23]

Concerning these prohibitions, it should be remembered that memorization of texts (as well as the reading of texts) was done out loud. The texts that any given monk might be practicing in this manner might well reflect on the reputation of the monastery as a whole in the eyes of the laity. All the *vinayas* contain provisions restricting monks from practicing certain kinds of texts. Often, as in the *Mahīśāsaka vinaya* passage above, the barred texts are simply referred to as "heretical texts" (外書). Most likely, this term refers to non-Buddhist texts such as the Vedas. The *Theravāda vinaya* equivalent to this rule prohibits specifically the recitation of *lokāyata* texts.[24] The *Sarvāstivāda vinaya,* however, prohibits the practice of any text not relevant to the occupation of a monk, adding "poetry and military treatises" to the prohibition.[25] The important point here is that the *vinaya* legal code contained standards that obliged the memorization of certain texts while proscribing others. The *Mahāsāṅghika vinaya* is typical on this point. It breaks the rule into two parts. The more serious offense occurs when a monk abandons authorized texts and only works on unauthorized texts, whereas the monk who learns unauthorized texts in addition to the normal text load, is guilty of a lesser offense.

> What is the abandonment of sūtra [捨經論]? The whole sūtra (*piṭaka*) has nine genres.[26] If a monk says, "I abandon these scriptures," this is called the abandonment of the discipline. If he says, "I have abandoned sūtras and *śāstras* in the past or (will abandon them) in the future, "this is not called abandonment of the discipline, rather, he incurs a heavy fault. If he has not given weight to past or future sūtras and *śāstras,* and directly says he abandons the sūtras, this is called abandonment of discipline. There are others of heretical paths and they likewise have their treatises. If (a monk) really wants to abandon these (the Buddhist) treatises (for them), it is called abandonment (of the discipline). [The case of] one who (embraces) those treatises (without abandoning Buddhist treatises) is not called abandonment of discipline; (but) he incurs a heavy fault.[27]

The scope of the regulation stipulates that the monk is to have reverence specifically for the nine genres of the *Sūtra Piṭaka* and is not to abandon them. In part, this regulation may stem from a concern about maintaining the doctrinal consensus in the monastery, as discussed in Chapter 3. In light of the *Mahīśāsaka* passage, we might suspect that the reputation of the monastery as a whole in the eyes of the laity was also tied to what texts monks memorized (at least in the eyes of the author of that text).

Although perhaps not statistically significant, the *vinaya* rules concerning memorization seem to coincide with the types of manuscripts found in monasteries in Central Asia. The manuscripts found in monasteries along the Silk Route (at least until the fifth century) are texts that could easily be classified as *buddhavacana*. Medical treatises and grammar books have also been found by the German expeditions, but these can be justified on pragmatic grounds. Even the so-called Spitzer Manuscript, discovered at the Ming-öi, at Qizil (c. 250 C.E.), which contains a lengthy discussion of Vaiśeṣika philosophy, can be justified under the *Sarvāstivāda vinaya* (probably the *vinaya* that was in use at Qizil) as an aid to refuting heterodox systems.[28]

A monk could memorize (and, presumably, copy down) a text that was not considered *buddhavacana*—even a heterodox text. What mattered was the motivation. Only the *Mahīśāsaka vinaya* and the *Sarvāstivāda vinaya* permitted a monk to take the time to memorize a text considered heterodox, and then *only if it was treated as a heterodox text*. Although these rules would not necessarily proscribe the study and memorization of Mahāyāna *sūtras*, they do demonstrate that the monastery as a whole had a stake in how a monk spent his time. The standard that authorized the memorization of certain texts and not others would form a minimum standard of acceptance for Mahāyāna to meet, especially in monasteries where labor was limited or where there was a grudge against Mahāyāna. For a monk memorizing a Mahāyāna *sūtra* to avoid liability, the *sūtra* would have to be considered to be "word of the Buddha" or part of one of the nine genres of *sūtra*. (Rules like this may explain in part why Mahāyānists chose to designate their texts as *vaipulya*, one of the nine genres, discussed further in Chapter 5.)

In either case, only those texts categorized as *sūtra piṭaka* or "word of the Buddha" would be assured of oral preservation in the monastery. If Mahāyāna texts were not so categorized in a particular monastery, their continued memorization would not have been part of the institutional commitment of the monastery and their transmission could not be assured for any significant period of time. At worst, those who spent their time memorizing Mahāyāna *sūtras* could be accused of "abandoning *sūtra*."

Book Copying

If Mahāyānists had difficulty preserving their texts through the usual oral mechanisms, perhaps they bypassed memorization altogether by putting their texts into writing—a thesis set forth by Richard Gombrich. Gombrich turns his attention to the passages in Mahāyāna *sūtras* that deal with the "cult of the book" (i.e., the numerous passages in Mahāyāna *sūtras* that promise merit to anyone who copies them down as a book) to argue that these same passages hint at the special preservation needs of early Mahāyānists.[29] He claims, in short, that literacy played a causative role in the rise of Mahāyāna.

> This hypothesis can be simply stated. It is that the rise of the Mahāyāna is due to the use of writing. . . . (T)he early Mahāyāna texts owe their survival to the fact that they were written down; any earlier texts which deviated from or criticized the canonical norms . . . could not survive because they were not included among the texts which the Saṃgha preserved orally.[30]

Following an earlier work by Lance Cousins, Gombrich first says that Buddhist "canonical" literature meets the criteria (derived largely from

Walter Ong) for the kinds of works that have been preserved orally. Buddhist canonical works make extensive use of "mnemonic lists, stock passages (clichés) and redundancy."[31] The significance of the oral character of Buddhist texts for Gombrich lies in the fact, reported by many scholars, that oral traditions tend to be remarkably adept at preserving texts from generation to generation with little corruption. In order for such oral preservation to take place, however, there has to be a degree of institutional organization and commitment to the labor of textual preservation. In the Buddhist case, oral preservation required countless hours of repetition and training.

Combining the conservative nature of oral preservation with the need for a formal institutional commitment to make it work, Gombrich contends that any text noticeably different from the existing (oral) canon would have no chance of being preserved by that mechanism. Because Mahāyāna texts had not originally been included among the corpus of texts that monks were already committed to preserving, Mahāyānists could not count on this method of preservation. His solution: Mahāyānists wrote their *sūtras* into books in order to bypass the mechanism of oral preservation. He explains Schopen's passages as a kind of celebration of the newly invented technology of writing.

> My feeling is that these texts preserve a sense of wonder at this marvelous invention which permits an individual's opinions or experiences to survive whether or not anyone agrees or cares. In a sense, they are celebrating their own survival. *Scripta manent* goes the Latin tag: "Writings survive." But perhaps only the Buddhists wrote panegyrics on it.[32]

Gombrich is aware, of course, that the preservation of written texts is not problem-free.

> It may be objected that written works too may perish, and are likely to do so unless an institution guards them. To this I would agree. . . . Certainly the great majority of Mahāyāna—indeed, of all later Buddhist—works were lost in their original versions in Indian languages. But many did survive long enough to be translated into Chinese and/or Tibetan, and that is all that my hypothesis requires. A single manuscript in a monastic library, studied by no one, could be picked up and read, even translated, by a curious browser or visiting scholar.[33]

In order for Gombrich's thesis to hold, textual preservation would have to have less stringent standards than oral preservation. This may well have been the case in some monasteries, for laws have teeth only if they are invoked. If, however, the legitimacy of Mahāyāna were a point of contention in a monastery (as it was in Nāgārjuna's monastery), *vinaya* rules would have a bearing on the replication and transmission of books. In this regard, *pācattika* rule number six is important to our study not only as an indicator of the standards for oral preservation but because the practice it describes may have extended to the *written* transmission of texts as well. In other words, the copying of texts may well have been a group activity, with one monk reciting the texts word by word while other monks copied what they heard. Furthermore, just as it was *buddhavacana* texts that monks were obliged to memorize orally, we can infer that the category of "word of the Buddha" would also govern which texts were to be reproduced graphically.

In fact, this is exactly what the *Dharmagupta vinaya* commentary indicates on the same rule. Where the *Mahāsāṅghika vinaya* has specific prohibitions against a monk's reciting a text to an unordained person to encourage him or her to repeat it, the *Dharmagupta vinaya* contains an additional prohibition against a monk's reciting a text of dharma one word at a time while another (unordained) person writes it down.

> "A sentence of dharma" means *buddhavacana,* which is the sound heard from the Buddha, that which is said by celestial beings, or sayings of all heavenly beings. If a monk teaches this to a non-ordained person, (so that they) recite it together—one teaching two teaching three teachings. *Whether teaching by mouth, or teaching by writing,* if it is clear and distinct that is a *pācattika* infraction. Further, (even if) it is not taught clearly and distinctly that is a *duṣkṛta.* Sons of *devas,* sons of *asuras,* sons of *yakṣasas,* sons of *nāgas,* sons of *gandharvas* and animal births can become converted. One teaching, two teachings three teachings; (teaching the) teachings clearly and distinctly or not clearly and distinctly is a *duṣkṛta.* If a teacher teaches without saying, "I will speak and finish and then and you may speak," that is a *duṣkṛta.* If one (teaches in this manner) to a nun, it is a *pācattika* infraction. (If one) teaches (in this manner to) a preceptor [*śikṣamāṇā,* 式叉摩那] a *śrāmeṇera* or a *śrāmeṇerī* (i.e., novices) it is also a *duṣkṛta.* Thus the correct teaching [是謂] becomes a sin. It is not a sin when I speak and finish and then you say it, or one person finishes reciting it and then one person writes it [一人誦竟一人書].[34]

The *Dharmagupta vinaya* commentary retains the same spirit as that of the *Mahāsāṅghika vinaya*. The type of texts covered by the rule is still "word of the Buddha." What is added to the *Dharmagupta vinaya* rule is simply a prohibition against transcribing from dictation. Since the prohibition against transcribing is merely an amendment or a specialized application of the first proscription, the copying of scripture could be done in a group setting in the same manner as that of oral memorization. By extension, "word of the Buddha" was the category that determined which texts Buddhist monks were obligated to copy down in written form.

If we imagine the *Mahāsāṅghika vinaya* scenario of the Building-Duty monk's teaching recitation to the group of boys, replace the unordained youths with ordained monks,[35] and imagine those monks writing down sentences of a sūtra after it had been dictated by the Building-Duty monk, then we might have a picture of how some of the British Library texts were reproduced (the British Library collection probably came from a Dharmagupta monastery, after all). In this scenario, it would have been the Building-Duty monk in our story who would have scrawled *likhidago* across the text after he was finished reciting it.

The category of "word of the Buddha" certainly appears to determine both the texts to be copied as well as the texts to be memorized. Other *vinayas* confirm this assumption. As discussed below, the *Mūlasarvāstivāda vinaya* states that part of the money from a monk's estate after his death is to go to the *dharma* (as opposed to the *saṅgha*) for the purpose of copying "word of the Buddha."[36]

The absence of any explicit discussion concerning which texts were to be copied may simply be due to the fact that the monks considered written copying of texts an extension of the practice of *sūtra* recitation. Because the commitment to textual preservation embodied in that rule turns on the category of "word of the Buddha," it is obvious what was at stake in the Mahāyānists' contention that Mahāyāna *sūtras* are "word of the Buddha." Monks would not be obligated to copy a text (like a Mahāyāna *sūtra*) that was not considered to have that status. The status of "canon" in second-century Indian monasteries would have functioned in the same manner as it would throughout Buddhist history. Stephen Teiser's comment on the advantages of canonicity in medieval China serve equally well in this respect.

> Canonical status was an assurance not only of textual authenticity—that a scripture transmitted accurately the words of the Buddha, or that a treatise propounded an interpretation acceptable to the highest echelons of the Buddhist Church—but also of physical survival. Non-

canonical Buddhist texts from the medieval period do survive, but in very small proportion to their historic numbers. By contrast, texts placed in the Buddhist canon were copied regularly with high levels of funding and were disseminated widely.[37]

Scripture as Property

What if a Mahāyānist monk wished to teach his disciple to memorize a Mahāyāna *sūtra* or simply slipped his personal copy to the disciple? If the other monks were inclined to use the law code against the Mahāyānists, the teacher could be accused of "abandoning the *sūtra*," since the Mahāyāna text could be construed as outside "the nine sections of *sūtra*" or could even be construed as a text of an "heterodox path." Even if opposition to Mahāyāna was not so technically articulated, the private transmission of an already written text from preceptor to disciple would have also been a problematic strategy for the long-term survival of Mahāyāna. So long as the copying and storage of Mahāyāna *sūtras* was left up to the initiative of individual monks, the reproduction of Mahāyāna texts would never be seen as a corporate responsibility. As such, the Mahāyānists could never be assured that the texts they copied would be recopied in perpetuity. On the contrary, each generation of Mahāyānists would have to copy or memorize the Mahāyāna *sūtras* individually (in addition to his assigned tasks), and each would have to privately solicit his successor in the task. Any failure to secure the next transmission could result in the loss of the *sūtra*.

Even assuming that Mahāyāna monks were not prohibited from engaging in the financial transactions necessary to reproduce texts such as acquiring pens and paper, hiring scribes, or buying books, once the completed sūtra was in their possession it would have fallen under the monastic rules dealing with property.[38] The type of property under which the book was classified would determine how it would be treated. Buddhist monastic law generally defined three types of property. The first might best be called "cultic property." In other *vinayas* it is designated "property of the Buddha" (佛物), although the *Mahāsāṅghika vinaya* uses the term "property of the *stūpa*" (塔物)—which seems to include any item used in worship or ritual. The second category is the property of the *saṅgha* (僧物), including the monastery buildings, beds, and boats. The last category of property under Buddhist monastic law is private property (我物), such as any small items that a monk might own: his robes, bowl, a mat, a needle, needle-case.

From the ritual burial of the scrolls of the British Library collection, we know that some monasteries quite early on considered written sūtras as falling into the category of "property of the Buddha." However, because the *Mahāsāṅghika vinaya* is silent on the matter of books, it is not clear how they were classified in this sect. The details of their treatment must be inferred by an examination of Mahāsāṅghika property law in general and by a comparison with the *vinayas* from other Buddhist traditions. The most fundamental property distinction in Buddhist monastic law is that between personal and corporate property. Early Buddhist scriptures speak of monks having recourse to only "four requisites" (Pali, *parikkhāra*; Sanskrit, *pariṣkāra*): robes, shelter (alt. bedding), food, and medicine. The rationale behind this list is to demonstrate that a monk lives without luxury and with the bare necessities. Later, another list of eight requisites (with some variations) comes into prominence with a different rationale: three robes, a bowl, a filter, needle and thread, and a razor (or scissors), and a belt.[39] The difference between the two lists consists not just in the additional items but in what has been omitted. The list of eight items consists of those things that a monk actually owns and might use from day to day. They may be obtained directly from a donor or be bequeathed from one monk to another at the time of death. Regardless of how these items are acquired, they are items that a monk may own and dispose of as he wishes. What is missing from the list of eight are food, shelter, and bedding. In most cases, these items were given to the monk for his use but, in fact, belonged to the *saṅgha* and were not his to dispose of.[40] The *Mahāsāṅghika vinaya* offers a glimpse of what the distinction between corporate and individual property meant in context in the following passage:

> "Heavy property" [重物]. The Buddha was staying at Śrāvastī. At that time all the monks were selling the *saṅgha's* bedding [床褥]. (The proceeds were) either lent to people or to kept for private enjoyment [私受用]. The Bhikṣus, accordingly, went and asked the Bhagavat (about this). The Buddha said, "Tell that monk to come." After the monk came, the Buddha inquired of the monk, "Sir, is this really true or not?" He replied, "it is true, Bhagavat." The Buddha said, "After today, it is not permitted for a monk to sell the *saṅgha's* bedding (or) to lend it or to keep it for his own property and use." (He) called a gathering of the *saṅgha* and forbade (such) sale, or lending to someone for personal use. If (something is) sold or rented for personal use that is a violation of the *vinaya* (*vinayātikrama*). What are called, "heavy goods"? Beds and cushions, iron utensils, clay utensils, wood utensils, bamboo utensils, just as they were discussed at

length in the rules concerning the prohibition against theft, these are classed "heavy property." A donor gives (*viz.*) bedding, chairs,[41] woolen rugs, huts, boats, cloth, belts, razors, keys, umbrellas, fans, leather shoes, needle cases, scissors to cut the fingernails, knives, and bathing pots to the *saṅgha*. Among these, the beds and cushions, chairs and boats are instances of this heavy property and must go to the *saṅgha* of the four directions. The remaining are light goods [輕物] (and) must be divided (among the monks).[42]

This passage presents the difference between the *saṅgha's* property (here designated as "heavy property") and personal property ("light property") in terms of a distinction between "ownership" and "possession." Ownership, as in modern jurisprudence, entails the right to dispose of the property freely, whereas possession is simply the right to use something granted by an owner minus the right to dispose of it (i.e., to sell, trade, or destroy it). A Buddhist monk may *possess* many items, but he does not have the right to lend, sell, or give them away, nor can he take possession of them without the consent of the owner (in this case, the monastery). To treat an item of corporate property as one's own constituted a *niḥsargika-pāccatika* offense as described in the *Mahāsāṅghika prātimokṣa:*

If a monk knows something belongs to the *Saṅgha* and turns it to his own (use), that is a *niḥsargika pāccatika*. The Bhikṣu who does so accordingly should confess.[43]

Vinaya literature describes a third type of property that is separate but functionally similar to property of the *saṅgha:* "property of the Buddha" [佛物]. According to Jacques Gernet:

as a result of the growth of the Buddhist cult a new development becomes discernible: the construction of sanctuaries and reliquaries and the making of statues modified the original conception of the property of the *saṅgha* as primarily communal. It was no longer their status as communal goods but rather their sanctity that qualified these new acquisitions as part of the religious patrimony, designated as property of the Buddha (*fo-wu*), whereas the property of the *saṅgha* (*seng-wu*) was restricted to the communal possessions of the bhikṣu. The property of the Buddhist Church, then, was of a dual nature: it comprised communal as well as sacred goods, with the emphasis shifting between these two aspects of *ch'ang-chu* [i.e., permanent] property.[44]

Whereas unlawfully appropriating property of the *saṅgha* as one's own was a *niḥsargika pāccatika* (an infraction requiring confession and relinquishment of the appropriated item), the separation of the *saṅgha*'s property from cultic property was much more rigid. Any monk caught using the property of the Buddha (or, in the case of the *Mahāsāṅghika vinaya*, "property of the *stūpa*") for the purposes of the *saṅgha* or selling the Buddha's property to purchase property of the *saṅgha* was guilty of a *parājika*, an offense requiring expulsion.[45]

What kind of property would books be considered? Although books are not discussed as property in the *Mahāsāṅghika vinaya*, we find a clue as to how they were treated in the *Mūlasarvāstivāda vinaya*'s account of the distribution of a dead monk's things. When a monk dies, only the "light goods"—that is, his personal property—may be divided among the other monks. Items that are owned by the *saṅgha* return to the *saṅgha* even though they were in the possession of an individual monk when he was alive. In cases of inheritance in monastic legal literature, it becomes clear that the *saṅgha* only has a responsibility to preserve and maintain those items that it owns and those items belonging to the Buddha. Of key importance is the fact that the *Mūlasarvāstivāda vinaya*, alone among all surviving *vinayas*, discusses the treatment of a dead monk's books.

> Concerning gems: Having removed them . . . , two piles should be made. The first is for the dharma (and) the second is for the *saṅgha*. With that for the dharma, Word of the Buddha is to be copied, or it is to be applied to the Lion Throne. That which is for the *saṅgha* is to be divided by the monks. Regarding books: books which are Word of the Buddha do not divide, but (these) are to be placed in the storeroom of the *Saṅgha* of the Four Directions. Books and treatises of others are to be sold by the monks and (the money) distributed.[46]

Here, the proceeds from the sale of a dead monk's things are to be divided in two. One portion goes to the *saṅgha*, not as corporate property in this case but, rather, devolving to the individual monks. The other portion goes to the *dharma*. In this instance, *dharma* stands for cultic property, since the text seems to be indifferent as to whether the money goes to the lion throne (a cultic object) or to the copying of "word of the Buddha books" (*buddhavacana pustakā*). It should be emphasized that *only* texts considered "word of the Buddha" merit the categorization of cultic property and subsequent preservation in the corporate storage space (i.e., the storage room of the *saṅgha* of the four directions). Books that are not "word of the Buddha" are treated just like any other item of personal property and sold. The monastery only had a responsibility to see that its monetary value was shared among the monks. Such a sale would permanently remove such books from circulation within the monastery.

Here we have another piece of the puzzle of the transmission of Buddhist texts. The archaeological evidence from Pakistan and Central Asia indicates that institutionally sanctioned textual reproduction and storage in the monastic library was available to texts whose religious status warranted a ritual burial equal to that of a holy relic. The *Mūlasarvāstivāda vinaya* commentary asserts that only those texts deemed to be "word of the Buddha" were to be placed in the monastic library. Hence, we may infer that a text's status as *cultic property* dictated its eligibility for storage in the library as well as for ritual burial. Conversely, *buddhavacana* texts would not have been considered private property even if they were in the possession of an individual monk. Such texts would have been treated as property of the Buddha and kept in a storeroom for common use.

At critical junctures any book that was not considered "word of the Buddha" would have been vulnerable to decisions made by the *saṅgha* as a whole. Although individual monks might have possessed and preserved their own private copies of Mahāyāna *sūtras,* the problem for the preservation of these *sūtras* lies in the passing of the *sūtra* from one monk to another after the monk dies. As private property, individually owned Mahāyāna *sūtras* (if they were not considered "word of the Buddha" by the host monastery) would have been treated as personal property for the purposes of inheritance. The Mahāsāṅghika legal system had certain provisions under which any monk disinclined toward Mahāyāna could block the transfer of a dead monk's possessions to his disciple.[47] This is a subtle point and so the *Mahāsāṅghika vinaya's* rules on inheritance are quoted here at some length.

A. If a monk falls ill or dies [*parinivṛtta*] no one should be sent to shut his door. If there is a live-in disciple [共行弟子, *sārdha vihārika-śiṣya*] or a disciple who lives nearby [依止弟子, *ante-vāsika*] who is moral [持戒, *śīlavat*] and trustworthy. (That disciple should) get the key. If that person is not trustworthy, (the *saṅgha*) should retain the key and it should then be given to the *saṅgha's vaiyyāvṛtykara* [僧知事人, lit. "the person who knows the affairs of the *saṅgha*]. (Either the disciple or the *vaiyyāvṛtykara* should) perform the final blessings [供養舍利] and thereafter arrange for the actual bringing forth of the robe (and other) items. If there is a live-in disciple who is moral and trustworthy then he may be assigned to bring it forth. If he is not a trustworthy person, then the *vaiyyāvṛtykara* should be assigned to bring it forth.

B. If a monk makes this speech: "I meet these (criteria) and am also the possessor of his robe and bowl." [我此中亦有衣鉢者] [The *saṅgha*] should examine person before them (and that person's) upholding of morality. The trustworthy person should (be allowed to) receive the monk's things. The untrustworthy person should not be granted (them). If he is a person whose trustworthiness is evident *sākṣāt-krīya* [證明] (he) should be granted (these items from) the deceased.

C. Thereafter the *saṅgha* should receive. Receiving is of three kinds. They (the monks) receive according to a formal motion (receiving by [羯磨] *karma* = *saṅghakarma* = a formal act of the *saṅgha*), they receive according to division, or they receive by exchange. "Receiving by a formal motion," means: the one making the motion (i.e., the *karmin* [羯磨人]) should make this speech: "Gentlemen [大德] of the *saṅgha,* listen! A certain monk has deteriorated and passed on. There is a box [所有, *bhāṇḍaka*] (containing) his robe and bowl and remaining sundries. We should publicly [現前, *sakṣāt?*] distribute them." If the *saṅgha* (deems the time) appropriate, then the *saṅgha* should have a public proceeding for that certain monk (so that other monks may) receive. (The monk should) speak thus: "Gentlemen! *Saṅgha,* listen! A certain named monk has fallen ill and died. His possessions are his robe and bowl and surplus assorted items. The *saṅgha* should divide them publicly. The *saṅgha* now publicly possesses his robe, bowl and surplus assorted items. For him, let the other monks receive the said monk's possessions. May all of you Gentlemen (please) accept this." (He will then) take the robe (etc.) and distribute them (in the name of) that monk (so that others will) receive (his goods). Acceptance means the *saṅgha* is silent. If they do not accept they speak up accordingly. After the *Saṅgha* in its entirety accepts, they take possession of said robe (etc.) and distribute them in the name of that monk until there is nothing left. The *saṅgha* (must) accept this in silence from beginning to end. This *(saṅgha) karma* is carried out like this. This is called "reception through a formal act."

D. "Receiving by parts" means: "To make a division and afterward reciting: "each one take for themselves and divide." This is called receiving through division.

E. "Receiving through exchange" means: exchanging with each other." This is called receiving through exchange. If four monks dwell in another village. And one monk becomes ill. Three

> monks ought to receive. [They] should make this speech: "Elders [長老],[48] Such-and-such a monk became ill and died. There is his robe (etc.). (These possessions) should be divided in front of the *saṅgha*. [But] this place has no *saṅgha*. We should divide (his possessions) publicly." If three monks reside there, and one monk becomes sick then two monks should receive. [They] ought to make this speech: Insofar as this place has no *saṅgha*, we should publicly receive (his possessions). If two monks dwell together and one monk becomes sick (and dies), the other monk should get custody. He should state his intention aloud (to himself), saying: "A certain named monk became sick and died. There are his robes and bowl that should be divided in front of the *saṅgha*. This place has no *saṅgha*. I should obtain it."[49]

This rule falls into five parts corresponding to the above five paragraphs. Paragraph A concerns the transmission of the dead monk's possessions to the monk's disciple. Clearly, the inheritance of the master's belongings to his disciple was more than a simple transfer of goods—it was also, to an extent, a transfer of authority. This transaction is therefore subject to the most careful scrutiny of the *saṅgha*. As this part of the rule indicates, being a disciple does not automatically entitle one to the master's possessions. It merely entitles the disciple to the privilege of performing the last rites and bringing the master's belongings before the entire *saṅgha*. Even then, the disciple only earns this privilege if the *saṅgha* as a whole deems him worthy. If he is deemed unworthy for any reason, he does not even receive the key to his master's cell. This rule attempts to guard against a disciple's simply appropriating his master's possessions without the knowledge of the *saṅgha*.

Paragraph B concerns a case where a disciple has somehow already acquired his master's belongings. In this case, the ultimate decision of whether or not the disciple can keep these items is left up to the judgment of the *saṅgha*. The remaining three rules concern the distribution of a monk's property after his immediate disciple has obtained his inheritance.

Paragraph C explains the formal, almost parliamentary procedure by which the distribution of the deceased's items is proposed, ratified, and only then implemented. The point of the official act of the *saṅgha* (*saṅgha-karma*) is to make all transactions as public as possible.

Paragraph D suggests that after the disciple has claimed his inheritance, the remainder of the items could be claimed by any monk so long as the appropriation was made public. If, however, a monk wished to make the distribution of goods subject to the approval of the *saṅgha*, he could always make a formal motion that the monk's belongings be distributed in a formal act of the *saṅgha*. In this formal allocation, any monk could be barred from receiving his share of a dead monk's possessions if there were other monks who objected.

The potential impact of Mahāsāṅghika property rights on the continued presence of Mahāyāna written texts in the monastery is obvious. Under this scenario, Mahāyānists would not be able to rely upon transmission of their scriptures from master to disciple. If there were monks who did not approve of Mahāyāna, they could demand that the dead monk's items be distributed by a formal proceeding and then object to the *sūtras'* being given to monks that they knew were Mahāyānists. If a monk was found already to be in possession of a *sūtra* previously owned by the deceased, the *saṅgha* could again intervene. The only scenario in which the transmission of property from one monk to another at death could not be strictly regulated would have been in "monasteries" with fewer than five monks (paragraph E). Although many such monasteries may have hosted Mahāyānists, Mahāyānists could hardly depend on such monasteries to copy and house their sūtras in the long term.

Such rules concerning property illuminate the relationship between the practice of textual reproduction and the content of a text, since only those texts demonstrating conformity to the standard of "word of the Buddha" would be assured of preservation. Although it is unlikely that any of the monasteries in Nāgārjuna's area followed the *Mūlasarvāstivāda vinaya*, and the *Mahāsāṅghika vinaya*, for its part, never mentions what to do with books,[50] the criterion that the *Mūlasarvāstivāda vinaya* uses to determine the preservation of a book seems to be a natural extension of regulations present in all the other *vinayas*. Any item that has cultic use (statues, paintings, and "*stūpa* property") was always considered to be owned by the monastery and could not be owned by individual monks. In light of discussions in the *Dīgha Nikāya* and *Aṅguttara Nikāya* concerning "word of the Buddha" discussed in Chapter 3, it seems natural that "word of the Buddha" so defined would be used as the criterion by which texts would be considered cultic property. In short, though Mahāyāna *sūtras* may have in fact found their way into Buddhist monasteries, their status as "word of the Buddha" had real consequences for their continued presence in the monastery.

Monasteries at the time of Nāgārjuna would have had working libraries, and these libraries had to be maintained from the material resources and labor of the monastery itself. All copying was done "in house." There is no evidence that Buddhist manuscripts were copied by hired scribes in Mahāsāṅghika monasteries or that text copying was sponsored by the laity at this early date. Thus text copying was probably much more of a zero-sum game in second-century Mahāsāṅghika monasteries than it would be later on, when (or in Mūlasarvāstivādin monasteries, where) hiring scribes and text sponsoring were common practices. If one text was being copied, this meant that another was not. Monasteries with limited resources would have to establish priorities for determining which texts were copied. By the same token, these same monasteries would have felt most severely the burden of Mahāyānists' demand to have Mahāyāna *sūtras* replicated. It is in this context that the idea of a "canon" takes on a functional definition.

The preceding discussion of Mahāsāṅghika law has revealed two categories denoting textual legitimacy: "the nine genres of the *Sūtra* (*Piṭaka*)" and "word of the Buddha." Texts considered to fall into these categories were sanctioned to be taught, memorized, copied, and stored as cultic property. At best, texts that were not considered to fall into these categories were not preserved as part of an ongoing institutional commitment. At worst, such texts were removed from the monastery, and the monks who spent time memorizing them were subject to sanctions.

Because the status of Mahāyāna *sūtras* as "word of the Buddha" was disputed, Mahāyānists could not take for granted the common productive apparatus of the monastery when it came to the maintenance of their *sūtras*. At this point, the situation for early Mahāyānists looks bleak. Their presence in the monastery would have added an additional burden to the copying tasks of the monastery. Put another way, the demand for Mahāyāna texts would have detracted from the available labor to maintain the "standard collection" of the monastic library. Any monk wishing to block the reproduction of Mahāyāna texts could always bring the charge of "splitting the *saṅgha*" against the Mahāyānists to attempt to shut them down, and archaeological evidence suggests that these tactics may have been somewhat successful in preventing Mahāyāna from flourishing in Indian monasteries for at least the first four or five centuries of its existence.

Mahāyāna Strategies: The *Ratnāvalī* and *Dharmadāna*

How could Mahāyānists hope to circumvent these legal obstacles? The best strategy, of course, would be to convince other monks that Mahāyāna *sūtras* were indeed "word of the Buddha." This is the primary strategy of Nāgārjuna—and for good reason (as discussed in Chapter 5). If Nāgārjuna could convince the other monks in his monastery that Mahāyāna *sūtras* were "word of the Buddha," then he could be assured that Mahāyāna texts would be replicated in perpetuity in the same manner as any other canonical text.

Convincing other Buddhists that Mahāyāna was "word of the Buddha" was not the Mahāyānists' only recourse. Nāgārjuna's works provide particularly useful examples of other early Mahāyāna strategies to secure their texts. The *Ratnāvalī* contains a lengthy section instructing the king on charity. Nāgārjuna tells the king to provide the *saṅgha* with images of the Buddha, *stūpas* and *vihāras,* along with the wealth necessary for their upkeep.[51] The Buddha images "sitting on lotuses" were discussed in Chapter 2, but it should be noted here that Nāgārjuna requests that they be "adorned with all precious substances." To *stūpas,* the king is to give "gold and jeweled friezes," "silver flowers, diamonds, corals, pearls, emeralds, cats eye gems, and sapphires,"[52] musical instruments and lamps.[53] For the monks and nuns living in the monastery, he is also to give medicine,[54] and "seasonally appropriate food and drink."[55] What is of key importance is that in all of Nāgārjuna's requests for resources, he presents Buddhism as a unitary whole. Not once does he request any goods or services to be granted specifically to Mahāyānists. Mahāyānists in Nāgārjuna's monastery did not receive or dispose of wealth *as Mahāyānists.* The organizational channels by which Mahāyānists obtained their resources were the same channels through which all monks received their resources—no special allocation was requested based on *yāna* affiliation.

Among the requests listed in the *Ratnāvalī,* Nāgārjuna asks the king to donate Buddhist scriptures and the means for reproducing Buddhist scriptures. Jeffrey Hopkins translates verse 238 of *Ratnāvalī* as follows:

> You [the king] should make donations of pages and books of the word of the King of Subduers and of the treatises that they give rise to, along with their prerequisites, pens and ink.[56]

Here again, Nāgārjuna requests a certain kind of donation, making no distinction between Mahāyānists and non-Mahāyānists. It is somewhat frustrating that the Sanskrit corresponding to this verse is missing because the Tibetan and the Chinese translations point to two different processes. The texts to be copied are designated in the Tibetan translation as "word of the *Munīndra* and the treatises they give rise to," whereas the Chinese is more interpretive: "*Āgamas* of the Buddha and the *śāstras.*" Where the two versions differ concerns what the king is to do. The Tibetan has a series of nouns (word of the Munīndra, pens, paper, ink) as the direct object of the imperative "donate" (*sbyin par mdzod*). Paramārtha's Chinese translation appears to instruct the king to provide 施

for the copying (書寫) and the recitation (讀誦) of the texts. The first version has the king donating completed texts to the monastery, while the second has the king merely giving the monastery requisites for its own copying tasks. The differences between the two translations are probably a function of the attempt by the Tibetan translators to get seven syllables per line and of the Chinese to achieve five syllables per line. Although obtaining the "original" text is not possible, neither translator took Nāgārjuna to be requesting that the king donate specifically *Mahāyāna sūtras* and *śāstras*. This passage shows that the institutional channels for the acquisition and production of scriptural materials did not acknowledge Mahāyāna scriptures as a separate category needing special sources of funds or an allocation of labor earmarked just for Mahāyāna texts. Yet this request would have also included Mahāyāna *sūtras* since his request for "word of the Silent Lord (*Munīndra*)" is clearly an allusion to the category of "word of the Buddha," and later in the text (verse 382) he makes a point of claiming of Mahāyāna *sūtras: bauddham idaṃ vacaḥ* (these are "word of the Buddha").

The idea of the "gift of *dharma*" has, of course, a long precedent in Buddhist sūtra literature. Perhaps the earliest reference can be found in the *Aṅguttara Nikāya*:

> O monks, there are two gifts. What are these two? The material (*āmisa*) and the spiritual (*dhamma*) gift. These are the [two] gifts. O monks, of these two gifts, the spiritual gift is the foremost.[57]

Elsewhere, Nāgārjuna claims that giving the means to study the *dharma* is the greatest gift.[58] The gift of *dharma* (*dharmadāna*) appears in a number of Mahāyāna sūtras under the perfection of giving (*dānapāramitā*). In all these contexts the gift of *dharma* is interpreted as the gift of spiritual instruction by which the monks reciprocate the material donations made by the laity. Nāgārjuna, while remaining close to the wording of the texts, reverses its intention. Here, he asks a layperson to donate the *dharma* (albeit materially) to the monks in the form of books.

By simply requesting that the donor give Mahāyāna *sūtras* to his monastery, Nāgārjuna circumvents the objections of other monks to Mahāyāna. If the Mahāyāna *sūtras* were not copied down by monks in Nāgārjuna's monastery but were received as donations, then the monastery's designation of these texts as un-*buddhavacana* would be superfluous because of a technicality in *Mahāsāṅghika* law. Immediately after the *Mahāsāṅghika vinaya* passage treating heavy and light property quoted earlier is the following discussion.

> If (there is a donor who) says that all (the donated property) should be completely distributed (among the monks), then (the *saṅgha*) must follow the donor's intent that it be distributed [i.e., the property becomes the personal property of each monk]. If (there is a donor who) says that it all must be given to the *Saṅgha* of the Four Directions [i.e., it becomes property of the *saṅgha*], then it must not be distributed. Requests are of two kinds: The first (is a request for) the *saṅgha*. The second is for private goods. That request obtains various kinds of donations. (Requests) for the *Saṅgha* obtain items which come to the *Saṅgha*. Afterwards, requests for personal items obtain items that go exclusively to oneself [presumably these would be light goods]. If beds and chairs are many and pots are few, then one should certainly speak to the donor to make this known. (The donor will) exchange [得轉] the beds and chairs to produce pots. If pots are many (the donor?) may also trade them for beds and chairs in the same manner. If there are broken utensils they may be melted down to make a big one. The (product) will be classed as heavy property.[59]

The passage demonstrates that the ownership in the Mahāsāṅghika system was a three-tiered affair. On the one hand, to the monks, the monastery was owner of all the heavy goods that the monk used from day to day. An individual monk might request these items from the laity, but, since they were heavy goods, he would be making the request on behalf of the *saṅgha*. To use these items, the monk would have to approach the monastic officer in charge of the distribution of goods. The monk was forbidden to sell or barter these items because he was merely possessor, not owner, of these items. Note, however, that the ownership rights of the monastery *vis-à-vis* donated goods was also not absolute. Since the ultimate point of donation is for the merit of the donor and since this merit accrued to that donor only if the donated items were used, the donor of an item retained a covenential relationship with the monastery that the donated items would be used. The donor retained the ultimate say in how goods were treated and could demand that donated goods be put to use. Such rules can also be found in the *Mūlasarvāstivāda vinaya*. According to Schopen:

> A monk is one who accepts gifts so others can make merit, and he is obligated to do so by the authority of the Buddha. . . . Acceptance of movable property . . . was not, or came to be thought not, sufficient to generate the full complement of the donor's merit. Like *vihāras,* all

such property had not only to be accepted, but to be used, and the monks, again, were under obligation to do so; they were under obligation to ensure that the donor was not denied the "merit resulting from use."[60]

Nāgārjuna's request that the king donate Buddhist texts in general qualifies as a request from the *saṅgha*. The items obtained from this request, therefore, would all qualify as property of the *saṅgha*. By the same token, if Nāgārjuna could persuade the king to include Mahāyāna scriptures among the books donated, then his monastery would have been obligated to use and maintain them even if individual monks in the monastery objected to their presence. To neglect them in any way would be tantamount to withholding from the king the merit he was due from his donation—probably not a good idea!

Nāgārjuna not only requests that the king provide texts and writing supplies to the monasteries, but he also informs the king of the merit that he would accrue if he memorized and taught the *dharma* himself. Thus, in verse 296:

> Through acting for the doctrine,
> Remembering books of doctrine and their meaning,
> And through stainless giving of the doctrine
> You will attain memory of your continuum of lives.[61]

The Tibetan of this verse has what is to be memorized as *chos gźuṅ* (probably a translation of the Sanskrit *dharmagrantha*). The Chinese is more specific: the king is to memorize the doctrine (正法, *saddharma*) in both its sentences and meanings (句義, *padārtha*). The verse places this activity on equal footing with the gift of *dharma* (*chos kyi sbyin pa* = *dharmadāna*). Again, this request is curious in light of the specific rule in all the *prātimokṣa* prohibiting monks from teaching the unordained to memorize and recite the *dharma* word for word. Nāgārjuna seems to be inserting a specifically Mahāyāna strategy for textual reproduction into his letter. According to the "strong reading" of *Mahāsāṅghika vinaya* passage dealing with this rule (see above), a monk cannot teach a layperson to recite or memorize a passage of *dharma* (here defined as "word of the Buddha"). Yet if a particular monastery had not accorded Mahāyāna *sūtras* with the status of "word of the Buddha," it would have no grounds for suit if a monk taught a layperson to memorize and teach others a Mahāyāna *sūtra*.

This is a small point, and yet the Mahāyānists would have had their opponents on the horns of a legal dilemma: if the opponents denied that Mahāyāna was "word of the Buddha," there would be no prohibition on teaching the laity to recite it or to write it down. But if the opponents declared Mahāyāna *sūtras* to be "word of the Buddha," then the *sūtras* would have to fall among the rest of the *sūtras* that were routinely copied by the monastery.

5
On the Parasitic Strategies of Mahāyāna

THE EUROPEAN AND ASIAN species of cuckoo are what is known as "brood parasites." The female lays her eggs in the nests of other birds, who, in turn, raise her chicks as their own. A successful cuckoo can pass its eggs off as those of another species so that the other species will provide the labor and material resources necessary to raise the young to adulthood. The simple fact that Mahāyānists were writing and copying unsanctioned scripture was potentially divisive. To alleviate tensions they would have had to convince the readers that their texts were *buddhavacana,* or "word of the Buddha." Mahāyānists employed a strategy similar to the cuckoo, by presenting their texts and ideas as "word of the Buddha." If the Mahāyānists could succeed in passing their *sūtras* off as "word of the Buddha," the host monastery would be obligated to preserve and reproduce Mahāyāna texts in perpetuity just as they would any other *buddhavacana* text. This chapter examines two strategies used by Mahāyānists to evoke the authority of "word of the Buddha" for their texts. The first strategy is simply a type of camouflage, presenting Mahāyāna texts so as to fit the description of *buddhavacana* texts. The second strategy is to evoke the authority of *buddhavacana* texts through the use of allusion. This second strategy is more sophisticated than the first and, like the strategy of the cuckoo bird, aims at a more pervasive transformation of the reading practices of the host monastery to better accommodate the interests of the newcomer.

Camouflaging as "Word of the Buddha," part I: "Thus Have I Heard . . ."

The most obvious strategy that Mahāyānists employed to convince their readers that Mahāyāna sūtras were "word of the Buddha" can be found at the beginning of virtually every Mahāyāna *sūtra*. Almost all Mahāyāna *sūtras* begin with the phrase "Thus have I heard at one time . . ." A common interpretation of this phrase is as an allusion to the first Buddhist Council (*saṅgīti*), where the *Tripiṭaka* was allegedly recited by Ānanda and its contents were (at least in the legend) agreed upon.[1] The use of this phrase is explicitly recommended in one Mahāyāna treatise. The author of the *Dazhidulun* (大智度論),[2] translated at the beginning of the fifth century, quotes from a Mahāyāna *sūtra* as follows (in Lamotte's translation).

> As for the precious basket of the law (*dharmaratnapiṭaka*) compiled during the three incalculable eons (*asaṃkhyeyakalpa*), it must be begun with the following formula: "It is thus that I heard at one occasion (*evaṃ mayā śrutam ekasmin samaye*); the Buddha resided in such-and-such region, such-and-such country, such-and-such grove . . ." Why [this introduction]? In the time of the Buddhas of the past (*atītabuddha*) the sūtras all began with this formula; in the time of the Buddhas of the future (*anāgatabuddha*) the sūtras will all begin with this formula. Finally, the Buddhas of the present (*pratyutpannabuddha*), at the moment of their Parinirvāṇa, also teach this formula. Henceforth, after my Parinirvāṇa, the sūtras must also begin with the formula: *Evaṃ mayā śrutam ekasmin samaye.*[3]

By stating that all *sūtras* composed after the death of the Buddha must also begin with the phrase "thus have I heard," the author of this passage has the Buddha tell other potential composers of Mahāyāna *sūtras* to couch Mahāyāna ideas in a familiar form: to make them look like all other Buddhist *sūtras*. Indeed, many Mahāyāna *sūtras* tend to be hybrid texts, that is, they combine traditional form with subtly innovative content in order to increase the likelihood of acceptance as "word of the Buddha."

Camouflaging as "Word of the Buddha," part II: Mahāyāna as *Vaipulya*

Mahāyānists further evoke the aura of "word of the Buddha" through their designation of Mahāyāna *sūtras* as *vaipulya sūtras*. In this same vein,

Mahāyāna itself was sometimes referred to as *Vetullavāda* (Pali) or *Vaipulyavāda* (Sanskrit). The Pali historical tradition refers to the Mahāyānists under the former name. Mahāyānists themselves also referred to their own *sūtras* as *vaipulya sūtras*. For example, Kumārajīva writes that the "profound *vaipulya sūtras*" (方等深奧經) that the *Nāga* king gives Nāgārjuna marks the beginning of Mahāyāna.[4] It is not accidental that Mahāyānists chose this designation for their *sūtras,* since it is also the name of one of the accepted genres of scripture.[5] Indeed, Asaṅga explicitly includes the *Bodhisattvapiṭaka* (an early Mahāyāna text) in the *vaipulya* limb of the twelve limbs of scripture in his *Bodhisattvabhūmi*.[6] By placing their *sūtras* within an already existing (and already authoritative) category of scripture, Mahāyānists were attempting to insinuate their texts into the common Buddhist canon.

Clearly, non-Mahāyāna texts were already considered to belong to this category, so why would Mahāyānists have chosen *this particular* category on which to stake their claims of legitimacy?[7] The term *vaipulya* is usually glossed as "extended," being derived from √*pul,* meaning "to be great" or "to be heaped up," but one nuance of this term is often missing from the standard lexicons, namely, an "elaboration" or "thematic exploration." This sense of the term is used in later *purāṇic* literature. There, the combination *vipuli* + √*kṛ* is often used in the sense of a sanctioned expansion on an authoritative text. So, for instance, the *Śrīmad Bhagavataṃ* contains the following.

> idaṃ bhāgavataṃ nāma yanme bhagavatoditam| saṃgraho 'yaṃ vibhūtīnāṃ tvam etad vipulīkuru||
>
> This [Purāṇa] called "Bhagavataṃ" was spoken to me by God ["Bhagavata" = Viṣṇu]. It is a compendium of [God's] manifestations (*vibhūti*). Make an expansion on it.[8]

Similarly, the *Devī Bhagavatāpurāṇa* includes the claim that the *purāṇa* itself is "an expansion [*vipulī*] made by students and their students."[9] In these contexts, "making an expansion" amounts to the author elaborating on an existing text. The "elaboration" thus created is neither exactly the same as the original, nor does it break away from the original. An analogy can be drawn to classical Indian music. The backbone of a north Indian *rāga* is a *ṭhāṭ* consisting of seven notes, of which at least five must be used. For any *rāga* that is played, these notes form the backbone, a constant touchstone throughout the piece, and yet the musician is allowed a certain amount of freedom in the way these notes are played and in the different patterns of ascending and descending sequences. The *rāga* remains "classical" even though it is simultaneously unique every time it is played. Following this analogy, the Purāṇas choose to present their teachings as *vipula* to downplay their innovations. Even though many of them were written toward the end of the first millennium C.E., they attempt to pass themselves off as *purāṇa* (i.e., "old") through the manipulation of already well-established tropes.

Buddhist *Vaipulya sūtras* must also touch on a standard set of doctrinal "notes," and it is from these notes that they derive their authority. They differ from other authoritative texts in that they expand on these notes in a particular direction (discussed below) and explore the subtle and profound nuances lying hidden in the original doctrines. This appears to have been the understanding of this genre even in some non-Mahāyāna sources such as the *Mahāvibhāṣā* (c. second century).

> What is Vaipulya [方廣]? It is said to be all the sūtras corresponding to elaborations on [廣説] the meanings of exceedingly profound dharmas. Such as the fifty-three sūtra, the Brahmā-jāla sūtra, the Māyā-jāla sūtra, the five aggregates, the six sense-spheres, the Mahā-nidāna sūtra, etc.[10]

Here, the *Mahāvibhāṣā* defines *vaipulya* not just as "extensive," but as expanding on (廣説; lit. "explaining at length") certain topics. Just as in the *Śrīmad Bhagavatam's* use of the phrase *vipuli-kṛta,* 廣説 is used in the *Mahāvibhāṣā* in the imperative mood. For example, 謂 . . . 餘廣説如本論 (lit. "teach an additional expansion according to the root text").[11] The topics to be expanded on are both *sūtras* (the *Brahmājāla/Māyājāla sūtras*) as well as the standard teaching lists (the five *skandhas,* etc.). As texts that expand on classical themes, Mahāyāna *sūtras* seem to fit even the non-Mahāyāna definition of the *vaipulya* category as an "expansion." Indeed, as Lamotte has pointed out, at least one Sarvāstivādin master acknowledged that the "Prajñā teachings" (般若説, the *Prajñāpāramitā Sūtras?*) belonged in this category.[12] It is perhaps not insignificant that the Pali canon avoids the use of the word *vaipulya* as the designation of the genre and instead uses the term *vedalla,* defined in the commentaries as "receiving joy," thereby attempting to close the loophole that might allow Mahāyāna texts to enter.[13]

For those who remained unconvinced by the camouflage, some *sūtras* adopt an additional measure to prevent opponents from voicing their reservations. Many of these *sūtras* curse those who do not believe that Mahāyāna *sūtras* are "word of the Buddha." For example, the *Aṣṭasāhasrikā Prajñāpāramitā* mentions that some reject the Perfection of Wisdom and its teaching of the omniscience (*sarvajñā*) of the Buddha on the grounds that "it is not the Buddha's word."[14] For them, the Buddha predicts a suffering in hell so horrible that those even hearing of the punishment should "beware lest hot blood spurt out of their mouths."[15] Similarly, the *Laṅkāvatāra Sūtra* labels those who doubt that Mahāyāna texts are "word of the Buddha" *icchantika,* or those who will never be capable of attaining nirvāṇa.

> How does [the *icchantika*] abandon all good roots? By slandering the *Bodhisattva Piṭaka* which amounts to committing a sin of speech. [S/he] says, "This is not according to the sūtra, the vinaya [or] the [Buddha's] enlightenment."[16]

Mahāyāna and Its Message

Not all Mahāyāna strategies to pass off their texts as "word of the Buddha" were as cosmetic or polemic as those discussed above. Indeed, some of their methods display a degree of philosophical subtlety. However, before this investigation of the ways that Mahāyāna camouflaged its message to appear to conform to *buddhavacana* texts continues, it is necessary to identify what that message was and how it may have differed from the standard Buddhist fare. Granted, no single set of theses applies to all Mahāyāna texts. However, a trend emerges within some Mahāyāna works that seems to have been defining of the genre for Nāgārjuna. This trend is used below as a provisional definition of Mahāyāna in order to show what he was trying to persuade his readers to accept. Note that the Mahāyāna trajectory described here is provisional and does not necessarily apply to all Mahāyāna authors and texts, nor does it exhaust the significance of Mahāyāna for Nāgārjuna.

Several scholars have noted that Indian Buddhist texts present two apparently conflicting interpretations of the insight that leads to enlightenment. Lambert Schmithausen discusses these conflicting interpretations as they are played out in the early sūtra tradition and connects them to the prevailing trends in *abhidharma* literature as well as to trends in Mahāyāna.[17] His discussion is lengthy and goes into more detail than is necessary here. In brief, he identifies two trends in descriptions of the Buddha's enlightenment experience corresponding to the two fundamental practices of Buddhist meditation: *vipaśyanā* (reasoned analysis) and *śamatha* (calming meditation).

The first of these, *vipaśyanā,* can be found in *sūtras* such as the *Dharmacakraparivartana sūtra,*[18] which explain "liberating insight"[19] to consist of an understanding of the negative aspects of saṃsāra embodied in the four noble truths. According to this sūtra, suffering is to be known, its cause is to be cut off, the cessation of suffering (defined here as the utter absence of the cause of suffering) is to be witnessed directly, and the path is to be practiced. Knowledge of the four noble truths alone is said by the Buddha to be both necessary and sufficient for enlightenment.[20] Furthermore, in the sūtra, simply hearing the four noble truths is enough for Koṇḍañña to obtain the "pure and spotless eye of the truth" (i.e., to become a "stream-enterer"). In other words, he knows that "whatever is subject to the condition of origination, is subject also to the condition of cessation."[21] This insight is enough to earn him the honor of being the first person to be ordained by the Buddha. As the *Pali Vinaya* passage continues, all five of the Buddha's former disciples become ordained. He preaches one more sermon to them, this time on the five aggregates as being impermanent, suffering, and not-self. The Buddha concludes his sermon as follows.

> Considering this, O Bhikkhus, a learned, noble hearer of the word becomes weary of body, weary of sensation, wary of perception, weary of the *saṃskāras,* weary of consciousness. Becoming weary of all that, he divests himself of passion; by absence of passion he is made free; when he is free, he becomes aware that he is free; and he realizes that re-birth is exhausted; that holiness is completed; that duty is fulfilled; and that there is no further return to this world.[22]

What is significant about this articulation of liberating insight is that liberation is attained simply from the contemplation of the unsatisfactoriness of *saṃsāra*. No reference is made to the stages of absorptive meditation (*dhyāna* or *samādhi*) or to the positive experience of nirvāṇa.

A similar pattern is seen in the "Dīghanakha sutta" of the *Majjhima Nikāya,* in which the Buddha instructs the wanderer Dīghanakha to contemplate the body as "impermanent, as suffering, as a disease, as a tumour, as a dart, as a calamity, as an affliction, as alien, as disintegrating, as void, as not self."[23] Similarly, the Buddha teaches Dīghanakha to contemplate the three varieties of feeling (*vedanā*: pleasant, painful, and neither pleasant-nor-painful feelings) as "impermanent, conditioned, dependently arisen, subject to destruction, fading away and ceasing."[24] The Buddha then explains the importance of this knowledge for liberation.

> Seeing this, a well-taught noble disciple becomes disenchanted with pleasant feeling, disenchanted with painful feeling, disenchanted

> with neither-painful-nor-pleasant feeling. Being disenchanted, he becomes dispassionate. Through dispassion [his mind] is liberated. When it is liberated there comes the knowledge: "it is liberated." He understands: "Birth is destroyed, the holy life has been lived, what had to be done has been done, there is no more coming to any state of being."[25]

On hearing this sermon, Śāriputra considered what the Buddha had said and his mind was liberated from all *āśravas* (the *Majjhima Nikāya Aṭṭhakathā* says that he became an *arhant*).[26] At the same time, Dīghanakha attained a "spotless immaculate vision of the Dhamma," namely, an understanding of dependent-origination and, according to the *Majjhima Nikāya Aṭṭhakathā,* became a stream-enterer.

According to Schmithausen, texts in which the content of liberating insight consists of a rationally contemplated "truth" vary as to the content of that truth. As mentioned, the *Dharmacakraparivartana* claims this truth to be the four noble truths. In the *Samyutta Nikāya,* it is insight into the twelve links of dependent-origination (in their forward and reverse sequences) that provides the liberating content.[27] The "Dīghanakha sutta" combines the three marks of existence (impermanence, suffering, and non-self) and dependent-origination as the content that liberates Śāriputra and Dīghanakkha. Schmithausen notes that some early *abhidharma* texts, such as the *Śārīputrābhidharmaśāstra* and the *Paṭisambhiddāmagga,* assert that one can be liberated simply by insight into the selflessness of things.[28] The primary characteristic of these texts is that they place an emphasis on reasoned contemplation and analysis as the means of liberation and on *saṃsāra* as the primary focus of said contemplation. Schmithausen argues that these *sūtras* present the various truths as the content of liberating insight in order to present a rational connection between what the Buddha experienced and the fruit of the experience—namely, the destruction of the defilements (here *āśrava*). Still, the rationality of the case is not without problems. He points out that if one takes liberating insight to be described by the four noble truths (e.g., where it is said that *suffering* is to be known, *the arising of suffering* is to be cut off, *cessation* is to be directly realized, and the *path* is to be practiced), then, under the view that liberating insight concerns only the negative aspects of *saṃsāra,* a contradiction occurs insofar as cutting off the arising of suffering will be identical to the witnessing of *nirodha,* and therefore they cannot occur in two separate moments as stated by the texts. The second trend describing the Buddha's liberating experience as one of mental stabilization (*śamatha* or *samādhi*) can be found in *sūtras* like the "Nivāpa sutta" of the *Majjhima Nikāya*. These *sūtras* place liberating efficacy within a positive experience of nirvāṇa itself during the trance of the "cessation of feelings and apperception" (*saṃjñāveditanirodha*). This experience leads to final liberation. Schmithausen points out that the *sūtras* are ambiguous as to whether the liberating wisdom occurs in the state of *saṃjñāveditanirodha* itself or immediately afterward.[29] In either case, these sūtras make the trance of *saṃjñāveditanirodha* the driving force behind the destruction of the *āśravas*. There is some logic to this approach. *Saṃjñā* is the aggregate responsible for being aware of an object *as something*. Whereas *vijñāna* simply produces an awareness of a thing, *saṃjñā* produces an understanding of that awareness. For example, *vijñāna* registers the presence of a blue cup while *saṃjñā* is responsible for the understanding "it is a blue cup."[30] Here, it may be useful to think of *vijñāna* as perception or cognition while *saṃjñā* is more akin to *ap*perception or *re*cognition. Within the Buddhist *abhidharma* traditions, the six *vijñāna* perceive colors, sounds, and so on, while *saṃjñā* registers "signs" (*nimitta*, something of a cross between Kant's categories of the understanding and Pierce's signifier). A sign is a set of qualities that are the sufficient cause for the identification or recognition of an object. Thus, when one sees a woman indistinctly at a distance, the type of movement or the roundness of the form are sufficient to identify the person as "female" even if nothing else is known about her.

The faculty of *saṃjñā* is generally recognized as the source of ignorance as well as the basis for all wrong action.[31] This connection is couched in a context reminiscent of the twelve links of dependent-origination in the "Madhupiṇḍika sutta" of the *Majjhima Nikāyā*. The forward sequence (i.e., the arising of suffering, *anuloma-pratītyasaṃutpāda*) reads as follows.

> Dependent on the eye and forms, eye-consciousness arises. The meeting of the three is contact. With contact as a condition, there is feeling [*vedanā*]. What one feels, that one perceives [*sañjānāti*]. What one perceives, one thinks about [*vitakketi*]. What one thinks about, one mentally proliferates [*papañceti*]. With what one mentally proliferates as the source, perceptions and notions tinged by mental proliferation beset a man with respect to past, future, and present forms recognizable though the eye.[32]

Here, unlike in the twelve links of dependent-origination, the origin of the chain lies in the physical world instead of in ignorance. Nevertheless, the apperceptive faculty (*saṃjñā*) is said to be the immediate cause of all mental proliferation. Later in the sūtra, mental proliferation is shown to be the source not only of karma but of ignorance itself.

> Bhikkhus, as to the source through which perceptions and notions tinged by mental proliferation beset a man: if nothing is found there to delight in, welcome and hold to, this is the end of the underlying tendency to lust, of the underlying tendency to aversion, of the underlying tendency to views, of the underlying tendency to doubt, of the underlying tendency to conceit, of the underlying tendency to desire for being, of the underlying tendency to ignorance; this is the end of resorting to rods and weapons, of quarrels, brawls, disputes, recrimination, malice, and false speech; here these evil unwholesome states cease without remainder.[33]

With the deleterious function of *saṃjñā* in mind, we can now understand why the highest states of absorption (either *naiva-saṃjñā-nâsaṃjñâyatana* or *saṃjñā-veditanirodha*) can be said to destroy the *āśravas*. Since the *āśravas* have their root in *saṃjñā*, they cannot function in its absence. Furthermore, since it is the function of *saṃjñā* to perceive *nimitta*, the cessation of *saṃjñā* would be a state that can only be described as *animitta* or "the absorption of the signless deliverance of mind" (*animitta cetovimutta samāpatti*). In Theravādin and Sarvāstivādin texts, the signless absorption along with the emptiness absorption and the wishlessness absorption are usually depicted as states of mind that lead to nirvāṇa (they are called "gates of liberation" [*vimokṣa-mukha*]). For the most part, these traditions treat emptiness, signlessness, and wishlessness as characteristics of the mind in the highest states of *samādhi*, although they are identified as such only on subsequent reflection (identification of the state *as signless* could occur only after the faculty of *saṃjñā* had resumed).[34] A few places in the Pali tradition, however, treat emptiness, signlessness, and wishlessness as positive characteristics of nirvāṇa itself. For example, according to the "Mahāvedalla sutta" of the *Majjhima Nikāya*, the two conditions for the signless absorption are "non-attention to all signs and attention to the signless element."[35] Again, the significance of this description of deliverance lies in its contrast to the descriptions of deliverance based on the understanding of truths. In the descriptions of deliverance based on truth, it is the unsatisfactoriness of *saṃsāra* alone that leads to release. In the description of deliverance in the "Mahāvedalla sutta," it is precisely the *inattention* to saṃsāra and the sole attention to the "signless element" *as a positive phenomenon* that leads to enlightenment. Although this interpretation is relatively rare in the early sūtra literature, a few of the Pali commentaries[36] as well as some *abhidharma* treatises[37] explicitly refer to emptiness, signlessness, and wishlessness as characteristics of nirvāṇa itself. These texts may have been picking up on a trend that began with the Dharmaguptakas and certainly predates Nāgārjuna. The *Śāriputrābhidharmaśāstra* presents the connection between emptiness and signlessness and nirvāṇa as follows.

> What is the primary meaning of emptiness? It is said to be nirvāna. Accordingly Bhikṣus: contemplate nirvāṇa as emptiness [思惟涅槃空], as the understanding of emptiness [知空], as the liberation of emptiness [解空], and as the attainment of emptiness [受空]. In regard to what is it empty? [It is] empty of "I" and empty of "mine," empty of immutability. Like this, it is to be carefully discerned. Gaining an absorbed mind, [one] abides in right concentration [正住]. . . . What is the *samādhi* of signlessness [*animitta*] apart from the *samādhi* of emptiness? If there is a remaining *samādhi* taking part in nirvāṇa as its objective representation [境界, *ālambana* or *viṣaya*], this is called *animitta samādhi*. Again, *animitta samādhi:* The conditioned world has signs [行有相, *saṃskṛtanimittavat*]. Nirvāṇa is signless. The conditioned world has three signs: arising, staying and passing away. Nirvāṇa has three signs. Not arising, not staying, and not passing away. Thus the conditioned world has signs and nirvāṇa is signless.[38]

The problem with the approach represented by the "Mahāvedalla sutta," as has been discussed extensively by Paul Griffiths, is that there is no room in *saṃjñāveditanirodha* for reasoned analysis because such analysis relies on identification and recognition, and the one faculty capable of this activity (i.e., *saṃjñā*) has shut down.[39] Hence, if a positive, personal mystical experience is put forward as the content of the enlightenment experience, then there is no room for the four noble truths and no plausible explanation for abandoning *saṃsāra*. Indeed, as Schmithausen points out, the "Jhāna sutta" of the *Aṅguttara Nikāya* expressly states: "penetration into Liberating Insight (*āññā/aññā*) is only possible so far as one dwells in meditative absorption involving ideation (*saṃjñā*)."[40] Hence, even by the standards of the early sūtra tradition, the two descriptions of liberating insight represented in the *Nivāpa Sūtra* and the *Mādhupiṇḍika Sūtra* are mutually exclusive.

The existing sūtra collections deal with this problem in different ways. The first approach is to reconcile the two by creating a division of labor. Texts like the "Aṭṭakanāgara sutta" of the *Majjhima Nikāya* use the levels of absorptive meditation as a vehicle to gain access to all realms of reality. After awakening from each level attained through *dhyāna,* the monk is to reflect on his prior experience as conditioned and impermanent. After all of reality (even its highest levels) is understood to be conditioned and impermanent, that understanding causes the monk to abandon *saṃsāra* altogether. Even a text dealing with the *samādhi* par excellence, namely, the "Cūḷasūññata sutta," has the monk achieving the *animitta samādhi* first and he abandons all *āśravas* only after he subsequently reflects on the experience as conditioned and subject to cessation. Other sūtras, like the "Kīṭāgiri sutta" (also of the *Majjhima Nikāya*) claim that these two different approaches to nirvāṇa are adopted by people with different propensities. Some practitioners are inclined toward reasoned analysis. For them, the analysis of *saṃsāra* as unsatisfactory (*vipassana* meditation) will be sufficient, while those who are adept at higher states of absorption can be liberated through *samādhi.*

Thus the early sūtra tradition shows a dichotomy both in practice and in ontology. In practice there is, on the one hand, the path of reasoned analysis (employing the faculty of *saṃjñā*) aimed at fully comprehending the unsatisfactoriness of saṃsāra to produce detachment from it; and, on the other hand, absorptive meditation that attempts to curtail or even stop the activity of *saṃjñā* and (at least in the Theravāda tradition) turn the practitioner's attention toward the "deathless element" of nirvāṇa. Put another way, reasoned analysis correlates to *saṃsāra,* whereas absorptive meditation correlates to nirvāṇa. Furthermore, the rationale behind both types of practice seems to be the notion that *saṃsāra* and nirvāṇa are mutually exclusive. To withdraw from one is to attend to the other.

By the time of Nāgārjuna, this dichotomy was entrenched in the *abhidharma* literature of the early schools. In these texts, the division of labor becomes more articulated. Without going into detail, it suffices to say that both the Sarvāstivādins and the Theravādins divide the labor between *śamatha* and *vipaśyanā* by creating "a path of seeing" (*darśanamārga*) and a path of meditation (*bhāvanamārga*). They both employ long lists of defilements and then state which mental defilements are eliminated by the *darśanamārga* (i.e., by *vipaśyanā,* or reasoned analysis) and which are eliminated by *bhāvanamārga* (i.e., by *samādhi,* or mental pacification), so that the *arhant* becomes one who employs both types of practice to uproot all defilements without exception.

What is common in all these articulations of the path is that they deal with the contradictions between the negative meditation on the world as suffering, impermanent, and not-self, and the positive meditation on nirvāṇa as peaceful, and so forth, by somehow keeping these two meditations separate and relegating them to a sequence.

Mahāyāna

Mahāyāna, by contrast, distinguishes itself by fusing these two trends into one. According to Schmithausen:

> In Mahāyāna Buddhism such a distinction between the comprehension of Essencelessness (as the true nature of mundane factors) and the comprehension of the truth of Cessation (as the Cessation of all mundane existence ontologically anticipated from time immemorial) . . . is usually not made. This means that, from the point of view of content, the "positive" and the negative" tradition come to be fused (the accent, it is true, varying from system to system). With regard to its formal aspect, however, the Mahāyāna descriptions or theories of liberating insight . . . refer to a clearly mystical experience, which resembles *saṃjñāvedayitanirodha* or *nirodhasamāpatti* in its aspect of a mystico-existential anticipatory realization of Nirvāṇa, though it is usually clearly distinguished from it.[41]

Mahāyānists seem to have picked up on the trend begun in the *Śāriputrābhidharmaśāstra* and found in various places in Pali literature wherein emptiness is said to be a characteristic of nirvāṇa. With this key element in place, Mahāyānists like Nāgārjuna are now in a position to fuse the two practices as well as the ontological dichotomy. Many sūtras use "empty" as a negative adjective describing *saṃsāra*. Emptiness as regards *saṃsāra* signifies the understanding that no individual has a soul, whereas the emptiness signifying nirvāṇa (even though it is often described as knowledge of *anātman*) is contrasted with the first emptiness. In Mahāyāna (or at least Nāgārjuna's version of it), the doctrine of emptiness is the lynchpin attaching the emptiness of *saṃsāra* seamlessly to the emptiness of nirvāṇa.[42] As Nāgārjuna says:

> Saṃsāra . . . is nothing essentially different from nirvāṇa. Nirvāṇa is nothing essentially different from saṃsāra.
>
> The limits . . . of nirvāṇa are the limits of saṃsāra. Between the two, also, there is not the slightest difference whatsoever.[43]

Having united the ontological dichotomy, Mahāyānists like Nāgārjuna are then in a position to join the practice of analytical insight (usually associated with the negative analysis of saṃsāra) to the fruits of *samādhi* (especially that of *saṃjñāveditanirodha* and the *animitta samādhi*). On the surface, Nāgārjuna looks like an advocate of "dry insight meditation." His works usually contain lengthy analyses of the soullessness of the self and the selflessness of phenomena—all of which require the dedicated effort of *saṃjñā*. Furthermore, he makes no mention of the practice of the *dhyānas* even in his didactic texts such as the *Ratnāvalī*.

However, the situation seems to be otherwise if his his mode of analysis is carefully examined. In his *Mūlamadhyamakakārikā*, Nāgārjuna provides twenty-seven chapters of reasoned analysis refuting such things as causality, motion, the elements, and the aggregates. In each case, he takes the component parts of the thing under examination and asks the same questions. Is *x* identical to *y*? Is *x* different from *y*? Is *x* prior to *y*? Are *x* and *y* simultaneous? Can *x* be related to *y* if it is past, present or future? Can *x* be unrelated to *y*? The *Abhidharmakośa* lists ten *nimitta* that are nonfunctional in the *animitta samādhi* (the meditation without *nimitta*): the five sense-spheres (*āyatanas*), male and female, arising, staying and passing away.[44] Three of these characteristics in particular (arising, staying, and ceasing) are said to characterize conditioned reality (*saṃskṛta*, i.e., *saṃsāra*). Although its source is uncertain, the *Dazhidulun* adds two more *nimitta* to the list: identity and difference.[45] Combining these lists yields: form, sound, taste, smell, thoughts, arising, staying, passing-away, identity, and difference, in addition to maleness and femaleness. The first ten of these *nimitta* are the categories that ground all of Nāgārjuna's investigations in the *Mūlamadhyamakakārikā*. They also happen to be the *nimitta* by which the faculty of *saṃjñā* identifies *saṃsāra* as *saṃsāra*.

If Nāgārjuna can show that nothing can be identified unequivocally to be arising, staying, passing away, identical, or different, then he has shown the *nimitta* of *saṃsāra* to be *animitta:* in short, no different from nirvāṇa. At the same time, the process of reasoned analysis in Nāgārjuna's texts works against the transparent functioning of *saṃjñā* to grasp its accustomed categorical objects. Clearly, in Nāgārjuna's version of *vipaśyanā*, *saṃjñā* still functions. *Saṃjñā* as a faculty is left intact, while certain *saṃjñās* (i.e., concepts, the objective correlates to the faculty of *saṃjñā*) corresponding to specific *nimittas*) are disabled.

Although certainly not all Mahāyāna texts take Nāgārjuna's approach, the uniting of *śamatha* and *vipaśyanā* appears to be a theme even in Mahāyāna texts touting special *samādhis*. For example, one would expect Mahāyāna texts with *Samādhi* in the title, such as the *Samādhirāja/*

Candrapradīpasamādhi Sūtra or the *Śūraṅgamasamādhi Sūtra,* to place much more emphasis on meditative stabilization than on any particular ontological position. On the contrary, the *Samādhirāja Sūtra* teaches an almost seamless transition between the path of vision and the "king of *Samādhis*" that is the "manifesting the sameness of all dharmas."

> the Bodhisattva-Mahāsattva who strives for this *samādhi* and wishes to attain the Supreme Enlightenment speedily, should be an expert knower of the essence of the non-existence. . . . (He) ought to comprehend all the dharmas as being non-existent in their essence, as signless, markless, not originated nor disappearing, inexpressible by letters, void, quiescent from the outset, pure by their very nature . . . the Bodhisattva-Mahāsattva who is an expert knower of the essence of the non-existence is neither attracted nor repulsed nor infatuated by all the elements of sight, hearing [etc.] For what reason? Because he does neither perceive nor apprehend this dharma . . . Neither perceiving nor apprehending this dharma, he does not cling to all the elements of the threefold world, soon reaches this *samādhi* and speedily attains the Supreme Enlightenment.[46]

Earlier, the same text states, among the characteristics of the *samādhi* that it teaches, "This *samādhi* is the seeing of dharmas (*dharmadarśana*), the cultivation of the path (*mārgabhāvanā*) and the meeting with a *tathāgata*"—again blurring the boundary between the two practices.[47]

Stealing the Thunder: Mahāyāna's Allusions to *Buddhavacana*

Not all Mahāyānists had the same agenda as Nāgārjuna. Nevertheless, the above discussion shows just how close Mahāyānists' theses could come to doctrinal positions that their *confrères* already held. Yet, because these interpretations deal with the very content of the liberating experience of the Buddha himself and all his disciples, even a small deviation could give rise to controversy. The proximity of this strand of Mahāyāna to that already contained in the *Tripiṭaka* stems from the fact that it is a hybrid view derived from a reworking of existing positions. Indeed, the very hybridity of this facet of Mahāyāna facilitated an important strategy. Because the hybrid position echoed the explicit teachings of the sūtras, but was not identical to them, Mahāyānists could easily allude to texts already considered to be "word of the Buddha" as a strategy to pass off their texts as authoritative. The strategy of canonical allusion is used widely in Mahāyāna texts, including those by Nāgārjuna. The advantage of this strategy is that it not only allows new, Mahāyāna ideas to appear authoritative but reorients the reader's perspective on the original corpus so that the new (Mahāyāna) meaning may be read back into the target text. The retroactive effect of this strategy owes its impact to the nature of literary allusion itself.

In an old, but nonetheless useful definition, Ziva Ben-Porat explains literary allusion as:

> a device for the simultaneous activation of two texts. The activation is achieved through manipulation of a special signal: a sign (simple or complex) in a given text characterized by an additional larger "referent." This referent is always an independent text. The simultaneous activation of the two texts thus connected results in the formation of intertextual patterns whose nature cannot be predetermined.[48]

Although the totality of the intertextual patterns may not be predetermined (Ben-Porat is interested primarily in describing the poetic surplus of meaning that arises form intertextual patterns), some intertextual patterns could be predetermined—and indeed *were*—by the Mahāyānists who employed them as a rhetorical strategy to influence the reading practices of the (local?) Buddhist community. What is useful in this definition and Ben-Porat's subsequent discussion is the precision with which his terminology allows allusion. In a case of literary allusion, an alluding text contains a particular sign. The sign itself has both a place and a function within the world of the alluding text, and yet it also calls to mind a "marker," which is "always identifiable as an element or pattern belonging to another independent text."[49] The marker, in turn, functions as a metonym for the marked text that now functions according to the patterns set out by the alluding text.

> In its manifest belonging to a larger independent system (i.e., the evoked text) the marker maintains the metonymic structure of the relationship sign-referent which characterizes all allusions: an "object" is represented by one of its components or by one of the systems to which it belongs. . . . In terms of the end product, the formation of intertextual patterns, the marker—regardless of the form it takes—is used for the activation of independent elements from the evoked text. Those are never referred to directly.[50]

The metonymic function of allusion will be vital for the Mahāyānists. When a Mahāyāna text alludes to a text already considered to be "word of the Buddha," it evokes not only the specific words and ideas contained in the target text but also the genre of "word of the Buddha" texts as a whole. (In the *mahāpadeśas* (criteria used to determine textual authenticity), discussed in Chapter 3, a *sūtra* could be considered to be "word of the Buddha" if it compared favorably with the sūtras one already knew.)

Allusions to "Word of the Buddha" in the *Śālistambha Sūtra*

Two examples illustrate how allusion can successfully evoke "word of the Buddha" while changing its meaning. The first example has been pointed out by Ross Reat in his study of the *Śālistambhasūtra*, an early, ostensibly Mahāyāna sūtra. Near the beginning of this *sūtra*, Śāriputra says to Maitreya:

> [Mahāsattva: "Maitreya, here, today, the Lord,] looking upon a stalk of rice, spoke this aphorism to the monks: "Whoever, monks, sees the conditioned arising sees Dharma, and whoever sees Dharma sees the Buddha." Having said this the Lord became silent.[51]

On this passage, Reat makes the following observation:

> [The . . .] crucially Mahāyāna content of the *Śālistambha* is the introductory material which reveals that the sūtra is essentially a discourse on the progressive realization of Dharma-kāya Buddha. In paragraph two, the *Śālistambha* says: "Whoever, monks sees conditioned arising . . . ." The statement is incipiently Mahāyāna, but the terms are remarkably Theravādin. This passage is, in fact, a conflation of two well-known passages from the Pali suttas (M1:191 and S3:120). . . . From paragraph seven on, it is clear that the *Śālistambha* expresses a fundamental Mahāyāna position, but it does so in remarkably conservative, even quaint terms.[52]

To best understand this passage, it is necessary to look at the two passages to which it alludes. The first can be found in the "Mahāhatthipadopama sutta" (Greater Elephant's Footprint Sutta) of the *Majjhima Nikāya*, where Sāriputta says:

> Now this has been said by the Blessed One: "One who sees dependent origination sees the Dhamma; one who sees Dhamma sees dependent origination."[53]

This is a curious passage because, despite Śāriputra's testimony that these are the Buddha's words, this quotation does not appear anywhere else in the Pali canon. The second source comes from the "Vakkali sutta" of the *Saṃyutta Nikāya*. Here a terminally ill monk requests his personal attendant to bring a relic and a footprint of the Buddha so that he can revere it. The Buddha comes to him and says:

> Enough Vakkali! Why do you want to see this foul body? One who sees the Dhamma sees me; one who sees me sees the Dhamma. For in seeing the dhamma, Vakkali, one sees me; and in seeing me one sees the Dhamma.[54]

The syntactic similarities between the two target verses coupled with their common use of the verb *passati* (sees) serve as identifiable "markers" for which the syntax of the *Śālistambha* verse functions as a sign. In so doing, the passage activates the general authority of the passages, making them function in the new text as a metonym for "word of the Buddha" itself. In one sense, the new passage is technically "word of the Buddha" because the Buddha did, in fact, utter each and every one of these words, just not together. Notice, however, some of the doctrinal content of the marker texts is elided (or at least reconfigured) in the process of its recontextualization. If Reat is correct that this passage refers to the Mahāyāna doctrine of the *dharmakāya,* then the sense of the new construction is *opposite* that of the "Vakkali sutta." In the "Vakkali sutta," the terms *dharma* and "body" (*kāya*) are contrasted—the *dharma* is what is to be sought, not the body of the Buddha, which he says is "putrid" (*pūti*). Further on, the *Śālistambha Sūtra* repeats the statement that the one who sees the *dharma* "sees the unsurpassable Dharma-body [*anuttara-dharma-śarīra*], the Buddha, by exertion based on right knowledge in clear understanding of the noble Dharma." The term *dharma-śarīra* here is odd (as Reat also notes). Usually, the expression *dharma-kāya* is found in Mahāyāna works that refer to the Dharma-Body of the Buddha. *Kāya* can mean either a collection of things or a physical body (much like the Latin *corpus*), whereas *śarīra* is used exclusively for the physical body. The *Śālistambha's* choice of words perhaps implies that the Buddha's body is not so putrid after all.

Allusions to "Word of the Buddha" in the *Mūlamadhyamakakārikā*

The next example of Mahāyāna's use of allusion is less obvious, although crucial for understanding Nāgārjuna and his textual strategies. This example can be found in the *Aṣṭadaśasāhasrikā* or the *Pañcaviṃśatisāhasrikā Prajñāpāramitā Sūtra.*[55]

> And how does he wisely know conditioned co-production? He wisely knows it as neither production, nor stopping, neither cut off nor eternal, neither single nor manifold, neither coming nor going away, as the appeasement of all futile discoursings, and as bliss.[56]

It is most likely to this passage that Nāgārjuna refers in the opening stanza of his *Mūlamadhyamakakārikā:*

> I pay homage to the Fully Enlightened One whose true, venerable words teach dependent-origination to be the blissful pacification of all mental proliferation, neither production, nor stopping, neither cut off nor eternal, neither single nor manifold, neither coming, nor going away.[57]

As the introductory stanza of the *Mūlamadhyamakakārikā,* this stanza deserves careful scrutiny, because it introduces not only the subject matter of the entire work but also its strategy. Nāgārjuna begins by piously saluting the Buddha and then identifies him as one who teaches the doctrine of dependent-origination (*pratītyasamutpāda*). In those texts where conformity to *dharmatā* (reality) is listed among the criteria for "word of the Buddha" (as it is in the *Abhidharmakośa* and *Sphuṭārtha*), *dharmatā* is defined as dependent-origination. Hence, by stating at the outset that the text will be a treatise concerning dependent-origination, Nāgārjuna makes it clear that he will be writing about, or expanding upon (*vipula kṛtaṃ*), a theme central to the definition of "word of the Buddha."

The series of eight negations (noncessation, and so on) that follow has a rather complicated, if strategically significant, relationship to texts generally considered "word of the Buddha" by non-Mahāyānists. For Mahāyānists, the authority of this text would have presented no problem—the passage referred to is "word of the Buddha" because the Buddha uttered it in a Mahāyāna sūtra. However, if Nāgārjuna was in the minority and, as such, had to rely on the general Buddhist monastic apparatus for the preservation of his text, then he would have to convince non-Mahāyānists that what he was writing fell within their definition of "word of the Buddha." Why, then, would he place a Mahāyāna reference at the beginning of a treatise seeking to convince non-Mahāyānists? Why this passage in particular?

Although a more complete answer to this question is discussed below, in Chapter 7, a few important points may be made here. Nāgārjuna's selection of this passage for his opening, salutary verse (*nāmaskāra*) was far from arbitrary. This passage, like the *Śālistambha* passage discussed above, uses idiosyncratic words and syntax to activate a plurality of marker texts within the corpus of texts already considered "word of the Buddha." It splices together these elements in such a way as to produce (or defend) a new, Mahāyāna meaning within the new text as well as to enact a new interpretation retroactively onto the *buddhavacana* corpus. The new text may then be considered "word of the Buddha"—both because its style compares favorably to existing texts and because it would now be possible to see that the Mahāyāna meaning had always existed, albeit latently, in the original corpus. An illustration of the process is provided by the eight negations in the passage that Nāgārjuna references to identify the marker texts evoked by the passage.

Dependent-Origination in the Canon

The *locus classicus* in the Buddhist *sūtra* collection for material on dependent-origination is the *Nidāna Vagga* of the *Saṃyutta Nikāya,* or "chapter on cause," which contains ninety-three sections on dependent-origination. What seems to have been viewed as the standard[58] version of the law of dependent- origination is found in the opening *sūtra* of this section.

> And what, bhikkhus, is dependent origination? With ignorance as condition, volitional formations [come to be]; with volitional formations as condition, consciousness; with consciousness as condition, name-and-form; with name-and-form as condition, the six sense bases; with the six sense bases as condition, contact; with contact as condition, feeling; with feeling as condition, craving; with craving as condition, clinging; with clinging as condition, existence; with existence as a condition, birth; with birth as condition, aging-and-death, sorrow, lamentation, pain, displeasure, and despair come

> to be. Such is the origin of this whole mass of suffering. This, bhikkhus, is called dependent origination.
>
> But with the remainderless fading away and cessation of ignorance comes cessation of volitional formations; with the cessation of volitional formations, cessation of consciousness; with the cessation of consciousness, cessation of name-and-form; with the cessation of name-and-form, cessation of the six sense bases; with the cessation of the six sense bases, cessation of contact; with the cessation of contact, cessation of feeling; with the cessation of feeling, cessation of craving; with the cessation of craving, cessation of clinging; with the cessation of clinging, cessation of existence; with the cessation of existence, cessation of birth; with the cessation of birth, aging-and-death, sorrow, lamentation, pain, displeasure, and despair cease. Such is the cessation of this whole mass of suffering.[59]

In some *sūtras,* this formula is summarized as follows.

> Thus when this exists, that comes to be; with the arising of this, that arises. When this does not exist, that does not come to be; with the cessation of this, that ceases.[60]

These three formulae constitute the classical teaching of dependent-origination in terms of the four noble truths. The first sequence describes the arising (*samuppāda* or *saṃbhavati*) of suffering, the second sequence describes the cessation *(nirodha)* of suffering, and the third is a kind of summary formula.

In most non-Mahāyāna texts that teach dependent-origination, a prologue is appended to the above formula. The prologue itself is also idiosyncratic and formulaic, and there are many standard variations. In the prologue, several types of questions are asked and subsequently responded to negatively or critiqued as faulty. For example, in the "Kaccāyana sutta," Kaccāyana asks whether everything exists or not. In response, the Buddha states that the two responses "everything exists" and "everything does not exist" are two extremes and that dependent-origination is the middle between them. Alternately, the interlocutor will ask whether suffering comes from the self or from another. It is among these questions that the source for some of the negations listed in the *Prajñāpāramitā* verse is located.

Elsewhere is another interpretation that categorizes these types of question as mere subsets of a more fundamental question. An example of this is in the *Timbaruka sūtra*. After Timbaruka asks whether pleasure and pain are brought about by oneself or by another, the Buddha rewords the question as follows:

> Timbaruka, [if one thinks,] "The feeling and the one who feels it are the same," [then one asserts] with reference to one existing from the beginning: "Pleasure and pain are created by oneself." I do not speak thus. But, Timbaruka, [if one thinks,] "The feeling is one, the one who feels it is another," [then one asserts] with reference to one stricken by feeling: "Pleasure and pain are created by another." Neither do I speak thus. Without veering towards either of those extremes, the Tathāgata teaches the Dhamma by the middle: "With ignorance as condition, volitional formations [come to be]."[61]

Here, the stock question of something originating "from itself" is seen as a question that assumes a continuous, unchanging self, whereas the question of something originating "from another" is seen as a question that assumes a completely discontinuous self. The *Timbaruka* sūtra subsumes these two types of question under the categories of *śāśvata* (eternality) and *ucchedatā* (disruption). This connection is made explicit in the "Acelakassapa Sūtra":

> Kassapa, [if one thinks,] "The one who acts is the same as the one who experiences [the result]," [then one asserts] with reference to one existing from the beginning: "Suffering is created by oneself." When one asserts this, this amounts to eternalism. But, Kassapa, [if one thinks,] 'The one who acts is one, the one who experiences [the result] is another, [then one asserts] with reference to one strictly by feeling: "Suffering is created by another." When one asserts this, this amounts to annihilationism. Without veering towards either of these extremes, the Tathāgata teaches the Dhamma by the middle: With ignorance as condition, volitional formations [come to be].[62]

The Pali views the pair *uccheda/śāśvata* as the overarching category of which the other pairs are merely subsets. In his commentary on this verse, Buddhaghosa (fifth century) adds the dichotomy of "being/non-being" as a subcategory of *ucchedavāda* and *śāśvatavāda*. A similar commentary occurs on the "Kaccāyana sutta." In Buddha's dialogue with Kaccāyana, "the right view" is defined as the middle way between the two extremes of being and non-being.

[Text:] This world, Kaccāna, for the most part depends upon a duality—upon the notion of existence and the notion of nonexistence. But for one who sees the origin of the world as it really is with correct wisdom, there is no notion of nonexistence in regard to the world. And for one who sees the cessation of the world as it really is with correct wisdom, there is no notion of existence in regard to the world.[63]

[Buddhaghosa's commentary:] "This is one extreme" [means] this is a deceptive extreme, a bad extreme [but] is primarily "eternity." "This second extreme" [means] this is the second. "Everything is non-existent" is the second false and bad extreme, the so-called view related to arising. It has the meaning of "disruption." The rest of this is clear.[64]

Even here, what would seem to be two unrelated extremes (being/non-being) are explained under the rubric of eternality and disruption.[65] That all false views fall under the heading of *śāśvata* or *uccheda* is not so clear in the other *nikāyas,* such as "Brahmajāla Sūtra" in the *Dīgha Nikāya*. Nevertheless, even there some commentators understood the sixty-two false views mentioned to fall under the rubric of eternality and disruption.[66]

Thus, when the *Prajñāpāramitā* verse states that dependent-origination is neither eternality nor disruption, the statement evokes not only the texts that have the words *śāśvata* and *ucchedatā* in them but also the entire group of texts that regard dependent-origination as the middle between two extremes.

Although the *sūtras* mentioned above seem to take the two extremes of eternality and disruption as the two most fundamental views, at least one *sūtra* tries to make this schema more complete by adding "unity" and "plurality" to the list. Thus, in the "Lokāyatika Sūtra" of the *Saṃyutta Nikāya:*

At Sāvatthī. Then a brahmin who was a cosmologist approached the Blessed One . . . and said to him:

"How is it, Master Gotama: does all exist?"

"'All exists': this, brahmin, is the oldest cosmology."

"Then, Master Gotama, does all not exist?"

"'All does not exist': this, brahmin, is the second cosmology."

"How is it, Master Gotama: is all a unity [*ekatta*]?"

"'All is a unity': this, brahmin, is the third cosmology."

"Then, Master Gotama, is all a plurality [*puthutta*]?"

"'All is a plurality': this, brahmin, is the fourth cosmology."

Without veering towards either of these extremes, the Tathāgata teaches the Dhamma by the middle . . . [the twelve links of dependent-origination follow].[67]

"Unity" (*ekārtha*) and "plurality" (*nānārtha* = *puthutta*) are, of course, also included in the *Prajñāpāramitā* list of negations. Hence, at least four out of the eight negations in the *Prajñāpāramitā* verse target actual passages discussing dependent-origination in the *Saṃyutta Nikāya*. When compared to the mass of sūtras dealing with dependent-origination, the formulaic nature of these prologues stands out. *Sūtras* dealing with dependent-origination are expected to begin with the denial of contradictory extremes and subsequently to teach dependent-origination as the middle way between both extremes and to end with a recitation of the twelve links of dependent-origination. The pattern is repeated to such an extent that it becomes an easily recognizable cliché. The pattern and its repetition, which originally served as an aid to memorization, become a marker to be evoked by later Mahāyānists in order to activate texts that were universally agreed to be "word of the Buddha." The presence of the pairs eternality/disruption and unity/plurality in regard to dependent-origination in the *Prajñāpāramitā* should be more than enough to allude to dependent-origination. Why then add the remaining two pairs?

The Unconditioned in the Canon

The four remaining negations in the *Prajñāpāramitā* passage are: "nonceasing," "nonarising," "noncoming," and "nongoing." The reader familiar with Buddhist literature would be aware that, although the Buddha claims dependent-origination to be *anucchedaṃ, aśāśvataṃ, anekārthaṃ,* and *anānārthaṃ,* nowhere in the extant (non-Mahāyāna) *sūtra* literature does he say that dependent-origination is "nonarising," "nonceasing," "noncoming," or "nongoing." Since dependent-origination is often said to be a description of the way that suffering arises (*utpāda*), it seems counterintuitive to say that it is "nonarising" (*an-utpāda*). On the contrary, it is likely that any monk would recognize "nonarising, nonceasing, etc." as more closely related to the Buddha's sermons on nirvāṇa in the *Udāna*.[68] Since "arising," "ceasing," "coming," and "going" are attributes of *saṃsāra* (conditioned reality, or *saṃskṛta*), nirvāṇa (considered in most non-Mahāyāna schools as unconditioned, or *asaṃskṛta*) should be their polar opposite. Indeed, in many verses in the *Udāna* the unconditioned realm of nirvāṇa is explicitly said to be not arising, not ceasing, not coming, and not going.

Consider the following verse from the Pali *Udāna*.

> There is, monks, that base [*tadāyatana*] wherein there is neither earth, nor water, nor fire, nor wind, nor that base consisting of endless space, nor that base consisting of infinite consciousness, nor that base consisting of nothingness, nor that base consisting of neither perception nor non-perception, nor this world, nor the next world, nor both sun and moon. There too [*tad*[*āyatana*] . . .], monks, I do not speak either of coming (*na āgatiṃ*), or going,[69] or remaining, or falling, or arising. This is (quite) without foundation, (quite) without occurrence, quite without object. This alone is the end of *duḥkha*.[70]

A parallel verse, though not identical, appears in the Sanskrit *Udāna Varga*.

> Don't like what will perish, what is born, arisen, and originated, is fabricated, composite and unstable and arises from the stream of food. Happiness is the peace on the basis of renunciation and rough and subtle investigation, (when) every misery is stopped and composites are at peace. O monks! with clairvoyance I see (it) does not abide anywhere. For it does not abide in the earth, the water, the fire or the wind. It does not abide in the source of boundless space,[71] in the source of boundless consciousness, in the source of nothingness, or in the source of neither existence nor non-existence of discrimination. And it does not abide in this world or the next, on the moon or on the sun. There is no observation of it. O monks! I do not state that going and coming exist there, for there is no abiding. I do not state that there is transmigration for there is no arising. The end of misery, is then, like this.[72]

From the standpoint of this *Udāna,* the negations, "noncoming," or "nongoing," are to indicate the unconditioned nature of nirvāṇa. The *Udāna* passage is typical of passages advocating a "positive, mystical" content of *samādhi* as discussed by Schmithausen.[73] The *Udāna* verse begins with the list of the stages of concentration beginning with elemental *kasiṇa* meditations and progressing up through the eight *dhyānas,* or "absorptions." Classically, the eight meditations are taught as follows: (1) one reflects on the unsatisfactoriness of the present situation; (2) one enters into the concentration that is empty of those distractions; (3) one becomes absorbed into that level of attainment; and (4) one emerges from the concentration and reflects on the degree of subtlety of the experience.

Upon reflection, one is to notice two things: the absence of what was present in the previous state, and the positive qualities of the present state. That which one perceives with regard to the meditative state is the resulting fruit of the concentration.[74]

The highest level of meditation (*dhyāna*) in the early canon is the point at which one is no longer cognizant of the "sign" (*nimitta*) of anything, whether it be infinite space, infinite consciousness, nothingness itself or neither-consciousness-nor-non-consciousness. The idea is for consciousness (which is conditioned) to come as close as possible to the unconditioned (i.e., *nirvāṇa* with no *nimitta*) in order to be able to perceive it.

The Theravāda commentaries on this passage interpret nirvāṇa as the "cause" (the commentary reading *āyatana* as *kāraṇaṃ*) of the experience, much in the same way that an actual (relatively permanent) barn is the "cause" of the (relatively fleeting) visual perception of a barn.[75] According to this model, the significance of the negations attributed to nirvāṇa in the *Udāna* is that they deny all the characteristics of conditionedness—the quintessence of *saṃsāra*. This point is further clarified in the following verse, again from the Pali *Udāna*.

> There exists, monks, that which is unborn, that which is unbecome, that which is uncreated, that which is unconditioned. [*ajātaṃ abhūtaṃ akata asaṇkhataṃ*]. For if there were not, monks, that which is unborn, that which is uncreated, that which is unconditioned, there would not be made known here the escape from that which is born, from that which is become, from that which is created, from that which is conditioned. Yet, since there exists, monks, that which is unborn, that which is uncreated, that which is unconditioned, there is therefore made known the escape from that which is born, from that which has become, from that which is created, from that which is conditioned.[76]

The Sanskrit version of the *Udāna* conveys the same point.

> O monks! the unborn, unoriginated, unfabricated, uncompounded, unarising exists. Birth, origination, fabrication, mental production, composition, and interdependent arising exist. O monks! were the unoriginated, unfabricated, uncompounded, and unarising not to exist, I would not state that there is the definite emergence from birth, fabrication, mental production, composition, and interdependent arising. O monks! it is because the unborn, unoriginated, un-

> fabricated, uncompounded, unarising exists that I state there is the definite emergence from birth, fabrication, mental production, composition, and interdependent arising.[77]

Here again nirvāṇa and *saṃsāra* are mutually exclusive. *Saṃsāra* is born, originated, and compounded, while nirvāṇa is unborn, unarisen, and uncompounded. The latter is exclusively "unconditioned," while the former is exclusively "conditioned." The passage also explicitly states that this unconditioned state is the opposite of "interdependent arising." Combined in the *Prajñāpāramitā* verse, the second and third sets of negations (*anucchеda, aśāśvata,* etc.) apply to the conditioned realm of *saṃsāra* that is governed by dependent-origination. The first and fourth sets of negations (the denials of arising, destruction, coming-into-being, going-out-of-being) would classically refer to nirvāṇa in contradistinction to *saṃsāra*.

If the reader of the *namaskāra* were steeped in Mahāyāna literature s/he would probably be aware of the *Udāna* texts,[78] but would also be aware that the negations that are most often applied to the higher states of absorption are claimed to be characteristics of reality itself (*tattva* or *dharmatā*) in Mahāyāna literature. Whereas the common Buddhist literature had made much of the dichotomies of nirvāṇa/*saṃsāra* and unconditioned/conditioned, the Mahāyāna *sūtras* undermined the dichotomy and drew attention to the nonduality of reality that underlay the distinction itself by applying the negations indicative of unconditionedness to that which is conditioned.

This shift, however, did not happen all at once. Alhough it is difficult to date the early Mahāyāna *sūtras* relative to one another, it is possible to ascertain the range of opinions around Nāgārjuna's time. The thinking of the Mahāyāna sūtras appears to have progressed toward the position represented in the *Prajñāpāramitā* passage that Nāgārjuna cites.

In *Prajñāpāramitā* literature, when one sees the conditioned as unconditioned (or sees *saṃsāra* as nirvāṇa), one attains omniscience or "all-knowledge" *(sarvajñatā)*, which is the understanding of all *dharmas*.[79] In the *Aṣṭasahāśrika Prajñāpāramitā,* this "all-knowledge" is described in almost exactly the same terms as the experience of nirvāṇa was in the *Udāna* (the parallel section is in italics):

> All-knowledge is immeasurable and unlimited. . . . That is not attainment [*prāptir*], or reunion [*abhisamayo*], or getting there [*adhigamo*]; not the path [*mārgo*] or its fruit [*mārgaphalaṃ*]; not cognition [*jñānaṃ*], or consciousness [*vijñānaṃ*]; *not genesis* [*utpatti*], *or destruction* [*vināśo*], *or production* [*utpado*], *or passing away* [*vyayo*], *or*

> *stopping* [*nirodho*], *or development* [*bhāvanā*] *or annihilation* [*vibhāvanā*]. *It has not been made by anything* [*kenacitkṛtaṃ*], *it has not come from anywhere* [*kutaścidāgataṃ*], *it does not go anywhere* [*kvacid gacchati*], *it does not stand in any place or spot* [*nāpi kvaciddeśe nāpi kvacitpradeśe sthitam*]. . . . But what is immeasurableness that does not lend itself to being fully known by anything [*na sāśakyākenacidabhisaṃboddhum*], be it form, or any *skandha,* or any of the six perfections. Because form is all-knowledge, and so are the other *skandhas,* and the six perfections.[80]

The italicized text indicates the cognition of all-knowledge as not rising (*utpāda*) and not ceasing (*nirodha*) (which corresponds to the Pali *na cutiṃ na upapattiṃ*), and it is also described as noncoming, nongoing, and nonstaying (which corresponds to the Pali *n' eva āgatiṃ vadāmi na gatiṃ na ṭhitiṃ*). As in the *Udāna,* these negations apply to a mental state, but unlike in the *Udāna,* the experience is indicative of the way that all things are *independent of thought.*

Here, then, are the beginnings of the context in which the Mahāyāna can claim that all *dharmas* are "emptiness" (*śūnyatā*), as well as the beginnings of the claim that *saṃsāra* is nirvāṇa. "Emptiness," instead of being one of the three characteristics of nirvāṇa (*à la* the "emptiness," "signless," and "wishless" absorptions), is now a description of the way that *saṃsāra* is already. For example, it is claimed in the *Kāśyapa Parivārta Sūtra:*

> Furthermore, Kāśyapa, the real investigation of dharmas, does not make dharmas empty because of emptiness, [rather] dharmas are already empty. [It] does not make dharmas signless due to the signless [rather] dharmas are already signless. [It] does not make dharmas wishless due to the wishless [rather] dharmas are already wishless. [It] does not make dharmas unformed (*anabhisaṃskāra*) by not forming them them [rather] dharmas are already unconditioned (*anabhisaṃskṛta*). Similarly, [it] does not make dharmas unarisen due to not giving rise to them, [rather] dharmas are already unarisen. And [it] does not make dharmas unproduced things (*ajātī*) due to not producing [them], [rather] dharmas are already unproduced. Nor [does it] make dharmas unperceived (*agrāhyā*) due to lack of perceiving them, [rather] dharmas are already unperceived. And *anāsrava* dharmas do not make dharmas *anāsrava* [i.e. dharmas devoid of the "intoxicants" of desire, desire for existence, views and ignorance], rather dharmas are already *anāsrava*. Insofar as, [one] does not make

essenceless dharmas by means of an essence, dharmas are simply essenceless. Similarly, insofar as there is no essencelessness of dharmas as an essence [in itself] and insofar as no essence is found, such indeed is the investigation, O Kaśyapa, that is said to be the true investigation of dharmas and to be the middle way.[81]

The *Aṣṭasāhasrikā Prajñāpāramitā* includes the example of the five aggregates (again, something characteristic of *saṃsāra*) being described as being "emptiness," "signless," and "wishless."

SUBHUTI: Would there be a reason to assume that the skandhas are immeasurable?
THE LORD: Yes, there would be.
SUBHUTI: Of what is that term "immeasurable" a synonym?
THE LORD: Of Emptiness, of the Signless, of the Wishless.
SUBHUTI: Is it a synonym only of those and not of the other dharmas?
THE LORD: Have I not described all dharmas as "empty"?
SUBHUTI: As simply empty has the Tathāgata described all dharmas.
THE LORD: And, being empty, they are also inexhaustible. And what is emptiness that is also immeasureableness. Therefore then, according to ultimate reality, no distinction or difference can be apprehended between these dharmas. As talk have they been described by the Tathāgata. One just talks when one speaks of "immeasurable," or "incalculable," or "inexhaustible," or of "empty," or "signless," or "wishless," or "the Unaffected," or "Non-production," "nobirth," "non-existence" . . . "cessation," or "Nirvāṇa." This exposition has by the Tathāgata been described as the consummation of his demonstrations.[82]

Like the previous passage quoted, this passage describes what would normally be taken as something firmly rooted in *saṃsāra* (the aggregates) and characterizes it in the same way as nirvāṇa (emptiness, signless, wishless).

The section of the *Aṣṭasāhasrikā Prajñāpāramitā* that is the most directly relevant to the *Mūlamadhyamakakārikā*'s *namaskāra* is the following, where dependent-origination is seen as "nonextinction."

SUBHUTI: How should a Bodhisattva consummate the perfection of wisdom?
THE LORD: Through the non-extinction [*akṣāyatva*] of form, etc. Through the non-extinction of ignorance, of the karma-formations, of consciousness, of name and form, of the six sense fields, of con-

tact, of feeling, of craving, of grasping, of becoming, of birth, of decay, and death, of grief, lamentation, pain, sadness, and despair. In this manner, the Bodhisattva surveys conditioned co-production in such a way that he avoids the duality of the extremes. He surveys it without seeing any beginning, end or middle. To survey conditioned co-production in such a manner, that is the special dharma of the Bodhisattva seated on the terrace of enlightenment. When he thus surveys conditioned co-production, he acquires the cognition of the all knowing.[83]

Just as in the early canon, this passage instructs the aspirant to mentally review the twelve links of dependent-origination, recalling the negations, so as to avoid the extreme views. Here, however, dependent-origination is seen as noncessation. The characteristics that marked *saṃsāra* (i.e., being destructible, *kṣayatva*) are now denied it in the same way that they are denied to nirvāṇa (hence, *akṣayatva*) in the *Udāna* passage. This changes the purpose of the formula of dependent-origination radically. In the early canon, one meditated on the twelve links in order to see reality as it is and thereby cultivate a revulsion toward it, but never is it denied that dependent-origination describes the arising and ceasing of things.[84] This suggests by implication that, in the Mahāyāna, one is to look on dependent-arising *itself* as nirvāṇa, and hence as nonarising and nonceasing.

As seen in the *Aṣṭasāhasrikā Prajñāpāramitā*, all *dharmas* are said to be non-arising (*na utpāda*), noncessation (*na nirodha*), noncoming (*na kutaścidāgataṃ*), nongoing (*na kvacid gaccati*). Elsewhere in the same text, dependent-origination is said to be nondestructible (*akṣayatva*). It is not, then, much of a leap to combine the two (as happens in Nāgārjuna's *namaskāra* passage), and say that dependent origination is not just nondestructible, but is nonceasing (etc.) as well.

Incidentally, not only does the way that the *namaskāra* combines these extremes cause the Mahāyāna interpretation of emptiness *qua* dependent origination to be read back into the canon (thus making it conform to *sūtra*—the first *mahāpadeśa*), but such a procedure also has implications for "non-contradiction with *dharmatā*" (the third *mahāpadeśa*). The common interpretation of *dharmatā* regards it as a synonym for dependent-origination.[85] By extension the Mahāyānist interpretation presents *dharmatā* to be emptiness as well.

Lamotte has shown how this interpretation affects the Mahāyāna reading of the "Gārava sutta" of the *Saṃyutta Nikāya* in the *Dazhidulun*. The *Dazhidulun* quotes and apparently revises the passage where the Buddha acknowledges that he became enlightened by knowing *dharma*. It substitutes the word *prajñāpāramitā* (a synonym for emptiness) for the word *dharma* in its revision.[86] The end result echos the opening stanzas of Nāgārjuna's *Mūlamadhyamakakārikā*.

> The Dharma of the Buddhas is the True Nature of dharmas (*dharmāṇāṃ dharmatā*). This True Nature is without arising, without destruction, without interruption, without permanence, without unity, without plurality, without arrival or departure, without support, non-existent, the same as Nirvāṇa.[87]

In sum, there are four extremes—*uccheda, śāśvata, ekārtha,* and *nānārtha*—the negation of which is taken as both representative and exhaustive of dependent-origination in the early canon. The remaining four extremes mentioned in Nāgārjuna's *Prajñāpāramitā* passage are either equivalent to, or synonymous with, the terms that signify "unconditioned-ness" in the commonly accepted Buddhist texts: *utpāda, nirodha, āgama,* and *nirgama*. These terms are also applied to the way that all *dharmas* are said to exist in the Mahāyāna *sūtras*. If these terms are viewed as markers activating certain target texts among the common Buddhist corpus, the arrangement of these negations presents a specifically Mahāyāna strategy for reading scripture in a way that leads to the specifically Mahāyāna doctrine of the sameness of *saṃsāra* and nirvāṇa.

In light of the foregoing, the *namaskāra* of the *Mūlamadhyamakakārikā* may now be seen as a model of how dependent-origination is presented in the entire work. On the one hand, from the common Buddhist point of view, dependent-origination is *saṃsāra* and the characteristics of the upper levels of concentration point to nirvāṇa. On the other hand, from the Mahāyāna point of view, the fact that dependent-origination is said to be characterized by all four indicates that the unconditioned is immanent within the conditioned.

The discussion here is not meant to imply that Mahāyānists devised this ontology by splicing together different canonical texts. Rather, given their commitment to the "sameness of all *dharmas*," Mahāyānists justify their stance by splicing together components from authoritative texts, thereby staying within the purview of "word of the Buddha." Furthermore, by downplaying the distinction between *saṃsāra* and nirvāṇa and by making emptiness accessible to reasoned analysis, Nāgārjuna makes nirvāṇa appear within the range of lay Buddhist capabilities. Whether or not this was an intended consequence is difficult to determine. What can be said about the Mahāyāna stance is that it "generalizes" emptiness, to use a term coined by Gregory Schopen. As Schopen defines it, "generalization" is a process in which

> a specialized attainment associated with a specific group and attainable through limited and specialized means has been transformed into a generalized 'benefit' open to all and available through a broad range of basic religious activities. This process . . . appears in fact to be one of the most characteristic elements of that "movement" we now call "the Mahāyāna."[88]

Schopen refers here to the power to remember past lives (*jātismara*), which is one of the powers attained through *samādhi*. He argues that, in Mahāyāna texts, this power is made available to the laity through the efforts of Mahāyāna virtuosi. It seems that a similar argument can be made for Nāgārjuna's treatment of the "emptiness gate of liberation" (*śūnyatā-vimokṣamukha*). What was once solely the provenance of meditation specialists is now generalized in such a way as to be (theoretically, at least) available to anyone capable of reasoned analysis. Nāgārjuna's presentation of emptiness as logically attainable would place this attainment within the purview of an educated layperson. The difference between Nāgārjuna's case and the examples cited by Schopen lies primarily in the fact that the Mahāyāna teachings (the books?) are what are made indispensable in Nāgārjuna's case and not the Mahāyāna virtuoso.

However, this is not to argue that Mahāyāna sūtras are somehow more "pro-laity" than other sūtras but, rather, that many Mahāyāna communities (specifically Nāgārjuna's) desperately needed lay support. As argued in Chapter 4, ensuring that Mahāyāna sūtras were copied was one of Nāgārjuna's primary concerns. Hence, making the Buddhist goal appear within reach of an educated layperson (such as the king) would serve his strategy of convincing the king to stay neutral toward Mahāyāna and perhaps even to supply the monastery with Mahāyāna *sūtras*.

Application of the Strategy in the *Mūlamadhyamakakārikā*

The juxtaposition of references from divergent sources in order to produce a different reading of the texts alluded to (such as in the *namaskāra*) is a practice that occurs throughout the *Mūlamadhyamakakārikā*. Although there are many examples of this kind of interplay between texts, the present discussion focuses on Nāgārjuna's reference to the "Kaccānagotta sutta" in chapter 15 of the *Mūlamadhyamakakārikā,* as one example. In order to show how the *Mūlamadhyamakakārikā*'s placement of the canonical reference relative to the rest of the argument affects the meaning, Buddhaghosa's Theravāda commentary on the same verse is used here to provide a contrasting interpretation. The text of the "Kaccānagotta sutta" itself reads:

> This world, Kaccāna, for the most part depends on a duality–upon the notion of existence and the notion of nonexistence. But for one who sees the origin of the world as it really is with correct wisdom, there is no notion of nonexistence in regard to the world. And for one who sees the cessation of the world as it really is with correct wisdom, there is no notion of existence in regard to the world.[89]

Buddhaghosa's commentary on this passage clarifies the terms.

> "This is one extreme" [means] this is a deceptive extreme, a bad extreme [and] is primarily "eternalism." . . . "Everything is non-existent" is the second false and bad extreme, a so-called "view related to arising." It is the meaning of "disruption" [*uccheda*]. The rest of this is clear.[90]

Here, the extremes of being/nonbeing are explained under the rubric of eternalism and disruption. Indeed, as seen in the Pali commentary on the *Nidānavagga* (the chapter of the canon that contains the "Kaccānagotta sutta"), all extreme views fall under these two overarching categories of eternality (*śāśvata*) or disruption (*uccheda*).[91] Even in the *suttas* that add "unity" and "plurality" to the list, such as the "Lokāyatika" *sutta*,[92] the commentary reduces these extremes again to the extremes of eternality and annihilationism.[93] In short, the Theravādins understood the extremes of eternalism and annihilationism as fundamental to all the analyses of the *Nidānavagga* and read all the passages in light of this assumption.

Nāgārjuna's reference to this *sūtra* comes just over half way through chapter 15. Verses 1 to 5 state the problem of being and nonbeing in terms of the reciprocal pair "own-being" (*svabhāva*) and "other-being" (*parabhāva*). The reasoning of the chapter draws out the various *reductio ad absurdum* arguments in order to demonstrate the radical interdependence (and hence emptiness) between the terms. These first five verses contain nothing to indicate any connection to the *Nidānavagga*.

Verses 6 and 7, however, both allude to the *Nidānavagga*. Verse 6 states:

"[t]hose who see [*paśyanti*] the concepts of self-nature, other nature, existence or non-existence do not perceive [*paśyanti*] the real truth in the Buddha's teaching."[94] This is an allusion to the "Mahāhatthipadopama sutta," where the saying "the one who sees dependent-origination sees dharma" is attributed to the Buddha. The second part of Nāgārjuna's verse is merely the negative formulation of the canonical verse.

Verse 7 explicitly refers to the "Kaccānagotta sutta":

> According to the Instructions to Kātyāyana, both existence and non-existence are criticized by the Blessed One who opposed being and non-being.[95]

The placement of the scriptural reference in relation to the argument of mutual dependence provides a context for understanding the quotation. From the demonstration that everything is empty, it follows that neither being nor nonbeing exist. The *Kaccānagotta* reference is there to make evident the connection between the absence of being and nonbeing and canonical teachings of dependent-origination. The reference to the "Mahāhatthipadopama sutta" further contextualizes the absence of being and nonbeing into discussions of dependent-origination as liberating insight.

Significantly, in the final two verses of chapter 15, Nāgārjuna presents an interpretation of the verse in keeping with that of the Theravādins; absence of being and nonbeing implies the absence of eternalism and annihilationism. In so doing, he does not deny what was probably a common interpretation of this verse. On the contrary, the way that he structures this chapter presents the Mahāyāna teaching of emptiness as the logical ground on which the more common interpretation must rely.

Allusions to "Word of the Buddha" in the *Ratnāvalī*

The same procedure is used in Nāgārjuna's defense of the six *pāramitā* in the *Ratnāvalī* (discussed in Chapter 3). And, again, when Nāgārjuna splices together Buddhist (canonical) texts in the *Ratnāvalī,* more than just the justification of Mahāyāna sūtras is at stake. In fact, his use of common Buddhist *sūtras* in the *Ratnāvalī* does not argue for the superiority of Mahāyāna *sūtras* over common sūtras. Rather, as he goes on to demonstrate, Mahāyāna consists in a more profound way of reading the common *sūtras.* By reading common Buddhist texts in such a way as to produce

Mahāyāna readings, Nāgārjuna can establish Mahāyāna doctrines as "word of the Buddha," such that they do not contradict commonly held scripture.

For example, chapter 1 of the *Ratnāvalī* launches into an argument analyzing the person in terms of the six elements (*dhātus*). The argument begins on familiar turf—there is no *ātman* because the person can be broken down into its elemental parts. Nāgārjuna proceeds to analyze the elements in terms of their relationship to one another. In this, his argument applies the idiosyncratic procedure made famous in his *Mūlamadhyamakakārikā* of asking whether the elements could exist separately or together, or both, and so on, demonstrating the emptiness of the elements thereby. This exercise concludes as follows.

> This mode [of refutation] is also to be applied
> To colors, odors, tastes, and objects of touch;
> Eye consciousness and form;
> Ignorance, action, and birth;
> Agent, object, and action,
> Number, possession, cause and effect
> Time, short, and long, and so forth,
> Name and name-bearer as well.
> Earth, water, fire, wind,
> Long, short, subtle, and coarse,
> As well as virtue and so forth are said by the Subduer
> To be ceased in consciousness.

The scripture referred to here is the "Kevaddha sutta" of the *Dīgha Nikāya*.[96] In this *sūtra,* a monk asks all the gods, "Where do the four elements . . . cease without remainder?" None of the gods have an answer to this question, and so he turns to the Buddha for an answer. The Buddha responds that the question is not properly worded. Instead, the question that should be asked is,

> Where do earth, water, fire and air no footing find? Where are long and short, small and great, fair and foul—Where are "name and form" wholly destroyed?

The answer is:

> Where consciousness is signless, boundless, all luminous. That's where earth, water, fire, and air find no footing. There both long and

> short, subtle and coarse, fair and foul [*subhāsubha*]. There "name and form" are wholly destroyed. With the cessation of consciousness this is all destroyed.[97]

It is significant that here, at the first place in the *Ratnāvalī* where Nāgārjuna refers to the Mahāyāna doctrine of emptiness, he illustrates it with an allusion to a scripture that would have been known by any Buddhist.

Of course, the teaching of the "Kevaddha sutta" and what Nāgārjuna does with it are not necessarily equivalent. The ostensible equivalence is only achieved through juxtaposing a logical argument with a scriptural allusion. Because the terms suggested for substitution in the logical argument are the same terms and in the same order as those of the "Kevaddha sutta," these terms are *marked* as scriptural. Anyone familiar with the scripture would recognize the sequence along with the phrase "ceased in consciousness." Yet there is a disjuncture between the context of the "Kevaddha sutta" and Nāgārjuna's logical argument. The argument shows a logical necessity to the emptiness of each of the terms. These elements are therefore empty all the time whether or not one realizes it. In the "Kevaddha sutta," the elements are ceased in consciousness only at the highest states of absorption. Indeed, this seems to have been a common rhetorical strategy for Mahāyāna in general—to use terms and concepts that are already well established for describing high states of meditative absorption (such as emptiness, signlessness, wishlessness) and to apply those terms to reality regardless of one's mental state. The *Ratnāvalī* could have illustrated this doctrine of emptiness with any number of Mahāyāna *sūtras* and achieved a better fit. The fact that Nāgārjuna chose to use a common Buddhist text for his purpose can be explained only by a need to show that the Mahāyāna doctrine can be read in a non-Mahāyāna text. In doing so, not only does he show that Mahāyāna sūtras do not contradict generally accepted Buddhist texts, but that the truth of the latter actually depends on the truth of the former. As such, Mahāyāna's status as "word of the Buddha" is secured, thereby assuring the preservation of Mahāyāna texts in the monastery. Second, by adopting a strategy found in a Mahāyāna sūtra, Nāgārjuna activates a well-known Mahāyāna text to undergird his interpretation of Mahāyāna—showing it to be "orthodox" Mahāyāna and thereby also "word of the Buddha" for those already steeped in Mahāyāna. As a result, a chain of copyists of Nāgārjuna's text has continued in an unbroken line from his day to our own.

6

Abhidharma and Sectarian Identity

"WORD OF THE BUDDHA" was an institutional category authorizing which texts would be preserved and replicated. "Word of the Buddha" therefore becomes both the site and the objective of Mahāyāna's struggle. If the word *Tripiṭaka* is substituted for *buddhavacana,* we can see how far we have come in our investigation of Nāgārjuna's strategy. Chapters 3 and 4 showed how Nāgārjuna appeals to the authority of the *Vinaya Piṭaka* to pre-empt any legal action taken against the Mahāyānists. Chapter 5 examined his appeal to the *Sūtra Piṭaka* portion of the *Tripiṭaka* and highlighted his attempt to make Mahāyāna appear to conform to sūtras held sacred by all Buddhists. Nevertheless, Nāgārjuna could not succeed by merely appearing to conform to "the *Tripiṭaka*" in the abstract. Mahāyānists would have had to show that their teachings were consistent with the actual reading practices of the sects of which they were members. To take an example from the West, Christian sects today agree, for the most part, on the contents of the Bible, but they differ passionately over how to read it. The same situation applied to the Buddhist sects in the second century.

This chapter argues that the differences between the *Abhidharma Piṭakas* of the various Buddhist sects reflect sectarian differences in how the *Sūtra Piṭaka* was to be read. Although the *Sūtra Piṭakas* and *Vinaya Piṭakas* of the various sects have some differences, they are minor compared to the differences between their *Abhidharma Piṭakas*. The *Abhidharma Piṭakas* of the various schools become the locus for the drawing of doctrinal boundaries between Buddhist sects. For this reason, it would have been incumbent upon Mahāyānists to show that their Mahāyāna conformed to the *Abhidharma Piṭaka* of the sects in which they lived. This chapter examines the doctrinal stances adopted by key Buddhist sects in their *abhidharma* collections at the time of Nāgārjuna, in order to show the doctrinal standards he would have to live up to.

Buddhists in the early centuries of the Common Era understood the various sects not just to have separate legal identities (i.e., holding separate *upoṣadha* and ordination ceremonies) but also to have distinct doctrinal identities. According to the early Buddhist doxographical works (discussed in Chapter 1), each Buddhist sect could be identified by the set of theses to which it adhered. There are two sources for our knowledge of the doctrinal identities of the early Buddhist sects. The first comprises works such as Vasumitra's *Saṅghabhedoparacanacakra*—doxographical works that simply list the theses adhered to by each sect. The second consists of the works of *abhidharma* belonging to each sect. The two appear to be connected since most of the theses listed by Vasumitra can be found in existing *abhidharma* texts. Indeed, it is possible that Vasumitra used the *abhidharma* collections at his disposal to compile his *Saṅghabhedoparacanacakra*.

From Sūtra to Sect

The *abhidharma* genre was a natural outcome of the sūtra tradition. Indeed, the early sermons of the Buddha made copious use of numerical lists, probably to facilitate memorization. In a monastic culture that stressed memorization, it was natural to group the sermons within a given collection according to the number of items in its primary list. The quintessential example of this is the *Aṅguttara Nikāya* (= *Ekottarāgama* preserved in Chinese). After the sermons became associated with one another by virtue of the enumeration they contain, the lists themselves could be discussed independently of any particular sermon that contained them. The collection of these discussions became the *abhidharma*.

Six lists fundamental to all Buddhist ontology and epistemology became formalized in *abhidharma* literature: the four noble truths, the twelve links of dependent-origination, the five *skandha* (aggregates), the twelve *āyatana* (sense spheres), the eighteen *dhātu* (elements), and the six *indriya* (faculties). Even outside of specifically *abhidharma* literature, the centrality of these lists for the Mahāsāṅghika is shown by the fact that they are mentioned in the *Mahāsāṅghika vinaya's* definition of *buddhavacana* (translated in Chapter 3). These lists are referred to again in the *Abhisamācārikā* section of the *Mahāsāṅghika vinaya,* which discusses what a preceptor is to teach a novice monk: "the beneficial elements, the aggregates, the sense fields and dependent-origination."[1] Within *abhidharma* literature, however, the authority of these lists becomes paramount. The Theravāda *Petakopadeśa* even goes so far as to claim: "There is no sermon, no verse, no prose which is not demonstrated in one of these six [sets of] teachings."[2] Harivārman claims that his *Satyasiddhiśāstra* should be studied because it discusses the five aggregates, the twelve links of dependent-origination, and the eighteen elements.[3]

In raising these six lists, the *abhidharma* writers were on solid ground as far as the *sūtra* tradition was concerned, because each of these lists is well represented in Buddhist sūtra traditions. Nevertheless, the *abhidharmists*—like the Mahāyānists who came after them—also had to establish that their writings were "word of the Buddha." The task seems to have been complete by the time the Mahāyānists first came on the scene. As early as III C.E., an inscription from Mathurā mentions a nun named Buddhamitra, who knew the *Tripiṭaka* and was a resident disciple (*antevāsinī*) of the monk Bala, who also knew the *Tripiṭaka*.[4] The third basket (*piṭaka*) can refer only to the *Abhidharma Piṭaka,* although we cannot be certain from the inscription which one is referred to here. *Abhidharma* texts appear in the earliest collections of Buddhist manuscripts and even predominate in the third-century collections from central Asia.[5]

Significantly, early *abhidharma* texts contain the same strategies that Mahāyānists use. For example, just as early Mahāyāna texts always inform the reader of the *sūtra*'s placement during the "First Buddhist Council," the authors of *abhidharma* texts also ascribe the origins of their texts to an equally authoritative setting. Perhaps the oldest *abhidharma*-type text is the "Saṅgīti sutta" found in the *Dīgha Nikāya*. There, the monk Śāriputra (an important interlocutor in *buddhavacana* texts) notes the disarray of the Jain religious order over disagreements concerning the teachings of their founder. To prevent a similar situation among Buddhists, he gathers the monks together to rehearse the seminal teachings of the Buddha. Many scholars have noted that those schools that utilized an *abhidharma* collection did so either with the understanding that it was compiled by one of the Buddha's top disciples, Mahākaśyapa or Kātyāyana, or with the understanding that it was taught by the Buddha himself to his mother in Tuṣita heaven immediately after his enlightenment.[6] For example, the Pali *Nettipakaraṇa* ends with a passage informing the reader that Mahākaccāyana (the *dharma*-heir of the Buddha) was the one who recited the text at the first council (as does the *Peṭakopadesa*).

Early *abhidharma* texts are also careful to shadow the content of the *sūtra* collection in order to show that their doctrines do not deviate from the accepted norm. They accomplish this by copious references to *sūtras*. The earliest *abhidharma* texts embed their *abhidharma* lists between quotations from the *Sūtra Piṭaka* that form a "*suttanta* matrix"[7] For example, the *Dharmaskandha* (a Sarvāstivādin *abhidharma* text, which, according to Frauwallner, is among the earliest)[8] produces a long series of scriptural quotations for each technical term. The length and number of these quotations indicate that the topics themselves serve merely as headings for a kind of anthology or "best of the Buddhist scriptures" collection. So long as its project was to summarize the doctrines of the *sūtra* collections, the *abhidharma* had little room for innovation.

As the *abhidharma* becomes a more established genre, it begins to move away from a strict adherence to the *sūtras*. Whereas the earliest *abhidharma* texts of each tradition tend to look quite similar (compare, for example, the *Śāriputrābhidharma* of the Dharmagupta with the *Dharmaskandha* of the Sarvāstivādins and the *Vibhaṅga* of the Theravādins), the later *abhidharma* texts of each tradition develop new theories and introduce new technical terms in an attempt to answer questions not addressed in the *sūtras*. After the *abhidharmists* introduced new technical terms to address problems in the *sūtras*, the *abhidharma* collections that they were composing began to diverge doctrinally. Thus, only with the production of *abhidharma* literature did the Buddhist sects begin to take on distinct doctrinal identities.

The *Abhidharma* Collections of the *Theravāda*

Two complete *abhidharma piṭakas* and fragments of others have survived. One of the complete collections belongs to the Theravādins in the south. It consists of seven main texts (along with the usual commentaries, i.e., the *aṭṭhakathā* and the *mūla*- and *anuṭīkā* commentaries) and a handful of "extracanonical" works. The main *abhidharma* texts are the *Dhammasaṅgaṇi, Vibhaṅga, Dhātukathā, Puggalapaññatti, Kathāvatthu, Yamaka,* and *Paṭṭhāna*. As to the relative dates of these texts, Buswell and Jaini put the matter succinctly:

> Text-critical analysis indicates that these books were composed in three stages. The earliest stage saw the compilation of the *Puggalapaññatti* and at least some sections of the *Dhammasaṅgaṇi* and *Vibhaṅga*. These three texts contain extensive quotations from the sūtras and, while the method of analysis in the latter two texts is obviously of later origin, their principle concern is to explain points of controversy in the *Nikāyas*. Hence, their overall approach is more indicative of this prim-

itive stage of development. The middle period saw the composition of the *Dhātukathā* and *Kathāvatthu*. A dialectical approach is commonly followed in these two texts, in which doctrine is taught through a complex series of questions and answers. The final period of development of the canonical books includes the uniquely Theravāda texts, *Yamaka* and *Paṭṭhāna*, Both employ an extremely advanced catechetical style that is all but incomprehensible to non-Abhidharmikas.[9]

Important later commentaries on these texts are the *Peṭakopadeśa, Paṭisaṃbhidhāmagga, Nettipakaraṇa, Vimuttimagga, Visuddhimagga*, and *Abhidhammatthasaṅgaha*.

Sarvāstivāda

The Sarvāstivādins in the north also claimed seven texts as authoritative: the *Jñānaprasthāna, Prakaraṇapāda, Vijñānakāya, Dharmaskandha, Prajñāptibhāṣya, Dhātukāya*, and *Saṅgītiparyāya*. Although the traditional ordering of these texts places the *Jñānaprasthāna* first, modern scholars place it last, dividing the development of the tradition into three phases as well. Again, Buswell and Jaini comment.

> Considerable controversy reigns among modern scholars concerning the authorship and chronology of these various texts . . . Ryogon Fukuhara, the scholar who has made the most exhaustive study of the Sarvāstivādin *Abhidharma* canon, has given what is perhaps the most plausible ordering of the canonical texts: *Saṅgītiparyāya* and *Dharmaskandha* in the earliest group; *Prajñaptibhāṣya, Dhātukāya*, and *Vijñānakāya*, and *Prakaraṇapāda* in the middle group; followed by the latest of the canonical works, the *Jñānaprasthāna*.[10]

Historically, these works have tended to be overshadowed by the commentaries on the *Jñānaprasthāna*. The most famous of these commentaries are the massive *Mahāvibhāṣā* (which according to legend, was compiled at a council convened by Kaṇiṣka c. second century), the *Saṃyuktābhidharmahṛdaya*, the *Abhidharmakośa*, and *Bhāṣya* by Vasubandhu, the *Abhidharmakośasphuṭārtha* by Yaśomitra, and the *Nyāyānusāra* by Sanghabhadra.

Other Texts

In addition to these two main groups of texts are independent works that were originally part of larger collections. From the Pudgalavādin sects, the three existing texts are available only in Chinese translation. The first two are the 三法度論 (*Sānfǎdùlùn*, T. 1506 = **Tridharmakaśāstra*) and the 四阿鋡暮抄序 (*Sìāhánmùchāoxù*, T. 1505): These are really two different versions of the same text, since the latter contains the title 三法度 in its last line.[11] The third is the 三彌底部論 (*Sānmídibùlùn*, T. 1649 = **Sāṃmitīyanikāya-śāstra*).[12] Other important *abhidharma* texts include the 舍利弗阿毘曇論 (*Shèlìfóāpítánlùn*, T. 1548 **Śāriputrābhidharma*, an early text usually ascribed to the Dharmagupta sect) and the 成實論 (T. 1646, **Satyasiddhiśāstra* by Harivārman—a Bahuśrutīya).[13] There is also at least one Mahāyāna *abhidharma* text: the *Abhidharmasammuccaya* by Asaṅga, not discussed here.

Abhidharma Innovations: *Saṃsāra*, Nirvāṇa, and *Mārga*

As vast as *abhidharma* literature is, the important doctrinal differences between the sects coalesce around relatively few issues raised by the *sūtra* tradition. The most fundamental of these revolve around the relationship between *saṃsāra* and nirvāṇa. All schools of Indian philosophy recognize the existence of something absolute that exists without conditions and is eternal or timeless. For the Sāṃkhya, this is *puruṣa*, for the Vedānta it is *ātman/brahman*, and for the Jains it is *adharma*. For the Buddhists, nirvāṇa falls into this category. The world that we (the unenlightened) acknowledge and move about in is usually placed in contradistinction to the absolute. For the (non-Mahāyānist) Buddhist, all that is not nirvāṇa is *saṃsāra*—*saṃsāra* being distinguished from nirvāṇa by the characteristics of suffering and impermanence.[14] The two realms of *saṃsāra* and nirvāṇa are not just different; they are defined as opposites with no middle ground in between. Consider again the verse from the *Udāna* discussed in Chapter 5:

> There exists, monks, that which is unborn, that which is unbecome, that which is uncreated, that which is unconditioned [*ajātaṃ abhūtaṃ akata asaṇkhataṃ*]. For if there were not, monks, that which is unborn, that which is uncreated, that which is unconditioned, there would not be made known here the escape from that which is born, from that which is become, from that which is created, from that which is conditioned. Yet, since there exists, monks, that which is unborn, that which is uncreated, that which is unconditioned, there is therefore made known the escape from that which is born, from that

which has become, from that which is created, from that which is conditioned.[15]

This verse presents a philosophical problem. The sense of the verse is that because there is a nirvāṇa (the opposite of *saṃsāra*), there must be such a thing as an escape from *saṃsāra*. The problem is that *saṃsāra* is described as *jātāṃ, bhūtam, kata,* and *sankhaṃ* while nirvāṇa is described as its opposite: *ajātaṃ, abhūtaṃ, akata,* and *asankhaṃ*. The principle of bivalance (a.k.a. *tertium non datur*) states that between *A* and *not-A* there can be no third term, and yet Buddhism as a religion does introduce a third term—namely, the karma, a category under which falls all the practices used to convey one from *saṃsāra* to nirvāṇa.

In fact, Buddhist philosophy has three important elements whose role *vis-à-vis saṃsāra* and nirvāṇa begin to create problems. The first, as stated above, is karma. Karma is generally considered in the *sūtra* tradition to fall into the category of *saṃsāra* because it is one of the important agents of change over time. Somehow, through the elimination of bad karma and through the accumulation of merit and insight, one is able to abandon *saṃsāra* and achieve nirvāṇa. The problem, as Nāgārjuna points out in his investigation of nirvāṇa (*Mūlamadhyamakakārikā,* chapter 25), revolves around the question of how a vehicle that is thoroughly conditioned can produce a state that is unconditioned. The other two problematic elements are related to karma, namely, the person leaving *saṃsāra* and achieving nirvāṇa as well as the practices used to travel from *saṃsāra* to nirvāṇa. These three—karma, the owner of karma, and the path—must either straddle or leap across the conditioned/unconditioned divide.[16] Each is originally part of conditioned reality, but must stand in a meaningful relation to unconditioned reality in order for Buddhist soteriology to be possible. It is in the attempt to articulate a meaningful relationship of these three terms to both saṃsāra and nirvāṇa that the *abhidharma* literature begins to diverge from the sūtra tradition.

Karma, *Kartṛ*, and *Mārga*

The importance of this divergence cannot be overestimated, as the doctrinal identities of Buddhist sects coalesced around this very issue. According to Thomas Dowling:

> In certain cases it is apparent that concern with karma doctrine or vocabulary explanatory thereof played a distinctly causal role in sectari-

an evolution. In other cases it is safer to say that the concern for an intelligible karma vocabulary was one among many complex factors that helped give decisive shape and substance to already distinct or emerging sectarian positions.[17]

The teachings of the *sūtra* tradition about karma, the owner of karma, and the path are fairly simple. Karma takes its place among the five aggregates as the aggregate of *saṃskāra,* which in turn is defined as volition (*cetanā*). In the twelve links of dependent-origination, *saṃskāra* is the second limb, conditioned only by ignorance.

The *sūtra* teaching of the owner of karma is somewhat more complicated. Early Buddhist *sūtras* are generally clear that there is no such entity answering to the description of the brahmanical *ātman*. They are equally emphatic that karma, the foundation of morality, exists. Yet to affirm the existence of karma involves the tacit assumption that reference to the karma possessor is in some sense meaningful. In the sermons teaching dependent-origination, the Buddha advocates a middle way, denying both the thesis that everything exists (i.e., has an abiding essence or "soul") and the thesis that nothing exists (i.e., that there is no continuity among impermanent things). The owner of karma, therefore, can be said to be neither a permanent entity nor nonexistent.

To articulate the sense in which statements concerning the owner of karma are meaningful, the sūtra tradition embarks on a tentative foray into language theory. The problem for the *sūtra* tradition was how to understand the status of a word (i.e., "self," *ātman*) whose object does not really exist and yet whose use in religious instruction was indispensable. The brahmanical philosophies, for the most part, held that words that produce distinct cognitions refer to real things. The Mīmāṃsikā held that the spoken word was a temporal manifestation of an atemporal and eternal reality.[18] Even the Nyāya-Vaiṣeśikā, who generally held that words obtained their meanings through convention, believed that words must have a one-to-one correspondence with extramental entities in order to be meaningful. Words really refer to things in Nyāya. It for this reason that the Naiyāyikā (and later Buddhist logicians) could not accept *reductio ad absurdum* arguments as independent arguments because the subject term of such arguments does not exist. One important implication of the Naiyāyika stance on language was that, because self-referential language (such as the word "I") implies the identity of an entity over time, there must be an enduring substance to which these words refer. That substance is a soul, or *ātman*. The Naiyākika commitment to the existence of verbal referents reflected a realism leading to the defense of universals and of wholes existing independent of their parts.

Buddhism, in contrast to these other philosophies, developed India's first theories of nominalism—both in the weak sense of maintaining that some words do not refer to existing entities and (especially for Dharmakīrti) in the strong sense of denying the existence of the universals to which words refer.[19] Although an explicit rejection of universals (*jāti*) *à la* Dharmakīrti does not occur in the *sūtras,* the sūtras include two versions of the first kind of nominalism. The first version amounts to the view that some words are just words (i.e., they do not have referents in either the external or internal worlds). Implied in these discussions is the sense that any commitment to the existence of entities named by words leads to trouble. For example, the "Hastipadottama sutta" (The Greater Discourse on the Simile of the Elephant's Footprint) of the *Majjhima Nikāya* says:

> Friends, just as when a space is enclosed by timber and creepers, grass, and clay, it comes to be termed "house," so too, when a space is enclosed by bones and sinews, flesh and skin, it comes to be termed "material form."[20]

This discussion is similar to a discussion held between the monk Nāgasena and King Milinda in the *Milindapañho*:

> I, reverend Nāgasena, am not telling a lie, for it is because of the pole, because of the axle, the wheels, the body of the chariot, the yoke, the reins, and because of the goad that "chariot" exists as a denotation [*sankhā*], appellation [*samaññā*], designation [*paññatti*], as a current usage [*vohāro*], as a name [*nāmaṃ*].[21]

Implicit in these sūtras is the understanding that terms like "material-form/color" (*rūpa*) or "chariot" do not denote independently existing reals, but are mere words used to denote the assemblage of a multiplicity of factors. The multiplicity of components really are present, but the unity to which the word "chariot" refers is not. Such designations may be useful in a conventional sense, but they do not denote real objects in any ultimate sense. The *Milindapañho* passage especially emphasizes that "chariot" exists only as a word. There is no one-to-one correspondence between the word and any one real particular in the world. Some early *Abhidharma* texts pick up on this nominalist trend specifically as it applies to the notion of the individual. For example, the *Śāriputrābhidharma,* picking up on "Hastipadottama sutta," states:

> Again, monks, contemplate in this manner: the person [人 = *pudgala?*] has eye, ear, nose tongue body and mind. The convention [假名, *saṅketa*] is a word used for the person. The eye, ear, nose tongue body and mind are not the person. Apart from eye, ear, nose tongue body and mind there is no person. If, in the same fashion, a dharma really arises, really stays and really passes away, a verbal convention designates (the arising, staying, and passing away) as "the person." Like a house having roof-beam, rafter, wall, is conventionally designated as "house." The beams, etc are not the house (and yet) without the roof-beam, etc, there is no house. If, in the same fashion, a dharma really arises, really stays and really passes away, a verbal convention designates (the arising, staying, and passing away) as the "house." . . . Just as in the "Elephant's Footprint [*Hastipadottama*] sutta" it is said. "Monks, conditioned by the timber, bamboo, and conditioned by the rope empty space is enclosed, (and all this) is the designation for "hut." Monks, just like this, conditioned by the back, the muscle, the blood, flesh, and skin (all) enclosing empty space, and we have the designation, "I." Just like this [it is] a device [方便, *upāya*]. Know this dharma to be impermanent and to arise according to conditions.[22]

The *Śāriputrābhidharma* probably uses the term *saṅketa* (convention) to indicate the nominal status of the *pudgala,* to follow the "Hastipadottama sutta." Most *abhidharma* texts, however, refer to nominal entities using a synonym for *saṅketa: prajñapti* ("designation" also translated as 假名).[23]

The second version of Buddhist nominalism can be seen in the "Mahānidāna sutta" of the *Dīgha Nikāya.*

> By whatever features, characteristics, signs or summarized descriptions there is a concept of the body of sentience (i.e., in a "living being," in everyday language); in the absence of these features, etc., there could be no contact discerned between the designation and the body of matter (of the "same" "living being"). By whatever features, etc., there is a concept of the body of matter; in the absence of these features, etc., there would be no contact discerned between the resistance (i.e., the matter) and the body of sentience. In the absence of the features, etc., by which there is a concept of both the body of sentience and the body of matter, there would be discerned neither contact of the designation nor contact of the resistance.[24]

In the passages from the "Hastipadottama sutta" and the *Milindapanha* quoted above, the words "chariot" and "being" stand in an almost arbitrary relationship to the collocation of parts that they designate. The *Mahānidāna* passage, by contrast, points to *causal* relationship between the perceiver's designation and certain functions (i.e., its "features, characteristics, signs, or summarized descriptions") of the referent. Here, the designation, as a kind of verbal-awareness, is seen as a product of a set of real external factors, and it disappears when those factors are not present. In this sense, the *prajñapti* is not a mere word but, rather, the product of a whole knowledge-producing event, to which the word is a contributing condition. Despite an apparent distaste for nominal entities, Buddhism has always had a place for verbally informed cognition in its tradition of meditation (consider, for example, the practice of verbally noting the object of meditation during *śamatha* meditation).

The contrast between the *Mahānidāna* passage and the "Hastipadottama" passage suggests that the verbal world is two-tiered: some words refer to unitary reals (i.e., *dharmas*), such as "color" (*rūpa*), and other words do not, such as "chariot" (*ātman*). What begins in Buddhist sūtras as a simple denial of the existence of an entity corresponding to the word *ātman* develops into a theory of nominalism tied to a theory of causality. The word *ātman* in brahmanical discourse denotes a singular entity. For Buddhists, there is no *ātman* because there is no *single cause* of the cognition *ātman*. The (false) cognition corresponding to the word *ātman* is a single effect produced by multiple causes and conditions working in concert. The overdetermination of the verbal cognition makes it false. The wise person sees that words denoting persons (*pudgala*) simply serve as an index to what is, in reality, a plurality of everchanging phenomena. As seen below, most of the *abhidharma* traditions come to interpret single, noncomposite phenomena (such as color) as ultimately true or ultimately existent (*paramārthasat*) on account of its irreducibility. But composite entities are said to exist as conventional designation (*prajñaptisat*) because they can be analyzed into ultimately existing components.

Two important sets of categories are now established. The categories of *saṃsāra* and nirvāṇa cast the world in terms of "conditioned-ness" and "unconditioned-ness," while the categories of linguistic referents cast things in terms of their "ultimate" versus "conventional" existence or truth. The problem with this scenario is that it leads to a tendency to overlay a dichotomy of "true" and "false" over the already problematic dichotomy of "conditioned" and "unconditioned." The set of causes and conditions producing the cognition of the "person" is nothing other than the set of causes and conditions constituting *saṃsāra,* and yet "the person" does not denote an entity that is ultimately real. However, the experience of *ātman's* absence is constitutive of the experience of nirvāṇa itself insofar as the liberation through "emptiness" (one of the characteristics of nirvāṇa) is synonymous with the realization of *anātman*.[25] This leaves the doctrine of *anātman* somehow equated with nirvāṇa, even though the person coursing through *saṃsāra* is already said to lack *ātman*. The task for *abhidharmists* will be to determine how the levels of truth apply to the states of *saṃsāra* and nirvāṇa.

Pudgalavāda

One of the first schools of *abhidharma* to tackle this issue appears to have been the Pudgalavādins. Their solution to bridge the conditioned/unconditioned divide was to depict karma, the owner of karma, and the practices of the Buddhist path as *hybrid entities* that, by their very nature, straddle the divide.

Avipranāśa

The Pudgalavādins argued that karma was a composite entity consisting of several temporal components and one atemporal one. Following the Buddhists *sūtras,* they claimed that mental *saṃskāras* (mental formations corresponding to karma) were of the nature of volition. Vocal and bodily karma, however, consisted only of the motion (*gati*) that could be observed. The motion itself is conditioned and therefore impermanent. The Pudgalavādins were, however, aware that the Buddha also taught the persistence of karma. In this the Pudgalavādins appealed to a text that was also considered authoritative by the Sarvāstivādins: "[Karma] does not perish, even after hundreds of millions of cosmic eras. When the complex [of conditions] and [favorable] times come together, they ripen for their author."[26] One particular subsect of Pudgalavādins—the Saṃmitīyas—took the imperishability of karma to be one thing and the causes and conditions of karma to be another. They posited the existence of an entity called, appropriately enough, the "indestructible" (*avipranāśa*), separate from the karma itself. This "indestructible" acts like a blank sheet of paper on which the actions (karma) are written. According to the *Sanmidibulun* (ostensibly the only surviving text of the Saṃmitīyas themselves):

> What is the goal of ones own activity [自作]? It is in order to experience [the results of that action].[27] What is the significance of one's own karma [自業]? It is one's allotment in life [分]. What is the reason? Because (the results of the action) do not go to another. There

> is an accumulation [*sheng* 生, *upacaya*][28] (of the fruit of action). Why? It is the means (by which karma is transmitted). It (the accumulation) exits in the domain of compounded things [行, *saṃskṛta*]. Why? Because it is conditioned by others. It is an imperishable thing [不滅, *avipraṇāśadharma*]. Why? It (the result) is experienced (long after the instigating action has disappeared). (And) because (the result) is the manifestation (of a latent past action). (And) because (as stated in the sūtra) actions (*karman*) accomplished in this world are not perishable.[29]

According to later sources, the *avipranāśa* is itself morally indeterminate (*avyākṛta*) while the effects that it conveys across time are good or bad depending on the moral quality of the action committed.[30] This position is articulated in Vasubandhu's representation of the Saṃmitīya opponent in his *Karmasiddhiprakaraṇa:*

> one should admit that the two actions, bodily and vocal action, good or bad, deposit (*ādadhati*) in the psycho-physical series (*skandhasaṃtāna*) a separate dharma, existing in and of itself (*dravyasat*) and classed among things not associated with the mind (*cittaviprayuktasaṃskāra*). For some, this dharma is called increase (*upacaya*); for others "without extinction" (*avipranāśa*). By reason of this dharma, one realized (*abhinirvṛt-*) the future agreeable or disagreeable fruit. In order that this should equally be mental action (*manaḥ karman*), one should admit the existence of this dharma. If not (*anyatra*), when another mind arises and when the mental action has disappeared (*nivṛtta*), if this particular dharma were not deposited in the mental series (*cittasaṃtāna*), how could one realize the future fruit? Thus it is necessary (*niyatam*) to admit the existence of such a dharma.[31]

Notice that although karma is said to be "without extinction," it is very much a part of conditioned (*saṃskṛta*) reality and as such is neither identical to nor different from the one to whom it belongs.

Pudgala and *Prajñapti*

Whereas the doctrine of *avipraṇāśa* may have been a doctrine peculiar to the Saṃmitīya subsect, all Pudgalavādins affirmed the existence of the *pudgala* (the person) as karma-possessor. Like other Buddhists, they also affirmed that the *pudgala* was essentially a *prajñapti*.[32] In contrast to other Buddhists, however, they did not consider this grounds for its dismissal (i.e., it was not considered to be a "mere" designation). The salient feature of the Pudgalavādin position was that they believed the *pudgala* to be "ultimate and true" and yet indeterminate and a *prajñapti* at the same time. For any other school of *abhidharma*, these three characteristics would be mutually exclusive—either something existed substantially, ultimately and truly, or it did not exist and was a mere word. Yet, in the Pudagalvādin school, *prajñapti* was considered a mode of existence that allowed for a hybrid entity whose ontological status was indeterminate (*avacya*) in relation to the totality of relations comprising it.

The benefit of this move was an easy explanation of the doctrine of karma, because the *pudgala* could serve as the entity that transmigrates from life to life and to whom karma belongs. This solution, unfortunately, created a problem of its own insofar as the Pudgalavādins' *pudgala* came very close to the brahmanical doctrine of *ātman* from which the Buddhists were trying to distance themselves. This problem was perhaps exacerbated by the fact that the Pudgalavādins had no compunction about using words like *ātman* and *jīva* as synonyms for their concept of *pudgala*.[33] However, in order to preempt objections of their fellow Buddhists, the Pudgalavādins had to describe this new concept in such a way as to distinguish it from an *ātman* while appearing consistent with "word of the Buddha." Their early texts emphasize that the *pudgala* as a *prajñapti* was neither identical to nor different from the aggregates. By contrast, the brahmanical *ātman* was considered a substance (*dravya*) responsible for, but ultimately separate from, the functions of perception, motion, and so on.

The key to understanding the Pudgalavādins' position lies in their peculiar use of the term *prajñapti* itself. The Pudgalavādins maintained that *pudgala* is *prajñapti* in three different ways: it is a designation "depending on" (some basis—*upādāya prajñapti*),[34] or it can be a designation of a state of transmigration[35] or of a state of cessation.[36] All *abhidharma* schools assert that the individual is designated based upon his body (*rūpa*), feelings, perceptions, and so on. The concept or verbal understanding that arises from this knowledge-event is usually classed as designation "depending on" a certain basis. Most schools regard this statement as meaning that the person is *nothing other than* the aggregates. The Pudgalavādins, however, regard the kind of dependence denoted by the gerund "depending on" (*upādāya*) as entailing neither an identity nor a difference between the thing depending and the object of the dependence. Hence, the person designated depending on certain aggregates is neither identical to nor different from those aggregates.

According to the Saṃmitīyas:

> It is asked, what is said to be the person [*pudgala*]? Answer: The Buddha said that there are three kinds of *pudgala*. What are the three kinds of *pudgala*? *Pudgala* designated in reference to its basis [*āśraya*, 依], *pudgala* designated according to its transmigration [度], and *pudgala* designated according to its cessation [滅]. What is the person designated according to its basis? Answer: according to the *buddha-vacana*, [the Buddha] said to [跋婆耶, Vātsyaya?]: "A certain *saṃskāra* is said to be the basis [of the designation of the person]. That certain [*saṃskāra*] is said to lie in this and is said to be the basis [for the person] just like the example of fire [and fuel]. . . . Just like the acquisition of form and the person acquiring form—the person and the form cannot be said to be different. Nor can the form be declared to be a different form [from the form that makes up the person]. A different [person would] acquire a [different] form and on the basis of that form would acquire a different name on the basis of the person and form [resulting in two separate people]. If the person is said to be this form or that self, this would indeed constitute what is called "belief in the self" [*ātmadṛṣṭi*]. If the person is said to be form, then the self, by means of this [form] would be in excess of the five aggregates of the person. As was said before, this would be accomplished in excess. Again it is said, if the person acquires the form of a person or a different form that would be called *parātmadṛṣṭi*. If the person is said to be different than the self, then by this excess, the person is different than the five aggregates.[37]

and later:

> That "the person who acquires the physical form" is merely a synonym . . . for "the physical form" is not a true explanation. If the explanation of the person is that "physical form" and "person who acquires physical form" are merely synonyms, this constitutes wrong view. Wrong view is the error of stating that there is no self. What has been said previously establishes that this is an error. Therefore there are the three errors [i.e., that the self is physical form, that the self is different from physical form, and that there is no self.]. So identity and difference . . . are wrong views.[38]

The *pudgala* is designated based on the aggregates *or* upon its past lives, *or* can be so designated in relation to its ultimate extinction. Especially in the latter two cases, the designation is made on the basis of factors different from the current configuration of aggregates constituting the individual. This threefold scheme amounts to three different perspectives on the way that identity is constituted. The reason for the different perspectives lies in the needs of the perceiver. The *Tridharmakhaṇḍaka* claims that these three views can be applied as the antidotes to three different false views. *Upādāya prajñapti* (designation depending on) remedies the false views of both essentialism (*astidṛṣṭi*) and nihilism (*nāstidṛṣṭi*), while the designation of transmigration remedies the false view of annihilationism (*ucchedadṛṣṭi*) and designation of extinction remedies the false view of eternalism (*śāśvatādṛṣṭi*).[39] By stating that both the belief in the identity of the *pudgala* and the aggregates and the belief in their difference constitute "wrong view," the *Saṃmitīyanikāyaśāstra* references the sūtra passages on dependent-origination wherein identity and difference (*ekārtha* and *nānārtha*) are said to be two extremes and a wrong view. The middle path is said to be dependent-origination. By alluding to the passages on dependent-origination, it not only appropriates canonical authority for its own theory, but ties the concept of *upādāya prajñapti* to that of dependent-origination.

Analogies: Fire and Fuel, Tree and Shadow

The concept of *upādāya prajñapti* is usually used in conjunction with the doctrine of the five aggregates; the soul does not exist because it is merely a designation depending on the five aggregates. Again, the most common simile used to illustrate the point is that of the chariot being designated on the basis of its wheels, axle, and so on. This example demonstrates that *prajñapti* is usually used for a designation based on *its own* parts. The Pudgalavādins could not follow this practice because to do so would make the *pudgala* vacuous, a mere designation. Instead, they adopted two other analogies. The most commonly cited is that of fuel and fire. A second is the analogy of a tree and its shadow mentioned in the *Katthāvatthu*. The Pudgalavādins argued that fire and fuel can be conceived as neither entirely the same nor entirely different.[40] The significant point in both analogies is that they are examples of a thing depending on factors that, from one point of view, belong to it and, from another, are external to it. The shadow is designated as a shadow depending on the tree, not on its own parts. This allows for the quasi independence of the *pudgala*. According to Leonard Priestley,

> The[*Katthāvatthu*] commentary makes it clear that the [tree and shadow] analogy is the Pudgalavādin's. (It also refers to the analogy

of fire and fuel.) But the shadow, although identifiable only by reference to the tree, does not consist of the tree; the tree is only what it derives from. So here again the analogy would indicate that the *pudgala* derives from the aggregates but does not consist of them.[41]

Priestley devotes an entire chapter to an exploration of both the textual precedent and the philosophical warrant for the Pudgalavādin's use of *prajñapti* in this manner. His primary aim in that chapter is to find justification for the Pudgalavādins' use of the word *prajñapti* to indicate an entity that is both true and ultimate. For this to happen, the Pudgalavādins must expand the meaning of *prajñapti*. Either the *pudgala* must refer to a noncomposite (ultimate in the sense of being irreducible to other elements) entity, or the category of ultimacy must be expanded to include composite entities. His justification for this move is both subtle and complex and unfortunately is difficult to summarize briefly. For our purposes it suffices simply to say that the Pudgalavādins had an expanded definition of both *prajñapti* (as discussed above) and ultimacy.

The Five Categories and the Two Truths

To accommodate the ambiguity of their articulation of the *pudgala* within the category of truth, the Pudgalavādins created a separate category in their *abhidharma* system just for the *pudgala*. Accordingly, they divided their ontology into five categories:[42] past, future, present, unconditoned (*asaṃskṛta*), and ineffable.[43] The first three (past things, present things, and future things) comprise all the things that constitute *saṃsāra*. These three categories include all conditioned entities such as the *skandhas,* the *dhātu,* and the *āyatanas*. The fourth category was the category of unconditioned things (*asaṃskṛta* = unmanifest or unconditioned). Only nirvāṇa falls into this category. The fifth category is simply called "ineffable" (*avācya*), and it is here that the Pudgalavādins place the *pudgala*. This fifth category functions as the middle between the usual *abhidharma* categories of conditioned phenomena (*saṃskṛta dharmas*) and unconditioned phenomena (*asaṃskṛta dharmas*). By positing a middle category, the Pudgalavādins can assert that, although *pudgala* is categorically distinct from aggregates (which are *saṃskṛta*), it cannot for that reason be equated with a soul *ātman* (which the Brahmanical schools would place under the *asaṃskṛta* category).

The Pudgalavādin *Abhidharma* puts a definite spin on the sūtra tradition in their claims that karma persisted because of *avipraṇāśa* (in the case of the Saṃmitīyas) and in claiming that *pudgala* was neither *saṃskṛta* nor *asamskṛta* (in the case of all Pudgalavādins). Yet the payoff for these maneuvers was sufficient to warrant such a move. As previously discussed, in positing an *avipraṇāśa,* the Saṃmitīyas could appeal to the words of the Buddha saying that karma was indestructible. By claiming that the *pudgala* was existent, they could meaningfully talk about the owner of karma while at the same time be able to explain how this owner could move from *saṃsāra* to nirvāṇa.

In positing the existence of a separate category of "ineffable" entities, the Pudgalavādins took as their cue the ten *avyākṛtāṇi* (unanswerable questions) of the Buddha.[44] These indeterminable points appear in multiple places in Buddhist scripture. In the *Dīgha Nikāya,* for example, a certain wanderer named Poṭṭhapāda asks the Buddha a long list of questions, the last five of which the Buddha does not answer: (1) whether the person's self and their perception are the same thing or two different things, (2) whether or not the world is eternal, (3) whether or not the world is infinite, (4) whether or not the *jīva* is the same as the body, and (5) whether the Tathāgata does or does not exist after death, both or neither.

> "Well, Lord, does the Tathāgata exist after death? Is only this true and all else false?" "I have not declared that the Tathāgata Exists after death" "Well, Lord, does the Tathāgata not exist after death, . . . both exist and not exist after death? . . . neither exist nor not exist after death?" "I have not declared that the Tathāgata neither exists nor does not exist after death, and that all else is false."

When asked why he refuses to answer, the Buddha says:

> "Poṭṭhapāda, that is not conducive to the purpose, not conducive to Dhamma, . . . not the way to embark on the holy life; it does not lead to disenchantment, to dispassion, to cessation, to calm, to higher knowledge, to enlightenment, to Nibbāna. That is why I have not declared it."
>
> But, Lord, what has the Lord declared? "Poṭṭhapāda, I have declared: 'This is suffering, this is the origin of suffering, this is the cessation of suffering, and this is the path leading to the cessation of suffering.'"[45]

In context, the Buddha's response asserts pragmatic concerns over theoretical ones. He does not answer questions concerning the relationship between the *jīva* and the body or the ontological status of the Tathāgata, and so on, because these issues are irrelevant to liberation.

The Pudgalavādins appealed to passages like this one to argue that the *pudgala* (certainly a synonym for *jīva*) is in some sense real, but that its relation *vis-à-vis* the aggregates or cessation made the exact nature of its existence ineffable. As the *pudgala* falls into a category that is neither *saṃskṛta* nor *asaṃskṛta,* it is neither in *saṃsāra* nor in nirvāṇa. Hence, the *pudgala* known as the "Tathāgata" can be said neither to exist nor not to exist after his *parinirvāṇa.* In short, by defining *pudgala* as ineffable, the Pudgalavādins were able to explain karma and the status of the Buddha after death without falling into the trap of positing an unchanging soul. The following is an account of their beliefs as related in the *Satyasiddhiśāstra.*

> The advocate of the Pudgala pleads in favour of its existence: The soul exists because amongst the four modes of answering the question the fourth one is *Sthapanīya,* i.e., avoiding the answer to the question. Examples: Does the Tathāgata exist after death, or does he not exist after death? This question should not be answered or decided. Since this mode of answering has been upheld, we must accept the existence of the soul.[46]

By appealing to the ten ineffable points in support of the *pudgala,* the Pudgalavādins made an important shift. In order to turn *pudgala* into a technical term, they had to transform the canonical category of ineffability from a pragmatic category of theoretical topics to be avoided to an ontological category consisting of the ineffable (*avācya*) *pudgala.* The *pudgala* is categorized as ineffable, not just because it is designated in reference to a basis, but because its designation is overdetermined in reference to multiple bases. According to the *Tridharmakaṇḍaka:*

> What is ineffable [不可說, *avācya*]? Reply: the designation of [*prajñapti,* 施設] the basis [受, *upādāna*], past life [受過, *pūrva-bhāva*] and cessation [滅, *nirodha*] are ineffable. The basis [i.e., the aggregates] is a *prajñapti.* Past life is a *prajñapti.* Cessation is a *prajñapti.* When there is something not understood, it is correct to say it is indescribable and not known [*avācya, ajñāna*]. *Upādāya prajñapti* [受施設] [means]: sentient beings [眾生, *sattva? pudgala?*] are already based on the *skandhas, dhātu* and *āyatanas.* It is mentally constructed [計, *parikalpyate*] to be either identity or difference. The *prajñapti* of the past life is said to be conditioned by prior existence of *skanda, dhātu* and *āyatana.* Like where it is said: "I, at a certain time, was called "Govinda" [瞿旬陀].[47] . . . The *prajñapti of nirodha* [occurs]: when, after cessation, one speaks of [that person's] causes or basis

[i.e., the *skandhas*]. Like where it is said, "The *Bhagavant* has died" [般涅槃, *parinirvṛtate*].[48]

The Pudgalavādins thus find warrant for the creation of a separate category of indeterminate entities in commonly held Buddhist scriptures. The Buddhist texts dealing with the ten *avyākṛta* questions are not, however, the only scriptural source from which the Pudgalavādins draw. There is also a structural similarity between the way the ten *avyākṛta* questions are framed (especially the questions concerning the Tathāgata) and the *lemmata* denied at the beginning of discussions of dependent-origination (e.g., the "Lokāyatika sutta": "everything exists, does not exist, is a unity, is a plurality").

The fact that the Pudgalavādins tie the ineffability of *prajñapti* entities to both "depending on" (*upādāya*) and to being neither the same nor different from entities on which they depend allows them to allude to authoritative Buddhist texts on dependent-origination that claim a dependently originated entity to be neither a unity nor a plurality, and so on. In so doing, they can claim to avoid the extremes of eternalism and nihilism so emphasized in the *Nidāna Saṃyutta*. Again, from the *Tridharmakhaṇḍaka:*

> Conception (or designation) according to appropriation: when the sentient being has appropriated the aggregates, elements and spheres, it is thought to be the same[as them] or apart [from them].
>
> Conception (or designation) according to the past: it is conceived on the basis of past aggregates, elements, and spheres, as when it is said, "I was at that time Kuśendra . . ."
>
> Conception (or designation) according to cessation: when they have ceased, it is conceived on the basis of those appropriations, as when it is said, "The Fortunate One has attained Parinirvana."
>
> Moreover, conception (or designation) according to the past precludes the annihilation of the sentient being. Conception (or designation) according to cessation precludes permanence. Conception (or designation) according to appropriation precludes its nonexistence. Conception (or designation) according to non-appropriation precludes its existence.[49]

In this passage, the misunderstanding of the *pudgala* as being either identical or different from its substrate (the aggregates, the sense spheres, and the elements) leads to continued appropriation and continued cycling through *saṃsāra*.[50] Apparently, some Pudgalavādins allowed the logic of "neither the same as nor different" to seep into other parts of their system.

Bhavya, in his *Nikāyabhedavibhaṅgavyākhyāna,* records two theses held by the Vātsīputrīyas stating that "nirvāṇa can neither be said to be one with all dharmas nor divided [from them]. Nirvāṇa can neither be said to be existent nor non-existent."[51] Although no other source mentions these theses, they should not be surprising. To say that nirvāṇa is neither identical to nor different from *dharmas* is entailed in the statement that the person is neither identical nor different from the aggregates, on one hand, and from *nirodha,* on the other.

Sarvāstivāda

Past, Present, and Future Exist

The Pudgalavādins developed the concept of *pudgala* in a particular direction to avoid certain philosophical problems in explaining karma and rebirth. The importance of the latter two teachings for this school was so great that they were willing to risk being perceived as teaching the existence of a soul. For the Sarvāstivādin *abhidharmists,* the ontological commitment to the utter absence of a perduring soul was initially too strong to venture anything like the Pudgalavādin's *pudgala.* Their solution to the problem of karma was twofold: first, they contended that past, present and future objects all exist; second, they also posited the existence of a special kind of "unmanifest matter" (*avjñaptirūpa*) to be the bearer of karma.

The Sarvāstivādin argument for the existence of objects in the past, present, and future first appears in the *Vijñānakāya.* In its first chapter, the opponent (a certain Maudgalyāyana) states that only present objects exist, but not those in the past or the future. Against this claim, the unnamed Sarvāstivādin interlocutor makes the following statement:

> ONE WILL ASK HIM: Yes or no, are there those people who saw, who see, who will see that attachment, the root of suffering is bad?
> HE RESPONDS: Yes.
> [ASK:] The attachment, the object of this view, is it past, future, present?

If he responds that the attachment, the object of this view, is past, one should tell him: "The past exists." He cannot say that the past does not exist. To maintain that the past does not exist is illogical. If he responds that the attachment is future, one should tell him, "The future exists." He cannot say that the future does not exist. To maintain that the future does not exist is illogical. If he responds that the attachment, the object of this view, is present, one should tell him: "There is therefore, in one person [*pudgala*], two simultaneous thoughts; the thought [which is] the object of the view [namely, the thought of the attachment] and the thought [which is] the subject of the view [namely, the thought that views the attachment]. This is inadmissible. If he doesn't admit that, in one person, there would be two simultaneous thoughts, one that is seen and one that sees, then he cannot say that one who sees the present is illogical.[52]

The Sarvāstivādin makes essentially the same argument for many different topics, for example, attachment and karmic retribution, the eye and its object. In every case, the form of the argument is as follows: The Sarvāstivādin begins with a passage from a Buddhist *sūtra,* asking whether the opponent agrees that the *sūtra* has been "well said, well taught." After the opponent agrees, the Sarvāstivādin takes the subject under discussion (usually some sort of faculty) and inquires into the temporal status of its object. In every case, it is shown that the faculty being examined can only have a past or a future object. The faculty with a present object would involve the contradiction of the simultaneous existence of an active and passive faculty registering the same object or the simultaneous existence of cause and effect.

By arguing that past present and future objects exist, the Sarvāstivādin can explain how an action performed in the past can have an effect far in the future without having to posit a persisting entity that bears the karma through time. The action committed at time t^1 is indeed impermanent and is not perceived after it is ended. Since the past exists in some sense, according to this theory, it can be the object of perception at time t^2 through the faculty of memory or through the "divine eye" of a Buddha. More important, just as past actions can be the basis for subsequent recollections, so too can past actions be the basis for future karmic results.

Svabhāva

To make this theory more complete, the Sarvāstivādins had to add more technical terms to their lexicon. The *Vijñānakāya's* argument against the Pudgalavādin's *pudgala* has the Pudgalavādin ask what the object of the meditation on loving-kindness (*maitryālambana*) could be if it is not the *pudgala.* The Sarvāstivādin response is crucial, although its implications would only be worked out in subsequent texts. The Sarvāstivādin responds:

> The dharmas have a *svabhāva* [essence] and are existent; they receive the metaphorical designation *sattva,* they are living; in this sense, the loving-kindness has as its object the series of grasped *skandhas*.[53]

Implicit in this statement is the same distinction between what is merely nominal (i.e., the *sattva*) and what is real (the *skandhas*) found in the *sūtras.* What the Sarvāstivādins add is a criterion for what constitutes the "real." *Dharmas* are real (as opposed to merely nominal) to the extent that they have essence (*svabhāva*).

The implications of this statement seem to have been ignored in the *Jñānaprasthāna* but are taken up in the *Mahāvibhāṣā.* If, according to the *Vijñānakāya,* real objects are said to exist by virtue of their *svabhāva,* then it is by virtue of this same *svabhāva* that objects exist in the past, present, and future. The essence of an entity is not a product of causes and conditions, but is unchanging.[54]

To make this theory plausible, and to turn the common Sanskrit term *svabhāva* into a technical term, the Sarvāstivādins had to distinguish two senses of "existence." In English as in Sanskrit, "existence" usually implies "*present* existence." The distinction that would become orthodoxy among Sarvāstivādins was the theory of Vasumitra distinguishing two senses of existence. A thing has an unchanging essence (*svabhāva*) by which it is identified. This persists regardless of whether it is past present or future. It also has a function (*kāritra*) that is produced by a set of causes and conditions and exists only in the present. It is by virtue of a thing's function that it is known to be past, present or future.

> the Bhadanta Vasumitra says: ". . . It is in the function of the activity (*kāritra*) that the periods are distinguished, and, from this point of view, the sense of the period (or path) is: 'going' [*marche*]. That is to say: the 'conditioned things' (*saṃskṛtadharmas*), when they have no more activity, are said to be 'future'; 'present,' when they have activity; 'past,' when their activity is destroyed. . . . According to this principle, the *rūpa* that is no longer *rūpaṇa* . . . is said to be future; present when it has *rūpaṇa;* past when the *rūpaṇa* is destroyed. The same for the four other *skandhas.*"[55]

Here the author makes a curious move. The *svabhāva* of a thing is its substance (*dravya*), and yet this essence is quite different from those functions that allow the object to be perceived (solidity, sound, color, smell, etc.), as these functions can only operate in the present. It is the *kāritra,* the dharma's function that allows for such awareness. In this sense, all objects must exist not just as nouns but also as verbs. Here we see that *rūpa* (material form) exists as a substance in the past, present, and future and as the activity of "being tearable" (*rūpaṇa*) only in the present.

Person and Language: *Prajñapti* vs. *Dravya*

Using a more rigorous criterion for existence, the Sarvāstivādins dismissed the Pudgalavādin argument for the existence of *pudgala*. For all its criticism of the Pudgalavādin's doctrine of the *pudgala* as bearer of karma, the Sarvāstivādins themselves posited an array of entities that served essentially the same function. In the Sarvāstivāda system, that function is largely carried out by entities such as, *avijñptirūpa* (unmanifest matter) or *anuśaya* (dormant *dharmas*). The difference between the Sarvāstivādin postulation of these entities and the Pudgalavādins is not that one postulates an enduring bearer of karma and the other does not but, rather, that the Sarvāstivādins devised a mechanism to explain why some *dharmas* are manifest and others are not. They did not need to devise a neither-identical-nor-different category.

The weak point in the Pudgalavādin arguments for the existence of *pudgala,* then, was precisely the ambiguity that the school exploited to steer clear of the extremes of nihilism and eternalism. For example, *pudgala* was always classed by the Pudgalavādins as a special in-between category (of which it was the only member). It was neither *saṃskṛta* nor *asaṃskṛta,* neither identical nor different from the aggregates, and so forth. The *Vijñānakāya* objects that the Buddha never taught such in-between categories and hence the Pudgalavādins would have to choose: *pudgala* had to be one or the other but could not be a separate category.[56] The Pudgalavādins agreed with other Buddhists that *pudgala* was a *prajñapti,* but claimed that existence as a *prajñapti* did not mean nonexistence. On the contrary, the *pudgala* occupied its own category of existence. Using a solid criterion of what constituted existence, the Sarvāstivādins tried to force the Pudgalavādins to choose whether *pudgala* was substantial (really existent, which would make it identical to a soul) or *prajñapti* (and thereby a mere word). Just as the *Vijñānakāya* makes the Pudgalavādin choose between *saṃskṛta* and *asaṃskṛta,* Vasubandhu, in his *Abhidharmakośa,* argues that there are two categories of terms—those that "existed as substance" (*dravyasat*) and those that "existed as [mere] designation" (*prajñaptisat*). The first category includes all things that could be considered concrete, atomic particulars. The second category consists of collective terms like "army" or "forest." With these two options, he tries to force the Pudgalavādins to admit that *pudgala* belonged to the *prajñaptisat* category and hence admit it as a mere designation.

As time went on, the Sarvāstivādins drew more sophisticated distinctions concerning existence. Saṅghabhadra (fifth century) argued that nominal entities did exist, but he was careful to distinguish this kind of existence from substantial existence. He defines existence in general as "that which produces cognition" and then distinguishes nominal existence from substantial existence on the basis of the way in which this cognition comes about.

> Here is my definition: "The real character of the existent is to engender the idea (*buddhi*) of the capacity of the object. The existent is of two kinds: *dravyasat* (*che-yeou*), that which exists as a thing, (that which exists in itself); *prajñaptisat,* that which exists by virtue of designation: these two categories, in effect, correspond to the ultimate truth (*paramārthasatya*) and the truth of experience (*saṃvṛtisatya*). When the idea is produced with regard to a thing without dependence [on other things] this thing is *dravyasat.* When it is produced with regard to a thing in dependence [on other things], that thing is *prajñaptisat,* for example, a jug or an army. [The idea of color refers to an entity, to a certain thing; the army doesn't exist except as a designation for the soldiers, etc.][57]

Saṅghabhadra's distinction between the two types of *prajñaptisat* entities as well as his correlation of *prajñaptisat* entities with worldly truth (*saṃvṛtisatya*) and *dravyasat* entities with ultimate truth (*paramārthasatya*) would become a commonplace not only in Sarvāstivādin literature, but in late Theravāda works as well.[58]

A Mahāsāṅghika Abhidharma Piṭaka?

The preceding discussion is from the *abhidharma* collections that have survived either in manuscript form or in translation. What is available today, however, represents only a small portion of *abhidharma* texts that Buddhists used. Since it is likely that Nāgārjuna spent at least a portion of his career in a Mahāsāṅghika monastery, it would be helpful inquire into the *abhidharma* collection(s) used by the Mahāsāṅghikas. Unfortunately, although the doxographical texts ascribe many theses to the Mahāsāṅghikas,[59] there is no surviving collection of *abhidharma* materials that can be identified as a *Mahāsāṅghika Abhidharma Piṭaka.* The first issue that must be resolved, then, is whether the Mahāsāṅghikas even had an *abhidharma* collection.[60] This is a concern because the Pali *Dīpavaṃsa* claims that the Mahāsāṅghikas did not.[61] The *Mahāsāṅghika-vinaya* is ambiguous on this issue. Certain passages explicitly refer to three collections—*sūtra, vinaya,* and *abhidharma* (阿毘曇).[62] Yet in three separate places in the *Mahāsāṅghika Vinaya* the word *abhidharma* is said to be nothing other than the nine categories of *sūtra* in the same way that the term *abhivinaya* is sometimes used for the *prātimokṣa*.[63] In this reading, the Mahāsāṅghikas should have no separate *abhidharma piṭaka*.

The preponderance of evidence, however, suggests that the Mahāsāṅghikas did have an *abhidharma piṭaka,* or at least some sects of it did. An inscription on a pillar from Nāgārjunakoṇḍa recording a donation to the *ācaryas* of the Apāramahāvīnaseliya sect (= Aparaśaila), dated to the sixth year of the reign of Virapurisadata (mid-third century[64] mentions a certain "Bhadānta Ānanda who was a disciple of the teachers of the Āryasaṅgha, and who were teachers of the *Dīgha-Majhima-Nikāyās* and the *pañcamātuka*."[65] The term *mātuka* in the inscription is a Prakrit equivalent of the Sanskrit *mātṛkā,* one of the synonyms for the *abhidharma*. Rao notes that *mātṛkā* can also denote the *vinaya,* but that, whereas the *Theravāda-vinaya* has five sections, the *Mahāsāṅghika-vinaya* does not. Hence, the "five-(sectioned)-*mātṛkā*" probably refers to the *abhidharma*. Harivarman's *Satyasiddhiśāstra* (c. 250–350 C.E.) mentions a text that Śāstri translates as "the *Ṣad-pāda-abhidharma-Loka-prajñapti*."[66] At the beginning of the fifth century, Faxian claims to have found a copy of a Mahāsāṅghika *abhidharma* text in a monastery at Paṭaliputra.[67] Finally, in the seventh century Xuanzang encounters two Mahāsāṅghika monks while visiting a country not far from Dhānyakaṭaka and studies Mahāsāṅghika *abhidharma* with them.

> The Master of the Law, whilst in this country, met with two priests, the first named Subhūti, the second Sūrya: both of them eminent for explaining the *Tripiṭaka* according to the Mahāsaṅghika school. . . . The Master of the Law [i.e., Xuanzang] on this account remained there several months studying the *Mūlābhidharma* and other *śāstras,* according to the Mahāsaṅghika School. They also studied the various *śāstras* of the Great Vehicle under the direction of the Master of the Law. And so becoming bound together in mind they all went in company to pay reverence to the sacred places of their religion.[68]

All this leads to the conclusion that the Mahāsāṅghikas had an *abhidharma piṭaka* that may have had five or six, rather than seven, parts. In addition, the Mahāsāṅghika monks of Xuanzang's time who were in possession of this *Mahāsāṅghika Mūlābhidharma* were not Mahāyānists, although they were apparently open to being instructed in it.

Mahāsāṅghika Theses

The tenets actually housed in the Mahāsāṅghika *abhidharma* collection would have varied somewhat from sect to sect. The early doxographies record the main subsects of the Mahāsāṅghika to be the Ekavyāvahārika, the Gokulika (alt. Kukkula), the Bahuśrutīya,[69] the Prajñaptivāda,[70] and the Caitika.[71] The *Samayabhedoparacanacakra* of Vasumitra adds the Lokottaravādin, the Uttaraśaila, and the Aparaśaila subsects to the list, while the *Mañjuśrīparipṛcchā* omits the Prajñaptivādins. Of these subsects, only one text is purported to be of the Bahuśrutīya sect, namely, the *Satyasiddhiśāstra* of Harivārman. Unfortunately, the *Satyasiddhiśāstra* postdates Nāgārjuna and furthermore is a doubtful representative of the school.[72] Although a representative Mahāsāṅghika *abhidharma* text is no longer available, the outlines of the theories it may have contained can nevertheless be pieced together from the testimonies of the early doxographies, starting with the *Samayabhedoparacanacakra*.

According to Vasumitra, three of the Mahāsāṅghika sects were doctrinally indistinguishable: the Ekavyāvahārika, the Gokulika, and the Lokottaravādins. Forty-eight theses are held in common by these three schools, and an additional nine theses were adopted later. Most of these theses do not concern us here. The brief treatment found in Vasumitra's treatise does, however, offer enough information to assess the differences between the Mahāsāṅghikas and the other schools concerning the fundamental doctrines of the *saṃsāra* and nirvāṇa, karma, the owner of karma, and the path to nirvāṇa.

The first area in which the Mahāsāṅghikas differ from the other schools is in the number of *dharmas* considered unconditioned. Other schools regarded the noble truth of suffering, the arising of suffering, and the noble path as part of conditioned (*saṃskṛta*) reality or *saṃsāra*. Only cessation (*nirodha*) among the truths and empty space were generally considered unconditioned. By contrast, the Mahāsāṅghikas did not allow the four noble truths to be so neatly categorized. According to Vasumitra, the Mahāsāṅghikas believed that there were nine unconditioned (*asaṃskṛta*) *dharmas* (無為法):

a) *Pratisaṃkhyā-nirodha* or "extinction (which is realized) by the discriminating (lit. enumerating) (power of wisdom)."

b) *Apratisaṃkhyā-nirodha,* or "extinction (which is) not (realized) by the discriminating (power of wisdom)."
c) *Ākāśa,* or "space"
d) *Ākāśānantyāyatana,* or "realm of infinity of space."
e) *Vijñānāntyāyatana,* or "realm of infinity of intelligence."
f) *Ākiñcanyāyatana,* or "realm of nothingness."
g) *Naivasaṃjñā-nāsaṃjñāyatana,* or "realm where there is neither consciousness nor unconsciousness."
h) *Pratītya-samutpādāṅgikatva,* or "law of causation."
i) *Aryamārgāṅgikatva,* or "law of the *āryan* paths."[73]

The first three in this list are identical to that of the Sarvāstivādins. The Mahāsāṅghikas include among the unconditioned the four formless realms (*d-g*) that one enters in the four highest *dhyānas.* This is curious, since texts such as the "Cūḷasūññata sutta" of the *Majjhima Nikāya* have the meditator reflect on these states upon awakening and pronounce them unsatisfactory because they are conditioned. The last two present even more difficulties. Masuda's translation reproduced above is from Xuanzang's version. A more literal translation would be: "Number eight—the characteristic or the essence of the limbs of dependent-origination. Number nine: the characteristic or essence of the limbs of the noble path."[74] The character 性 can be translated as *lakṣaṇa* or *svabhāva,* or, as Masuda renders it, as a simply abstract ending like *-tā* or *-tva.* Bareau translates the whole compound back into Sanskrit as *pratītyasamutpādāṅgasvabhāva.* By using this ending, Xuanzang in effect bifurcates dependent-origination and the noble path. It is through meditation on dependent-origination that one comes to see the unsatisfactoriness of *saṃsāra* and abandon it. The noble path also must be conditioned, otherwise no one could practice it. Hence, dependent-origination and the noble path stand for the conditioned process of the arising of suffering and the cessation of suffering respectively. Nevertheless, *the fact of* dependent-origination and the noble eightfold path is not subject to any conditions or qualifications. Its essence is unconditioned. By splitting these two terms, Xuanzang allows dependent-origination and the noble path to be conditioned, whereas their natures are unconditioned.

Xuanzang's translation is clever, but unfortunately it is not confirmed by any of the earlier or later translations. Both the Qin dynasty translation (anonymous) and Paramārtha's translation of (presumably) the same text simply have "the limbs of dependent-origination" and "the limbs of the noble path,"[75] as does Dharmākara's Tibetan translation and possibly Vinītadeva's commentary.[76] The conclusion that the Mahāsāṅghikas held the limbs of dependent-origination and the limbs of the noble eightfold path to somehow be unconditioned in the same sense that *nirodha* and empty space are unconditioned is unavoidable. Neither Vasumitra's treatise nor its commentaries explain how this is possible.

The one available clue is from Vasubandhu's *Abhidharmakośa,* in which he raises this issue.

> Certain schools maintain that dependent-origination is unconditioned, *asaṃskṛta,* because the Sūtra says: "Whether Tathāgatas appear, whether Tathāgatas do not appear, this nature of dharma of the dharmas is stable." This thesis is true or false depending on the manner in which one interprets it. If one wants to say that it is always by reason of *avidya,* etc., which are producing the *saṃskāras,* etc., and not by reason of another thing, and is not without a cause; and that, in this sense, *Pratītyasamutpāda* is stable, eternal (*nītya*): then we approve. If one wants to say that there is a certain eternal dharma named *Pratītyasamutpāda,* this opinion is inadmissible. Because the *utpāda,* the production or birth, is a characteristic of the conditioned (*saṃskṛtakakṣaṇa*); an eternal dharma, as *utpāda* would be or *Pratītyasamutpāda* according to this hypothesis, wouldn't be a characteristic of transitoriness, of conditionenedness.[77]

The translations of Vasumitra's treatise are clearer on several other points regarding the nature of dharmas, especially as they relate to the debates over karma. The Mahāsāṅghikas did not go along with the Sarvāstivādin theory of dharmas existing in the past present and future. Specifically, they denied that anything existed in the past or the future and furthermore denied the past and future to be substances. Nor did they posit an enduring entity like the Pudgalavādins.[78] On the contrary, they held that there was a continuity of development (*saṃtāna*) that carried change through time. Although other schools, such as the Sarvāstivādins and the Theravādins, also had a doctrine of continuity to explain the transmission of karma from cause to effect, they posited a stream of substantially and temporally discrete (i.e., momentary) *dharmas* with each succeeding one being the effect of its predecessor. For this model to function, each *dharma* would have to disappear before the next could arise. Against this articulation, the Mahāsāṅghikas' notion of "stream" was not broken into discrete moments. To illustrate this, they used the example of a seed growing into a sprout.

Paramārtha and Xuanzang's versions of this thesis are virtually identical: "The seed is nothing other than the sprout."[79] The term *jí* (即) is used here in the sense that the seed and the sprout are two different aspects of the same thing. The Qin dynasty translation differs substantially from the other two: "The mental seed is nothing other than the *upādāna* [取]."[80] *Upādāna* is the usual translation of 取, and I have left the Sanskrit untranslated because of the wide range of its possible meanings. *Upādāna* here can mean either "substratum" or "grasping."[81] Hence, this phrase can be rendered as either "the mental seed is nothing other than its substratum (i.e., the mind)" or "the mental seed is nothing other than its grasping." The differences between the Qin translation and the other two are intriguing, but the point seems to be that, for the Mahāsāṅghikas, karmic causality functioned on a smooth continuum, not by discrete moments, as the Sarvāstivādins asserted. Kuiji, in his commentary on Xuanzang's translation, explains this thesis as follows.

> (The Mahāsāṅghikas) admit that *rūpas* (exist) for a long time without creation and destruction. Therefore the substances of seeds change and become sprout: not that when the seeds are destroyed, the sprouts come into existence. Other schools (maintain that when) the seeds perish there come into being sprouts. Therefore (the view of the other schools) is not the same as the view of the Mahāsāṅghikas (lit. this).[82]

There are some hints that the Mahāsāṅghikas diverged from the other schools on the matter of the content of liberating insight as well. As discussed in Chapter 5, the Theravādins and the Sarvāstivādins seem to have given equal importance to the roles of analytical investigation (*vipaśyanā*) and mental pacification (*śamatha*) by placing them in separate but equal parts of the path (*darśana* and *bhāvanā mārgas,* respectively). As these two paths are articulated in these traditions, *bhāvanā-mārga* culminates in the complete suppression of cognitive recognition (*saṃjñā*), while the *darśana-mārga* uses precisely this same faculty to analyze reality.

The brief comments in Vasumitra's work imply that the division between *darśana* and *bhāvanā mārgas* was not so strict in the Mahāsāṅghika. On the one hand, there is the thesis "Even in the state of the *samāhita* (等引) one can utter words (lit., there is an utterance of speech): there is also a subdued mind (調伏心) and also a quarrelsome mind (諍作意)."[83] Furthermore, it was apparently a tenet of the Mahāsāṅghikas that *samādhi* was not even a necessary component of liberating insight. The Mahāsāṅghikas held that "Through the instrumentality (*prayoga*) of wisdom (*prajñā*) one annihilates suffering and is also capable of obtaining the final beatitude (*sukha*)."[84] Hence, for the Mahāsāṅghikas, the power of correctly guided *saṃjñā* alone is capable of producing liberation and that *saṃjñā* is still present even in the higher states of absorption.

Bahuśrūtīya Theses

Vasumitra says little of the Bahuśrūtīya other than the fact that they believed that Arhants can be fallible and that five teachings were ultimately true (*paramārthasat*): (1) impermanence, (2) suffering, (3) emptiness, (4) selflessness, and the (5) peace of nirvāṇa.[85]

Prajñaptivāda Theses

None of the theses ascribed to the Mahāsāṅghikas mentions much of the distinction between real and nominal entities that so occupied the debates between the Vatsīputrīyas and the Sarvāstivādins. However, one rather obscure subsect of the Mahāsāṅghikas, the Prajñāptivādins, did seem preoccupied with these issues. Very little is known of this sect other than what is written by Vasumitra and Bhavya and passing references in a handful of other sources. The name appears nowhere in votive inscriptions, and the only source as to their whereabouts comes from Taranātha, who tells us that they existed in Maghada during his lifetime (c. ninth to tenth centuries).[86] Perhaps the Prajñaptivādins were another lineage within the greater fold of the Mahāsāṅghika, similar to the Ekavyāvahārikas and the Gokulikas—separate at one time and subsequently all but swallowed up by the larger sect. The problem is further complicated by the fact that sources diverge in their presentation of which theses the sect actually held. According to Xuanzang's translation of the *Samayabhedoparacanacakra*, the Prajñaptivādins held that:

1) Suffering is not the *skandhas*.
2) The twelve *āyatana* are not ultimately real (真實, *paramārthasat*).
3) *Zhūxíng* (諸行, either latent impressions *samskāras* or conditioned reality *saṃskṛta*—see below) is interdependently (相待展轉, *anyonyāpekṣa*) constructed (和合, *sāmagrī*). It (i.e., the *zhūxíng*) is a *prajñapti* for suffering.
4) There is no heroic effort (無士夫用, *puruṣa-kāra?*).
5) There is no untimely death—the previous *karman* (先業) accrues to the (overall) karmic accumulation (which in turn) acts as the cause for the different maturation.

6) The fruit ripens due to merit, which is the cause of gaining the Noble Path.
7) The path cannot be cultivated (修, *bhāvanā*). The path cannot be destroyed (壞).[87]

Dharmākara's Tibetan translation is quite close to Xuanzang's.

1) Suffering is not an aggregate.
2) The *āyatanas* are not comprehended (*yoṅs su ma rigs pa dag*).[88]
3) Suffering (occurs) by means of the *saṃskāras* that are reciprocally designated (*anyonya-prajñapti-phan tshun btags pa*).
4) The agent of the entities does not exist.
5) There is no untimely death—it is attained by previous karma. The fruition that is established arises due to the accumulation of karma.
6) By giving rise to all-knowledge along with merit, one attains the path.
7) The path is not to be performed with contemplation. The path is not destroyed.[89]

The two earlier translations—that of Paramārtha and the Qin dynasty translation—diverge from the later translations in the number of theses held as well as in their presentation of the theses themselves. The Qin dynasty translation is somewhat more difficult than the later translations, and it seems to record only four out of the seven theses (the theses are numbered to match the theses of Xuanzang's version).

3) If it is said that all *skandha* (陰) are without karma, then all (*skandhas*) will not comprise the *samskāras*. They are (therefore) interdependently designated (*anyonya-prajñapayati*).[90]
5) The ignorant person's affairs do not produce an untimely death due to the source of karma by which is obtained the accumulation of karma, which is the origin of the arising of all suffering.
6) According to karma accrued, he accrues merit and virtue and gives rise to the noble path.
7) The path is neither cultivated (*bhāvanā*) nor and is not destroyed (*na pranāśayati?* 不失).[91]

Aside from the fact that his is the only translation to designate this school Vibhajyavāda instead of Prajñaptivāda, Paramārtha's version seems to be a bridge between the Qin dynasty translation and the later translations.

1) Suffering is not in the *skandhas*.
2) All *āyatanas* are not achieved (成就).
3) All *yǒu wéi* (again, this could translate either *saṃskāra* or *saṃskṛta*) dharmas are interdependently designated and are the reason the word *duḥkha* is established.
4) There is no person (*pudgala?*) who is an agent (無人功力).
5) Accumulation is the cause for the fruit and is able to produce karma. All suffering follows karma's arising.
6) The noble path is due to the acquisition of merit and virtue.
7) The noble path is attained without *bhāvana*.[92]

Let us examine these theses one by one. All three translations agree that, for the Prajñāptivādins, suffering was not an aggregate. Masuda gives the following explanation.

> The *Fa Jen* says that the present proposition is aimed at the Sarvāstivādins who claim that sufferings are *skandhas* . . . The Sanskrit *skandha* signifies etymologically multitude, group, etc. but as a technical term it implies the five elements of a being. According to the Prajñaptivādin these elements have no potent power in themselves to cause suffering to a man. Suffering comes into being when two *saṃskāras* combine together.[93]

It is a bit more difficult to reconcile the three translations of the second thesis. The *āyatanas* are either not achieved, not ultimately true, or not understood. the *Fa ren* explains that the *āyatanas* are not ultimately true because they are the products of the aggregation of *skandhas*. Hence they would exist as a *prajñapti* instead of an ultimately existing thing.[94]

The third proposition is both the most important and the most problematic. It is important because it is the proposition from which the sect derives its name. It is problematic because each translation presents it differently. The difficulty begins with the subject of the thesis. I have left the subject of Xuanzang's and Paramārtha's Chinese versions untranslated since the terms they chose are ambiguous. Paramārtha's subject is 有為法, while Xuanzang chooses to translate it as 諸行. The problem is that both of these terms could be translations of either *saṃskāra* ("mental formations" consisting of the *citta-samprayukta dharmas*—one of the five aggregates) or *saṃskṛta* (conditioned reality = *saṃsāra* itself—as opposed to unconditioned elements like *nirodha*). Although all *dharmas* contained in the *saṃskāra* aggregate are conditioned (*saṃskṛta*), not all conditioned *dharmas* belong to the *saṃskāra* aggregate. The Qin dynasty translation clearly uses the term 諸行 for *saṃskāra* because it is in a discussion of the five aggregates. Yet the Qin version of this thesis is structurally so different from the other translations as to make it unclear whether it is the same thesis.

> If it is said that all *skandha* [陰] are without karma, then all [*skandhas*] will not comprise the *samskāras*. They are (therefore) interdependently designated *anyonya-prajñapayati*.

The thesis seems to be arguing against those who would take the five aggregates as ultimately existent entities.[95] Against this, the Prajñaptivādin contends that, if that were the case then karma could not pertain to the five aggregates since karma is the very essence of conditionality and change. If karma does not pertain to the five aggregates, then the fourth aggregate (*saṃskāra*) could not be an aggregate, since the fourth aggregate is considered the locus of karma. Because it is contradictory to say that the fourth aggregate is not one of the five aggregates, the five aggregates ultimately must not exist. The solution is presented in the following sentence, "They are (therefore) interdependent [展轉] designations [施設] [probably something like *anyonya-prajñapti*]." Just as the Vatsīputrīyas and the Sarvāstivādins used the concept of *prajñapti* (designation of a collectivity) to describe the nominal character of the *pudgala*, the Prajñaptivādins argue that the aggregates themselves are equally designations of a collectivity. Furthermore, whereas the Sarvāstivādins argue that the *pudgala* is merely a denomination based on the aggregates, the Prajñaptivādins claim that the aggregates are designated not on the basis of smaller components, but by virtue of their reciprocal relationship with one another.

Xuanzang's and Paramārtha's translations are briefer and lose some of the sense of the Qin dynasty translation. Paramārtha says that 有為 *dharmas* are designated interdependently (again *anyonya-prajñapti*—and thus are not ultimately true) and that this state is the basis on which the word "suffering" is established. Paramārtha's version seems to shift the emphasis from the *skandhas* being *prajñaptisat* entities to suffering being composite and hence not ultimately real (*contra* Bahuśrūtīya thesis number 2, listed above) but, rather, based on the interdependent designation of something else (the 有為 *dharmas*). Xuanzang's translation has the 諸行 being interdependently constructed 相待展轉和合 (full stop), and such the construction makes suffering a *prajñapti*. Dharmākara's Tibetan translation is not significantly different from Paramārtha's translation to warrant comment, although a note should be made regarding Wassiliew's translation of Dharmākara. He renders it as "alle Taten sind in Folge ihrer gegenseitigen Verbindung qualvoll."[96] While *btags pa* can sometimes translate the Sanskrit *bhandana* (= Wassiljew's *Verbindung*),[97] the more usual translation of *prajñapti* is confirmed by the three Chinese translations of 施設 (Qin dynasty), 假 (Paramārtha), and 假名 (Xuanzang). Each of these Chinese terms is an acceptable translation of *prajñapti*, and none of them can translate *bhandana*. If the Chinese and the Tibetan translations are compared, there is no option but to translate the technical term in the thesis as something like *anyonya-prajñapti*.

Returning to the issue of the subject term of the thesis, the problem remains as to whether Paramārtha and Xuanzang's translations argue that only mental formations (*samskāras*) are *anyonya-prajñapti* or whether all conditioned *dharmas* (*saṃskṛta*) are so constructed. In this case, the precision of Tibetan grammar can clarify an ambiguity in the Chinese. Whereas 有為法 and 諸行 could be translated as either *saṃskāra* or *saṃskṛta*, Dharmākara's *'du byed rnams* can *only* translate as *saṃskāras*. The Tibetan term *'dus byas* is usually reserved for *saṃskṛta*. But this is not the end of the story. Bhavya's *Nikāyabhedavibhaṅgavyākhyāna* (extant only in Tibetan translation) contains two different versions of this thesis. The first reads: "Suffering exists by the *anyonya-prajñapti* of conditioned things [*'dos byas—saṃskṛta*]."[98] The second reads: "Mental formations [*'dus byed—saṃskāras*] are *anyonya-prajñapti*."[99] As both versions occur in the same text (and both in Tibetan), there is no ambiguity. We may conclude that, at least at the time of Bhavya, two different versions existed of the same thesis: one in which the Prajñaptivādins hold that *saṃskāras* are interdependently designated, and another in which all conditioned things (all *saṃskṛta* dharmas, i.e., all things in *saṃsāra*) are so designated, a fact that leads to suffering. The ambiguity on this point in Paramārtha and Xuanzang's translations demands that we remain open to the possibility that the subject of both is *saṃkṛta* in the sense of conditioned existence generally and not just the *saṃskāra* aggregate.

The next thesis mentioned by Vasumitra concerns the mechanism of the transmission of karma. Thankfully, the various translations are close enough to one another to offer a clear picture of what the Prajñaptivādins were after. All the versions agree that action in the past accumulates and that this accumulation is the basis for the future fruition. One is tempted to take the "karmic accumulation" as a technical term in the same manner as the *avipranāśa* of the Saṃmitīyas. Indeed, the *Saṃmitīya Nikāya Śāstra* gives *upacaya* (accumulation) as a synonym for *avipranāśa*.[100] Buddhaghosa's fifth-century *Katthāvatthu Aṭṭhakathā* mentions the doctrine of *kammūpacaya* held by "the Andhakas and the Saṃmitīyas." According to this theory, the accumulation of karma is separate from karma and was "dissociated from consciousness [*cittavippayutto* = *cittaviprayukta*] indeterminate or ineffable [*abyākato* = *avyākṛta*] and objectless [*anārammaṇa* = *anālambana*]."[101] Because many who lived in the Andhra area were Mahāsāṅghikas, it is possible that Buddhaghosa was referring here to a Prajñaptivādin theory. In any case, the Qin dynasty translation as well as that of Xuanzang and Dharmākara use this mechanism of karma to explain why there is no such thing as an accidental death.

The last two theses, according to Vasumitra, both concern the path. Apparently, the Prajñaptivādins believed that it was one's merit ripening the karmic fruit that allows him to attain the noble path, and that the path cannot be meditated upon nor can it be destroyed. It is difficult to say, without corroborating evidence, whether this thesis was meant to de-emphasize the role of absorptive meditation (*bhāvanā-mārga*) or whether it is simply a rearticulation of the Mahāsāṅghika thesis that the path is unconditioned.

Most scholars who study *abhidharma* material are occupied primarily with that of the Theravādins and the Sarvāstivādins because their texts are still extant and good editions of the Indic originals are available. Much less is known about the *abhidharma* literature of other Buddhist schools, simply because the resources are less accessible. By looking at the available sources, it is clear that the Pudgalavādins and the Mahāsāṅghikas had well-established doctrines that differed considerably from those of the other schools. This literature provided alternative theories on the relationship between *saṃsāra* and nirvāṇa, the mechanism of karma and the ultimate status of entities. A full understanding of Nāgārjuna requires an understanding of the theories with which he was working. Although the preceding treatment of *abhidharma* literature is by no means exhaustive, it provides sufficient background for understanding some of the doctrinal stances that Nāgārjuna takes.

7
Nāgārjuna and the *Abhidharma*

IN ORDER TO ESTABLISH MAHĀYĀNA on a firm footing in his monastery, Nāgārjuna would have to demonstrate to his *confrères* that the adoption of Mahāyāna would augment the doctrinal positions current in the monastery in which he resided. It is useful to emphasize this because it has become a commonplace in modern scholarship on Mahāyāna to state that one of Mahāyāna's prime objectives was to refute "the *abhidharmists*." The following statement of Musashi Tachikawa is typical:

> While adhering to the original standpoint of Early Buddhism that all things are impermanent, Mahāyāna Buddhism propounded by means of its own original methodology the non-reality of the world in contrast to the methods of *Abhidharma* Buddhism which had sought to define the world as existent and possessing a specific structure.[1]

There is certainly something to this. Even the *Zhonglun*, one of the earliest commentaries on the *Mūlamadhyamakakārikā*, presents Mahāyāna in general as a reaction against the *abhidharma*.

> After the Buddha's decease, in the second five hundred years of the patterned Dharma, men's faculties became dulled, they became deeply attached to all dharmas, and sought for settled, fixed characteristics in the twelve causal links, the five *skandhas*, the twelve *āyatanas*, the eighteen realms, and so on. They did not know the Buddha's intention and were merely attached to words and letters. Hearing the utter empti-

> ness taught in the Mahāyāna-Dharma they did not know the reason for things being empty, and so conceived doubts and views, such as, "If all things are utterly empty, how can you differentiate sin and merit, karmic recompense and so on? If this were so, there would be no worldly truth and no truth of the supreme meaning." They seized hold of the characteristic of "emptiness" and produced voracious attachments, generating all sorts of errors about utter emptiness. It was for such reasons as these that the Bodhisattva Nāgārjuna composed his Middle Treatise.[2]

Although he does not mention *abhidharma* by name, the author of the *Zhonglun* does little to disguise the target of his ire. In fact, none of the extant commentaries on Nāgārjuna's *Mūlamadhyamakakārikā* show much appreciation for *abhidharma* literature, although the *Zhonglun*'s reaction to it is especially vituperative.

In light of what has been said in the preceding chapters, however, the simple picture of Mahāyāna's blanket denial of *abhidharma* is problematic. If the *abhidharma* literature of a given Buddhist school comprised its authoritative interpretation of "word of the Buddha," then how could Mahāyānists debunk it without relinquishing hard-earned legitimacy in the eyes of other monks? More to the point, Nāgārjuna is stereotyped (largely on the basis of the last verse of the *Mūlamadhyamakakārikā* and the *Virgrahavyāvartanī*) as a kind of philosophical pugilist refuting all views and having no thesis of his own. How could a Mahāyānist like Nāgārjuna refute the very *abhidharma* tenets held dear by his fellow monks without undermining himself? The commentaries on the *Mūlamadhamakakārikā* were probably written at times and in places in which Mahāyāna was on a better footing. The authors of these commentaries presumably had different institutional needs and commitments than Nāgārjuna did—the groundwork already having been lain by the master himself. Given the precarious situation of early Mahāyāna (outlined in Chapter 1), we should at least be open to the possibility that Nāgārjuna was not simply trying to refute the teachings of *abhidharma* literature. A far more complex relationship to *abhidharma* is proposed here.

In light of the possibility that the doctrines of multiple schools might enter into his works, it is also possible that Nāgārjuna's position *vis-à-vis abhidharma* is neither a blanket denial nor a blanket acceptance. Nāgārjuna's arguments entertain certain *abhidharmic* standpoints while refuting others. Indeed, the view of Nāgārjuna's strategies is incomplete without an untangling of the *abhidharma* references in his works and a determination of how he positions Mahāyāna in relation to them. As should be clear from previous chapters, Mahāyāna's survival depended far more on making friends than on conquering enemies. For this reason, Nāgārjuna's arguments should be examined in terms of the *alliances that they forge* instead of merely whom they attack. For example, Nāgārjuna at times argues against the Sarvāstivādins, but he is doing so in the presence of an invisible onlooker—his home monastery. Furthermore, although Nāgārjuṇa does refute the "views" of some schools, a close reading of his texts will show that he carefully avoids attacking others. The *abhidharma* arguments that he upholds provide a better picture of the doctrinal atmosphere of the monastery in which he lived and how he sought to get into their good graces.

Nāgārjuna and the Sarvāstivādin *Abhidharma*

The most obvious *abhidharma* references in Nāgārjuna's works are clearly his attacks on certain Sarvāstivādin tenets. These attacks occur primarily in the *Mūlamadhyamakakārikā*. The clearest reference to Sarvāstivāda *abhidharma* occurs in the first chapter in the second and third verses.

> 2 Four only are the conditions of arising: cause, objective basis, the immediately preceding condition, and the decisive factor; there is no fifth condition . . .
>
> 3 If there are conditions, things are not self-existent; if there is there is no self-existence there is no other-existence.[3]

The four conditions (*pratyayā*) listed in the order of "primary causal, appropriating or objectively extending, sequential or contiguous, and dominantly extending conditions" (*hetu, ālambana, anantara,* and *ādhipatyeya*) occurs nowhere in the *sūtra* literature and does not occur anywhere in Theravādin *abhidharma* literature. It does appear in two of the Sārvāstivādin *abhidharma* texts: the *Vijñānakāya*[4] and the *Prakaraṇapāda*.[5] With one or both of these texts as the target for Nāgārjuna's arguments in this chapter, we may tentatively assume that Nāgārjuna was not writing in a Sarvāstivādin monastery.[6]

Contrary to the opinion of the author of the *Zhonglun,* however, Nāgārjuna's involvement even with *abhidharma* literature is far more complicated than one of simple opposition. Nāgārjuna may have opposed certain notions in the Sarvāstivādin *abhidharma,* but he does not eschew all *abhidharma*. Chapter 5 of the *Ratnāvalī* lists fifty-seven moral faults that Nāgārjuna claims come from a text called the *Kṣudravastuka*. Yukihiro

Okada and Michael Hahn have pointed out that both the *Vibhaṅga* of the Theravādins and in the *Dharmaskandha* of the Sarvāstivādins contain a chapter called *Kṣudravastu* (雜事品 = Pali *Khuddakavattu*).[7] Although a core number of terms are shared by the two texts, the order of the terms in the *Ratnāvalī* is identical to that in the *Dharmaskandha*. For this reason, Okada and Hahn conclude that the Sarvāstivādin *Dharmaskandha* is the best match for the list of fifty-seven in Nāgārjuna's.[8] There is no indication in the *Ratnāvalī* discussion that follows that Nāgārjuna does anything but recommend the study and application of these topical lists (*mātṛkā*). He tells the king, "With vigor you should definitely realize those renowned as the fifty-seven."[9] Thus, while one of Nāgārjuna's works attacks Sarvāstivāda *abhidharma* literature, another appears to support it. This discrepancy requires an explanation.

If Nāgārjuna had lived in a Mahāsāṅghika monastery when he wrote the *Ratnāvalī,* then why would he quote a Sarvāstivādin *abhidharma* text favorably when he had attacked other texts of the same school in his other work? One answer may be that the texts cited in the *Ratnāvalī* may not have been exclusively Sarvāstivādin texts. Scholars who have looked at the basic *abhidharma* texts of the Sarvāstivādins and the Theravādins have noticed that many of the texts seem to have parallels in the other schools. So, for instance, the *Dharmaskandha* of the Sarvāstivādins "closely parallels . . . the Pali *Vibhaṅga* and the first half of the *Śāriputrābhidharmaśāstra*."[10] Similarly, the *Saṅgītiparyāya* is counted as one of the early Sarvāstivādin *abhidharma* texts but is also found in Theravāda and Dharmagupta recensions,[11] and a version of it has also been found at Bāmiyān, a Mahāsāṅghika stronghold.[12] Hence, whereas different schools may have had characteristic collections (at least as far as the early *abhidharma* works are concerned), these works did not necessarily differ considerably from the early works of another school.

The reason for the relative conformity of early *abhidharma* works is not hard to discern. As discussed in Chapter 6, early *abhidharma* texts are concerned with justifying themselves as "word of the Buddha." Consequently, they tend to stick close to the *sūtras*—usually by inserting their topical lists in a "*suttanta* matrix." As we move away from the early texts and *abhidharma* becomes more established, the *abhidharma* treatises begin to be less strictly tied to their *sūtra* moorings. Perhaps, when Nāgārjuna quotes from the *Kṣudravastu,* he is quoting from a Mahāsāṅghika *version* of the *Dharmaskandha/Vibhaṅga*. After all, these versions are not identical—the Sarvāstivādin *Dharmaskandha* has seventy-six *doṣas,* not fifty-seven.

Only the latest two of the Sarvāstivādin "seven-section *abhidharma*" (i.e., the *Vijñānakāya* and the *Prakaraṇapāda*) include the argument that the past, present, and future exist. None of the other five Sarvāstivāda root texts contain this doctrine. Finally, it is only in these two texts that the term *svabhāva* becomes a technical term denoting that part of a *dharma* that exists unchanging in the past, present, and future. Thus it would be possible for Nāgārjuna to refute the Sarvāstivādin doctrine of the four causes and their doctrine of *svabhāva* while *not* dismissing the *abhidharma* project as a whole. Under this interpretation, the *Mūlamadhyamakakārikā* can be read as attacking only two of Sarvāstivāda's latest *abhidharma* root-texts or perhaps their commentaries while upholding a no-longer-extant Mahāsāṅghika *Abhidharma* text (one resembling the *Dharmaskandha*) in the *Ratnāvalī*.

The *Mūlamadhyamakakārikā* and the *Abhidharma* of the Mahāsāmghikas

Most commentators on Nāgārjuna's works have failed to take into consideration the possibility that Nāgārjuna may be positioning himself in relation to more than one corpus of *abhidharma* literature. His references to Sarvāstivādin *abhidharma* literature are the most obvious because theirs is one of the few *abhidharma* collections that has survived. Nevertheless, we cannot conclude that the Sarvāstivādin *abhidharma* was the only *abhidharma* system of importance to him. His take on the positions of some of the other schools can perhaps best be seen in chapter 17, "The Investigation of Karma and Its Fruit" (*Karmaphala Parīkṣā*). In this chapter Nāgārjuna places Mahāyāna into conversation with two different systems of *abhidharma*. With reference only to Nāgārjuna's verses, the chapter may be organized as follows.

- Verses 1–5 introduce certain basic teachings related to karma such as self-restraint, kindness, benevolence (verse 1); Karma of thought and karma of action (verse 2–3); Karma of speech, action, and abandonment, each of which can be either manifest and unmanifest, virtuous or unvirtuous (verse 4–5).
- Verse 6 problematizes the teaching of karma by raising the question of how karma can be spoken of as persisting without falling into either the trap of eternalism (*śāśvatāvāda*) or annihilationism (*ucchedavāda*). These verses emphasize that the apparent continuity of karma is a function of the mind.
- Verses 7–10 respond to the problematic of verse 6 by positing the construct of a "stream" (*saṃtāna*) of *dharmas*. This stream becomes

the substratum for karmic effects while the individual *dharmas* making up the stream remain evanescent.

- Verse 11 introduces the ten paths of pure action.
- Verses 12–20 refute the example of the sprout and seed introduced in verse 7 and introduce another construct, karma as *avipraṇāśa*. The verses declare that this *avipraṇāśa* is an appropriate conceptualization praised by the Buddhas (verse 13), it is originally indeterminate *avyākṛta* (verse 14), it cannot be simply abandoned by the path of seeing but must be abandoned through absorptive meditation, it avoids the faults of eternalism and annihilationism (verses 15–19). Verse 20 states that the Buddha taught the dharmas of emptiness, the fact that *saṃsāra* is neither eternalism nor annihilationism and that karma does not perish (*avipranāśa*).[13]
- Verses 21–33 argue that if karma were to have *svabhāva,* then it would indeed fall into the trap of eternalism and annihilationism, but its emptiness means that it is unarisen, and as it is unarisen it does not fall into the trap of eternalism and annihilationism.

This chapter attempts to reconcile an apparent conflict in scripture. The *Āgamas* teach the persistence and inevitability of karma, on one hand, while they teach that all conditioned (*pratītyasamutpanna*) things avoid the two extremes of eternalism and annihilationism, on the other. Nāgārjuna introduces the Āgamic teachings of karma in verses 1 through 5 and raises the apparent conflicting teaching in verse 6. The commentaries are consistent in identifying verses 7 through 11 as a solution proposed by one non-Mādhyamika school and verses 12 through 20 as belonging to another such school. Unfortunately, the commentaries (including Avalokitavrāta's subcommentary) are equally consistent in not identifying the schools to which these approaches belong.

The first school addresses the problem by introducing the metaphor of the seed and sprout and posits a stream (*saṃtāna*) of dharmas as the substratum that gives rise to karmic effect. Lamotte identifies this speaker as a "Sautrāntika" on the basis of the use of the seed-and-sprout metaphor.[14] Unfortunately, this identification offers little assistance since the Sautrāntikas left no physical trace of themselves—no inscriptions, no cache of manuscripts, nothing to locate them either geographically or historically.[15] Hence, it is uncertain that they were anywhere where Nāgārjuna was and unclear why he would reference their doctrines. The Sautrāntikas were not, however, the only school to use this analogy. As discussed in Chapter 6, the seed-and-sprout metaphor is also ascribed to the Mahāsāṅghikas in the *Samayabhedoparacanacakra*. The Mahāsāṅghikas used the seed-sprout metaphor as a tool to demonstrate that the relationship of karmic cause to karmic fruit was one of a continuum, not of the series of substantially and temporally discrete entities that the Sarvāstivādins claimed it to be.

If Nāgārjuna had been interested in refuting every *abhidharmika* thesis, verse 12 might be expected to be Nāgārjuna's refutation of the stream theory of karmic action. Instead, he has another school criticize the approach of the Mahāsāṅghikas. Nāgārjuna never returns to the seed-and-sprout analogy to refute it. That Nāgārjuna would not directly critique a Mahāsāṅghika doctrine makes sense on two levels. First, nothing in Mahāsāṅghika doctrine inherently would oppose the Mahāyāna doctrine of emptiness because Mahāsāṅghikas never adopted a theory of *svabhāva*, and at least some Mahāsāṅghikas (e.g., the Prajñaptivādins) held that all conditioned *dharmas* were *prajñaptisat* entities anyway. Nāgārjuna would have no reason to refute the Mahāsāṅghika stream theory so long as the stream and the person based on it are acknowledged to be empty. He could certainly argue, as Candrakīrti does, that a seed can develop into a sprout only if it is empty of its own essence. Second, if Nāgārjuna had been a resident in a Mahāsāṅghika monastery when he wrote the *Mūlamadhyamakakārikā*, he would not want to refute one of their theses on the chance that he might offend his fellow monks.

The *Mūlamadhyamakakārikā* includes other instances that appear cater to Mahāsāṅghika tastes as well. From what little is known of the Mahāsāṅghika *abhidharma*, it appears that some of the basic tenets of the *Mūlamadhyamakakārikā* mesh well with doctrines that some of the Mahāsāṅghikas held. Nāgārjuna begins the *Mūlamadhyamakakārikā* with a quotation from a *Prajñāpāramitā* text (as noted in Chapter 5). In the quotation the Buddha teaches that dependent-origination is "non-arising and non-ceasing." This makes dependent-origination essentially unconditioned (*asaṃskṛta*). This equation may seem at odds with scripture, and for many schools of Buddhism it would have been problematic (see, for example, Vasubandhu's objection in volume 5 of the *Abhidharmakośa*, discussed in Chapter 6). However, if the theses that the Mahāsāṅghikas adhered to are considered, Nāgārjuna's quotation of this passage appears to be especially well thought out. For the Theravādins and the Sarvāstivādins, dependent-origination is the epitome of *saṃsāra*. Yet, as discussed in Vasumitra's *Samayabhedoparacanacakra*,[16] a Mahāsāṅghika audience would have been comfortable with the idea that dependent-origination itself was unconditioned. By quoting the *Prajñāpāramitā* passage containing the eight negations in his opening verse, Nāgārjuna begins on what appears to be common ground for the Mahāsāṅghikas.

At this point, let me offer a word of caution. The Mahāsāṅghikas' teachings of dependent-origination and emptiness were not identical to the Mahāyāna (or even the Mādhyamika) teachings. The Mahāsāṅghika notion of emptiness is tied to discussions of absorptive meditation (*samādhi*) and does not venture out into discussions of the way that things are in themselves. Even Nāgārjuna's notion of the absoluteness of dependent-origination was noticeably different from that of the Mahāsāṅghikas. Bhāvaviveka points out that even those non-Mahāyānists who do believe that dependent-origination was unconditioned did not agree with the Mahāyāna articulation of this theory. At one point in the *Prajñāpradīpa,* Bhāvaviveka has a "Sautrāntika" claim that the "Śrāvakayānists" also believe that dependent-origination is "non-arising/non-ceasing" and so forth. Bhāvaviveka then lists reasons why their claim for the unconditioned nature of dependent-origination differs from that of the Mādhyamika.

> *Objection:* Some of [our] fellow Buddhists (*sva-ūthya*), who wish to negate the composition *(ārambha)* of [this] treatise, say: Dependent origination, characterized by non origination, etc., is unconditioned *(asaṃskṛta).* Therefore, it is established for our own position (*pakṣa*) also; and it is not the case that [your] doctrine of dependent-origination is not shared by the Śrāvakas. Therefore it is not appropriate [for Nāgārjuna] to compose [this] treatise.

> Bhāvaviveka responds:

> *Answer:* [Our doctrine of dependent origination is not shared by the śrāvakas] [1] because [we] teach dependent origination, characterized by non origination, etc., by means of negation, and [2] because there is no inference for showing that unconditioned dependent origination exists. If [you] suppose that origination from definite causal conditions is just unconditioned, [that is not so] because origination has been negated; therefore it is not possible that [being unconditioned] is a property[*dharma*] of that [origination]. [Moreover] [Thesis:] Origination is not unconditioned, [Reason:] because it possesses a cause, [Example:] like continuation [*sthiti*]. By inference, that [unconditioned dependent origination] does not exist; therefore it is not the case that [this treatise] is not appropriate.[17]

Thus, whereas some non-Mahāyānists saw dependent-origination as unconditioned, the later Mādhyamikas distinguished themselves from these by claiming that if origination did exist it would be conditioned.

Origination, however, is empty, according to the Mādhyamika, and only then can it be unconditioned.

Whether or not Nāgārjuna's use of a particular doctrine is identical to its non-Mahāyāna context is not the point. The point is that Nāgārjuna uses doctrines with the greatest similarity to those of his audience as the focal point of his arguments. He does this in order to best effect a shift in the way his audience reads their own tradition. The Mahāsāṅghikas never said that *saṃsāra* is not different from nirvāṇa (as Nāgārjuna does), but they left open the way to this statement by saying that dependent-origination is unconditioned. Nor did the Mahāsāṅghikas claim that all *dharmas* are empty of their own nature, but again, they left open the possibility with their discussions of emptiness in meditation.

Nāgārjuna may have tried to capitalize on Mahāyāna's doctrinal similarities to the creeds that his audience already held. Mahāsāṅghikas were quite comfortable with discussions about emptiness, though, again, a slightly different version of emptiness than the one Nāgārjuna was advocating. This is evident in the *Mahāsāṅghika vinaya*. In the section defining "word of the Buddha," the text mentions the teaching that "all dharmas are suffering, *empty,* impermanent and not self."[18] This statement on its own is not sufficient to place Nāgārjuna in the Mahāsāṅghika camp. Most schools of Buddhism hold the teaching of emptiness to be an important doctrine in one way or another. Most regard "emptiness" as a synonym for selflessness. However, the Mahāsāṅghikas were open to blurring the distinction between conditioned and unconditioned reality in a manner quite similar to Nāgārjuna (as seen in Chapter 6). Furthermore, there seems to be a parallel between the path implicit in the *Mūlamadhyamakakārikā* and that of the Mahāsāṅghikas. Nāgārjuna's version of Mahāyāna melds the fruit of absorptive meditation (i.e., the pacification of *saṃjñā*) with the method of contemplative meditation (i.e., analysis of reality using the concepts from *saṃjñā*). Note that the *Mūlamadhyamakakārikā* consists of twenty-seven chapters of *reasoned arguments*. There certainly seems to be a connection between the correct functioning of reason and the attainment of mental pacification. For example, after one of his typical logical analyses of the relationship between a characteristic and the characterized thing in Chapter 5, the last two verses implicitly connect the preceding discussion to the ultimate goal of a pacified state of mind.

> Therefore, space is not an entity, non-entity, characterization or characteristics. The rest of the other five *dhātus* can be treated in the same manner as space.

> Those of low intelligence (i.e., inferior insight) who see only the existence and non-existence of things cannot perceive the wonderful quiescence (*upaśamaṃ śivaṃ*) of things.[19]

Although the connection between analytical conviction and the pacification of mental proliferation (*prapañca*) is only implied here, it is significant that Nāgārjuna only discusses reasoned analysis in his works and does not encourage the traditional stages of *dhyāna* even in the *Ratnāvalī*. The Mahāsāṅghikas may well have been open to Nāgārjuna's approach to reasoned analysis, because they believed that one could attain the goal through *prajñā* alone and that *saṃjñā* functions even in the highest states of absorption.

The Mahāsāṅghikas were not the only Buddhist sect that may have been receptive to Mahāyāna. At least one other school, the Dharmaguptas, taught a version of emptiness that comes close to the Mahāyāna version.[20] The one surviving *abhidharma* text of the Dharmagupta school is the *Śāriputrābhidharmaśāstra*. According to Shingyo Yoshimoto:

> This text is one of the oldest Abhidharma texts in India. . . . This text has some common contents and thought with *Vibhaṅga* and *Prakaraṇapāda*. Perhaps the root of this text may be the text of the Vibhajyavādins before it split into Theravāda, Kāśyapīya, Mahīśāsaka, and so on. But the dominant view of the scholastic affiliation of the extant text is that it may have belonged to the Dharmaguptaka.[21]

In its discussion of the emptiness absorption (空定, *śūnyatā samādhi*), the *Śāriputrābhidharmaśāstra* contains a list of six kinds of emptinesses: internal emptiness (内空), external emptiness (外空), internal and external emptiness (内外空), emptiness of emptiness (空空), great emptiness (大空), and ultimate emptiness (第一義空).[22] Although the Dharmaguptas were apparently not the only ones to use lists of emptinesses (the *Mahāvibhāṣā* ascribes a similar lists to the Sarvāstivādin's own *Prajñaptiśāstra*),[23] this particular list of six emptinesses seems to have been a favorite among Mahāyānists other than Nāgārjuna. The list is included verbatim in the lists of emptinesses found in some rather prominent Mahāyāna *sūtras*, such as the *Pañcaviṃśati-sāhasrikā Prajñāpāramitā*,[24] and the *Śatasāhasrikā Prajñāpāramitā*.[25] Curiously, this list is not found in the *Aṣṭasāhasrikā Prajñāpāramitā*. Since this list is unique to the *Śāriputrābhidharmaśāstra* (it does not appear in the *Prakaraṇapāda* or the *Vibaṅga*), perhaps the authors of the *Pañcaviṃśati-Sāhasrikā Prajñāpāramitā* and the *Śatasāhasrikā*

Prajñāpāramitā were writing to an audience familiar with Dharmagupta doctrine, while the author of the *Aṣṭasāhasrikā Prajñāpāramitā* was not. By the same token, given the fact that Nāgārjuna never uses any of these terms in his works (imagine how much mileage he could have derived from a term like "the emptiness of emptiness"!), his audience likely was not Dharmagupta.

The *Mūlamadhyamakakārikā* and the *Prajñaptivādins*

The fit between Nāgārjuna's logical method and the theses of the Mahāsāṅghikas (detailed in Chapter 6) appears even tighter if his method of argumentation is seen in light of the theses of the Prajñaptivādins. The Prajñaptivādins held that (depending on how it is read) suffering is *prajñapti* based on conditioned entities that are themselves reciprocally designated (*anyonya prajñapti*). Other schools of Buddhism had lists of types of *prajñapti,* but, as far as I am aware, no school held a doctrine of "reciprocal-designation" (*anyonya prajñapti*) apart from the Prajñaptivādins.

Although he never states so explicitly, many of Nāgārjuna's arguments arguably aim to reveal the phenomena they investigate to be *prajñaptis* with no substantial basis whatsoever. In his study of Nāgārjuna's argumentation, David Burton makes exactly this claim.

> emptiness (the absence of *svabhāva* of entities) appears to mean both that entities are dependently arisen (*pratītyasamutpanna*) and that they do not have foundational existence (*dravyasat*). Which is to say that all dependently arisen entities have merely conceptually constructed existence (*prajñaptisat*). Thus the entities which dependently arise are like a dream.[26]

and elsewhere:

> It can be argued, therefore, that Nāgārjuna means that dependently arisen entities do not have *svabhāva* in the Abhidharma sense, i.e., they are not *dravyasat.* Which is to say that they are *prajñaptisat.* (In Abhidharma terms these are the only possible categories. Whatever is not *dravyasat* must be *prajñaptisat*). This would explain why the dependently arisen entity which arises without *svabhāva* cannot be called 'arisen.' That is, there are no real, *dravya,* dependently arising

entities. All dependently arising entities are conceptually constructed (*prajñapti*) and in this sense their arising is unreal.[27]

Here Burton claims that Nāgārjuna is exploiting the fact that all conditioned dharmas (defined by their *svabhāva*) arise according to causes and conditions to argue that all *dharmas* are composite and thus *prajñaptisat*. Under this interpretation, all *dharmas* are nothing but composite *prajñapti* and there are no foundational substances or essences anywhere.

Burton's assessment is essentially correct, but it is the *manner* in which he is correct that is relevant to this study. Under Burton's reading, Nāgārjuna tries to demonstrate that what other Buddhists see as ultimately existing (i.e., irreducible) *dravyasat* entities are in fact just designations for composite *prajñaptisat* entities. Most Buddhist schools believed that at least the aggregates (*skandha*) and the atomic elements (*dhātu*) were ultimately existent entities. Vasubandhu summarizes the distinction between ultimate existence and conventional existence in his *Abhidharmakośabhāṣya*.

The Blessed One proclaimed four truths; he has also declared two truths, the relative truth [*saṃvṛtisatya*], [and] the absolute truth. What are these two truths?

[Verse 4] The idea of the pot comes to an end when the pot is destroyed; the idea of water comes to an end, by the mind [*buddhi*] analyzing the water. The pot and the water, and everything they resemble exist relatively. The rest exist absolutely.

If the idea of a thing disappears [*na pravartate*] when that thing is broken into pieces, that thing exists relatively [*saṃvṛtisat*], for example, a pot: the idea of the pot disappears when it is reduced to shards. If the idea of a thing disappears when with the mind one dissolves [*apohyān dharmān*] the thing, that thing should be regarded as existing relatively; for example, water. If, in the water, we take and remove the dharmas such as color, etc. the idea of water disappears.

That which is different is the absolute truth. When a thing is broken down or dissolved by the mind, the idea of that thing continues, that thing exists absolutely [*paramārthasat*]; for example *rūpa;* one can reduce the *rūpa* to atoms, one can withdraw by the mind the flavor and the other dharmas, and the idea of the essential nature of *rūpa* persists. The same goes for sensation, etc.[28]

Yaśomitra's commentary on this passage is helpful.

> There are two examples to illustrate the two meanings of "division" [*bheda*]. The pot etc. [are broken down] due to being split by violence [*upakramabheda*]. Water, etc. are [broken down] due to being split by the mind [*buddhibheda*]. [The second type of splitting is mentioned] because it is not possible to remove [*apakarṣaṇa*] flavor, etc. by violence in the case of water, etc. Alternately, there are [another] two kinds of conventionally existing [*saṃvṛti*] entities; conventionally existing entities that are based in [*vyapāśraya*] other conventionally existing entities and conventionally existing entities that are based on substantial entities.[29]

According to Vasubandhu, a thing qualifies as conventionally existing if it can be broken down. The "breaking down" (*bheda*, lit. "splitting") can either be a physical dismemberment, as in the case of pots and chariots, or it can be a mental "breakdown" as a kind of analysis. What does it mean to break down something mentally? One denies or mentally removes an element from the thing to see if its existence is still conceivable. Vasubandhu identifies what is removed as the *apohya dharma*. *Apoha*, from *apa-* (away) + √*ūh* (thrust), can mean either physically removing or logically denying.[30] Yaśomitra paraphrases the process using the term *apakarṣaṇa*. Like *apoha*, the term *apakarṣaṇa* comes from the verb √*kṛṣ* (to draw away, to take away, or to draw out).[31] The prefix *apa-* strengthens the sense of "away from," hence *apakarṣaṇa* means "taking away," "removing," or "denying." If one mentally conjures up an image of water and then imagines flavor and all the other concomitant characteristics of water removed from it, the image disappears.

Paramārtha, in his commentary on this passage explicitly equates the category of conventional existence with the category of *prajñaptisat* and goes on to describe three ways that a thing can exist as a *prajñapti*.

> If the idea of a thing does not occur any more after the thing has been smashed, that thing exists conventionally [*saṃvṛtisat*] When the pot is reduced to fired earth, the idea of the pot does not occur any more apart from that fired earth. Therefore, things such as the pot exist as a metaphorical designation (*prajñapti*) for the figure . . . In the second place, if the idea of a thing does not occur any more when, by the mind, one removes from that thing the other dharmas, that thing exists conventionally, like water. If, from the water, one removes with the mind the color, the flavor, the elements (*mahābhūta*), etc., the idea of the water is no longer produced. Therefore the things such as water exist as a metaphorical designation in com-

> bination (*tsiu tsi, samavāya?*). In the third case, it is by the names, phrases and syllables . . . that one expresses the *paramārtha,* the real thing; it is due to the names that there is produced a relative flavor of *paramārtha.*[32]

Although all of the above accounts postdate Nāgārjuna, they each articulate a test by which a given *dharma* is classed as *saṃvṛtisat* or *paramārthasat*/*prajñaptisat* or *dravyasat.* All accounts agree that a thing is a *prajñapti* if it can be either physically broken (*upakramabheda*) or cognitively dissected (*buddhibheda*) through the mental extraction of some factor necessary but not identical to the thing itself.

Clearly, Nāgārjuna is attempting the latter procedure in his *Mūlamadhyamakakārikā.* According to the above definitions, the threshold criteria by which conventional truth is distinguished from ultimate truth is whether the concept under investigation remains intact after a foreign but necessary factor is identified and mentally removed. When he investigates the concept of *rūpa* in the chapter 4 of his *Mūlamadhyamakakārikā,* Nāgārjuna applies the exact same procedure to the aggregates. The opening two verses read as follows.

> 1 Material form [*rūpa*] separated from the efficient cause [*kāraṇa*] cannot be conceived. Moreover, separated from material form the efficient cause cannot be seen.
>
> 2 If material form is separated from efficient cause, then it follows that form will be without a cause. However, nowhere is there a thing existing without a cause.[33]

The term that Inada translates as "efficient cause" (*kāraṇa*) might better be translated as "material cause." Qingmu's *Zhonglun* commentary (T. 1564) on the first verse illustrates the relationship with the analogy of threads and a cloth.

> As for "cause of form," it is like threads being the cause of cloth. If you take away the threads, there is no cloth, and if you cast away the cloth, there is no thread. The cloth is like form, the threads are like its cause.[34]

Similarly, Candrakīrti glosses material form (*rūpa*) as *bhautika:* "that which is made of the elements [*bhūta*]."[35] He glosses *kāraṇa,* then, as "the four elements." Thus, in the first two stanzas, material form and material cause stand in relation to each other as *bhūta* and *bhautika.* Put in this stark manner, it is certainly reasonable to say that a material thing (*bhautika*) cannot be conceived apart from the material element or elements that comprise it any more than a cloth can be conceived apart from its threads. Put in the language of the Sarvāstivāda texts quoted above, Nāgārjuna is breaking down the concept of *rūpa* mentally by removing one of its factors, namely, its material cause. On this analysis, the concept of *rūpa* is no longer conceivable apart from the concept of its material cause. By the above definitions, Nāgārjuna has shown that *rūpa* ultimately does not exist at all, but is only conventionally existent. To the extent that the material cause is a necessary feature for the concept of *rūpa* to occur, *rūpa* is a *prajñapti*, not a *dravya*. To use Paramārtha's typology, Nāgārjuna's analysis shows *rūpa* to be a "*prajñapti* in combination."

So far so good. Nāgārjuna follows a method of analysis to which the Sarvāstivādins would have no objection, and by verse 5 he arrives at the conclusion that the *rūpaskandha* is a *prajñaptisat* entity. This is not surprising since collectivity is implied in the very word *skandha*. But it is *how* the components occur in relation to one another that reflects innovation. Consider: why did Nāgārjuna chose to mentally "draw out" material cause in his analysis? In the example given in the *Abhidharmakośabhāṣya,* only features that might be considered "accidental" are mentally excluded from the thing through analysis. The Sarvāstivādins might object that the material cause that Nāgārjuna excerpts is essential to *rūpa* itself and therefore hardly an accidental property. The key lies in Nāgārjuna's verse 6.

> It is untenable that the effect [*kārya*] will resemble the efficient cause [*kāraṇa*]. Again, it is untenable that the effect [*kārya*] will not resemble the efficient cause [*kāraṇa*].[36]

Although verses like this have been the cause of numerous headaches for modern logically inclined interpreters of Nāgārjuna,[37] Nāgārjuna's subtle shift in terminology offers a clue as to what he is doing. The verses up to this point had examined the relationship between *rūpa* (form) and *kāraṇa* (cause). Verse 6 slips in *kārya* (future passive participle of √*kṛ* [to make, lit. "that which is to be caused," i.e., effect]) for *rūpa*.

The pair *kārya/kāraṇa* make explicit the relationship that Nāgārjuna wants to make evident in *rūpa/kāraṇa*. If the concept of *rūpa* as the thing that is caused is no longer possible when its *kāraṇa* or cause is removed, then the concept of *rūpa* is a *prajñapti* brought about by some kind of combination of the cause and effect. In the *kārya/kāraṇa* pair, if either *kāraṇa* or *kārya* are removed through *apakarṣaṇa,* the remaining concept is no longer possible. The relationship between the two is not a temporal relationship but one of reciprocal necessity. If one mentally removes the concept of "cause," there can be no concept of "the caused (thing)" any more than if one removes the concept of the "caused (thing)" the concept of the cause can no longer occur. Hence, each of the two exists as a *prajñapti* depending on the other one reciprocally. In the *Vigrahavyāvartanī,* Nāgārjuna illustrates this type of relationship with the analogy of "father and son."[38] The son exists as a son only by virtue of the father. The father exists as a father only by virtue of the son. "Father" and "son" could then be said to be designated reciprocally (*anyonya prajñapti*).

We now have three things. There is the *dharma*, *rūpa* that is a *prajñapti* depending on two other *prajñaptis—kārya* and *kāraṇa*. The latter two *prajñaptis,* however, are designated depending on each other, thus the three are each *prajñaptis* based on a necessary relationship to something else within the triad. And yet the system does not seem to require an ultimate basis in something substantial. This triadic structure is surely reminiscent of the Prajñaptivādins thesis that all conditioned (*saṃskṛta*) *dharmas* are reciprocally designated (*anyonya prajñapti*) and that suffering is designated on this basis. That his argument would have been acceptable to the Prajñaptivādins is further aided by the fact that one of their cardinal theses, according to Vasumitra, was that none of the aggregates (e.g., *rūpa*) existed ultimately in the first place. Hence, Nāgārjuna is arguing for a thesis that the Prajñaptivādins already held, using a concept of *prajñapti* that they were already using.

But surely the conundrum that Nāgārjuna raises could be solved by admitting a simple identity between the material cause and the form, in the same way that the cloth is nothing other then the threads that comprise it. The *Abhidharmakośa* example excludes accidental factors from *rūpa,* such as taste, in order to prove that it is ultimate. By removing matter from *rūpa,* isn't Nāgārjuna essentially trying to remove *rūpa* from *rūpa*?

The next chapter of the *Mūlamadhyamakakārikā* moves on to the concept of *dhātu* (the elements) itself. Here again, *dhātu* cannot be conceived apart from the reciprocally designated concepts of characteristic (*lakṣaṇa*) and that-which-is-to-be-characterized (*lakṣya*), and the latter two cannot be conceived apart from each other. Nāgārjuna shows thereby that a *dharma* the Sarvāstivādins thought to be ultimately existing (space) is, in fact, composite. The *Mūlamadhyamakakārikā* uses this structure of argumentation in many chapters. Musashi Tachikawa catalogues all the ways that Nāgārjuna distributes his terms in the *Mūlamadhyamakakārikā.* His list contains the arguments of many earlier chapters involving the interplay between reciprocally designated groups of words.[39]

CHAPTER	TERMS
II	*gata/agata/gamyamāna/gantṛ/gati*
	"that which has been traversed"/"that which has not yet been traversed"/"that which is currently being traversed"/"goer"/"going"
III	*darṣaṇa/draṣṭṛ*
	"sight"/"seer"
IV	*kārya/kāraṇa*
	"that which is to be caused"/"cause"
V	*lakṣya/lakṣaṇa*
	"that which is to be characterized"/"the characteristic"
VI	*rāga/rakta*
	"passion"/"the impassioned one"
VII	*utpāda/utpanna/anutpanna/utpadyamāna*
	"arising"/"the arisen"/"the not yet arisen"/"the arising thing"
	sthitabhāva/ asthitabhāva/tiṣṭhamāna
	"the thing that has stood"/"the thing that has not yet stood"/"the standing thing"
	niruddha/aniruddha/nirudhyamāna
	"the extinguished"/"the not yet extinguished"/"the thing being extinguished"
VIII	*karma/kāraka*
	"action"/"agent"
XXIII	*kleśa/kliṣṭa*
	"the defilement"/"the defiled"

The key to Nāgārjuna's method in the arguments that distribute their terms in this fashion appears to lie in the fact that, for any verbal noun, the passive participle will be entailed in the verbal noun but will not be identical to it. "A killer" implies that there is "something killed," but there is a huge difference between killing and being killed.

Indeed, the fact that Nāgārjuna founds his apparent paradoxes on these kind of reciprocal relations is tacitly recognized by Candrakīrti. In a brief comment on verse 8 of chapter 6 ("Investigation of Passion and the Impassioned"), Candrakīrti states that one of the reasons that the opponent has difficulties establishing either the simultaneity or the priority of *rāga* and *rakta* is that they have each other as a basis (*itaretarāśraya*). Here, Mervyn Sprung's translation gets the sense of the passage.

> It being thus clear that the opponent's proof is established on a reciprocal relationship, which of the two is the basis of proof and which is the proven? [Nāgārjuna's verse 9:] "That is to say if separateness does not exist, simultaneity cannot establish it; but if separateness does exist then what simultaneity can you have in mind."[40]

Although Candrakīrti does not elaborate on this remark, he seems to suggest that the opponent will get nowhere trying to establish either simultaneity or priority when the two terms are reciprocally dependent.

My primary aim in this chapter is to explain why Nāgārjuna made the philosophical choices that he did, not to demonstrate the validity of his arguments. Nevertheless, some of Burton's difficulties with Nāgārjuna's methodology can be cleared up by the above discussion. One of Burton's concerns is that Nāgārjuna showed that all *dharmas* exist as *prajñapti,* but only by conflating the teaching that some *dharmas* are dependently originated with the teaching that some things are *prajñaptisat,* thereby doing violence to both doctrines and making philosophical moves that would not have been acceptable within the Sarvāstivāda *abhidharma* system. Burton states his objection:

> Nāgārjuna says . . . that the dependent origination of entities is incompatible with their possession of *svabhāva.* Taken at face-value, this means simply that all entities dependently arise, and therefore they do not have independent existence. However—and this is a crucial point—in Abhidharma philosophy the dependent origination of some entities, i.e., *saṃskṛta dharma-s* is said to be actually compatible with their possession of *svabhāva*. In other words, according to Abhidharma thought possession of *svabhāva* does not entail independent existence.
>
> For the Ābhidharmika, *svabhāva* is attributed to *dharma-s* because *dharma-s* are independent of causes and conditions in a specific sense. Dharma-s are not dependent upon parts for their existence. The *dharma-s* are the foundational components of the world. They are not further analyzable into constituents, and they are the constituents of all other entities. These *dharma-s* are, for the Ābhidharmikas, "ultimate truths" (*paramārthasatya*), and have "substantial" or primary existence (*dravyasat*).[41]

And later:

> It is arguable, however, that Nāgārjuna's general tendency to equate lack of *svabhāva* with dependence on causes and conditions, rather than specifically with dependence on parts, indicates a subtle shift in the meaning of *svabhāva*.[42]

In other words, by claiming that dependently originated entities lacked *svabhāva* and were *prajñaptisat* or conventionally existing entities, Nāgārjuna was making a move that was not warranted by the *abhidharma* system that he critiqued. Lack of *svabhāva* could be proved in that system only if the *dharma* can be shown to have parts, and to call the causes and conditions of dependent-origination "parts" is to do violence to the very notion of "parts." Hence, "the Ābhidharmikas" would always keep the concept of dependently originated entities (*pratītyasamutpanna*) separate from the concept of dependently designated entities (*prajñaptisat*).

Several points need to be made here. The first is that the definition of *upādāya prajñapti* as "a thing being designated on its parts" is only one definition of that term, and not one that is necessarily emphasized in the *Abhdharmakośa* and its commentaries. All that the *Abhidharmakośa* and its commentaries seem to be saying is that if, when one mentally removes a factor from a given concept, that concept is no longer possible, then the concept is not an ultimately existing *dharma*. In fact, as Leonard Priestley has ably demonstrated, there were several definitions of what constitutes a *prajñapti* in Sarvāstivādin and Theravādin *abhidharma* literature.[43] Of course, *prajñapti* is commonly defined as a designation based on its own parts like a chariot based on the wheels, and so on. However, other definitions of *upādāya prajñapti* are broader than this and include designations based on things that are not necessarily internal parts. For example, in the Theravādin *Puggalapaññatti Aṭṭhakathā:*

> There, in the case of [the person, who is really] *rūpa, vedana,* etc., just like *rūpa, vedāna,* etc. are either identical or different [from the person], the essence [of the person] is not apprehended truly and ultimately. [So too] (the person *satta*) is considered as having done a deed (*kāraṇa*) by means of and *depending on* [*upādāya*] the aggregates divided into rūpa, vedāna, etc. [Or] the chariot, the house, the fist (are designated) *depending on* (their respective) parts bound together. [Or] the pot, the cloth (are designated) *depending on* each *rūpa,* etc. [Or] time and space (are designated) *depending on* the revolution of the sun and the moon. [Or] the one considered to have acted on ac-

> count of and *depending on* each of the elements and the benefits of meditation has established the "learning sign" and the "counterpart sign" by each aspect. The same goes for the so-called *upādāya prajñapti*. It is a designation through that which is to be designated, not through what has already been designated. Moreover, it (the *upādāya prajñapti*) is a designation of that object, (hence) it is (classed as) "a designation of what does not exist.[44]

Burton understands Nāgārjuna's argument as demonstrating that all things are *prañaptisat,* but that Nāgārjuna's argument fails because the model of *upādāya prajñapti* that he seems to be employing does not fit the analogy of the chariot and its parts. The passage from the *Puggalapaññatti Aṭṭhakathā,* however, amply demonstrates that Buddhists at the time had a broader notion of the concept than is illustrated in that one analogy. Certainly the revolution of the sun and the moon cannot be considered "parts" of time in the same way that an axel is part of a chariot. Nor can the external meditation object be considered "part" of the internal meditative object. Yet both of these are said to be *prajñaptis* depending on something.

As for Burton's claim that the doctrine of *prajñapti* and that of dependent-origination must be kept separate, he may be correct as far as the twelve links of dependent-origination go. However, it seems that a more important articulation of dependent-origination for Nāgārjuna is found in its summary from the *Saṃyutta Nikāya:*

> Thus when this exists, that comes to be; with the arising of this, that arises. When this does not exist, that does not come to be; with the cessation of this, that ceases.[45]

Here dependent-origination is stated in terms of the necessary *conditions* for something to be. This does indeed seem to lie at the heart of the very criterion that Sarvāstivādins used to determine whether or not an entity ultimately existed.

Another of Burton's objections can be addressed in light of the Prajñaptivādin's concept of *anyonya prajñapti.* Burton worries that Nāgārjuna's demonstration that all *dharmas* are *prajñaptisat* leads to an infinite regress (*anavasthā*).

> Conceptually constructed entity *z* might be constructed on the basis of *y*. *Y* might also be constructed on the basis of *x*. And so on. But at some point this regress must stop. Not everything can be a product of conceptual construction, because 'conceptual construction' re-

quires a basis or material which is not itself conceptually constructed. To claim otherwise would be to advocate that the entire world is created *ex nihilo!*[46]

Part of Burton's objection can be answered, although probably not to his satisfaction, by the doctrine of reciprocal designation. *Rūpa* and so forth are designated on the basis of *kārya/kāraṇa*. But because these two are designated based on each other, like two sheaves of reeds leaning one against the other (to use a metaphor commonly associated with dependent-origination) there is no regress. This is a not a temporal relationship of causal dependency but an atemporal relationship of conditional necessity. No further element is necessary.

Fortunately, Nāgārjuna did not have to convince the Sarvāstivādins that they were defeated. If the thesis presented here is correct, all he needed to do was to convince the monks in his home monastery that the Sarvāstivādins were defeated. This is why the standards of the Prajñaptivādins become important. The Sarvāstivādins may not have accepted that conditioned entities could exist as reciprocally designated, but the Prajñaptivādins did.

It would not serve Nāgārjuna's purposes simply to echo Prajñaptivādin doctrine, nor am I arguing that he did. Indeed, in places the *Mūlamadhyamakakārikā* critiques reciprocality. Consider the following verses from the "Investigation of Fire and Fuel":

9 If fire is dependent on fuel and fuel is dependent on fire, which of the two arises prior, that on which fire is dependent or that on which fuel is dependent? . . .

10 One thing is established as dependent on the very thing which is dependent on it. If what is to be dependent is posited as already existing, which depends on which? . . .

11 How can a supposedly dependent entity be dependent if it does not exist? On the other hand it does not make sense that an existing entity should be dependent on a dependent entity.[47]

Verse 9 raises the question of mutual dependency and reduces it to a matter of two separate causalities. As Candrakīrti alludes to in his commentary on "Passion and the Impassioned One," neither priority nor simultaneity can be established in a case where each thing has its basis in the other reciprocally. Despite a lack of evidence that the Prajñaptivādins took their *anyonya prajñapti* this far, it can be surmised that Nāgārjuna wanted them to take it this far, in order for them to see that their doctrine entails emptiness.

The *Mūlamadhyamakakārikā* and the Pudgalavāda *Abhidharma*

Chapter 17 Revisited

However, just because the *Mūlamadhyamakakārikā* shows some affinities to Mahāsāṅghika doctrine, we cannot assume that the Mahāsāṅghikas were its only intended audience. Authors seldom have only one reader in mind, and it is possible that Nāgārjuna knew that his treatise would also be read by sects other than the Mahāsāṅghikas. Evidence of this can be seen again in *Mūlamadhyamakakārikā,* chapter 17. As mentioned above, Nāgārjuna himself never refutes the metaphor of the seed and sprout in chapter 17. In verse 12 of that chapter, he has another speaker object that the Mahāsāṅghika's metaphor (*kalpanā*) of the seed, and the sprout is not appropriate to explain karma. The new speaker claims that a more appropriate metaphor would be one that comes from the *Āgamas* themselves. Here the doctrine of the "indestructible" (*avipraṇāśa)* is introduced. It is appropriate because "it has been praised by the Buddhas, *pratyekabuddhas* and the *śravakas*" (i.e., it is "word of the Buddha").[48] Again, the commentaries are mostly silent as to the identity of this new speaker. Avalokitavrāta comes closest to identifying this school when he says that the doctrine of *avipraṇāśa* is put forth by "someone from the outskirts of the Vaibhāṣikas."[49] In light of the discussion in Chapter 6, however, this doctrine could belong either to the Saṃmitīyas, for whom it was a signature doctrine,[50] or to the Prajñaptivādins and the "Andhakas," who had a version of this theory under the name *upacaya* (accumulation). The Saṃmitīyas seem to be the best choice. Because the speaker of verses 12 through 20 reprimands the speaker of verses 7 through 11, we have to assume the speakers were understood to be of two different schools.

At this point, a problem emerges. Nāgārjuna has just introduced theories of the way that karma works belonging to two different Buddhist sects. In his response (verses 21 through 33) he would be expected to refute both positions. Indeed, he could have easily dispensed with the seed-sprout theory using arguments similar to the ones he uses in chapter 8. By the same token, he could have just as easily refuted the theory of *avipraṇāśa* by questioning the relationship between the karma and the *avipraṇāśa* that bears it. His response in verses 21 through 33 does neither. Instead, he discusses the implications that would accrue if karma had an essence (*svabhāva*). The problem is that it is not immediately obvious how, or even if, Nāgārjuna's arguments establishing karma's lack of *svabhāva* pertain to either of the prior points of view. Neither the Sautrāntikas nor the Mahāsāṅghikas in their articulation of the first position ever assumed the seed or sprout to have *svabhāva*. Indeed, the *Abhidharmakośa* records the Sautrāntika theory of *bīja* as being in opposition to the Sarvāstivādin's own theory of karma.[51]

The same goes for the Saṃmitīya/Prajñaptivādin theory of *avipraṇāśa/upacaya*. Any entity labeled "indestructible" would seem to lend itself to notions of substantiality, just like the notion of *svabhāva*. Nevertheless, little evidence points to the Saṃmitīyas as taking *avipraṇāśa* to be a substance, and *no* evidence indicates that they held anything like the Sarvāstivādin doctrine of *svabhāva*. It should be remembered that the Sarvāsitvādins came up with the notion of *svabhāva* in the *Vijñānakāya* as a response to the *pudgalavādins'* theory of karma (just as the Mahāsāṅghika theory of karmic continuity was a response to the same Sarvāstivādin *svabhāva* theory). The characteristics of this *avipraṇāśa* as listed in the various sources seem to point in the other direction. Although the *Saṃmitīya Nikāya Śāstra* itself is of little help, Nāgārjuna himself has its proponent in verse 14 claim that this *avipraṇāśa* is *avyākṛta*.[52] Whereas commentaries like Candrakīrti's *Prasannapadā* take this to mean that the *avipraṇāśa* is *morally* neutral, if the doctrine does indeed come from the Saṃmitīyas, this *avyākṛta* is better read as "indeterminate" (the Vātsīputrīya's fifth category of existence called *avyākṛta* (ineffable, i.e., that which is neither conditioned nor unconditioned). This is especially so since the Mahāsāṅghikas did not admit the existence of such a thing as moral neutrality. This interpretation would fit both with the Pudgalavādins' own statements about *pudgala* as the substratum of karma and with Buddhaghosa's statement that it is *anārammaṇa* (objectless).

The only dissenting voice is that of Vasubandhu, who in his *Karmasiddhiprakaraṇa* states that the *avipraṇāśa* is "a separate dharma, existing in and of itself (*dravyasat*) and classed among things not associated with the mind (*cittaviprayuktasaṃskāra*)."[53] Although Avalokitavrāta and Buddhaghosa agree that it is dissociated from the mind, Vasubandhu's statement that the *avipraṇāśa* exists *dravyatas* (substantially) does not seem to fit. Indeed, it is questionable whether this sentence was in the original text. The sentence in question occurs in the Tibetan translation that Lamotte uses, as well as in Xuanzang's seventh-century translation.[54] The sentence is noticeably absent, however, in the earliest extant translation, that of Bimuzhixian (毘目智仙), finished in 541.

How can the fact that Nāgārjuna's arguments in verses 21 through 33 seem to miss their mark be explained? Was Nāgārjuna merely making a "straw-man" argument, was he simply not very familiar with the Pudgalavādins' doctrines, or was he giving his own views of karma in these verses? Some modern translators, such as David Kalupahana, take verses 12 through 20 as Nāgārjuna's own position, contending that, since the indestructibility of karma is "word of the Buddha," Nāgārjuna cannot argue against it.[55] I cannot go along with this position, because the term *avipranāśa* itself, along with the way that Nāgārjuna speaks about it, is idiosyncratically Saṃmitīya. The only possible explanation is that Nāgārjuna wishes to show that the Saṃmitīya position is possible *if and only if* they acknowledge the Mahāyāna thesis of emptiness. Indeed, Nāgārjuna's statement in chapter 24, verse 14, may be regarded as a statement of Nāgārjuna's objective.

> All things make sense [*yujyate*] for him for whom the absence of being [*śūnyatā*] makes sense. Nothing makes sense for him for whom the absence of being does not make sense.[56]

In other words, Nāgārjuna's response to the Saṃmitīyas in this chapter (as with his response to the Mahāsāṅghikas throughout) is an attempt to forge an alliance with the school.

A clearer picture of what Nāgārjuna might be doing emerges in his *Śūnyatāsaptati* and its (auto?) commentary. Verse 33 of the *Śūnyatāsaptati* also raises the issue of *avipraṇāśa* (Tibetan, *chud mi za ba*), and in that text there can be no question that this verse represents the opinion of the opponent. Indeed, verses 33 through 34 of the *Śūnyatāsaptati* closely mirror the structure and themes of chapter 17 of the *Mūlamadhyamakakārikā*.[57] The verses and their commentary are as follows:

33 The Blessed one, the teacher has taught of karma's existence, karma's essence, karma's fruit, and the essence of the karma of sentient beings. He has taught that karmas are *avipranāśa*.

> From the Āgamas of the Bhagavat, karma and the fruit of karma are also taught to be not identical [*yaṅ rnam pa du ma–anekadhā*]. Nor are karmic actions taught to be without fruit. It is also said that karma is indestructible [*chud mi za ba–avipranāśa*] and that sentient beings are not said to be the owner of karma [*das bdag gir bya ba*]. This has also been said (by the Buddha). If this is the case then karma and the fruit of karma (must) exist.

34 Due to the fact that *svabhāva* is taught to not exist, that karma which is non-arising is not destroyed. The grasping of self produces karma. But the grasping of its increase is due to *vikalpa*.

> Due to the fact that the *svabhāva* of karma is taught to not exist, as something non-arising it is not perishing [*de 'jig pa med–avināśa*]. Furthermore, grasping at self, karma arises. Because of that, karma, when it arises due to the grasping of self [*ātmagrāha*], it also arises from mental discrimination [*vikalpa*].[58]

In verse 34 and its commentary, Nāgārjuna uses a strategy similar to the strategies discussed in Chapter 3, which examined the verse from the *Ratnāvalī* identifying the Mahāyāna term "emptiness" with the common Buddhist term *kṣaya* to show that Mahāyāna is none other than "word of the Buddha."[59] Here, Nāgārjuna is taking up another term—this one considered "word of the Buddha" by the Saṃmitīyas. Instead of directly refuting the Saṃmitīya doctrine of *avipranāśa,* he reinterprets it. Karma is "imperishable" (*avipranāśa*) because it is "nonarisen" (*anutpāda*, a Mahāyāna synonym for emptiness).

Nāgārjuna's position *vis-à-vis* the doctrine of *avipraṇāśa,* as in the case of Mahāsāṅghika *abhidharma,* is thus not one of either opposition or adoption but of *rehabilitation.* Although it is not possible to know whether at the time the Saṃmitīyas found Nāgārjuna's solution to their taste, his treatment of their doctrine in this chapter is relatively noncombative compared to his treatment of Sarvāstivādin doctrines elsewhere. If he had written the *Mūlamadhyamakakārikā* to a Saṃmitīya audience, he would have needed to show that Mahāyāna supported their doctrines against the Sarvāstivādins in order to secure monastic reproduction of Mahāyāna *sūtras*. As a strategy, this works something along the lines of "the enemy of my enemy is my friend." Because the Sarvāstivādins attacked the doctrine of *pudgala* in many works dating from this period, Nāgārjuna's ability to defeat their arguments is more likely to have been a demonstration of his allegiance to the Saṃmitīyas than a threat to the Sarvāstivādins (who, in their literature, seem to have mostly ignored both Nāgārjuna and the Mahāyānists). Although he probably could not take the Saṃmitīya doctrines at face value, he does show how the doctrine of *avipraṇāśa* would be acceptable (and safe from the Sarvāstivādin criticism) if and only if they adopt the Mahāyāna doctrine of emptiness.

Other Pudgalavādin Connections

Further evidence links some early Mahāyānists and Mahāyāna *sūtras* with the Pudgalavādins. For example, as Bhikkhu Pāsādika has pointed out, *avipraṇāśa* as a technical term is used in the *Tathāgataguhyasūtra* (a Mahāyāna text) cited in the *Sūtrasammuccāya* (attributed to Nāgārjuna).[60] It should also be noted in this regard that the commentator on the Pudgalavāḍin *Tridharmakhaṇḍaka* (T. 1506) is said to have been a Mahāyānist who "considered the work of Shan-hsien as [a work in which] the idea is profound and simple, but its expression still hidden"[61]—so there does seem to be a Mahāyāna/ Pudgalavāda connection (tenuous though it may be).

Indeed, other chapters of the *Mūlamadhyamakakārikā* make better sense if read from a Pudgalavādin perspective. Tilmann Vetter was perhaps the first to point out that some of Nāgārjuna's arguments do not exactly refute, but might actually exploit, a Pudgalavādin position (after a fashion). Vetter argues that the subjects dealt with in the first part of the *Mūlamadhyamakakārikā* simply critique a notion of an individual self that is not sect-specific.[62] Beginning in chapter 9 of the *Mūlamadhyamakakārikā*, however, he begins to discern a specifically Pudgalavādin element entering into Nāgārjuna's argumentation. Noting that, according to their opponents, the Pudgalavādins believed that the *pudgala* was neither identical nor different from the aggregates, Vetter finds this doctrine echoed in chapters 9, 10, 18, 23, and 27 of the *Mūlamadhyamakakārikā*.

Beginning with the *Mūlamadhyamakakārikā*'s "Investigation of the Prior State" (alternately titled "*Upādāna* and *Upadātṛ*"), Vetter raises the question of whether or not the one who senses exists prior to the senses. In essence the chapter asks the same kind of question as the Pudgalavādins did concerning the *pudgala's* relation to the aggregates. The chapter ends with the statement:

> Of an entity which does not exist prior to, concomitantly, or posterior to the functions of seeing, etc. the notions of existence and nonexistence are unnecessary.[63]

He also points to the last verse of chapter 10, the "Investigation of Fire and Fuel." Chapter 10 has been traditionally looked at as a refutation of the Pudgalavādin theory of *pudgala* because the relationship between fire and fuel was a favorite illustration of that school.

Throughout the chapter, Nāgārjuna examines the different possibilities of how fire and fuel could be related. Nāgārjuna's investigation ends with a position in which the empirical person is neither identical nor different from its empirical functions. His conclusions are best summed up in the last three verses.

14 Again, fire is not wood nor is it in something else than wood. Fire does not contain wood. There is neither wood in fire nor fire in wood.

15 By means of the analysis of fire and wood, the total relationship between *ātman* and *upādāna* and along with [it] the (notions of) earthen jar and cloth, etc. have all been explained without fail.

16 Insofar as I am concerned, those who speak about the reality of entities and who assign them distinct existences cannot be considered to be truly knowledgeable of the (Buddha's) teachings.[64]

Nāgārjuna shows that fire and fuel cannot be related in any of the five ways expressed in verse 14. The last verse castigates those who speak about entities as "distinct" (*pṛthak pṛthak*). Ostensibly, this chapter has been understood to refute the existence of the *pudgala* based on the analogy of fire and fuel. The problem is that, although the Pudgalavādins maintained that the *pudgala* was real, they never claimed that it was "distinct." Furthermore, there is no indication that they ever believed that fire and fuel (or *pudgala* and the aggregates for that matter) were related in any of the ways that Nāgārjuna discusses. The Pudgalavādins (at least the early school), in short, maintained that the *pudgala* existed as a *prajñapti,* not as a *svabhāva*. Again, it is questionable that the arguments presented in this chapter refute any doctrine that the Pudgalavādins actually held, or if in fact they simply rehabilitate the Pudgalavādin position so as to not conflict with Mahāyāna theories. If the analogy between fire and fuel is seen as an analogy of the relationship between *pudgala* and the *skandhas* (the Pudgalavādin view), then Nāgārjuna has actually moved toward establishing the Pudgalavāda case, not refuting it. The Pudgalavādins argued that the *pudgala* is neither the same nor different from the *skandhas*. All schools claimed that there was neither identity nor difference between the *pudgala* and the aggregates. Where the Pudgalavādins part company is when they claim that the *pudgala* is nevertheless "true and ultimate," while other schools view the "neither same nor different" relationship as an indication that the *pudgala* is nothing but a word—only the aggregates exist. In regarding fire and fuel as interdependent, Nāgārjuna is not reducing the existence of the fire to that of the fuel. Nor does he, for that matter, claim that the fire is "true and ultimate," but the position of emptiness that he articulates is far more accommodating of the possibility of *pudgala* than that of competing schools.

It should be noted, however, that Nāgārjuna takes his examination of this relationship well beyond any extant Pudgalavādin argument. Whereas the *Saṃmitīya Nikāya Śāstra* passage discussed in Chapter 6 merely introduces the example of fire and fuel—saying that they are neither the same nor different—Nāgārjuna (echoing the *Cūḷavedallasutta* of the *Majjhima*

Nikāya)[65] raises objections to every conceivable description of the relationship between the two. One cannot help calling the relationship "indescribable." It is difficult to see how the Pudgalavādins could object to any of these statements. Vetter also points to passages in other chapters in which Nāgārjuna explicitly denies *both* the belief in the self *and* the belief that there is no self. Thus, chapter 27 includes the statement:

> Indeed, [*ātman*] can be neither different from the-basis-which-is-relied-upon [*upādāna,* i.e., the aggregates], nor is it identical to it. A not-relied-upon-basis [*anupādāna*] does not exist, nor does it [the *ātman*] not exist.[66]

And in chapter 23, verse 3:

> The existence and non-existence of *ātman* can never be established. How then could existence and non-existence of defilements be established apart from the *ātman*?[67]

Both passages seem to reiterate the Pudgalavādin position that the person is neither the same nor different from the things on which it depends. Vetter ends his analysis with chapter 18, the "Investigation of *Ātman.*" In that chapter, Nāgārjuna makes the following statements.

> 1. If the bifurcated self [*ātman*] is constitutive of *skandhas,* it will be endowed with the nature of origination and destruction. If it is other than the *skandhas* it will not be endowed with the latter's characteristics.
>
> 2. Where the bifurcated self does not exist, how could there be a self-hood (*atmīya*)? From the fact that the bifurcated self and self-hood are (in their basic nature) quiescence, there is no self-identity (mama) or individuality (*ahaṃkāra*).
>
> 3. Any entity without individuality and self-identity does not exist. Whosoever sees (it with) non-individuality and non-self-identity cannot see or grasp (the truth).
>
> 4. Grasping ceases to be where, internally and externally, (the ideas of) individuality and self-identity are destroyed. From the cessation of grasping the cessation of birth also follows.
>
> 5. There is *mokṣa* [release or liberation] from the destruction of karmic defilements which are but conceptualization. These arise from mere conceptual play [*prapañca*] which are in turn banished in *śūnyatā.*

6. The Buddhas have provisionally employed the term *ātman* and instructed on the true idea of *anātman*. they have also taught that any (abstract) entity as *ātman* or *anātman* does not exist.

10. Any existence which is relational is indeed neither identical nor different from the related object. Therefore, it is neither interruption nor constancy.[68]

This chapter is the most important for Vetter because in it Nāgārjuna explicitly ties what he reads as Pudgalavādin-type statements about the aggregates being neither identical nor different from the *ātman* to the doctrine of dependent-origination as the middle way between the extremes of eternality and annihilation, identity and difference. Finally, this chapter also ties the rejection of the two extremes to the pacification of mental proliferation (*prapañca*) in the Mahāyāna notion of emptiness.

So how does Vetter explain the presence of all these references to Pudgalavāda in Nāgārjuna's *Mūlamadhyamakakārikā*? He mostly skirts the issue, concerning himself instead with demonstrating that Nāgārjuna is still primarily interested in negating all views.

> Any concept of Buddhist teaching and any good general concept is a suitable vehicle for the overcoming of all conceptualizations. The concept of the person or the self seemed to Nāgārjuna to be equally suitable to provide a connection to the old formula of dependent origination [*pratītyasamutpāda*] of suffering, and for that reason also to the old conception of the arising of enlightenment, namely through the negation [*Aufhebung*] of certain conditions of suffering.[69]

As far as he goes, Vetter is correct to say that Nāgārjuna remains an advocate of emptiness despite an apparent nod toward the Pudgalavāda. However, Nāgārjuna may come closer to Pudgalavādin doctrine than Vetter indicates because, as mentioned in Chapter 6, the *Saṃmitīya Nikāya Śāstra* also connects the doctrine of the *pudgala* as being neither the same nor different from the aggregates to the common Buddhist notion of dependent-origination being the middle way between the extremes of eternality, annihilation, and so forth. Thus Nāgārjuna's merging of the concepts of dependent-origination and the doctrine of *prajñapti* may not have attracted any attention in the Pudgalavādin camp. Of course, one could argue that Nāgārjuna's teaching about emptiness also indicates that the *ātman* itself is empty and would therefore be perceived to undermine the Pudgalavādins' belief that the soul somehow existed. In his defense, it should be pointed out that the Saṃmitīyas had no problems connecting the doctrine of *anātman* to that of emptiness (just like any other school). The *Saṃmitīya Nikāya Śāstra* equates "me" (*ahaṃkāra*) with the *pudgala* and "mine" (*mamaṃkāra*) with the aggregates and indicates that the doctrine of emptiness means that there can be neither me nor mine nor both.

> Emptiness (*śūnyatā*) is the absence of Me and Mine (*ahaṃkāra-mamaṃkāra*) and of both, the absence of these three things is what is called emptiness (*śūnyatā*). . . . How can me and mine not exist when the Blessed One has said, "At that time, I was the Brahmin Sunetra"? He also said: "Monk, my hand appears in space." It cannot be this (since) Me and Mine are conventional designations (*chia hsao* [*sic*], 假號, *prajñapti*.) However if the five aggregates (*skandha*) are considered, the self (*ātman*) would be Me (*ahaṃkāra*). That the Blessed One never admitted. If the objects (*ching-ch'ien* 境界, *viṣaya?*) are considered as possessions, that would be Mine (*mamaṃkāra*). That the Buddha did not admit either. As it is said in the *Shêng fa yin ching* 聖法印經 (*Āryadharmamudrāsūtra*):[70] Emptiness (*śūnyatā*) is contemplation of the empty (*śūnya*)." Hence, emptiness (*śūnyatā*) and Me and Mine (*ahaṃkāramamaṃkāra*) can be established together. That is why there is no error. That is what is named "emptiness."[71]

Thus far it appears that, although the Pudgalavādins not have made the exact same arguments that Nāgārjuna made, neither would they have had much to object to in his arguments. In other words, the Pudgalavādins may have been another audience open to Nāgārjuna's style of argumentation.

Other Chapters

In addition to the chapters discussed by Vetter, other chapters of the *Mūlamadhyamakakārikā*, on a close reading, seem to cater to Pudgalavādin predilections as well. As mentioned above in the discussion of chapter 4 (the "Investigation of *Skandha*"), Nāgārjuna extracts two components from *rūpa* in order to show that it is a *prajñapti*. The first is, of course, the material cause, *kāraṇa*. The second is *rūpa* itself—here seen as the "effect" *kārya*. Under the chariot/parts analogy of *prajñapti*, the *rūpa skandha* would be a *prajñapti*, while the material cause would be the substance on which the designation is based. The chariot/parts analogy does not seem to provide an adequate model for Nāgārjuna's method of argumentation in this chapter. Nāgārjuna seems to be saying that, in order for the material cause to also be a *prajñapti*, it must in some sense have the *rūpa* as a necessary condition for its existence. Following Qingmu's analogy of the cloth and its threads, one is tempted to read the debate here in terms of the relation between parts and the whole. Normally, the whole is thought of as just a name and as having no existence removed from the parts. Yet, verse 4 asserts that the parts (the *kāraṇa*) *are* dependent on the whole just as much as the reverse is true.

> 4 When material-form exists, its cause is untenable. Moreover, even when material form does not exist, its cause is (likewise) untenable.[72]

In this verse, the whole must enjoy a kind of quasi-existence, or, at least, it must enjoy the same status that the material cause enjoys. Although this kind of reasoning may or may not have been acceptable to a Sarvāstivādin, it certainly would have been acceptable to a Pudgalavādin, because the *pudgala* itself is neither identical nor separate from the aggregates. Furthermore, whereas the chariot is a designation based on its own parts, the preferred Pudgalavādin metaphor for the relationship between the *pudgala* and its component parts was that of fire and fuel. The *pudgala* is designated depending on something that can neither be said to be "its own" or "another's" parts (if the word "parts" is even still applicable).

The term *pudgala* itself appears in only four verses of the *Mūlamadhamakakārikā:* three verses in chapter 12 and one in chapter 16. The verses in chapter 12 simply insert the word *pudgala* into the scriptural formulae teaching dependent-origination. Instead of asking (as it is asked in the "Timbaruka *sūtra*" of the *Saṃyutta Nikāya*) whether suffering is self-caused or other caused, Nāgārjuna asks whether suffering is born from one's own *pudgala* or from another. In the context of a lengthy allusion to *buddhavacana* texts dealing with dependent-origination, the conclusion here is less a refutation of the Pudgalavādin theory of *pudgala* than simply a proof that *pudgala* is dependently originated. If, as seems to be the case, Nāgārjuna was arguing against the Sarvāstivādin position in the *Vijñānakāya,* these verses could actually serve as a Vātsīputrīya rebuttal to one of the Sarvāstivādin arguments. Furthermore, because the *pudgalavādins* believed that *pudgala* was neither *saṃskṛta* nor *asaṃskṛta,* it is difficult to determine how they could object to this way of presenting the problem.

The two verses that complicate the hypothesis of the Pudgalavādin audience are verses 2 and 3 of chapter 16, "Investigation of Bondage and Liberation," which deals with two theories concerning transmigration. The first (verse 1) is that the *saṃskāras* transmigrate; the second (verses 2 and 3) is that it is the *pudgala* that transmigrates.

2 The *pudgala* transmigrates. If it is sought in five ways in the aggregates, sense-fields, and elements, it does not exist. What will transmigrate?[73]

3 [The thing] transmigrating from substratum [*upādāna*] to substratum would be ubiquitous [*vibhāva*]. What is a ubiquitous thing without a substratum? How will it transmigrate?[74]

The commentaries consistently ascribe these verses as Nāgārjuna's own position against the *pudgalavādins,* but, as is the case in chapter 10, the Pudgalavādins explicitly say that *pudgala* is not in the aggregates, and so on. Indeed, as shown in Chapter 6, according to the Pudgalavādins, there is no escape from *saṃsāra* so long as one thinks that the *pudgala* is identical to the *skandhas* or thinks that the *pudgala* is other than the *skandhas.* In pointing out that the *pudgala* does not exist in any of the five relationships to the *skandhas,* Nāgārjuna is just taking their argument one step farther.

My translation above is meant to be the most straightforward reading of the verse. The first two words form a complete sentence, "*pudgala* transmigrates." The second sentence begins with a conditional clause, "IF it is sought in five ways, (THEN) it does not exist." Even if one does not wish to break the sentence there, the phrase *pañcadhā mṛgyamāno* stands in apposition to *pudgalaḥ*. Thus Nāgārjuna is not saying that "the *pudgala* does not exist." Rather, the Sanskrit says that "the *pudgala* that is being searched for in the fivefold (manner) in the aggregates, sense-spheres and elements, does not exist." This leaves open the possibility that some other kind of *pudgala* (perhaps an empty one) is *not* nonexistent. The verse here never questions whether the *pudgala* transmigrates. All this verse indicates is that, *if* the *pudgala* does transmigrate, it may not do so in any of the five relations that are explored in chapter 10. Again, it is difficult to see exactly how a Pudgalavādin could object unless Nāgārjuna actually said that the *pudgala* was nonexistent (which he does not say). If anything, Nāgārjuna is trying to convince the audience that *pudgala* is empty, which is another matter entirely.

There is some discrepancy between the Chinese translation and the Tibetan translation of the following verse. The Chinese translation of the first two *pāda* reads: "If something transmigrates from a body to a body, it will be bodiless."[75] The Tibetan reads: "If there is revolution from substratum to substratum, [the *pudgala*] would not exist."[76] The discrepancy turns on the translation of the word *vibhava*. The usual Sanskrit translation of *vibhava* is "powerful, rich . . . being everywhere, omnipresence."[77] Buddhist texts will sometimes use *vibhava* with the added sense of "nonexistence." Typically, the latter usage occurs in the context of the two extreme views of existence and nonexistence (*bhava* and *vibhava*).[78] For example, the *Dīgha Nikāya Aṭṭhakathā* explains that *bhava* is equated with the extreme of "eternity" (*sasata*), while *vibhava* is equated with "annihilation." (*uccheda*).[79] The first sense of omnipresence seems to be behind Qingmu's translation of "without a body" (無身). The Tibetan translation, by contrast, is *srid med pa* (lit. "without being" or "nonexistent"), which has the second connotation. It is a difficult to see how transmigration from one set of aggregates to another would entail nonexistence. But even if this approach is taken, *pudgala* being *vibhava* would have to be an undesired consequence (equal to *ucchedavāda*), not a statement of doctrine. It is one thing to say that *pudgala* is nonexistent; it is quite another to say that the (apparent) *pudgala* is obliterated at death and that there is no continuity from one lifetime to another. Hence, even in the Tibetan rendering, verse 3 makes no claim that the *pudgala* is nonexistent.

According to Candrakīrti, what is at stake in this verse is the question of the status of the *pudgala* in between lifetimes. His commentary says:

> Here, the one who transmigrates from the substratum [*upādāna*] of a man to the substratum of a god either has abandoned the man's substratum or, should he transmigrate, he has not abandoned (it). If it is said that so long as he transmigrates, he abandons (the substratum of a man), then due to abandoning the previous substratum and due to being without (any) substratum in the intermediate state [*antarāla*], he will be *vibhava*. *Vibhava* means the state [*bhava*] of death/dispersal [*vigata*] of (someone).[80]

In this context, Qingmu's reading of the verse seems more plausible. When not attached to a particular substratum (read "body"), the *pudgala* would have to be nonlocalized, that is, ubiquitous. How can a ubiquitous thing transmigrate? The solution, of course, is never to imagine the *pudgala* as separate from its substratum any more than one would envision it to be identical to its substratum. And, in fact, the Pudgalavādins held precisely this thesis. According to Vasumitra, one of the theses that the Pudgalavādins put forward was: "Things (dharma) cannot transmigrate [*saṃkrānti*] from one world to the other . . . apart from the *pudgala*. They can be said to transmigrate along with the *pudgala*."[81] In other words, there is no indication that the Pudgalavādins believed that the *pudgala* transmigrated without *dharmas* in the first place. The *pudgala* could be said to be ubiquitous only if it were cut off from accompanying *dharmas*. But this premise would have been a "wrong view," according to the Pudgalavādins. Hence, Nāgārjuna again may have just established a thesis to which the Pudgalavādins would probably have subscribed.

Chapter 16 seems to drop the specifically Pudgalavādin doctrine after verse 3. Nāgārjuna's own position (from verses 8 and 10) seems to be that, whatever it is that transmigrates, it can be neither bound nor freed (i.e., in neither *saṃsāra* nor nirvāṇa). For the Sarvāstivādins, this would present a problem because *saṃskṛta* and *asaṃskṛta* are the only two categories of existence. Yet Nāgārjuna's argument in this chapter seems to support the Pudgalavādin claim that, in order for enlightenment to be possible, the entity to be enlightened must fall into neither category (or fall into their fifth category—the ineffable).

Finally, in chapter 25, the "Investigation of Nirvāṇa," Nāgārjuna argues in verses 5 and 6 that nirvāṇa is neither conditioned (*saṃskṛta*) nor unconditioned (*asaṃskṛta*) and in verse 10 he states: "The teacher (Buddha) has taught the abandonment of the concepts of being and nonbeing. Therefore, nirvāṇa is properly neither (in the realm of) existence nor nonexistence."[82] In this chapter, Nāgārjuna's presentation of nirvāṇa resembles the Pudgalavāda articulation of the *pudgala*. Indeed, as Priestley points out, the Pudgalavādins themselves appear to have made this same connection.

> As we know from many of our sources, the *pudgala* is neither the same as the *dharmas* of the five aggregates nor different from them. According to Bhavya, the Vātsīputrīyas held that "Nirvana cannot be said to be the same as all *dharmas* or different from them" (P5256, 68c6; P5640, 255c3). It would seem, then, that as the *pudgala* and Nirvana are both non-different from the same *dharmas* (those of the five aggregates being included in "all *dharmas*"), the *pudgala* and Nirvana ought to be non-different from each other; and in fact the Pudgalavādin in the *Katthāvatthu* is represented as denying that the aggregates, Nirvana and the *pudgala* are three separate things (KV 1.1.226). If the *pudgala* and Nirvana are not really different from each other, then as long as Nirvana exists, the *pudgala* cannot be said to be non-existent.[83]

Certainly, no Pudgalavādin text that I am aware of claims, as Nāgārjuna does later in the chapter, that "there is not the slightest difference" between *saṃsāra* and nirvāṇa. The important point for our purposes is the fact that a Pudgalavādin audience would have no problem with many of the steps that Nāgārjuna takes to get to that point.

Thus, through my own observations along with those of Vetter and

Priestley, it is clear that some elements may have appealed to (or at least not offended) a Pudgalavādin audience in chapters 4, 9, 10, 12, 16, 18, 25, and 27 of the *Mūlamadhyamakakārikā*—in other words, in almost a third of the chapters in the book.

Prajñāptir upādāya

The hypothesis of a Pudgalavādin audience for the *Mūlamadhyamakakārikā* allows us to make sense of one of the stickier issues of that text. The troublesome passage is found in verse 18 of chapter 24, the "*Āryasatya Parīkṣā*." This verse, which was made famous by Huiwen and Zhiyi,[84] reads as follows.

> That which is dependent-origination, that is what we call emptiness.
> It is *prajñaptir-upādāya* and this indeed is the middle way.[85]

I have left the phrase *prajñaptir-upādāya* untranslated for purposes of discussion. Grammatically, the word *upādāya* (depending on) requires an accusative object.[86] The absence of an accusative object in the verse to which *upādāya* may refer suggests that the phrase might be used in a technical sense. As seen in Chapter 6, most schools of *abhidharma* had a concept of *upādāya prajñapti,* but many features of Nāgārjuna's use of this term in relation to emptiness and dependent-origination conform more closely to a Pudgalavādin usage than to that of any other school. It is possible, then, that Nāgārjuna could have adopted this term to better address monks of this school.

In the early Mādhyamika works available, little comment is made concerning this *prajñāptir upādāya.* Neither the *Akutobhayā* nor the *Buddhapālitavṛtti* nor the *Zhonglun* comment on the term at all. Bhāvaviveka merely glosses the term as *upādānam upādāya prajñaptiḥ* ("[It is] a *prajñapti* that relies on what is relied upon")—a true statement, though not a helpful one.[87] Candrakīrti's discussion is more elaborate.

> This emptiness of essence, [*svabhāva*][88] is *prajñaptir upādāya.* That very same emptiness is established to be *prajñaptir upādāya.* The chariot is designated to be chariot parts depending on the wheel, etc. Regarding that, the designation based on something's own parts does not occur as a *svabhāva.* And whatever does not occur as (having) *svabhāva,* that is emptiness. Emptiness, which has the characteristic of the non-arising of *svabhāva,* is established as the middle path. For the

one who (maintains) the non-arising of *svabhāva,* there is no existence. And for what is not-arisen as *svabhāva,* there is no non-existence because there is no destruction [*vigama*]. Hence, it has been said that emptiness, which has the characteristic of the non-arising of all *svabhāva* due to the absence [*rahitatva*] of the two extremes of existence and non-existence, is the middle path. "*Śūnyatā, upādāya prajñapti,* (and) the middle way" these are distinctive notions [*viśeṣa-saṃjñā*] of *pratītyasamutpāda.*[89]

This discussion of the term *upādāya prajñapti* seems straightforward enough. It is simply the "designation" (*prajñapti*) of a thing "depending on" (*upādāya*) its own parts. Notice also that emptiness, *upādāya prajñapti,* and the middle way are all placed on the same level as the special conceptions of dependent-origination.

Candrakīrti's gloss of *prajñaptir-upādāya* as a dependency of a designation on its own parts is somewhat problematic for reasons that David Burton has pointed out. There is some question as to what extent Nāgārjuna can be said to analyze entities into "their own parts" in order to establish that they are *prajñaptisat* by showing that they are dependently originated. Furthermore, under such a definition, it is difficult to see how *upādāya prajñapti* could relate to dependent-origination.

Let's return to the Pudgalavādin use of the term *upādāya prajñapti.* As discussed in Chapter 6, the Saṃmitīyas' own *Saṃmitīya Nikāya Śāstra* uses the metaphor of fire and fuel to explain how the *pudgala* is an *upādāya prajñapti.* Indeed, the importance of this term for the Saṃmitīyas is reinforced by the fact that, as Leonard Priestley points out, the original title of the *Saṃmitīya Nikāya Śāstra* was probably the *Upādāya Prajñapti Śāstra.*[90] As opposed to the metaphor of the chariot and its parts, the Saṃmitīya's metaphor is introduced to illustrate that the *pudgala* and its necessary contributing factors are neither identical nor different. Like the fire or the shadow, the *pudgala* depends on the aggregates but is not composed of them—thus the actual status of *pudgala* is ineffable. It will be recalled that the same text used the negation of sameness and difference, existence and nonexistence to connect the concept of *upādāya prajñapti* to that of dependent-origination.

Hence, if Nāgārjuna tended to merge the concept of *upādāya prajñapti* with that of dependent-origination, a Pudgalavādin audience would probably not have objected. Of course, Nāgārjuna's presentation of *upādāya prajñapti,* though most likely inspired by the Pudgalavādins, cannot be conflated with the presentation of the Pudgalavādins. Nāgārjuna seems to be most interested in the constructed nature of things on which the identity is founded. As discussed above, his use of the term may well be colored with the Prajñaptivādin notion of *anyonya prajñapti*. Nevertheless, like the Pudagalavādins, he apparently intends *upādāya prajñapti* to indicate that there is neither identity nor difference of composite thing and component parts, as well as for the connotation of ineffability that stems from such a relationship. Furthermore, if he can show that all identities come to awareness as sets of mutually interdependent relations, then he can show that no identity ever exists independently and he has made the cornerstone of the Mahāyāna case.

Paramārthasatya and Emptiness

The examination of Nāgārjuna's chapter 24 brings up another issue that may be resolved in light of certain Pudgalvādin theses. Verse 8 states:

> The teaching of the Dharma by the various Buddhas is based on two truths; namely, the relative (worldly) truth and the absolute (supreme) truth.[91]

Presumably, the Mahāyāna teaching of emptiness falls under the category of ultimate truth. Nāgārjuna might have been able to justify this move in the eyes of the Mahāsāṅghikas through the connection between emptiness and dependent-origination that he asserts in verse 18. As discussed above, the Mahāsāṅghikas held that dependent-origination was an unconditioned *dharma* and hence (presumably also) ultimately existent. The problem with justifying the ultimate nature of emptiness in the eyes of other schools who did not accept that dependent-origination was unconditioned would lie in his identification of emptiness as *upādāya prajñapti*. The term *prajñaptisat* connotes constructedness or compositeness and is usually seen as the antonym of the ultimate truth, *paramārthasat*. Verse 18 may be read such that the identification of "emptiness" with *upādāya prajñapti* simply indicates that "emptiness" is a mere word to which one should not get too attached (i.e., the word "emptiness" ultimately does not exist at all, even if its referent does). There are some good reasons to read the verse this way (this way of reading it meshes well with Paramārtha's category of *prajñapti* of manifestation discussed above). However, from the Pudgalavādin point of view, another way to understand the relationship between the concept of emptiness is the concept of *upādāya prajñapti* and the ultimate truth. Namely, the Pudgalavādins, perhaps alone among all Buddhist schools, did not define an ultimate truth as something not constructed or irreducible. The Pudgalavādins had three truths. According to the *Tridharmakhaṇḍaka:* "The truths are practical (等 *deng*, 俗數 *sushu*), characteristical (相 *xiang*), and ultimate (第一義 *diyiyi*)."[92] Although the practical and characteristical truths correspond to other school's use of the terms "worldly convention" (*lokavyavahāra*) and "conventional truth" (*saṃvṛtisat*), the Pudgalavādin definition of ultimate truth differs from that of the other schools: "The final stopping of action, speech and thought is called ultimate truth. Action is bodily activity; speech is verbal activity; thought is mental activity. If these three have finally ceased, that is called ultimate truth, which means Nirvana (T. 1506, 24c16–25a5)."[93] Thus, from the Pudgalavādin perspective, emptiness's status as a *prajñapti* would not have barred it from the category of an ultimate truth. By the same token, statements such as chapter 18, verse 5, cited above ("There is *mokṣa* . . . from the destruction of *karmaic* defilements which are but conceptualization. These arise from mere conceptual play . . . which are in turn banished [*nirudhyate*] in *śūnyatā*")[94] would have made the case for emptiness being an ultimate truth according to the Pudgalavādin definition.

In sum, the *Mūlamadhyamakakārikā* engages at least three *abhidharma* collections in conversation: the Sarvāstivādin's, the Mahāsāṅghika's, and the Pudgalavādin's. If he attacks specific Sarvāstivādin positions, it is most likely because he is trying to show his allegiance to one or both of the other two. Further, if my interpretation of Nāgārjuna's *abhidharma* references is correct, then in the *Mūlamadhyamakakārikā* Nāgārjuna appropriates and rehabilitates certain key concepts from the Mahāsāṅghika and Pudgalavādin (especially the Saṃmitīya) *abhidharma* and uses these key terms and concepts to find fault with the Sarvāstivādin's concept of *svabhāva*. This strategy should not be seen as an attempt to get the Sarvāstivādins to change their minds but, rather, as an attempt to cement an alliance between Nāgārjuna's Mahāyānists and their host monasteries.

The *Ratnāvalī*

The doctrinal configuration in the *Mūlamadhyamakakārikā* and perhaps the *Śūnyatāsaptati* is noticeably different in other works ascribed to Nāgārjuna. To the extent that Nāgārjuna's use of the term *upādāya prajñapti* was influenced by the Pudgalavādins, the Pudgalavādin influence is absent from three particular works: the *Lokātītastāva* and the *Acintyastāva* (both are devotional hymns to the Buddha) as well as the *Vigrahavyāvartanī* (which is a rebuttal to objections against his philosophy). Each of these texts makes reference to *Mūlamadhyamakakārikā,* chapter 24, verse 18. Consider the following:

Lokatītastava, verse 22:

The [fact of] dependent origination is exactly what You think of as emptiness. O, Your incomparable lion's roar is that no independent thing exists![95]

Acintyastava, verse 40:

The fact of dependent co-origination is exactly what you maintain to be emptiness. Of that kind is the true principle [*saddharma*] and the Tathāgata is like that.[96]

Vigrahavyāvartanī

I adore that incomparable Buddha . . . who taught Voidness, Dependent-Origination and the Middle Way as equivalent.[97]

All three verses equate emptiness with dependent-origination, but elide references to *upādāya prajñapti*. Because at least the *Vigrahavyāvartanī* was written after the *Mūlamadhyamakakārikā,* Nāgārjuna's decision to omit any reference to *upādāya prajñapti* might indicate a change in circumstances.

The *Ratnāvalī* makes no mention of *upādāya prajñapti*. Thus it is not surprising that this work also differs from the *Mūlamadhyamakakārikā* in that it directly attacks the Pudgalavādin doctrine of the *pudgala*.

Ask the Sāṃkhyas, the followers of Kaṇaḍa, Nirgranthas, and *the worldly proponents of a person and aggregates,* whether they propound what passes beyond "is" and "is not."

Thereby know that the ambrosia of the Buddhas' teaching is called profound, and exclusive doctrine passing far beyond "is" and "is not."[98]

Nāgārjuna's use of the term *pudgalaskandhavādin* is most likely a variation on the more common designation: *pudgalavādin*.[99] The *Ratnāvalī* contains no references to the doctrine of *avipranāśa,* and at least one verse (chapter 1, verse 82) appears to refute the Pudgalavādin's analogy of fire and fuel, instead of supporting it.

Further comparison of the *Ratnāvalī* with the *Mūlamadhyamakakārikā* reveals that, despite numerous specific references to Sarvāstivādin doctrines in the latter, the number of references to specific Sarvāstivādin doctrines in the former is practically nil. Second, despite the absence of references to the doctrine of momentariness in the *Mūlamadhyamakakārikā,* the *Ratnāvalī* does include references to this doctrine. In *Ratnāvalī* chapter 1, verses 66–70:

66 If always changing, how are things non-momentary? If not changing, how can they be altered in fact?
67 Do they become momentary through partial or complete disintegration? Because an inequality is not apprehended, this momentariness cannot be admitted either way.
68 If momentary, then it becomes entirely non-existent; hence, how could it be old? Also if non-momentary, it is constant; hence how could it be old?
69 Just as a moment has an end, so a beginning and a middle must be considered. Thus due to this triple nature of a moment, there is non momentary aiding of the world.
70 Also the beginning, middle, and end are to be analyzed like a moment. Therefore beginning, middle, and end are also not [produced] from self or other.[100]

In these verses, Nāgārjuna argues that momentariness can be neither affirmed nor denied—thereby avoiding any direct contradiction with the school that advocates momentariness. In his summary verse, verse 70, he alludes to the canonical passages discussing dependent-origination as a production neither from one's self nor from another. In doing so, he ties the doctrine of momentariness to authoritative discussions of dependent-origination, a move that allows him to suggest that the doctrine of momentariness is valid only if those moments are empty. In other words, his audience must accept the Mahāyāna doctrine of emptiness to make their own doctrines coherent.

Although many schools subscribed to the doctrine that all things are momentary,[101] it is significant that the two schools listed by Buddhaghosa as holding this doctrine were the Pūrvaśailya and Aparaśailyas, the two most prominent schools of the lower Krishna River Valley while Nāgārjuna was writing the *Ratnāvalī.*[102] Because Nāgārjuna treats the doctrine of momentariness in the *Ratnāvalī* in the same manner as he treats the doctrine of *pudgala* in the *Mūlamadhyamakakārikā,* it is reasonable to surmise that the holders of this doctrine had taken the place of the Pudgalavādins as the ones whom Nāgārjuna needed to convince.

Conclusion: Toward the Outline of a Career

THIS BOOK AIMS TO DEMYTHOLOGIZE Nāgārjuna. However, the intent of my "demythologization" differs slightly from that of Rudolf Bultmann.[1] My intention is not to rescue universal elements from the myth of Nāgārjuna but, rather, to rescue Nāgārjuna from an overemphasis on his universality. True, the Nāgārjuna of interest in the present discussion is precisely the one that has been obscured by myth. Yet the myth that needs to be undermined is not the myth of traditional Buddhist hagiography, but the modern academic myth of Nāgārjuna. A reference to Roland Barthes should further clarify what is meant here by "myth."

> It is now possible to complete the semiological definition of myth in a bourgeois society: *myth is depoliticized speech.* One must naturally understand political in its deeper meaning, as describing the whole of human relations in their real, social structure, in their power of making the world; one must above all give an active value to the prefix *de-*: here it represents an operational movement, it permanently embodies a defaulting . . . Myth does not deny things, on the contrary, its function is to talk about them; simply it purifies them, it makes them innocent, it gives them a natural and eternal justification, it gives them a clarity which is not that of an explanation, but a statement of fact. . . . In passing from history to nature, myth acts economically: it abolishes the complexity of human acts, it gives them the simplicity of essences, it does away with all dialectics, with any going back beyond what is immediately visible, it organizes a world without

contradictions because it is without depth, a world wide open and wallowing in the evident, it establishes a blissful clarity: things appear to mean something by themselves.[2]

The two myths under examination here are the those of "Nāgārjuna the Mahāyānist" and "Nāgārjuna the philosopher." To call these two epithets myths is not to deny that Nāgārjuna was a Mahāyānist or, for that matter, that he was a philosopher. If anything, he was both. Instead, these labels gloss over and naturalize attributions that were probably the results of well-thought-out struggle. Yet this is precisely why Nāgārjuna's identity as a Mahāyānist philosopher should be taken not as a pre-existing given, but as an identity that he is in the process of forging through his writings. Nāgārjuna weaves a Mahāyāna identity out of the threads already available. The "Mahāyāna" that is the end result is not a mere description. It is, rather, a hybridity won by hard negotiation, and it is precisely this performative nature that must not be overlooked.

The statement "Nāgārjuna was a Mahayanist" is a modern academic myth, not because it is false, but because it is too easy. Explanatory power is lost in exchange for ease of categorization. Any third grader could state that matter is related to energy using the equation $E = mc^2$. Yet what is elided in the ease with which the third grader recites the formula is precisely the struggle in deriving it. But anyone who goes through the trouble of deriving the formula for himself will have a fundamentally different perspective on its truth, even if the result is the same. Someone who knows the formula's derivation will also know the limits of the formula's applicability, the exceptions, and so on. By the same token, the present discussion in no way contradicted the common knowledge that Nāgārjuna was a Mahāyānist and a philosopher. However, the circumstances under which Nāgārjuna wrote suggested certain limitations on the way we interpret his philosophy . To take an obvious example, until someone can provide an alternate explanation of Nāgārjuna's institutional context, the reading of Nāgārjuna as refuting "the *abhidharma*" (or even refuting all theses) is unlikely.

This book investigates Nāgārjuna's contributions to Mahāyāna, not just as a philosophical movement but as a Buddhist institution. Nāgārjuna's task was more difficult than it may first appear. The issue can be reduced to a single question: given that Nāgārjuna was a monk who had taken vows in a specific Buddhist sect, and given that he was a Mahāyānist, how did he manage to champion a heterodox movement without violating any of his vows, incurring legal sanctions, or otherwise alienating his peers? Throughout, the discussion presented monastic and civil law as an opportunity structure—one that forms both the constraints over Mahāyāna and a vital source of power for securing necessary resources.

Nāgārjuna appears to have taken a two-pronged approach to facilitating the acceptance of Mahāyāna. One approach involved garnering the lay support. If Nāgārjuna could convince the king not to intervene in a debate within the *saṅgha,* then those opposed to Mahāyāna would cease to have the authority of the state behind them. Similarly, if Nāgārjuna could convince the laity to donate Mahāyāna texts to the monastery, then the other monks would be obliged to maintain them. As the laity were the final arbiters in any dispute and were the source of the monastery's material livelihood, convincing the laity of the validity of Mahāyāna would go a long way toward ensuring its survival.

The second prong of Nāgārjuna's approach targets the monks themselves. The monks of his home monastery would have been familiar with Buddhist sūtra literature as well as with the sectarian literature contained in the *abhidharma* collections. Nāgārjuna had to convince this audience that his own writings, as well as the writings of Mahāyāna in general, were *buddhavacana* to guarantee their survival. Chapter 5, in particular, shows how Nāgārjuna authorized the stewardship of Mahāyāna treatises by demonstrating that the Mahāyāna doctrine of emptiness underlies and makes possible the statements concerning dependent-origination in Buddhist scripture. Nāgārjuna ties the doctrine of emptiness to the doctrine of dependent-origination through the similarities between the structure of his arguments for emptiness and the structure of discussions of dependent-origination in the *Tripiṭaka.*

The strategy employed here is refined further by examining Nāgārjuna's use of the theses found in *abhidharma* literature in order to address the issue of Nāgārjuna's sectarian affiliations. Although Nāgārjuna's references to and refutations of Sarvāstivādin *abhidharma* theories are well documented, an examination of references to the theses of other Buddhist sects indicates that Nāgārjuna tries to highlight affinities between Mahāyāna doctrine and that of the Mahāsāṅghikas (especially the Prajñaptivādins) and the Saṃmitīyas. He attacks Sarvāstivādin theories precisely to show his allegiance to the latter two schools.

This book brings together the doctrinal, legal, and rhetorical strategies of Nāgārjuna's works. Nāgārjuna's writings are far from the mere collections of abstract arguments that early Western scholars took them to be. On the contrary, couched within his philosophical writings are the very legal, logical, and textual strategies that ensured the survival of Mahāyāna beyond its nascent stage.

Let me now suggest some directions for future research. Chapter 2 locates the composition of Nāgājuna's *Ratnāvalī.* If we can locate the composition of some of his other writings, then we will begin to have the outlines of the career of Nāgārjuna—not just as a philosopher, but as a monk. The *abhidharma* literature reviewed in Chapter 6 and Nāgārjuna's strategies with regard to Buddhist sectarian literature provide key evidence to further pinpoint other important settings of his career.

If it had been important for Nāgārjuna to support (or not offend) the Pudgalavādin position in the *Mūlamadhyamakakārikā* and *Śūnyatāsaptati,* and not important for him to support Pudgalavādins in the *Lokātītastava, Acintyastava, Vigrahavyāvartanī,* and *Ratnāvalī,* then we can begin to ask questions about the development of his career as a product of the intersection between doctrines and geography.

After a thorough analysis and comparison of the styles of the *Mūlamadhyamakakārikā* and the *Ratnāvalī,* Tillman Vetter concludes:

> The observations [of the stylistic differences] are not so strong as to force us to deny the authenticity to the *Ratnāvalī,* but if it was composed by Nāgārjuna, it is difficult to imagine that it was written in the same period as the *Kārikās.*[3]

This being the case, we might imagine that the *Mūlamadhyamakakārikā* and the *Śūnyatāsaptati* (let us call these group A texts) were written at a substantially different time than the *Lokātītastava, Acintyastava, Vigrahavyāvartanī,* and *Ratnāvalī* (let us call these group B texts). We may look at the doctrinal positions given importance in each text set as an indication of where the text was written. This assumes, of course, that the most relevant audience for any writing is the one that has the most power over the author, that is, the audience that is geographically local.

Chapter 2 established that the *Ratnāvalī* was written in the lower Krishna River Valley at the end of the second century. This hypothesis is certainly not contradicted by the doctrinal evidence found in the missive. The *Ratnāvalī* contains references to what was probably a Mahāsāṅghika *abhidharma* treatise as well as a reference to the doctrine of momentariness (held by the Pūrvaśaila and Aparaśailas) and an apparent refutation of *pudgala* (there is no evidence of Pudgalavādins in the south until one gets to the Western Deccan). It contains, however, virtually no references to the Sarvāstivādins, which corresponds to their absence in the Eastern Deccan.

There is no reason to assume that Nāgārjuna spent his entire career in one place. Hence we should look for a different location for the writing of the group A texts, such as the *Mūlamadhyamakakārikā* and the *Śūnyatāsaptati*. To begin with, both works try to rehabilitate Mahāsāṅghika doctrines as well as the doctrine of *avipraṇāśa*. The presence of the Mahāsāṅghikas was felt throughout the Deccan, not only in the Krishna River Valley but also in the Western Deccan.[4] That being the case, the analogy of the seed and sprout could have been one used by monks anywhere in the Deccan. The same cannot be said for the doctrine of *avipraṇāśa*. Although the Andhakas (Sanskrit, Andhras) mentioned by Buddhaghosa are represented in early Purāṇic literature, as "originally a Vindhyan tribe, indigenous to the Deccan,"[5] it is quite possible that the specific Andhras to which Buddhaghosa refers were the Dharmottarīyas and the Bhadrayānīyas, both subschools of the Vātsīputrīyas. The presence of the Dharmottarīyas is testified in two second-century inscriptions from Karle and one inscription from Junnar, while the Inscriptions from Kanheri and Nāsik record Sātavāhana patronage of the Bhadrayānīyas as early as Vāsiṣṭhīputra Pulomā (130–150 C.E.).[6] If Nāgārjuna had written the *Mūlamadhyamakakārikā* in the Western Deccan, then it is understandable that he would have to deal gingerly with the Vātsīputrīya theories—especially if they had the ear of the king. This latter detail may help to explain why the *Mūlamadhyamakakārikā*, in chapter 17, verse 21, takes care to show how the Mahāyāna doctrine of emptiness does not contradict the teaching of *avipraṇāśa* and does not extend the same treatment to the seed and spout analogy of the Sautrāntika/Mahāsāṃghikas. Under this scenario, Nāgārjuna would have written the *Mūlamadhyamakakārikā* and the *Śūnyatāsaptati* in the Western Deccan and then moved to the Eastern Deccan toward the end of the Sātavāhana dynasty. Incidentally, this would mean that he essentially followed the royal center as it moved from west to east.

Although this scenario has much to recommend it, it has one nagging problem with respect to Nāgārjuna writing his early works in the Western Deccan. There is evidence there of the presence of Mahāsāṅghikas as well as Bhadranīyas and Dharmottaras, but not of Mahāyāna during his lifetime. Furthermore, there is no evidence of Sarvāstivādin influence as far south as the Deccan during this period. One wonders why Nāgārjuna would choose to attack Sarvāstivādin texts to demonstrate his allegiance to the Vātsīputrīyas and the Mahāsāṅghikas if there were no Sarvāstivādin threat in the vicinity. Similarly, where did he learn of Mahāyāna to begin with?

We are now looking for a "best fit" between a place in India and the doctrines that Nāgārjuna attempts to co-opt in the Group A texts. Is there evidence somewhere, during the second century, of the presence of the Mahāsāṅghikas, the Pudgalavādins, the Sarvāstivādins, and a budding Mahāyāna all at the same time? Tentatively, I would like to suggest one such place. In Mathurā on the Lion capital inscription, dating from the time of Śoḍāsa in the Kuṣaṇa era, is an inscription recording a rivalry between the Mahāsāṅghikas and the Sarvāstivādins. The latter school had sent a prominent debater to Mathurā to teach the Mahāsāṅghikas the truth.[7] Better yet, the only inscription mentioning the Saṃmitīyas during the Kuṣaṇa era also hails from Mathurā.[8] Furthermore, the *Saṃmitīyanikāyaśāstra* (T. 1649) actually uses Mathurā as an example in one of its discussions—further suggesting a connection between the Saṃmitīyas and Mathurā.[9]

Finally, Mathurā is one of the earliest sites south of the Silk Route where there is any evidence for the existence of Mahāyāna during the Kuṣaṇa era. That evidence is found in a lone inscription dating from the second century, recording the donation of an image of Amitabhā Buddha.[10] The existence of the statue of Amitābha at Mathurā should also cause a reconsideration of the authenticity of those texts, such as the *Twelve-Gate Treatise,* that discuss the worship of Amitābha. Equally important as its testimony to the presence of Mahāyāna in second-century India are Gregory Schopen's observations on the significance of the Mathurā inscription for the character of early Mahāyāna. Noting that the votive formula does not seem significantly different from those of other Buddhist schools, and noting as well that this would be the first and the last representation of Amitābha for centuries, Schopen states:

> the setting up of the earliest known image of a Mahāyāna Buddha was undertaken for a purpose which was specifically and explicitly associated with established non-Mahāyāna groups. This, in turn, would strongly suggest that the concern with Amitābha which produced our inscription in the 2nd century A.D. was not only, as we have seen, very limited and uninfluential—a minor preoccupation—it also was not a part of a wholly independent movement. It expressed itself half in old and established idioms, and half in not yet finished new formulae that would come to characterize not a cult of Amitābha, but the Mahāyāna as a whole; it dictated the production of a new image, but for—in part at least—an old and established purpose.[11]

The context that Schopen describes for the budding Mahāyāna in Mathurā is roughly the context that this present discussion supports as implied by Nāgārjuna's writings. Nāgārjuna's writings show signs of a Mahāyāna that is not independent, not established in any secure way. It is a Mahāyāna that has some features of its own, but still has to borrow heavily on the authority of pre-existing forms of authority to maintain its position.

Appendix: The Authorship of the *Ratnāvalī*

FEW SCHOLARS HAVE SERIOUSLY QUESTIONED Nāgārjuna's authorship of the *Ratnāvalī*. Nevertheless, because it plays such an important role in the argument of the present book, a brief overview of the evidence for its authorship is offered here. In general, there are two approaches to ascribing texts to Nāgārjuna. Some take the conservative approach and use only the *Mūlamadhyamakakārikā* and perhaps the *Vigrahavyāvartanī*, because these are the only two texts whose authenticity is unassailable (largely because their authorship is axiomatic).[1] If, however, we are willing to entertain the possibility that Nāgārjuna wrote more than two texts during his career then we must rely on other types of data to determine the authenticity of those texts. The following examines attributions of the *Ratnāvalī* in other works, its logical and doctrinal content, its references to *sūtras*, and its poetics. Although none of this evidence provides absolute proof of Nāgārjuna's authorship of this text, the weight of the evidence certainly points in that direction.

Attributions in Other Works

Nāgārjuna's authorship of the *Ratnāvalī* has been well attested in India, China, and Tibet at least as far back as the sixth century.[2] Paramārtha first translated the work into Chinese in the sixth century, although he does not name its author. Quotations from the work are scattered throughout Buddhist literature.[3] The earliest explicit attribution of this text to Nāgārjuna is in Bhāvaviveka's *Tarkajvālā,* where he quotes verses 35 to 39 from the chapter 5 of the *Ratnāvalī,* introducing them by saying, "the great teacher, Ārya Nāgārjuna said . . ."[4] Although the dates for Bhāvaviveka are even more elusive than those for Nāgārjuna, it seems safe to place him in the sixth century[5]—perhaps as a slightly younger contemporary of Paramārtha. Candrakīrti (seventh century) quotes the *Ratnāvalī* sixteen times in his *Prasannapadā*[6] and five times in his *Madhyamakāvatāra.* Although he never explicitly ascribes it to Nāgārjuna in these works, La Vallée Poussin notes that the *Ratnāvalī* verse quoted after chapter 25, verse 3, of the *Mūlamadhyamakakārikā* "est citée *Nāmasaṃgītiṭīkā,* A.D. 96, où la *Ratnāvalī* est attribuée à Nāgārjuna."[7] Similarly, Haribhadra, in his eighth-century *Prajñāpāramitopadeśaśāstra,* Śāntarakṣita, in his *Madhyamakālaṃkāravṛtti,* and Prajñākaramati (c. end of eighth–beginning of ninth centuries), in his *Bodhicaryāvatārapañjikā* quote from it, but without attribution.[8] It is clear from the number and the context of these quotations that the *Ratnāvalī* was a text held in great esteem by the Mādhyamika school. It is not clear what, if any, conclusions should be drawn from the fact that so many early scholars felt comfortable quoting it without attribution. Candrakīrti surely knew about Bhāvaviveka's attribution of the text to Nāgārjuna, and if he does not repeat the former's attribution, neither does he deny it. In the eighth century, Jñānagarbha and Klu'i rgyal mtshan as well as the team of Vidyākaraprabha and sKa ba dPal brtsegs both explicitly attribute their translations of the *Ratnāvalī* to Nāgārjuna in their colophons, as does Ajītamitra, author of the ninth-century commentary on the work. In short, the work is attributed to Nāgārjuna as early as the sixth century, and this attribution is repeated in the eighth and ninth centuries. Although these attributions might seem late, it should be kept in mind that (other than a brief remark by Kumārajīva) Bhāvaviveka is the earliest extant source that mentions any other texts that Nāgārjuna wrote.

Doctrine and Logic in the Ratnāvalī

The doctrinal and logical content of the *Ratnāvalī* compares favorably with that of the *Mūlamadhyamakakārikā.* The *Ratnāvalī* is a very different text from the *Mūlamadhyamakakārikā* and presumably speaks to a different audience. Nevertheless, it contains points of striking similarity to the *Mūlamadhyamakakārikā.* In general, both works are committed to a Mahāyāna teaching of emptiness. Both works, moreover, share a similarity in the topics dealt with as well as the way these topics are treated. For instance, both works have lengthy refutations of the three times (past present and future)[9] as well as arguments about antecedent states of being.[10] The rather peculiar treatment of nirvāṇa as being neither *bhāva* nor *abhāva* occurs in both works[11] as does the teaching that *saṃsāra* is somehow not different from nirvāṇa.[12]

The topics discussed, however, do not help determine authorship because a rehearsal of topics is precisely what determines a school of thought. To determine authorship, we must isolate those elements that are likely to be idiosyncratic by determining those elements that were unlikely to have been emulated by his followers. Three areas of Nāgārjuna's writing in the *Mūlamadhyamakakārikā* appear to be matters of individual style, rather than modes of discourse characteristic of the early Mādhyamika school: logical syntax, use of scripture, and metrics. These elements are present in the *Ratnāvalī*, yet absent in the works of Nāgārjuna's closest disciple (and the one most likely to imitate him), Āryadeva.

Although examples of truly logical arguments are fewer in the *Ratnāvalī* than in the *Mūlamadhyamakakārikā*, the *Ratnāvalī* has a few passages whose unusual logical syntax is remarkably similar to prominent verses in the *Mūlamadhyamakakārikā*. Consider *Ratnāvalī*, chapter 4, verse 56:

> Past and future objects and the senses are meaningless, [due to the preceding argument]. So too are present objects since they are not distinct from these two.[13]

Compare this to the familiar verse from *Mūlamadhyamakakārikā*, chapter 2:

> What has been traversed is not being traversed. What has not yet been traversed is not being traversed. What is being traversed, apart from what has been traversed and what is not yet traversed, is not being traversed.[14]

Both passages appeal to the law of excluded middle to eliminate a third term that common sense indicates must exist. Although Āryadeva treats similar topics in his *Catuḥśataka* and *Śataśāstra*, he consistently avoids expressing the same ideas in this form.[15] Both the *Mūlamadhyamakakārikā* and the *Ratnāvalī* also contain verses displaying a rather unusual syntax of the form "if *a* not *b*; if not *a* also not *b*." For example, *Mūlamadhyamakakārikā* chapter 20, verse 15:

Without partaking of a union, how could cause give rise to an effect? But again, with the partaking of a union, how could cause give rise to an effect?[16]

Compare this to *Ratnāvalī,* verse 68:

If momentary, then it becomes entirely non-existent; hence how could it be old? Also, if non-momentary, it is constant; hence, how could it become old?[17]

Again, this way of phrasing the issue is unusual, and I can find no examples of it in the writings of Āryadeva. This way of phrasing an issue was evidently peculiar to Nāgārjuna and not a way of expressing a thought characteristic of the early Mādhyamika school more broadly.

Sūtra References in the *Ratnāvalī*

The *Mūlamadhyamakakārikā* and the *Ratnāvalī* both give a prominent position to the same *sūtras* and make use of those scriptures in remarkably similar ways.[18] Taking the most obvious examples, some version of the "Pārileyyaka sutta,"[19] where the Buddha states that some questions are unanswerable (*avyākṛta*), is alluded to in many places in both works.[20] Similarly, the teaching that *dharmas* are beyond existence and nonexistence from the "Kaccāyanagotta sutta" plays a prominent role in the *Mūlamadhyamakakārikā*[21] and also can be seen in several places in the *Ratnāvalī.*[22] Both works also include allusions to the Buddha's reluctance to teach as told in the "Āryaparyeṣana sutta."[23] That any Buddhist of the early centuries of the Common Era would allude to these *sūtras* is not unusual, but the way that these two texts employ these two *sūtras* to justify the teaching of emptiness seems to be a distinguishing feature of these texts.

However, one reference to a *sūtra* in both the *Mūlamadhyamakakārikā* and the *Ratnāvalī* seems to have been unknown even to the early Mādhyamika tradition. Consider *Mūlamadhyamakakārikā,* chapter 18, verse 6:

The Buddhas have provisionally employed the term *ātman* and instructed on the true idea of *anātman.* They have also taught that any . . . entity as *ātman* or *anātman* does not exist.[24]

Compare this with *Ratnāvalī,* chapter 2, verse 3:

Thus neither the self nor non–self are said to be apprehended as real.
Therefore the Great Subduer rejected views of self and non-self.[25]

Whenever Nāgārjuna says something like "the Buddha says . . ." the Indian commentaries assume that he has a specific *sūtra* in mind. Of the three earliest extant commentaries, the *Akutobhayā* and the *Buddhapālitavṛtti* are the most conscientious about identifying the source of Nāgārjuna's references. The curious fact about their comments on *Mūlamadhyamakakārikā,* chapter 15, verse 6, however, is that, although they both assume that Nāgārjuna is referring to a specific scripture here, they nevertheless seem hard-pressed to identify it. They both quote the "Sāleyyaka sutta" of the *Majjhima Nikāya* as the source of this *Mūlamadhyamakakārikā* verse. The text that they both quote is from a sermon in which the Buddha is explaining to a group of Brahmins which activities of body speech and mind lead to good destinies and which lead to foul. Among the thoughts leading to a foul rebirth are the thoughts: "this world does not exist. The other world does not exist. Beings who are spontaneously produced do not exist, etc."[26] The *Akutobhayā* and *Buddhapālitavṛtti* take this passage as describing different dispositions of converts (*gdul bya* = *vineya*) upon entering the order. The teachings of self and nonself are to be seen as antidotes to a specific false view. This is a bit of a commentarial stretch considering the passage's original context. The "Sāleyyaka sutta" never mentions *ātman* and *anātman* as beliefs to be abandoned. The question remains as to why these early commentaries did not find a better proof-text. Certainly, stanzas 22, 93, or 154 of the *Suttanipāta's Aṭṭhakavagga* would have been a better choice. An answer is suggested by the commentaries of Bhāvaviveka and Candrakīrti. Neither Bhāvaviveka nor Candrakīrti identify the *Suttanipāta* as the source of this quote. Both consider its source to be a Mahāyāna text, although they identify two different texts. Bhāvaviveka quotes from the *Suvikrāntavikrāmin Sūtra,*[27] while Candrakīrti quotes from the *Kāśyapaparivarta Sūtra.*[28] What is significant here is the textual histories of these two *sūtras*. According J. W. de Jong, the former text is fairly late—the *terminus ante quem* coinciding only with the dates of Bhāvaviveka (sixth century).[29] In other words, there is no evidence that the *sūtra* existed prior to Bhāvaviveka, who mentions it in the sixth century, and hence it is unlikely that Nāgārjuna's commentators (much less Nāgārjuna himself) could have quoted from it. The story is different with the *Kāśyapaparivarta*. It is, by all accounts, one of the oldest Mahāyāna texts, or at least it is one of the earliest to have reached China. The oldest translation into Chinese is ascribed to a certain Lóujiāchàn (婁迦讖) during the second century C.E.[30] Hence, it is historically quite possible that this is the *sūtra* to which Nāgārjuna is referring.

The passage in question, however, does not occur in this earliest translation.[31] It does occur in the next extant translation (anonymous), completed sometime between 265 and 420.[32] If Nāgārjuna is indeed referring to this passage, then we have to conclude that, during the first few centuries of the Common Era, some manuscripts of the *Kāśyapaparivarta* contained this verse and some did not. Whether or not Nāgārjuna was referring to this verse or one from the *Suttanipāta*, the case of the *Kāśyapaparivarta* is illustrative of the status of many texts in early India. Buddhist monks had access to Buddhist scriptures, but not all Buddhist monks had access to all Buddhist scriptures. Moreover, just because a monk had access to a Buddhist scripture, we cannot assume that he had access to the same version that was available to other monks. The fact that Nāgārjuna refers to a scripture with which other members of the early Mādhyamika school were unfamiliar means that access to his version of that scripture was limited to a few members of the early school—perhaps even limited to Nāgārjuna alone since Āryadeva makes no references to this passage. The fact that the *Ratnāvalī* refers to a *sūtra* of which other early Mādhyamikas seem to have been unaware increases the likelihood that Nāgārjuna wrote it.

The Poetic Style of the *Ratnāvalī*

The final aspect of Nāgārjuna's work under discussion here is the issue of his poetic style. The main work on this issue to date is by Tilmann Vetter, who in a 1992 article analyzed the statistics of the *Ratnāvalī's* metrics and use of conjunctions in comparison with the same statistics from the *Mūlamadhyamakakārikā*. His findings are, not surprisingly, inconclusive. The metrics of the *Ratnāvalī* do not diverge significantly from those of the *Mūlamadhyamakakārikā*,[33] and although the use of certain particles[34] and compounds does differ significantly,[35] he nevertheless concludes:

> Concluding these remarks on style we might state: The observations are not so strong as to force us to deny the authenticity to the *Ratnāvalī*, but if it was composed by Nāgārjuna, it is difficult to imagine that is was written in the same period as the *Kārikās*.[36]

Nothing in Vetter's statistics seriously challenges Nāgārjuna's authorship of the *Ratnāvalī*, and in fact his analysis provides with an important suggestion. If the *Ratnāvalī* was written later in Nāgārjuna's life than the *Mūlamadhyamakakārikā,* we might be able to explain some of the slight divergences between the two texts. Sanskrit was probably a second language for Nāgārjuna, and certainly the highly stylized metrical version used in his works was developed over years of practice. In ordinary speech, the use of compounds would have been less frequent—the conjunctive task having been taken over by particles. As the author's poetic style developed over the years, the facility with making compounds would presumably increase. Vetter's statistics, then, seem to indicate that the *Ratnāvalī* is a more mature work poetically, if not philosophically. If, then, Nāgārjuna did write the *Ratnāvalī,* he probably did so later than the *Mūlamadhyamakakārikā.*

This hypothesis gains support from at least two arguments in the *Ratnāvalī* that are not in the *Mūlamadhyamakakārikā.* The first of these concerns the doctrine of momentariness. *Ratnāvalī,* verse 63, begins a discussion of the three times. The argument is similar to those in the *Mūlamadhyamakakārikā* until verse 66, when the discussion shifts to the status of the moment (*kṣaṇa*). Verses 66 through 70 refute the possibility of momentariness in much the same way as each of the three times is refuted in the *Mūlamadhyamakakārikā.* This argument is significant in light of the importance that this notion would play in the future of Buddhist philosophy (especially in the works of Dignāga, Dharmakīrti, and Ratnakīrti) as well as the fact that the concept is wholly absent from the *Mūlamadhyamakakārikā.* The other argument in the *Ratnāvalī* that goes beyond the *Mūlamadhyamakakārikā* is the one asserting that the object of desire must be a false construction because the image one attaches to is unitary whereas the senses that actually perceive it are fivefold.[37]

The latter argument seems to have been picked up by Āryadeva (in his *Catuḥśataka*),[38] although he avoids arguments against momentariness in the *Śatakaśāstra.* There can be little question, however, of Āryadeva's having written the *Ratnāvalī.* Although Vetter's statistical analysis of the *Ratnāvalī's* style is inconclusive concerning Nāgārjuna's authorship, it nevertheless rules out Āryadeva as the author.

> It may be noteworthy that the 303 lines of the Sanskrit fragments of Āryadeva's *Catuḥśataka* as edited by Karen Lang . . . contain only a percentage of 2.3% *vipulā* (7 on a total of 303 lines), and only *ma-vipulā.* Āryadeva, so it seems, may be safely eliminated as a possible author of the *Ratnāvalī.*[39]

Overall, then, the evidence supporting Nāgārjuna's authorship of the *Ratnāvalī* is strong. It is ascribed to Nāgārjuna by multiple sources beginning in the sixth century and shows an affinity for common Mādhyamika doctrine. Finally, the *Ratnāvalī* contains many of the peculiar stylistic elements found in the *Mūlamadhyamakakārikā* that are not found in other authors of the early Mādhyamika school, such as Āryadeva, Buddhapālita, and the author of the *Akutobhayā*.

Notes

Notes to the Introduction

1. Paul Williams, *Mahāyāna Buddhism: The Doctrinal Foundations* (New York: Routledge, 1989), p. 194.
2. Kenneth Inada, *Nāgārjuna, A Translation of His Mūlamadhyamakakārikā with an Introductory Essay* (Delhi: Sri Satguru, 1993), p. 39.
3. Ibid., p. 84.
4. John Lofland, *Social Movement Organizations* (New York: Aldine de Gruyter, 1996), pp. 2–3.
5. Ibid., p. 4.
6. See Lofland's definition above.
7. John McCarthy and Mayer Zald, "Resource Mobilization and Social Movements: A Partial Theory," *American Journal of Sociology* 82, no. 6 (May 1977): 1220–1221.
8. Ibid., pp. 1216–1217.
9. Ibid., p. 1221. McCarthy and Zald get this term from R. H. Turner, "Determinants of Social Movement Strategies," in *Human Nature and Collective Behavior: Papers in Honor of Herbert Blumer*, Tamotsu Shibutani, ed. (Englewood Cliffs, NJ: Prentice Hall, 1970), pp. 145–164.
10. For a good discussion of the strengths and weaknesses of Resource Mobilization Theory, see Herbert Kitschelt, "Resource Mobilization Theory: A Critique," in *Research on Social Movements: The State of the Art in Europe and the USA*, Dieter Rucht, ed. (Frankfurt am Main: Campus; Boulder: Westview Press, 1991), pp. 323–347; and Mayer Zald, "The Continuing Vitality of Resource Mobilization Theory: Response to Herbert Kitschelt's Critique," in ibid., pp. 348–354.

11. Herbert Kitschelt, "Political Opportunity Structures and Political Protest: Anti-Nuclear Movements in Four Democracies," *British Journal of Political Science* 16, no. 1 (January 1986): 58.
12. Ibid.
13. Ibid., pp. 59–60.
14. See U.S. code, Title 1, 106b (available at http://frwebgate.access.gpo.gov).
15. Kitschelt, "Political Opportunity Structures," p. 66.
16. There are some who question whether Nāgārjuna was a Mahāyānist at all. See A. K. Warder, "Is Nāgārjuna a Mahāyānist?" in *The Problem of Two Truths in Buddhism and Vedānta,* Mervyn Sprung, ed. (Dordrecht: Reidel, 1973), pp. 78–88; and David Kalupahana, *Mūlamadhyamakakārikā of Nāgārjuna: The Philosophy of the Middle Way* (Albany: State University of New York Press, 1986), p. 5. Both scholars base their claim on the absence of any direct quotation of a Mahāyāna *sūtra* in Nāgārjuna's main text, the *Mūlamadhyamakakārikā*. The main problem with this argument is that the opening verses of that work are a quotation from the *Aṣṭādaśaprajñāpāramitā Sūtra*. For more on this passage see Chapter 5.
17. Steven Collins, "On the Very Idea of the Pāli Canon," *Journal of the Pāli Text Society* 15 (1990): 90.
18. For an extended discussion of this list and the twelve-limbed canon, see Etienne Lamotte, *History of Indian Buddhism,* Sara Webb-Boin, trans. (Paris: Peeters Press, 1988), pp. 144ff.
19. Collins, "The Very Idea of the Pāli Canon," p. 93.
20. See José Cabézon, "Vasubandhu's *Vyākhyāyukti* on the Authenticity of Mahāyāna Sūtras," in *Texts in Context,* Jeffrey Timm, ed. (Albany: State University of New York Press, 1992), p. 227; and Vasubandhu, *L'Abhidharmakośa de Vasubandhu,* Louis de La Valleé Poussin, trans., *Mélanges chinois et bouddhiques* 16, no. 5: 251–252.
21. See Collins, "On the Very Idea of the Pāli Canon," p. 104.
22. Collins presents this argument in ibid., p. 98.
23. Ibid., p. 99.
24. Homi Bhabha, *The Location of Culture* (New York: Routledge Press, 1994), p. 2.

Notes to Chapter 1

1. The general scholarly consensus is that Nāgārjuna lived sometime around the second or third century. This rather broad range suffices for the purposes of this chapter, although subsequent chapters will require considerably more precision. Chapter 2 narrows his dates and place of residence.
2. Jan Nattier, *A Few Good Men: The Bodhisattva Path According to the Inquiry of Ugra (Ugraparipṛcchā)* (Honolulu: University of Hawai'i Press, 2003), pp. 191–192. This problem of the definition of Mahāyāna in Western scholarship is also addressed by Jonathan Silk in "What, If Anything, Is Mahāyāna Buddhism?

Problems of Definitions and Classifications," *Numen* 49, no. 4 (2002): 355–405.

3. Even the "earliest" of the *sūtras* that use the word Mahāyāna do not seem to feel any obligation to define the term. They assume that the audience already knows what it means.
4. For a discussion of each of these authors' contributions, see Jonathan Silk, "The Origins and Early History of the Mahāratnakūṭa Tradition of Mahāyāna Buddhism with a Study of the Ratnarāśisūtra and Related Materials" (Ph.D. dissertation, University of Michigan, 1994), pp. 1–14.
5. See Stephen Kent, "A Sectarian Interpretation of the Rise of Mahāyāna," *Religion* 12, no. 4 (1982): 311–332.
6. Gregory Schopen, "The Mahāyāna and the Middle Period in Indian Buddhism: Through a Chinese Looking-Glass," *Eastern Buddhist,* n.s. 32, no. 2 (2000): 20.
7. Akira Hirakawa, "The Rise of Mahāyāna Buddhism and Its Relationship to the Worship of Stūpas," *Memoirs of the Research Department of the Toyo Bunko* 22 (1963): 57–69.
8. Ibid., pp. 69–73.
9. Ibid., pp. 73–79. Ulrich Pagel has pointed out some flaws in this argument: "[Hirakawa's argument] raises several problems. First, the five moral precepts do not correspond to the first five elements of the ten virtuous paths of actions but have counterparts in the *śikṣāpadas.* Second, for the *Ugraparipṛcchā* on which much of his claim rests (p. 94), the *pañcaśīlas* are enjoined for laymen—not recluses. Third, not even the *daśasīla* and the *daśakuśalakarmapathas* correspond exactly in order and contents. All this indicates that the situation was much more complex than suggested by Hirakawa and that we cannot speak of a direct, verbatim borrowing between the morality of the *śrāvakas* and bodhisattvas" (*The Bodhisattvapiṭaka* [Tring, UK: Institute for Buddhist Studies, 1998], p. 165n205).
10. Hirakawa, "The Rise of Mahāyāna," pp. 79–84.
11. He cites passages in the *Saddharmapuṇḍarīka,* the *Upāyakauśalya-paripṛcchā,* the *Vyākaraṇa-paripṛcchā,* the *Puṇyaparyāya-paripṛcchā,* the *Bhaiṣajyarājapūrvayoga-paripṛcchā,* and the *Tathāgatāyuṣpramāṇa-paripṛcchā* (ibid., pp. 85–89).
12. Ibid., pp. 98–100.
13. Ibid., p. 99.
14. "If the *saṅgha* was not permitted access to the offerings made to the Buddha *stūpa,* it was only natural that they oppose the worship and offering to the *stūpa*" (ibid., p. 99).
15. Ibid., pp. 96–97.
16. Hirakawa does say that Mahāyāna is more Buddha-centered than its *non-mahāyāna* counterpart, although he never contrasts the practice of worship with the practice of meditation.
17. Schopen, "The Mahāyāna and the Middle Period," pp. 20ff.
18. In a note published in *Journal Asiatique* 1 (1912): 622.

19. Sir Charles Eliot, *Hinduism and Buddhism* (London: Routledge and K. Paul, 1957), 3:220n7.
20. Ibid., p. 220.
21. Eliot makes a few brief remarks on the similarities between Kṣitigarbha and the Zoroastrian angel Srosh. See ibid., p. 221.
22. Etienne Lamotte, "Sur la formation de Mahāyāna," in *Asiatica,* U. Schneider, ed. (Leipzig: O. Harrassowitz, 1954), pp. 386ff.
23. Lamotte's *purvapakṣa* is in ibid., pp. 386–389. I address his examination of Nāgārjuna's place of residence in Chapter 2.
24. Ibid., pp. 390–391.
25. I argue against his hypothesis in Chapter 2.
26. Ibid., p. 392.
27. Xinru Liu, *Ancient India and Ancient China* (Delhi: Oxford India Paperbacks, 1997), pp. 93–94.
28. Paul Harrison, "Who Gets to Ride in the Great Vehicle: Self-Image and Identity Among the Followers of the Early Mahāyāna," *Journal of the International Association of Buddhist Studies* 10, no. 1 (1987): 72.
29. Ibid., p. 73.
30. On Mahayanists and their settled life in the *Maitreyamahāsiṃhanāda sūtra,* see Gregory Schopen, "The Bones of a Buddha and the Business of a Monk: Conservative Monastic Values in an Early Mahāyāna Polemical Tract," *Journal of Indian Philosophy* 27 (1999): 279–324.
31. This *sūtra* seems to be primarily interested in how to be a "good monk" in a monastery. See Silk, "Origins and Early History," *passim.*
32. The *Mahāsāṅghika vinaya* also explicitly includes the forest-dwelling monks under the jurisdiction of monastic officials. For example, the *Abhisamacācārikā* states that anyone who shirks work in the monastery on account of being a forest dweller is guilty of an "infraction of the discipline" (T. 1425, 504a10–12); for a translation of this passage, see Silk, "Origins and Early History," p. 239. Furthermore, in the *Mahāsāṅghika vinaya* account of Dravya Mallaputra, the monks are seated at mealtime according to their monastic vocations. In this account, the forest-dwellers all sit together—apparently in the same refectory as the other monks. See ibid., p. 242.
33. This is somewhat ambiguous, because the text also states that one can take the *pratimokṣa* vow as a layperson. See Mark Tatz, *Asaṅga's Chapter on Ethics with the Commentary of Tsong-kha-pa, the Basic Path to Awakening, the Complete Bodhisattva* (Lewiston, NY: Edwin Mellen Press, 1986), p. 48.
34. Shizuka Sasaki, "A Study on the Origin of Mahāyāna Buddhism," *Eastern Buddhist* n.s. 30, no. 1 (1997): 98.
35. Hajime Nakamura, "Mahāyāna Buddhism," in *Encyclopedia of Religion,* M. Eliade, ed. (New York: Macmillan, 1987), p. 461.
36. Nalinaksha Dutt, "Notes on the Nāgārjunikoṇḍa Inscriptions," *Indian Historical Quarterly* 7, no. 3 (1931): 639.
37. B. S. L. Hanumantha Rao, *Religion in Andhra: A Survey of Religious Develop-*

ments in Andhra from Early Times up to A.D. 1325 (Guntur: Welcome Press, 1973), p. 100.

38. Lamotte, "Sur la formation du Mahāyāna," pp. 384–385.
39. B. S. L. Hanumantha Rao et al., *Buddhist Inscriptions of Andhradesa* (Secunderbad: Ananda Buddha Vihara Trust, 1998), p. 39.
40. Sir Monier Monier-Williams, *Sanskrit-English Dictionary* (Delhi: Motilal Banarsidass, 1982), *s.v.*
41. Dinesh Chandra Sircar, *Indian Epigraphical Glossary* (Delhi: Motilal Banarsidass, 1966), *s.v.*
42. Ibid., p. 151.
43. "gaccha kulaputra ayamihaiva dakṣiṇāpathe samudravetālyāṃ nālayurnāma janapadaḥ|" (P. L. Vaidya, *Gaṇḍavyūhasūtra* [Darbhanga: Mithila Institute, 1960], p. 85).
44. According to Demiéville, Buddhabhadra arrived in Chang'an in 408 and, according to the first line of the text, he translated it during the Eastern Jin dynasty, which ended in 420 (Demiéville et al., *Répertoire du canon bouddhique sino-japonais,* Fascicule Annexe du *Hobogirin* [Paris: L'Académie des inscriptions et Belles-Lettres, Institut de France, 1978], p. 238).
45. T. 279, 687c9.
46. Hirakawa lists *dhanya* as one of the definitions of 福. See Akira Hirakawa, *Buddhist Chinese-Sanskrit Dictionary* (Tokyo: Reiyukai, 1997), *s.v.*
47. See Lore Sander, "The Earliest Manuscripts from Central Asia and the Sarvāstivāda Mission," in *Corolla Iranica,* Ronald Emmerick and Dieter Weber, eds. (Frankfurt am Main: Peter Lang, 1991), pp. 133–150.
48. See Aurel Stein, *Ancient Khotan, Detailed Report of Archaeological Explorations in Chinese Turkestan, Carried Out and Described Under the Orders of H. M. Indian Government by M. Aurel Stein* (Oxford: Clarendon Press, 1907).
49. Lore Sander, "A Brief Paleographical Analysis of the Brāhmī Manuscripts in Volume I," in *Buddhist Manuscripts in the Schøyen Collection,* J. Braarvig, ed. (Oslo: Hermes, 2000), p. 288.
50. Ibid., p. 291. It shares many peculiarities with the example catalog number 27 from Qizil (see Lore Sander and Ernst Waldenschmidt, eds., *Sanskrithandschriften Aus Den Turfanfunden* [Stuttgart: Franz Steiner Verlag, 1965], 1:291, table 10).
51. Richard Salomon, *Ancient Buddhist Scrolls from Gandhāra: the British Library Kharosthī Fragments* (Seattle: University of Washington Press, 1999), p. 178.
52. For a summary, see Sander and Waldenschmidt, *Sanskrithandschriften Aus Den Turfanfunden*, 8:224–225.
53. Sander, "Earliest Manuscripts," pp. 135–136.
54. See ibid., *passim.*
55. See Stein, *Ancient Khotan,* vol. 1, *passim.*
56. Jiang Zhongxin, ed., *Sanskrit Lotus Sūtra Fragments from the Lüshun Museum Collection* (Lüshun and Tokyo: Lüshun Museum, 1997).
57. Prods Oktor Skjærvø, *Khotanese Manuscripts from Chinese Turkestan in the*

British Library: A Complete Catalogue with Texts and Translations (London: British Library, 2002), p. lxxiii.

58. Ibid., p. lxx.
59. Gregory Schopen, "The Inscription on the Kuṣān Image of Amitābha and the Character of the Early Mahāyāna in India," *Journal of the International Association of Buddhist Studies* 10, no. 2 (1987): 124.
60. One other inscription from the Gandhara region might refer to Amitābha, although Schopen and Salomon have recently put forward some strong arguments against this reading. See Gregory Schopen and Richard Salomon, "On an Alleged Reference to Amitābha in a Kharoṣṭhī Inscription on a Gandhāran Relief," *Journal of the International Association of Buddhist Studies* 25, nos. 1–2 (2002): 3–31.
61. Richard Salomon, "A Stone Inscription in Central Asian Gāndhārī from Endere (Xinjiang)," *Bulletin of the Asia Institute,* n.s. 13 (1999): 2.
62. Ibid., p. 4.
63. Ibid., p. 10; asterisks, in the original, indicate Salomon's conjectures.
64. According to Boyer, the majority of the letters found at Niya were written between 239 and 265 C.E. Auguste Boyer and Edward Rapson, eds., *Kharoṣṭhi Inscriptions Discovered by Sir Aurel Stein in Chinese Turkestan* (Oxford: Clarendon Press, 1920–1929), p. 373.
65. The inscription mentions the *cozbo* Samasena who governed under King Mahiri, the successor of Aṃogha. See Christopher Atwood, "Life in Third-fourth Century Cadh'ota: A Survey of Information Gathered from the Prakrit Documents Found North of Minfeng (Niyä)," *Central Asiatic Journal* 35 (1991): 196.
66. Thomas Burrow, *A Translation of the Kharoṣṭhi Documents from Chinese Turkestan* (London: Royal Asiatic Society, 1940), pp. 79–80.
67. *Derge, bka' 'gyur,* vol. 54, *tha.*
68. Fredrick William Thomas, "Some Notes on the Kharoṣṭhī Documents from Chinese Turkestan," *Acta Orientalia* 12 (1934): 60.
69. See especially chapter 12 of the *Suvarṇabhāsottama sūtra;* translated in Ronald Emmerick, *The Sūtra of Golden Light* (Oxford: Pāli Text Society, 1996), pp. 57–62.
70. Richard Salomon, "A Fragment of a Collection of Buddhist Legends, with a Reference to King Huvikṣa as a Follower of the Mahāyāna," in *Buddhist Manuscripts,* Jens Braarvig, ed. (Oslo: Hermes, 2002), 3: 255.
71. Ibid., p. 261.
72. Gregory Schopen, "Mahāyāna in Indian Inscriptions," *Indo-Iranian Journal* 21 (1979): 10.
73. Ghulam Yazdani, "Notes on the Painted and Incised Inscriptions of Caves XXXXVI," in *Ajaṇṭā: The Colour and Monochrome Reproductions of the Ajanta Frescoes Based on Photography* (London: Oxford University Press, 1935), part iv, pp. 111–124.

74. R. Mukherji and Sachindra Kumar Maity, "Nālanda Stone-Slab Inscription of the Time of Mahipāladena," in *Corpus of Bengal Inscriptions Bearing on History and Civilization of Bengal* (Calcutta: Firma K. L. Mukhopadhyay, 1967).
75. Dinesh Candra Sircar, "Some Inscriptions from Bihar," *Journal of the Bihar Research Society* 37 (1951): 9–10; idem, "Jaynagar Image Inscription of Year 35," *Journal of the Bihar Research Society* 41 (1955): 143–153; A. Banerji-Sastri, "Ninety-three Inscriptions on the Kurkihar Bronzes," *Journal of the Bihar Research Society* 26 (1940): 240.
76. D. C. Bhattacharya, "A Newly Discovered Copperplate from Tippera [The Gunaighar Grant of Vainyagupta: Year 188 Current (Gupta Era)]," *Indian Historical Quarterly* 6 (1930): 45–60; N. K. Bhattasali, *Iconography of Buddhist and Brahmanical Sculptures in the Dacca Museum* (Dacca: Rai S. N. Bhadra Bahadur, 1929), pp. 25–26.
77. V. N. Aiyar, "Inscribed Buddhist Image from Gopalpur," *Epigraphia Indica* 18 (1925–1926): 73–74.
78. D. R. Sahni, *Catalogue of the Museum of Archaeology at Sārnāth* (Calcutta, 1914); V. V. Mirashi, "Sarnath Stone Inscription of Karna: (Kalachuri) Year 810," in *Inscriptions of the Kalachuri-Chedi Era* (Octamund, 1955), p. 276.
79. R. G. Bhandarkar, "On Two Copper Plates from Valabhī," *Indian Antiquary* (February 2, 1872): 45.
80. N. N. Law, "Some Images and Traces of Mahāyāna Buddhism in Chittagong," *Indian Historical Quarterly* 8 (1932): 139–158.
81. See Richard Cohen, "Discontented Categories: Hīnayāna and Mahāyāna in Indian Buddhist History," *Journal of the American Academy of Religion* 63, no. 1 (1995): 10–11.
82. "pravaramā(ma)hāyāna-yāyinaḥ paropāsaka" (Mukherji and Maity, "Nālanda Stone-Slab Inscription," p. 209).
83. The inscription from the Dacca Museum is dated on paleographic grounds to the tenth or eleventh centuries (Law, "Some Images and Traces of Mahāyāna Buddhism in Chittagong," p. 25), whereas the copperplate inscription from Tippera dates to December 13, 506 (Bhattacharya, "A Newly Discovered Copperplate," p. 47).
84. Bhandarkar, "On Two Copper Plates from Valabhī," pp. 45–46
85. Bhattacharyya, "A Newly Discovered Copperplate," p. 54.
86. Gregory Schopen, "Two Problems in the History of Indian Buddhism: The Layman/Monk Distinction and the Doctrines of the Transference of Merit," in *Bones, Stones, and Buddhist Monks: Collected Papers on Archaeology, Epigraphy, and Texts of Monastic Buddhism in India*, Schopen, ed. (Honolulu: University of Hawai'i Press, 1997), p. 30.
87. Gregory Schopen, "The Phrase '*sa pṛthivīpradeśaś caityabhūto bhavet*' in the *Vajracchedikā*: Notes on the Cult of the Book in Mahāyāna," *Indo-Iranian Journal* 17 (1975): 180.
88. Schopen, "Mahāyāna in Indian Inscriptions," p. 11.

89. Schopen, "Two Problems in the History of Indian Buddhism," p. 32.
90. Tilmann Vetter, "On the Origin of Mahāyāna Buddhism and the Subsequent Introduction of *Prajñāpāramitā*," *Asiatische Studien* 48, no. 4 (1994): 1252n25.
91. Yao-ming Tsai, "Searching for the Origins of Mahāyāna and Moving Toward a Better Understanding of Early Mahāyāna" (Ph.D. dissertation, University of California, 1997), pp. 110–111.
92. Richard Cohen, "Kinsmen of the Son: *Śākyabhikṣus* and the Institutionalization of the Bodhisattva Ideal," *History of Religions* 40, no. 1 (2000): 1–31.
93. Vaslii Wassiljew, *Der buddhismus, seine Dogmen, Geschichte und Literatur,* Anton Schiefner, trans. (St. Petersburg: Kaiserliche Akademie der Wissenschaften, 1860), p. 245.
94. Cohen, "Kinsmen of the Son," p. 7n13.
95. "[siddham] deyadharmmo 'yaṃ śākyabhikṣom aparaśaila. i . . . nīyasya mātāpitṛ . . . [u]tranya.[o] [sa]rvvasatvānām anuttara[jñā]nāvāptaye saurupyasaubhāgyaguṇopapaṃnā guṇendriye bhāsvaradīptayas te bhavaṃti te nayanābhirāmā ye kārayaṃtī[ha] ji[nasya] biṃbaṃ" (Cohen, "Discontented Categories," p. 11 and note 16).
96. Cohen, "Discontented Categories," pp. 6–7.
97. Peter Schalk has argued this in a series of articles. For a summary of his findings and references to his work, see Anne Monius, *Imagining a Place for Buddhism* (New York: Oxford University Press, 2001), pp. 5–7 and note 14.
98. James Legge, *A Record of Buddhistic Kingdoms* (New York: Dover, 1965), p. 17. In his edition appended to the end of the translation, this passage can be found on p. 4.12: 於僧 伽藍 僧 伽藍 名瞿摩帝是大乘寺。 The presence of Mahāyāna in Khotan suggests that Mahāyāna may have also been a presence in Kashmir at this time, since most accounts say that Buddhism came to Khotan from there. See Baij Nath Puri, *Buddhism in Central Asia* (Delhi: Motilal Banarsidass, 1987), pp. 52ff. In this regard, some scholars suspect a Mahāyāna influence on the *Ekottarāgama* (T. 125), which is said to have come from Kashmir. For a discussion of this question, see Paul Demiéville, "La *Yogācārabhūmi* de Saṅgharakṣa," *Bulletin de l'Ecole française d'Extrême Orient* 44, no. 2 (1954): 373–376.
99. Robert H. Matthews, *Matthews' Chinese English Dictionary,* rev. American ed. (Cambridge: Harvard University Press, 1947), *s.v.*
100. Faxian mentions this monastery twice (Legge, *A Record of Buddhistic Kingdoms,* pp. 26, 36; Chinese, pp. 26.11–12, 35.12).
101. Ibid., Chinese, pp. 12.7–8; 12.10; 16.5.
102. He mentions them in passing in his discussion of the various *vinayas* (Legge, *A Record of Buddhistic Kingdoms,* p. 98).
103. Ibid., pp. 18–19.
104. Ibid., Chinese, p. 14.8.
105. Ibid., pp. 44–46.
106. Junjirō Takakusu, *A Record of the Buddhist Religion as Practiced in India and the Malay Archipelago* (A.D. 671–695) (Oxford: Clarendon Press, 1896), pp. 14–15.

則律撿不殊 制五扁通修四諦若禮菩薩讀大乘經名之為大不行斯 事號之為小 (T. 2125, 205c10–13).

107. Takakusu, *A Record of the Buddhist Religion*, p. 7.

108. Ibid., p. 14. 其四部之中 大乘小乘區分不定(T. 2125, 205c8).

109. For example, he tells of Mahāyāna monasteries at Udyāna whose monks were experts in the five *vinayas* (Dharmagupta, Mahīśāsaka, Kāśyapīya, Sarvāstivādin, and Mahāsāṅghika) (Thomas Watters, *On Yuan Chwang's Travels in India 629–645 A.D.*, T. W. Rhys Davids and S. W. Bushell, eds. [New Delhi: Asian Educational Services, 1988], 1:226).

110. 千人習學大乘上座部法律儀清肅戒行貞明(T. 2087, 918b 13–14).

111. Lamotte, *History of Indian Buddhism*, p. 540; cf., for example, T. 2087, p. 918b 14–15.

112. Lamotte, *History of Indian Buddhism*, p. 540.

113. 大乘小乘兼功習學。(T. 2087, 896b 6–7).

114. Lamotte, "Sur la formation du Mahāyāna," p. 392.

115. Lamotte has summarized quite a number of these histories in ibid., pp. 517–548.

116. T. 1465, 900c ff.

117. For the dates of the translations, see note 118.

118. T. 2032. There are some problems with this attribution. Most catalogues state that the translator is Paramārtha, but an anonymous editor placed a note at the end of the work suggesting that it might also be by Kumārajīva. Demiéville discusses both sides of the issue in his "Les Versions chinois du *Milindapañha*," *Bulletin de l'Ecole française d'Extrême Orient* 24, no. 1 (1924): 48n1. Regardless of the identity of the translator, the first translation was likely to have been completed sometime during one of the Qin dynasties of the Sixteen Kingdoms period. Masuda simply refers to the period of its composition as "the Ch'in [= Qin] dynasty (351–431 C.E.)" on the basis of an inserted note stating: "Sthavira means the school [of those people who] sit above, [i.e., the elders] in the word of Ch'in [秦言]" (Jiryō Masuda, "Origin and Doctrines of Early Indian Buddhist Schools," *Asia Major* 2 [1925]: p. 6n1; see T. 2032, 18a14). Since this translation cannot be firmly attributed to Kumārajīva, I will refer to it simply as *the* "Qin dynasty translation" although technically the years 351 to 431 comprise the Former Qin (前秦, 351–394 C.E.), the Later Qin (後秦, 384–417 C.E.), and the Western Qin (西秦, 385–431 C.E.). Note that the Qin dynasty of this text should not be confused with the much earlier Qin dynasty (221 B.C.E.–206 B.C.E.).

119. André Bareau, *Les sectes bouddhiques du petit véhicule* (Paris: Ecole française de l'Extrême Orient, 1955), p. 21.

120. T. 1545, 510c–512a.

121. The five theses are: "1) Arhats can be led astray by others, that is, have seminal emissions during their sleep. . . . 2) Arhats are still subject to ignorance, not defiled ignorance (*avidya*) . . . but undefiled ignorance (*akliṣṭa ajñāna*), a residue of their former passions . . . 3–4) Arhats are still subject to doubt

(*kāṅkṣā*) and can be informed by others . . . 5) Entry into the Buddhist Path (*mārga*) can be accompanied by a vocal utterance (*vacībheda*)" (Lamotte, *History of Indian Buddhism*, pp. 274–275). The various accounts of this schism have been summarized in Jan Nattier and Charles Prebish, "Mahāsāṃghika Origins: The Beginnings of Buddhist Sectarianism," *History of Religions* 16, no. 3 (1977): 237–272.

122. Nattier and Prebish, "Mahāsāṃghika Origins," p. 240.
123. Hermann Oldenberg, *The Dīpavaṃsa: An Ancient Buddhist Historical Record* (London: Williams and Norgate, 1879), pp. 140–141.
124. Ibid., pp. 141–142.
125. John Holt, *The Buddha in the Crown* (New York: Oxford University Press, 1991), pp. 63–64.
126. Cf. Gunapala Piyasena Malalasekera, *Dictionary of Pāli Proper Names* (New Delhi: Munshiram Manoharlal, 1983), *vetullavāda*, *s.v.*
127. *Vetullavāda* is first mentioned with respect to the purge of Goṭhābhaya; see *Mahāvāṃsa: mūla evam Hindī rūpāntara,* Rāmakumāra Tripāthī et al., eds. (Varanasi: Bauddha Ākara Granthamālā, 1996), p. 558.
128. Legge, *A Record of Buddhistic Kingdoms*, pp. 100–111.
129. Cf. ibid., pp. 16–21, 41.
130. Demiéville, "Versions chinois du *Milindapañha*," p. 48n1.
131. T. 468, 501a19–28.
132. "Um diese Zeit der weise Vasumitra, (chines.: der wahre) Çākja-Bhikschu, von grossem Geiste und von der Weisheit eines Bodhisattva, begabt mit einem scharfsinnigen Verstand, machte sich mit sorfältiger Untersuchung an die Reinigung der verschiednen Theorien (chines.: welche die Welt beunruhigt hatten), und verfasste folgende Deduction: *Das Buddha Wort ist in allen Werken enthalten, welche die gespaltenen Schulen anerkennen. Der Gegenstand (der Lehre) des Ārjaçātīja (der vier Wahrheiten) enthält alles in sich, was von dem Buddha gelehrt (und dieses findet sich in diesen Werken) wie Gold im Sande*" (Wassiljew, *Der Buddhismus,* pp. 245–246; emphasis added).
133. 三論玄義 (T. 1852, pp. 8–9).
134. The *Sanrongengi Kenyūshū*, T. 2300, especially pp. 450–460.
135. Paul Demiéville, "L'Origine des sectes bouddhiques d'après Paramārtha," *Mélanges chinois et bouddhiques* 1 (1931): 16–64.
136. Cf. Lamotte, *History of Indian Buddhism*, pp. 274–285.
137. Demiéville, "L'origine des sectes bouddhiques," pp. 37–38. This passage is not quoted by Jizang, but is found in Chūkan (see T. 2300a27ff.).
138. Demiéville, "L'origine des sectes bouddhiques," pp. 40–42. See T. 1852, 8c16ff.
139. Chūkan's commentary lists more *sūtras*: *Avataṃsaka*, *Nirvāṇa*, *Śrīmālā*, *Vimalakīrti*, *Suvarṇaprabhāsa*, *Prajñā* (T. 2300, 459b11–12; trans. in Demiéville, "L'origine des sectes bouddhiques," p. 43).
140. 此部將華嚴般若等大乘經雜三藏中說之(T. 1852, 8c18–19).
141. Chūkan's version does not mention Ānanda's recitation as the authorizing feature but claims, instead, that the *Tripiṭaka* was actually uttered by the Buddha

while the Mahāyāna *sūtras* were "tous oeuvres d'hommes." See Demiéville, "L'origine des sectes bouddhiques," p. 43.

142. Apparently, some Mahāyānists would meditate on Buddhas of other world systems in order to be able to visit those Buddhas in a trance or in a dream. It is from the lips of these dream or trance Buddhas that the Mahāyānists claim to have heard the Mahāyāna *sūtras* expounded. This kind of justification for the creation of Mahāyāna *sūtras* is referred to in the *Pratyutpanna-buddha-saṃmukhāvasthita-samādhi Sūtra*:

"Just as the above-mentioned dreaming persons, who think of themselves as dwelling in space, do not think 'night' and do not think 'day,' and their faculty of sight is not obstructed by walls nor obscured by darkness, so it is, Bhadrapāla, with the *bodhisattvas* who perform an act of thought like this. . . . Without having obtained divine vision, the *bodhisattvas* see the Buddha Amitābha; without having obtained divine hearing, they hear the *sūtra*/dharma expounded by the Buddha Amitābha . . . Simply staying in this world as before, they see the Buddha, the *Tathāgata* Amitābha, and hear him expounding the Dharma. As they have heard it they take it up. The *bodhisattvas* then wake from this concentration, and then expound widely to others the Dharma as they have heard it" (Paul Harrison, *The Samādhi of Direct Encounter with the Buddhas of the Present* [Tokyo: International Institute for Buddhist Studies, 1990], p. 33n4; cf. T. 419, 922a17–27).

143. Demiéville translates this as "les principes de la Voie (au principes logiques tao li: siddhānta, nyāya" for Jizang's version and as "les principes logiques (siddhānta?)" in Chūkan's version. Jizang's tells us that one can justify the Mahāyāna *sūtras* by 量道理, while Chūkan has 擇道理. The problem, of course, is that the characters 道 (*dao*) and 理 (*li*) are overdetermined in Chinese religious traditions. If this were a Daoist or Confucianist text we would translate it as "choose or determine the way and the principle." *Li*, however, can also mean "reason" or "logic"—terms that probably did not have ready cultural equivalents in the Chinese language of Paramārtha's day.

144. The Arhant is unnamed in Jizang's version. The name is found only in Chūkan, T. 2300, 460c9–10.

145. Demiéville, "L'origine des sectes bouddhiques," pp. 48–49; T. 2300, 460c17–22.

146. 故參涉大乘意也 (T. 2300, 460c22).

147. See Masuda, "Origin and Doctrines," pp. 35–36.

148. He quotes Āryadeva's *Catuḥśātaka*, verse 33 at T. 1646, 298b14, and alludes to it throughout section 127. Paramārtha's assessment is confirmed by Daoxuan later on, that while the work is predominantly Hīnayānist, it is colored throughout with fully developed Mahāyāna ideas (see Junjirō Takakusu, *Essentials of Buddhist Philosophy*, Wing Tsit Chan and Charles A. Moore, eds. [Delhi: Motilal Banarsidass, 1987), p. 76]). Harivarman says: "The fulfillment of six *pāramitās*, charity, etc. leads to the suprememost Enlightenment (*anuttara-samyak-sambodhi*). The good action done in a slightly inferior form leads to the Enlightenment of Pratyekabuddha, and the action in a still inferior form leads

to the enlightenment of the Śrāvaka" (T. 1646, 291b24–26). Later he says, "The person that has awakened Bodhi-citta causing Śūnyatā is salutable by the Arhans" (*Satyasiddhiśāstra of Harivarman,* N. Aiyaswami Śāstri, ed. and trans. [Baroda: Oriental Institute, Maharaja Sayajirao University, 1975–1978], p. 200). On the whole, it is difficult to imagine that the *Satyasiddhiśāstra* was representative of the Bahuśrutīyas and seems, rather, to have been the idiosyncratic work of its author, Harivarman.

149. Demiéville, "L'origine des sectes bouddhiques," pp. 60–61; Chūkan, T. 2300, 465b22ff.

150. The *Dharmgupta vinaya* mentions the recitation of mantras at T. 1428, 754b7–8. It should be noted, however, that the use of mantras was by no means an identifying feature of Mahāyāna. They can also be found in the Pāli canon; e.g., *Cūḷavagga,* verse 6, vol. 5, p. 6, and the "Āṭānāṭiya sutta" of the *Dīgha Nikāya*.

151. T. 1852, 9c23–4. In fact, the extant translation of the *Satyasiddhiśāstra* also mentions a canon consisting of five parts, but they are *Sūtra*, *Vinaya*, *Abhidharma*, *Samyukta,* and *Bodhisattvapiṭaka.* See, for example, paragraph 183, which warns the practitioner to not put off practicing the path. The practitioner thinks aloud: "I ought to slowly cultivate the path. First [I] should study *Sūtra*, *Vinaya* (比尼), *Abhidharma*, *Kṣudrakapiṭaka* and *Bodhisattvapiṭaka*, and [then] the wide array of non-Buddhist texts. [I should then] accumulate many disciples." Cf. *Satyasiddhiśāstra of Harivarman,* N. Aiyaswami Sastri, ed. and trans. (Baroda: Oriental Institute, Maharaja Sayajirao University, 1975–1978), p. 427. 我徐當修道 先當讀誦修多羅比尼阿毘曇雜藏菩薩藏廣綜外典多畜弟子 (T. 1646, p. 352c, 1. 14–16). André Bareau gives two other citations (297c and 300b) but these seem to be incorrect (*Les sectes*, p. 296). For a discussion of the referent of the term *bodhisattvapiṭaka*, see Pagels, *The Bodhisattvapiṭaka*, pp. 7–36.

152. The Dharmagupta list of Āgamas is mentioned at T. 1428, 967b19ff. Mahāyāna is mentioned in the preface and in a story beginning at T. 1428, 779c22ff

153. Buddhayaśas also translated the *Akāśagarbha Sūtra*, T. 405, 虛空藏菩薩經. And he is said to have learned both Mahāyāna and Hīnayāna treatises in 出三藏記集 (T. 2145, 102a25–6).

154. 曇無德部。體大乘三藏(T. 1428, 567a26).

155. Peter Skilling, "Citations from the Scriptures of the 'Eighteen Schools' in the *Tarkajvāla,*" in *Bauddhavidyāsudhākaraḥ: Studies in Honour of Heinz Bechert on the Occasion of His 65th Birthday,* Petra Kieffer-Pülz and Jens-Uwe Hartmann, eds. (Swisttal-Odendorf: Indica et Tibetica Verlag, 1997), pp. 606–607.

156. "'dir ñan thos kyi theg pa pa dag na re theg pa chen po ni saṅs rgyas kyi bka' ma yin te| sde pa bco brgyad kyi khoṅs su ma gtogs pa'i phyir dper na graṅs can la sogs pa'i bstan pa bźin no źes zer ba'i gtan tshigs, de'i don kyaṅ ma grub pa ñid yin te| 'di ltar dge 'dun phal chen sde ñid kyi sde snod kyi gźi chen po źes bya ba'i khoṅs su theg pa chen po 'di yaṅ gtogs te| de (san) nas sa bcu pa'i mdo daṅ pha rol tu phyin pa 'i mtshan ñid dag 'byuṅ ba'i phyir daṅ| dge 'dun

phal chen sde ñid kyi śar gyi ri bo'i sde dań nub kyi ri bo'i sde dag las kyań 'bral ('phral)? skad du| śes rab kyi pha rol tu phyin pa la sogs pa theg pa chen po 'i mdo dag 'byuń ba'i phyir ro|" (Peking *bsTan 'Gyur*, 97:290, 321a1–4). I should also note that Candrakīrti, at the end of his *Madhyamakāvatāra*, claims that the *Lokānuvārtana sūtra* (ostensibly a Mahāyāna *sūtra*) was in use by the Pūrvaśailyas. See Paul Harrison, "Sanskrit Fragments of a Lokottaravādin Tradition," in *Indological and Buddhist Studies,* L. Hercus et al., eds. (Canberra: Australian National University, Faculty of Asian Studies, 1982), p. 26.

157. See Atwood, "Life in Third-Fourth Century Cadh'ota," p. 174.
158. Vidya Dehejia, "The Collective and Popular Basis of Early Buddhist Patronage: Sacred Monuments, 100 B.C.–A.D. 250," in *The Powers of Art,* B. S. Miller, ed. (Delhi: Oxford University Press, 1992), pp. 37–38.
159. T. 1425, 336c5.
160. We don't know the gender of the donor of the Tippera grant.
161. Published in 515 C.E. For a discussion of the date of the *Jusanzang jiji*, see Erik Zürcher, *The Buddhist Conquest of China: The Spread and Adaptation of Buddhism in Early Medieval China* (Leiden: E.J. Brill, 1972), p. 10.
162. 彼土小乘學者。乃以聞王。云漢地沙門乃以婆羅門書或亂真言 (T. 2145, 41c29–42a1).
163. Zürcher, *Buddhist Conquest*, p. 63.
164. Mark Twain, *Following the Equator*, Pudd'nhead Wilson's New Calendar (Avon, CT: Limited Editions Club, 1974).

Notes to Chapter 2

This chapter has been adapted from my "Nāgārjuna and the *Ratnāvalī:* New Ways to Date an Old Philosopher," *Journal of the International Association of Buddhist Studies* 25, nos. 1–2 (2002): 209–262.

1. Although I have yet to find any scholar who seriously questions the authenticity of the *Ratnāvalī,* I have included a discussion of its authorship in the Appendix.
2. Max Walleser, *The Life of Nāgārjuna from Tibetan and Chinese Sources* (reprint, Delhi: Nag, 1979), p. 1. The original article appeared in *Asia Major,* Introductory Volume. Hirth Anniversary Volume (London, Probsthain, 1923), pp. 421–455.
3. Ian Mabbett, "The Problem of the Historical Nāgārjuna Revisited," *Journal of the American Oriental Society* 118, no. 3 (1998): 332.
4. Etienne Lamotte, *The Teaching of Vimalakīrti (Vimalakīrtinirdeśa),* Sara Boin, trans. (Oxford: Pāli Text Society, 1994), p. xcvii.
5. T. 2047, 龍樹菩薩傳, lit. "The Chronicle of the Bodhisattva Nāgārjuna." The rest of this chapter refers to it simply as the *Biography.*
6. Roger Corless, "The Chinese Life of Nāgārjuna," in *Buddhism in Practice,* Donald Lopez, ed. (Princeton: Princeton University Press, 1995), p. 531.

7. Richard H. Robinson, *Early Mādhyamika in India and China* (reprint, Delhi: Motilal Banarsidass, 1978), p. 25.
8. Here I follow Jan Nattier's translation of the term. See Jan Nattier, *Once Upon a Future Time: Studies in a Buddhist Prophesy of Decline* (Berkeley: Asian Humanities Press, 1991), pp. 86–89.
9. Hakuju Ui, *The Vaiśeṣika Philosophy According to the Daśapadārtha-Śāstra*, 2nd ed. (Varanasi: Chowkhamba Sanskrit Series Office, 1962), p. 43. For Ui's discussion of Nāgārjuna's date, see pp. 42–46.
10. Using a similar method, one could try to come up with a date for Nāgārjuna's birth based on the testimony of works such as the *Laṅkāvatāra Sūtra*, the *Mahāmegha Sūtra*, or the *Mañjuśrīmūlatantra*, which claim that Nāgārjuna was born four hundred, seven hundred, and four hundred years after the Buddha's Parinirvāṇa, respectively. Unfortunately, since we know nothing of the authors of these texts, we do not know when they thought the Buddha's *parinirvāṇa* was. Hence, these dates are of little use.
11. Guṇavarman was born in India in 367 and arrived in China in 431. See Demiéville et al., *Répertoire du canon bouddhique sino-japonais*, p. 252 (*q.v.* "Gunabatsuma").
12. T. 1672, p. 745b13.
13. T. 2125, p. 227c14–15.
14. Ibid. Mabbett, using Pulleyblank, renders this in its Central Middle Indic equivalent as *sa-ta-ba-xa-na^h*. See Mabbett, "The Problem," p. 336.
15. For a brief biography of Paramārtha, see Demiéville et al., *Répertoire du canon bouddhique sino-japonais,* p. 276.
16. T. 2087, p. 929a27.
17. Rao et al., *Buddhist Inscriptions of Andhradesa*, p. 54.
18. Ibid., p. 109.
19. A total of eight Sada/Sāta kings are mentioned in inscriptions: Śrī Sada(sāta), Sivamaka Sada (Vaddamanu), Mānasada, Mahāsada, Asaka Sada, Aira Asaka Sada, Siri Mahasada and Siva Sada. Concerning their territory I. K. Sarma identifies Mahiṣaka with the Maisolia region (ibid., pp. 109–110).
20. Ajītamitra, in the beginning of his commentary on the *Ratnāvalī* says: "de la 'dir btsun pa 'phags pa klu sgrub 'jig rten mtha' dag la phan par bźed pas rgyal po bde spyod kyi dbaṅ du mdzad nas dam pa'i chos rin po che'i phreṅ ba dgod pa'i ṅes pa mdzad de dam pa'i spyod pa daṅ mthun par|" (*Die Ratnāvalīṭīkā des Ajitamitra,* Yukihiro Okada, ed. [Bonn: Indica et Tibetica Verlag, 1990], p. 1).
21. Nāgārjuna, *Golden Zephyr: Instructions from a Spiritual Friend,* L. Kawamura, trans. (Berkeley: Dharma, 1975), p. 93.
22. This was suggested by Jan W. de Jong in his "Review of J. Hopkins and Lati Rimpoche, trans., *The Precious Garland and the Song of the Four Mindfulnesses*," *Indo-Iranian Journal* 20 (1978): 137.
23. *Tārānātha's Geschichte des Buddhismus in Indien,* Anton Scheifner, trans. (St. Petersburg, 1869), p. 2n2.
24. Mabbett, "The Problem," p. 341.

25. In addition to Mabbett's article, I recommend Phyllis Granoff, "Jain Biographies of Nāgārjuna: Notes on the Composing of a Biography in Medieval India," in *Monks and Magicians: Religious Biographies in Asia,* Phyllis Granoff and Koichi Shinohara, eds. (Oakville, ONT: Mosaic Press, 1988), pp. 45–61, and David G. White, *Alchemical Body: Siddha Traditions in Medieval India* (Chicago: University of Chicago Press, 1996), pp. 62–77.
26. This is mentioned by Xuanzang. See Watters, *On Yuan Chwang's Travels*, p. 201; Bāṇa, see Bāṇa, *The Harṣa-Carita of Bāṇa,* Edward B. Cowell and Frederick William Thomas, trans. (Delhi: Motilal Banarsidass, 1961), p. 252; Jain sources including the *Prabandhakośa,* see *Prabandha Kośa,* Jina Vijaya, ed. (Śāntiniketan: Adhisṭhāta-siṅghī Jaina Jñānapīṭha, 1991), p. 84; and the *Prabandha Cintāmaṇi,* see Merutuṅgācārya, *Prabandha Cintāmaṇi of Merutuṅgācārya,* Jinavijaya Muni, ed. (Śāntiniketan: Adhisṭātā Siṅghī Jaina Jñānapīṭha, 1933), part I, p. 119; Abhāyadatta's Lives of the 84 Siddhas, see Abhayadatta, *Masters of Mahāmudrā: Songs and Histories of the Eighty-Four Buddhist Siddhas,* Kenneth Dowman, trans. (Albany: State University of New York Press, 1984), p. 115; the *Rasendra Maṅgala,* see White, *Alchemical Body,* p. 155; Bu-ston, see Bu-ston, *History of Buddhism in India and Tibet,* Eugene Obermiller, trans. (1932; reprint, Delhi: Sri Satguru Press, 1986), p. 127; and Tārānātha, see *Tārānātha's History of Buddhism in India,* D. Chattopadhyaya, trans. (Calcutta: K. P. Bagchi, 1970), p. 109.
27. On this site see Stein's note: "*Ṣaḍarhadvana,* 'the wood of the six Saints,' if rightly identified by the glossator as (*Harvan grāme*), is the modern village *Hārvan,* situated about one and a half miles to the N.W. of the gardens of Shālimār near Śrīnagar. On the hill-side to the south of Hārvan ancient remains have come to light in the shape of highly ornamented brick pavements, which were dug up in the course of excavations conducted at the site in connection with the new Śrīnagar waterworks." See Sir Mark Aurel Stein, *Kalhaṇa's Rājataraṅgiṇī: A Chronicle of the Kings of Kaśmīr* (Srinagar: Verinag, 1961), p. 31n173. Could *Ṣaḍarhadvana* be used in this story because it is a homonym for "Sātavāhana"?
28. Corless, "The Chinese Life," p. 528.
29. This passage does not appear in the earliest version of the *Laṅkāvatāra* translated by Guṇabhadra in 443 C.E. It does appear in the versions translated by Bodhiruci (trans. 513 C.E.) and Śikṣānanda (trans. 700–704). The passage in question, according to Walleser, may have been added in the fifth century C.E. because the section in which it appears contains a verse referring to Maurya, Gupta, and Nanda kings of the Kāli Yuga.
30. Translated by Jeffrey Hopkins in *Buddhist Advice for Living & Liberation: Nāgārjuna's Precious Garland* (Ithaca: Snow Lion, 1998), p. 13. There are only three substantial differences between this prophecy and that of the *Laṅkāvatāra Sūtra:* (1) the number of years that he appears after the Buddha's *parinirvāṇa* increases to four hundred years and his life-span increases to six hundred years, (2) no place name is indicated, and (3) he is the transmitter of the

Mahāmayūrī mantra. The *Laṅkāvatāra* is probably the earlier of the two, and what can be said of it can also be said of the *Manjuśrī Mūlatantra* as far as its testimony of Nāgārjuna is concerned.

31. Hopkins cites nineteenth-century Mongolian scholar Nga-wang-bel-den (b. 1797), who in his discussion of Jam-yang-shay-ba's work "gives *be da* (misprinted as *pe da*) and identifies the place as Vidarbha (*be dar bha*)" (ibid., p. 10, note a). Alternatively, P. S. Shastri suggests that this "Vedalya" could also be "Dehali," which is a site near Nāgārjunakoṇḍa, the site of Vijaya Sātkarṇi's capital. See Inguva Karthikeya Sarma, *Studies in Early Buddhist Monuments and Brāhmī Inscriptions of Āndhradeśa* (Nagpur: Dattsons, 1988), p. 17. See also Mabbett, "The Problem," p. 335n32.
32. Watters, *Yuan Chwang's Travels,* p. 201. Watters, by using two different Chinese glosses, reasons that *Polomolokili* is probably a transliteration of *Bhrāmara-gīri* (Bee-peak), which is confirmed by the 黑蜂 (Black Bee) translation. He cites Beal's reasoning that Black Bee is a synonym for the Goddess Durgā or Pārvatī, and hence *Polomolokili* is some form of *Parvata* (lit., "mountain"). James Burgess, following this lead, identifies Nāgārjuna's abode with Śrī-Parvata, a well-known mountain on the Krishna River in modern-day Andrha Pradesh (ibid., p. 208).
33. See Karen Lang, *Āryadeva's Catuḥśataka: On the Bodhisattva's Cultivation of Merit and Knowledge* (Copenhagen: Akademisk Forlag, 1986), p. 7.
34. Jain legends of Nāgārjuna have been discussed extensively in Granoff, "The Jain Biographies."
35. Alberuni (writing in 1030) mentions that Nāgārjuna lived at a Gujarati site, "Fort Daihak" near Somnath, one hundred years before his writing. See Mabbett, "The Problem," p. 338.
36. This is called "Ḍhaṅka" in Merutuṅgācārya, *Prabandha Cintāmaṇi,* p. 119, and "Śatruñjaya" in the *Prabandha Kośa,* p. 84.
37. Bu-ston, *History of Buddhism,* p. 127.
38. Abhayadatta, *Buddha's Lions: The Lives of the Eighty-Four Siddhas,* James Robinson, trans. (Berkeley: Dharma, 1979), p. 75.
39. As both Bu-ston and Tārānātha assert.
40. This attribution can be found in the *Tantra Mahārṇava.* See White, *Alchemical Body,* p. 113.
41. Lamotte, "Sur la formation du Mahāyāna," p. 388 (emphasis added).
42. The multiple Nāgārjuna hypothesis has been most seriously criticized by Jan-Yün Hua, in "Nāgārjuna, One or More? A New Interpretation of Buddhist Hagiography," *History of Religions* 10 (1970): 139–153.
43. White mentions some of these other Nāgārjunas. Xuanzang met one of the disciples of Nāgārjuna, "who looked thirty despite his seven hundred years." Similarly, some texts of a much later date are written by authors named Nāgārjuna. The first of these is the *Yogaśataka* datable to the seventh or ninth century. Similarly, the fourteenth-century *Rasendra Maṅgala* is ostensibly by a "Śrīman Nāgārjuna" (White, *Alchemical Body,* p. 75).

44. Ibid., p. 164.
45. Corless, "The Chinese Life," p. 528.
46. Both the *Mūlamadhyamakakārikā* and the *Ratnāvalī* are certainly Buddhist works. The *Ratnāvalī* (verses 61–62) discusses the superiority of Buddhism to Sāṃkhya, Vaiśeṣika, and Jainism insofar as none of these have a teaching that is beyond existence and nonexistence. Similarly, in verse 237 Nāgārjuna tells the king not to revere other religious specialists (*Tīrthikas*).
47. *Nandi: Prakrit Text, Sanskrit Rendering, Hindi Translation, Comparative Notes and Various Appendixes,* A. Mahaprajna, ed. (Ladnun, Rajasthan: Jain Visva-Bharati Institute, 1997), p. 9.

    V. 35 "kāliyasuya-aṇu-ogassa dhāre dhāre ya puvvāṇaṃ| himaṃvatakhamā-samaṇe vaṃde ṇāgajjuṇāyariё||"

    V. 36 "miü-maddava-saṃpaṇṇe aṇupuṃvvi vāyagattaṇaṃ patte| oha-suya-samāyāre nāgajjuṇavāye vaṃde||"
48. Natubhai Shah, *Jainism: The World of the Conquerors* (Portland: Sussex Academic Press, 1998), p. 17.
49. Demiéville has *Suviśuddhaprabhābhūmi.* See Paul Demiéville, "Sur un passage du *Mahāmeghasūtra,*" appendix 2 of "Les Versions chinois du *Milindapañha,*" *Bulletin de l'Ecole française d'Extrême Orient* 24, no. 1 (1924): 218.
50. "ye śes 'byuṅ gnas 'od."
51. "yaṅ 'phags pa sprin chen po stoṅ phrag bcu gñis pa las kyaṅ| kun dga' po li tsa byi gźon nu sems can thams cad kyis mthoṅ na dga' ba źes bya ba 'di ni ṅa mya ṅan las 'das nas lo bźi brgya lon pa na klu źes bya ba'i dge sloṅ du gyur nas ṅai bstan pa rgyas par rab tu bstan te| mthar gyi sa rab tu daṅ ba'i od ces bya ba'i 'jig rten gyi khams su de bźin gśegs pa dgra bcom pa yaṅ dag par rdzogs pa'i saṅs rgyas ye śes 'byuṅ gnas 'od ces bya bar 'gyur ro źes gsuṅs so| de'i phyir 'dis luṅ phyin ci ma log par ṅes par grub bo||" (Candrakīrti, *Madhyamakāvatāra par Candrakīrti,* Louis de La Valée Poussin, ed. [Osnabruck: Biblio, 1970], p. 76).
52. Translation by 曇無讖 = ("Dharmakṣema"), an Indian monk who arrived in China in 412. See Demiéville et al., *Répertoire du canon bouddhique sino-japonais,* p. 243.
53. 是大菩薩大香象王 (T. 387, p. 1100a7–8).
54. This is Demiéville's reconstruction. See Demiéville, "Sur un passage," p. 225.
55. "The one who at that time was the *nāga* king Mahāvīrya is now the Licchavi, Priyadarśana, and will become the Bhikṣu who protects the dharma." 時王精進龍王者.即令 樂見梨車.是樂見梨車.即是未來護法比丘 (T. 387, p. 1100b5–6). See Demiéville, "Sur un passage," p. 228.
56. Demiéville, "Sur un passage," p. 227; T. 387, pp. 1099c–1100a.
57. The *Mahābherīhārakaparivarta Sūtra* does give a name to this monk, but that name is "Mindful." See Hopkins, *Advice,* p. 15. Similarly, the name "Nāgārjuna" is nowhere mentioned in the corresponding prophecy in the *Suvarṇaprabhāsottama Sūtra.* See *Suvarṇaprabhāsottamasūtra: Das Goldglanz-Sūtra: Ein Sanskrittext des Mahayana-Buddhismus,* Johannes Nobel, ed. (Leiden: E.J. Brill, 1950), pp. 12–17.

58. The Sanskrit is from Mabbett's reconstruction. See Mabbett, "The Problem," p. 337.
59. Ibid.
60. Bu-ston, *History of Buddhism,* p. 129.
61. Ibid., pp. 129–130.
62. Granoff, "Jain Biographies," p. 47.
63. Ibid., p. 48.
64. Stein, *Kalhaṇa's Rājataraṅgiṇī,* p. 33.
65. See ibid., n184. "K. refers here to the legend told in the *Nīlamata* (vv. 325 *sq.*) regarding the liberation of the land from the Piśācas. The latter . . . occupied Kaśmīr under a sentence of Kāśyapa during the six months of winter, while men lived there for the remaining six months only, and emigrated each year before the month of Āśvayuja. The deliverance of the country from the Piśācas and the excessive cold was effective after four Yugas through the observance of the rites which Candradeva, and old Brahman, descended from Kāśyapa, had learned from the Nīla Nāga . . . The story told by K[alhana] in i. 178–184 is obviously in particulars a mere rechauffé of the ancient legend. The charitable comparison between the Piśācas and the Bauddhas leaves no doubt as to the source from which K. borrowed it."
66. For example, Rājaśekhara Sūri uses this term in his *Prabandha Kośa,* p. 85.
67. Granoff, "Jain Biographies," pp. 49–50.
68. This theme also shows up (predictably) in tantric stories related to Nāgārjuna. White mentions two such incidents; one in the *Rasendra Maṅgala,* where Nāgārjuna promises the Goddess Prajñāpāramitā that he will turn Śrīparvata into gold. On the other hand, in a fourteenth-century Telegu work, the *Navanātha* by Gauraṇa, the credit for this feat is given to Nāgārjuna's student (also named Nāgārjuna). See White, *Alchemical Body,* p. 166.
69. Watters, *Yuan Chwang's Travels,* 2:201.
70. In Xuanzang's account the length of the Sātavāhana king's life is also tied to Nāgārjuna's, but no elixir is mentioned.
71. Granoff, "Jain Biographies," p. 47.
72. Ibid., p. 57.
73. The way to the association of Nāgārjuna with Gujarat is opened by his identification with the Surāṣṭrian monk in the *Mahāmegha Sūtra* (Mt. Śatruñjāya is in Bhavnagar district, Gujarat).
74. White, *Alchemical Body,* p. 70.
75. James Roland Ware, *Alchemy, Medicine, and Religion in the China of* A.D. 320: The Nei P'ien of Ko Hung (Cambridge: MIT Press, 1966), p. 16.2a. Perhaps, the earliest reference to an invisibility potion in an Indic source can be found in Bāṇabhaṭṭa's seventh-century play *Kādambarī.* See White, *Alchemical Body,* p. 49.
76. See Karen Lang's translation of Candrakīrti's *Catuḥśatakavṛtti:* "Āryadeva was born on the island of Siṃhala as the some of the Siṃhala king. In the end he

renounced his status as crown thre prince and entered the religious life. He then traveled to southern India and became Nāgārjuna's disciple" (*Four Illusions: Candrakīrti's Advice to Travelers on the Bodhisattva Path* [New York: Oxford University Press, 2003], p. 112).

77. K. Satcidananda Murti, *Nāgārjuna* (New Delhi: National Book Trust, 1971), p. 50.
78. Robinson, *Early Mādhyamika,* p. 72.
79. In this connection, however, it should be mentioned that Xuanzang visited Dhānyakaṭaka and did not hear any stories about Nāgārjuna. This case is different from that of Nālanda insofar as Nālanda was still a vibrant university when he visited there (hence, one should expect some institutional memory of a former master to survive), whereas many of the monasteries around Dhānyakaṭaka were deserted. See Watters, *Yuan Chwang's Travels,* p. 214.
80. Anne Macdonald suggests that the description of the stupa at Dhānyakaṭaka is influenced at least in part not by what was there to be seen but by the *Kalacakra Tantra*'s versions of mandalas of Vajradhatu and Dharmadhatuvagisvara ("Le Dhanyakataka de Man-Luns guru," *Bulletin de l'Ecole française d'Extrême Orient* 57 [1970]: 187).
81. Wooden images of the Buddha are also mentioned in verse 2 of the *Suhṛllekha:* "Just as the wise ones will respect a statue of the Sugata, even though it be made of wood [and] however [unadorned] it may be, so in the same manner, although this composition of mine may be pitiful, may you not criticize it, for it is based on the Sublime Teaching." See Nāgārjuna, *Golden Zephyr,* p. 6. Guṇavarman's translation does not specifically mention wood, but refers to a "Buddha image which is carved and painted" (T. 1672, 刻畫造佛像, p. 745b14). However, since Nāgārjuna's authorship of this text is more difficult to defend, my inquiry is limited to the relevant verses of the *Ratnāvalī.*
82. Translation of these verses is from Hopkins, *Advice,* pp. 124–125 and 159. There is no Sanskrit available for any of these verses.

    Tibetan: "saṅs rgyas sku gzugs mchod rten daṅ| gtsug lag khaṅ dag gus tshul du| śin tu rgya chen gnas mal sogs| rgya chen phyug pa bsgrub par mdzod||" (v. 231).

    Variant readings: 231c [Narthang and Peking] *gnas lam* vs. *gnas mal*, in Chone, Derge, and in Rgyal tshab rje's commentary on the *Ratnāvalī* (in Nāgārjuna, *Nagārjuna's Ratnāvalī: Vol. I, The Basic Texts (Sanskrit, Tibetan, Chinese),* Michael Hahn, ed., Indica et Tibetica series, vol 1 [Bonn: Indica et Tibetica Publications, 1982], p. 78).

    佛像及支提 殿堂拄持廟 最勝多供具 汝應敬成立 (T. 1656, 498b26–27).
83. v. 232. "rin chen kun las bgyis pa yi| saṅs rgyas sku gzugs dbyibs mdzes śiṅ| legs par bris pa padma la| bźugs pa dag kyaṅ bgyid do stsol||" (Nāgārjuna, *Nagārjuna's Ratnāvalī*).

    Variations: v. 232b Narthang and Peking have *legs śiṅ* whereas Chone and Derge have *mdes śiṅ*. v. 232d; Narthang and Peking have two lines: "bźugs pa dag la rin po che| kun gyis brgyan pa bgyid du gsol|.” The Chone and Derge versions, however, are confirmed by Rgyal tshab rje and Paramārtha's translation (below) (Nāgārjuna, *Nagārjuna's Ratnāvalī*, p. 78).

John Dunne and Sarah McClintock write: “The Zhol, Narthang and Peking editions of a slightly different reading. Following those editions, the verse would read as follows: “From all kinds of precious substances, please make well drawn and beautifully proportioned images of buddhas seated upon lotuses and adorned with all kinds of gems” (Nāgārjuna, *The Precious Garland: An Epistle to a King*, Dunne and McClintock, trans. [Boston: Wisdom, 1997], p. 118n50). My thanks to John Dunne and Wisdom Press for providing me with a copy of this translation.

Paramārtha's translation:

坐寶 (var. Ming mss. 實) 連花上 好色微妙畫 一切金寶種 汝應造佛像 (T. 1656, p. 498b28–28).

84. Both Dunne and McClintock and Hopkins translate *sku gzugs* as “icon,” which is certainly acceptable. For our purposes, however, “icon” could refer to any of a number of nonanthropomorphic representations of the Buddha (such as the empty throne, the *Buddhapāda*) prevalent in India until the third century C.E. It should be noted that a more literal translation for *sku gzugs* would be “body-image.” Since the word *sku* is the respectful form for *lus* = “body,” it is implied that the image the king is to go in front of is an image of the Buddha's body. The phrase is unequivocal in Paramārtha's Chinese translation: 為此因及果| 現前佛支提 (Therefore, rise up determined and appear before a Buddha or caitya).

85. v. 465. “de phyir sku gzugs mchod rten gyi| spyan sṅa 'am yaṅ na gźan yaṅ ruṅ| tshigs su bcad pa ṭi śu 'di| ñin gcig bźin yaṅ dus gsum brjod||” (Nāgārjuna, *Ratnāvalī*, p. 155).

為此因及果| 現前佛支提 日夜各三遍 願誦二十揭 (T. 1656, 504b 12--13).

86. Paul Harrison writes, “there can be no doubt that by the second century C.E. some Buddhists were indeed practicing a form of *buddhānusmṛti* that . . . included detailed visualization of the physical body of the Buddha, and was accompanied by the use of images. The principle evidence for this is provided by the Mahāyāna *Pratyutpanna-buddha-saṃmukhāvasthita-samādhi-sūtra* . . . the first translation of which was made by the Indo-Scythian Lokakṣema in 179 C.E.” (“Commemoration and Identification in *Buddhānusmṛti*,” in *In the Mirror of Memory: Reflections on Mindfulness and Remembrance in Indian and Tibetan Buddhism*, Janet Gyatso, ed. [Albany: State University of New York Press, 1992], p. 220). Ju-hyung Rhi points out several other early Mahāyāna sources in which the act of constructing Buddhas sitting on lotuses leads to better rebirth as an *upapāduka*. His references are: the *Sumatidārikaparipṛccha* (T. 334, 76c; translated by Dharmarakṣa, c. late third century), *Vimaladatta-paripṛcchā* (T. 338, 94c-95a; also translated by Dharmarakṣa), and the *Bodhisambhāraśāstra* attributed to Nāgārjuna himself (T. 1660, 536c). See Ju-hyung Rhi, “Gandhāran Images of the 'Śrāvastī Miracle': An Iconographic

Reassessment" (Ph.D. dissertation, University of California, 1991), pp. 144–145 and notes 8–9.

Regarding the ritual use of these images, it is interesting to note that although Mahāyāna *sūtras* such as the *Ugradattaparipṛcchā* and the late *Bodhisattvaprātimokṣa* mention a Mahāyāna ritual like the one that Nāgārjuna describes in the *Ratnāvalī*, the *Ratnāvalī* is the only text that instructs the adherent to stand in front of a statue or *stūpa* and not to stand in front of a (human monk?) Mahāyāna bodhisattva.

87. Although the controversies surrounding the dates and chronology of the Sātavāhana dynasty are far from over, this chapter uses the dates provided by Shastri. See Ajay Mitra Shastri, *The Satavahanas and the Western Kshatrapas: A Historical Framework* (Nagpur: Dattsons, 1998), p. 131. Since I am fixing Nāgārjuna's dates to the reign of Yajña Śrī, the dates of the former should be adjusted to correspond to discoveries concerning the date of the latter.

88. See Walter Spink, *Ajaṇṭā to Ellora* (Ann Arbor: Marg, 1967), pp. 7–8. There is one notable exception that perhaps proves the point. Marilyn Leese has documented two anthropomorphic images of the Buddha at cave 3 at Kaṇheri. These images (which she takes pains to prove were carved during the reign of Yajña Śrī) are quite small, only about a foot high, and are placed at the top of a pillar so as to be inconspicuous. She attributes their small size to their being modeled after portable images procured through trade with the north. See Marilyn Leese, "The Early Buddhist Icons in Kaṇheri's Cave 3," *Artibus Asiae* 41, no. 1 (1979): 93. Madhukar Keshav Dhavalikar, however, attributes their small stature to another motive: "[The Kaṇheri Buddha images] have been carved on the top of the pillar. No one can normally see it and it therefore seems highly likely that the sculptor had stealthily carved it without the knowledge of the donor" (*Later Hinayana Caves of Western India* [Poona: Deccan College Postgraduate and Research Institute, 1984], p. 66). Dhavalikar takes this as proof positive that the Buddha image had made it to the western Deccan by the end of the second century, perhaps in order to support his claim that some of the shrine niches found at Kaṇheri may have contained wooden images of the Buddha. In any case, the fact remains that no such images have been found. This, coupled with the avoidance of any open anthropomorphic representation of the Buddha in stone or in paint, leaves us with the impression that whereas the Buddha image may have been known at this time, its representation was considered somehow distasteful.

89. See Ajay Mitra Shastri, "The Closing Phase of the Sātavāhana Power and Allied Issues," in his *Early History of the Deccan* (Delhi: Sundeep Prakashan, 1987), pp. 38–44.

90. Himanshu P. Ray, *Monastery and Guild: Commerce Under the Sātavāhanas* (Delhi: Oxford University Press, 1986), p. 40.

91. See Ramesh C. Sharma, *Buddhist Art of Mathurā* (Delhi: Agam Kala Prakashan, 1984), pp. viii–ix.

92. *Divyāvadānam,* P. L. Vaidya, ed. (Darbhanga: Mithila Institute of Post-graduate Studies and Research in Sanskrit Learning, 1959), p. 466.
93. "The priests and the laymen in India make Kaityas or images with earth, or impress the Buddha's image on silk or paper, and worship it with offerings wherever they go. Sometimes they build stupas of the Buddha by making a pile and surrounding it with bricks. They sometimes form these stupas in lovely fields, and leave them to fall in ruins. Any one may thus employ himself in making the objects for worship. Again when the people make images and Kaityas which consist of gold, silver, copper, iron, earth, lacquer, bricks, and stone, or when they heap up the snowy sand . . . , they put in the images or Kaityas two kinds of śāriras. The relics of the teacher, and the Gāthā of the chain of causation" (Takakusu, *A Record of the Buddhist Religion*, pp. 150–151).
94. Dhavalikar, *Later Hinayana Caves,* p. 51.
95. Elizabeth Rosen Stone, *The Buddhist Art of Nāgārjunakoṇḍa* (Delhi: Motilal Banarsidass, 1994), pl. 187.
96. These phases are actually a revision of the ones first proposed by Sivaramamurti, "Amaravati Sculptures in the Madras Government Museum," *Bulletin of the Madras Government Museum* 4 (1956): 26–32.
97. Anamika Roy, *Amarāvatī Stūpa: A Critical Comparison of Epigraphic, Architectural, and Sculptural Evidence* (Delhi: Agam Kala Prakashan, 1994), p. 132.
98. For a discussion of these seats, see ibid., pp. 136–137.
99. Roy, *Amarāvatī Stūpa,* p. 138.
100. For examples of this motif, cf. Nilakanth Purushottam Joshi and Ramesh Chandra Sharma, *Catalogue of Gandhāra Sculptures in the State Museum, Lucknow* (Lucknow: State Museum, 1969); Sarla D. Nagar, *Gandhāran Sculpture: A Catalogue of the Collection in the Museum of Art and Archaeology, University of Missouri-Columbia* (Columbia: Museum of Art and Archaeology, 1981).
101. See Nagar, *Gandhāran Sculpture.* There are, perhaps, some early exceptions from Sikri, which Sir John Marshall dates to the first century C.E. See Sir John Hubert Marshall, *The Buddhist Art of Gandhara: The Story of the Early School, Its Birth, Growth, and Decline* (Karachi: Department of Archaeology and Museums, Government of Pakistan, 1973), p. 56 and plate 50.
102. See Sharma, *Buddhist Art of Mathurā,* plates.
103. Ananda K. Coomaraswamy, *Elements of Buddhist Iconography* (New Delhi: M. Manoharlal, 1972), p. 39. Precursors to the *padmapīṭha* can be found earlier. For example, the State Museum of Lucknow has an image of Hāritī whose feet rest on a square base decorated with lotus petals. See Joshi and Sharma, *Catalogue of Gandhāra Sculptures,* fig. 68 (accession num. 47.105). At Bharhut, there are two medallions with reliefs of Śrī Lakṣmi standing on a lotus rising out of a *pūrṇa-ghaṭa* and a *yakṣī* standing on a lotus. See Benimadhab Barua, *Barhut: Aspects of Life and Art* (Calcutta: Indian Research Institute Publications, 1934–1935), book 3, pls. LXVI. 79, LXVII. 80 and LXVIII. 81. Similarly (and perhaps related), there is a beautiful image of the Buddha's mother, Māyā, sitting on a lotus (also rising out of a *pūrṇa-ghaṭa*) from Sāñchī. See Sir

John Marshall and Alfred Foucher, *Monuments of Sāñcī* (Delhi: Swati, 1982), vol. 2, pl. 41.

104. The same dates are also concluded by Robert Knox for the pieces in the British Museum. Cf. Robert Knox, *Amaravati: Buddhist Sculpture from the Great Stūpa* (London: British Museum Press, 1992), pp. 60 and 139–140.
105. See Roy, *Amarāvatī Stūpa,* appendix 4, table 4.
106. Cf. ibid., tables 3 and 4.
107. Roy describes this piece as follows: "The carving on this fragment is divided into three panels. The uppermost shows a *stūpa* surmounted by an umbrella and the lower panels show the haloed figure of the Buddha on a lotus pedestal. Between the second and the third panels there are two inscriptions belonging to two different periods. One belongs to the first century B.C., while the other belongs to the seventh century A.D. Moreover, the sculpture does not belong to the period of either of the inscriptions. It seems that the first inscription was engraved on the plain octagonal pillar in the first century B.C., and that this pillar was then recarved in the third century A.D. Subsequently, in the seventh century A.D. another inscription was engraved on it" (ibid., p. 152).
108. Ibid., p. 198.
109. Knox, *Amaravati,* p. 141.
110. H. Sarkar, "Some Early Inscriptions in the Amarāvatī Museum," *Journal of Ancient Indian History* 4, nos. 1–2 (1971): 8.
111. H. Sarkar, "Nāgārjunakoṇḍa Prakrit Inscription of Gautamīputra Vijaya Sātakarṇi, Year 6," *Epigraphia Indica* 36 (1965–66): 273–275. Other inscriptions refer to Nāgārjunakoṇḍa as "Vijayapūri." Cf. Jean Philippe Vogel, "Prakrit Inscriptions from a Buddhist Site at Nāgārjunakoṇḍa," *Epigraphica Indica* 20 (1929–1930): 22.
112. For the dates of the Ikṣvāku kings, see H. Sarkar, "The Nāgārjunakoṇḍa Phase of the Lower Kṛṣṇā Valley Art: A Study Based on Epigraphical Data," in *Indian Epigraphy: Its Bearing on the History of Art,* F. Asher and G. S. Gai, ed. (New Delhi: American Institute of Indian Studies, 1985), p. 31.
113. Stone, *Nāgārjunakoṇḍa,* p. 17.
114. Ray, *Monastery and Guild,* p. 40.
115. Rao, *Buddhist Inscriptions of Andhradesa,* p. 10.
116. Ibid., pp. 174–175.
117. The southernmost Dharmaguptaka inscription located so far was found at Mathurā. For a recent discussion of the Dharmaguptakas and their location, see Salomon, *Ancient Buddhist Scrolls from Gandhāra*, pp. 167–169.
118. Rao, *Buddhist Inscriptions of Andhradesa,* pp. 156–157.
119. Ibid., p. 201.
120. Ibid., pp. 214–216.

Pṛthivi(vi) Śrī-Mūlarājaḥ sva-vishaya-vāsinaḥ sarvvān = evam = ājñāpayati . . . yadhā(thā) [||] viditam = astu bhavatām may = ātmīya-priya-tanay-ānugraharttam (thaṃ) Tāṇḍikoṇda tat = pratishṭhāpita –śākya-bhikshu-mahāvihāra-ni vāsinaḥ catur-ddiś = āryya-vara-bhikshu saṃghasya chīvara-śayy = asana-glāna-pratyaya-bheshajya-parishkār-opabhogāya Tālupaka-vishaye Tāṇḍikoṇḍa-chu[r]p pāṭuppuḍu- Velkoṇḍa-kuriki.

Notes to Chapter 3

1. Schopen, "The Mahāyāna and the Middle Period in Indian Buddhism," p. 19.
2. Nattier points out that the *Ugradattaparipṛcchā,* in particular, lacks not only the kind of defensiveness that is often found in other Mahāyāna works but the usual merit incentives to copy the book. This would suggest that the author(s) of the *Ugra* were quite comfortably ensconced in their monastery, wherever that was. See especially Jan Nattier, *A Few Good Men: The Bodhisattva Path According to the Inquiry of Ugra (Ugraparipṛcchā)* (Honolulu: University of Hawai'i Press, 2003), p. 185. One might also say the same about the *Ratnārāśī Sūtra.*
3. Schopen, "The Mahāyāna and the Middle Period in Indian Buddhism," pp. 6–7.
4. Presumably, one could make the same case for works by Aśvaghosa, a contemporary of Nāgārjuna.
5. Schopen, "The Mahāyāna," p. 8.
6. Ibid.
7. Ibid.
8. Although, at certain points some *vinayas* appear to be renegotiating the boundaries of secular and monastic law. For an interesting discussion of this negotiation, see Gregory Schopen, "Monastic Law Meets the Real World: A Monk's Continuing Right to Inherit Family Property in Classical India," *History of Religions* 35, no. 2 (1995).
9. Gregory Schopen, "Archaeology and Protestant Presuppositions in the Study of Indian Buddhism," *History of Religions* 31, no. 1 (1991).
10. Gregory Schopen, "Archaeology and Protestant Presuppositions in the Study of Indian Buddhism," in *Bones, Stones, and Buddhist Monks: Collected Papers on the Archaeology, Epigraphy, and Texts of Monastic Buddhism in India,* Schopen, ed. (Honolulu: University of Hawai'i Press, 1997), p. 4.
11. See ibid., p. 5.
12. See, for example, Gregory Schopen, "The Good Monk and His Money in a Buddhist Monasticism of 'The Mahāyāna Period,'" *Eastern Buddhist,* n.s. 32, no. 1 (2000): 85–105.
13. For references see M. B. Voyce, "The King's Enforcement of the Vinaya Piṭaka: The Purification of the Saṅgha Under Asoka (C.B.C. 269–232)," *Zeitschrift für Religions und Geistesgeschichte* 37, no. 1 (1985): 38. See also his discussion of *vinaya* as law on p. 53.
14. Ibid., p. 38n5.
15. See Chapter 2.

16. T. 1425, 492a7–9.
17. Leo Strauss, *Persecution and the Art of Writing* (reprint, Chicago: University of Chicago Press, 1988), p. 24.
18. A note concerning the date and provenance of this text is useful at this point. Although multiple manuscripts of the *Mahāsāṅghika Prātimokṣa* have been found, the full text of the *Mahāsāṅghika vinaya* survives only in the Chinese translation by Faxian and Saṅghabhadra completed at the beginning of the fifth century. There is one (Hybrid) Sanskrit manuscript of the *Abhisamācārika* section, corresponding to the Chinese translation, T. 1425, pp. 300a ff. The only other Sanskrit manuscript are two fragments dating from the sixth century found in the Schøyen collection. See Seishi Karashima, "A Fragment of the Prātimokṣa-Vibhaṅga of the Mahāsāṅghika-Lokottaravādins," in *Buddhist Manuscripts in the Schøyen Collection,* Jens Braarvig, ed. (Oslo: Hermes, 2000), pp. 1: 233–241, and idem, "Two More Folios of the Prātimokṣa-Vibhaṅga of the Mahāsāṃghika-Lokottaravādins," in *Buddhist Manuscripts in the Schøyen Collection,* vol. 3, Jens Braarvig, ed. (Oslo: Hermes, 2002), pp. 215–228. Faxian records that he discovered this manuscript in a Mahāyāna monastery in Paṭaliputra, but that his manuscript had originally been copied at the Jetavana-vihāra sometime earlier (see T. 1425, 548b1 ff.). As to the date of the *Mahāsāṅghika vinaya* itself, it could not have been completed before the first century C.E., since it mentions the practice of covering Buddhist monuments with silk banners and flags (presupposing a silk trade) and mentions the practice of bathing the image of the bodhisattva (which presupposes the existence and use of statues of the Buddha). Although we are not secure in dating all portions of it until the beginning of the fifth century, there is evidence that this *vinaya* and its commentary was in use in the second century. That this *vinaya* was in use in the Lower Krishna River Valley has been argued by B. S. L. Hanumantha Rao: "It seems that *Mahāvinayadhara* [in a Dhānyakaṭaka inscription] does not mean the great Master of *Vinaya.* It is probable that *Mahāvinaya* was the Text of the *Mahāsāṅghikas.* The term *Mahāvinayadhara* occurs in several of the Dhānyakaṭaka inscriptions and in one record, the sect living at Dhānyakaṭaka is clearly mentioned as *pūrva mahāvinaśeliyas* . . . If read together, the terms *Mahāvinayadhara* and *Mahāvinayaśeliyas,* suggest that there was a text known as *Mahāvinaya.* The masters of the Text were *Mahāvinayadharas* and the Sailas who followed it were *Mahāvina(ya)śeliyas*" (*Buddhist Inscriptions of Andhradesa,* p. 51).
19. The five *anantarīya karma* are listed in the *Mahāvyutpatti* as: (1) matricide, (2) killing an arhant, (3) patricide, (4) splitting the *saṅgha,* and (5) spilling the blood of a Buddha. See Unrai Wogihara, ed., *The Sanskrit-Chinese Dictionary of Buddhist Technical Terms Based on the Mahāvyupatti* (Tokyo: Sankibo, 1959), p. 79.
20. Vasubandhu, *L'Abhidharmakośa de Vasubandhu*, p. 218.
21. Charles Prebish, *Buddhist Monastic Discipline* (Delhi: Motilal Banarsidass, 1996), p. 56.

22. Ibid., pp. 56 and 58; *Prātimokṣasūtram of the Lokottaravādimahāsāṅghika School,* Nathmal Tatia, ed. (Patna: Kashi Prasad Jayaswal Research Institute, 1976), p. 10.
23. The so-called *adhikaraṇaśamatha, viz.*: confrontation, majority rule, exemptions for mental defect and "covering over with grass."
24. *Majjhima Nikāya,* V. Trenckner and R. Chalmers, eds. (London: Pāli Text Society, 1888–1925), 2:247; translated as *The Middle Length Discourses of the Buddha,* Ven. Ñāṇamoli and Ven. Bodhi, trans. (Boston: Wisdom, 1995), pp. 855–856.
25. Heinz Bechert, "The Importance of Aśoka's So-Called Schism Edict," in *Indological and Buddhist Studies,* L. Hercus et al. (Canberra: Australian National University, 1982), p. 65.
26. Williams, *Mahāyāna Buddhism,* pp. 4–5 (emphasis added).
27. *The Vinaya Piṭakam, One of the Principle Buddhist Holy Scriptures in the Pāli Language,* Hermann Oldenberg, ed. (London: Williams and Norgate, 1879–1883), 2:204.
28. "adhammaṃ dhamoti dīpentīti -ādisu aṭṭhārasasu bhedakaravatthūsu suttantapariyāyena tāva dasa kusalakammapathā dhammo. dasa akusalakammapathā adhammo. tathā cattāro satipaṭṭhānā cattāro sammappadhānā cattāra iddhipādā pañcindriyāni pañcabalāni satta bojjhaṅgā ariyo atthaṅgiko maggoti sattatiṃsa bodhipakkhiyadhammā dhammo nāma" (Buddhaghosa, *Samantapāsādikā: Buddhaghosa's Commentary on the Vinaya Pitaka,* J. Takakusu and M. Nagai, eds. [London: Pāli Text Society, 1947–1976], 6:1277).
29. Nattier and Prebish, "Mahāsāṅghika Origins and the Beginnings of Buddhist Sectarianism," p. 241.
30. For references to the six *anudharma,* see Franklin Edgerton, *Buddhist Hybrid Sanskrit Dictionary* (reprint, Delhi: Motilal Banarshidass, 1993), *s.v.*
31. T. 1425, 281c12–21.
32. Although later than Nāgārjuna, Vasubandhu notes in the *Vyākhyāyukti* that even among non-Mahāyānists there were textual variations from sect to sect. According to José Cabézon's translation: "it is clear that even in the *Śrāvakayāna* the word of the Buddha is incomplete. Even the authorized editions (*yang dag par bsdus pa'i gzhi bo*) which are composed by the four arhants such as Mahākaśyapa, etc., have degenerated, for the various sects (*sde pa*) have disparate ways of setting for the scriptures, of dividing them into chapters, and so forth. . . . What is more, even in one sect, one and the same *sūtra* will oftentimes have different passages and chapters" ("Vasubandhu's *Vyākhyāyukti* on the Authenticity of the Mahāyāna Sūtras," p. 227).
33. I-Ching, *Chinese Monks in India: Biography of Eminent Monks Who Went to the Western World in Search of the Law During the Great T'ang Dynasty,* Latika Lahiri, trans. (Delhi: Motilal Banarsidass, 1986), pp. 54–55; T. 2066, 5c27–8.
34. T. 1425, 328a3–14.
35. For example, a *bahuśrutīya* monk is the first authority listed in the *Dīgha*

Nikāya version of the *mahāpadeśā* quoted above. The *bahuśrutīya* is also included in many of the standard lists of monastic vocations.

36. For a translation and discussion of Aśoka's Kauśāmbhī pillar inscription, see Bechert, "The Importance of Aśoka's So-called Schism Edict," p. 62ff. For a discussion of the convergence between *vinaya* law and *Dharmaśāstra* on this matter, see also Voyce, "The King's Enforcement of the Vinaya Pitaka."
37. Pānduraṅga Vāmana Kāne, *History of Dharmaśāstra* (Poona: Bhandarkar Oriental Research Institute, 1968–1975), 3:158 (emphasis added).
38. For a description of the kingdom, see Atwood, "Life in Third-fourth Century Cadh'ota," pp. 166–169.
39. Burrow, *Translation of the Kharoṣṭhi Documents*, p. 95.
40. Given the types of infractions listed, we may assume that these are *vinaya* rules and not *kriyākarma*.
41. The *Cūḷavagga* adds that he had been a "vulture torturer" (*gaddhabādhin*) before becoming a monk. The Mahāsāṅghika account lacks this detail.
42. 如來説法我知。世尊説障道法。習此法不能障道 (T. 1425, 367a9–10); cf. "tathāhaṃ bhagavatā dhammaṃ desitaṃ ājānāmi yathā yeme antarāyika dhamma vuttā bhagavatā te paṭisevato nālaṃ antarāyāyā 'ti|" (*Vinaya piṭakam*, 2:25).
43. T. 1425, 367b25–28.
44. 諸比丘應諫。是比丘作是言。長老。汝莫謗世尊。謗世尊者不善。世尊不作是語。世尊説障道。實能障道。汝捨此惡事。諸比丘諫是比丘。故堅持不捨。如是第二第三諫。捨者善。若不捨。僧應與作舉羯磨。已得波夜提 (T. 1425, 367b16–21).
45. Prebish, *Buddhist Monastic Discipline*, p. 82 (Sanskrit added); "yo puna bhikṣurjānan bhikṣuṃ tathā utkṣiptaṃ samagreṇa saṅghena dharmeṇa vinayena yathāvādiṃ tathākāiṃ tām pāpikām dṛṣṭiṃ apratinissarantaṃ akṛtānudharmaṃ saṃbhuñjeya vā saṃvaseya vā sahagāraśayyāṃ va kalpeya, pācattikaṃ|" (*Prātimokṣasūtram*, p. 23). This rule appears as *pācattika* rule no. 69 in the *Theravāda-vinaya* and no. 56 in the *Mūlasarvāstivāda-* and in the *Sarvāstivāda-vinayas*. (See Prebish, *Buddhist Monastic Discipline*, p. 143.)
46. The issue of *buddhavacana* and the constitution of scriptural authority in Buddhism was first treated by Etienne Lamotte in his "La Critique d'authenticité dans le bouddhisme," in *India Antiqua: A Volume of Oriental Studies Presented by His Friends and Pupils to Jean Philippe Vogel, C.I.E., on the Occasion of the Fiftieth Anniversary of His Doctorate* (Leiden: E.J. Brill, 1947), pp. 213–222. This discussion has been updated and extended to the appropriation of this category by Mahāyānists and Vajrāyānists in an excellent article by Ronald Davidson in his "Introduction to the Standards of Scriptural Authority in Indian Buddhism," in *Chinese Buddhist Apocrypha*, Robert Buswell, ed. (Honolulu: University of Hawai'i Press, 1990), pp. 291–325. Much of the following discussion of *buddhavacana* has already been covered in these two sources.
47. 法者。世尊所説。世尊所印可。世尊説者。世尊自説印可者。諸弟子説世尊印可 (T. 1425, 367b22–24).

48. 法者佛所說佛印可。佛所說者。佛口自說。佛印可者。佛弟子餘人所說佛所印可(T. 1425, 336a21–24). Cf. Lamotte, "Critique d'authenticité," p. 216.
49. We find a parallel to these criteria in *Dharmaśāstra* works such as the *Yajñavalkyasmṛti*.
50. See *Dīgha Nikāya*, T.W. Rhys Davids and J.E. Carpenter, eds. (London: Pāli Text Society, 1889–1910), 2:124ff., and T. 1, 17c; *Aṅguttara-nikāya*, Rev. Richard Morris, ed. (London: H. Frowde for the Pāli Text Society, 1885–1910), 2:167. Lamotte lists the following references: *Mūlasarvāstivādavinaya* (T. 1451, 389b–c), the *Dīrgha Āgama* (T. 1, 17c), three versions of the *Mahāparinirvāna sūtra* (T. 5, 127a; T. 6, 182c; and T. 7, 195c); and *Tseng yi a han* (T. 125, 652b).
51. George D. Bond, "Two Theravāda Traditions of Meaning of 'The Word of the Buddha,'" *Maha-Bodhi* 83, nos. 10–12 (1975): 406.
52. *The Long Discourses of the Buddha: A Translation of the Dīgha Nikāya*, trans. Maurice Walshe (Boston: Wisdom, 1995), p. 255 (Pāli added); trans., cf. *Dīgha Nikāya*, 2:124, and T. 1, 17c. It is also found in the *Mūlasarvāstivāda Vinayavastu*, T. 1451, 389b–c.
53. *mātikādharo* = Sanskrit *mātṛkādhara*; this could also refer to the *prātimokṣa*.
54. See Gregory Schopen, "On Monks, Nuns, and 'Vulgar' Practices: The Introduction of the Image Cult into Indian Buddhism," in *Bones, Stones, and Buddhist Monks*, p. 243.
55. Of course, the opposite holds as well. If a monastery considered its canon closed and its contents not up for discussion, Mahāyānists would have to adopt the kind of combative strategies that one finds in, say, the *Saddharmapuṇḍarikā Sūtra*.
56. See Davidson, "Introduction to the Standards of Scriptural Authority," p. 301.
57. Vasubandhu, *L'Abhidharmakośa*, 9:251–252. This criterion for *buddhavacana* does not appear in the *Dīgha* passage or in the *Aṅguttara*. It does, however, figure prominently in most of the later discussions of *buddhavacana*.
58. "*na kilaitad buddha-vacanam* iti. kenāpi adhyāropitāny etāni sūtrāṇīti abhiprāyaḥ. *sarva-nikāyāntareśv* iti Tāmraparṇīya-nikāy'ādiṣu. *na ca sūtraṃ bādhate*. na ca sūtrāntaraṃ bādhate. na ca sūtrāntaraṃ virodhayati. *na dharmatā bādhata* iti pratītyasamutpāda-dharmatāṃ" (Yaśomitra, *Sputārthā Abhidharmakośavyākhyā by Yaśomitra*, Unrai Wogihara, ed. [Tokyo: Sankibo Buddhist Book Store, 1971], 2:705). Text in italic is from Vasubandhu.
59. Davidson, "Introduction to the Standards of Scriptural Authority," p. 301.
60. Gregory Schopen, "Counting the Buddha and the Local Spirits In: A Monastic Ritual of Inclusion for the Rain Retreat," *Journal of Indian Philosophy* 30 (2002): 360.
61. A formal speech to commence the rain retreat can also be found in the *Mahīśāsaka vinaya* (T. 1421, 129a15–19), the *Mahāsāṅghika vinaya* (T. 1425, 450c8–17), and in the *Sarvāstivāda vinaya* (T. 1435, 173b18–c1). The *Theravāda vinaya* does not have an equivalent speech, and although there is such a speech in the *Dharmaguptaka vinaya* (T. 1428, 830c 7–11), it is placed in the mouths of the six *vargikā bhikṣus*.

62. For a definition of the 四大教 see T. 1, 18a10–23; and T. 1716, 812a29–b3.
63. T. 1425, 492a7–19.
64. 有二比丘作制限。當共受經。當共誦經。後不受不誦者得越比尼罪(T. 1425, 252b9–10).
65. Tatz, *Asaṅga's Chapter*, pp. 59–60; cf. Asaṅga, *Bodhisattvabhūmi: A Statement of Whole Course of the Bodhisattva (Being the Fifteenth Section of Yogācārabhūmi)*, Unrai Wogihara, ed. (reprint, Tokyo: Sankibo Buddhist Bookstore, 1971), pp. 152–153.
66. Tatz, *Asaṅga's Chapter*, p. 61; Asaṅga, *Bodhisattvabhūmi*, pp. 153–154.
67. Tatz, *Asaṅga's Chapter*, p. 62; Asaṅga, *Bodhisattvabhūmi*, pp. 155–156.
68. Tatz, *Asaṅga's Chapter*, pp. 62–63; Asaṅga, *Bodhisattvabhūmi*, p. 156.
69. The part of the line describing the bodhisattva scriptures is missing from the Sanskrit. Wogihara supplies the Tibetan as: "byaṅ chub sems dpa'i mdo sde'i sde snod las kyaṅ bsgrims te| mñam pa 'am| yaṅ na byaṅ chub sems dpa'i mdo sde'i sde snod kyi ma mo bsdus pa 'di las kyaṅ mñan te| 'di ltar bcom ldan 'das kyis mdo sde de daṅ de dag tu byaṅ chub sems dpa' rnams kyi bslab a'i gźi stoṅ phrag du ma gsuṅs pa dag bsgrub pa'i phyir de kho na bźin du bslab par bya'o|" (Asaṅga, *Bodhisattvabhūmi*, p. 156n1).
70. Tatz, *Asaṅga's Chapter*, pp. 65–66.
71. This phrase appears several times. Regarding the practice of worshiping the Tathāgatas and Mahāyāna books, see Tatz, *Asaṅga's Chapter*, p. 67; Asaṅga, *Bodhisattvabhūmi*, p. 162. For similar references, see Schopen, "Counting the Buddha," pp. 382–383n17.
72. Hopkins, *Buddhist Advice*, pp. 144–145.

> 80 "dānaśīlakṣamāvīryadhyānaprajñākṛpātmakam| mahāyānamataṃ tasmin kasmād durbhāṣitaṃ vacaḥ||"
>
> 81 "parārtho dānaśīlābhyāṃ kṣāntyā vīryeṇa cātmanaḥ| dhyānaṃ prajñā ca mokṣāya mahāyānārthasaṅgrahaḥ||"
>
> 82 "parā[tmahita]mokṣārthāḥ saṃkṣepād buddhaśāsanam| te ṣaṭpāramitāgarbhās tasmād bauddham idaṃ vacaḥ||" (Nāgārjuna, *Nāgārjuna's Ratnāvalī*, pp. 122–124)

73. "āvilattā, bhikkhave, udakassa| evamevaṃ kho, bhikkhave, so vata bhikkhu āvilena cittena attatthaṃ vā ñassati paratthaṃ vā ñassati ubhayatthaṃ vā ñassati uttariṃ vā manussadhammā alamariyañāṇadassanavisesaṃ sacchikarissatīti netaṃ ṭhānaṃ vijjati|" (*Aṅguttara-nikāya*, 1:9).
74. Cf. Nāgārjuna, *Nāgārjuna's Ratnāvalī,* pp. 126–127: Sanskrit: "anutpādo mahāyāne pareṣāṃ śūnyatā kṣayaḥ| kṣayānutpādayoś caikyam arthataḥ kṣamyatāṃ yataḥ||"; Tibetan: "theg pa che las skye med bstan| gźan gyi zad pa stoṅ pa ñid| zad daṅ mi skye don du ni| gcig pas de phyir bzod par gyis||"
75. Translation: *The Long Discourses of the Buddha*, p. 405; "Kicca bhikkhave bhikkuno balasmiṃ? Idha bhikkhave bhikkhu āsavānaṃ khayā anāsavaṃ cetovimutti paññāvimuttiṃ diṭṭhava dhamme sayaṃ abhiññāsaccikatva upasampajja viharati. Idaṃ kho bhikkhave bhikkuno balasmiṃ" (*Dīgha Nikāya*, 3:78).

76. Translation: *The Middle Length Discourses,* 1143; *Majjhima Nikāya*, 3:294ff. For a good discussion of this verse and others related to it in the Pāli canon, see Nancy McCagney, *Nāgārjuna and the Philosophy of Openness* (Lanham, MD: Rowman & Littlefield, 1997), pp. 53–56.
77. Translated from Baron A. von Stael-Holstein, *The Kāśyapaparivarta: A Mahāyānasūtra of the Ratnakūṭa Class* (1926; reprinted, Tokyo: Meicho-Fukyū-Kai, 1977), p. 94. Cf. partial translations by Garma Chang et al., ed. and trans., *A Treasury of Mahāyāna Sūtras: Selections from the Mahāratnakūṭa Sūtra* (Delhi: Motilal Banarsidass, 1996), p. 395; Etienne Lamotte, *Le Traité de la grande vertu de sagesse. Mahāprajñāpāramitāśāstra (Traduction chinoise de Kumārajīva)* (Louvain: Institut orientaliste, Bibliothèque de l'Université, 1970–1981), 3:1227n2.
78. Luis Gómez, "Proto-Mādhyamika in the Pāli Canon," *Philosophy East and West* 26, no. 2 (April 1976).
79. Kalupahana, *Mūlamadhyamakakārikā of Nāgārjuna*, p. 5.
80. Nāgārjuna, *Nāgārjuna's Ratnāvalī*, p. 118, verses 4.67ff., e.g., "bodhisattvasya saṃbhāro mahāyāne tathāgataiḥ| nirdiṣṭaḥ sa tu saṃmūḍhaiḥ pradviṣṭaiś caiva nindyate||"
81. Cf. "tad dveṣī tena dahyate|" (4.70, in ibid.).
82. The faith and hatred types are a reference to a common Buddhist typology of persons. For the purposes of meditation, people are divided into three major types corresponding to the three root afflictions: greed (*rāga*), hate (*dveṣa*), and delusion (*moha*). In some texts, these types are made parallel to the three humor types in Āyurvedic medicine. See, for example, the fragment at the beginning of T. 617. For other references, see Demiéville, "La *Yogācārabhūmi* of Saṅghadeva," p. 359n2. Some texts, such as the *Nettipakaraṇa,* also develop numerous subtypes.
83. "śrāddho 'pi durgṛhītena dviṣyāt kruddho 'thavetaraḥ| śrāddho 'pi dagdha ity uktaḥ kā cintā dveṣabandhure||" (Nāgārjuna, *Nāgārjuna's Ratnāvalī*, p. 120).
84. Prebish, *Buddhist Monastic Discipline*, p. 92. "yo puna bhikṣu bhikṣusya duṣṭo doṣāt kupito anāttamano amūlakena saṅghātiśeṣeṇa dharmeṇānudhvaṃseya, pācattikaṃ|" (*Prātimokṣasūtram*, p. 28).
85. "388. Tathāgatābhisaṃdhyoktāny asukhaṃ jñātum ity ataḥ ekayānatriyānoktād ātmā rakṣya upekṣayā|"

    "389. Upekṣayā hi nāpuṇyaṃ dveṣāt pāpaṃ kutaḥ śubham mahāyāne yato dveṣo nātmakāmaiḥ kṛto 'rhati|" (Nāgārjuna, *Nāgārjuna's Ratnāvalī*, p. 126).
86. S. Candra Das, *Tibetan-English Dictionary* (reprint, Delhi: Motilal Banarsidass, 1995), *s.v.*
87. "saṅs rgyas kyi bka' la btaṅ sñoms byas pas ni ñes par mi 'gyur ro" (Ajitamitra, *Die Ratnāvalīṭīkā des Ajitamitra*, p. 131).
88. Kāne, *A History of Dharmaśāstra*, 3:172.
89. For biographical details of Asaṅga and Vasubandhu, see the introduction to Stefan Anacker, *Seven Works of Vasubandhu* (Delhi: Motilal Banarsidass, 1984).
90. Text: "buddhavacanasyedaṃ lakṣaṇaṃ yatsūtre 'vatarati vinaye saṃdṛśyate

dharmatā ca na vilomayati| na caivaṃ mahāyānam, sarvadharmaniḥ-svabhāvatvopadeśāt| tasmānna buddhavacanamiti . . . avataratyevedaṃ svasmin mahāyānasūtre svasya ca kleśasya[kleśaḥ?] vinayaḥ[vinaye]saṃdṛśyate| yo mahāyāne bodhisatvānāṃ[sic] kleśaḥ uktaḥ| vikalpakleśāhi bodhisatvāḥ[sic]| audāryagāmbhīryalakṣaṇtvācca| na dharmatāṃ vilomayatyaithava iha dharmatāmahābodhiprāptaye|" (Asaṅga, *Mahāyānasūtrālaṃkāra*, S. V. Limaye, trans. and ed. [Delhi: Sri Satguru, 1992], pp. 9–10). Thanks are due to Mario D'Amaro for assistance with this passage.

Notes to Chapter 4

1. T. 1425, 510b09–16.
2. See Collins, "On the Very Idea of the Pāli Canon," p. 95.
3. For the probable location of the find spot for these scrolls, see Salomon, *Ancient Buddhist Scrolls from Gandhāra,* p. 20; for the date of these scrolls, see ibid., pp. 141–155; and for their affiliation with the Dharmaguptas, see ibid., pp. 166–177.
4. Ibid., pp. 77–86.
5. Ibid., p. 81.
6. Ibid., pp. 54–55. It is uncertain whether the copyists were monks whose duty it was to copy texts or whether the monastery employed (lay) scribes (*kāyastha*) for this purpose. I assume the former, although (as Salomon points out on page p. 54) the *Mūlasarvāstivada vinaya* mentions the allocation of money to hire (lay) scribes for the copying of *sūtras*.
7. Ibid., p. 83.
8. Ibid., p. 36.
9. T. 1425, 237a3–7.
10. The Sanskrit has *grāhayitavya,* a causative potential participle of the verb √*grah* ("to grasp, to acknowledge" or "to learn"). Singh and Minowa translate this sentence as: "As long as the resident monk is ordained by the preceptor, the twofold vinaya has to be accepted" (Sanghasen Singh and Kenryo Minowa, ed. and trans., "A Critical Edition and Translation of *Abhisamācārikā Nāma Bhikṣu-Prakīrṇakaḥ,*" *Buddhist Studies, Department of Buddhist Studies, University of Delhi* 12 [March 1988]: 137). Thereafter, they translate *grāhayitavya* as "to be accepted." While grammatically correct, the problem with this translation is that it presents the *vinaya* rules as something that a monk may pick and choose from. If we were to employ their translation, a monk could choose to acknowledge only the four *pārājika* rules and abandon the rest of the monastic rules. Faxian's Chinese translation, on the other hand, consistently translates *grāhayitavya* as 教誦 ([the monk should be] taught to recite [x number of rules]). Apparently, he understood *grāhayitavya* in the sense of "is to be learned." Since learning was done by reciting out loud in order to memorize the texts, I have chosen to translate *grāhayitavya* as "is to be learned." In other

words, a monk would have to accept all of the *vinaya* rules, but he may only have to memorize a small amount of the actual text. This translation also works better with *pārayati* (to learn, to master) in the following line.

11. This sentence is missing from the Chinese.
12. The Chinese simply says "the nine sections of *sūtra*" without listing the nine.
13. The Chinese has 受經時 (when to study) and then adds 共誦時 (when to chant together), which is not in the Sanskrit.
14. Translated from the edited portion of Singh and Minowa, "A Critical Edition and Translation of *Abhisamācārikā Nāma Bhikṣu-Prakīrṇakaḥ*," p. 101; cf. T. 1425, 501c22–502a2.
15. The phrase 喡喡 (*wei wei*) is used by Faxian in an onomatopoeic sense to denote a weird noise. He uses it at a later point to refer to the sound that some misbehaved monks make to scare other monks. See T. 1425, 379c13ff.
16. T. 1425, 336c6–14. This section has also been translated by Seishi Karashima in "Two More Folios of the Prātimokṣa-Vibhaṅga," p. 220. The rule contained in the last line is found in the Prātimokṣa of the Mahāsāṅghikas. See Prebish, *Buddhist Monastic Discipline,* p. 74; "yo puna bhikṣuranupasampannaṃ pudgalaṃ padaśo dharmaṃ vaceya, pācattikaṃ" (*Prātimokṣasūtram,* p. 19). The rule is virtually the same in all *vinayas* except that in the *Theravāda vinaya* it appears as rule number four.
17. Sylvain Lévi translates 不遮 as as "qu'ils ne comprennent pas" ("Sur la récitation primitive des textes bouddhiques," *Journal Asiatique,* ser. II, vol. 5 [1915]). The sense is, instead, that they are not to chant without a break or without showing restraint.
18. Presumably, this sentence refers to the conferring of lay precepts. Despite the fact that the commentary at this point seems to be more concerned with the decorum of the teaching process, teaching the *sūtras* themselves to laypersons would still be a violation of the rule.
19. T. 1425, 336c19–337a12. This section has been partially translated by Lévi ("Sur la récitation primitive des textes bouddhiques," pp. 422–423) as well as by Karashima ("Two More Folios," pp. 220–221). I have used my own translation here in order to highlight the possible Sanskrit equivalents in this passage. Karashima's article includes an edition of a newly discovered Sanskrit folio corresponding to this passage. What is curious is that, while the Sanskrit clearly reflects the same rule, there is no close correspondence between the Sanskrit and any portion of Faxian's Chinese translation.
20. Venerable Kumāra Bhikku, personal communication, December 17, 2003.
21. See Lévi, "Sur la récitation primitive des textes bouddhiques," p. 420.
22. For a comparison between the *vinayas* on this point, see Ernst Frauwallner, *The Earliest Vinaya and the Beginnings of Buddhist Literature,* L. Petech, trans. (Rome: Istituto Italiano per il Medio ed Estremo Oriente, 1956), p. 83.
23. T. 1421, 174b7–12. The *Sarvāstivāda vinaya* also allows the memorization of heterodox texts for the purpose of refuting other sects. See T. 1435, 274a25–b11.
24. "bhagavato etamattham ārocesum| na bhikkhave lokāyatam vācetabbam| yo

vāceyya āpatti dukkaṭassā'ti||" (*Vinaya Piṭakam, One of the Principle Buddhist Holy Scriptures in the Pāli Language,* Hermann Oldenberg, ed. [London: Williams and Norgate, 1879–1883], 2:139).

25. 佛言。從今諸比丘。若有學誦外書文章兵法者。突吉羅(T. 1435, 274a26–27).
26. The nine sections of the *Sūtra Piṭaka* are listed at T. 1425, c11–12, and in the Sanskrit edition of the *Abhisamācārikā.* See note 14 above.
27. 彼諸外道亦有經論。若實欲捨此經論。假言捨。彼經論者。是不名捨戒。得偷蘭罪(T. 1425, 237a15–22). Cf. the *Dharmagupta vinaya,* T. 1428, 571b.
28. Eli Franco, "The Oldest Philosophical Manuscript in Sanskrit," *Journal of Indian Philosophy* 31 (2003): 21.
29. See Schopen, "The Phrase '*sa pṛthivīpradeśaś caityabhūto bhavet*' in the *Vajracchedikā.*"
30. Richard Gombrich, "How the Mahāyāna Began," *Buddhist Forum* 1 (1990): 21.
31. Ibid., p. 22.
32. Ibid., p. 29.
33. Ibid.
34. T. 1428, 639a16–24.
35. The monk in the *Mahāsāṅghika vinaya* may not have been completely at fault. The *vinaya* lists five *sūtras* that are specifically to be taught to novices (T. 1425, 337a1–3), one of which comes from the *Sutta Nipāta.* For a good discussion of these texts, see Salomon, *Ancient Buddhist Scrolls,* pp. 158–163.
36. Stephen Teiser, *The Scripture on the Ten Kings and the Making of Purgatory in Medieval Chinese Buddhism* (Honolulu: University of Hawai'i Press, 1994), p. 80.
37. Ibid.
38. Imagine, for example, a monk copying a *sūtra* like the *Perfection of Wisdom in 100,000 Lines* or the *Avataṃsaka Sūtra.* The amount of paper required to copy one of these *sūtras* alone would be enough to attract unwanted attention from the monk in charge of the distribution of supplies.
39. For references, see T. W. Rhys Davids and S. W. Stede, *Pāli-English Dictionary* (reprint, Delhi: Motilal Banarsidass, 1993), s.v.
40. Gernet reports that, according to Daoxuan's commentary on the *Dharmagupta vinaya,* property of the *saṅgha* consisted of: "1. Estates 2. Victuals 3. Clothing, medicines, and utensils used in the cells 4. Light goods bequeathed by deceased monks." See Jacques Gernet, *Buddhism in Chinese Society* (New York: Columbia University Press, 1995), p. 68.
41. 俱攝 (*jù zhé*). Literally this would mean something like "both pleats," which is not very helpful. A better interpretation reads these characters phonetically. *Jù* can mean "together," but when it is used phonetically, it often serves for the Indic *ku* or *ko* sounds. For examples, see Hirakawa, *Buddhist Chinese-Sanskrit Dictionary*, 俱 *s.v.* Hence, 俱攝 probably represents the sounds *ko* + *che* = *koccha.* According to the *PTS Dictionary: koccha*: "some kind of seat or settee, made of bark, grass or rushes Vin. II.149; IV.40" (Rhys Davids and Stede, *Pali-English Dictionary*, *s.v.*). A *koccha* can also be a comb, although in context *koccha*

as an item of furniture seems more appropriate. The phonetic reading of these characters is confirmed by the fact that later editions all have the word as 俱執" *jù zhí*." See, T. 1425, 478, note 25.

42. T. 1425, 478b28–c9. For "boat," the Taishō edition has 杭, which makes sense. Later editions render this as 枕 (pillow). See ibid., note 27. I have gone with the standard edition, since it makes more sense that a boat would be heavy property.
43. T. 1425, 324a28. Cf. Prebish, *Buddhist Monastic Discipline,* p. 72, rule number 30; "yo puna bhikṣurjānan sāṃghikaṃ lobhaṃ saṃghe pariṇatamātmano pariṇāmeya nissargikapācattikaṃ" (*Prātimokṣasūtram,* p. 18).
44. Gernet, *Buddhism in Chinese Society,* p. 69.
45. T. 1425, 251c22ff.
46. "ratnānāṃ muktā varjayitvā maṇivaiḍūryadkṣiṇāvartaparyantāni tu dvau bhāgau kartavyānīti eko dharmasya dvītīyaḥ saṃghasya| yo dharmasya tena buddhavacanaṃ lekhayitavyam| siṃhāsane copayoktavyam| yaḥ saṃghasya sa bhikṣubhirbhājayitavyaḥ| pustakānāṃ buddhavacanapustakā avibhajya cāturdiśāya bhikṣusaṃghāya dharaṇakoṣṭhikāyāṃ prakṣeptavyāḥ| bahiḥ-śāstrapustakā bhikṣubhirvikrīya bhājayitavyāḥ|" (*Gilgit Manuscripts,* Nalinaksha Dutt, ed. [Delhi: Sri Satguru, 1984], vol. 3, pt. 2:143). For a discussion of this passage, see Gregory Schopen, "Doing Business for the Lord," *Journal of the American Oriental Society* 114, no. 4 (1994): 531. See also the parallel discussion in Yijing: T. 2125, p. 230c13ff., and Takakusu, *A Record of the Buddhist Religion,* p. 192.
47. This situation would have been different under different monastic laws. For instance, the *Mahīśāsaka vinaya* allows for a monk to make prior arrangements for his belongings before his death. See Gernet, *Buddhism in Chinese Society,* p. 86.
48. From the context, it is not clear whether the elders of the main *saṅgha* are intended or the village elders.
49. T. 1425, 479b23–c23.
50. The *Mahāsāṅghika vinaya* does contain a section discussing what to do with the belongings of deceased monks (T. 1425, p. 478c25 ff). In this section, the phrase 依. . . 鉢雜物 (the monk's robe, bowl and sundry things) stands in for all his personal effects. Books are never mentioned specifically.
51. "saṅs rgyas sku gzugs mchod rten daṅ| gtsug lag khaṅ dag gus tshul du| śin tu rgya chen gnas mal [Zhol has "la"] sogs| rgya chen phyg pa bsgrub par mdzod|" (*Nāgārjuna's Ratnāvalī,* p. 78, verse 231).
52. Nāgārjuna, *Nāgārjuna's Ratnāvalī,* verses 233–234, p. 78. Note that he makes no reference to the "seven jewels" so common in northern literature at the time. For a good discussion of the *sapta-ratna,* see Liu, *Ancient India,* p. 92ff.
53. Nāgārjuna, *Nāgārjuna's Ratnāvalī*, p. 90, verses 292–293.
54. Ibid., verse 291. He is to give the "five essentials," viz., sugar/molasses, ghee, honey, sesame oil, and salt (Hopkins, *Buddhist Advice,* p. 132 note b).
55. Hopkins, *Buddhist Advice*, verse 244, p. 126.

56. Ibid., p. 125. "thub dbaṅ gsuṅ daṅ des byuṅ ba'i| gźuṅ rnams bri daṅ glegs bam ni| snag tsha dag daṅ smyu gu dag| sṅon du 'gro ba sbyin par mdzod|" (Nāgārjuna, *Nāgārjuna's Ratnāvalī,* p. 79).

Paramārtha: 佛阿含及論。書寫讀誦施。亦惠祇筆墨。汝應修此福(T. 1656, 498c11–12).

57. See Pagels, *The Bodhisattvapiṭaka,* p. 146n118, for references.

58. "gaṅ la chos don gaṅ med na| śin tu ñan thag gyur pa de| de yi mod la bde stsal na| de las sbyin mchog ma mchis so||" (Nāgārjuna, *Nāgārjuna's Ratnāvalī*, p. 84, verse 262).

59. T. 1425, 478c19–25.

60. Gregory Schopen, "The Lay Ownership of Monasteries and the Role of the Monk in Mūlasarvāstivādin Monasticism," *Journal of the International Association of Buddhist Studies,* 19, no. 1 (1996): 115. A similar rule is in the *Mahāsāṅghika vinaya,* T. 1425, 312a29ff.

61. Hopkins, *Buddhist Advice,* p. 133; "chos kyi ched daṅ de bźin du| chos gźuṅ don dag dran pa daṅ| chos kyi sbyin pa dri med pas| tshe rabs dran pa 'thob par 'gyur||" (Nāgārjuna, *Nāgārjuna's Ratnāvalī,* p. 91); 令他憶法事。及正法句義。 或淨心施法。故感宿命智 (T. 1656, 500a13–14).

Notes to Chapter 5

1. The speaker, under this interpretation, would be Ānanda himself. For a different interpretation, see Jonathan Silk, "A Note on the Opening Formula of Buddhist Sūtras," *Journal of the International Association of Buddhist Studies* 12, no. 1 (1989): 158–163.

2. This text has been ascribed to Nāgārjuna, although many have challenged this ascription. See Etienne Lamotte, *Der Verfasser des Upadeśa und seine-Quellen* (Gottingen: Vandenhoeck and Ruprecht, 1973). The work is, nevertheless, an early Mahāyāna work written before the fifth century, when Kumārajīva translated it. Its encyclopedic nature makes it an invaluable resource, even if its provenance and date remain uncertain.

3. Lamotte, *Le Traité*, 1:86–87; T. 1509, 66c13–67a4.

4. T. 2047, 184c10–11.

5. Pāli sources list this ***aṅga*** as ***vedalla***, but Chinese translations such as the *Mahāsāṅghika-vinaya* point toward the term *vaipulya*. See T. 1425, 281c12–22 (方廣); cf. Singh and Minowa, "A Critical Edition and Translation of *Abhisamācārikā*," p. 101.

6. Pagels, *The Bodhisattvapiṭaka*, p. 11 (he cites Asaṅga, *Bodhisattvabhūmi: A Statement of Whole Course of the Bodhisattva (Being the Fifteenth Section of Yogācārabhūmi),* Unrai Wogihara, ed. [reprint, Tokyo: Sankibo Buddhist Bookstore, 1971], p. 96.1–5). Also see ibid., p. 11n10. Asaṅga's *Yogācārabhūmi* itself may be an attempt to co-opt an established genre of ***buddhavacana***. According to Demiéville, *Yogācārabhūmi* was a genre of Buddhist anthologies on meditation that originally had nothing to do with Mahāyāna. The fact that Asaṅga

names his work *Yogācārabhūmi* indicates a strategic reinterpretation of the genre in Mahāyāna terms. For a good discussion of this genre prior to Asaṅga, see Demiéville, "La Yogācārabhūmi de Saṅgharakṣa," *passim*.

7. The standard list from Pāli commentarial literature contains: the *Cūḷavedalla*, *Mahāvedalla*, *Sammādiṭṭhi*, *Saṅkhārabhājaniya*, *Mahāpuṇṇama* (all from the *Majjhima Nikāya*), and the *Sakkapañha* (from the *Dīgha Nikāya*). See Lamotte, *History of Indian Buddhism*, p. 144.
8. *Mahārṣīvedavyāsapraṇitam Śrīmadbhāgavatamahāpurāṇam*, Krishashanker Shastri, ed. (Vārānasī: Śrīvidyāhitanidhisadasyāh, 1966–1968), 2:336 (book 2, chapter 7, verse 51); translation by author.
9. "śiṣyapraśiṣyadvāreṇa tadeva vipulīkṛtam." *Devī Bhagavatāpurāṇa*, quoted in Giorgio Bonazzoli, "Remarks on the Nature of the Purāṇa-s," *Purāṇa* 25, no. 1 (1983): 84.
10. T. 1545, 660a27–29.
11. T. 1545, 269c22.
12. Lamotte, *History of Indian Buddhism*, p. 146; T. 1545, 660a29. In his insightful history of Yogācāra, Ronald Davidson has argued that the doctrinal content of early Yogācāra texts appear to have been primarily elaborations on Sarvāstivāda Abhidharma themes, taking them in the direction of the *Prajñāpāramitā Sūtras*. See Ronald Davidson, "Buddhist Systems of Transformation: *Āśraya-parivṛtti* Among the Yogācāra" (Ph.D. diss., University of California, 1985), chapter 5. Despite this, it appears that Mahāyānists were not very successful in establishing their *sūtras* within the Sarvāstivādin canon until at least the sixth or seventh centuries, when Mahāyāna texts were placed alongside Sarvāstivādin texts in the stūpa at Gilgit. Further, as Davidson himself points out, Yogācāra does not seem to have been known as a separate school until the second half of the fifth century (p. 141).
13. E.g., "sabbepi vedañca tuṭṭhiñca laddhā laddhā pucchitasuttantā vedallanti veditabbaṃ" (Buddhaghosa, *The Aṭṭhasālinī, Buddhaghosa's Commentary on the Dhammasanganī*, Edward Müller, ed. [London: H. Frowde for the Pāli Text Society, 1897], p. 26).
14. Edward Conze, *The Perfection of Wisdom in Eight Thousand Lines & Its Verse Summary* (Delhi: Sri Satguru, 1973; reprinted 1994), p. 139.
15. Ibid., p. 140.
16. T. 670, 487b21–23; cf. Daisetz Teitaro Suzuki, *The Laṅkāvatāra Sūtra* (Delhi: Munshiram Manoharlal, 1999), p. 59.
17. Lambert Schmithausen, "'Liberating Insight' and 'Enlightenment' in Early Buddhism," in *Studien zum Jainismus und Buddhismus,* Klaus Bruhn und Albrecht Wezler, eds. (Wiesbaden: Franz Steiner Verlag, 1981), pp. 199–250.
18. *Vinaya Piṭakam,* 1:10ff.
19. This is Schmithausen's term.
20. *Vinaya Piṭakam,* 1:11.
21. *Vinaya Texts*, Part I, T. W. Rhys Davids and H. Oldenberg, trans. (reprint, Delhi: Motilal Banarsidass, 1996), p. 97.

22. Ibid., p. 101; *Vinaya Piṭakam,* 1:14.
23. *The Middle Length Discourses*, p. 605; "anicco dukkhato rogato gaṇḍato sallato aghato ābādhato parato palokato suññato anattato" (*Majjhima Nikāya*, 1:500).
24. "aniccā saṅkhatā paṭiccasamuppannā khayadhammā vayadhammā virāgadhammā nirodhadhammā" (ibid.).
25. *The Middle Length Discourses,* p. 606.
26. Buddhaghosa, *Papañcasūdanī Majjhimanikāyṭṭthakathā of Buddhaghosācariya,* J. H. Woods, D. Kosambi and I. B. Horner, eds. (London: Pāli Text Society, 1922–1938), 3:209.
27. Schmithausen cites T. 1548, 595a3ff., and *Paṭisambhidāmagga*, Arnold C. Taylor, ed. (London: Pāli Text Society, 1979), 2:105.
28. Schmithausen, "Liberating Insight," pp. 216–217.
29. For an excellent discussion of *saṃjñā* and its relation to *vijñāna* (from which this example comes), see Paul Williams, "Some Aspects of Language and Construction in the Madhyamaka," *Journal of Indian Philosophy* 8 (1980): 15.
30. See, e.g., *Majjhima Nikāya,* 2:231, and Vasubandhu, *L'Abhidharmakośa,* 5:144.
31. Translation, *The Middle Length Discourses,* p. 203, Pāli added; text: "Cakkuñcā-cakkhuviññāṇaṃ rūpe ca uppajjhati cakkhiññāṇaṃ tiṇṇaṃ saṅgati phasso. Phassapaccayā vedanā. Yaṃ vedeti, taṃ sañjānāti. Yaṃ sañjānāti taṃ vitakketi. Yaṃ vitakketi taṃ papañceti. Yapapañcasaññāsaṅakhānidānaṃ purisaṃ papañcasaññāsaukhā samudācaranti atītānāgatapaccuppannesu cakkhuviññeyyesu rūpesu" (*Majjhima Nikāya,* 1:111–112).
32. Translation, *The Middle Length Discourses,* pp. 201–202; text: *Majjhima Nikāya,* 1:109–110.
33. E.g., see the "Cūḷasuññata sutta" (*Majjhima Nikāya,* sutta number 121)
34. "sabbanimittānañca amanasikāro animittāya ca dhātuyā manasikāro" (*Majjhima Nikāya,* 1:296).
35. The *Majjhima Nikāya Aṭṭhakathā* on the "Mahāvedalla sutta" glosses the *animitta dhātu* as *nibbāna*. In the *Sutta Nipāta Aṭṭhakathā*, emptiness, signlessness and wishlessness are explicitly said to be characteristics (*lakkhana*) of *nibbāna*. See *Sutta-nipāta Commentary: Being Paramatthajotikā,* Helmer Smith, ed. (London: Luzac for the Pāli Text Society, 1966–1972), 2:41.
36. According to the *Abhidharmakośa, animitta* is said to be the object of the absorption having nirvāṇa for its object. (See Vasubandhu, *L'Abhidharmakośa,* 5:185.) These three are also said to be the three aspects of *nibbāna* in the *Abhidhammatthāsanghaha* of Anuruddha: "Tathā suññataṃ animittaṃ appaṇihitaṃ c'āti tividhaṃ hoti ākārabhedena" (Anuruddha, *A Manual of Abhidhamma being Abhidhammattha Saṅgaha of Bhadanta Anuruddhācariya,* 4th ed. [Kuala Lumpur: Buddhist Missionary Society, 1979], p. 312).
37. T. 1548, 633a28–b7.
38. See Paul Griffiths, *On Being Mindless* (La Salle: Open Court Press, 1991).
39. Schmithausen, "Liberating Insight," p. 229. The *sūtra* to which he refers is in *The Aṅguttara-nikāya,* Rev. Richard Morris, ed. (London: H. Frowde for the Pāli Text Society, 1885–1910), 4:422ff. He also notes that, although there does

not seem to be a Chinese equivalent to this verse, it is cited in the *Abhidharmasammucchaya* and bhāṣya as well as at T. 1602, 576c11ff. (= Āryaśāsanaprakaraṇa? ostensibly also by Asaṅga).

40. Schmithausen, "Liberating Insight," p. 247.
41. For references to other Mahāyāna *sūtras* in which *saṃsāra* is identified with nirvāṇa, see Jikido Takasaki, "Saṃsāra eva nirvāṇaṃ," in Jonathan Silk, ed., *Wisdom, Compassion, and The Search for Understanding: The Buddhist Studies Legacy of Gadjin M. Nagao* (Honolulu: University of Hawai'i Press, 2000), pp. 333–346.
42. Inada, *Nāgārjuna,* p. 158.
43. Vasubandhu, *L'Abhidharmakośa,* 5:185.
44. Lamotte, *Le Traité,* 3:1216; T. 1509, 206b6–7.
45. Konstantin Régamey, *Philosophy in the Samādhirājasūtra* (Delhi: Motilal Banarsidass, 1990), pp. 63–65. Mahāyāna literature is far from univocal on this point, however. For a short survey on a range of Mahāyāna approaches to *samādhi,* see Etienne Lamotte, *The Śūraṅgamasamādhisūtra: The Concentration of Heroic Progress,* Sara Boin-Webb, trans. (Surrey, UK: Curzon Press, 1998), pp. 11–38.
46. See Jonathan Silk, "The King of Samādhis: Chapters I–IV," in Luis Gomez and Silk, *Studies in the Literature of the Great Vehicle: Three Mahāyāna Buddhist Texts* (Ann Arbor: Collegiate Institute for the Study of Buddhist Literature and Center for South and Southeast Asian Studies, 1989), p. 55.
47. Ziva Ben-Porat, "The Poetics of Literary Allusion," *PTL: A Journal for Descriptive Poetics and Theory of Literature* 1 (1976), 107–108. My thanks to Benjamin Sommer for pointing me to this source.
48. Ibid., pp. 108–109.
49. Noble Ross Reat, *The Śālistambha Sūtra* (Delhi: Motilal Banarsidass, 1993), p. 27.
50. Ibid., p. 3.
51. *The Middle Length Discourses,* p. 283.
52. *Connected Discourses of Buddha,* Bhikkhu Bodhi, trans. (Somerville, MA: Wisdom Press, 2000), 1:939; "alaṃ vakkali. kiṃ te iminā pūtikāyena diṭṭhena, yo kho vakkali, dhammaṃ passati, yo maṃ passati so dhammaṃ passati, dhammaṃ hi vakkali, passanto maṃ passati. maṃ passanto dhammaṃ passati" (*The Samyutta-nikāya of the Sutta-piṭaka,* Léon Feer, ed. [London: H. Frowde for the Pāli Text Society, 1884–1904], 3:119).
53. The textual history of this passage is difficult. On the one hand, the passage appears in the fifth- to sixth-century manuscript of the *Aṣṭadaśasāhasrika P.P.* found in the Gilgit stūpa. Curiously, it does not appear in the Chinese translations of the *Pañcaviṃsatisāhasrika P.P.* by Dharmarakṣa and Mokṣala (T. 222 and 221 respectively; both third century) or in that by Kumārajīva (T. 223, fifth century) or Xuanzang (T. 220, seventh century). Although this passage also does not appear in Xuanzang's translation of the *Aṣṭadaśasāhasrika P.P.* it is

possible that it was originally part of another Prajñāpāramitā collection and then added to the *Aṣṭadaśasāhasrika P.P.* at a later date.

Conze's somewhat disparaging remarks on the state of Prajñāpāramitā literature at Gilgit is telling:

> It is rather hard to explain rationally how such an astonishing mixture could have been deposited in the Gilgit Stupa. There is the enormity of a scribe who calmly omits 30 leaves without any break in pagination. . . . There is the equally remarkable enormity of his changing from the version in 25.000 Lines to the version in 18.000 Lines . . . without telling anybody about it. And then there is the amazing coincidence that the subsidiary Ms contains a high proportion of the omitted and lost pages. With some diligence the existing material will therefore allow us to produce a text of the Large P.P Sutra as it circulated in the 5th or 6th century." (*The Gilgit Manuscript of the Aṣṭadaśasāhasrikāprajñāpāramitā: Chapters 70 to 82 Corresponding to the 6th, 7th, and 8th Abhisamayas,* Edward Conze, ed. [Rome: Istituto Italiano per il Medio ed Estremo Oriente, 1974], p. xv)

We have to consider, however, whether the state of the manuscripts found at Gilgit was due less to the "enormity" of a single scribe than to a different attitude about what constitutes a "book."

54. Edward Conze, *The Large Sūtra on Perfect Wisdom With the Divisions of the Abhisamāyālaṅkāra* (Berkeley: University of California Press, 1975), p. 595. This translation is identical to his translation of the same passage from the *Aṣṭadaśasāhasrikā P.P.* (Conze, *Perfection of Wisdom in Eight Thousand Lines,* p. 189). In the latter he also provides an edition of the manuscript. The Sanskrit reads: "kathaṃ ca pratītyasamutpādaṃ prajānāti. evam anirodhato 'nucchedato 'śāśvatato 'nekārthato 'nānārthato 'nāgamato na nirgamataḥ prapañcoparamataḥ śivaṃ pratītyasamutpādaṃ prajānāti" (ibid., p. 66). Both in his *Large Sūtra on Perfect Wisdom* and in his *Aṣṭadaśasāhasrika P.P.*, Conze notes the similarity of this verse to the opening verse of the *Mūlamadhyamakakārikā*. Strangely, this connection has not caught the attention of other scholars—most notably Kalupahana who maintains that Nāgārjuna never refers to a Mahāyāna *sūtra*. See Kalupahana, *Mūlamadhyamakakārikā of Nāgārjuna*, p. 5; see also Warder, "Is Nāgārjuna a Mahāyānist?" pp. 78–88.

55. "anirodham anutpādam anucchedam aśāśvatam| anekartham ananartham anāgama amanirgamam |yaḥ pratītyasamutpāda prapañcopaśamam śivam| deśayāmāsa saṃbuddhataṃ vande vadatāṃ varaṃ||" (Candrakīrti, *Prasannapadā*, p. 11).

"gaṅ gis rten ciṅ 'brel par 'byuṅ| 'gag pa med pa sgye med pa| chad pa med pa rtag med pa| 'oṅ ba med pa 'gro med pa|| tha dad don min don cig min| spros pa ñer źi źi bstan pa| rdzogs pa'i saṅs rgyas smra rnams kyi| dam pa de la phyag 'tshal lo||"

不生亦不滅 不常亦不斷 不一亦不異 不來亦不出 能說是因緣 善滅諸戲論 我稽首禮佛 諸說中第一 (T. 1564, 1b14–17)

56. Although there were certainly variations, this seems to have been taken as standard by Nāgārjuna and his contemporaries. For a discussion of the variations in the canon, see Louis de La Valeé Poussin, *Théorie des douze causes* (Gand: E. Van Goethem, 1913), pp. 1–5.
57. *The Connected Discourses,* 1:533–534; *Saṃyutta-Nikāya*, 2:1–2.
58. *Saṃyutta-Nikāya*, 2:28; also *Majjhima Nikāya*, 1:262–263.
59. *The Connected Discourses,* 1:549.
60. Ibid., 1:546–547; text: "so karoti so paṭisamvediyatīti kho kassapa ādito sato sayaṃkataṃ dukkhanti iti vadaṃ sassatam etam pareti|| añño karoti añño paṭisaṃvediyatīti kho kassapa vedanābhitunnassa sato paraṃkataṃ dukkhanti iti vadam ucchedam etam pareti|| ete te kassapa ubho ante anupagamma majjhena tathāgato dhammam deseti||" (*Saṃyutta-Nikāya*, 2: 20).
61. *The Connected Discourses,* 1:544; *Saṃyutta-Nikāya*, 2:17.
62. "ayaṃ eko anto ti esa eko nikat' anto, lāmak' anto paṭhamaṃ sassataṃ ayaṃ dutiyo anto ti| esa dutiyo| sabbaṃ n' atthī ti uppajjanaka-diṭṭhi-sankhāto nikat' anto lāmak' anto dutiyako ucchedoti attho.|| Sesam ettha uttānam evāti" (Buddhaghosa, *Sāratthа-Ppakāsinī*: *Buddhaghosa's Commentary on the Saṃyutta-Nikāya* [London: Pāli Text Society, 1932], p. 34).
63. Nāgārjuna's assumption that *bhāva* entails the inability to change may be justified by reference to passages such as this. This assumption is not, however, limited to Buddhist texts. Cf. "nā'sato vidyate bhāvo nā'bhāvo vidyate sataḥ ubhayor api dṛṣṭo'ntas tv anayos tattvadarśibhiḥ|" (Franklin Edgerton, *The Bhagavad Gīta* [Cambridge: Harvard University Press, 1952], p. 16).
64. Cf. Yaśomitra, *Spuṭārthā*, pp. 265ff. It looks as if he relates all sixty-two views back to belief in *ātman*, which is in turn a product of the two extremes (*śāśvānta* and *ucchedānta*).
65. *The Connected Discourses,* 1:584–585. Pāli added from *Saṃyutta-Nikāya*, 2:76–77.
66. The presence of these negations in this text is especially important because of the wide provenance of this text. The *Udāna* verses in question can be found in Pāli (undated) and in four Chinese versions. The earliest of these was translated anonymously in the third century. Verses from the *Udāna* have been found among the earliest manuscripts found in Central Asia, e.g., the Subaši manuscript has been dated to the third century C.E. See Sander, "The Earliest Manuscripts from Central Asia," p. 147.
67. *Na gatiṃ*. The Commentary glosses this as *na gamanaṃ* as in "not going or coming from life."
68. Translation: *The Udāna*, Peter Masefield, trans. (Oxford: Pāli Text Society, 1994), p. 165; text: "atthi bhikkhave tat āyatanaṃ, yattha n'eva paṭhavī na āpo na tejo na vāyo na ākāsā nañcāyatanaṃ na viññāṇā nañcāyatanaṃ na ākiñcaññāyatanaṃ na nevasaññānāsaññāyatanaṃ n'āyaṃ loko na paraloko ubho candimasūriyā, tad amhaṃ bhikkhave *n' eva āgatiṃ vadāmi na gatiṃ na ṭhitiṃ na cutiṃ na upapattiṃ, appatiṭṭhaṃ appavattaṃ anārammaṇam eva taṃ, es' ev' anto dukkhassā 'ti*" (*Udāna*, Paul Steinthal, ed. [London: Pāli Text Society, 1885], p. 80; emphasis added).

69. "nam mkha' mtha' yas skye mched (ākāśānantyāyatana)."
70. Gareth Sparham, *The Tibetan Dhammapada* (New Delhi: Mahāyāna, 1983), pp. 102–103. Sparham's translation is from the Tibetan, but the Tibetan reads close to the Sanskrit.
71. For references see Schmithausen, "Liberating Insight," p. 227n100.
72. Cf. the "Cūḷasuññata sutta" of the *Majjhima Nikāya* and chapter 10 of the *Visuddhimagga*.
73. Passage as follows:

> *That base (tadāyatanaṃ)*: that cause (*kāraṇaṃ*). . . . For nibbāna is spoken of as a base in the sense of a cause on account of its being an object-condition [*ārammaṇa-ppaccaya-bhāvato*] for the knowledges associated with the paths and their fruitions and so on, just as visible forms and so forth constitute the objective-conditions for eye-consciousness and so on. And, thus far, has the Lord made known to those monks the existence, in its highest sense [*paramatthato*], of the unconditioned element [*asaṅkhatāya dhātuyā*]. This is a positive inference concerning Dhamma [*dhamma-nayo*] in the present case: since conditioned things are found to exist here, there has to be an unconditioned element too, on account of there (always) being an opposite [*paṭipakkhattā*] of those things that have an own-nature [*sabhāva-dhammānaṃ*]. (Peter Masefield, trans., *Udāna Commentary, Sacred Books of the Buddhists* [Oxford: Pāli Text Society, 1995], p. 1012; Pāli added)

74. Translation: *Udāna*, Masefield, trans., p. 166; "atthi bhikkhave ajātaṃ abhūtaṃ akataṃ asaṃkhataṃ, no ce taṃ bhikkhave abhavissa ajātaṃ abhūtaṃ akataṃ asaṇkhataṃ, na yidha jātassa bhūtassa katassa saṇkhatassa nissaraṇaṃ paññāyetha. yasmā ca kho khikkhave atthi ajātaṃ abhūtaṃ akataṃ asaṃkhataṃ, tasmā jātassa bhūtassa katassa saṇkatassa nissaraṇaṃpaññāyatī'ti" (*Udāna*, Steinthal, ed., pp. 80–81).

    Also, cf.: "Jātaṃ bhūtaṃ samuppannaṃ kataṃ saṇkhatam-addhuvaṃ|. jarāmaraṇasaṇkhataṃ roganīḷaṃ pabhaṇguṇaṃ| āhāranettippabhavaṃ nālaṃ tad-abhinandituṃ|| Tassa nissaraṇaṃ santaṃ atakkā vacaraṃ dhuvaṃ| ajātaṃ asamuppannam asokaṃ virajaṃ padaṃ| nirodho dukkhadhammāṇaṃ saṇkhārūpasamo sukho ti||" (*Iti-Vuttaka*, Ernst Windisch, ed. [reprint, London: Oxford University Press, 1966–72], pp. 37–38)
75. Sparham, *The Tibetan Dhammapada*, p. 102; cf. *Udānavarga de Subaši: Edition critique du manuscrit sanskrit sur bois provenant de Subaši,* H. Nakatani, ed. (Paris: Collège de France, Institut de civilisation indienne, 1987), pp. 75–76.
76. It seems to be the case that in Mahāyāna literature a basic knowledge of common Buddhist literature is assumed, whereas the reverse is not true.
77. "The Omniscience in regard to the Objects [*vastu*] of the Empirical World, which is possessed by the Buddha and the Bodhisattva, and likewise is accessible to the Hīnayānist saint, the Śrāvaka and the Pratyekabuddha [*sarva-jñāta—thams cad śes pa ñid* or *vastu-jñāna—gzi-śes*]. It is a kind of knowledge which is conformable to the faculty of understanding of the Hīnayānist, and represents the cognition of all the empirical objects from the standpoint of

their non-relation to a real and independent individual Ego" (Eugene Obermiller, *Prajñāpāramitā in Tibetan Buddhism*, H. S. Sobti, ed. [Delhi: Classics India Publications, 1988], p. 56).

78. Translation: Conze, *The Perfection of Wisdom in Eight Thousand Lines*, p. 191; text: *Aṣṭāsāhasrikā Prajñāpāramitā: With Haribhādra's Commentary Called Āloka*, P. L. Vaidya, ed. (Darbhanga: Mithila Institute, 1960), p. 151.

79. According to the *Mahāvyutpatti*: *pratyavekṣa* is one of the five knowledges for a Buddha: (1) *Dharma-dhātu-viśuddhi;* (2) *Ādarśa-jñānam;* (3) *Samatā-jñanam;* (4) *Pratyavekṣaṇa-jñānam;* and (5) *Kṛtyānusthāna-jñānam*. See Unrai Wogihara, ed., *The Sanskrit-Chinese Dictionary of Buddhist Technical Terms Based on the Mahavyutpatti* (reprint, Tokyo: Sankibo, 1959), p. 8.

80. "punar aparaṃkāśyapa dharmāṇāṃ bhūtapratyavekṣā yan na śunyatāyā dharmāśūnyākaroti dharmāeva śūnyā| yan nānimittena dharmān animittān karoti dharmācaivānimittāḥ yan nāpraṇihitena dharmāpraṇihitān karoti dharmā evāpraṇihitāḥ . . . evaṃ yan ma svabhāvena dharmāsvabhāvatā dharmāṇāṃ yat svabhāvaṃ nopalabhate yā evaṃ pratyavekṣā iyam ucyate kāśyapa madhyamā pratipad dharmāṇāṃ bhūtapratyavekṣāḥ" (Baron A. von Stael-Holstein, *The Kāśyapaparivarta: A Mahāyānasūtra of the Ratnakūṭa Class* [1926; reprinted, Tokyo: Meicho-Fukyū-Kai, 1977], p. 94). The passage goes on to claim that *dharmas* are just "unconditioned" (*anābhisaṃskṛta*), "unarisen" (*anutpāda*), "unborn" (*ajāta*), "ungrasped" (*agrāhya*), "without a basis" (*anāśrava*), and "without self-nature" (*asvabhāva*). This section, however, seems to have been unknown to Candrakīrti (see Candrakīrti, *Mūlamadhyamakakārikās (Mādhyamikasūtras) de Nāgārjuna avec la Prasannapadā commentaire de Candrakīrti*, Louis de La Vallée Poussin, ed. (Osnabruck: Biblio, 1970), pp. 248–249). Although the *sūtra* itself is quite old, perhaps these other negations were not in all versions.

81. Conze, *Perfection of Wisdom in Eight Thousand Lines*, p. 211.

82. *Aṣṭasāhasrikā Prajñāpāramitā*, p. 231.

83. "But for the one who sees the origin of the world as it really is with correct wisdom, there is no notion of nonexistence in regard to the world. And for one who sees the cessation of the world as it really is with correct wisdom, there is no notion of existence in regard to the world" (*The Connected Discourses*, p. 544).

84. See, for example, the *Nettippakaraṇa's* discussion of conformity to *dharmatā* in its discussion of the *mahāpadeśas*: "tāni padabyañjanāni . . . katamissaṃ dhammatāyaṃ upanikkhipitabbāni| paṭiccasamuppāde|"; "The words and syllables [of the new teaching in question]—what is the *dharmatā* onto which they are to be overlaid [for purposes of comparison]? Onto dependent-origination" (*The Netti-pakarana, with Extracts from Dhammapāla's Commentary,* E. Hardy, ed. [London: H. Frowde for the Pāli Text Society, 1902], p. 22).

85. Etienne Lamotte, "The Gāravasutta of the Saṃyutta Nikāya and Its Mahāyānist Developments," *Journal of the Pāli Text Society* 9 (1981): 136–137.

86. Ibid., p. 139.

87. Gregory Schopen, "The Generalization of an Old Yogic Attainment in Medieval Mahāyāna Sūtra Literature: Some Notes on *Jātismara*," *Journal of the International Association of Buddhist Studies* 6, no. 1 (1983): 133.
88. Translation, *The Connected Discourses,* 1:544.
89. "Ayaṃ eko anto ti, esa eko nikat' anto, lāmak' anto, paṭhamaṃ sassataṃ. Ayaṃ dutiyo anto ti, esa dutiyo. Sabbaṃ n' atthīti, uppajjanaka-diṭṭhi-sankhāto nikat' anto, lāmak' anto dutiyako, ucchedo to attho. Sesam ettha uttānam evāti" (Buddhaghosa, *Sārattha-Ppākasinī*, p. 34).
90. Cf. Yaśomitra, *Sputārtha*, p. 265ff. It looks as if he relates all sixty-two views (from the "Brahmajāla sutta"?) to belief in *ātman,* which is in turn a product of the two extremes (*śāśvānta, ucchedānta*).
91. Sander and Waldenschmidt, "The Earliest Manuscripts from Central Asia," p. 147.
92. Commentary runs as follows:

    > "Unity": He asks [if it is] one essence, a permanent essence. "Diversity": He asks [if it is] a different essence [*nānā-sabhāva*] than formerly, after having been first with the state of a human or a god, etc., and then afterward not (to be)—after having been destroyed. All this exists, all is unity, these two are also eternalist view: everything does not exist, everything is diversity, these two are disruption view. Thus it is to be known.

    Text: "Ekattan ti, eka-sabhāvaṃ. Nicca-sabhāvam evāti pucchati. Puthuttan ti, purima-sabhāvena nānā-sabhāvaṃ, devamanussādi-bhāvena paṭhamaṃ hutvā-pacchāna hotīti uchenaṃ sandhāya pucchati. Evam ettha sabbam atthi, sabbam ekattan ti, imādve pi sassata-diṭṭhiyo: sabbaṃ n' atthi, sabbaṃ puthuttan ti, imādve uccheda-diṭṭhiyo ti veditabbā" (Buddhaghosa, *Sārattha-Ppākasinī*, p. 76).
93. Inada, *Nāgārjuna*, p. 99.
94. Ibid.
95. Hopkins, *Buddhist Advice*, pp. 106–107.
96. This is also referred to at *Yuktiṣaṣtika*, v. 34. See Christina Anna Scherrer-Schaub, *Yuktiṣaṣṭikāvṛtti: Commentaire . . . la soixantaine sur le raisonnement, ou Du vrai enseignement de la causalité par le Maître indien Candrakīrti* (Brussels: Institut Belge des Hautes Etudes Chinoises, 1991), p. 252. Especially see her fascinating note 492 (pp. 252–259) on the apparent *citta-mātra* content of this verse and the debates over it.
97. *Long Discourses*, pp. 179–180.

Notes to Chapter 6

1. "Śekhayitavyo dhātukauśalyaṃ skandhakauśalyam āyatanakauśalyaṃ pratītyasamutpādakauśalyaṃ|" (Singh and Minowa, "A Critical Edition and Translation of *Abhisamācārikā*," p. 105; cf. translation, p. 141).
2. "Natthi taṃ suttaṃ vā gāthā vā byākaraṇaṃ vā imesuma channaṃ dhammā-

naṃ aññatarasmiṃ na saṃdissati" (*The Petakopadesa,* Arabinda Barua, ed. [London: Ceylon Daily News Press for the Pāli Text Society, 1949], p. 98).

3. "[One] should study this treatise in order to get knowledge of the person and the dharmas. As it is said in the sūtras: The world has two [types of] people: One is wise [and] one is stupid. If one does not properly distinguish the dharmas of the aggregates, the dhātu, all the āyatanas, the [links of] dependent-origination, cause and effect, etc. then one is, called a stupid person."
   應習此論。所以者何。學習此論得智人法。如經中說。世有二人。一謂智人。一謂愚人。若不善分別陰界諸入十二因緣因果等法是名愚人 (T. 1646, 249a13–16).
4. "bhi[kṣu]sya balasya trepiṭakasya antevāsi[nī]ye bhikṣuṇīye tre[piṭakā]ye buddhamitrāye" (Dinesh Chandra Sircar, *Select Inscriptions Bearing on Indian History and Civilization* [Delhi: Motilal Banarsidass, 1965], p. 153).
5. Sander and Waldenschmidt, "The Earliest Manuscripts from Central Asia and the Sarvāstivāda Mission," p. 133.
6. Robert Buswell and Padmanabh Jaini, "The Development of Abhidharma Philosophy," in Encyclopedia of Indian Philosophies: Volume VII Abhidharma Buddhism to 150 A.D., Karl Potter, ed. (Delhi: Motilal Banarsidass, 1996), pp. 80–82.
7. This felicitous phrase was borrowed from ibid., p. 96.
8. Frauwallner claims that the similarities between the Dharmaskandha and the Vibhanga of the Pāli school are too numerous and idiosyncratic to be coincidental. Therefore, the two texts date from a time prior to the split between Sarvāstivāda and Theravāda. He concludes that it is the earliest abhidharma text after the Saṅgītiparyāya. See Ernst Frauwallner, Studies in Abhidharma Literature and the Origins of Buddhist Philosophical Systems, Sophie Francis Kidd, trans. (Albany: State University of New York Press, 1995), pp. 17–21.
9. Buswell and Jaini, "The Development of Abhidharma Philosophy," pp. 90–91.
10. Ibid., p. 102.
11. Thich Thien Chau, The Literature of the Personalists of Early Buddhism, Sara Boin-Webb, trans. (Delhi: Motilal Banarsidass, 1999), p. 19.
12. For excellent discussions of these works, see two articles by Thich Thien Chau, "The Literature of the Pudgalavādins," *Journal of the International Association of Buddhist Studies* 7, no. 1 (1984): 7–16; and "Les Réponses des Pudgalavādin aux critiques des écoles bouddhiques," *Journal of the International Association of Buddhist Studies* 10, no. 1 (1987): 33–54. See also his *Literature of the Personalists*.
13. Leonard Priestley informs me that the title of this text is better rendered as *Tattvasiddhi* since the character 實 is regularly used for *tattva,* while *satya* is translated as 諦. I have maintained the usual translation of the title throughout this chapter in order to avoid confusion, since this is how Shastri reconstructs the title in his translation, to which I refer below.
14. *Anātman* is also a characteristic of *saṃsāra,* but since it is also a characteristic of nirvāṇa it is not included here as a distinguishing characteristic.

15. See Chapter 5, notes 73 and 74.
16. These three elements have been discussed at length by Etienne Lamotte in his *Karmasiddhiprakaraṇa: The Treatise on Action by Vasubandhu,* Leo Pruden, trans. (Berkeley: Asian Humanities Press, 1988), pp. 15–17.
17. Thomas Dowling, "Karma Doctrine and Sectarian Development," in *Studies in Pāli and Buddhism: A Memorial Volume in Honor of Bhikkhu Jagdish Kashyapa,* A. K. Narain, ed. (Delhi: B. R. Publication Corporation, 1979), p. 83.
18. See, for example, Jaimini on *Mīmāṃsā Sūtra* 1.1.5.
19. The best treatment of Dharmakīrti's theories of nominalism in recent literature is Georges Dreyfus, *Recognizing Reality: Dharmakīrti's Philosophy and Its Tibetan Interpretations* (Albany: State University of New York Press, 1997).
20. *Majjhima Nikāya,* 1:191; *Middle Length Discourses,* p. 283.
21. Translation: I. B. Horner, *Milinda's Questions* (London: Luzac, 1963), 1:37 (cf. *The Milindapañho, Being Dialogues Between King Milinda and the Buddhist Sage Nāgasena: The Pāli Text,* V. Trenckner, ed. [London: Royal Asiatic Society, 1928], p. 27). For a parallel passage, see *Saṃyutta Nikāya,* 1:135 and 169–170; *Dīgha Nikāya,* 1:202.
22. T. 1548, 626c8–20.
23. The *Papañcasūdanī* glosses *saṅkhaṃ* (*saṅketa*) as *prajñaptimātra*: "agāraṃtveva saṅkhaṃ gacchatīti agāranti paṇṇattimattaṃ hoti|" (2:229).
24. *Dīgha Nikāya,* 2:62ff., translated in A. K. Warder, "The Concept of a Concept," *Journal of Indian Philosophy* 1, no. 1 (1971): 183.
25. See *Majjhima Nikāya,* 1:297–298; "And what, friend, is the deliverance of mind through voidness? Here a bhikkhu, gone to the forest or to the root of a tree or to an empty hut, reflects thus: 'This is void of a self or of what belongs to a self.' This is called the deliverance of mind through voidness" (*Middle Length Discourses,* p. 394).
26. "na praṇaśyanti karmāṇi kalpakoṭiśatair api| sāmagrīm prāpya kālaṃ ca phalanti khalu dehinām||" (Lamotte, *Karmasiddhiprakaraṇa,* p. 16). According to La Valée Poussin, this verse is cited nine times in the *Divyāvadāna,* once in the *Bodhicāryāvatāra* and once in the *Abhidharmakośavākya* (Candrakīrti, *Mūlamadhyamakakārikās (Mādhyamikasūtras) de Nāgārjuna,* p. 324n1).
27. Here, I have taken 義 (*yi*) as "meaning/purpose" (as a translation for the Sanskrit *artha*), following Chau (*Literature of the Personalists,* p. 189). As an alternate reading, one might also take *yi* as "righteousness" and read the sentence as "It is in order to experience [the results of] righteousness." The former reading is preferable because not all actions are righteous.
28. The Chinese of this passage is anything but clear. One could certainly translate *sheng* as the more usual "birth" or "lifetime" (*jāti*). However, the following sentences only make sense if we take it to be a technical term denoting accumulated-but-not-yet-manifest karma similar to that in the *ālayavijñāna* of the (later?) Yogācārins.
29. In this translation, I have followed that of Chau, *The Literature of the Personalists,* p. 189; T. 1649, 462a13–16.

30. Nāgārjuna also mentions the neutrality of *avipranāśa* in the *Mūlamadhyamakakārikā,* chapter 17, verse 14. See also Candrakīrti, *Mūlamadhyamakakārikās (Mādhyamikasūtras) de Nāgārjuna,* p. 318.
31. Lamotte, *Karmasiddhiprakaraṇa, p. 55.*
32. This is stated as the first Vātsīputrīya thesis in Vasumitra's *Samayabhedoparacanacakra*. For a discussion of this thesis in the different versions of this text, see Leonard Priestley, *Pudgalavāda Buddhism: The Reality of the Indeterminate Self* (Toronto: University of Toronto, Centre for South Asian Studies, 1999), pp. 53–55. Priestley convincingly argues that the Pudgalavādins abandoned the thesis that the pudgala was a *prajñapti* around the time of Vasubandhu and adopted the thesis that it was a substance. See ibid., p. 87.
33. Ibid., p. 83.
34. 依說, T. 1649, 466b2, 受教授, T. 1505, 10a8, 受施設, T. 1506, 24b1. Chau gives the Sanskrit equivalent of this term as either *āśrayaprajñapta* (Chau, *The Literature of the Personalists,* p. 143) or *upādānaprajñapti* (ibid., p. 145). Unfortunately, since there is no existing Sanskrit for these passages, the reconstruction could go either way. Hirakawa lists the gerund *upādāya* as a Sanskrit equivalent for both 依 and 受, while the noun *upādāna* is listed as an equivalent for neither (Hirakawa, *Buddhist Chinese-Sanskrit Dictionary s.v.*). Priestley (*Pudgalavāda Buddhism,* p. 72) notes that Kumārajīva often uses the character 受 to translate *upādāya* in his translation of Nāgāruna's *Mūlamadhyamakakārikā* (though for some reason, not at 24.18; see T. 1564, 33b13). He also notes that the Theravāda commentaries discuss *upādāpaññatti* as a type of *prajñapti* and that the "concept of the person, which is based on the five aggregates, is understood to be a concept of this type." Hence, there is good reason to translate this phrase as *upādāyaprajñapti.* Curiously, Paramārtha's translation of Vasumitra alone mentions the three *prajñapti,* though his understanding appears to be different: "There are three kinds of *prajñapti* [假]. The first is the group of the *prajñapti* of wholes [一切]. The second is the collection of *prajñapti* of parts [一分]. The third is the group of *prajñapti* (relating to) *nirodha*/nirvāṇa [滅度]" (T. 2033, 21c22–23).
35. The three texts differ most regarding the interpretation of this term. 度說, T. 1649; T.1505, 10a12 uses the term 方便教授 (*upāya-prajñapti*) to the same effect. T. 1506 discusses the concept without a technical term. See Chau, *The Literature of the Personalists,* pp. 162–164.
36. 滅說, T. 1649; 滅教授, 1505, 10a20; 滅施設, 1506, 24b1.
37. T. 1649, 466a28–b14. The Chinese here is far from clear. Cf. Chau, *The Literature of the Personalists,* p. 143, and Priestley, *Pudgalavāda Buddhism,* pp. 62–63.
38. Priestley, *Pudgalavāda Buddhism,* p. 64.
39. Chau, *The Literature of the Personalists,* p. 186; T. 1506, 24a29–b8.
40. For references to this analogy, see Chau, *The Literature of the Personalists,* p. 35; T. 1649, 466b6; *Satyasiddhiśāstra,* p. 73; Vasubandhu, *L'Abhidharmakośa,* 5:234–237; cf. Vasubandhu, *Abhidharmakośabhāṣyam,* Prahlāda Pradhāna, ed. (Patna: Kāśīprasadajāyasavāla-Anuśīlan-Institute, 1975), pp. 471–472. For another use of

the term *upādāyaprajñapti* in the sense of a dependent thing being neither identical to nor different from its component parts, see Yaśomitra, *Abhidharmakośasphuṭārthā,* pp. 148–149.

41. Priestley, *Pudgalavāda Buddhism,* p. 128.
42. See, for example, Vasubandhu, *L'Abhidharmakośa,* 5:237; *Abhidharmakośabhāṣyam,* Pradhāna, ed., p. 473.
43. *Satyasiddhiśāstra,* p. 74. Cf. Chau, "Réponses des Pudgalavādin," p. 42; Lamotte, *Le Traité,* 1:43; Chau, *The Literature of the Personalists,* pp. 158–161.
44. *Dīgha Nikāya,* 1:187–188; *Majjhima Nikāya,* 1:157, 426, 484; *Saṃyutta Nikāya,* 3:213ff., 258; 4:286, 391; 5:418.

    The ten questions are: (1–2) Is the world eternal or not? (3–4) Is the world infinite or not? (5–6) Is the person (alternately *jīva* or *puruṣa*) identical to the body or not? (7–10) Does the Tathāgata exist, not exist, both or neither?
45. *Long Discourses,* p. 164.
46. *Satyasiddhiśāstra,* p. 69.
47. A reference to the "Mahāgovinda sutta" of the *Dīgha Nikāya.*
48. T. 1506, 24a29–b5. Parts of this passage have been translated into French by Chau, "Réponses des Pudgalavādin," pp. 35 and 37.
49. Priestley, *Pudgalavāda Buddhism,* pp. 56–57; cf. Chau, "Réponses des Pudgalavādin," pp. 38–39; T. 1506, 24a30–b7.
50. See Priestley's comment in ibid., p. 57.
51. Enga Teramoto and Tomotsugu Hiramatsu, eds. and trans., *Vasumitra's Samaya-Bhedoparacana-cakra, Bhavya's Nikāyabheda-Vibhaṅga-Vyākhyāna and Vinītadeva's Samaya-Bhedoparacana-cakrasya-Nikāya-Bhedopadarśana-Nāma-Saṅgraha: Three Tibetan Texts* (Kyoto: Mokudosha, 1935), p. 730. Tibetan canon, Peking edition, p. 183a.
52. Louis de La Valée Poussin, "La Controverse du temps et du Pudgala dans le Vijñānakāya," in *Etudes asiatiques oubliées à l'occasion du 25e anniversaire de l'Ecole française de l'Extrême Orient* (Paris: Ecole française de l'Extrême Orient, 1925), 1:346–347.
53. Ibid., p. 367, right before 13a (translated from the French).
54. This is stated in the *Mahāvibhāṣā*: "Parce qu'il y a causes et conditions, étant déjà nés, ils naissent. C'est à dire: tous les dharmas possèdent déjà leur nature propre, car chaque futur réside dans son caractère essentiel (*svabhāvalakṣaṇa*). Possèdant déjà une nature propre, ils sont déjà nés: ce n'est pas que leur nature propre soit née des causes et conditions" (Louis de La Vallée Poussin, "Documents d'Abhidharma," *Mélanges chinois et bouddhiques* 5 [July 1937]: 15).
55. La Valée Poussin, "Documents," p. 12 (translated from the French); see also Vasubandhu, *L'Abhidharmakośa,* 1:24.
56. See Fumimaro Watanabe, *Philosophy and Its Development in the Nikāyas and Abhidhamma* (Delhi: Motilal Banarsidass, 1983), p. 197; see also *Abhidharmakośa,* 5:233ff.
57. La Valée Poussin, "Documents," pp. 28–29.
58. Different types of *prajñapti* (Pāli, *paññatti*) are distinguished in the commen-

taries of Buddhaghosa. Buddhadatta's *Abhidhammāvatāra* (fifth century) comes quite close to Saṅghabhadra's position, as he distinguishes the two types of *prajñapti* as *paññāpetabba* ("requiring to be made understood") and *paññāpana* ("making understood"). This distinction is made by Ānanda (tenth century) in his *Mūlaṭīkā*. Dhammapāla II and Anuruddha II explicitly tie this distinction to the two truths (*saṃvṛtisatya/ paramārthasatya*) in their works. For references, see Warder, "The Concept of a Concept," pp. 191–193.

59. For a summary of Mahāsāṅghika theses, see Bareau, *Les Sectes bouddhiques du petit véhicule*, pp. 55–106.
60. For this discussion, I have relied heavily on ibid., pp. 55–56.
61. Lamotte, *History of Indian Buddhism*, p. 181; *Dīpavaṃsa*, p. 37.
62. E.g., T. 1425, 295a26.
63. T. 1425, 340c5, 475c14, and 501c24–25. This last passage has a parallel in the *Abhisamācārika-Dharma* which spells out what the nine categories of scripture are: "abhidharmmo nāma navavidho sūtrānto sūtraṃ geyaṃ vyākaraṇaṃ gāthā udānaṃ itivṛttakaṃ jātakaṃ vaipulyādbhutādharmmā." See Chapter 3, note 17.
64. For a discussion of the dates of the Ikṣvāku kings, see Stone, *The Buddhist Art of Nāgārjunakoṇḍa*, pp. 4–9.
65. Text: "āchariyānaṃ Aparamahāvinaseliyānaṃ suparigahitaṃ imaṃmahāchetiya navakaṃma(ṃ) Paṃnagāma vathavānaṃdigha—majhima- pa(ṃ)chamātuka - osaka vāchakānam āchariyānaṃ Ayira—haṅghānaṃ [ṃ] a(ṃ)tevāsikena Dīgha-majhima-nikāya- dharena bhajamt [sic]- Ānaṃdena nithapitaṃ imaṃ navakamaṃ mahāchetiyaṃ" (Rao et al., *Buddhist Inscriptions of Andhradesa*, p. 140); Vogel, "Prakrit Inscriptions from a Buddhist Site," p. 17.
66. *Satyasiddhiśāstra*, p. 234; 六足阿毘曇樓炭 (T. 1646, 300b28).
67. Legge, *A Record of Buddhistic Kingdoms*, p. 99.
68. Hwu Li, *The Life of Hiuen-Tsiang*, S. Beal, trans. (reprint, San Francisco: Chinese Materials Center, 1976), p. 137; 法師在其國逢二僧。一名蘇部底。二名蘇利耶。善解大眾部三藏。法師因就停數月。學大眾部根本阿毘達摩等論。彼亦依法師學大乘諸論。遂結志同行巡禮聖跡。自此西行千餘里至珠利耶 (T. 2053, 241b27–c2).
69. The Later Qin dynasty translation of the *Samayabhedoparacanacakra* (T. 2032) omits any reference to the Bahuśrutīyas arising out of the Mahāsāṅghikas. See André Bareau, "Le Cycle de la formation des schismes (*Samayabhedoparacanacakra*) de Vasumitra," *Journal Asiatique* 242, no. 2 (1954): 236n6.
70. Paramārtha's translation of the *Samayabhedoparacanacakra* renders this school as *Vibhahyavādin* (分別說部) (ibid., p. 237n1 and 3). See, for example, T. 2033, 20b1–2.
71. These can be found in the *Dīpavaṃsa*, the *Nikāyabhedavibhaṅga* of Bhavya, and the *Śāriputraparipṛcchāsūtra*.
72. See Chapter 1, note 150.
73. Masuda, "Origin and Doctrines," p. 29.

74. 八緣起支性。九聖道支性 (T. 2031, 15c27).

75. 八十二因緣生分。九八聖道 (T. 2033, 20c29–30); 十二緣 起支道支 (T. 2032, 8c04–5). See Bareau, "Le Cycle," p. 244n3.

76. Vasumitra: "rteṅ ciṅ 'brel bar 'byuṅ ba rnams daṅ| lam ni 'dus ma byas kyi dṅos po" (Teramoto and Hiramatsu, *Vasumitra's Samaya-Bhedoparacana-cakra,* p. 7). Vinītadeva has a similar list, although the translation is somewhat garbled; see ibid., p. 42, and André Bareau, "Trois traités sur les sectes bouddhiques attribués . . . Vasumitra, Bhavya et Vinītadeva," *Journal Asiatique* 244, no. 2 (1956): 194–195, esp. note 4.

77. *L'Abhidharmakośa,* 2:77. Cf. *Abhidharmakośabhāṣyam,* Pradhanāna, ed., p. 137. La Valée Poussin cites many sources attributing this theory both to the Mahāsāṅghikas and to the Mahīśāsakas. See *L'Abhidharmakośa,* 2:77n1.

78. As Ronald Davidson points out, however, a curious passage in the *Mahāyānasaṃgraha* states that the Mahāsāṅghikas ascribed to the existence of a *mūlavijñāna* (Tibetan, "rtsa ba'i rnam par śes pa"; Chinese, 根本識) (Davidson, "Buddhist Systems of Transformation," p. 107n10); cf. Asaṅga, *La Somme du grand véhicule d'Asaṅga (Mahāyānasaṃgraha),* Etienne Lamotte, ed. and trans. (Louvain-la-Neuve: Université de Louvain, Institut orientaliste, 1973), 1:7 and 2:27; T. 1594, 134a24. None of the other sources mention this thesis.

79. 種即為芽 (T. 2031, 16a8–10); 種子即是芽 (T. 2033, 21a11).

80. 想種子即是取 (T. 2032, 18c10–11).

81. See Edgerton, *Buddhist Hybrid Sanskrit Dictionary, s.v.*

82. Masuda, "Origin and Doctrines," p. 34n1.

83. Ibid., p. 23, and Bareau, "Le Cycle," pp. 241–242 = T. 2031, 15c15. The other translations offer some different interpretations and probably represent different versions of the original. See Bareau, "Le Cycle," p. 242n1. 禪定中聞亦有言說。亦調伏心。亦攝受思惟 (T. 2032, 18b23); "In *samādhi* there are words and speech to make the mind subdued and to allow comprehension (*parigraha*)"; 若心在定。 亦得有語折伏心恆有。相壞心恆有。是故凡夫有上下 (T. 2033, 20c16–18); "If the mind resides in *samādhi* it obtains possession of words to either subdue 折伏 the mind perpetually or to help ruin the mind perpetually. Therefore, the common person is either superior or inferior." Alternately, Bareau has: "La pensée disciplinée existe toujours. La pensée de destruction mutuelle existe toujours. C'est pourquoi, chez les profanes (*pṛthagjana*), il y a [des degrés] superieurs et inférieurs" ("Le Cycle," p. 242n1). Dharmākara's translation has: "mñam par bźag pa'i tshig brjod pa yod do" (Teramoto, *Vasumitra's Samaya-Bhedoparacana-cakra,* p. 6), "Words are spoken in (the state of) *samāhita.*"

84. Masuda, "Origin and Doctrines," p. 24, and Bareau, "Le Cycle," p. 243 (incl. note 3). Cf. 智慧方便得離生死。亦得安樂(T. 2032, 18b27); "Wisdom is a means to attain freedom from birth and death and to attain beatitude"; 般若相應滅苦 (T. 2033, 20c22); "Suffering is annihilated depending on Prajñā." Dharmākara: "sdug bsṅal spaṅs pa'i phyir śes rab kyi sbyor ba daṅ| bde ba'i yo

byad do||" (Teramoto, *Vasumitra's Samaya-Bhedoparacana-cakra,* p. 6); "The application of wisdom is due to the cutting off of suffering and it is the basis for bliss."

85. Masuda, "Origin and Doctrines," pp. 35–36, and Bareau, "Le Cycle," pp. 246–247.
86. Bareau, *Les Sectes bouddhiques,* p. 86.
87. T. 2031, 16a17–20.
88. Two editions of this text have *ma regs pa* (do not touch), which Teramoto corrects to *ma rigs pa* (are not comprehended), on the basis of the Chinese versions. See his "Corrective Table of Vasumitra's *Samaya-bhedoparacana-cakra,*" in Teramoto and Hiramatsu, *Vasumitra's Samaya-Bhedoparacana-cakra,* p. 48.
89. Ibid., pp. 8–9.
90. Bareau tries to divide this thesis in three, presumably to make it fit with the other versions (Bareau, "Le Cycle," p. 247nn3–5). This does not work very well, so I keep to the structure of the Qin text itself.
91. T. 2032, 18c18–23.
92. T. 2033, 21a19–24.
93. Masuda, "Origin and Doctrines," p. 36n3.
94. Ibid., n4.
95. It is not entirely clear who advocated this position. It is possible that it was held by the Bahuśrutīyas, since Harivarman treats the aggregates (or at least their functions) as uncomposite for the purposes of analyzing composite things. Harivarman, like Saṅghabhadra, equates *prajñaptis* with conventional truth and the *dharmas* with ultimate truth. A *prajñapti,* like a person or a pot, is negated because it is reducible to its component parts. As in his discussion on matter, he maintains that the sense data corresponding to the *skandhas* cannot be so reduced and therefore they are truly considered to be *dharma*.

    "Empirical things like pitcher, etc. are nominally existing but not substantially. For, . . . in the world of nominalism concepts come into play but not in the world of the absolute; People say that it is the colour of the pitcher, but do not say that it is the colour's colour. Nor is it the feeling's colour. . . . [and later] Nominal thing is achieved depending on another thing; e.g., *ghaṭa* is depending on the colour, etc. (*rūpādi*). The absolute thing is not so, e.g., feeling. The nominal thing discharges different functions, lamp, e.g. illuminates as well as burns. The feeling, e.g., feels and does not cognize. The term, chariot is employed in an assemblage of the wheel, etc. but the term, *rūpa,* etc. is not employed in any such object (*padārtha*). The constituents of chariot are factors of chariot and the term chariot is not there. Thus, the character of chariot is nominal" (*Satyasiddhiśāstra,* pp. 337–338).
96. V. P. Vasilyev, *Der buddhismus, seine Dogmen, Geschichte und Literatur* (St. Petersburg: Kaiserliche Akademie der Wissenschaften, 1860), p. 269.

97. See Lokesh Candra, *Tibetan-Sanskrit Dictionary* (Kyoto: Rinsen Book Company, 1990), *s.v.*
98. "'dus byas rnams phan tshun btags pa ñid kyis sdug bsṅal ba yin no źes smra ba'iphyir btags par smra ba pa'o|" (Teramoto and Hiramatsu, *Vasumitra's Samaya-Bhedoparacana-cakra,* p. 19). Bareau has: "Il y a douleur (***duḥkha***) parce que les pomposés (*saṃskṛta*) ne sont que désignation (*prajñaptireva*) mutuelle (*anyonya*)." The negative sense that he gives to *anyonyaprajñapti* ("*nothing but* mutual designation") is missing in the Tibetan. See Bareau, "Trois traités," p. 169.
99. "'du byed rnams ni phan tshun btags pa yin no| yaṅ sdug bsṅal ni don dam par ro|" (Teramoto and Hiramatsu, *Vasumitra's Samaya-Bhedoparacana-cakra,* p. 25). W. W. Rockhill, following Wassiljew, translates the phrase *phan tshun btags pa as* "bound together" (*The Life of the Buddha* [London: Trübner, 1884], p. 189), as does Bareau ("mutuellement liés") (Bareau, "Trois traités," p. 176), despite the fact that he translates the same term as *prajñapti* in the earlier version of the Prajñaptivādin theses. For these reasons I have not followed any of these translations.
100. See note 28 above.
101. "idāni kammūpacayakathā nāma hoti. tattha yesaṃ kammūpacayo nāma kammato añño cittavippayutto abyākato anārammaṇoti laddhi seyyathāpi andhakānañceva sammitiyānañca; to sandhāya aññaṃ kammanti pucchā sakavādissa, paṭiññā itarassa. atha naṃ "yadi kammato añño kammūpacayo, phassāditopi aññena phassūpacayādinā bhavitabban"ti codetuṃ añño phassoti -ādimāha. itaro laddhiyā abhāvena paṭikkhipati" (*Kathāvatthuppakarana-aṭṭhakathā: Included in Pañcappakarana-atthakathā, Named Paramatthadīpanī,* N. A. Jayawickrama, ed. [London: Pāli Text Society, 1979], p. 158).

Notes to Chapter 7

1. Musashi Tachikawa, *An Introduction to the Philosophy of Nāgārjuna,* Rolf W. Giebel, trans. (Delhi: Motilal Banarsidass, 1997), p. 1.
2. Brian Bocking, *Nāgārjuna in China: A Translation of the Middle Treatise* (Lewiston, NY: Edwin Mellon Press, 1995), pp. 104–105; T. 1564, 1b29ff.
3. Mervyn Sprung, *Lucid Exposition of the Middle Way: The Essential Chapters from the Prasannapadā of Candrakīrti* (London: Routledge & Kegan Paul, 1979), pp. 65–66. There are so many translations of the verses of Nāgārjuna's ***Mūlamadhyamakakārikā*** that it is not necessary for me to offer new translations of all of these verses. Unfortunately, most of the published translations are uneven in their accuracy. This chapter alternates between the translations of Kenneth Inada and Mervyn Sprung, unless there is some reason for me to offer my own translation.
4. T. 1539, 547b22–c4.
5. T. 1541, 45b6–7, and T. 1542, 712b12–13.

6. It is, of course, possible that he is arguing against the *Mahāvibhāṣā* itself, but since the date of that text is problematic (tied as it is to the rather shaky date of Kaniṣka), I will avoid making this assumption. In any case, there is no question that the *Vijñānakāya* was written well before Nāgārjuna.

   Nāgārjuna attacks other specifically Sarvāstivādin theories as well. One the deserves special mention in this regard is the Sarvāstivādin notion of "secondary characteristics" (*anulakṣaṇa*). See Vasubandhu, *L'Abhidharmakośa,* 2:224ff. and note 3. The Sarvāstivādins held that for certain characteristics pertaining to conditioned reality, there were characteristics of those characteristics, namely: the arising of arising, the endurance of endurance, the decay of decay and the impermanence of impermanence. Nāgārjuna refutes these secondary characteristics in chapter 7 of the *Mūlamadhyamakakārikā.* Candrakīrti mentions that the Saṃmitīyas also held this doctrine. Unfortunately, this is not confirmed in any other source, so we do not know if this was an important doctrine for them at the time of Nāgārjuna (*Prasannapadā,* p. 148). My thanks to Leonard Priestly for pointing this out.
7. Yukihiro Okada and Michael Hahn, "Zur Quelle der 57 Fehler in der Ratnāvalī des Nāgārjuna," *Indo-Iranian Journal* 28 (1985): 125.
8. See the concordance in ibid., pp. 128–130.
9. Hopkins, *Buddhist Advice,* p. 149.
10. Buswell and Jaini, "The Development of Abhidharma Philosophy," p. 103.
11. Christian Lindtner, "Saṅgīti Paryāya," in *Encyclopedia of Indian Philosophies: Volume VII Abhidharma Buddhism to 150 A.D.,* Karl Potter, ed. (Delhi: Motilal Banarsidass, 1996), p. 203.
12. Puri, *Buddhism in Central Asia,* p. 216.
13. My thanks to Ulrich Kragh for his help in unraveling this last verse.
14. For an excellent discussion of the Sautrāntikas, see Lamotte, *Karmasiddhiprakaraṇa,* pp. 25–32.
15. Lamotte mentions a few candidate inscriptions from Bhārhut and Sāñcī but notes, "it is doubtful whether the term *sautrāntika* used by these inscriptions designates an adherent of the *Sautrāntika* school" (*History of Indian Buddhism,* p. 524n6).
16. T. 2031, 15c27; T. 2032, 18c04–5; T. 2033, 20c29.
17. William Ames, "Bhavaviveka '*Prajñāpradīpa*': A Translation of Chapter 1, Examination of Causal Conditions (*Pratyaya*)," *Journal of Indian Philosophy* 21, no. 3 (1993): 219.
18. T. 1425, 336c19–28. See above, Chapter 4, note 19, for a discussion of this passage.
19. Inada, *Nāgārjuna,* pp. 58–59.
20. Although, as noted in Chapter 2, it is difficult to determine when they actually did adopt Mahāyāna scriptures.
21. Shingyo Yoshimoto, "Śārīputrābhidharmaśāstra," in *Encyclopedia of Indian Philosophies: Volume VII Abhidharma Buddhism to 150 A.D.,* Karl Potter, ed. (Delhi: Motilal Banarsidass, 1996), p. 317.

22. T. 1548, 633a11–12; see also Bareau, *Les Sectes,* p. 198.
23. 施設. Citation at T. 1545, 540a20–22. The *Prajñaptiśāstra* is the name of one of the early *abhidharma* texts of the Sarvāstivādins. According to Potter, although some texts correspond to this name extant in Tibetan, "it is doubtful whether any of it remains in existence" (*Encyclopedia of Indian Philosophies: Abhidharma Buddhism to 150 A.D.*, p. 217). There is also a text by this name in Chinese translation (T. 1538). It does not, however, contain the discussion of emptiness referred to in the *Mahāvibhāṣa.* The Dharmagupta list is also mentioned without attribution at T. 1545, 37a13ff.
24. T. 221, 13b6ff.
25. T. 220, 290c17–18.
26. David Burton, *Emptiness Appraised: A Critical Study of Nāgārjuna's Philosophy* (Richmond, UK: Curzon Press, 1999), pp. 35–36.
27. Ibid., p. 99.
28. Vasubandhu, *L'Abhdharmakośa,* 4:139–41; idem, *Abhidharmakośabhāṣyaṃ,* p. 334.
29. Yasomitra, *Sputārthā,* 2:524; cf. Vasubandhu, *L'Abhdharmakośa,* 4:140n1.
30. Monier-Williams, *Sanskrit-English Dictionary, s.v.* It is, of course, the latter sense that Dignāga and Dharmakīrti make famous.
31. Ibid., *s.v.*
32. Vasubandhu, *L'Abhdharmakośa,* 4:140n1. Cf. T. 1559, 268c17–20.
33. Inada, *Nāgārjuna,* pp. 54–55.
34. Bocking, *Nāgārjuna in China,* p. 139.
35. Candrakīrti, *Prasannapadā,* p. 123.
36. Inada, *Nāgārjuna,* p. 55; Sanskrit added.
37. See especially Claus Oetke, "Pragmatic Implicatures and Text—Interpretation (The Alleged Error of the Negation of the Antecedent in the *Mūlamadhyamakakārikās*)," *Studien zur Indologie und Iranistik* 16 (1992): 185–233; and Johannes Bronkhorst, "Nāgārjuna's Logic," in *Bauddhavidyāsudhākaraḥ: Studies in Honour of Heinz Bechert on the Occasion of His 65th Birthday,* Petra Kieffer-Pülz and Jens-Uwe Hartmann, eds. (Swisttal-Odendorf: Indica et Tibetica Verlag, 1997), pp. 29–37.
38. See Nāgārjuna. *The Dialectical Method of Nāgārjuna (Vigrahavyāvartanī),* Kamaleswar Bhattacharya, trans., E. H. Johnston and Arnold Kunst, eds. (Delhi: Motilal Banarsidass, 1978), p. 123.
39. The following table is summarized from Tachikawa, *Philosophy of Nāgārjuna,* pp. 37–45, table 1.
40. Sprung, *Lucid Exposition,* p. 113. Cf. "nanvevaṃ sati itaretarāśrayāyāṃ siddhau sthitāyāṃ kasyedānīṃ siddhau satyāṃ kasya siddhirastu|" (Candrakīrti, *Prasannapadā,* p. 141).
41. Burton, *Emptiness Appraised,* p. 90.
42. Ibid., p. 93.
43. Priestly devotes all of his chapter 9 to discussing the varieties of *prajñapti.*
44. "Tattha yo rūpavedanādīhi ekattena vā aññattena vā rūpavedanādayo viya sacci-

kaṭṭhaparamatthena anupalabbhasabhāvopi rūpavedanādibhede khandhe upādāya nissāya kāraṇaṃ katvā sammato satto. Tāni tāni aṅgāni upādāya ratho gehaṃ muṭṭhi uddhananti ca; te teyeva rūpādayo upādāya ghaṭo paṭo; candasūriyaparivattādayo upādāya kālo, disā; taṃ taṃ bhūtanimittañceva bhāvanānisaṃsañca upādāya nissāya kāraṇaṃ katvā sammataṃ tena tenākārena upaṭṭhitaṃ uggahanimittaṃ paṭibhāganimittanti ayaṃ evarūpā upādāpaññatti nāma. Paññapetabbaṭṭhena cesā paññatti nāma, na paññāpanaṭṭhena. Yā pana tassatthassa paññāpanā, ayaṃ avijjamānapaññattiyeva" (Buddhaghosa, *Puggala-paññatti and Puggala Paññatti-Aṭṭhakathā,* Richard Morris, Dr. Georg Landsberg, and Mrs. Rhys Davids, eds. [London: Luzac for the Pāli Text Society, 1972], p. 173).

45. *Connected Discourses of Buddha,* 1:552.
46. Burton, *Emptiness Appraised,* pp. 109–110.
47. Sprung, *Lucid Exposition,* pp. 136–138.
48. "Imāṃ punaḥ pravakṣyāmi kalpanāṃ yātra yojyate| buddhaiḥ pratyekabuddaiśca śrāvakaiścānuvarṇitāṃ||" (Candrakīrti, *Prasannapadā,* p. 317, v. 13).
49. "bye brag tu smra ba rnams kyi grub pa'i 'mtha" (Avalokitavrāta, *Śes rab sgron mahi rya-cher ḥgrel-pa* [*Prajñāpradīpa-ṭīkā*], Peking *bsTan 'Gyur,* vol. 97, #5259, p. 40a4). According to Vasumitra, the Saṃmitīyas and the Vātsīputrīyas came out of the Sthavīra branch that included the Sarvāstivādins (Bareau, *Les Sectes,* p. 18).
50. See Chau, *The Literature of the Personalists,* pp. 188–189; T. 1649 462a 13–16.
51. See Vasubandhu, *L'Abhidharmakośa,* 4: 242–244.
52. Its status as *cittaviprayukta* is confirmed by Buddhaghosa. See Chapter 6, note 101.
53. Lamotte, *Karmasiddhiprakaraṇa,* p. 55.
54. T. 1609, 783b21.
55. Kalupahana comments on verse 14: "Here a debt and karma are compared to an imperishable promissory note. The metaphor . . . is used by Nāgārjuna to illustrate the doctrine of karma as described in one of the most popular and authoritative statements in the Indian Buddhist tradition. . . . The statement runs thus: Karmas do not perish even after hundreds of millions of aeons. Reaching the harmony of conditions and the appropriate time, they produce consequences for human beings" (*Mūlamadhyamakakārikā of Nāgārjuna,* pp. 250–251). It is one thing to say, as the verse cited by Kalupahana does, that karma is indestructible. It is quite another to say, as the Saṃmitīyas did, that the indestructibility of karma is something separate from the karma itself. See also *Katthāvathu,* pp. 519ff.
56. Sprung, *Lucid Exposition,* p. 235.
57. Nāgarjuna. *sToṅ pa ñid bdun cu pa'i 'grel pa* (*Śūnyatāsaptativṛtti*). Peking *bsTan 'Gyur*, vol. 95, # 5231, p. 131b8ff.
58. "'dir smras pa| las gnas pa ni bcom ldan gsuṅs|| bla ma las bdag 'bras bu daṅ|| sems can las bdag bya ba daṅ|| las rnams chud za min par gsuṅs|| bcom ldan

'das kyis mdo sde dag las las daṅ las kyi 'bras bu yaṅ rnam pa du mar yoṅs su bstan| las rnams 'bras bu med pa ma yin par yaṅ gsuṅs| las rnams chud mi za ba daṅ| sems can rnams ni las bdag gir bya ba ma yin no|| źes kyaṅ gsuṅs te| de lta bas na| las daṅ las kyi 'bras bu yod do|| 'dir bshad pa, gaṅ phyir raṅ bźin med bstan pa|| de phyir de ma skyes pa las| mi 'jig bdag 'dzin de las skye|| de skyed 'dzin de'ang rnam rtog las||gang gi phyir las raṅ bźin med par bstan zin pa de'i phyir ma skyes pas ni de 'jig pa med do|| gźan yaṅ, bdag 'dzin de las skyes|| de'i phyir las ni bdag tu 'dzin pas bskyed la| de yaṅ rnam par rtog pa las byuṅ ṅo||" (ibid., 131b8–132a4). My sincere thanks to Ulrich Kragh for pointing out this verse to me.

59. "The non-arising [*anutpādo*] that [is taught] in the Mahāyāna—that emptiness [*śūnyatā*] is the "extinction" [*kṣaya*] of others [i.e., of other Buddhists]. Hence be accepting [of Mahāyāna] because of the unity of the meaning/purpose [*artha*] of cessation and non-arising!" (Nāgārjuna, *Ratnāvalī*, p. 126).
60. Bhikkhu Pāsādika, "The Concept of Avipraṇāśa in Nāgārjuna," in *Recent Researches in Buddhist Studies: Essays in Honor of Professor Karunadassa* (Colombo, Sri Lanka, and Hong Kong: Y. Karunadasa Felicitation Committee with the Chi Ying Foundation, 1997), p. 518. Pāsādika notes, however, that the term also appears in other versions of the same text.
61. Chau, *The Literature of the Personalists,* p. 35.
62. Tilmann Vetter, "Zum Problem der Person in Nāgārjunas Mūla-Madhyamaka-Kārikās," in *Offenbarung als Heilserfahrung im Christentum, Hinduismus, und Buddhismus,* Walter Strolz and Shizuteru Ueda, eds. (Freiburg: Herder Press, 1982), pp. 167–185.
63. Inada, *Nāgārjuna,* p. 79.
64. Ibid., p. 84.
65. *Majjhima Nikāya,* 1:300.
66. "evaṃ nānya upādānna copādānameva saḥ| ātmā nāstyanupādānaḥ nāpi nāstyeṣa niścayaḥ||" (Candrakīrti, *Prasannapadā,* pp. 578–579). Inada translates *upādāna* as "perceptual clinging," reading it as one of the twelve links of dependent origination. Here however, it refers to the aggregates that are the basis for the word *ātman*. Cf. Inada, *Nāgārjuna,* p. 166.
67. Inada, *Nāgārjuna,* p. 137.
68. Ibid., pp. 113–115.
69. Vetter, "Zum Problem der Person," p. 178.
70. A *sūtra* by this name exists in the Tibetan canon, though not in the Chinese. Cf. *Chos kyi phyag rgya* Sde ge, # 203.
71. Chau, *The Literature of the Personalists,* pp. 135–136; T. 1506, 19a13–20.
72. Inada, *Nāgārjuna,* p. 55.
73. "pudgalaḥ saṃsarati cetskandhāyatanadhātuṣu| pañcadhā mṛgyamāṇo 'sau nāsti kaḥ saṃsariṣyati||" (Candrakīrti, *Prasannapadā,* p. 284). Inada's translation is problematic. For some reason he takes the *pañcadā mṛgyamāno* to be the *pañcagati* or the five realms of existence (Inada, *Nāgārjuna,* p. 102). All the com-

mentaries connect this phrase to the fivefold investigation from chapter 10. "pudgalaḥ saṃsarati cetskandhāyatanadhātuṣu| pañcadhā mṛgyamāṇo 'sau nāsti kaḥ saṃsariṣyati||" (Candrakīrti, *Prasannapadā,* p. 284).

74. "upādānādupādānaṃ saṃsaran vibhavo bhavet| vibhavaścānupādānaḥ kaḥ sa kiṃ saṃsariṣyati||" (ibid.).

75. Bocking, *Nāgārjuna in China,* p. 252; 若從身至身 往來即無身 (T. 1564, 20c22–23).

76. "ñe bar len pas ñer len par| 'khor na srid pa med par 'gyur|" (Candrakīrti, *Prasannapadā,* p. 284n5).

77. Monier-Williams, *Sanskrit-English Dictionary, s.v.*

78. E.g., *Dīgha Nikāya,* 3:212.

79. Buddhaghosa, *The Sumaṅgala-vilāsinī, Buddhaghosa's Commentary on the Dīgha Nikāya,* T. W. Rhys Davids and J. Estlin Carpenter, eds. (London: H. Frowde for the Pāli Text Society, 1886–1919), p. 978. Nāgārjuna himself uses *vibhava* in this sense in other chapters, e.g., chapter 25, verse 10.

80. "iha manuṣyopadānāddevopādānaṃ gacchan parityajya vā manuṣyopādānaṃ devopādānaṃ gacchedaparityajya vā| Yadi tāvatparityajya gacchatītyucyate, tadā pūrvopādānasya parityāgāduttarasya cānupādānāttadantarāle vibhavaḥ syāt| vigato bhavo yasyeti vibhavaḥ| [bhavaḥ] pañcopādānaskandhāḥ, tadrahitaḥ syat|" (Candrakīrti, *Prasannapadā,* p. 285).

81. Masuda, "Origin and Doctrines," p. 55.

82. Inada, *Nāgārjuna,* p. 156.

83. Priestley, *Pudgalavāda Buddhism,* p. 110.

84. See Paul Swanson, *Foundations of T'ien-t'ai Philosophy: The Flowering of the Two Truths Theory in Chinese Buddhism* (Berkeley: Asian Humanities Press, 1989), chapter 8.

85. "yaḥ pratītyasamutpādaḥ śūnyatāṃ tāṃ pracakṣmahe| sā prajñaptirupādāya pratipatsaiva madhyamā||" (Candrakīrti, *Prasannapadā,* p. 503).

86. Edgerton, *Buddhist Hybrid Sanskrit Dictionary, s.v.*

87. Cf. Gadjin Nagao, *Mādhyamika and Yogācara,* Leslie Kawamura, trans. (Albany: State University of New York Press, 1991), pp. 192–193.

88. *Svabhāva* is missing in Tibetan.

89. Candrakīrti, *Prasannapadā,* p. 504.

90. Priestley, *Pudgalavāda Buddhism,* p. 72.

91. Inada, *Nāgārjuna,* p. 146.

92. Priestley, *Pudgalavāda Buddhism,* p. 105.

93. Ibid., p. 106.

94. Inada, *Nāgārjuna,* p. 114.

95. "yaḥ pratītyasamutpādaḥ śūnyatā saiva te matā| bhāvaḥ svatantro nāstiīti siṃhanādas tavātulaḥ|" (text and trans. from Christian Lindtner, *Nāgārjuniana: Studies in the Writings and Philosophy of Nāgārjuna* [Delhi: Motilal Banarsidass, 1990], pp. 135–136).

96. "yaḥ pratītyasamutpādaḥ śūnyatā saiva te matā| tathāvidhaś ca saddharmas tat samaś ca tathāgataḥ||" (ibid., pp. 152–153).

97. "yaḥ śūnyatāṃ pratītyasamutpādaṃ madhyamāṃ pratipadaṃ ca | ekārthāṃ nijagāda praṇamāmi tamapratimabuddham ||" (Bhattacharya, *Vigrahavyāvartanī,* p. 70; translation, ibid., p. 138).
98. 61. "sasāṃkhyaulukyanirgranthapudgalaskandhavādinam| pṛccha lokaṃ yadi vadaty astināstivyatikramam|| 62. dharmayautakam ity asmān nāstyastitvavyatikramam| viddhi gambhīram ity uktaṃ buddānāṃ śāsanāmṛtam||" (text in Nāgārjuna, *Ratnāvalī,* p. 26; translation in Hopkins, *Buddhist Advice,* p. 102, emphasis added).
99. Ajitamitra, is of little help here. See *Ratnāvalīṭīkā,* p. 50: 'di la gaṅ zag daṅ phuṅ por smra ba'i ṅaṅ tshul yod pas na de dag ni de dag tu smra ba'o|
100. Hopkins, *Buddhist Advice,* p. 103.
101. Bareau lists the Pūrvaśaila, Aparaśaila, Sarvāstivād'ns, Mahīśāsaka, Vātsīputrīya, and Kāśyapīya (*Les Sectes,* p. 286).
102. Buddhaghosa, *Kathāvatthu Aṭṭhakathā,* p. 198.

Notes to Conclusion

1. See, for example, his essay "The Problem of Demythologizing," in *The Hermeneutics Reader*, Kurt Mueller-Vollmer, ed. (New York: Continuum Press, 1985).
2. Roland Barthes, *Mythologies,* Annette Lavers, trans. (New York: Noonday Press, 1972), p. 143.
3. Tilmann Vetter, "On the Authenticity of the *Ratnāvalī,*" *Asiatische Studien* 46, no. 1 (1992): 504.
4. Lamotte, *History of Indian Buddhism,* pp. 524–526.
5. Vijay Nath, *Purāṇas and Acculturation: A Historico-Anthropological Perspective* (New Delhi: Munshiram Manoharlal, 2001), p. 79.
6. Chau, *The Literature of the Personalists,* pp. 16–17.
7. See Puri, *Buddhism in Central Asia,* p. 103.
8. Daya Ram Sahni, "Seven Inscriptions from Mathurā," *Epigraphia Indica* 19 (1927–29): 67.
9. Chau, *The Literature of the Personalists,* p. 100.
10. See Schopen, "The Inscription on the Kuṣān Image."
11. Ibid., pp. 122–123.

Notes to Appendix

1. See, for example, Warder, "Is Nāgārjuna a Mahāyānist?" p. 79. Warder claims that the authenticity of any other texts "has not been established beyond doubt and we ought not to assume it."
2. Christian Lindtner states that the *Ratnāvalī* is ascribed to Nāgārjuna by Bhavya, Candrakīrti, and Śāntarakṣita, "and many other later authors." See Lindtner, *Nāgārjuniana,* p. 163.
3. Hahn, building on earlier work by Lindtner and De Jong, compiles a partial

list. See Nāgārjuna, *Nagārjuna's Ratnāvalī,* pp. 9–10 and 19–20. The discussion that follows is based on his list.

4. Lindtner, *Nāgārjuniana,* p. 163n156; "slob dpon chen po 'phags pa na ga rdsu nas ji skad du" (Peking *bsTan 'Gyur,* vol. 96, #5256, p. 145a).
5. For a discussion of this date, see Shotaro Iida, *Reason and Emptiness: A Study in Logic and Mysticism* (Tokyo: Hokuseido Press, 1980), pp. 6–12.
6. For page numbers see Nāgārjuna, *Nagārjuna's Ratnāvalī,* p. 10.
7. Candrakīrti, *Prasannapadā,* p. 524n4.
8. Haribhadra cites *Ratnāvalī* verse 98 in his *Abhisamayālaṃkārāloka*. See Haribhadra, *Abhisamayālaṃkār'alokā Prajñāpāramitāvyākhyā,* Unrai Wogihara, ed. (Tōkyō: Tōyō Bunko, Hatsubaijo Sankibō Busshorin, 1973), p. 66.
9. *Ratnāvalī,* verses 1.63–5 and 2.8–15. Compare with similar arguments in *Mūlamadhyamakakārikā,* chapters 2, 5, 7, 9, 11, 19, 20, and 27.
10. *Ratnāvalī,* verse 47, dealing with prior and simultaneous production (*prāg-* and *sahajāta*) echoes the argument about antecedent states of being in chapter 9 and the discussion of previous and simultaneous causes in *Mūlamadhyamakakārikā,* chapter 6 (there the terms are *pūrva-* and *saha-bhāvaṃ*).
11. Cf. *Ratnāvalī,* chapter 1, verse 42, with arguments in *Mūlamadhyamakakārikā,* chapter 25.
12. Cf. *Ratnāvalī,* chapter 1, verses 41 and 64, with *Mūlamadhyamakakārikā,* chapter 25, verses 19–20.
13. Hopkins, *Buddhist Advice,* p. 141; "bdag phan ci daṅ ci bya źes| ji ltar khyed la gus yod pa| gźan phan ci daṅ ci bya źes| de bźin khyod ni gus par mdzod||" (Nāgārjuna, *Nāgārjuna's Ratnāvalī,* p. 83).
14. "gataṃ na gamyate tāvad agataṃ naiva gamyate| gatāgatavinirmuktaṃ gamyamānaṃ na gamyate||" (Candrakīrti, *Prasannapadā,* p. 92).
15. Cf. "jāyate 'stīti niṣpanno nāstīty akṛta ucyate| jāyamāno yadābhāvas tadā ko nāma sa smṛtaḥ||" (*Catuḥśataka,* verse 374); trans.: "About the completed it is said, 'It exists'; about the uncompleted it is said,' It does not exist.' When the process of arising is non-existent, what, indeed, is it said to be?" (Lang, *Āryadeva's Catuḥśataka,* pp. 142–143). See also *Śataśāstra,* chapter 8, in Giuseppe Tucci, *Pre-Dignāga Buddhist Texts from Chinese Sources* (Baroda: Oriental Institute, 1929), pp. 65–72.
16. Inada, *Nāgārjuna,* p. 122. Another example is in chapter 6, verse 5.
17. Hopkins, *Buddhist Advice,* p. 103. See also chapter 1, verse 88.
18. Lintner gives a long list of *sūtra* citations in the *Ratnāvalī,* in *Nāgārjuniana,* p. 163n159.
19. *Samyutta Nikāya,* 3:94–99; see also the "Poṭṭhapāda sutta" of the *Dīgha Nikāya,* pp. 187–189.
20. *Ratnāvalī,* chapter 1, verse 73, chapter 2, verses 5, 6, and 15, and *Mūlamadhyamakakārikā,* chapter 22, verse 14, and chapter 27.
21. It is mentioned by name in the *Mūlamadhyamakakārikā,* chapter 15, verse 7.
22. *Ratnāvalī,* chapter 1, verses 38, 42, 46, and 71.
23. *Ratnāvalī,* chapter 1, verse 3, and *Mūlamadhyamakakārikā,* chapter 24, verse 12.

24. Inada, *Nāgārjuna,* p. 115; "ātmety api prajñapitam anātmetyapi deśitaṃ| buddhair nātmā na cānātmā kaścid ity api deśitaṃ||" (Candrakīrti, *Prasannapadā,* p. 355).
25. Hopkins, *Buddhist Advice*, p. 109; cf. Nāgārjuna, *Nāgārjuna's Ratnāvalī*, p. 40.
26. "gdul ba [sic] gaṅ dag la 'jig rten 'di med do 'jig rten pha rol med do|| sems can brdzus te skye ba med do sñam pa'i lta ba de lta bu byuṅ bar gyur pa de dag gi bdag med par lta ba bzlog pa'i phyir bdag go zhes kyang gtags par gyur to||" (Clair W. Huntington, "The 'Akutobhayā' and Early Indian Madhyamaka" [Ph.D. dissertation, University of Michigan, 1986], p. 432).

    "de la gdul bya gaṅ dag la 'jig rten 'di med do| 'jig rten pha rol med do| sems can rdzus te skye ba med do sñam pa'i lta ba de lta bu byuṅ bar gyur ba|" (Buddhapālita, *dBu ma rtsa ba'i 'grel pa buddha p'ali ta [Buddhapālitamūlamadhyamakavṛtti],* Peking *bsTan 'Gyur*, vol. 95, #5242, p. 273b).

    Cf. "natthi ayaṃ loko natthi paro loko natthi mātā natthi pitā natthi sattā opapātikā" (*Majjhima Nikāya,* 1:287).
27. "de ltar yaṅ ji skad du rab kyi rtsa la gyis rnam par gnon pa| gjugs ni bdag gam bdag med pa ma yin no| de bźin du tshor ba daṅ| 'du śes daṅ| 'du byed rnams daṅ| rnam par śes pa yaṅ| bdag gam bdag med pa ma yin no|" (Bhāvaviveka, *dBu ma rtsa ba'i 'grel pa shes rab sgron ma [Prajñpradīpamūlamadhyamakavṛtti],* Peking *bsTan 'Gyur,* vol. 95, #5253, p. 233a).
28. "yathoktam āryaratnakūṭe| ātmeti kāśyapa ayam eko'ntaḥ| nairātmyam ity ayaṃ dvitīyo'ntaḥ| yad etad anayorantayor madhyaṃ tadarūpyam anidarśanam apratiṣṭham anābhāsam–avijñaptikam aniketam iyam ucyate Kāśyapa madhyamā pratipaddharmāṇāṃ bhūtapraty avekṣeti||" (Candrakīrti, *Prasannapadā*, p. 358). This is virtually identical to a passage in the *Kāśyapaparivarta.* Cf. Stäel-Holstein, *The Kāśyapaparivarta*, p. 87, para. 57.

    Translation: "Ego is one extreme, egolessness is the other, and [the two-in-one of] ego-egolessness is the middle, which is formless, shapeless, incognizable, and unknowable. [To realize] it is called the middle way, the true insight into all dharmas" (Chang et al., *A Treasury of Mahāyāna Sūtras*, p. 394).
29. Jan Willem de Jong, "Notes on Prajñāpāramitā Texts: The *Suvikrāntavikrāmiparipṛcchā,*" in *Prajñāpāramitā and Related Systems: Studies in Honor of Edward Conze*, Louis Lancaster, ed. (Berkeley: Berkeley Buddhist Studies, 1977), p. 187.
30. Stäel-Holstein, *Kāśyapaparivarta*, p. ix.
31. Ibid., p. 87, para. 57.
32. Ibid., p. ix.
33. "The total number of *vipulā* forms in the *Kārikās* is 160, which is 18% of a total of 884 lines. The 14.4% in the *Ratnāvalī* does not diverge significantly from this figure, though the higher number *of ra-vipulā* in the *Kārikās* and the occurrence of other *vipulā* forms should be kept in mind" (Vetter, "On the Authenticity of the *Ratnāvalī*," p. 501).
34. "*Ca, eva, api, iti, vā, punaḥ* and *tu*" (ibid., p. 501).
35. Vetter finds that the density of particles in the Sanskrit fragments of the *Ratnāvalī* is about half of that in the *Mūlamadhyamakakārikā*. Furthermore, in

the *Mūlamadhyamakakārikā* 79 percent of the verses do not contain compounds, while in the *Ratnāvalī* only 51.1 percent do not contain compounds. See ibid., p. 503.

36. Ibid., p. 504.

37.

> When [all] five senses, eye and so forth
> [Simultaneously] apprehend their objects
> A thought [of pleasure] does not refer [to all of them]
> Therefore at that time they do not [all] give pleasure.
> Whenever any of the [five] objects is known
> [As pleasurable] by one of the [five] senses,
> Then the remaining [objects] are not so known by the remaining [senses]
> Since they then are not meaningful [causes of pleasure] (Hopkins *Buddhist Advice,* p. 140).

Cf. Nāgārjuna, *Nāgārjuna's Ratnāvalī*, p. 112.

38. See Lang, *Āryadeva's Catuḥśataka*, p. 109 (chapter 11, verse 18).

39. Vetter, "On the Authenticity of the *Ratnāvalī*," p. 501.

Bibliography

Note: T. = *Taishō shinshu daizokyo*. Junjirō Takakusu and Kaigyoku Watanabe, eds. 85 vols. Tokyo: Taishō issaikyo kankokai, Taishō 13–Showa 7, 1924–1932. Also available as: *Chinese Electronic Tripitaka Series*. CD-ROM. Taipei: Chinese Buddhist Electronic Text Association, 2002.

Chinese Editions

T. 1 長阿含經. *Dīrgha āgama*. Translated by Buddhayaśas.

T. 5 佛般泥洹經. *Mahāparinirvāṇa Sūtra*. Translated by Báifǎzǔ.

T. 6 般泥洹經. *Mahāparinirvāṇa Sūtra*. Anonymous translation (c. 317–420).

T. 7 大般涅槃經. *Mahāparinirvāṇa Sūtra*. Translated by Faxian.

T. 125 增壹阿含經. *Ekottarāgama*. Translated by Gautama Saṅghadeva.

T. 220 大般若波羅蜜多經. *Mahāprajñāpāramitāsūtras* (a compendium of eleven *Prajñāpāramitā* texts). Translated by Xuanzang.

T. 221 放光般若經. *Pañcaviṃśatisāhasrikāprajñāpāramitā*. Translated by Mokṣala.

T. 222 光讚經. *Pañcaviṃśatisāhasrikāprajñāpāramitā*. Translated by Dharmarakṣa.

T. 223 摩訶般若波羅蜜經. *Pañcaviṃśatisāhasrikāprajñāpāramitā*. Translated by Kumārajīva.

T. 294 羅摩伽經 *Gaṇḍavyūha*. Translated by Shèngjiān 聖堅.

T. 334 須摩提菩薩經 *Sumatidārikaparipṛcchā*. Translated by Dharmarakṣa.

T. 338 離垢施女經 *Vimaladattaparipṛcchā*. Translated by Dharmarakṣa.

T. 387 大方等無想經. *Mahāmeghasūtra*. Translated by Dharmakṣema.

T. 419 拔陂菩薩經. *Pratyutpannabuddhasaṃmukhāvasthitasamādhisūtra*. Anonymous translation c. 25–220 C.E.

T. 468 文殊師利問經. *Mañjuśrīparipṛcchā*. Translated by Saṅghabhara.

T. 670 楞伽阿跋多羅寶經. *Laṅkāvatārasūtra*. Translated by Guṇabhadra.

T. 1421 彌沙塞部和醯五分律. *Mahīśāsaka vinaya*. Translated by Buddhajīva.

T. 1425 摩訶僧祇律. *Mahāsāṅghika vinaya*. Translated by Buddhabhadra and Faxian.

T. 1428 四分律. *Dharmaguptaka vinaya*. Translated by Buddhayaśas.

T. 1435 十誦律 *Sarvāstivāda vinaya*. Translated by Puṇyatara, Dharmaruci, and Kumārajīva.

T. 1451 根本説一切有部毘奈耶雜事. *Mūlasarvāstivāda vinayakṣudrakavastu*. Translated by Yijing.

T. 1465 佛説目連所問經. *Śāriputrapariprcchā*. Anonymous translation c. 317–420 C.E.

T. 1505 四阿鋡暮抄解. Vasubhadra. (Sanskrit uncertain; Priestley translates title as *Selections and Explanations from the Four Āgamas*). Translated by Kumārabhuddhi.

T. 1506 三法度論. Vasubhadra. *Tridharmakhaṇḍaka*. Translated by Gautama Saṅghadeva.

T. 1509 大智度論. (Attributed to Nāgārjuna) *Mahāprajñāpāramitopadeśa*. Translated by Kumārajīva.

T. 1538 施設論 *Prajñapti Śāstra*. Translated by Dharmapāla.

T. 1539 阿毘達磨識身足論. Vasumitra. *Vijñānakāya*. Translated by Xuanzang.

T. 1541 眾事分阿毘曇論. Vasumitra. *Prakaraṇapāda*. Translated by Guṇabhadra.

T. 1542 阿毘達磨品類足論. Vasumitra. *Prakaraṇapāda*. Translated by Xuanzang.

T. 1545 阿毘達磨大毘婆沙論. *Mahāvibhāṣā*. Translated by Xuanzang.

T. 1548 舍利弗阿毘曇論. *Śāriputrābhidharmaśāstra*. Translated by Dharmayaśas and Dharmagupta.

T. 1559 阿毘達磨俱舍釋論 Vasubandhu, *Abhidharmakośa Śāstra*. Translated by Paramārtha.

T. 1564 中論. Qingmu. *Madhyamakaśāstra* [= *Mūlamadhyamakakārikā*]. Translated by Kumārajīva.

T. 1594 攝大乘論 Asaṅga. *Mahāyānasaṃgraha*. Translated by Xuanzang.

T. 1602 顯揚聖教論. (Attributed to) Asaṅga. *Āryaśāsanaprakaraṇa*. Translated by Xuanzang.

T. 1609 大乘成業論 Vasubandhu. *Karmasiddhiprakaraṇa*. Translated by Xuanzang.

T. 1646 成實論. Haribhadra. *Satyasiddhiśāstra*. Translated by Kumārajīva.

T. 1649 三彌底部論. *Saṃmitīyanikāyaśāstra*. Anonymous translation c. 350–431 C.E.

T. 1656, 寶行王正論. Nāgārjuna. *Rājaparikathāratnamālī* [= *Ratnāvalī*]. Translated by Paramārtha.

T. 1660 Nāgārjuna (attributed). *Bodhisambhāra Śastra*. Translated by Zìzái 自在.

T. 1672, 龍樹菩薩為禪陀迦王説法要偈. Nāgārjuna. *Suhṛllekha*. Translated by Guṇavarman.

T. 1716 妙法蓮華經玄義. Zhiyi.

T. 1852 三論玄義. Jizang.

T. 2031 異部宗輪論. Vasumitra. *Samayabhedoparacanacakra*. Translated by Xuanzang.

T. 2032 十八部論. Vasumitra. [lit. "*Aṣṭadaśanikāyaśāstra*"] *Samayabhedoparacanacakra*. Translated by Kumārajīva? [and Paramārtha]

T. 2033 部執異論. Vasumitra. *Samayabhedoparacanacakra*. Translated by Paramārtha.

T. 2047 龍樹菩薩傳. Kumārajīva.

T. 2053 大唐大慈恩寺三藏法師傳. Huili and Yensong
T. 2066 大唐西域求法高僧傳. Yijing.
T. 2087 大唐西域記. Xuanzang.
T. 2125 南海寄歸內法傳. Faxian.
T. 2145 出三藏記集. Sengyu.
T. 2300 三論玄義檢幽集. Chūzen.

Tibetan Editions

Ajitamitra. *Die Ratnāvalīṭīkā des Ajitamitra.* Yukihiro Okada, ed. Bonn: Indica et Tibetica Verlag, 1990.

Avalokitavrata. *Śes rab sgron mahi rya-cher 'grel-pa* (*Prajñāpradīpa-ṭīkā*). Peking *bsTan 'Gyur,* vols. 96–97, #5259.

Bhāvaviveka. *dBu ma'i snying po'i 'grel pa rtog ge 'bar ba (Tarkajvāla).* Peking *bsTan 'Gyur,* vol. 96, #5256.

———. *dBu ma rtsa ba'i 'grel pa shes rab sgron ma (Prajñāpradīpamūlamadhyamakavṛtti).* Peking *bsTan 'Gyur,* vol. 95, #5253.

Buddhapālita. *dBu ma rtsa ba'i 'grel pa buddha p'ali ta (Buddhapālitamūlamadhyamakavṛtti).* Peking bsTan 'Gyur, vol. 95, #5242.

Candrakīrti. *Madhyamakāvatāra par Candrakīrti.* Louis de La Valée Poussin, ed. Bibliotheca Buddhica, vol. 9. Osnabruck: Biblio, 1970.

Nāgārjuna. *sToṅ pa ñid bdun cu pa'i 'grel pa* (*Śūnyatāsaptativṛtti*). Peking *bsTan 'Gyur*, vol. 95, # 5231.

'Phags pa chos kyi phyag rgya zhes bya ba theg pa chen po'i mdo (*Āryadharmamudrānāmamahāyāna Sūtra*). Peking *bsTan 'Gyur*, vol. 34, #869.

Teramoto, Enga, and Tomotsugu Hiramatsu, ed. and trans. *Vasumitra's Samaya-Bhedoparacana-cakra, Bhavya's Nikāyabheda-Vibhaṅga-Vyākhyāna and Vinītadeva's Samaya-Bhedoparacana-cakrasya-Nikāya-Bhedopadarśana-Nāma-Saṃgraha: Three Tibetan Texts.* Kyoto: Mokudosha, 1935.

Wogihara, Unrai, ed. *The Sanskrit-Chinese Dictionary of Buddhist Technical Terms Based on the Mahavyutpatti.* Reprint. Tokyo: Sankibo, 1959.

Indic Editions

The Aṅguttara-nikāya. Rev. Richard Morris, ed. London: H. Frowde for the Pāli Text Society, 1885–1910.

Asaṅga. *Bodhisattvabhūmi: A Statement of Whole Course of the Bodhisattva (Being the Fifteenth Section of Yogācārabhūmi).* Unrai Wogihara, ed. Reprint. Tokyo: Sankibo Buddhist Bookstore, 1971.

Aṣṭasāhasrikā Prajñāpāramitā: With Haribhādra's Commentary Called Āloka, P. L. Vaidya, ed. Buddhist Sanskrit Texts Series no. 4. Darbhanga: Mithila Institute, 1960.

Buddhaghosa. *The Aṭṭhasālinī, Buddhaghosa's Commentary on the Dhammasangaṇī,* Edward Müller, ed. London: H. Frowde for the Pāli Text Society, 1897.

———. *Kathāvatthuppakarana-atthakathā: Included in Pañcappakarana-aṭṭhakathā, Named Paramatthadīpanī,* N. A. Jayawickrama, ed. London: Pāli Text Society, 1979.

———. *Papañcasūdanī Majjhimanikāyṭṭthakathā of Buddhaghosācariya.* J. H. Woods, D. Kosambi and I. B. Horner, eds. 5 vols. London: Pāli Text Society, 1922–1938.

———. *Puggala-paññatti and Puggala Paññatti-Aṭṭhakathā.* Richard Morris, Dr. Georg Landsberg, and Mrs. Rhys Davids, eds. London: Luzac for the Pāli Text Society, 1972.

———. *Samantapāsādikā: Buddhaghosa's Commentary on the Vinaya Pitaka.* J. Takakusu and M. Nagai, eds. 8 vols. London: Pāli Text Society, 1947–1976.

———. *Sārattha-Ppakāsinī: Buddhaghosa's Commentary on the Saṃyutta-Nikāya.* Pāli Text Society Text Series, vol. 119. London: Pāli Text Society, 1932.

———. *The Sumaṅgala-vilāsinī, Buddhaghosa's Commentary on the Dīgha Nikāya.* T. W. Rhys Davids and J. Estlin Carpenter, eds. London: H. Frowde for the Pāli Text Society, 1886–1819.

Candrakīrti. *Mūlamadhyamakakārikās (Mādhyamikasūtras) de Nāgārjuna avec la Prasannapadā commentaire de Candrakīrti.* Louis de La Vallée Poussin, ed. Bibliotheca Buddhica, vol. 4. Osnabruck: Biblio, 1970.

Dīgha Nikāya. T.W. Rhys Davids and J.E. Carpenter, eds. 3 vols. London: Pāli Text Society, 1889–1910.

Divyāvadānam. P. L. Vaidya, ed. Darbhanga: Mithila Institute of Post-graduate Studies and Research in Sanskrit Learning, 1959.

The Gilgit Manuscript of the Aṣṭadaśasāhasrikāprajñāpāramitā: Chapters 70 to 82 Corresponding to the 6th, 7th, and 8th Abhisamayas. Edward Conze, ed. Rome: Istituto Italiano per il Medio ed Estremo Oriente, 1974.

Gilgit Manuscripts. Nalinaksha Dutt, ed. Bibliotheca Indo-Buddhica series, vols. 1–4. Delhi: Sri Satguru, 1984.

Haribhadra. *Abhisamayālaṃkār'alokā Prajñāpāramitāvyākhyā.* Unrai Wogihara, ed. Tōkyō: Tōyō Bunko, Hatsubaijo Sankibō Busshorin, 1973.

Itivuttaka. Ernst Windisch, ed. London: Pāli Text Society, 1889. Reprint. London: Luzac for the Pāli Text Society, 1966–1972.

Mahārṣīvedavyāsapraṇitam Śrīmadbhāgavatamahāpurāṇam. Krishashanker Shastri, ed. Vārānasī: Śrīvidyāhitanidhisadasyāh, 1966–1968.

Mahāvāṃsa: mūla evam Hindī rūpāntara. Rāmakumāra Tripāthī et al., eds. Varanasi: Bauddha Ākara Granthamālā, 1996.

Majjhima Nikāya. V. Trenckner and R. Chalmers, eds. 4 vols. London: Pāli Text Society, 1888–1925.

Merutuṅgācārya. *Prabandha Cintāmaṇi of Merutuṅgācārya.* Jinavijaya Muni, ed. Śāntiniketan: Adhiṣṭātā Siṅghī Jaina Jñānapīṭha, 1933.

The Milindapañho, Being Dialogues Between King Milinda and the Buddhist Sage Nāgasena: The Pāli Text. V. Trenckner, ed. London: Royal Asiatic Society, 1928.

Nāgārjuna. *Nāgārjuna's Ratnāvalī: Vol. I, The Basic Texts (Sanskrit, Tibetan, Chinese).* Michael Hahn, ed. Indica et Tibetica series, vol 1. Bonn: Indica et Tibetica Publications, 1982.

Nandi: Prakrit Text, Sanskrit Rendering, Hindi Translation, Comparative Notes and Various Appendixes. A. Mahaprajna, ed. Ladnun, Rajasthan: Jain Visva-Bharati Institute, 1997.

The Netti-pakarana, with Extracts from Dhammapāla's Commentary. E. Hardy, ed. London: H. Frowde for the Pāli Text Society, 1902.

Paṭisambhidāmagga. Arnold C. Taylor, ed. 2 vols. London: Pāli Text Society; distributed by Routledge & Kegan Paul, 1979.

The Petakopadesa. Arabinda Barua, ed. London: Ceylon Daily News Press for the Pāli Text Society, 1949.

Prabandha Kośa. Jina Vijaya, ed. Śāntiniketan: Adhisṭhāta-siṅghī Jaina Jñānapīṭha, 1991.

Prātimokṣasūtram of the Lokottaravādimahāsāṅghika School. Nathmal Tatia, ed. Patna: Kashi Prasad Jayaswal Research Institute, 1976.

The Samyutta-nikāya of the Sutta-piṭaka. Léon Feer, ed. 5 vols. London: H. Frowde for the Pāli Text Society, 1884–1904.

Singh, Sanghasen, and Kenryo Minowa, ed. and trans. "A Critical Edition and Translation of *Abhidamācārikā Nāma Bhikṣu-Prakīrṇakaḥ.*" *Buddhist Studies, Department of Buddhist Studies, University of Delhi* 12 (March 1988): 81–143.

Sutta-nipāta Commentary: Being Paramatthajotikā. Helmer Smith, ed. 3 vols. London: H. Milford for the Pāli Text Society, 1916–1918.

Suvarṇaprabhāsottamasūtra: Das Goldglanz-Sūtra: Ein Sanskrittext des Mahayana-Buddhismus. Johannes Nobel, ed. Leiden: E. J. Brill, 1950.

Udāna. Paul Steinthal, ed. London: Pāli Text Society, 1885.

Udānavarga de Subaši: Edition critique du manuscrit sanskrit sur bois provenant de Subaši. H. Nakatani, ed. Paris: Collège de France, Institut de civilisation indienne, 1987.

Vasubandhu. *Abhidharmakośabhāṣyam.* Prahlāda Pradhāna, ed. Patna: Kāśīprasada-jāyasavāla-Anuśīlan-Institute, 1975.

The Vinaya Piṭakam, One of the Principle Buddhist Holy Scriptures in the Pāli Language. Hermann Oldenberg, ed. 5 vols. London: Williams and Norgate, 1879–1883.

Yaśomitra. *Sputārthā Abhidharmakośavyākhyā by Yaśomitra.* Unrai Wogihara, ed. 2 vols. Tokyo: Sankibo Buddhist Book Store, 1971.

General Modern Sources

Abhayadatta. *Buddha's Lions: The Lives of the Eighty-Four Siddhas.* James Robinson, trans. Berkeley: Dharma, 1979.

———. *Masters of Mahāmudrā: Songs and Histories of the Eighty-Four Buddhist Siddhas.* Kenneth Dowman, trans. Albany: State University of New York Press, 1984.

Aiyar, V. N. "Inscribed Buddhist Image from Gopalpur." *Epigraphia Indica* 18 (1925–1926): 73–74.

Ames, William. "Bhāvaviveka '*Prajñāpradīpa*': A Translation of Chapter 1, Examination of Causal Conditions (*Pratyaya*)." *Journal of Indian Philosophy* 21, no. 3 (1993): 209–259.

Anacker, Stefan. *Seven Works of Vasubandhu.* Delhi: Motilal Banarsidass, 1984.

Anuruddha. *A Manual of Abhidhamma being Abhidhammattha Saṅgaha of Bhadanta Anuruddhācariya,* 4th ed. Kuala Lumpur: Buddhist Missionary Society, 1979.

Asaṅga. *Mahāyānasūtrālaṃkāra.* S. V. Limaye, trans. and ed. Bibliotheca Indo-Buddhica Series, vol. 94. Delhi: Sri Satguru, 1992.

———. *La Somme du grand véhicule d'Asaṅga (Mahāyānasaṃgraha).* 2 vols. Etienne Lamotte, ed. and trans. Louvain-la-Neuve: Université de Louvain, Institut orientaliste, 1973.

Atwood, Christopher. "Life in Third-fourth Century Cadh'ota: A Survey of Information Gathered from the Prakrit Documents Found North of Minfeng (Niyä)." *Central Asiatic Journal* 35 (1991): 161–199.

Banerji-Sastri, A. "Ninety-three Inscriptions on the Kurkihar Bronzes." *Journal of the Bihar Research Society* 26 (1940): 236–251.

Bāṇa. *The Harṣa-Carita of Bāṇa.* Edward B. Cowell and Frederick William Thomas, trans. Delhi: Motilal Banarsidass, 1961.

Bareau, André. "Le Cycle de la formation des schismes (*Samayabhedoparacanacakra*) de Vasumitra." *Journal Asiatique* 242, no. 2 (1954): 234–266.

———. *Les Sectes bouddhiques du petit véhicule.* Paris: Ecole française de l'Extrême Orient, 1955.

———. "Trois Traités sur les sectes bouddhiques attribués à Vasumitra, Bhavya et Vinītadeva." *Journal Asiatique* 244, no. 2 (1956): 167–200.

Barthes, Roland. *Mythologies.* Annette Lavers, trans. New York: Noonday Press, 1972.

Barua, Benimadhab. *Barhut: Aspects of Life and Art,* book 3. Calcutta: Indian Research Institute Publications, 1934–1935.

Bechert, Heinz. "The Importance of Aśoka's So-Called Schism Edict." In *Indological and Buddhist Studies,* L. Hercus et al., pp. 61–68. Canberra: Australian National University, 1982.

Ben-Porat, Ziva. "The Poetics of Literary Allusion." *PTL: A Journal for Descriptive Poetics and Theory of Literature* 1 (1976): 105–128.

Bhabha, Homi. *The Location of Culture.* New York: Routledge, 1994.

Bhandarkar, R. G. "On Two Copper Plates from Valabhī." *Indian Antiquary* (February 2, 1872): 45–46.

Bhattacharya, D. C. "A Newly Discovered Copperplate from Tippera [The Gunaighar Grant of Vainyagupta: Year 188 Current (Gupta Era)]." *Indian Historical Quarterly* 6 (1930): 45–60.

Bhattasali, N. K. *Iconography of Buddhist and Brahmanical Sculptures in the Dacca Museum.* Dacca: Rai S. N. Bhadra Bahadur, 1929.

Bocking, Brian. *Nāgārjuna in China: A Translation of the Middle Treatise.* Lewiston: Edwin Mellon Press, 1995.

Bond, George D. "Two Theravāda Traditions of Meaning of 'The Word of the Buddha.'" *Maha-Bodhi* 83, nos. 10–12 (1975): 402–413.

Bonazzoli, Giorgio. "Remarks on the Nature of the Purāṇa-s." *Purāṇa* 25, no. 1 (1983): 77–113.

Boyer, Auguste, and Edward Rapson, eds. *Kharoṣṭhi Inscriptions Discovered by Sir Aurel Stein in Chinese Turkestan.* Oxford: Clarendon Press, 1920–1929.

Bronkhorst, Johannes. "Nāgārjuna's Logic." In *Bauddhavidyāsudhākaraḥ: Studies in Honour of Heinz Bechert on the Occasion of His 65th Birthday,* Petra Kieffer-Pṃlz and Jens-Uwe Hartmann, eds., pp. 29–37. Swisttal-Odendorf: Indica et Tibetica Verlag, 1997.

Bultmann, Rudolf. "The Problem of Demythologizing." In *The Hermeneutics Reader*, Kurt Mueller-Vollmer, ed., pp. 248–255. New York: Continuum Press, 1985.

Burrow, Thomas. *A Translation of the Kharoṣṭhi Documents from Chinese Turkestan.* London: Royal Asiatic Society, 1940.

Burton, David. *Emptiness Appraised: A Critical Study of Nāgārjuna's Philosophy.* Richmond, UK: Curzon Press, 1999.

Bu-ston. *History of Buddhism in India and Tibet.* Eugene Obermiller, trans. Bibliotheca Indo-Buddhica, no. 26. 1932. Reprint. Delhi: Sri Satguru Press, 1986.

Buswell, Robert, and Padmanabh Jaini. "The Development of Abhidharma Philosophy." In *Encyclopedia of Indian Philosophies: Volume VII Abhidharma Buddhism to 150 A.D.,* Potter, ed., pp. 73–120.

Cabézon, José. "Vasubandhu's *Vyākhyāyukti* on the Authenticity of Mahāyāna Sūtras." In *Texts in the Context of Traditional Hermeneutics in South Asia,* Jeffrey Timm, ed., pp. 221–243. Albany: State University of New York Press, 1992.

Candra, Lokesh. *Tibetan-Sanskrit Dictionary.* Kyoto: Rinsen Book Company, 1990.

Candra Das, S. *Tibetan-English Dictionary.* Reprint. Delhi: Motilal Banarsidass, 1995.

Chang, Garma, et al., ed. and trans. *A Treasury of Mahāyāna Sūtras: Selections from the Mahāratnakūṭa Sūtra.* Delhi: Motilal Banarsidass, 1996.

Chau, Thich Tien. *The Literature of the Personalists of Early Buddhism.* Sara Boin-Webb, trans. Delhi: Motilal Banarsidass, 1999.

———. "The Literature of the Pudgalavādins." *Journal of the International Association of Buddhist Studies* 7, no. 1 (1984): 7–16.

———. "Les Réponses des Pudgalavādin aux critiques des écoles bouddhiques." *Journal of the International Association of Buddhist Studies* 10, no. 1 (1987): 33–54.

Cohen, Richard. "Discontented Categories: Hīnayāna and Mahāyāna in Indian Buddhist History." *Journal of the American Academy of Religion* 63, no. 1 (1995): 1–25.

———. "Kinsmen of the Son: *Śākyabhikṣus* and the Institutionalization of the Bodhisattva Ideal." *History of Religions* 40, no. 1 (2000): 1–31.

Collins, Steven. "On the Very Idea of the Pāli Canon." *Journal of the Pāli Text Society* 15 (1990): 89–126.

Connected Discourses of Buddha. Bhikkhu Bodhi, trans. 2 vols. Somerville, MA: Wisdom Press, 2000.

Conze, Edward. *The Large Sūtra on Perfect Wisdom with the Divisions of the Abhisamāyālaṅkāra.* Berkeley: University of California Press, 1975.

———. *The Perfection of Wisdom in Eight Thousand Lines & Its Verse Summary.* Delhi: Sri Satguru, 1973; reprinted 1994.

Coomaraswamy, Ananda K. *Elements of Buddhist Iconography.* New Delhi: M. Manoharlal, 1972.

Corless, Roger. "The Chinese Life of Nāgārjuna." In *Buddhism in Practice,* Donald Lopez, ed., pp. 525–531. Princeton: Princeton University Press, 1995.

Davidson, Ronald. "Buddhist Systems of Transformation: *Āśraya-parivṛtti* Among the Yogācāra." Ph.D. dissertation, University of California, 1985.

——. "Introduction to the Standards of Scriptural Authority in Indian Buddhism." In *Chinese Buddhist Apocrypha,* Robert Buswell, ed., pp. 291–325. Honolulu: University of Hawai'i Press, 1990.

Dehejia, Vidya. "The Collective and Popular Basis of Early Buddhist Patronage: Sacred Monuments, 100 B.C.–A.D. 250." In *The Powers of Art,* B. S. Miller, ed., pp. 35–45. Delhi: Oxford University Press, 1992.

de Jong, Jan Willem. "Notes on Prajñāpāramitā Texts: The *Suvikrāntavikrāmiparipṛcchā.*" In *Prajñāpāramitā and Related Systems: Studies in Honor of Edward Conze,* Louis Lancaster, ed., pp. 187–202. Berkeley: Berkeley Buddhist Studies, 1977.

——. "Review of J. Hopkins and Lati Rimpoche, trans., *The Precious Garland and the Song of the Four Mindfullnesses* (London, 1975)." *Indo-Iranian Journal* 20 (1978): 137–138.

Demiéville, Paul. "L'Origine des sectes bouddhiques d'après Paramārtha." *Mélanges chinois et bouddhiques* 1 (1931): 16–64.

——. "Sur un passage du *Mahāmeghasūtra,*" appendix 2 of "Les Versions chinois du *Milindapañha.*" *Bulletin de l'Ecole française d'Extrême Orient* 24, no. 1 (1924).

——. "Les Versions chinois du *Milindapañha.*" *Bulletin de l'Ecole française d'Extrême Orient* 24, no. 1 (1924).

——. "La Yogācārabhūmi de Saṅgharakṣa." *Bulletin de l'Ecole française d'Extrême Orient* 44, no. 2 (1954): 339–436.

Demiéville, Paul, et al. *Répertoire du canon bouddhique sino-japonais,* Fascicule Annexe du *Hobogirin.* Paris: L'Académie des inscriptions et Belles-Lettres, Institut de France, 1978.

Dhavalikar, Madhukar Keshav. *Later Hinayana Caves of Western India.* Poona: Deccan College Postgraduate and Research Institute, 1984.

Dowling, Thomas. "Karma Doctrine and Sectarian Development." In *Studies in Pāli and Buddhism: A Memorial Volume in Honor of Bhikkhu Jagdish Kashyapa,* A. K. Narain, ed. Delhi: B.R. Publishing Corporation, 1979.

Dreyfus, Georges. *Recognizing Reality: Dharmakīrti's Philosophy and Its Tibetan Interpretations.* Albany: State University of New York Press, 1997.

Dutt, Nalinaksha. "Notes on the Nāgārjunikoṇḍa Inscriptions." *Indian Historical Quarterly* 7, no. 3 (1931): 633–653.

Edgerton, Franklin. *The Bhagavad Gīta.* Cambridge: Harvard University Press, 1952.

——. *Buddhist Hybrid Sanskrit Dictionary.* Reprint. Delhi: Motilal Banarsidass, 1993.

Eliot, Sir Charles. *Hinduism and Buddhism,* vol. 3. London: Routledge and K. Paul, 1957.

Emmerick, Ronald. *The Sūtra of Golden Light.* Oxford: Pāli Text Society, 1996.

Franco, Eli. "The Oldest Philosophical Manuscript in Sanskrit." *Journal of Indian Philosophy* 31 (2003): 21–31.

Frauwallner, Ernst. *The Earliest Vinaya and the Beginnings of Buddhist Literature.* L. Petech, trans. Rome: Istituto Italiano per il Medio ed Estremo Oriente, 1956.

———. *Studies in Abhidharma Literature and the Origins of Buddhist Philosophical Systems.* Sophie Francis Kidd, trans. Albany: State University of New York Press, 1995.

Gernet, Jacques. *Buddhism in Chinese Society.* New York: Columbia University Press, 1995.

Gombrich, Richard. "How the Mahāyāna Began." *Buddhist Forum* 1 (1990): 21–30.

Gomez, Luis. "Proto-Mādhyamika in the Pāli Canon." *Philosophy East and West* 26, no. 2 (April 1976): 137–165.

Gomez, Luis, and Jonathan Silk, eds. *Studies in the Literature of the Great Vehicle: Three Mahāyāna Buddhist Texts.* Ann Arbor: Collegiate Institute for the Study of Buddhist Literature and Center for South and Southeast Asian Studies, 1989.

Granoff, Phyllis. "Jain Biographies of Nāgārjuna: Notes on the Composing of a Biography in Medieval India." In *Monks and Magicians: Religious Biographies in Asia,* Phyllis Granoff and Koichi Shinohara, eds., pp. 45–61. Oakville, ONT: Mosaic Press, 1988.

Griffiths, Paul. *On Being Mindless.* La Salle: Open Court Press, 1991.

Harivarman. *Satyasiddhiśāstra of Harivarman.* N. Aiyaswami Śāstri, ed. and trans. Baroda: Oriental Institute, Maharaja Sayajirao University, 1975–1978.

Harrison, Paul. "Commemoration and Identification in *Buddhānusmṛti.*" In *In the Mirror of Memory: Reflections on Mindfulness and Remembrance in Indian and Tibetan Buddhism,* Janet Gyatso, ed. Albany: State University of New York Press, 1992.

———. *The Samādhi of Direct Encounter with the Buddhas of the Present.* Tokyo: International Institute for Buddhist Studies, 1990.

———. "Sanskrit Fragments of a Lokottaravādin Tradition." In *Indological and Buddhist Studies.* L. Hercus et al., eds., pp. 211–234. Canberra: Australian National University, Faculty of Asian Studies, 1982.

———. "Who Gets to Ride in the Great Vehicle: Self-Image and Identity Among the Followers of the Early Mahāyāna." *Journal of the International Association of Buddhist Studies* 10, no. 1 (1987): 67–89.

Hirakawa, Akira. *Buddhist Chinese-Sanskrit Dictionary.* Tokyo: Reiyukai, 1997.

———. "The Rise of Mahāyāna Buddhism and Its Relationship to the Worship of Stūpas." *Memoirs of the Research Department of the Toyo Bunko* 22 (1963): 57–69.

Holt, John. *The Buddha in the Crown.* New York: Oxford University Press, 1991.

Hopkins, Jeffrey. *Buddhist Advice for Living & Liberation: Nāgārjuna's Precious Garland.* Ithaca: Snow Lion, 1998.

Horner, I. B. *Milinda's Questions.* London: Luzac, 1963.

Huntington, Clair W. "The 'Akutobhayā' and Early Indian Madhyamaka." Ph.D. dissertation, University of Michigan, 1986.

I-Ching. *Chinese Monks in India: Biography of Eminent Monks Who Went to the West-*

ern World in Search of the Law During the Great T'ang Dynasty. Latika Lahiri, trans. Delhi: Motilal Banarsidass, 1986.

Iida, Shotaro. *Reason and Emptiness: A Study in Logic and Mysticism.* Tokyo: Hokuseido Press, 1980.

Inada, Kenneth K. *Nāgārjuna, A Translation of His Mūlamadhyamakakārikā with an Introductory Essay.* Delhi: Sri Satguru, 1993.

Jan Yün-Hua. "Nāgārjuna, One or More? A New Interpretation of Buddhist Hagiography." *History of Religions* 10 (1970): 139–153.

Jiang Zhongxin, ed. *Sanskrit Lotus Sūtra Fragments from the Lüshun Museum Collection.* Lüshun and Tokyo: Lüshun Museum, 1997.

Joshi, Nilakanth Purushottam, and Ramesh Chandra Sharma. *Catalogue of Gandhāra Sculptures in the State Museum, Lucknow.* Lucknow: State Museum, 1969.

Kalupahana, David. *Mūlamadhyamakakārikā of Nāgārjuna: The Philosophy of the Middle Way.* Albany: State University of New York Press, 1986.

Kāne, Pānduraṅga Vāmana. *History of Dharmaśāstra.* 5 vols. 2nd edition. Poona, Bhandarkar Oriental Research Institute, 1968–1975.

Karashima, Seishi. "A Fragment of the Prātimokṣa-Vibhaṅga of the Mahāsāṃghika-Lokottaravādins." In *Buddhist Manuscripts in the Schøyen Collection,* Jens Braarvig, ed., pp. 233–241. Oslo: Hermes, 2000.

——. "Two More Folios of the Prātimokṣa-Vibhaṅga of the Mahāsāṃghika-Lokottaravādins." In *Buddhist Manuscripts in the Schøyen Collection,* vol. 3, Jens Braarvig, ed., pp. 215–228. Oslo: Hermes, 2002.

Kent, Stephen. "A Sectarian Interpretation of the Rise of Mahāyāna." *Religion* 12, no. 4 (1982): 311–332.

Kitschelt, Herbert. "Political Opportunity Structures and Political Protest: Anti-Nuclear Movements in Four Democracies." *British Journal of Political Science* 16, no. 1 (January 1986): 57–85.

——. "Resource Mobilization Theory: A Critique." In *Research on Social Movements: The State of the Art in Europe and the USA,* Dieter Rucht, ed., pp. 323–347. Frankfurt am Main: Campus; Boulder: Westview Press, 1991.

Knox, Robert. *Amaravati: Buddhist Sculpture from the Great Stūpa.* London: British Museum Press, 1992.

Lévi, Sylvain. "Sur la récitation primitive des textes bouddhiques." *Journal Asiatique,* ser. II, vol. 5 (1915): 401–447.

La Valée Poussin, Louis de. "La Controverse du temps et du Pudgala dans le Vijñānakāya." In *Etudes asiatiques oubliées à l'occasion du 25e anniversaire de l'Ecole française de l'Extrême Orient,* 1:346–347. Paris: Ecole française de l'Extrême Orient, 1925.

——. "Documents d'Abhidharma." *Mélanges chinois et bouddhiques* 5 (July 1937): 15.

——. *Theorie des douze causes.* Gand: E. Van Goethem, 1913.

Lamotte, Etienne. "La Critique d'authenticité dans le bouddhisme." In *India Antiqua: A Volume of Oriental Studies Presented by His Friends and Pupils to Jean Philippe Vogel, C.I.E., on the Occasion of the Fiftieth Anniversary of His Doctorate,* pp. 213–222. Leiden: E.J. Brill, 1947.

——. "The Gāravasutta of the Saṃyutta Nikāya and Its Mahāyānist Developments." *Journal of the Pāli Text Society* 9 (1981): 127–144.

——. *History of Indian Buddhism*. Sarah Boin-Webb, trans. Louvain: Peeters Press, 1988.

——. *Karmasiddhiprakaraṇa: The Treatise on Action by Vasubandhu*. Leo Pruden, trans. Berkeley: Asian Humanities Press, 1988.

——. *The Śūraṃgamasamādhisūtra: The Concentration of Heroic Progress*. Sara Boin-Webb, trans. Surrey, UK: Curzon Press, 1998.

——. "Sur la formation de Mahāyāna." In *Asiatica: Festschrift F. Weller*, U. Schneider, ed., pp. 377–396. Leipzig: O. Harrassowitz, 1954.

——. *The Teaching of Vimalakīrti (Vimalakīrtinirdeśa)*. Sara Boin, trans. Oxford: Pāli Text Society, 1994.

——. *Le Traité de la grande vertu de sagesse. Mahāprajñāpāramitāśāstra (Traduction chinoise de Kumārajīva)*, vols. 1–5. Louvain: Institut orientaliste, Bibliothèque de l'Université, 1970–1981.

——. *Der Verfasser des Upadeśa und seine-Quellen*. Gottingen: Vandenhoeck & Ruprecht, 1973.

Lang, Karen. *Āryadeva's Catuḥśataka: On the Bodhisattva's Cultivation of Merit and Knowledge*. Copenhagen: Akademisk Forlag, 1986.

——. *Four Illusions: Candrakīrti's Advice to Travelers on the Bodhisattva Path*. New York: Oxford University Press, 2003.

Law, N. N. "Some Images and Traces of Mahāyāna Buddhism in Chittagong." *Indian Historical Quarterly* 8 (1932) 139–158.

Leese, Marilyn. "The Early Buddhist Icons in Kaṇheri's Cave 3." *Artibus Asiae* 41, no. 1 (1979): 83–93.

Legge, James. *A Record of Buddhistic Kingdoms*. New York: Dover, 1965.

Li, Hwu. *The Life of Hiuen-Tsiang*. S. Beal, trans. Reprint. San Francisco: Chinese Materials Center, 1976.

Lindtner, Christian. *Nāgārjuniana: Studies in the Writings and Philosophy of Nāgārjuna*. Delhi: Motilal Banarsidass, 1990.

——. "Sangīt Paryāya." In *Encyclopedia of Indian Philosophies: Volume VII Abhidharma Buddhism to 150 A.D.*, Potter, ed., pp. 203–216.

Liu, Xinru. *Ancient India and Ancient China*. Delhi: Oxford India Paperbacks, 1997.

Lofland, John. *Social Movement Organizations*. New York: Aldine de Gruyter, 1996.

The Long Discourses of the Buddha: A Translation of the Dīgha Nikāya. Maurice Walshe, trans. Boston: Wisdom, 1995.

Mabbett, Ian. "The Problem of the Historical Nāgārjuna Revisited." *Journal of the American Oriental Society* 118, no. 3 (1998): 332–346.

Macdonald, Anne. "Le Dhanyakataka de Man-Luns guru." *Bulletin de l'Ecole française d'Extrême Orient* 57 (1970): 169–213.

Malalasekera, Gunapala Piyasena. *Dictionary of Pāli Proper Names*. New Delhi: Munshiram Manoharlal, 1983.

Marshall, Sir John Hubert. *The Buddhist Art of Gandhara: The Story of the Early*

School, Its Birth, Growth, and Decline. Karachi: Department of Archaeology and Museums, Government of Pakistan, 1973.

Marshall, Sir John, and Alfred Foucher. *Monuments of Sāñcī,* vol. 2. Delhi: Swati, 1982.

Masefield, Peter, trans. *Udāna Commentary, Sacred Books of the Buddhists,* vol. 43. Oxford: Pāli Text Society, 1995.

Masuda, Jiryō. "Origin and Doctrines of Early Indian Buddhist Schools." *Asia Major* 2 (1925): 1–75.

Matthews, Robert H. *Matthews' Chinese English Dictionary.* Rev. American ed. Cambridge: Harvard University Press, 1947.

McCagney, Nancy. *Nāgārjuna and the Philosophy of Openness.* Lanham, MD: Rowman & Littlefield, 1997.

McCarthy, John, and Mayer Zald. "Resource Mobilization and Social Movements: A Partial Theory." *American Journal of Sociology* 82, no. 6 (May 1977): 1212–1241.

The Middle Length Discourses of the Buddha: A New Translation of the Majjhima Nikaya. Ven. Ñāṇamoli and Ven. Bodhi, trans. Boston: Wisdom, 1995.

Mirashi, V. V. "Sarnath Stone Inscription of Karna: (Kalachuri) Year 810." In *Inscriptions of the Kalachuri-Chedi Era*, pp. 275–278. Corpus Inscriptionum Indicarum, IV pt. 1. Octamund, 1955.

Monier-Williams, Sir Monier. *Sanskrit-English Dictionary.* Reprint. Delhi: Motilal Banarsidass, 1982.

Monius, Anne. *Imagining a Place for Buddhism.* New York: Oxford University Press, 2001.

Mukherji, Ramaranjan, and Sachindra Kumar Maity, eds. *Corpus of Bengal Inscriptions Bearing on History and Civilization of Bengal.* Calcutta: Firma K. L. Mukhopadhyay, 1967.

Murti, K. Satcidananda. *Nāgārjuna.* New Delhi: National Book Trust, 1971.

Nagao, Gadjin. *Mādhyamika and Yogācara.* Leslie Kawamura, trans. Albany: State University of New York Press, 1991.

Nagar, Sarla D. *Gandhāran Sculpture: A Catalogue of the Collection in the Museum of Art and Archaeology, University of Missouri-Columbia.* Columbia: Museum of Art and Archaeology, 1981.

Nāgārjuna. *The Dialectical Method of Nāgārjuna (Vigrahavyāvartanī).* Kamaleswar Bhattacharya, trans. E. H. Johnston and Arnold Kunst, eds. Delhi: Motilal Banarsidass, 1978.

——. *Golden Zephyr: Instructions from a Spiritual Friend.* L. Kawamura, trans. Berkeley: Dharma, 1975.

——. *The Precious Garland: An Epistle to a King.* John Dunne and Sarah McClintock, trans. Boston: Wisdom, 1997.

Nakamura, Hajime. "Mahāyāna Buddhism." In *Encyclopedia of Religion,* M. Eliade, ed., pp. 457–472. New York: Macmillan, 1987.

Nath, Vijay. *Purāṇas and Acculturation: A Historico-Anthropological Perspective.* New Delhi: Munshiram Manoharlal, 2001.

Nattier, Jan. *A Few Good Men: The Bodhisattva Path According to the Inquiry of Ugra (Ugraparipṛcchā).* Honolulu: University of Hawai'i Press, 2003.

——. *Once Upon a Future Time: Studies in a Buddhist Prophesy of Decline.* Berkeley: Asian Humanities Press, 1991.

Nattier, Jan, and Charles Prebish, "Mahāsāṃghika Origins and the Beginnings of Buddhist Sectarianism." *History of Religions* 16, no. 3 (1977): 237–272.

Obermiller, Eugene. *Prajñāpāramitā in Tibetan Buddhism.* Vol. 3, H. S. Sobti, ed. Classics India Religion and Philosophy Series. Delhi: Classics India Publications, 1988.

Oetke, Claus. "Pragmatic Implicatures and Text–Interpretation (The Alleged Error of the Negation of the Antecedent in the *Mūlamadhyamakakārikās*)." *Studien zur Indologie und Iranistik* 16 (1992): 185–233.

Okada, Yukihiro, and Michael Hahn. "Zur Quelle der 57 Fehler in der Ratnāvalī des Nāgārjuna." *Indo-Iranian Journal* 28 (1985): 123–134.

Oldenberg, Hermann. *The Dīpavaṃsa: An Ancient Buddhist Historical Record.* London: Williams and Norgate, 1879.

Pagels, Ulrich. *The Bodhisattvapiṭaka.* Tring, UK: Institute for Buddhist Studies, 1998.

Pāsādika, Bhikkhu. "The Concept of Avipraṇāśa in Nāgārjuna." In *Recent Researches in Buddhist Studies: Essays in Honor of Professor Karunadassa.* Colombo, Sri Lanka, and Hong Kong: Y. Karunadasa Felicitation Committee with the Chi Ying Foundation, 1997.

Potter, Karl, ed. *Encyclopedia of Indian Philosophies: Volume VII Abhidharma Buddhism to 150 A.D.* Delhi: Motilal Banarsidass, 1996.

Prebish, Charles. *Buddhist Monastic Discipline.* Delhi: Motilal Banarsidass, 1996.

Priestley, Leonard. *Pudgalavāda Buddhism: The Reality of the Indeterminate Self.* Toronto: University of Toronto, Centre for South Asian Studies, 1999.

Puri, Baij Nath. *Buddhism in Central Asia.* Delhi: Motilal Banarsidass, 1987.

Régamey, Konstantin. *Philosophy in the Samādhirājasūtra.* Delhi: Motilal Banarsidass, 1990.

Rao, B. S. L. Hanumantha. *Religion in Andhra: A Survey of Religious Developments in Andhra from Early Times up to A.D.* 1325. Guntur: Welcome Press, 1973.

Rao, B. S. L. Hanumantha, et al. *Buddhist Inscriptions of Andhradesa.* Secunderbad: Ananda Buddha Vihara Trust, 1998.

Ray, Himanshu P. *Monastery and Guild: Commerce Under the Sātavāhanas.* Delhi: Oxford University Press, 1986.

Reat, Noble Ross. *The Śālistambha Sūtra.* Delhi: Motilal Banarsidass, 1993.

Rhys Davids, T. W., and S. W. Stede. *Pāli-English Dictionary.* Reprint. Delhi: Motilal Banarsidass, 1993.

Rhi, Ju-hyung. "Gandhāran Images of the 'Śrāvastī Miracle': An Iconographic Reassessment." Ph.D. dissertation, University of California, 1991.

Robinson, Richard H. *Early Mādhyamika in India and China.* Reprint. Delhi: Motilal Banarsidass, 1978.

Rockhill, W. W. *The Life of the Buddha.* London: Trübner, 1884.

Roy, Anamika. *Amarāvatī Stūpa: A Critical Comparison of Epigraphic, Architectural, and Sculptural Evidence.* Delhi: Agam Kala Prakashan, 1994.

Sahni, D. R. *Catalogue of the Museum of Archaeology at Sārnath.* Calcutta, 1914.

Sahni, Daya Ram. "Seven Inscriptions from Mathurā." *Epigraphia Indica* 19 (1927–28): 65–69.

Salomon, Richard. *Ancient Buddhist Scrolls from Gandhāra: The British Library Kharoṣṭhī Fragments.* Seattle: University of Washington Press, 1999.

——. "A Fragment of a Collection of Buddhist Legends, with a Reference to King Huvikṣa as a Follower of the Mahāyāna." In *Buddhist Manuscripts,* Braarvig, ed., 3:255–267.

——. "A Stone Inscription in Central Asian Gāndhārī from Endere (Xinjiang)." *Bulletin of the Asia Institute,* n.s. 13 (1999): 1–13.

Sander, Lore. "The Earliest Manuscripts from Central Asia and the Sarvāstivāda Mission." In *Corolla Iranica: Papers in Honour of Prof. Dr. David Neil MacKenzie on the Occasion of His 65th Birthday on April 8th, 1991,* Ronald Emmerick and Dieter Weber, eds., pp. 133–150. Frankfurt am Main: Peter Lang, 1991.

Sander, Lore, and Ernst Waldenschmidt. "A Brief Paleographical Analysis of the Brāhmī Manuscripts in Volume I." In *Buddhist Manuscripts,* Braarvig, ed. (2000), pp. 285–300.

——. *Sanskrithandschriften aus den Turfanfunden.* Stuttgart: Franz Steiner Verlag, 1965.

Sarkar, H. "The Nāgārjunakoṇḍa Phase of the Lower Kṛṣṇa Valley Art: A Study Based on Epigraphical Data." In *Indian Epigraphy: Its Bearing on the History of Art,* F. Asher and G. S. Gai, ed., pp. 29–35. New Delhi: American Institute of Indian Studies, 1985.

——. "Nāgārjunakoṇḍa Prakrit Inscription of Gautamīputra Vijaya Sātakarṇi, Year 6." *Epigraphia Indica* 36 (1965–1966): 273–275.

——. "Some Early Inscriptions in the Amarāvatī Museum." *Journal of Ancient Indian History* 4, nos. 1–2 (1971): 8.

Sarma, Inguva Karthikeya. *Studies in Early Buddhist Monuments and Brāhmī Inscriptions of Āndhradeśa.* Nagpur: Dattsons, 1988.

Sasaki, Shizuka. "A Study on the Origin of Mahāyāna Buddhism." *Eastern Buddhist* n.s. 30, no. 1 (1997): 79–113.

Satyasiddhiśāstra of Harivarman. N. Aiyaswami Sastri, ed. and trans. Baroda: Oriental Institute, Maharaja Sayajirao University, 1975–1978.

Scherrer-Schaub, Christina Anna. *Yuktiṣaṣṭikāvṛtti: Commentaire . . . la soixantaine sur le raisonnement, ou Du vrai enseignement de la causalité par le Maître indien Candrakīrti.* Mélanges Chinois et Bouddhiques, vol. 25. Brussels: Institut Belge des Hautes Etudes Chinoises, 1991.

Schmithausen, Lambert. "'Liberating Insight' and 'Enlightenment' in Early Buddhism." In *Studien zum Jainismus und Buddhismus,* Klaus Bruhn und Albrecht Wezler, eds., pp. 199–250. Wiesbaden: Franz Steiner Verlag, 1981.

Schopen, Gregory. "Archaeology and Protestant Presuppositions in the Study of Indian Buddhism." *History of Religions* 31, no. 1 (1991): 1–22.

——. "Archaeology and Protestant Presuppositions in the Study of Indian Buddhism." In *Bones, Stones, and Buddhist Monks: Collected Papers on Archaeology, Epig-*

raphy, and Texts of Monastic Buddhism in India, Schopen, ed., pp. 1–22. Honolulu: University of Hawai'i Press, 1997.

———. "The Bones of a Buddha and the Business of a Monk: Conservative Monastic Values in an Early Mahāyāna Polemical Tract." *Journal of Indian Philosophy* 27 (1999): 279–324.

———. "Counting the Buddha and the Local Spirits In: A Monastic Ritual of Inclusion for the Rain Retreat." *Journal of Indian Philosophy* 30 (2002): 359–388.

———. "Doing Business for the Lord." *Journal of the American Oriental Society* 114, no. 4 (1994): 527–554.

———. "The Generalization of an Old Yogic Attainment in Medieval Mahāyāna Sūtra Literature: Some Notes on *Jātismara.*" *Journal of the International Association of Buddhist Studies* 6, no. 1 (1983): 109–147.

———. "The Good Monk and His Money in a Buddhist Monasticism of 'The Mahāyāna Period.'" *Eastern Buddhist*, n.s. 32, no. 1 (2000): 85–105.

———. "The Inscription on the Kuṣān Image of Amitābha and the Character of the Early Mahāyāna in India." *Journal of the International Association of Buddhist Studies* 10, no. 2 (1987): 99–137.

———. "The Lay Ownership of Monasteries and the Role of the Monk in Mūlasarvāstivādin Monasticism." *Journal of the International Association of Buddhist Studies* 19, no. 1 (1996): 81–126.

———. "Mahāyāna in Indian Inscriptions." *Indo-Iranian Journal* 21 (1979): 1–19.

———. "The Mahāyāna and the Middle Period in Indian Buddhism: Through a Chinese Looking-Glass." *Eastern Buddhist,* n.s. 32, no. 2 (2000): 1–25.

———. "Monastic Law Meets the Real World: A Monk's Continuing Right to Inherit Family Property in Classical India." *History of Religions* 35, no. 2 (1995): 101–123.

———. "On Monks, Nuns, and 'Vulgar' Practices: The Introduction of the Image Cult into Indian Buddhism." In *Bones, Stones, and Buddhist Monk,* Schopen, ed., pp. 238–257.

———. "The Phrase *'sa pṛthivīpradeśaś caityabhūto bhavet'* in the *Vajracchedikā:* Notes on the Cult of the Book in Mahāyāna." *Indo-Iranian Journal* (1975): 147–181.

———. "Two Problems in the History of Indian Buddhism: The Layman/Monk Distinction and the Doctrines of the Transference of Merit." In *Bones, Stones, and Buddhist Monks,* Schopen, ed., pp. 23–55.

Schopen, Gregory, and Richard Salomon. "On an Alleged Reference to Amitābha in a Kharoṣṭhī Inscription on a Gandhāran Relief." *Journal of the International Association of Buddhist Studies* 25, nos. 1–2 (2002): 3–31.

Shah, Natubhai. *Jainism: The World of the Conquerors.* Portland: Sussex Academic Press, 1998.

Sharma, Ramesh Chandra. *Buddhist Art of Mathurā.* Delhi: Agam Kala Prakashan, 1984.

Shastri, Ajay Mitra. "The Closing Phase of the Sātavāhana Power and Allied Issues." In *Early History of the Deccan,* Shastri, ed., pp. 38–44. Delhi: Sundeep Prakashan, 1987.

——. *The Satavahanas and the Western Kshatrapas: A Historical Framework.* Nagpur: Dattsons, 1998.

Silk, Jonathan. "The King of Samādhis: Chapters I–IV." In *Studies in the Literature of the Great Vehicle,* Gomez and Silk, ed., pp. 11–87.

——. "The Origins and Early History of the Mahāratnakūṭa Tradition of Mahāyāna Buddhism with a Study of the Ratnarāśisūtra and Related Materials." Ph.D. dissertation, University of Michigan, 1994.

——. "A Note on the Opening Formula of Buddhist Sūtras." *Journal of the International Association of Buddhist Studies* 12, no. 1 (1989): 158–163.

——. "What, If Anything, Is Mahāyāna Buddhism? Problems of Definitions and Classifications." *Numen* 49, no. 4 (2002): 355–405.

Sircar, Dinesh Chandra. *Indian Epigraphical Glossary.* Delhi: Motilal Banarsidass, 1966.

——. "Jaynagar Image Inscription of Year 35." *Journal of the Bihar Research Society* 41 (1955): 143–153.

——. *Select Inscriptions Bearing on Indian History and Civilization.* Delhi: Motilal Banarsidass, 1965.

——. "Some Inscriptions from Bihar." *Journal of the Bihar Research Society* 37 (1951): 1–13.

Sivaramamurti. "Amarāvatī Sculptures in the Madras Government Museum." *Bulletin of the Madras Government Museum* 4 (1956): 26–32.

Skjærvø, Prods Oktor. *Khotanese Manuscripts from Chinese Turkestan in the British Library: A Complete Catalogue with Texts and Translations.* London: British Library, 2002.

Skilling, Peter. "Citations from the Scriptures of the 'Eighteen Schools' in the *Tarkajvāla.*" In *Bauddhavidyāsudhākaraḥ: Studies in Honour of Heinz Bechert on the Occasion of his 65th Birthday,* Petra Kieffer-Pülz and Jens-Uwe Hartmann, eds., pp. 605–614. Swisttal-Odendorf: Indica et Tibetica Verlag, 1997.

Sparham, Gareth. *The Tibetan Dhammapada.* New Delhi: Mahāyāna, 1983.

Spink, Walter. *Ajaṇṭā to Ellora.* Ann Arbor: Marg, 1967.

Sprung, Mervyn. *Lucid Exposition of the Middle Way: The Essential Chapters from the Prasannapadā of Candrakīrti.* London: Routledge & Kegan Paul, 1979.

Stael-Holstein, Baron A. von. *The Kāśyapaparivarta: A Mahāyānasūtra of the Ratnakūṭa Class.* 1926. Reprint. Tokyo: Meicho-Fukyū-Kai, 1977.

Stein, Aurel. *Ancient Khotan, Detailed Report of Archaeological Explorations in Chinese Turkestan, Carried Out and Described Under the Orders of H. M. Indian Government by M. Aurel Stein.* 3 vols. Oxford: Clarendon Press, 1907.

——. *Kalhaṇa's Rājataraṅgiṇī: A Chronicle of the Kings of Kaśmīr.* Srinagar: Verinag, 1961.

Stone, Elizabeth Rosen. *The Buddhist Art of Nāgārjunakoṇḍa.* Delhi: Motilal Banarsidass, 1994.

Strauss, Leo. *Persecution and the Art of Writing.* Reprint. Chicago: University of Chicago Press, 1988.

Suzuki, Daisetz Teitaro, trans. *The Laṅkāvatāra Sūtra.* Delhi: Munshiram Manoharlal, 1999.

Swanson, Paul. *Foundations of T'ien-t'ai Philosophy: The Flowering of the Two Truths Theory in Chinese Buddhism.* Berkeley: Asian Humanities Press, 1989.

Tachikawa, Musashi. *An Introduction to the Philosophy of Nāgārjuna.* Rolf W. Giebel, trans. Delhi: Motilal Banarsidass, 1997.

Takakusu, Junjirō. *Essentials of Buddhist Philosophy.* Wing Tsit Chan and Charles A. Moore, eds. Delhi: Motilal Banarsidass, 1987.

——. *A Record of the Buddhist Religion as Practiced in India and the Malay Archipelago (A.D. 671–695).* Oxford: Clarendon Press, 1896.

Takasaki, Jikido. "Saṃsāra eva nirvāṇaṃ." In *Wisdom, Compassion, and The Search for Understanding: The Buddhist Studies Legacy of Gadjin M. Nagao,* Jonathan Silk, ed., pp. 333–346. Honolulu: University of Hawai'i Press, 2000.

Tāranātha's Geschichte des Buddhismus in Indien. Anton Scheifner, trans. St. Petersburg, 1869.

Tāranātha's History of Buddhism in India. D. Chattopadhyaya, trans. Calcutta: K. P. Bagchi, 1970.

Tatz, Mark. *Asaṅga's Chapter on Ethics with the Commentary of Tsong-kha-pa, the Basic Path to Awakening, the Complete Bodhisattva.* Studies in Asian Thought and Religion, vol. 4. Lewiston, NY: Edwin Mellen Press, 1986.

Teiser, Stephen. *The Scripture on the Ten Kings and the Making of Purgatory in Medieval Chinese Buddhism.* Honolulu: University of Hawai'i Press, 1994.

Thomas, Fredrick William. "Some Notes on the Kharoṣṭhī Documents from Chinese Turkestan." *Acta Orientalia* 12 (1934): 37–70.

Tsai, Yao-ming. "Searching for the Origins of Mahāyāna and Moving Toward a Better Understanding of Early Mahāyāna." Ph.D. dissertation, University of California, 1997.

Turner, R. H. "Determinants of Social Movement Strategies." In *Human Nature and Collective Behavior: Papers in Honor of Herbert Blumer,* Tamotsu Shibutani, ed., pp. 145–164. Englewood Cliffs, NJ: Prentice Hall, 1970.

Tucci, Giuseppe. *Pre-Dignāga Buddhist Texts from Chinese Sources.* Baroda: Oriental Institute, 1929.

The Udāna. Peter Masefield, trans. Oxford: Pāli Text Society, 1994.

Ui, Hakuju. *The Vaiśeṣika Philosophy According to the Daśapadārtha-Śāstra.* 2nd ed. Varanasi: Chowkhamba Sanskrit Series Office, 1962.

Vaidya, P. L. *Gaṇḍavyūhasūtra.* Darbhanga: Mithila Institute, 1960.

Vasilyev, V. P. *Der buddhismus, seine Dogmen, Geschichte und Literatur.* St. Petersburg: Kaiserliche Akademie der Wissenschaften, 1860.

Vasubandhu. *L'Abhidharmakośa de Vasubandhu: traduction et annotations.* Louis de La Valeé Poussin, trans. *Mélanges chinois et bouddhiques* 16 (1972). Reprint. Brussels: Institut Belge des Hautes Etudes Chinoises, 1980.

Vetter, Tilmann. "On the Authenticity of the *Ratnāvalī.*" *Asiatische Studien* 46, no. 1 (1992): 492–506.

——. "On the Origin of Mahāyāna Buddhism and the Subsequent Introduction of *Prajñāpāramitā.*" *Asiatische Studien* 48, no. 4 (1994): 1241–1281.

——. "Zum Problem der Person in Nāgārjunas Mūla-Madhyamaka-Kārikās." In

Offenbarung als Heilserfahrung im Christentum, Hinduismus, und Buddhismus, Walter Strolz and Shizuteru Ueda, eds., pp. 167–185. Freiburg: Herder Press, 1982.

Vinaya Texts. T.W. Rhys Davids and H. Oldenberg, trans. Sacred Books of the East, vol. 13. Reprint. Delhi: Motilal Banarsidass, 1996.

Vogel, Jean Philippe. "Prakrit Inscriptions from a Buddhist Site at Nāgārjunakoṇḍa." *Epigraphica Indica* 20 (1929–1930): 1–36.

Voyce, M. B. "The King's Enforcement of the Vinaya Piṭaka: The Purification of the Saṅgha under Aśoka (C.B.C. 269–232)." *Zeitschrift für Religions und Geistesgeschichte* 37, no. 1 (1985): 38–57.

Walleser, Max. *The Life of Nāgārjuna from Tibetan and Chinese Sources.* Reprint. Delhi: Nag, 1979.

Warder, A. K. "The Concept of a Concept." *Journal of Indian Philosophy* 1, no. 1 (1971): 181–196.

——. "Is Nagarjuna a Mahayanist?" In *The Problem of Two Truths in Buddhism and Vedānta,* Mervyn Sprung, ed., pp. 78–88. Boston: Reidel, 1973.

Ware, James Roland. *Alchemy, Medicine, and Religion in the China of A.D. 320*: The Nei P'ien of Ko Hung. Cambridge: MIT Press, 1966.

Wassiljew, Vaslii. *Der buddhismus, seine Dogmen, Geschichte und Literatur.* A. Schiefner, trans. St. Petersburg: Kaiserliche Akademie der Wissenschaften, 1860.

Watanabe, Fumimaro. *Philosophy and Its Development in the Nikāyas and Abhidhamma.* Delhi: Motilal Banarsidass, 1983.

Watters, Thomas. *On Yuan Chwang's Travels in India 629–645 A.D.* T. W. Rhys Davids and S. W. Bushell, eds. New Delhi: Asian Educational Services, 1988.

White, David G. *The Alchemical Body: Siddha Traditions in Medieval India.* Chicago: University of Chicago Press, 1996.

Williams, Paul. *Mahāyāna Buddhism: The Doctrinal Foundations.* New York: Routledge, 1989.

——. "Some Aspects of Language and Construction in the Madhyamaka." *Journal of Indian Philosophy* 8 (1980): 1–45.

Yazdani, Ghulam. *Ajaṇṭā: The Colour and Monochrome Reproductions of the Ajanta Frescoes Based on Photography.* London: Oxford University Press, 1930–1955.

Yoshimoto, Shingyo. "Śārīputrābhidharmaśāstra." In *Encyclopedia of Indian Philosophies: Volume VII Abhidharma Buddhism to 150 A.D.,* Potter, ed., pp. 317–325.

Zald, Mayer. "The Continuing Vitality of Resource Mobilization Theory: Response to Herbert Kitschelt's Critique." In *Research on Social Movements,* Dieter Rucht, ed., pp. 348–354.

Zürcher, Erik. *The Buddhist Conquest of China: The Spread and Adaptation of Buddhism in Early Medieval China.* Leiden: E. J. Brill, 1972.

Index

Abhāyadatta 293–294
Abhayagiri monastery 12, 47
Abhidhammatthasaṅghaha 192, 315
Abhidhammāvatāra 326
abhidharma 11, 14, 18, 28, 40, 46, 108, 129, 157, 159, 160, 162–163, 188–189, 190–193, 213, 225, 265–266; Mahāsāṅghika 214–218; Prajñaptivāda 218–223; Pudgalavāda 193; 199–208; Sarvāstivāda 192; 208–214; Theravāda 191–192
Abhidharmakośa 12, 109, 165, 211, 216, 230, 239, 242, 246, 280, 303, 306, 315, 330
Abhidharmakośabhāṣya 96, 192, 235, 323
Abhidharmakośa Sputhārtha 170, 192, 196, 306
Abhidharmasammuccaya 193, 316
Abhisamācārikā 129, 189, 282, 303, 309–313, 321, 326
Abhisamayālaṃkārāloka 336
abhivinaya 129
accumulation. *See upacaya.*
Acintyastava 261–262, 267
Acts of suspension. *See utkṣepanīyakarma.*
adhikaraṇa 98, 102
Adhikaraṇaśamatha (settling disputes) 304
Afghanistan 22, 27, 40, 125
Agnipurāṇa 120
Ahura Mazda 20
Aiyar, V. N. 285
Ajaṇṭā 34, 37, 299
Ajītamitra 65, 120, 272, 292, 308
Ākāśa 215
Akāśagarbha sūtra 290
Ākāśānantyāyātana 215
Ākiñcanyāyatana 215
Akṣobhyavyūha 16
Akutobhayā 258, 275, 278, 337
ālayavijñāna 323
Al-beruni 66
Alchemy 73, 75–79
Alluru 87
Allusion 167
Amarāvatī 46, 61, 63, 82–4, 85–87, 300–301
Amitābhā Buddha 20–21, 31, 33, 269, 284, 289
ammonite (*musāragalva*) 22
Aṃogka, (King) 31, 33, 284
Aṅguttara Nikāya 109, 115, 146, 149, 162, 189, 306, 315
Ānanda 40, 50–51, 154
Anantamukhanirhāradhāraṇī 29
anantarīya karma (immediate sins) 303
anātman 131, 164, 186, 199, 218, 251–252, 274, 322
Andhaka 222, 245
Andhra Pradesh 3, 14, 21, 25–26, 58, 60, 64–69, 86–89, 125, 223, 282

animitta (signlessness) 161–162, 179, 180, 186–187, 315
animitta samādhi 163, 165
anitya 232
anudharma 304
anulakṣaṇa 330
Anuruddha 315
anuśaya 211
anyonya prajñapti 219, 221–222, 220, 234, 239, 243–244, 260, 328
apakarṣana 236, 239
Aparaśaila 38, 50, 53, 87–88, 213, 267, 335
apoha 235–236
Apratisaṃkhyā-nirodha 215
āraṇyakas 20, 103
Ariṣṭa (monk) 106–107
Āryadeva 52, 66, 273–274, 276–278, 289, 294, 296, 336
Aryamārgāṅgikatva 215
Āryaparyeṣana sutta 274
Aśoka 45, 49–50, 103–104, 305
āśrava (outflows) 159–163
Aśvaghoṣa 2, 62, 302
Asaṅga 113, 115, 121–122, 155, 193, 182, 307–309, 313–316, 327
asaṃskṛta (unconditioned dharmas) 175, 194, 198, 204–206, 211, 214–216, 230–232, 254, 257
astidṛṣṭi 202–203
Aṣṭadaśaprajñāpāramitā Sūtra 280, 316
Aṣṭadaśasāhastrikā Prajñāpāramitā 19, 25, 28, 31, 156, 178, 180–181, 233–234, 170
Āṭanāṭiya sutta 290
atman 193, 195, 198–199, 251, 274
Aṭṭakanāgara sutta 162
Aṭṭhakavagga 275
Aṭṭhasālinī 314
Atwood, Christopher 284, 291
avācya (ineffable) 204, 206
avadāna 32–33, 126–127
Avalokitavrata 53–54, 87, 229, 245–246, 332
Avataṃsaka 25, 27, 50
āveṇka dharmas 88
avijñaptirūpa (unmanifest matter) 208, 211
Avipranāśa 199–200, 204–205, 222, 229, 245–246, 248, 262, 268, 324, 333
avyākṛta 200, 223, 229, 246, 251, 274, 325
āyatana 129, 131, 165, 189, 190, 204, 206–207, 218–220, 224

bahuśrutīya 51–52, 87, 102–103, 108, 193, 214, 218, 221, 304–305, 327
Bairam Ali manuscript 127
Bāmiyān 27–30, 33, 227
Bāṇa 293, 296
Bandarkar 285
Bangladesh 39
Baopuzi 77
Bareau, André 44, 287, 290
Bargazya 22
Barhut 35
Barth, Auguste 18
Barthes, Roland 264
Bechert 18, 98, 101
being/non-being 173
Bengal 34, 39, 285
Ben-Porat, Ziva 167
Bhabha, Homi 14, 280
Bhadrayānīya 53, 87, 268
Bhagavad Gīta 318
Bhagavatāpurāṇa 314
Bhaiṣajyaguruvaiḍuryaprabharāja 29
Bhaiṣajyarājapūrvayogaparipṛcchā 281
Bhandarkar 34, 35
Bhaṭṭa Somadeva 66
Bharhut 300
Bharkaccha 42
Bhattacharya, D. C. 285
Bhattasali, N. K. 285
bhāvanā mārga 163, 217, 223
Bhāvaviveka 53–54, 124, 231, 271–272, 275
Bhavya 208, 218, 257, 316
Bodhgāya 42
Bhida 40
bhikṣunīs 40
Bihar 34, 285
Bimbisāra, (King) 82
Bimuzhixian 246
Biography of Nāgārjuna 69, 74–78
Bodhi tree motif 83
Bodhicāryāvatāra 323
Bodhicaryāvatārapañjikā 110, 272
Bodhiruci 293
Bodhisambhāraśāstra 298
bodhisattva 16, 19–20, 24, 26, 37, 40–41, 114; bodhisattva vow 24, 113
Bodhisattvabhūmi 24, 155, 307
Bodhisattvapiṭaka 25, 52–53, 112, 155, 157, 290
Bodhisattvaprātimokṣa 299
Bodhisattvayāna 23

Bond, George 306
Books 140; buying 139; copying 135–139; bookkeeping 124; books as property 139–147
Boyer, August 284
Brahmājāla sūtra 156, 174, 321
Brahman 193
Brahmī 28
Bronkhorst, Johannes 331
Buddha, footprint of the 169; image of 81–87; on lotuses 298
Buddhabhadra 27, 283
Buddhadatta 326
Buddhaghosa 99, 173, 184, 222–223, 263, 268, 314–315, 321, 332, 334
Buddhapālita 124, 278
Buddhapālitavṛtti 258, 275
buddhavacana (word of the Buddha) 11, 13, 107, 109–110, 116, 118–122, 130–131, 134–135, 138, 142–143, 146–149, 151, 153, 157, 166–168, 170–171, 175, 185, 188–190, 202, 225, 227, 247, 266, 288, 305–308
Buddhayaśas 52
building duty monk 56, 129, 138
Bultmann, Rudolf 264
Burrow, Thomas 31, 284
Burton, David 234, 241–244
Buston 21, 72, 76, 293, 296
Buswell, Robert 191–192
Bṛhatkathāmañjārī 66, 76

Cūḷasūññata sutta 163, 215
Cūḷavagga 99, 106, 290, 305
Cūḷavedallasutta 250
Cabézon, José 280, 304
Cadh'ota 284
Caitika 50, 87–88, 214
Candra Śrī 81, 86
Candrakīrti 21, 66, 71–74, 77, 124, 230, 237, 240, 244, 246, 456, 458–459, 272, 275, 291, 295–296, 320, 330
Candrapradīpasamādhi 166
canon 11–12, 138
Cīrāyus (king) 76–77
Catuḥśataka 66, 273, 277, 289, 294, 336
Catuḥśatakavṛtti 77, 296
Central Asia 22, 127, 134, 143
Chūkan 49, 51, 288–289
Chang, Garma 308
Chang'an 62–63, 78, 283
Chau, Thich Thien 322
Chebrolu 64
China 22, 25, 75, 125, 138
Chinese pilgrims 39–43
Chittagong 34, 285
Chronicles, Early Buddhist 43–48
Chronicles, Mahāyāna 48–54
Cipiyi 51
cittasamprayuktasaṃskāra 220
Cohen, Richard 34, 37–38, 285–286
Collins, Steve 11, 280
Confucianism 289
Conze, Edward 317
Coomaraswami, Ananda 84, 300
coral (*lohitikā*) 22
Corless, Roger 291, 293, 295
Cousins, Lance 135
Cox, Collette 125
cuckoos 153
cult of the book 16, 36, 114, 135

Dakṣināpatha 25, 66
Damdān-Uiliq 29
dāna 103
dānapāramitā 149
Daoism 289
Daoxuan 289
darśana mārga 163, 217
daśabālaśīla 19
daśabhūmi 16, 18
Daśabhūmika Sūtra 19, 53, 62
Das, Chandra 120
Davidson, Ronald, 110, 305–306, 314, 327
Dazhidulun 154, 165, 181
De Jong, J. W. 275, 292
Deccan 14, 26, 61, 63, 79–83, 86, 267–268
Dehejia, Vidya 55–6
Demiéville, Paul 49, 72, 283, 287–290, 292, 295, 308, 313–314
Demythologization 264, 335
Dependent origination (see *pratītyasamutpāda*)
Devī Bhagavatāpurāṇa 155
Devadatta 100–101
Dhaṅka (mountain) 76
dhammadharo 108
Dhammasaṅgaṇi 191
Ḍhaṅka (mountain) 77, 294
Dhānyakaṭaka (origin of name) 25–26, 43, 61, 63, 65, 67, 72, 77–78, 81–82, 84, 86, 297, 303

Dhānyākara 25
Dharanendra 74
Dharasena IV 34
Dharma pratirūpaka 63
Dharmaśāstra 91, 103–104, 120
Dharmacakra motif 83
Dharmacakraparivartana sūtra 157, 159
Dharmadāna 147–152
Dharmagupta 5, 17, 52, 87, 125, 191, 193, 227, 233–234, 287, 301, 309, 331
Dharmākara 215, 219, 221–223, 327
Dharmakīrti 196, 277
Dharmakāya 168
Dharmakṣema 295
Dharmarakṣa 62, 316
Dharmaskandha 191–192, 227, 322
dharmatā 109–110, 121, 170, 181, 320
Dharmottarīya 268
dhātu 189–190, 204, 206–207, 224, 232, 235, 239
Dhātukathā 191–192
Dhātukāya 192
Dhavalikar, M. K. 82, 299–300
dhūtaṅga 112
dhyāna 106, 165, 177, 215
Dīghanakha sutta 158
Dīgha Nikāya 107, 109, 117, 146, 174, 186, 190, 197, 205, 213, 290, 306; *Dīgha Nikāya Aṭṭhakathā* 256
Dignāga 277
Dīpavaṃsa 45, 47, 213, 326
Dīrgha Āgama 52, 114, 306
Divyāvadāna 82, 299, 323
donors 35
Dowling, Thomas 194
Dowman, Kenneth 293
Doxographies 43
dravya 210, 234, 238
Dravya Mallaputra 282
dravyasat 200, 211–212, 234–235, 237, 241, 246
Dreyfus, Georges 323
Dunhuang 29
Dunne, John 298
duḥkha 131, 218, 221, 232
Dutt, Nalinaksha 25, 282

Ehuvala Cāṃtamūla 86
eight *dhyānas* 176
Ekavyāvahārika 51, 214, 218
ekayāna 17
Ekottara Āgama 37, 52, 189, 286
elements (*bhūta*) 237–238
Eliot, Charles 20, 282
Emmerick, Ronald 284
emptiness. See *śūnyatā*.
Endere 29, 31–33, 36
eternalism/annihilationism 175, 184
Ethiopia 22

Faxian 21, 39–43, 47, 54, 124, 213, 303, 309
field of merit 103
fire and fuel analogy 203, 244, 249–250, 254
First Buddhist council 51, 94, 154, 190
five categories (of *pudgalavāda*) 204
five essentials 312
Five knowledges of the Buddha 320
five pure dharmas 94, 111
forest-dwelling monk 20, 24, 38, 102, 129, 282
four conditions (*pratyāya*) 226
four noble truths 41, 157, 159
Franco, Eli 311
Frauwallner, Ernst 191, 310, 322
Fukuhara, Ryogon 192

Gandhāra 29, 80, 83, 87, 124–127, 284, 300
Gaṇḍavyūha Sūtra 25, 27, 283
Gārava sutta 181
gātha chanting 131
gati (motion) 199
Gauraṇa 296
Gautamiputra Sātakarṇi 83
Gehong 77, 296
Gernet, Jacques 141, 311–312
Ghantasala 87
Gilgit 314, 316; Gilgit Manuscripts 312
Godāvarī 64, 67
Gokulika 214, 218
gold (*suvarṇa*) 22
Gomati monastery 39–40
Gombrich, Richard 135–137
Gdmez, Luis 118, 308
Gopalpur 34, 285
Govindavarman I 88
grāhayitavya 309
Granoff, Phyllis 74, 76, 293, 296
Guhyasamājatantra 78
guilds 93, 104
Gujarat 22, 34, 49, 67, 69–72, 76
Guṇabhadra 293

Guṇavarman 63, 65, 292, 297
Guntupali 64
Guntur district 26

Hahn, Michael 227
Haḍḍa 27, 125
Haribhadra 272, 336
Harisena 81
Harivārman 190, 193, 213–214, 289, 327
Harrison, Paul 23, 282, 289, 291, 298
Harṣa Carita 74, 293
Hārwan 67
Hastipadottama sutta 196–198
Hathigumpha 64
hatred type 119
heterodox books 133–134
Himalaya 66, 69
Himavant 70
hīnayāna 23, 40–41, 57, 115
Hindu 66, 77
Hirakawa, Akira 18–20, 24, 35–38, 54, 281, 283
Holt, John 47, 288
Hopkins, Jeffrey 148, 293
Hua, Jan-yün 294
Huichao 78
Huiwen 258
Huntington, C. W. 337
Huvikṣa 32–33, 66, 77

iccantika 157
Iida, Shotaro 336
Ikṣvāku 86, 326
Inada, Kenneth 279, 329
indriya 189
inheritance 142, 145–146
intertextuality 167
Investigation of *ātman* (*Ātmaparīkṣā*) 251
Investigation of bondage and liberation (*Bandhamokṣaparīkṣā*) 254
Investigation of Karma and Fruit (*Karmaphalaparīkṣā*) 228
Investigation of Passion and the impassioned one (Rāga parīkṣā) 244
Investigation of *skandha* (*Skandhaparīkṣā*) 253
Investigation of the Four Noble Truths (*Āryasatyaparīkṣā*) 258

Jainism 66, 69–70, 74–5, 77, 193, 262, 293–295
Jaini, Padmanabh 191
Jam-yang-shay-ba 294
Jātaka 46, 83, 127
Jaynagar 285
Jhāna sutta 162
Jiang Zongxin 283
jīva 205
Jizang 49–50, 288–289
Jñanagarbha 272
Jñānaprasthāna 192, 210
Junnar 87, 268
Jusanzang jiji 57, 291
Juṣka 66–67, 77

Kaccāna 174
Kaccānagotta sutta 184–185, 172, 274
Kādambarī 296
Kālacakra Tantra 78, 297
Kalhaṇa 21, 66–67, 293, 296
Kaliṅga 42, 64–65
Kālika scriptures 70
Kalupahana, David 118, 247, 280, 332
Kāmandakīyanītisāra 120
Kañchipūram 67
Kane, P. V. 104
Kanheri 82, 87, 268, 299
Kaniṣka 33, 66–67, 77, 79
Kannauj 40
Kant, Imanuel 160
Kanyakubja 42
Kaṇaḍa 262
kāraṇa/kārya 254
Karashima, Seishi 303, 310
kāritra 210
Karle 87, 268
karma 194–195, 199, 201, 204, 211, 214, 223, 228, 230, 246, 248
Karmasiddhiprakaraṇa 200, 246, 323
Karmavibhaṅga 30
kārya/Kāraṇa (material cause) 237–238
Kashgar 78
Kashmir 21–32, 66–67, 74, 78, 286
Kathāsaritsāgara 66, 76, 78
Kathāvatthu 21, 191–192, 203, 257
Kathāvatthu Aṭṭhakathā 222, 329
Kātyāyana 190
Kauśāmbhī 34
Kaukūlika 51
kavya 28
Kāśyapa 179
Kāśyapa Parivārta Sūtra 29–30, 117, 179, 275–276, 320, 337
Kāśyapīya 233, 287, 335
Kent, Stephen 18, 281
Kevaddha sutta 186–187
Khādalik 29
Kharoṣṭhī 31, 35, 125
Khotan 55, 57–58, 286

Khotanese 29–30
kings 103, 119, 266
Kitschelt 7–8, 11, 109, 279–280
Kīṭgiri sutta 163
Klu'i rgyal 272
Knox, Robert 85
Kośala 43, 66
koccha (chairs) 311
Kohmārī Mazar 28
Konow, Sten 35
Koṇḍañña 158
Krishna River 14, 72, 96
Krishna River Valley 87, 263, 268
kriyākarma 91, 93, 110–114, 305
Krorainia 32, 104
kṣayatva (momentariness) 181, 263
Kṣemendra 66
Kṣitigarbha 21, 282
Kṣudravastu 226–227
kuśala dharmas 130
Kuanyin 40
Kuča 29, 78
Kuiji 217
kulaputra 19
Kumāra Bhikkhu 310
Kumārajīva 44–45, 62–3, 66, 69–70, 75, 77–8, 155, 272, 287, 313, 316
Kumbha Sātkarṇi 81
kuśa grass motif 84
Kuṣaṇa 21–22, 27–28, 32–33, 83, 269

Lévi, Sylvain 20, 132, 310
Lahiri, Latika 102
laity 18–9, 24, 33, 103, 131, 133, 266; laity teaching sūtras 132
lakṣaṇa/lakṣya 239
Lamotte, Etienne 21, 27, 42–43, 55, 62, 67, 154, 156, 229, 246, 280, 282–283, 287–288, 291, 305–306, 308, 313, 316
Lang, Karen 277, 294, 296
Laṅkāvatāra sūtra 66, 71, 73, 157, 292–293
La Valée Poussin, Louis 18, 272, 280, 318
Law, N. N. 285
Leese, Marilyn 34, 299
Legge, James 39, 286, 288
libraries 146
Lindtner, Christian 335
Liu, Xinru 22, 282
Lofland, John 4, 5, 279
Lokakṣema 23
Lokānuvārtana Sūtra 291
Lokātītastāva 261–262, 267
lokavyāvahāra 261
Lokāyata texts 133
Lokāyatika sūtra 174, 184
Lokottaravāda 51, 214
lotus *pīṭha* 79–88, 300
Loujiachan (translator) 275
Loulan 104
Lṃders 92
Luoma gajing 27
Luoyang 28

Mabbett, Ian 60–61, 65, 72, 291–296
MacDonald, Anne 297
Mādhupiṇḍika Sutta 160, 162
Mādhya Pradesh 34
Madhyama Āgama 52
Madhyamakālaṃkāravṛtti 272
Madhyamakāvatāra 71, 272, 291, 295
Mādhyamika 60, 124, 231–232, 273, 278
Madhyāntavibhāga Bhāṣya 17
Maghada 21, 27, 218
Mahābhārata 67, 120
Mahābherīhārakaparivarta Sūtra 71, 295
Mahādeva 44–45, 49–51; five theses 287
Mahāhatthipadopama sutta 168, 185
Mahākaśyapa 190
Mahākaruṇāpuṇḍarīka 21
Mahāmadugalyāyana 40
Mahāmayurī 294
Mahāmegha Sūtra 71–74, 72, 79, 292, 295–296
Mahāmeghavāha Khāravela 64
Mahānidāna Sūtra 156, 197–198
mahāpadeśa (four great teachings) 107, 111–112, 168, 181, 305, 320
Mahāparinibbāna sutta 107
Mahāparinirvāṇa sūtra 306
Mahāprajñāpāramitopadeśa 18, 21
Mahāratnakūṭa 281
Mahāsāṅghika 3, 5, 14–15, 18, 36, 38, 45–46, 49–53, 87, 89, 96, 100, 124, 130, 147, 167, 212–218, 223, 227, 228–232, 245–248, 260, 266, 268–269, 287, 305, 326–327
Mahāsāṅghika Abhidharma 212, 228, 248
Mahāsāṅghika prātimokṣa 98, 141, 304, 308, 310
Mahāsāṅghika Vinaya 19,

40–41, 56, 93–96, 101–102, 104, 106–109, 111–112, 115, 119, 124–125, 127–129, 132–133, 138–139, 142–3, 146, 149, 151, 189, 213, 232, 282, 303, 311–313
Mahāsena 45
Mahāvaṃsa 45, 47
Mahāvastu 22
Mahāvedalla sūtra 161–162
Mahāvibhāṣā 44–45, 49, 156, 192, 210, 233, 325, 330–331
Mahāvihāra monastery 47
Mahāvyuttpatti 303, 320
Mahāyāna 135, 164
Mahāyāna chronicles 48ff.
Mahāyāna, working definition 17
Mahāyāna inscriptions 30–6
Mahāyāna origins 17
Mahāyāna Sūtras 23–25
Mahāyānasaṃgraha 327
"*mahāyāna-sthavira*" 42
Mahāyānasūtrālaṃkāra 110, 121, 309
Mahipāla I 34
Mahīśāśaka vinaya 111, 113–114, 306, 312
Mahīśāsaka 40, 46, 87, 233, 287, 327, 335
Maitreya 168
Maitreyamahāsiṃhanāda Sūtra 23
maitryālambana (meditation on loving-kindness) 209
Majjhima Nikāya 97–98, 117, 158, 160–163, 168, 196, 213, 215, 250, 275, 304, 315
Majjhima Nikāya Aṭṭhakathā 159
Mañjuśrī 20, 25–26, 40, 48
Mañjuśrīmūlakalpa 21
Mañjuśrīmūlatantra 26, 66, 292, 294
Mañjuśrīparipṛcchā 48–49, 214
Mūlamadhyamakakārikā 2, 15, 17, 60, 69, 89, 118, 165, 170, 180, 182, 184, 186, 194, 224–228, 230, 232, 237, 239, 247, 249, 251, 253–254, 258, 261–263, 267–268, 271–275, 277–280, 295, 317, 323, 330; and Mahāsāṅghika 228–234; and Prajñaptivāda 234–244; and Pudgalavāda 245–261; and Sarvāstivāda 226
Mūlasarvāstivāda sect 41, 147
Mūlasarvāstivāda vinaya 38, 92–93, 102, 109, 110–111, 138, 142, 146, 150, 306, 309
Mīmāṃsikā 195
Māṭarīputra Vīrapuruṣadatta 86–87
mantrapiṭaka 52
mantras 57, 290
Masefield, Peter 319
Masuda, Jiryŏ215, 220, 269, 287, 289
Mathurā 3, 33, 80, 83–84, 87, 190, 269
mātṛkā 213
mātṛkādhara 41, 306
Matsypurāṇa 120
Maudgalyāyana 51, 112, 208
Māyajāla sūtra 156
McCagney, Nancy 308
McCarthy, John 6, 279
McClintock, Sarah 298
medical treatises 134
Memorization 133
merchants 104
Merutuṅgācārya 293
Merv 27, 127
metrics 276–277
Milinda, (King) 196
Milindapañho 196–197
Ming-öi 134
Mokṣala 316
momentariness (see *kṣaṇikatva*)
Monius, Anne 286
Mukherji, R. 284
Murti, Satcidananda 297
Murtuq 29
Music 155
Myakadoni (Bellary dist.) 81
myth 264

Nāga 25, 70–79, 155
Nāgārjuna (Jain) 69–71; (Telugu Actor) 69
Nāgārjunakoṇḍa 81–84, 86–87, 92, 213, 282, 294, 300–301
Nāgārjuna's hagiography 65–69
Nāgārjuna's monastery 87–88
Nāgasena 196
naiva saṃjñānāsaṃjñāyatana or saṃjñāveditanirodha 161
Naivasaṃjñāsāsaṃjñāyatana 215

Nakamura, Hajime 24, 282
Nīlamata Purāṇa 74–75, 296
Nālanda 34, 39, 67–68, 77–78, 101, 285, 297
Nāmasaṃgītiṭīkā 272
ṭāṇamoli, Bhikkhu 98
Nandayapallem 64
Nandi sutta 70
Nanhai qigui neifazhuan (*Nanhai jigui neifa chuan*) 41, 63
Nāradasmṛti 121
Nāsik 22, 81, 87
nāstidṛṣṭi 203
Nath, Vijay 335
Nattier, Jan 16, 100, 280, 288, 292, 302
navakarmika 56
Navanātha 296
Netti Pakaraṇa 110, 190, 192, 308, 320
Nga-wang-bel-den 294
Nidāna Vagga 171, 184
Niddesa 46
Nigrantha (Jain) 262
niḥsargikapāccayaita offence 141
Nikāyabhedavibhaṅga 326
Nikāyabhedavibhaṅgavyākhyāna 208
Nikāya Saṅgaha 47
nimitta (sign) 160–161, 177; ten *nimitta* 177
nine genres of scripture 100, 129, 134, 139, 147
nirodha 159, 208, 214, 216
nirodhasamāpatti 164
nirvāṇa 163–164, 178, 182, 193–194, 198, 204–205, 208, 214, 223, 232, 257, 273
Nivāpa sutta 160, 162
Niya 28–29, 31–33, 36, 39, 104–105, 284
novice training 129
nyāya 289
Nyāyānusāra 192
Nyaya-Vaiṣeśikā 195

Obermiller, Eugene 320
Oetke, Claus 331
Ogha śruta 70
Okada, Yukihiro 227
Oldenberg, Hermann 45
Ong, Walter 136
opportunity structure 8, 11, 13, 109, 93, 266, 280

Pācattika offense 130, 137
Padaliptācārya 76
Pagel, Ulrich 281, 290, 313
Paithan 81
Pakistan 125, 143
Pañcavimsatisāhasrika Prajñāpāramitā 170, 233, 316
Papañcaśudhanī 315, 323
Paramārha (translator) 45, 49–52, 64–65, 82, 86–87, 100, 215–216, 219–222, 236, 238, 260, 271–272, 287, 289, 292, 326
paramārthasat 198, 212, 218, 235, 237, 241, 260
pāramitā 17, 19
paramopāsaka 36, 56
parātmadṛṣṭi 202
Pārileyyaka sutta 274
Parivāra 46
Parśvanātha Tīrthamkāra 74
Pāsādika Bhikkhu 248, 333
Paṭaliputra 39–41, 213, 303
Paṭisambhidāmagga 46, 159, 192, 315
Paṭṭhāna 191–2
pearl (*muktā*) 22
Peshāwar 87, 125
Petakopadeśa 190, 192, 322
Pierce, C. S. 160
Pitaputrasamāgama 25
Poṭṭhapāda 205
posatha 105
possession 141
Prabandha Kośa 296
Prabandhacintamani 75–76, 293
Prabandhakośa 293
Prajñā 233
Prajñākaramati 272
Prajñāpāramitā 23, 30, 33, 40, 48–49, 53–4, 58, 61, 74, 156, 172, 175, 178, 182, 230
Prajñāpāramitopadeśaśāstra 272, 313
Prajñāpradīpa 53, 231, 337
Prajñāpradīpaṭīkā 53
prajñapti 196–201, 203–204, 206, 211, 220–222, 234–235, 236, 238–242, 251, 253, 258, 261, 324, 325, 327, 331; *prajñaptisat* 198, 211–212, 221, 230, 234–238, 242–243
Prajñaptiśāstra 233, 331
Prajñāptibhāṣya 192
Prajñaptivāda 214, 218–223, 234, 239, 243–245
Prakaraṇapāda 226, 233
Prakrit 30
prapañca 160, 233, 251
Prasannapadā 246, 272
prātimokṣa 24, 28, 40, 42,

93, 100, 105–106, 113–114, 119, 129, 151, 213
Pratisaṃkhyānirodha 214
pratītyasamutpāda 129, 159, 160, 169–172, 174–175, 181, 190, 195, 215–216, 224, 231, 234, 242–243, 251, 258–259, 263, 266; in the Tripiṭaka 171–175
Pratyekabuddha 48, 49
Pratyutpannabuddhasaṃmukhāvasthitasamādhi Sūtra 289, 298
Prebish, Charles 98, 100, 288
preceptor (*upādhyāya*) 128
Priestley, Leonard 203–204, 242, 258, 322, 324, 331
Property, private 139; of Buddha 141; of saṅgha 139, 141; of the Buddha 139, 140; of the *stūpa* 139, 142, 146; "heavy property" 140–141, 150; "light property" 141–142, 150
Prysluski, Jean 18
Pudgala 109, 197–198, 200–203, 206–209, 212, 220–221, 246, 248–250, 254–257, 262–263, 267
Pudgalavāda 192, 199, 201, 204, 205, 209, 211, 216, 246–247, 249–251, 253, 255–263, 267, 269
Puggalapaññatti 191
Puggalapaññatti Aṭṭhakathā 242–243, 332
Pulleyblank, Edwin G. 292
Puḷumāvi I 81, 83; II 81, 86; III 86
Punjab 40
Puṇyaparyāyaparipṛcchā 281
Purāṇas 65, 67, 75, 85, 155–156
pure land 16
Puri, Baij Nath 286, 335
Pūrva śrutas 70
Pūrvaśaila 53, 87–88, 263, 267, 291, 335

Qarashar 29
Qin dynasty 4, 287; Qin dynasty translation 215, 217, 219
Qingmu 237, 254, 256
Qizil 27, 29, 134, 283

Rāhula 37, 40
Rājagīrika 87
Rājagṛha 50–51
Rājataraṅginī 21, 66, 73–74, 293, 296
Ramatīrtham 64
Rao, Hanumanathan 25–26, 282–283, 292, 303
Rapson, Edward 284
rasayāna (alchemy) 75
Rasendra Maṅgala 69, 293–294, 296
Raṣṭrapālaparipṛcchā 24
Ratnakīrti 277
Ratnārāśi Sūtra 23–24, 54, 281, 302
Ratnāvalī 58, 61, 63–65, 86, 79–91, 115–116, 119, 121–122, 145, 147–148, 165, 185–187, 226–227, 233, 248, 261–263, 267, 271–274, 276–278, 291, 295, 297–299, 308, 312–313
Ratnāvalīṭīkā 65, 308
Ray, Himanshu 38–39, 54, 299, 301
Ray, Reginald 20, 23
Reat, N. Ross 168–169
reductio ad absurdum arguments (*prasaṅgika*) 184, 195
Resource Mobilization Theory 6, 7–9, 279
Rhi, Ju-hying 298
Robinson, Richard 62, 197, 292
Rome 22
Roy, Anamika 83–84, 300–301
Rudrāyanāvadāna 82

Saddhamapuṇḍarīka 18, 22, 24–25, 29, 281, 306
Ṣaḍpāramitā 185
Sahni, D. R. 285
Śaka Sātkarṇi 81
śākyabhikṣu/śākyabhikṣunī 36–39, 88, 286
Śākyamitra 73
Sāleyyaka sutta 275
Śālistambha sūtra 168–171
Salomon, Richard 28, 31–33, 55, 126, 283–284, 301, 309
samādhi 161, 183, 231–2
Samādhirāja Sūtra 165–166, 316
Sāmagāma sutta 97
Samantapāsādikā 304
śamatha (calming meditation) 157, 163, 165, 198, 217
śamathādhikaraṇa (pacification of disputes) 102

samaya 93, 103
Samayabhedoparacanacakra 38, 44–45, 49–50, 53, 104, 189, 214, 218, 229–230, 326
Saṃdhinirmocana Sūtra 29
Saṃjñā 160–165, 217–218, 232–233
saṃjñāveditanirodha 160, 162, 164–165
Sāṃkhya 3, 53, 193, 262, 295
Saṃmitīya 3, 199–205, 222, 245–248, 251, 259, 261, 266, 330
Sammitīya Nikāya Śāstra (*Sanmidibulun*) 41, 193, 199, 222, 246, 250, 253, 259, 269
saṃsāra 157, 159, 163–165, 178, 182, 193–194, 198–199, 205, 207, 214–215, 220, 223, 232, 257
saṃskāra/saṃskṛta 219–220
saṃskāra skandha 195, 199, 202, 221–222, 254
saṃskṛta (conditioned nature) 165, 175, 200, 204, 210, 222, 239, 241, 254, 257
saṃtāna (stream) 200, 216, 228–230
saṃvid (compact) 104
saṃvṛtisat 212, 235–236, 261
Samyukta Āgama 52
Saṃyuktābhidharmahṛdaya 192
Saṃyutta Nikāya 159, 169, 171, 174, 175, 181, 207, 243, 254, 318
Sañchī 55–56, 300
Sander, Lore 28, 283
Sanfadulun (*Tridharmakaśāstra*) 193
Saṅghabhadra 48, 192, 212
saṅghabheda 18, 45, 49, 95–100, 102, 105, 116, 118–119, 121–122
Saṅghakarma 144
Saṅghāṭa Sūtra 30
saṅghātiśeṣa offense 96–97, 119
Sangim 29
Saṅgītiparyāya 192, 227, 322
Saṅgīti sutta 190
Saṅ jwei 63
Saṅkāśya (Samkassam) 40
Sanlun xuanyi 49
Śāntarakṣita 272
Sāratthappakāsinī 318, 321
sārddhevihārasmiṃ 128, 143
Śāriputra 40, 112, 159, 168, 169, 190
Śāriputrābhidharmaśāstra 159, 162, 164, 191, 193, 196–197, 227, 233
Śāriputraparipṛcchā 44–45, 100, 326
Sarkar, H. 301
Sārnāth 34, 39
Sarvajñādeva 65
Sarvāstivāda 3, 5, 9, 17, 19, 38, 40, 46, 100, 161, 163, 191–192, 199, 208–212, 215–218, 221, 223, 226–227, 230, 233, 238, 244, 246, 248, 254, 257, 261–262, 266–269, 283, 287, 322, 330–331, 335
Sarvāstivāda vinaya 111, 132–134, 306, 310
Sasaki, Shizuka 24, 54, 282
Sassanian empire 22
śāśvata (eternity) 173–174, 178, 203
Sata/Sada dynasty 64–65, 86, 292
Śatasāhasrikā Prajñāpāramitā 25, 233
Śataśāstra 273, 336, 277
Sātavāhana 61, 63–68, 72–82, 84, 86, 268, 299
Sātkarṇi 65
Śatruñjaya (Mountain) 67, 296
Satyasiddhiśāstra 52, 190, 193, 206, 213–214, 290, 322, 327
Saukhavastan 21
Sautrāntika 229, 231, 246, 268, 330
Schalk, Peter 286
Scherrer-Schaub, Christina 321
schism. See *saṅghabheda*.
Schmithausen, Lambert 157, 159, 162, 164, 176
schools 130
Schopen, Gregory 18, 20, 31, 34–39, 43, 54, 89–92, 110, 115–119, 136, 150, 183, 269, 281–286, 302, 306, 312
Schøyen collection 28–33
scribes (*kāyastha*) 126, 139, 309

Seed sprout analogy 230, 245–246
Sekoddesaṭika 26
Seng-jui 62
Seven jewels 22
Shah, Natubhai 295
Shan-hsien 249
Shan-Shan 31, 33, 35, 54–55
Sharma, Ramesh 299
Shastri, Ajay Mitra 81, 299
Shastri, P. S. 294
Shih Tao An 37
Siāhanmuchāoxu 193
Siddha 66–67
Siddhārthikas 53
sign (literary-semiotic) 167
signlessness (see *animitta*)
Śikṣānanda 27, 293
śikṣāpada (training rules) 113–114, 281
silk 22; silk banners 303
Silk, Jonathan 280–282, 313
Silk Route 27, 104, 134
silver (*rūpya*) 22
Sircar, D. C. 64, 283, 285
Śiva Skandha 84
Siva Śrī 83
Sivamakasada 83
Sivamakaskandha Gautamiputra 81
Sivaramamurti 300
sKa bad Pal brtsegs 272
skandha 129, 131, 189–190, 202–204, 206–210, 218–221, 235, 238, 249, 250, 253–255
Skilling, Peter 53, 290
Skjærvø, Oktor 29, 283
Smaller Sukhāvatī Sūtra 19
Social Movement theory 4–9
Sorčuq 27, 29
Sparham, Gareth 319
sphāṭika (quartz) 22
Spink, Walter 299
Spitzer Manuscript 134
Sprung, Mervyn 241, 329
śramāṇas 33
śrāvaka 16, 19, 24, 48–49, 290; *śrāvakayāna* 53, 120, 231
Śrī Laṅka 42, 47, 55
Śrīmad Bhagavatam 155–156
Śrīnagar 293
Śrī Parvata 67–68, 76–77, 294, 296
Srosh 282
Stāmbhana 77
Stāmbhana Tīrtha 74
Stein, Aurel 283, 293
Sthaviravāda 41, 45, 49
Sthūlāpatti offense 128
Stone, Elizabeth 300
Strauss, Leo 95, 303
stūpas 18–19, 35–36, 38, 55, 125, 148, 281, 300
Subaši 27, 318
Sudhana 25
suffering (see *duḥkha*)
Suhṛllekha 63, 65, 297
Sukhāvatī 19, 21
Sumaṅgala-vilāsinī 334
Sumatidārikaparipṛcchā 298
śūnyatā (emptiness) 16–17, 23, 116–117, 131, 161–162, 164, 179–182, 186–187, 199, 218, 225, 231–232, 244, 248, 251, 253, 259, 261, 263, 268, 272, 290; 12 emptinesses 233; emptiness gate 118, 183
Śūnyatāsaptati 247, 261, 267–268
Śūraṅgamasamādhi Sūtra 30, 166, 316
Surāṣṭra 69, 72
Surat 42
sūtradhāra 41
Sutrasammuccāya 248
Suttanipāta 129, 275–276, 311
Suvarnabhāsottama Sūtra 30, 32, 71, 284, 295
Suviśuddhaprabhābhūmi 295
Suvikrāntavikrāmin 275
svabhāva 210, 228–229, 235, 241–242, 245–248, 258–259
svabhāva parabhāva 184
svādhyaya 128
Śvetāmbara 70

Tachikawa, Musashi 224, 239
Takakusu, Junirō 18, 286, 289
Takasaki, Jikido 316
Takla Makan desert 28
Tamil Nadu 27
Tāranātha 21, 76, 218, 292
Tarkajvālā 53, 272, 290
Tathāgata 166, 205–207, 216
Tathāgataguhya Sūtra 25, 248
Tathāgatāyuṣpramāṇa-paripṛcchā 281

Tatz, Mark 113, 282
Taxila 22, 125
Teiser, Stephen 138
Ten *avyākṛtāṇi* 205, 206–207
Theravāda 9, 12, 87, 100, 131, 161, 163, 184–185, 190–191, 192, 212–213, 216–217, 223, 227, 230, 242, 322; *Abhidharma* 226; *Vinaya* 133, 158, 306
Third Jain council 70
Thirty seven *bodhipakṣā* 100
Thomas, Fredrick William 284
Three vehicles 88
Thus have I heard . . . 154
Timbaruka sutta 173, 254
Tippera 38, 56, 285, 291
Tokharian 20
Toyoq 29
tree and shadow analogy 203–204
Tridharmakandhaka 203, 206–207, 249, 261
trikāya 16
Tripiṭaka 4, 12, 13, 50–51
Tsai, Yao-ming 37–38, 286
Tucci, Giuseppe 336
Tummalagudem 88
Turkmenistan 27, 127
Turner, R. H. 279
Turuṣka 67
Tuṣita Heaven 21
Twain, Mark 57, 291

ucchedadṛṣṭi 203
ucchedatā (annihilationism) 173–174, 178
Udāna 175, 176–178, 181, 193, 318
Udyāna 287
Ugradattaparipṛcchā 19–20, 23, 280–281, 299, 302
Ui, Hakuji 63, 292
Ujjain 65, 85
Unconditioned (*asaṃskṛta*) 175–181
unity/plurality 174–175
universals (jāti) 196
untimely death 218–220
upacaya (accumulatiuon) 200, 222, 245–246
upādāya 207; *upādāya prajñapti* 201, 203, 206, 242–243, 258–262, 324–325
Upāli 51, 94, 99, 102, 111
Upāliparipṛcchā 23
upāsaka 103, 131–132
upāya 120
upāyakauśalya 23
Upāyakauśalyaparipṛcchā 281
upekṣā 90, 120
upoṣadha ceremony 113, 189
utkṣepanīyakarma (Act of suspension) 105–107
utkṣiptam 106
Uttar Pradesh 40
Uttaraśaila 50, 87, 214

Vaḍḍamanu 64
Vaiśālī 44
Vaiśālī council 100
Vaiśeṣika 134, 292, 295
Vaibhāṣika 245
vaiḍūrya (lapis lazuli) 22
Vaipulya sūtras 53, 72–73, 135, 154, 156
Vairothya (snake goddess) 76
Vaitulya 47
Vajjiputaka 45–47
Vākāṭaka dynasty 81
Vakkali sutta 169
Valabhī 34, 38–39, 49, 55–56, 70, 285
Vallabhipūr 34, 70
Varṣavastu 110, 132
Vāsiṣṭhīputra Pulomā 268
Vāsiṣṭhīputra Sātakarṇi 83
Vasubandhu 12, 17, 96, 109, 192, 200, 211, 216, 235–236, 246, 280, 303–304, 306, 308, 330
Vāsuki (Nāga king) 74
Vasumitra 38, 44–45, 49, 52, 100, 104, 189, 210, 214, 216–218, 222–223, 239, 256, 288, 324, 327, 329, 332
Vatsīputrīya 87, 109, 208, 218, 221, 246, 257, 268, 324, 335
vaṃsa 12
vayyāvṛtykara 143
vedalla 156
vedanā 158
Vedānta 193
Vedas 133
Velpur 64
Vengi 87
Vesali 45
Vessantara Jātaka 67
Vetter, Tilmann 37, 249, 251, 253, 257, 267, 276–277, 286, 337
vetullavāda/vaipulyavāda 47, 155
Vibhaṅga 191, 227, 233, 322
Vibhajyavāda 219, 233
vibhava 256
Vidarbha 66–67, 77–78, 81, 294
Vidyadhāra-piṭaka 53

Vidyākaraprabha 272
Vigrahavyāvartanī 225, 239, 261–262, 267, 271
vihārapāla 101
Vijaya Sātakarṇi 81, 86, 294
vijñāna 160
Vijñānakāya 192, 208, 210–211, 226, 246, 330
Vijñānāntyāyatana 215
Vimaladattaparipṛcchā 298
Vimalakīrtinirdeśa sūtra 30, 291
vimokṣamukkha 161
Vimuttimagga 192
Vinītadeva 215, 327
Vinaya Piṭaka 11, 13–14, 18–19, 38, 40–41, 45–46, 91–92, 188
vinayadhāra 41, 108
vipaśyana 157, 163, 217
vipaśyana 165
vipula 170
Virapurisadata 213
Viṣṇudharmottara 120
Voyce, M. B. 302
Vyākaraṇaparipṛcchā 281
Vyākhyāyukti 12, 280, 304

Walleser, Max 58, 291
Walshe, Maurice 107
Warder, A. K. 280, 326, 335
Ware, James Roland 296
Wassiljew, Vaslii 221, 286
Watters, Thomas 287, 293
White, David 76, 293–294
Williams, Paul 18, 98, 101, 279, 315
Wishlessness 161–162, 179, 180, 187
Word of the Buddha 53, 132. *See also buddha-vacana*
Writing 124

Xinjiang 29, 31, 33, 39
Xočo 29
Xuanzang 18, 21, 39, 41, 42–43, 45, 57, 64–66, 76, 78, 213, 215–223, 246, 293–294, 297, 316
Yajñavalkyasmṛti 104, 306
Yajña Śrī Satkarṇi 81, 84–86, 299
Yamaka 191–192
Yaśomitra 109–110, 192, 235–236, 306, 318, 321
Yazdani, Ghulam 284
Yijing 18, 39, 41–42, 63, 65, 78, 82, 101–102
Yogācāra 314
Yogācārabhūmi of Asaṅga 113, 286
Yogācārabhūmi of Saṅghadeva 308
Yogaśataka 69, 294
Yoshimoto, Shingyo 233
Yuktiṣaṣtikā 321

Zald, Mayer 6, 279
Zambasta, Book of 30
Zhiyi 258
Zhonglun 224, 225, 237
Zhushixing 57
Zürcher, Erik 57, 291
Zoroastrianism 20